Handbook for
Banking Strategy

WILEY PROFESSIONAL BANKING AND FINANCE SERIES
EDWARD I. ALTMAN, Editor

THE STOCK MARKET, 4TH EDITION
Richard J. Teweles and Edward S. Bradley

TAX SHELTERED FINANCING THROUGH THE R & D LIMITED PARTNERSHIP
James K. La Fleur

CORPORATE FINANCIAL DISTRESS: A COMPLETE GUIDE TO PREDICTING, AVOIDING, AND DEALING WITH BANKRUPTCY
Edward I. Altman

CREDIT ANALYSIS: A COMPLETE GUIDE
Roger H. Hale

CURRENT ASSET MANAGEMENT: CASH, CREDIT, AND INVENTORY
Jarl G. Kallberg and Kenneth Parkinson

HANDBOOK FOR BANKING STRATEGY
Richard C. Aspinwall and Robert A. Eisenbeis

Handbook for Banking Strategy

Edited by

RICHARD C. ASPINWALL
Vice President
The Chase Manhattan Bank, N.A.

and

ROBERT A. EISENBEIS
Wachovia Professor of Banking
University of North Carolina

A Wiley-Interscience Publication

John Wiley & Sons

New York • Chichester • Brisbane • Toronto • Singapore

Library of Congress Cataloging in Publication Data:

Main entry under title:
Handbook for banking strategy.

(Wiley professional banking and finance series)
"A Wiley-Interscience publication."
Includes index.
1. Bank management—Handbooks, manuals, etc.
2. Banks and banking—United States—Handbooks, manuals,
etc. I. Aspinwall, Richard C. II. Eisenbeis, Robert A.
III. Series.
HG1615.H35 1985 332.1'068 84-19487
ISBN 0-471-89314-5

Printed in the United States of America

10 9 8 7 6 5 4 3 2

Editorial Consulting Board

The editors received valuable advice on the organization of the *Handbook* and the selection of contributors. The list of distinguished editorial consultants includes representatives from private industry, government, and the academic community.

Contributors

EDWARD I. ALTMAN is professor of finance and chairman of the MBA program at New York University. He has been a visiting professor at the Hautes Etudes Commerciales and Universite de Paris-Dauphine in France, at the Pontificia Catolica Universidade in Rio de Janeiro, Brazil, and the Australian Graduate School of Management. He is editor of the *Journal of Banking and Finance* and two series, Contemporary Studies in Economics and Finance (JAI Press) and the Wiley Professional Banking and Finance Series (John Wiley & Sons). Altman has published several books and over 50 articles in scholarly finance, accounting, and economic journals. His primary areas of research include bankruptcy analysis and prediction, credit and lending policies, and capital markets. He has been a consultant to several government agencies, major financial and accounting institutions, and industrial companies, and has lectured to executives in North America, South America, Europe, and Asia.

RICHARD C. ASPINWALL is vice president in the National Positioning Group of The Chase Manhattan Bank, where his responsibilities cover issues of expansion, planning, and financial regulation. Before moving to that group, he was director of banking and financial market research in the Economics Group. Prior to joining Chase in 1970, he was an economist for the Federal Reserve Bank of New York, and he has also served as adjunct assistant professor in the Graduate School of Business at Columbia University. Aspinwall's primary research interests are in the fields of financial institutions, markets, and regulation. At Chase his research in these areas has been applied to asset/liability management, expansion, and strategic planning. He has written for a number of financial and economics publications. Aspinwall holds a bachelor's degree from the University of Michigan and a Ph.D. from Columbia University, where he concentrated in economics and finance.

ROBERT A. EISENBEIS is Wachovia Professor of Banking at the School of Business Administration at the University of North Carolina at Chapel

Hill. Prior to going to Chapel Hill in early 1982, he was senior deputy associate director in the Division of Research and Statistics at the Federal Reserve Board in Washington. In that position he was in charge of basic research and policy analysis of microbanking issues, including banking market structure and performance, proposed bank holding company acquisitions, mergers, new holding company activities, and consumer regulatory issues. He also served at the FDIC, where he was assistant director of research and chief of the financial and economic research section. Eisenbeis has published more than 30 articles in professional journals and is co-author of two books. Much of his research has been devoted to problems in banking and finance, including the application of classification procedures to such problems as loan review, bond evaluation, and problem bank identification. Eisenbeis serves on editorial advisory boards of the *Journal of Bank Research, Journal of Financial and Quantitative Analysis, Journal of Banking and Finance, The Journal of Economics and Business, The Journal of Financial Research,* and *The Journal of Financial and Quantitative Analysis.* He did his undergraduate work at Brown University and holds M.A. and Ph.D. degrees in economics from the University of Wisconsin.

MARK J. FLANNERY is associate professor of finance at the University of North Carolina. He previously taught at the University of Pennsylvania's Wharton School and served as research adviser to the Federal Reserve Bank of Philadelphia. He holds economics degrees from Princeton and Yale. His primary research interests are financial intermediaries and the effects of monetary policy. Flannery has published two books and numerous articles in professional journals, including work on unit banking restrictions, the effective maturities of bank assets and liabilities, and the effect of interest rate changes on the common stock of financial institutions. He has also designed and implemented a computer-based bank simulation game for classroom and management training uses.

BENJAMIN M. FRIEDMAN is professor of economics at Harvard University, where he teaches macroeconomics and monetary economics and conducts a seminar on monetary and fiscal policy. His recent research interests have centered primarily on financial markets and their effects on economic activity. Specific subjects have included the impacts of government deficits on U.S. capital formation, the role of money and credit targets in the conduct of U.S. monetary policy, the implications of private pension funds for corporate financial decisions, and the relative importance of various factors affecting interest rates. His work in these areas has been published widely. He also serves as director of financial markets and monetary economics research at the National Bureau of Economic Research, a director of the Private Export Funding Corporation, and associate editor of the *Journal of Monetary Economics*. In addition, he has served as a member of the National Science Foundation Subcommittee on Economics and as a trustee of the College Retirement Equities Fund. He is also a member of the Brookings Panel on Economic Activity and the Council on Foreign Relations. Friedman joined the Harvard faculty in 1972. Before that he was associated with Morgan Stanley & Co., investment bankers in New York. He has also worked in consulting or other capacities with the Board of Governors of the Federal Reserve System, the Federal Reserve Bank of New York, and the Federal Reserve Bank of Boston. Friedman received A.B., A.M., and Ph.D. degrees in economics from Harvard University; during his graduate study at Harvard he was Junior Fellow of the Society of Fellows. In addition, he received the M.Sc. in economics and politics from King's College, Cambridge, England, where he studied as a Marshall Scholar.

JOHN D. HAWKE, JR., is a partner in the firm of Arnold & Porter in Washington, D.C. He has specialized in matters relating to federal regulation of financial institutions. His practice involves the counseling and representation of banks and thrift institutions—as well as investors in financial institutions—in matters such as holding company formations and expansion, takeovers, enforcement proceedings, electronic banking, and regulatory and supervisory issues. Many of these involve actions before the Board of Governors of the Federal Reserve System, the Comptroller of the Currency, the Federal Deposit Insurance Corporation, and the Federal Home Loan Bank Board. Hawke also served as general counsel at the Board of Governors of the Federal Reserve System from 1975 to 1978. Since 1971, he has been an adjunct professor of law at the Georgetown University Law Center. He is also a member of the editorial advisory board of *Issues in Bank Regulation* and is chairman of the editorial advisory board of *Banking Expansion Reporter*. Hawke has written widely for legal and banking publications. He holds a B.A. from Yale University and an L.L.B. from the Columbia University School of Law, where he was editor-in-chief of the *Columbia Law Review*.

ARNOLD A. HEGGESTAD is William H. Dial professor of banking and chairman of the Department of Finance, Insurance, and Real Estate at the Graduate School of Business Administration, University of Florida. He has been at the University of Florida since 1974. Previously, he was financial economist for the Board of Governors of the Federal Reserve System in Washington, where he also served as visiting senior economist in 1983. Heggestad is currently director of the University of Florida Financial Institutions and Monetary Policy Center and educational director for the Florida School of Banking. He serves on the editorial board of *Bank Acquisition Report* and the *Review of Industrial Organization*. His research interests include bank financial management, mergers, and banking structure and regulation. Heggestad received his B.A. from the University of Maryland and his Ph.D. in economics from Michigan State University.

DAVID B. HUMPHREY is currently chief of the Financial Studies Section at the Board of Governors of the Federal Reserve System in Washington. He has been at the Board since 1975 and before that taught at Tulane and San Francisco State Universities for seven years. He received his Ph.D. in economics from the University of California (Berkeley) and has published some 30 professional articles, the most recent of which covered bank scale economies. His current research deals with costs, pricing, competition, and risk in the U.S. payments system.

JOHN H. KALCHBRENNER is senior vice president and chief economist at the Shawmut Bank of Boston, N.A. Previously he was a staff economist with the Board of Governors of the Federal Reserve System in Washington. He transferred to the Federal Reserve Bank of Chicago, where he served as a senior economist and assistant vice-president. He later returned to the Board of Governors and worked as an adviser and then associate director in the Division of Research and Statistics, with responsibilities for long-term research and econometric models. Kalchbrenner holds B.A. and M.A. degrees in economics from the University of Iowa and M.A. and Ph.D. degrees in economics from the University of Wisconsin.

EDWARD J. KANE is the Everett D. Reese Professor of Banking and Monetary Economics at Ohio State University. Previously he taught at Boston College, Princeton University, and Iowa State University and held visiting professorships at Istanbul University and Simon Fraser University. He has consulted for the Federal Deposit Insurance Corporation, the Federal Home Loan Bank Board, the Department of Housing and Urban Development, various components of the Federal Reserve System, and the Joint Economic Committee and Office of Technology Assessment of the U.S. Congress. Kane is a past president of the American Finance Association and a former Guggenheim fellow. In 1981 he won an Ohio State University Alumni Award for Distinguished Teaching. He has published widely in professional journals and serves currently on six editorial boards. Kane writes occasional columns for *The American Banker* and is a research associate of the National Bureau of Economic Research and a trustee and member of the finance committee of Teachers Insurance Annuity Association. Kane received a B.S. from Georgetown University and a Ph.D. from Massachusetts Institute of Technology.

GEORGE G. KAUFMAN is John F. Smith, Jr., professor of finance and economics at the School of Business Administration, Loyola University, Chicago. He received a B.A. from Oberlin College, an M.A. from the University of Michigan, and a Ph.D. in economics from the University of Iowa. He was a research fellow, economist, and senior economist at the Federal Reserve Bank of Chicago from 1959 to 1970. From 1970 to 1980 he was the John B. Rogers professor of banking and finance and director of the Center for Capital Market Research at the College of Business Administration, University of Oregon. He has been a visiting professor at the University of Southern California, Stanford University, University of California at Berkeley, and the Office of the Comptroller of the Currency. Kaufman also served as Deputy to the Assistant Secretary for Economic Policy of the U.S. Treasury. Kaufman's teaching and research interests are in financial economics, financial institutions and markets, and monetary policy, subjects on which he has published extensively. He served on the boards of directors of the American Finance Association and the Midwest Finance Association and as president of the Western Finance Association. Kaufman is currently on the editorial boards of three professional journals, *Journal of Financial and Quantitative Analysis, Journal of Bank Research,* and *Journal of Financial Research.* In 1982, he was elected a trustee of the Teachers Insurance Annuity Association and College Retirement Equity Fund (TIAA-CREF), the second largest private pension fund in the country.

SYDNEY J. KEY is an economist in the Federal Reserve Board's Division of International Finance, where she specializes in current issues in international banking. Key has worked on the Board's regulations providing for the establishment of international banking facilities in the United States and on implementation of the International Banking Act of 1978 and the Monetary Control Act of 1980. She is the author of a number of articles and papers on international banking facilities, the U.S. activities of foreign banks, and the International Banking Act of 1978. Key has also published articles on employee group pension plans and the federal tax treatment of married two-earner couples. She has testified before Congressional committees on the marriage tax penalty and was a member of the President's Interdepartmental Task Force on Women in 1979–80. Key obtained her A.B. in economics from Radcliffe College in 1966. She did her graduate work in economics at Harvard University and received an A.M. in 1969 and a Ph.D. in 1973.

REID NAGLE is vice chairman and chief administrative and financial officer of City Federal Savings and Loan Association, Piscataway, New Jersey. He joined City Federal in 1978 as vice-president in charge of economics and planning. Subsequently, he was named senior vice-president, responsible additionally for budgeting and financial hedging. In 1982 he was elected executive vice-president and chief financial officer. In that capacity, he was responsible for treasury, accounting, tax, and financial planning activities. Nagle was appointed to his current position in early 1984. He is the author of numerous articles relating to hedging with financial futures, alternative mortgage instruments, savings and loan asset/liability management, tax incentives for savings, capital requirements for financial institutions, and tax planning. Prior to joining City Federal, Nagle served as a consulting economist for the Maryland Department of Economic and Community Development, responsible for preparation of the state's annual economic report. Before that, he was task force investigator for the U.S. Senate Budget Committee and consultant to the National Savings and Loan League. Nagle did his undergraduate work at Georgetown University and received his M.A. and Ph.D. degrees in economics from the Johns Hopkins University.

CHRISTINE PAVEL is associate economist at the Federal Reserve Bank of Chicago. She has been with that institution since 1982. Her work has concentrated on competition and the effects of deregulation in the financial services industry. Pavel received her B.A. in economics from Duquesne University and is completing her M.B.A. at the University of Chicago.

BRUCE PETERSEN is vice president for securities portfolio and trading, City Federal Savings and Loan Association, Piscataway, New Jersey. Since joining City Federal in 1979, he has served in several capacities. In 1980 he was named marketing director for City Federal's consumer lending subsidiary, City Consumer Services. In late 1981 Petersen rejoined the parent company as cofounder and manager of financial hedging. The following year he was named assistant vice-president for risk management. His responsibilities in that capacity included the financial hedging program, balance sheet planning, and the asset/liability management staff. He also served as a member of City Federal's asset/liability management committee. In 1983 Petersen was named manager of financial planning, and a year later he assumed his current position. Petersen received an A.B.

in history and Russian studies from Princeton University and is currently pursuing an M.S. in statistics at New York University.

MANFERD O. PETERSON is professor and chairman of the Department of Finance, University of Nebraska-Lincoln. Peterson received his B.A. with honors in 1966 from Wisconsin State University-River Falls, a Master of Arts in economics in 1968 from Michigan State University, and in 1971 a Ph.D. in economics, also from Michigan State University. From 1970 to 1976 Peterson was a financial economist at the Federal Deposit Insurance Corporation in Washington, D.C. Peterson's primary teaching and research interests are in financial markets and institutions, and his work has been published in a number of scholarly journals. In addition, Peterson has presented papers to the American Statistical Association and has testified as an expert witness before the U.S. Senate Committee on Banking, Housing, and Urban Affairs.

RICHARD L. PETERSON is I. Wylie and Elizabeth Briscoe professor of bank management and finance, Texas Tech University, Lubbock. He was previously associate director of the Credit Research Center at Purdue University and, before that, financial economist in the Mortgage and Consumer Finance Section of the Division of Research and Statistics, Board of Governors of the Federal Reserve System. His major areas of research interest include bank and nonbank financial institutions, consumer credit, mortgage finance, and the economics of information and regulation—on all of which he has published widely.

ALMARIN PHILLIPS is Hower professor of public policy and management and professor of economics and law at the University of Pennsylvania. He was codirector of the President's Commission on Financial Structure and Regulation (Hunt Commission) and a member of the National Commission on Electronic Funds Transfer. Competition and regulatory policies constitute major research interests, and he has published widely on topics in these areas. Phillips received his B.S. and M.A. degrees from Pennsylvania and his Ph.D. from Harvard.

JERRY E. POHLMAN is senior executive vice president and chief economist at American Savings and Loan Association, the principal subsidiary of Financial Corporation of America (FCA). He is responsible for economic forecasting and analysis for American and FCA, corporate marketing, public affairs, and retail branch and sales operations. He is also a member of American's asset/liability management and executive committees. Prior to joining American Savings, Pohlman was senior vice president and chief economist at Coast Savings and, before that, California Federal Savings. He also served as professor of economics at the State University of New York at Buffalo, staff economist with the Cost of Living Council in Washington, and a principal with Arthur Young and Company in New York. Pohlman received his B.A. and M.A. degrees from the University of Iowa and his Ph.D. in economics from Cornell University.

HARVEY ROSENBLUM is vice president and associate director of the research department at the Federal Reserve Bank of Chicago, where he has been employed since 1970. Rosenblum is also visiting professor of finance at DePaul University, a position he has held since 1973. During 1977–78, he also served as visiting professor of finance at the University of Oregon. In addition, Rosenblum has served as an economic and management consultant to a variety of financial institutions. He received a B.S. degree from the University of Connecticut and M.A. and Ph.D. degrees in economics from the University of California at Santa Barbara. Rosenblum has done considerable research on competition in financial services and has published widely in leading scholarly journals. For many years he has been responsible for organizing the annual Conference on Bank Structure and Competition hosted by the Federal Reserve Bank of Chicago. His other duties include serving as monetary policy adviser to the bank's president, and he is the chief administrative officer of the economic research department.

ANTHONY M. SANTOMERO is Richard K. Mellon professor of finance and vice dean of the Graduate Division at the Wharton School of the University of Pennsylvania. He is also associate editor of the *Journal of Finance, Journal of Money, Credit and Banking, Journal of Banking and Finance, Journal of Financial Research,* and *Journal of Economics and Business.* Santomero has published widely on the demand for money, employment, and commercial bank soundness and capital adequacy. He has also consulted for major U.S. banks as well as for regulatory agencies. He is a member of the American Economic Association, the American Finance Association, and the European Finance Association. He received a Ph.D. in economics from Brown University.

DONALD T. SAVAGE is senior economist in the Financial Structure Section of the Division of Research and Statistics of the Board of Governors of the Federal Reserve System. Prior to his employment at the Federal Reserve Board in 1976, he taught economics at the University of Maine and Clark University. He is the author or coauthor of three economics textbooks and numerous articles on issues related to the structure of the U.S. financial system. His current research interests center on issues related to banking deregulation, especially interstate banking. Savage received a B.B.A. from the University of Massachusetts and a Ph.D. from the University of Wisconsin.

JOSEPH F. SINKEY, JR. is professor of banking and finance in the College of Business Administration at the University of Georgia, Athens. He has written numerous books and articles dealing with banking and finance. He is the book review editor for the *Journal of Banking and Finance,* an associate editor of the *Journal of Financial Research,* and reviewer for major banking and finance journals. From 1971 to 1976, Sinkey was a financial economist with the Division of Research of the Federal Deposit Insurance Corporation. He joined the University of Georgia in 1976. Sinkey has consulted for industry and government, has testified before the United States Senate, and has served as an expert witness in litigation. He received a B.A. in economics from St. Vincent College, Latrobe, Pennsylvania, and a Ph.D. in economics from Boston College.

ROBERT L. SLIGHTON is vice president and director for international forecasting in the Economics Group of The Chase Manhattan Bank. He joined Chase in 1976 from the Treasury Department, where he was Deputy Assistant Secretary for research in the office of the Assistant Secretary for International Affairs. In 1974–75 he served as the national intelligence officer for economics and energy for the Director of Central Intelligence. Prior to entering government, Slighton was a senior economist at the Rand Corporation and assistant professor of economics at Stanford University. He is the coauthor of *Structural Change in a Developing Economy.* Slighton received an A.B. in international affairs at Princeton University and a Ph.D. in economics at Johns Hopkins University.

ROBERT A. TAGGART, JR. is professor of finance at Boston University. He was previously a faculty member of Northwestern University's J.L. Kellogg Graduate School of Management and has held visiting positions at the Federal Reserve Bank of Boston and the Harvard Business School. He also serves currently as editor of *Financial Management* and as an associate editor of the *Journal of Financial and Quantitative Analysis.* Taggart's primary research interests are corporate finance and its application to financial institutions and other regulated industries. Recent publications have dealt with capital expenditure proposals under inflation, corporate capital structure theory for banking institutions, and secular patterns in the financing of U.S. corporations.

KEVIN E. VILLANI is senior vice president for financial and economic analysis and chief economist for the Federal Home Loan Mortgage Corporation. Previously, he was Deputy Assistant Secretary and chief economist for the Department of Housing and Urban Development. Villani was formerly an adjunct professor of finance at the Wharton School of Business of the University of Pennsylvania, and he currently teaches at George Mason University in Fairfax, Virginia. In addition, he is coeditor of the *Housing Finance Review,* and editor in chief of *Secondary Mortgage Markets.* Villani received a B.S. in mathematics from the University of Massachusetts and a Ph.D. in economics from Purdue University.

BENJAMIN WOLKOWITZ is vice president in Citibank's money market division, where he is responsible for directing marketing for the bank's financial futures brokerage operation and fixed income research. Prior to joining Citibank, Wolkowitz was the chief economist at the New York Futures Exchange. He also served as a section chief of the Financial Study Section in the Division of Research Statistics of the Board of Governors of the Federal Reserve System and taught economics at Tulane University. His current research interests relate to the management of interest rate risk exposure using futures, options, and other instruments and techniques. Recent publications have included work on futures and hedging as well as determinants of interest rates on fixed income invetments. Wolkowitz holds a Ph.D. degree in economics from Brown University.

Series Preface

The worlds of banking and finance have changed dramatically during the past few years, and no doubt this turbulence will continue through the 1980s. We have established the Wiley Professional Banking and Finance Series to aid in characterizing this dynamic environment and to further the understanding of the emerging structures, issues, and content for the professional financial community.

We envision three types of book in this series. First, we are commissioning distinguished experts in a broad range of fields to assemble a number of authorities to write specific primers on related topics. For example, some of the early handbook-type volumes in the series concentrate on the Stock Market, Investment Banking, and Financial Depository Institutions. A second type of book attempts to combine text material with appropriate empirical and case studies written by practitioners in relevant fields. An early example is a forthcoming volume on The Management of Cash and Other Short-Term Assets. Finally, we are encouraging definitive, authoritative works on specialized subjects for practitioners and theorists.

It is a distinct pleasure and honor for me to assist John Wiley & Sons, Inc. in this important endeavor. In addition to banking and financial practitioners, we think business students and faculty will benefit from this series. Most of all, though, we hope this series will become a primary source in the 1980s for the members of the professional financial community to refer to theories and data and to integrate important aspects of the central changes in our financial world.

EDWARD I. ALTMAN

Professor of Finance
New York University
Schools of Business

Preface

Events of the past decade have set in motion forces that are causing extensive changes in markets for financial services. These changes are being reflected in the pricing, content, delivery, and packaging of services. They also are being accompanied by shifts in the institutional composition of financial markets. These shifts include entry into service markets by new competitors and amalgamations within and between classes of institutions. Moreover, the effects of service and institutional changes also are raising new questions relating to regulation and supervision.

Nowhere is the pace of change more evident than in markets traditionally served by commercial banks. Not too many years ago, a bank was an institution chartered as a commercial bank. That is, to a considerable extent banking services were linked distinctly to banking institutions. In recent years, however, more and more banking services have been developed by others. Thrift institutions offer packages of services in many cases comparable to those offered by commercial banks. Moreover, a number of other financial entities, such as insurance companies, mutual funds, brokerage firms, and nonfinancial entities, also are offering services that are close substitutes for many of those available at traditional depository institutions. In addition, many users of services are pursuing do-it-yourself strategies which reduce roles for financial intermediaries.

In this light, the term *banking strategy* contained in the title applies not only to commercial banks, but also to those *services* for which depository institutions have been the predominant suppliers historically. Therefore, while there must be institutional identification in some of the more descriptive sections, an effort has been made to concentrate on *functions*.

The chapters written for this volume dissect these changes in financial institutions and markets and analyze their implications for both management strategies and public policy. The chapters are organized in four parts, beginning with a discussion of the role of intermediaries generally. The second part moves to analyses of major forces for change, and the third to analyses of specific manifestations of change in the markets served by banking institutions. The final part of the book treats major challenges to effective management. To repeat, the emphasis is on the underlying forces for change and the implications of these forces for the development of effective strategies.

The editors have benefited enormously in the development of this volume from the generous counsel of contributors and members of the Editorial Consulting Board. They are also deeply grateful to Mary Ascerno and Geraldine Hope at The Chase Manhattan Bank for their invaluable assistance.

RICHARD C. ASPINWALL
ROBERT A. EISENBEIS

New York, New York
Chapel Hill, North Carolina

Contents

1 The Role of Intermediaries in Fostering Economic Activity

Financial intermediaries increase the efficient functioning of economic units—such as households and business firms—by assuming certain risks in borrowing from surplus units and lending to deficit units. In addition, they offer customers benefits of joint production and distribution and economies of scale.

A discussion of the reasons why the roles of intermediaries are important serves as the introduction to the book. The two papers contained in this section approach this question from two general perspectives. One is to examine trends between intermediated and unintermediated flows of funds, as well as shifts in shares among major classes of intermediaries. Since this book is about banking (broadly defined to include commercial banks and thrift institutions), such entities are highlighted. The second emphasis is the identification of linkages between these changes and economic policies, especially fiscal and monetary. In connection with the latter, the policy issues under review are those aimed at broad economic activity. Questions relating to the conduct of banking activities—generally classed as regulatory or supervisory policies—are deferred for subsequent sections.

1 Financial Intermediation in the United States

Benjamin M. Friedman

The intermediating function provided by specialized institutions has always been a hallmark of well-developed financial markets. In the modern economy, almost everyone participates in the financial markets, and few economic events take place without their financial counterpart. The basic role of the financial markets is to enable millions of businesses and individuals to carry out, more easily and more efficiently, the interactions that their activities in the nonfinancial economy entail. Although in principle businesses and individuals could carry out their financial dealings directly, without the advantages of intermediary services, in most cases doing so would be inconsistent with the underlying reason for having and using financial markets in the first place. Intermediation renders financial transactions more efficient, and therefore increases the use that both businesses and individuals make of financial markets. In addition, in some instances financial intermediaries enable market participants to achieve objectives that would be unattainable in their absence.

This important role played by financial intermediation is typically not static. Throughout their history, financial markets have undergone a shift—away from direct transactions between nonfinancial borrowers and lenders, toward the intervention of financial intermediaries. In the United States, the development of the commercial banking system and the life insurance industry in earlier years, and more recently the great expansion of nonbank

This paper is based in part on my earlier contribution to *The American Economy in Transition,* edited by Martin Feldstein (Chicago: University of Chicago Press, 1980). I am grateful to Michael Burda and Jeffrey Fuhrer for research assistance and helpful suggestions.

deposit institutions and both private- and public-sector pension funds, have been important features of the development of the U.S. financial system. In addition, the roles played even by specific intermediary institutions change over time. The shifting requirements of the nonfinancial economy, the evolution of new communications and information processing technologies, changes in government regulations, and even independent financial innovations, all play a part in this dynamic process.

The goal of this chapter is to examine the structure of financial intermediation in the United States, both as it exists today and as it has evolved in the years since World War II.[1] The primary focus is on the role played by intermediation in general, and by specific kinds of intermediaries in particular, in fulfilling the financial markets' basic purpose of serving the needs of the nonfinancial economy.

The first section of this chapter, Rationales for Financial Intermediation, notes explicitly several of the main rationales underlying the use of financial intermediation. The second section, The Portfolio Behavior of Nonfinancial Investors, relates these considerations to the observed portfolio behavior of participants in the U.S. financial markets other than financial intermediaries, including especially the household sector. The third section, The Dominance of Financial Intermediation, quantifies the role of financial intermediaries, at the aggregate level, in the United States. The fourth section, The Role of Specific Intermediaries, details the respective roles of several specific kinds of intermediaries, including commercial banks, nonbank deposit institutions, life insurance companies and pension funds, and federally sponsored intermediaries. The last section briefly summarizes the chapter's principal points.

RATIONALES FOR FINANCIAL INTERMEDIATION

Three basic rationales typically motivate the reliance on financial intermediaries in the modern economy: benefits of size and specialization, when there are economies of scale in gathering information or in processing transactions; diversification of specific asset risks, when asset holders are risk averse; and pooling of liquidity or other risks, when asset holders themselves face uncertain contingencies.

Benefits of Size and Specialization

Many economic activities exhibit economies of scale, at least up to a point, and what takes place in the financial markets is no exception. At the simplest level, the data processing equipment needed to process many financial transactions efficiently is expensive. Acquiring it is out of the question for all but a few of the largest businesses. The obvious solution is sharing effected by reliance on specialized institutions.

An analogous argument applies to the human capital represented by the specific knowledge required either to operate sophisticated equipment or to perform the purely human aspects of financial transactions. The kinds of human capital involved in the services provided by financial intermediaries go well beyond mere transactions processing, however. The existence of assets bearing uncertain returns, due to either market or specific risk, creates a need for information-related activities. Holders of such assets must first discover the attendant risks, and then monitor them on an ongoing basis. These information costs are especially large in the case of negotiated loans like home mortgages, consumer credit, and bank loans to businesses, although some kinds of securities investments have similar characteristics. Once again, the obvious solution is for most asset holders to delegate these information-gathering and -monitoring costs to specialized third parties.

In some cases economies of scale are sufficiently great that assets simply become indivisible beyond set limits. Many kinds of investments available in today's financial markets have minimum transaction sizes. Real estate assets are a common example, as are participations in newly created business enterprises. In principle, of course, an investor could directly obtain a smaller unit size at some price, but in practice no one does so. In such cases the more straightforward and economically more sensible approach to such indivisibilities is to hold the relevant assets through intermediaries.

Diversification of Specific Asset Risks

Investors who are risk averse care not only about the most likely return associated with their asset holdings, but also about the uncertainty associated with that return. For a given level of uncertainty, of course, investors presumably prefer a higher expected return to a lower one. Conversely, for a given expected return, risk-averse investors prefer less uncertainty to more.

When different assets bear specific risks that are not perfectly correlated—as is the case, for example, among equity investments in different companies—investors can reduce the level of uncertainty associated with the return to their overall portfolios by holding a diverse mix of assets rather than only one. By doing so they can take advantage of the imperfect correlation among the individual asset returns, in effect exploiting the "law of large numbers" as some assets end up delivering higher than expected returns and others lower, to achieve a total portfolio return more likely to fall within any stated range above or below the associated expected return.

Such diversification is, in essence, the motivation behind mutual funds. A risk-averse investor is better off, in the sense of facing less uncertainty for a given expected return, holding a diversified portfolio of equities than holding just one stock. The same argument applies for mortgages, consumer and business loans, and a wide variety of other assets. Rather than betting on whether any single borrower will default, a risk-averse investor is in each case better off holding a portfolio of many such loans.

Because of indivisibilities and economies of scale in asset holding, however, this kind of diversification is not feasible for most individuals or for most nonfinancial businesses acting on their own. Few investors have sufficient capital even to acquire well-diversified equity portfolios consisting of round lots of each security. Fewer still have sufficient capital to acquire and service portfolios of mortgages or other loans. The obvious solution is to achieve the required diversification through intermediation. Financial intermediaries in effect transform assets, therefore, holding assets subject to specific risk while issuing against them claims in which these specific risks are largely diversified away.

Risk Pooling

Risks associated with their portfolios of financial assets are hardly the only kind of risks that individuals and businesses face in today's environment. At the individual level, people can lose their jobs, suffer expensive illnesses, have automobile accidents, or see their houses burned or burgled. Businesses face many of the same contingencies, as well as more directly business-connected risks such as weak market demand, delivery failures, or lawsuits.

The pooling of such risks via explicit insurance arrangements is a longstanding practice, and both life and casualty insurance have been familiar examples of financial intermediation for centuries. By insuring against a specific contingency, an individual or business in effect accepts a cost equal to the average incidence of that contingency within the insured population. Although it is possible to imagine such insurance taking place apart from any financial intermediation per se, in practice almost all insurance arrangements guarantee performance through the holding of financial reserves. Moreover, certain forms of life insurance have traditionally combined saving and risk-pooling features.

Risk spreading via financial intermediation goes well beyond insurance arrangements, however. Banks and other deposit intermediaries in effect pool the liquidity needs of many individual and business depositors. Just as risk pooling makes sense in an insurance context because it is highly improbable that all houses will burn or all automobiles will crash in any year, deposit intermediation is advantageous because not all depositors are likely to want to withdraw their funds on the same day, or even in the same week or month. Deposit intermediaries in effect exploit the imperfect correlation among depositors' uncertain liquidity requirements to achieve yet a further kind of asset transformation, holding portfolios that may consist mostly of highly illiquid assets while issuing against them claims that each depositor can rightly regard as fully liquid. Even some nondeposit intermediaries, such as open-ended mutual funds, perform an analogous transformation.

Because of these three basic economic effects achieved by the intermediation process—exploitation of economies of scale, diversification of specific asset risks, and risk pooling—the development of intermediation in general and of specific intermediary institutions has typically paralleled, and has often spurred, the evolution of modern financial markets.

THE PORTFOLIO BEHAVIOR OF NONFINANCIAL INVESTORS

The function of the financial markets in any economy is to provide for the needs of participants in the nonfinancial economy. On one side, individuals and businesses come to these markets to find financial resources, seeking to issue claims of various forms in exchange for those resources. At the same time, others come with resources to deploy, seeking to acquire in exchange for them some kind of claim on resources in the future. The unwillingness of some individuals and businesses to hold directly the claims that others issue creates the need for intermediation.

Households

In the United States, individuals are the principal *non*financial holders of assets that represent direct claims on other nonfinancial participants in the economy. Figure 1.1 shows that U.S. households have shifted the composition of their financial asset portfolios in important ways during the postwar period.[2] Households' aggregate holdings of deposit-type liabilities of financial intermediaries have grown continually from the early 1950s to the early 1980s, not only absolutely but in relation to overall nonfinancial economic activity (and personal income). Households' claims on insurance and pension reserves have also grown on balance during the postwar years, although here the growth has been less steady because of the effect of equity price changes on the valuation of these reserves. By contrast, households' direct holdings of nonintermediated debt have declined in relative terms almost continually since World War II, and their

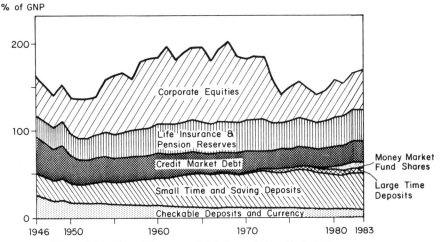

Figure 1.1. Financial assets of U.S. households, 1946–1983.

direct holdings of equity claims on business corporations have varied mostly with equity price fluctuations, exhibiting little overall relative trend.[3] Since the total size of households' financial asset portfolios in relation to the gross national product has also shown no overall trend—first declining during the immediate postwar years, then rising sharply in the 1950s, remaining steady through the 1960s, declining in the 1970s, and then rising again in the early 1980s—these patterns of growth and decline in comparison to the gross national product also correspond, for the postwar period as a whole, to growth or decline in shares of households' aggregate portfolio.

Households' increasing preference for claims on intermediaries has appeared even more pronounced from the perspective of their accumulation of financial assets. Table 1.1 provides an indication of U.S. households' portfolio preferences during the post–World War II period by presenting data, both in dollars and as percentage shares of households' total net acquisition of financial assets, showing the average volume of net acquisition of various specific asset categories. In order to abstract from year-to-year variations, yet still capture significant changes over time, the table presents these data in the form of averages for successive five-year periods (and the three-year average for 1981–1983).

The two features of households' investment behavior that stand out most sharply here are the dominance of deposits and life insurance and pension reserves throughout the postwar period, and the change that took

Table 1.1. Net Acquisitions of Financial Assets by U.S. Households

			Equities				Life Insurance and Pension Reserves	
	Total Assets	Currency and Deposits	Total	Investment Company Shares	Direct Holdings	Credit Market Debt		Other

Billions of Dollars

	Total Assets	Currency and Deposits	Total	Investment Company Shares	Direct Holdings	Credit Market Debt	Life Insurance and Pension Reserves	Other
1946–1950	$ 14.3	$ 3.4	$ 1.0	$ 0.2	$ 0.7	$ 1.2	$ 5.7	$ 3.1
1951–1955	21.8	9.7	1.2	0.5	0.7	3.3	7.6	−0.2
1956–1960	30.5	13.0	1.0	1.4	−0.4	6.5	10.6	−0.5
1961–1965	47.4	27.8	−1.3	2.1	−3.4	4.7	14.3	1.9
1966–1970	66.3	33.5	−3.5	3.9	−7.3	15.8	20.6	−0.1
1971–1975	125.1	80.5	−4.2	0.2	−4.4	25.0	34.0	−10.2
1976–1980	234.2	134.8	−5.7	0.7	−6.4	54.2	70.3	−19.4
1981–1983	339.2	186.9	−6.3	19.3	−25.6	66.8	120.6	−28.8

Percentage of Total Net Acquisitions

	Total Assets	Currency and Deposits	Total	Investment Company Shares	Direct Holdings	Credit Market Debt	Life Insurance and Pension Reserves	Other
1946–1950	100.0	23.9	6.4	1.6	4.8	8.1	39.9	21.7
1951–1955	100.0	44.5	5.7	2.3	3.4	15.3	35.1	−0.7
1956–1960	100.0	42.7	3.5	4.4	−0.9	20.6	34.6	−1.5
1961–1965	100.0	58.2	−2.8	4.4	−7.2	10.1	30.6	3.9
1966–1970	100.0	48.5	−5.1	6.0	−11.1	25.4	31.3	−0.2
1971–1975	100.0	65.9	−3.5	−0.3	−3.8	18.4	27.2	−8.0
1976–1980	100.0	58.2	−2.4	0.2	−2.6	22.4	30.0	−8.2
1981–1983	100.0	55.1	−1.9	5.7	−7.5	19.7	35.6	−8.5

SOURCE: Board of Governors of the Federal Reserve System.

NOTE: Data are averages of annual flows, in dollars and as percentages of annual total net acquisitions. Detail may not add to totals because of rounding.

place at the end of the 1950s in households' net investment in corporate equities. Except for the first few postwar years, U.S. households have consistently invested two-fifths or more of their financial saving in deposits and currency. In more recent years, except for the late 1960s, the fraction going into monetary instruments has been well in excess of one-half. The devotion of approximately one-third of financial saving to life insurance and pension forms has been a steady feature of household behavior ever since World War II.

Although U.S. households purchased more equity shares in corporations than they sold in every year during 1946–1957, so that the tripling in value of their direct equity holdings over this period represented the combined result of capital gains and positive net purchases, in every year since 1958 they have sold more direct equity shares than they have purchased. Capital gains have therefore accounted for more than all of the increase in total value of their direct equity holdings during this period. Moreover, allowing for the shift from direct ownership of equities to indirect ownership via mutual funds does not alter this picture of individuals' investment behavior. Households in the aggregate were net purchasers of mutual fund shares during the rise of that industry in the 1960s, and have been again during 1980–1983, but in neither period were mutual fund purchases sufficient to offset the liquidation of their direct equity holdings. During the 1970s households were net sellers of both direct equity holdings and mutual fund shares. Hence the conclusion stands that equity price movements have accounted for more than all of any increase in the value of individuals' equity holdings for the past quarter of a century. Because equity prices have fluctuated widely but shown little net gain since the mid-1960s, even in nominal terms, the aggregate equity portfolio of individuals in the United States has shown no trend movement in nominal value and has declined in relative value during the last decade and more.

This shift of individuals' investment flows away from equities during the second half of the postwar period probably reflects several considerations in addition to the economies-of-scale and diversification motives noted above as general advantages of intermediation. No doubt changing birth rates, age distributions, and income levels have all played some role. The increasing government provision of health, education, and income security benefits has also altered the objectives associated with saving for many people. The growing importance of workers' claims on future pension benefits, including job-specific pensions in both the private and public sectors and also Social Security, has especially changed many people's need to accumulate assets directly to finance their retirement.[4] Perceptions of the relative returns and risks associated with different assets, including both debt and equity securities, have also changed markedly during the postwar period. After the official unpegging of bond prices in 1951, fixed-income securities became subject to market risk in addition to inflation risk, and since the 1970s both inflation risk and market risk have increased dramatically. During most of the 1950s and 1960s renewed confidence in economic stability and prosperity lessened fears of any collapse of equity values comparable to that of 1929–1933, and in addition many people regarded equities as a "hedge" against price inflation.[5] Following the rapid acceleration of inflation and the poor performance of both equity prices and the U.S. economy during the 1970s, however, prevailing opinion became progressively more skeptical both of the economy's long-run growth prospects and of the usefulness of equities as an inflation hedge.[6]

Apart from equities, holdings of direct claims against other nonfinancial participants in the economy have always constituted a relatively small fraction of U.S. households' aggregate portfolios. As Table 1.1 shows, net acquisitions of such debt have accounted for less than one-fourth of households' financial saving throughout the postwar period. Against this background of households' aversion to holding direct claims in either debt or equity form, the need for financial intermediation is readily apparent.

Other Nonfinancial Investors

Although individuals are the dominant nonfinancial holders of direct claims on other nonfinancial participants in the U.S. economy, businesses also advance a substantial amount of direct credit, both to individuals in the form of installment and other consumer credit, and to each other in the form of trade credit and commercial paper. Even with the ready availability of business credit cards and charge accounts, however, commercial banks and finance companies have increasingly dominated the consumer credit field. The share of outstanding consumer credit owed to nonfinancial businesses (including corporations and others) has fallen from just over one-third in the early 1950s to just under one-sixth since the 1970s. In addition, business lending via purchases of nonfinancial commercial paper has remained relatively small, so that trade credit—typically equal to 15 to 18% of the gross national product, and mostly borrowed and lent within the corporate sector—remains the primary vehicle for businesses' holdings of direct claims on nonfinancial obligors.

Foreign investors have held a small but growing share of direct claims on nonfinancial participants in the U.S. economy throughout the postwar period.[7] The growth of foreign holdings was especially rapid during the 1970s, as the persistent U.S. balance of payments deficit transferred assets abroad, especially to member countries of the international oil cartel. This rapid growth proceeded from a small base, however, so that foreign holdings still represented less than 5% of all direct claims against U.S. non-financial obligors as of year-end 1983. Nevertheless, the concentration of foreign (especially foreign official) investments in specific instruments has made foreign holdings of somewhat greater importance in several U.S. markets. The year-end 1983 share of federal government securities held abroad, for example, was approximately one-tenth.

In sum, neither individuals nor other nonfinancial entities participating in the U.S. financial markets, including businesses and foreign investors, have shown much willingness to hold direct claims on U.S. individuals and businesses. Instead, they have largely left that task to financial intermediaries.

THE DOMINANCE OF FINANCIAL INTERMEDIATION

Figures 1.2 and 1.3 indicate the extent to which the increasing preference for claims on financial intermediaries by individuals (and, to a lesser extent, by other nonfinancial investors) has shifted to intermediaries the task of

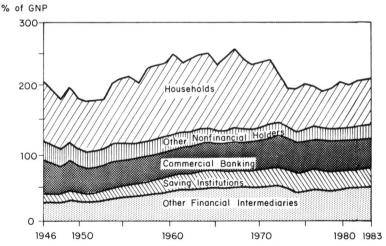

Figure 1.2. Holders of claims (including equities) against U.S. nonfinancial sectors, 1946–1983.

% of GNP

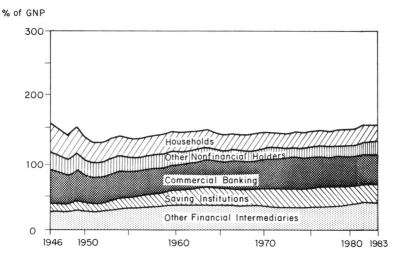

Figure 1.3. Holders of claims (excluding equities) against U.S. nonfinancial sectors, 1946–1983.

meeting the needs that nonfinancial participants in the economy have brought to the U.S. financial markets. As of 1983 individuals in the aggregate remained the largest single class of holders of all direct claims on nonfinancial borrowers and share issuers—but only by virtue of their continuing domination of the ownership of corporate equities, as the contrast between Figures 1.2 and 1.3 shows. On an overall basis, however, the household share either including or excluding equities has declined, as has the share held by all other nonfinancial investors. As the share of direct claims on nonfinancial entities held by all *non*financial investors has declined, the share held by financial intermediaries has correspondingly risen. Intermediaries' holdings first accounted for the majority of all direct claims outstanding in the U.S. financial markets (including equities) in 1969, and they have remained the majority ever since.

Table 1.2 presents flow data indicating the even stronger postwar dominance of intermediaries in meeting the new funds required each year by nonfinancial participants in the U.S. economy. The table shows data both in dollars and as percentage shares of all net funds extended to all nonfinancial sectors. As in Table 1.1, the data are in the form of five-year averages (and the three-year average for 1981–1983). Also as in Table 1.1, these data exclude equity capital gains, which constituted most of the increase in households' equity holdings until the late 1960s, and more than all of the increase since then.

Table 1.2. U.S. Credit Market Funds Advanced to Nonfinancial Sectors

					Financial Intermediaries			
	Total	Private-Domestic Nonfinancial Investors	Federal Government	Foreign	Total	Commercial Banks	Savings Institutions	Other
Billions of Dollars								
1946–1950	$ 12.2	$ 3.1	$ 0.3	$ 0.0	$ 8.8	$ 0.6	$ 2.7	$ 5.5
1951–1955	30.6	6.7	0.6	0.7	22.6	5.6	5.6	11.3
1956–1960	37.8	5.6	0.8	1.3	30.0	7.4	8.6	14.0
1961–1965	58.3	2.4	1.0	0.7	54.1	18.1	14.6	21.4
1966–1970	87.5	4.5	2.4	3.1	77.5	28.2	13.0	36.3
1971–1975	181.7	24.2	4.1	12.8	140.6	49.9	35.4	55.3
1976–1980	339.1	33.8	11.8	25.3	268.3	87.0	59.1	122.2
1981–1983	441.8	49.5	11.8	24.6	355.7	107.3	37.5	211.0
Percentage of Total Funds Advanced								
1946–1950	100.0	41.2	3.2	3.3	53.3	26.9	5.5	19.9
1951–1955	100.0	20.8	2.1	2.2	74.8	19.4	18.1	37.3
1956–1960	100.0	13.4	2.1	3.4	81.2	20.3	23.1	37.7
1961–1965	100.0	4.1	1.8	1.3	92.7	30.8	25.3	36.6
1966–1970	100.0	5.5	2.8	3.0	88.7	32.2	14.8	41.7
1971–1975	100.0	12.6	2.1	7.5	77.7	27.7	19.6	30.4
1976–1980	100.0	10.0	3.4	7.6	79.0	25.4	18.0	35.6
1981–1983	100.0	10.5	2.9	5.6	81.0	24.3	7.4	49.3

SOURCE: Board of Governors of the Federal Reserve System.

NOTE: Data are averages of annual flows, in dollars and as percentages of annual total funds advanced. Detail may not add to totals because of rounding.

Apart from accumulating capital gains on equities, individuals and other private domestic nonfinancial investors have played only a small role in meeting directly the needs that nonfinancial entities have brought to the U.S. financial markets.[8] Similarly, the role of the federal government has been consistently small in this context, and that of foreign investors has grown but remains small nonetheless. In part because of the growing fraction of nonfinancial sectors' needs that have come in the form of debt issued by private borrowers rather than government borrowers (at least until the 1980s),[9] as well as for other reasons related to financial innovation, nonfinancial investors have instead accumulated claims on intermediaries and have left to them the task of directly allocating the economy's financial resources. As Table 1.2 also shows, banks, savings institutions, and nondeposit intermediaries have all been significant participants in this process.

THE ROLE OF SPECIFIC INTERMEDIARIES

The advance of intermediation in the U.S. financial markets since World War II has hardly been uniform. The specialization of financial intermediaries has inevitably led to more important roles for some than for others, and more rapid growth for some than for others, as the needs and objectives of both borrowers and lenders have changed, and as government interventions have (intentionally or otherwise) favored first one kind of institution and then another.

Commercial Banks

The commercial banking system has long stood at the center of attention devoted to financial markets. Even today, despite several decades of increasing importance of nonbank intermediaries,[10] many kinds of discussions ranging from textbook descriptions of the economy to professional evaluations of monetary policy often proceed as if commercial banks were the only intermediaries in the U.S. financial markets. This emphasis on the commercial banking system is understandable in part, in view of the special role that banks play in the monetary policy process by virtue of their relationship to the Federal Reserve System. In addition, in the past commercial banks were more dominant in financial market activity than they are today. Earlier in this century banks' assets and liabilities dwarfed those of other intermediaries, and before passage of the Glass-Steagall Act in 1933 commercial banks also dominated the securities business.[11]

Table 1.3. Assets and Liabilities of U.S. Commercial Banks

	Financial Assets					Financial Liabilities			
	Total	Treasury Debt	Government Agency Debt	State and Local Debt	Loans	Total	Demand Deposits	Non-CD Time Deposits	CDs
Percent of GNP									
1946–1950	54.8	26.7	0.6	2.3	16.0	51.1	35.4	14.0	0.0
1951–1955	47.1	17.5	0.8	3.0	18.6	43.8	29.6	12.0	0.0
1956–1960	45.1	13.2	0.5	3.4	22.2	41.6	25.8	13.3	0.0
1961–1965	47.0	10.6	0.7	4.8	26.1	43.5	22.6	16.6	1.5
1966–1970	49.1	6.9	1.1	6.3	30.1	46.0	19.4	19.7	2.2
1971–1975	52.7	5.0	2.0	7.1	34.0	49.7	17.1	22.3	4.6
1976–1980	50.6	4.6	2.0	5.6	33.6	47.7	13.5	17.9	9.1
1981–1983	51.0	4.5	2.4	4.9	34.1	48.1	11.6	19.4	9.3
Percentage of Total Financial Assets									
1946–1950	100.0	48.3	1.1	4.3	29.5	93.2	64.6	25.4	0.0
1951–1955	100.0	37.1	1.6	6.5	39.6	93.0	62.8	25.6	0.0
1956–1960	100.0	29.1	1.1	7.5	49.4	92.3	57.1	29.7	0.1
1961–1965	100.0	22.2	1.6	10.3	55.8	92.7	47.8	35.5	3.3
1966–1970	100.0	14.0	2.3	12.8	61.4	93.6	39.4	40.1	4.4
1971–1975	100.0	9.4	3.9	13.3	64.6	94.3	32.1	42.3	9.0
1976–1980	100.0	9.1	4.0	11.1	66.6	94.2	26.7	35.4	18.1
1981–1983	100.0	8.7	4.7	9.7	66.9	94.3	22.6	38.0	18.3

SOURCE: Board of Governors of the Federal Reserve System

NOTE: Data are averages of year-end amounts, as percentages of annual fourth-quarter gross national product, seasonally adjusted at annual rates, and as percentages of annual year-end total assets. Detail may not add to totals because of rounding.

Until as recently as the early 1970s, commercial banks in the United States enjoyed a monopoly on the right to issue checkable deposits.

Since World War II, the U.S. commercial banking system has just about held its own in relation to the scale of nonfinancial economic activity, but it has not participated in the economy's overall postwar expansion of intermediation. The approximate stability of the banking system's relative size is apparent in Figure 1.3, and also in the more detailed data on commercial banks' assets and liabilities in relation to the gross national product presented in the upper half of Table 1.3. The total size of the banking system in relation to gross national product has shown essentially no trend during the postwar period. As Figure 1.4 shows, there has been little postwar trend in the "income velocity" of bank credit, which consists of most commercial bank earning assets. This relative stability stands in marked contrast to the prewar years when, over nearly a century, the size of the banking system continually grew in relation to the gross national product.[12]

Within the stability of the overall totals, however, the postwar years have also seen substantial shifts in composition on both sides of the banking system's balance sheet, as is clear from the percentage share data presented in the lower half of Table 1.3. Among bank assets, the most significant development during this period has been the postwar (really post-depression) recovery of bank loan portfolios, and hence the general resumption of banks' traditional role as "inside" intermediaries. In 1929 loans constituted 73% of bank credit. During the depression and then the

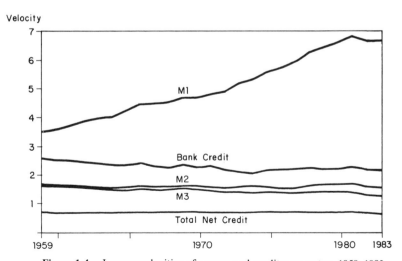

Figure 1.4. Income velocities of money and credit aggregates, 1959–1983.

war years, however, the falling off in private debt-issuing activity meant that, for all practical purposes, there was little or no loan business to be had. By contrast, the federal government was then issuing debt in record volume, and banks participated in financing it. By 1935 banks' securities investments exceeded their loan portfolios, and in 1945 investments constituted 79% of bank credit. Commercial banks simply were no longer very commercial. The years since 1946 have largely consisted of a reversal of the 1930–1945 pattern, with bank loans exceeding securities investments in 1957 for the first time in more than two decades, and standing again at 73% of total bank credit as of year-end 1983.

In rebuilding their loan portfolios and deemphasizing their investments, banks have both altered the mix of their lending business and changed the character of their securities holdings. Although banks remain a principal source of business credit, and commercial and industrial loans are still the largest single category of bank lending, these loans no longer dominate bank loan portfolios as they once did. Instead, mortgage credit and other consumer loans now comprise more than one-third of the total. Especially during the second half of the postwar period, the widespread use of bank-issued credit cards has been a major element in banks' development of their consumer lending business. Moreover, among business loans per se, the larger banks have increasingly become a major factor in the intermediate-term credit market through the use of explicitly longer-maturity loans (in some cases up to 10 years) and revolving credits of an implicitly ongoing nature. Total bank investments have grown slowly since World War II, but because of tax incentives banks have so concentrated their investments on state and local government issues that, for a few years in the early 1970s, they held more of these securities than of federal government debt.[13]

Among bank liabilities, the two most significant changes that have occurred during the postwar period have been the continual decline of demand balances and increase of time and saving deposits, relative to either total bank liabilities or gross national product, and the "liability management revolution" that has greatly increased the larger banks' reliance on "bought funds." As Figure 1.4 shows, the income velocity of the narrow M1 money stock, consisting of currency plus checkable deposits, has about tripled over the postwar years as a result of a combination of influences including economies of scale in the public's holding of cash balances, the secular rise in nominal interest rates, and the increasingly widespread use of credit cards and charge accounts.[14] This persistent trend increase in M1 velocity stands in sharp contrast to both the absence of any trend during 1910–1930 and the steeply declining trend during 1930–1945. Only the strong growth of time and savings deposits, including the new negotiable certificates of deposit that first came into existence in 1961, has accounted for the absence of much postwar trend in the income velocity of the broader M2 and M3. Total net credit, consisting of the outstanding debt of all U.S. obligors other than financial intermediaries, has also shown no velocity trend.

Large banks' growing use of such liabilities as certificates of deposit, federal funds, Eurodollar borrowings, commercial paper issues, repurchase agreements, and so on—instruments that in some cases represent the development of new financial markets since World War II—has not only changed banks' balance sheets but has also facilitated a major change in the feasible aggressiveness of bank lending practices. The enormous postwar expansion of bank loan portfolios, which banks have achieved in part through the competitive use of such devices as loan commitments and medium-term credits, would probably have been impossible if banks had simply continued to follow the classic practice of treating their deposits (and other liabilities) as determined by outside forces.

Finally, it is useful to point out explicitly that because of changes in commercial bank organization, especially during the 1960s, the representation of banks as having merely held their own during the postwar increase in the U.S. economy's reliance on financial intermediation relative to economic activity risks understating by a wide margin the growing overall presence of commercial banks in the financial system. After falling by more than one-half between 1920 and 1935, the number of American commercial banks has remained roughly steady at about 14,000. The number of bank branches, however, has risen from some 4,000 to over 39,000 during the postwar years, with most of this growth occurring since 1960. Moreover, especially since the 1970 Amendments to the Bank Holding Company Act and the 1980 Depository Institutions Deregulation and Monetary Control Act, banks have increasingly entered activities other than their traditional loan and deposit business. Most recently, these extensions of activity have included indirect participation in the securities brokerage business. Although their direct participation in financial intermediation has not kept pace with the rising postwar trend, commercial banks have increasingly enhanced their importance as more nearly full-service financial institutions.

Nonbank Deposit Institutions

As is clear from Figure 1.3, one group of intermediaries that has accounted for much of the post–World War II increase in U.S. financial intermediation has been the nonbank deposit institutions, including savings and loan associations, mutual savings banks, and credit unions. The public's strong demand for consumer-type time and savings deposits has enabled these institutions to grow rapidly, not just absolutely but in relation to economic activity, during most of the postwar period. Their growth has been great enough to offset the relative stagnation of the commercial banking system, so that the income velocities of the M2 and M3 money stocks have shown a modest downward trend. When extrapolated backward, this trend appears to have been a continuation of the downward trend associated with corresponding aggregates during the prewar era when nonbank deposit institutions were not of major importance.

Table 1.4 presents data for the individual deposit (or share) volume and combined asset holdings of the three major groups of nonbank deposit institutions, first in relation to gross national product and then as a share of the total assets of the three groups of institutions together. The postwar expansion of the savings and loan industry stands out clearly here. Between the early postwar years and the 1970s outstanding savings and loan shares more than quadrupled as a percentage of gross national product. By 1983 the amount of these shares was well over twice the amount of mutual savings bank deposits and credit union shares combined, and was almost equal to the amount of consumer-type time and savings deposits held at commercial banks. In comparison with mutual savings banks, the primary factor underlying the more rapid growth of savings and loan associations has probably been mere geography; mutual savings banks are overwhelmingly concentrated in a few states, especially New York and Massachusetts, which have experienced slower than average economic growth since World War II. In comparison with commercial banks, the primary factor at work has probably been the effect of government regulation, in that savings and loan associations did not face deposit interest rate ceilings until 1965 and enjoyed a 0.25% differential over commercial banks for many years thereafter. The growth of credit unions has been even faster than that of savings and loan associations, but credit unions constitute another example of rapid growth from a small base, and they remain by far the smallest of the three groups of institutions. Mutual savings banks are alone among the three groups in having failed to do more than grow in pace with economic activity. Although mutual savings banks were twice as large as savings and loan associations at the end of World War II, savings and loans were equal in size in 1954 and larger by a factor of four by 1983.

The history of nonbank deposit institutions in the United States since World War II has been in large part a story of evolving financial regulation, including restrictions on these intermediaries' liability issuing as well as their asset holding. Especially because these institutions operate under legal and regulatory constraints governing the disposition of their asset

Table 1.4.   Assets and Liabilities of U.S. Nonbank Deposit Institutions

	Combined Financial Assets			Liabilities by Institution		
	Total	Mortgages	Consumer Credit	Savings and Loan Shares	Mutual Savings Bank Deposits	Credit Union Shares
Percentage of GNP						
1946–1950	13.4	6.3	0.3	4.3	7.2	0.2
1951–1955	15.3	9.7	0.5	6.3	6.6	0.5
1956–1960	21.0	15.0	1.0	10.3	7.1	0.8
1961–1965	26.9	20.5	1.3	14.7	7.3	1.2
1966–1970	27.0	20.9	1.6	14.7	7.2	1.4
1971–1975	30.2	22.3	2.1	16.8	7.2	1.8
1976–1980	32.4	23.1	2.5	19.0	6.3	2.3
1981–1983	31.2	19.1	2.4	18.6	5.1	2.5
Percentage of Total Combined Financial Assets						
1946–1950	100.0	47.4	2.2	32.3	53.5	1.8
1951–1955	100.0	63.4	3.3	41.2	43.0	3.0
1956–1960	100.0	71.4	4.4	50.0	33.9	4.0
1961–1965	100.0	76.4	5.0	54.7	27.1	4.4
1966–1970	100.0	77.3	6.0	54.5	26.6	5.2
1971–1975	100.0	73.9	7.0	56.0	23.5	6.2
1976–1980	100.0	71.2	7.8	58.6	19.4	7.2
1981–1983	100.0	61.5	7.5	59.8	16.3	8.2

SOURCE: Board of Governors of the Federal Reserve System.

NOTE: Data are averages of year-end amounts, as percentages of annual fourth-quarter gross national product, seasonally adjusted at annual rates, and as percentages of annual year-end total combined financial assets. Detail may not add to totals because of rounding.

portfolios (although many of these constraints were eased by legislation in 1980 and 1982), their aggregate contribution to meeting the financial needs of nonfinancial participants in the economy has followed a fairly predictable pattern. Savings and loan associations and mutual savings banks both typically invest the majority of their assets in mortgages, so that these two groups together have become the nation's leading provider of mortgage lending. This dominance has lessened somewhat in recent years, however, especially with the increasing prominence of the federally sponsored mortgage pools. As of year-end 1983, savings and loan associations and mutual savings banks together held more than one-third of all outstanding mortgages, down from nearly one-half only a few years earlier. (By comparison, commercial banks held less than one-fifth of all outstanding mortgages as of 1983.) Credit unions have instead traditionally invested most of their assets in consumer installment loans, and as of 1983 they accounted for just over one-tenth of the outstanding consumer credit.

Private Nondeposit Intermediaries

As is also apparent from Figure 1.3, a significant part of the post–World War II increase in the U.S. economy's reliance on financial intermediation has stemmed from neither commercial banks nor nonbank deposit institutions but, instead, from intermediaries that issue only nondeposit claims. There are many forms of such intermediaries operating in the U.S. markets, but among the most familiar and important are life and casualty insurance companies, private- and public-sector pension funds, independent consumer finance companies and the "captive" finance companies of nonfinancial businesses, equity and money market mutual funds, real estate investment trusts, and securities brokers and dealers.

Table 1.5 presents data analogous to those shown above for the nonbank deposit institutions for three specific categories of U.S. nondeposit intermediaries:[15] life insurance companies, private pension funds, and state and local government pension funds. The reason for focusing particularly on these three kinds of institutions is not only that they are the largest of the nondeposit intermediaries but also that their postwar experience reflects interesting contrasts. Because the low returns paid on the savings component of ordinary life insurance have increasingly prompted the use of group and other term insurance policies, life insurance companies' total assets held and liabilities outstanding grew little relative to gross national product during the first half of the postwar period; and since then they have mostly been declining in relative terms. Moreover, the relative decline in these companies' life insurance business has been even more pronounced, in that their growth in recent years has consisted disproportionately of pensions that they manage for other businesses. As of year-

Table 1.5. Assets of U.S. Life Insurance Companies and Pension Funds

	Combined Financial Assets				Financial Assets by Institutions		
	Total	Equities	Corporate Bonds	Mortgages	Life Insurance Companies	Private Pensions	State and Local Government Pensions
Percentage of GNP							
1946–1950	24.6	0.8	8.2	4.3	21.2	1.9	1.4
1951–1955	26.3	1.6	10.8	6.5	20.8	3.3	2.2
1956–1960	31.8	3.4	13.2	8.3	22.3	6.2	3.3
1961–1965	36.0	6.1	14.3	9.1	22.3	9.2	4.5
1966–1970	36.8	8.3	14.0	9.0	20.6	10.8	5.4
1971–1975	35.1	10.2	12.9	6.7	18.4	10.4	6.4
1976–1980	33.2	8.7	12.5	5.4	17.0	9.3	6.8
1981–1983	36.5	9.7	11.9	5.1	17.8	10.5	8.2
Percentage of Total Combined Financial Assets							
1946–1950	100.0	3.3	33.4	17.4	86.4	7.7	5.9
1951–1955	100.0	6.0	41.1	24.9	79.1	12.6	8.3
1956–1960	100.0	10.6	41.4	26.1	70.0	19.4	10.5
1961–1965	100.0	17.0	39.7	25.3	62.0	25.6	12.4
1966–1970	100.0	22.6	38.1	24.3	55.9	29.3	14.8
1971–1975	100.0	29.0	36.7	19.6	52.4	29.5	18.1
1976–1980	100.0	26.2	37.8	16.3	51.4	28.0	20.6
1981–1983	100.0	26.5	32.6	13.9	48.7	28.8	22.5

SOURCE: Board of Governors of the Federal Reserve System.

NOTE: Data are averages of year-end amounts, as percentages of annual fourth-quarter gross national product, seasonally adjusted at annual rates, and as percentages of annual year-end total combined financial assets. Detail may not add to totals because of rounding.

end 1983 pension reserves constituted more than two-fifths of U.S. life insurance companies' total liabilities, up from less than one-tenth in the early postwar years.

By contrast, both private- and public-sector pensions have experienced extraordinarily rapid growth throughout these years.[16] Tax incentives at both the individual and corporate levels, business personnel policies aimed at reducing worker turnover, features of the collective bargaining process, and other corporate financial objectives have all combined to favor the mushrooming of private pension liabilities since World War II. During most of this period, however, businesses had (and many used) broad latitude to incur pension liabilities without funding them. The 1974 Employee Retirement Income Security Act subsequently specified minimum standards for the vesting of workers' rights to accumulated pension benefits and for employers' funding of vested pension liabilities. Even so, businesses retain important flexibility in choosing the actuarial assumptions underlying the calculation of future benefits, the minimum required amortization of unfunded vested benefits is very slow, and nonvested benefits require no funding at all. Consequently, many businesses continue to carry substantial amounts of unfunded liabilities, so that private pension funds' total assets as shown in Table 1.5 substantially understate their liabilities.[17] This understatement was especially great during the 1970s when many private pension funds' asset portfolios, more than half of which in the aggregate is invested in equities, suffered an erosion in market value.

State and local government pensions, including both teachers' and other employees' funds, have experienced similar postwar growth. Public-sector workers have the same tax incentive to use the pension mechanism to spread income beyond retirement as do private-sector workers. Although public-sector employers do not have the same tax incentives as do private businesses, in many cases the political process has favored the use of pension compensation over current compensation, especially when there is no pressure to raise tax or other revenues immediately to fund the accumulating pension liabilities. Hence public-sector pension funds have been and remain substantially underfunded, so that the asset data shown in Table 1.5 greatly understate their liabilities also.[18] The continued growth of public-sector pensions' assets during the 1970s, in contrast to that of private pensions, reflects merely the smaller share of assets invested in equities by public-sector funds' portfolios (about one-third in the aggregate) rather than any difference in funding practices.

The asset mix of these insurance and pension intermediaries—and hence their role in financing economic activity—has undergone important changes since World War II. Regulatory changes in the 1960s allowed many life insurance companies to increase the equity portion of their port-folios, and since the mid-1960s life insurers have largely withdrawn from direct home mortgage lending. State and local government pension funds and especially private pension funds have even more dramatically in-creased the equity share of their investments. Consequently, these non-deposit intermediaries have increasingly become a major source of both debt and equity funds for corporate businesses. As a result of these port-folio changes, together with the rapid growth of pensions and the (relative) stagnation of the commercial banking system, insurance companies and pension funds combined have increasingly dominated banks as holders of claims on the U.S. corporate business sector—despite banks' postwar emphasis on loans over investments in government securities. In the early postwar years these nondeposit intermediaries held only slightly more claims on the corporate sector than did commercial banks, but by the 1970s they held more than twice as much.

It is also important to distinguish the claims on business held by banks, which are overwhelmingly in the form of short- to medium-term loans, from the corresponding claims held by insurance companies and pension funds, which consist mostly of long-term debt and equity securities. These nondeposit intermediaries have traditionally held more than two-thirds of all outstanding corporate bonds, and in recent years they have also come to hold about one-sixth of all corporate equity. On a flow basis, these investors have been of even greater importance in providing long-term debt and equity capital to U.S. business corporations. In addition to ac-counting for much or all of the corporate sector's net long-term bond fi-nancing throughout the postwar period, since 1960 they have accounted for more than all of its equity financing, absorbing also the equity holdings liquidated by the household sector. In sum, businesses' equity and bond financing has become increasingly dominated by these nondeposit inter-mediaries. Given their high rates of portfolio turnover, especially in com-parison with individuals, equity and bond trading has become even more so.

Government-Sponsored Intermediaries

Another important change that has come about in the U.S. financial mar-kets since World War II has been the great increase in the federal gov-ernment's activities as an intermediary for (and also a guarantor of) private credit. "Off-budget" sponsored credit agencies like the Federal Home Loan Bank System and the Federal Intermediate Credit Bank were in operation before World War II, but the scale of their lending operations was small then. As of 1946, all of these agencies combined held only about $2 billion in assets, the majority of which consisted of agricultural loans, and they owed only $2 billion in liabilities. The focus of these agencies' activity turned more toward support for home building after the Federal National Mortgage Association began its lending operations in 1955, but as late as 1960, when their combined assets had reached $11 billion, their total agricultural credit outstanding still exceeded their total housing credit. Only since the 1960s, as the interaction of deposit interest rate ceilings with rising nominal interest rates led to the introduction of large-scale support for housing, did government financial intermediation begin to increase rapidly.

Table 1.6 presents data comparable to those shown above for other groups of intermediaries for the assets of the federally sponsored credit agencies and the even more recent mortgage "pools" like the Government National Mortgage Association and the Federal Home Loan Mortgage Corporation. Government-sponsored intermediation has grown rapidly, not just absolutely but in relation to gross national product. By 1983 these intermediaries held more than one-fifth of all outstanding home mortgages and more than two-fifths of all outstanding farm debt. Moreover, the total housing credit advanced by these intermediaries, which have grown especially rapidly since the onset of periodic disintermediation in the mid-1960s, includes not only direct purchases of mortgages but also Federal Home Loan Bank advances to savings and loan associations, so that the effective amount is even greater. Federally sponsored intermediaries accounted for 45%, 48%, 52%, and 100% of the total net extensions of single-family home mortgage credit in the high-disintermediation years 1969, 1970, 1974, and 1982, respectively.[19]

Federally sponsored intermediaries conduct their business much the way private intermediaries do, acquiring financial assets on either a loan or purchase basis, and in turn issuing their own liabilities. There are at least two important differences, however. One is that government intermediaries do not operate subject to the profit motive alone. While they typically pursue a profit objective, they do so within the limitations imposed by their charter to support areas of economic activity designated by Congress as public policy priorities.[20] The other key difference is that the liabilities of the mortgage pools and some of the sponsored credit agencies are directly guaranteed by the federal government and accordingly pay interest geared to that on federal government securities. Hence government intermediation also provides some degree of subsidy in the form of access to less expensive (because less risky, by virtue of the guarantee) credit.[21]

The federal government's role as a credit guarantor, which is not limited

Table 1.6. Assets of U.S.-Sponsored Credit Agencies and Mortgage Pools

	Combined Financial Assets			Housing Credit	Loans to Agriculture
	Total	Agencies	Mortgage Pools		
Percentage of GNP					
1946–1950	1.0	1.0	0.0	0.2	0.7
1951–1955	1.1	1.1	0.0	0.3	0.6
1956–1960	1.8	1.8	0.0	0.7	0.8
1961–1965	2.5	2.4	0.1	1.1	1.1
1966–1970	3.7	3.4	0.3	2.0	1.4
1971–1975	6.3	5.0	1.3	4.2	1.8
1976–1980	9.3	6.0	3.2	6.7	2.2
1981–1983	13.5	7.8	5.7	10.2	2.4
Percentage of Total Combined Financial Assets					
1946–1950	100.0	99.7	0.3	18.7	65.9
1951–1955	100.0	98.3	1.6	25.0	58.8
1956–1960	100.0	97.8	2.1	36.0	45.1
1961–1965	100.0	96.6	3.4	43.0	42.4
1966–1970	100.0	92.2	7.8	50.0	38.8
1971–1975	100.0	79.5	20.5	65.0	28.1
1976–1980	100.0	65.4	34.6	71.8	23.6
1981–1983	100.0	58.1	41.9	75.1	17.9

SOURCE: Board of Governors of the Federal Reserve System.

NOTE: Data are averages of year-end amounts, as percentages of annual fourth-quarter gross national product, at seasonally adjusted annual rates, and as percentages of annual year-end total combined financial assets. Detail may not add to totals because of rounding.

to the financial intermediation that it sponsors, is itself an important factor that has had great influence on the U.S. economy's reliance on financial intermediation. Deposit insurance provided by the Federal Deposit Insurance Corporation and the Federal Savings and Loan Insurance Corporation constitutes the most prevalent form of government-sponsored guarantee provided for a fee. It significantly alters the character of the liabilities that private-sector deposit intermediaries can offer. Other familiar government-sponsored agencies providing guarantees for a fee include the Veterans Administration, the Federal Housing Authority, the Overseas Investors Protection Corporation, the Security Investors Protection Corporation, and, most recently, the Pension Benefit Guarantee Corporation. The federal government has also sponsored large-scale loan guarantee programs for diverse borrowers ranging from college students and small businesses to the Lockheed and Chrysler Corporations and New York City. In all, the government's 1983 outstanding credit and credit guarantees—including direct loans, formally guaranteed loans, and other loans by federally sponsored lenders—totaled $848 billion, compared with $986 billion of direct federal debt obligations outstanding and held outside the federal government (including the Federal Reserve System).

This post–World War II growth in the U.S. economy's reliance on federal government intermediation, deposit insurance, and other credit guarantees has probably been to a great extent a counterpart of the government's waning role as a direct borrower. Given the substantial decline (relative to nonfinancial activity) in the federal government's outstanding debt, and the corresponding increase in the outstanding debt of private nonfinancial borrowers,[22] the U.S. financial markets have increasingly attempted to make private obligations more acceptable to the economy's ultimate wealth holders by converting them into government obligations via government insurance and credit guarantees. Along with the increase in private financial intermediation, the growth of government credit guarantees broadly defined—including some that are merely implicit—has enabled the U.S. financial system to absorb with substantial success the large postwar shift in the public versus private mix of the economy's debt.

SUMMARY

Intermediation is a hallmark of all highly developed financial systems, and the United States is no exception. The U.S. financial markets are heavily intermediated, and since World War II they have become progressively more so.

The principal forces that give rise to financial intermediation are benefits of size and specialization, the diversification of specific asset risks, and the pooling of even broader classes of risk. Each is a significant factor in accounting for the U.S. economy's reliance on intermediation. Since World War II, a further important factor has been the economy's continual shift away from government debt toward the debt of private nonfinancial entities including individuals and businesses. Nonfinancial investors (primarily individuals) have exhibited a strong preference for holding the debt of these nonfinancial borrowers via financial intermediaries rather than directly.

As the U.S. economy's reliance on financial intermediaries overall has increased during the postwar period, some specific kinds of intermediary institutions have grown more rapidly than others. Commercial banks have about held their own in relative terms, while steadily shifting their basic business back toward lending activities and away from securities investments. Nonbank deposit intermediaries have grown in relation to overall economic and financial activity, as the growth of savings and loan associations has more than offset the (relative) decline of mutual savings banks. Among private nondeposit intermediaries, life insurance companies have declined in relative terms while both public- and private-sector pension funds have shown exceptionally rapid growth. Finally, the federal government's participation in the financial intermediation process in the United States has also increased rapidly during these years, in part as a result of the pressures created by the economy's shift from government debt to private debt.

NOTES

1. See Goldsmith (1958, 1969) and Gurley and Shaw (1960) for an analysis of the prior experience.
2. The discussion here (and the data plotted in Figure 1.1 and used in Table 1.1 below) refers only to financial assets and hence excludes nonfinancial assets like houses and consumer durables. As of year-end 1983, households' nonfinancial assets, valued at replacement cost, totaled $4.8 trillion (of which $2.2 trillion was residential real estate), compared with $8.3 trillion of financial assets. The available current-value data on nonfinancial asset holdings are understandably weak.
3. Moreover, these data overstate households' direct equity holdings in that they do not separate holdings via mutual funds, which grew from 2% of total equity holdings on average during 1946–1950 to 6% on average during 1976–1980.
4. Feldstein (1974), for example, derived a large estimate of Social Security "wealth" (defined as the present discounted value of expected future benefits) and found evidence of a significant impact of Social Security on private saving behavior. Although this

work and the literature that has followed it have emphasized effects on total saving behavior, there is no reason to expect the composition of asset holding to remain invariant.

5. Some of the best-known examples of this thinking were Greenough (1951) and Advisory Committee (1969).

6. Lintner (1975), Modigliani and Cohn (1979), and Feldstein (1979), among others, have provided analyses of the failure of equity returns to keep pace with inflation.

7. A distinction documented by Hartman (1978) is that, within the category of long-term portfolio (as opposed to direct) investments, foreign investors have mostly bought U.S. equities while U.S. investors have mostly bought foreign debt securities.

8. Funds generated internally and retained by corporate businesses also represent a form of investment by the holders of equity shares in those corporations, of course. Given the large household ownership of equities, the incorporation of retained earnings in the data shown in Table 1.1 would greatly increase the share of funds "advanced" by nonfinancial investors, but would still leave intermediaries as the direct source of well over half of the total.

9. See Friedman (1980, 1982) for a discussion of the postwar increase in the role of private debt in the U.S. economy.

10. Gurley and Shaw (1960) first emphasized this phenomenon.

11. Following Glass-Steagall, commercial banks no longer engage on their own account in underwriting or broker–dealer activities for publicly offered corporate securities, although they do so for public-sector securities, and in recent years they have been increasingly involved in arranging direct placements of corporate securities. In addition, the trust departments of commercial banks continue to be the largest single factor in private asset management.

12. See the historical account given in Friedman and Schwartz (1963).

13. Banks' holdings of Treasury securities were essentially flat from 1946 until the swelling of the federal deficit in 1975, so that banks' portfolios of municipals have exceeded their portfolios of direct U.S. Treasury obligations ever since 1969. Except for 1974–1976 and 1980–1983, all the growth in banks' holdings of federal government debt has consisted of federal agency securities.

14. See Goldfeld (1973, 1976) for a review of the postwar evidence on money demand behavior.

15. In Table 1.5, however, the respective size of the three groups is indicated by their total assets because of the lack of historical data on pension funds' liabilities.

16. See Bodie and Shoven (1983) and Kotlikoff and Smith (1983) for a comprehensive survey of the role of pension funds in the U.S. economy.

17. Several of the papers in Bodie and Shoven (1983) investigate the nature of this underfunding. Although corporations are now required to report (as a footnote to the balance sheet) the difference between pension assets and liabilities for vested benefits, there is no easy way to discover the liability for nonvested benefits.

18. See again Kotlikoff and Smith (1983).

19. The mortgage market receives, as a net addition to available funds, less than all of the credit provided by the sponsored credit agencies and mortgage pools if they in turn sell their securities to investors who would otherwise have held deposits in thrift institutions; see the analysis of this question in Jaffee and Rosen (1979).

20. It is important not to draw this distinction too firmly, however. For example, savings and loan associations have a tax incentive to hold at least 82% of their asset portfolios in residential mortgages (or other qualified assets). Also, in the presence of deposit interest ceilings limiting the payout of earnings to holders of deposit shares, the role of the profit motive has never been clear in portfolio decisions of savings and loan associations or mutual savings banks.

21. See Penner and Silber (1973) for an analysis of the subsidy implicit in federal credit programs.

22. See again Friedman (1980, 1982).

REFERENCES

Advisory Committee on Endowment Management. *Managing Educational Endowments.* New York: Ford Foundation, 1969.

Bodie, Zvi, and Shoven, John B. *Financial Aspects of the United States Pension System.* Chicago: University of Chicago Press, 1983.

Feldstein, Martin S. "Social Security, Induced Retirement and Aggregate Capital Formation." *Journal of Political Economy,* September–October 1974, *82,* pp. 905–926.

———. "Inflation, Tax Rules, and the Stock Market." *Journal of Monetary Economics,* July 1980, *6,* pp. 309–331.

Friedman, Benjamin M. "Post-War Changes in the American Financial Markets." In M. S. Feldstein (Ed.), *The American Economy in Transition.* Chicago: University of Chicago Press, 1980.

———. "Debt and Economic Activity in the United States." In B.M. Friedman (Ed.), *The Changing Roles of Debt and Equity in Financing U.S. Capital Formation.* Chicago: University of Chicago Press, 1982.

Friedman, Milton, and Schwartz, Anna Jacobson. *A Monetary History of the United States, 1867–1960.* Princeton: Princeton University Press, 1963.

Goldfeld, Stephen M. "The Demand for Money Revisited." *Brookings Papers on Economic Activity,* 1973 (No. 3), pp. 577–638.

———. "The Case of the Missing Money." *Brookings Papers on Economic Activity,* 1976 (No. 3), pp. 683–730.

Goldsmith, Raymond W. *Financial Intermediaries in the American Economy Since 1900.* Princeton: Princeton University Press, 1958.

———. *Financial Structure and Development.* New Haven: Yale University Press, 1969.

Greenough, William C. *A New Approach to Retirement Income.* New York: Teachers Insurance & Annuity Association of America, 1951.

Gurley, John G., and Shaw, Edward S. *Money in a Theory of Finance.* Washington, D.C.: The Brookings Institution, 1960.

Hartman, David G. "Long-Term International Capital Flows and the U.S. Economy." Mimeographed. Cambridge: Harvard University, 1978.

Jaffee, Dwight M., and Rosen, Kenneth T. "Mortgage Credit Availability and Residential Construction." *Brookings Papers on Economic Activity,* 1979 (No. 3), pp. 333–376.

Kotlikoff, Laurence, and Smith, Daniel. *Pensions in the American Economy*. Chicago: University of Chicago Press, 1983.

Lintner, John. "Inflation and Security Returns." *Journal of Finance,* May 1957, *30,* pp. 259–280.

Modigliani, Franco, and Cohn, Richard A. "Inflation, Rational Valuation and the Market." *Financial Analysts Journal,* March–April 1979, pp. 24–44.

Penner, Rudolph G., and Silber, William L. "The Interaction between Federal Credit Programs and the Impact on the Allocation of Credit." *American Economic Review,* December 1973, *63,* pp. 838–852.

2 Financial Intermediation and Economic Policies

John H. Kalchbrenner

Much analysis of recent changes in United States financial structure has focused on the roles played by monetary policy, regulation, innovations by private institutions and individuals, and information technology. In this chapter, recent changes in financial intermediation are related to broad economic events over the past decade that transformed other markets as well.

The first section of the chapter contains a selective review of the economic history of this unsettled period. The interpretation of the record is in accord with the view that much of the apparent deterioration in the stability of economic relationships in the United States can be attributed in the first instance to a unique combination of shocks to the economy such as the OPEC oil price increases and economic policies pursued earlier. The second section of the chapter traces the responses of economic policy to these shocks, with the emphasis on monetary policy.

The second and third sections of the chapter suggest that combinations of economic dislocations and public policy responses served as catalysts to accelerate changes in economic behavior and market structure, some of which had much earlier antecedents. In turn, these induced changes in private-sector behavior had feedback effects that complicated the conduct of economic policy. A major result was the transformation of financial markets and regulatory policy. Emphasis in the third section is on the major responses in financial markets to the changing environment.

The final section of the chapter concerns the future relationships between depository institutions and economic policy. The chapter concludes with the view that relatively stable and essentially familiar economic behavior hinges on establishing a better balance between monetary and fiscal policy and avoidance of further major external shocks. Although significant adjustment problems remain in financial, product, and labor markets, little reason is seen to fear that financial markets and monetary policy will not be able to function effectively in what currently appears to be the likely future financial environment if a more stable environment is established. If greater stability is not achieved, continued problems are foreseen for both financial markets and economic policy.

THE BROADER SETTING

From several perspectives, the decade of the 1970s marked a period of deterioration of economic performance of the world economy. Major economic problems arose that proved to be persistent and seemingly intractable when attacked with the public policy instruments that had been used relatively effectively in earlier periods. Based on the poor record of economic achievement in recent years, analysts such as Magaziner and Reich (1982) have concluded that fundamental structural change has undermined the stability of previous economic relationships. Current macroeconomic analytical and policy tools are alleged to be inadequate to achieve stable, noninflationary growth without a major assist from more comprehensive direct governmental intervention in the economic process.

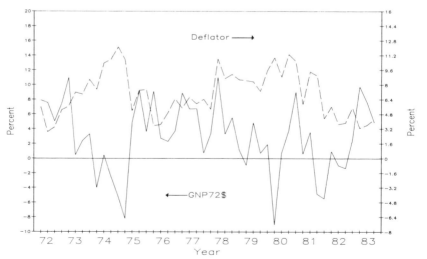

Figure 2.1.   Gross national product—72$; implicit GNP price deflator; percentage of change—SAAR. (*Source:* Shawmut Economics and DRI Data Base, reprinted with permission.)

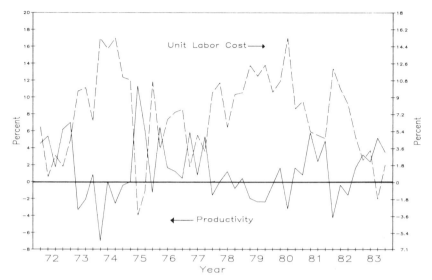

Figure 2.2. Productivity and unit labor cost; percentage of change—SAAR. (*Source:* Shawmut Economics and DRI Data Base.)

A growing body of economic analysis suggests a different conclusion, however, as exemplified by the studies presented at a recent Federal Reserve Bank of Kansas City conference (1983). Several studies suggest strongly that the problems of the 1970s were caused initially by a clustered series of shocks and previous economic policies. These analyses also suggest that the combined effects of the shocks and public policy responses induced changes in observed private-sector behavior that complicated the problem of setting public policy and further delayed adjustment. From this perspective, the decade was in many respects unique; the problems did not reflect pervasive structural market failures.

During the decade of the 1970s, the attainability of relatively stable growth of output and employment without accelerating inflation came into question. Growth in real output was erratic (Figure 2.1), manufacturing productivity growth deteriorated in the United States (Figure 2.2), and price stability seemed to be achievable only at the expense of unacceptably low levels of output and employment (Figures 2.1 and 2.3). The roller coaster pattern traced by attempts to control the situation has persisted for over a decade, as shown in Figure 2.1. The variants of incomes policies proposed by Okun, Tobin, Wallich, and others are attempts to find answers to this dilemma—the familiar problem of "stagflation"—that do not involve subjecting the economy to a protracted period of depressed activity. (For further discussion, see Tobin, 1983.) The more recent "industrial

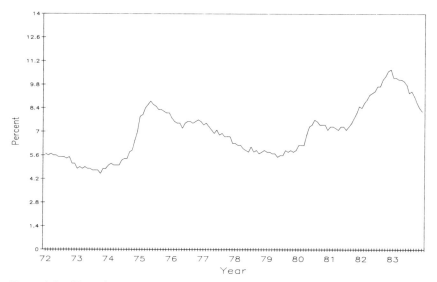

Figure 2.3.   Unemployment rate monthly. (*Source:* Shawmut Economics and DRI Data Base.)

policy'' proposals can be viewed as having the same objective, although pursued in a different manner.

An additional dimension related to the stagflation policy dilemma was the rational expectations challenge to prevailing macroeconomics in the mid-1970s. Lucas (1976), Sargent (1981), and others argued that the so-called neo-Keynesian synthesis was without well-grounded microeconomic foundations—particularly with respect to the acquisition and use of information. Policy analysis derived from neo-Keynesian analysis and its associated econometric models was rejected by these critics as presupposing nonrational behavior on the part of market participants. The debate within the economics profession set off by this counterview has continued into the 1980s.

Before proceeding, however, it is helpful to recount the unusual set of economic dislocations that occurred during this period. The more significant of these disruptions can be reduced ultimately to political actions that had far-reaching and long-lasting economic effects. Moreover, the economic problems mounted in an environment of political instability or unrest that persisted in much of the world.

As the decade began, the inflationary consequences of the conduct of the war in Vietnam, coupled with the financing of domestic expenditures, led to pressures that culminated in the adoption of the so-called new economic policy and the passage of the Economic Stabilization Act in 1971.

The latter entailed wage–price controls that proved largely ineffective in achieving their desired ends and were difficult to shed. The rigid-exchange-rate international monetary system adopted after World War II at Bretton Woods succumbed to growing international financial disequilibrium and was replaced by a managed-floating-exchange-rate system. The Nixon Administration also acknowledged that part of the inflation problem arose from the policies adopted to encourage rapid recovery from the 1969–1970 recession, which led to an excess demand situation (and doomed the prospects of success of the wage–price controls).

In the fall of 1973, OPEC raised oil prices fourfold. This act added further sharp inflationary pressures to the world economy, given the inability to adapt quickly to such a large price shock for a basic commodity. The problems were further compounded by rising food prices, stemming from worldwide food shortages, and depreciation of the dollar after exchange rates were permitted to float, which added to the pressures of rising import prices in the United States. (For further discussions of the effects of this convergence of economic shocks see the *Economic Report of the President,* 1981, Blinder, 1982, Eckstein, 1980, and Klein, 1983.)

Throughout most of 1973, unemployment remained slightly below 5% (see Figure 2.3), but the effects of steps toward restraint in monetary policy were already in evidence as several measures of economic activity showed signs of weakening. Inflation, as measured by the implicit GNP deflator,

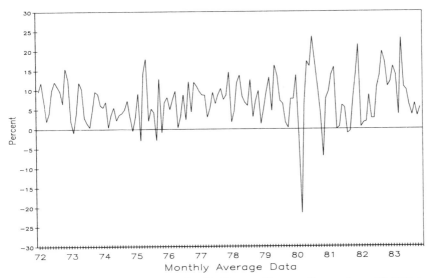

Figure 2.4. M1; percentage change—SAAR. (*Source:* Shawmut Economics and DRI Data Base.)

increased during 1973 from the 5% level at the beginning of the year to about 8% by the end of the year (as shown in Figure 2.1) and continued to increase to over 10% during 1974.

On a Unified Budget basis, the federal budget approached balance in 1973 (and was actually in surplus on the National Income Accounts basis). Monetary growth trended irregularly downward from 1972 to 1974 as did growth in real GNP (see Figures 2.1 and 2.4). Combined with the acceleration in the rate of inflation, "real" M1 and M2 declined significantly and market interest rates increased rapidly (except for a brief respite during the period of the oil embargo) to historically high levels (See Figure 2.5). Hobbled by rising inflation, shortages of energy, and restrictive monetary policy, the economy lapsed into serious recession.

After the economy recovered from the recession of 1974–1975, it soon became apparent that achieving the objective of stable growth of output and employment with reasonably stable prices would be difficult. As early as 1977 (again, see Figure 2.1) the rate of inflation had retraced about one-third of the reductions that occurred during the recession and appeared to be on a new higher plateau. Following a brief rebound after the recession, the rate of growth of productivity resumed a decline that lasted until the recession of 1980. Over the same period, growth in unit labor costs increased to over 10% (Figure 2.2).

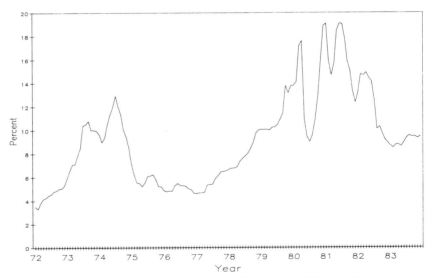

Figure 2.5. Federal funds rate; monthly average data. (*Source:* Shawmut Economics and DRI Data Base.)

The decline in the rate of growth of productivity has yet to be explained satisfactorily. In part, it reflected the adverse effects on capital investment of the uncertain energy supply, rising environmental and safety concerns, and the economic policies undertaken in the face of persisting inflation. Productivity was also affected to some degree by significant changes in the composition of the labor force.

Between 1970 and 1980, the labor force participation rate of adult women increased from about 45% to just over 50%. The participation rate for teenagers of both sexes increased from 50% to about 58% over the same period, as the post–World War II generation entered the labor force. Neither group of new entrants contained a high proportion of skilled workers. Growth in the total labor force was high relative to historical trends without an offsetting increase in capital spending. Consequently, the capital–labor ratio declined over the decade.

Changes in the patterns and volume of world trade were also important in the 1970s as the United States became a significantly more open economy during the decade. (The following relies on the work by Richardson, 1983. Also see Lawrence, 1983, and Bryant, 1980.) International trade grew from 4 to 6% of GNP in 1971 to 9 to 12% by the early 1980s. Total trade grew more rapidly than domestic activity over the same period, as world trade increased strongly for all industrialized nations after the 1974–1975 recession. During this period, less-developed countries became important trading partners of the developed nations, reflecting economic development that took place after World War II.

In addition to the overall growth in international trade as a percentage of GNP, the composition of trade has also been important to the behavior of the economy. Agricultural exports grew rapidly in the 1970s, and a significant proportion of U.S. exports consists of more technology-intensive capital goods. Both of these production categories are subject to more intense variation over business cycles and add to the apparent increase in instability of the domestic economy.

The agricultural sector was buffeted from four sources in recent years. Natural forces such as cold and drought, alternating with very good crop years, caused crop yields, prices, and incomes to vary substantially. The energy crisis depressed incomes by raising fuel, fertilizer, and chemical prices. Domestic recessions during the decade led to debt service and repayment problems. Finally, agricultural exports were affected by the increased extent to which agricultural trade became an arm of foreign policy. The most significant example was the Soviet grain embargo, imposed in early 1980.

Imports have become more competitive with goods that were previously a major part of domestic manufacturing, such as textiles, automobiles, and other consumer durable goods. This trend has caused difficult labor market adjustment problems that are not yet complete, and which were delayed by attempts to maintain growth in real incomes in the inflationary environment of the decade. Wachter and Wascher (1983) note that among the affected industries there have been substantial wage differentials. For industries such as steel and autos, which have large highly unionized labor forces with high relative wages, adjustment will continue to be a problem. For industries such as textiles, where the wages are lower relative to the U.S. average, adjustment seems to rest more on maintenance of aggregate growth in the economy to provide alternative employment opportunities.

Growing participation in world trade implies greater sensitivity of domestic economic activity to policies adopted by other nations and to economic fluctuations abroad. With it comes the need to find means of speeding adjustment of domestic labor, product, and financial markets to conditions that develop in world markets. An unfortunate side effect of the dislocations of the decade has been deterioration of the openness of international trade, as nations adopted a variety of protective measures and provided public subsidies to exports. These actions further increased the difficulty of maintaining stable and sustainable economic growth.

Against the background of these ongoing changes, renewed inflation became a serious concern by 1978. The Carter Administration and the Federal Reserve began to take actions intended to slow the pace of economic activity without causing recession. Monetary growth was reduced during the year and both short- and long-term interest rates rose significantly. The high employment budget shifted to surplus by the second half of 1979. But before these steps had time to have an effect on inflation, the OPEC nations acted again, doubling oil prices.

During 1979, real output growth slowed to just below 1%. Net exports were very strong following the depreciation of the dollar in 1977–1978 and the further depreciation subsequent to the Iranian revolution. Although the Revenue Act of 1978 reduced taxes in early 1979 and monetary growth accelerated during the first half of the year, real disposable income was virtually flat for the year.

Prices escalated rapidly during the year, with strong gains in food, housing, and energy prices. Internationally traded raw materials prices moved up sharply, particularly as the depreciation of the dollar increased and political tensions worsened in the Middle East. Market behavior suggested heightened inflationary expectations and speculative activity in precious metals and financial markets. By the end of 1979, the rate of inflation had increased to the 11% level reached in 1974.

In October 1979, as the economy slowed and another recession appeared likely, the operating procedures and the conduct of monetary policy were changed by the Federal Reserve. The changes adopted by the Federal Reserve are discussed in more detail in the next section.

Despite very sharp increases in interest rates subsequent to the monetary policy change, in the early months of 1980 the restrictive policy actions did not appear to be reducing economic turmoil. Variability of monetary growth increased sharply, growth of the consumer price index exceeded 15% during the first quarter, further speculative activity was in evidence, and fears of a "price explosion" followed by possible financial market collapse arose as credit demands remained very strong despite the record interest rate levels (see *Economic Report of the President,* 1981, 131–136).

In view of the deteriorating economic conditions, policy authorities decided that additional measures were called for, and selective credit controls were imposed in March. Subsequent to the imposition of selective credit controls, real output growth plummeted at a record rate and credit demand retrenched very sharply. Almost as quickly, interest rates fell and economic activity rebounded far more quickly than expected (see Figure 2.1).

Sharp variation in economic growth continued into 1981 as the Reagan Administration took office. Positive growth early in the year gave way to recession again toward year end. In order to contain the strength of the rebound from the recession of 1980 and to resist the continuing high rate of inflation, monetary policy once again turned highly restrictive in 1981. Interest rates again rose to new record levels, and productivity growth slumped after recovering in the latter part of 1980.

The economic recession of 1981–1982 was severe. Unemployment rose to almost 11% in December 1982 (see Figure 2.3), and real GNP growth declined 1.9% on an annual average basis from 1981 to 1982. The recession did have the desired effect on inflation, however. By year-end 1981, the rate of increase of the GNP deflator had declined to less than one-half that prevailing early in 1981. A sharp decline in unit labor costs was also recorded.

The recession extended to other nations as well, affecting industrialized and developing countries alike. One concomitant of the worldwide recession and the high interest rates was severe strain in international financial markets. The combination of reduced foreign exchange earnings and high interest rates forced a widespread rescheduling of international debt of developing nations, with adverse spillover effects on the creditors and the financial markets in the developed nations.

1983 was a recovery year, with sharply lower interest rates, continued low inflation, and strong consumer-led expenditure growth spurred by the sequential tax cuts provided in the Economic Recovery and Tax Act of

1981. The major negative factor during 1983 was the poor export performance resulting from slack worldwide demand and the sharp appreciation of the dollar that began in 1981 as monetary policy became restrictive.

The economic record of the 1980s hardly offers much evidence that the nation no longer faces the dilemma of choosing between growth in output and employment and restraint of inflation. By year-end 1983, the recessions of 1980 and 1981–1982 had reduced the rate of inflation and unit labor costs, real output and employment had increased strongly, and productivity growth increased. But these patterns are similar to those observed in earlier cycles. It remains to be seen whether an acceleration of inflation can be avoided as economic expansion continues. There are, however, significant differences between the monetary and fiscal policies of the 1970s and the situation in the 1980s, and private-sector perceptions of the problems seem to have changed for the better. These differences and some of their implications are discussed in the following sections.

ECONOMIC POLICY

Early in 1974, the Council of Economic Advisers acknowledged that it would take some time to reduce the rate of inflation under the circumstances that had developed. But, perhaps with more hope than conviction, the council also believed the private sector would adjust quickly to the large changes in relative energy prices brought on by OPEC actions. Transition aid was to be provided by an accommodative fiscal policy, and a resumption of economic growth with reduced inflation was expected later in the year.

However, the problems of adjustment, the degree of monetary restraint that was imposed, and the difficulty of modifying fiscal policy were all underestimated. Fiscal policy remained tighter than desired as inflation persisted at higher than projected levels, raising nominal incomes and revenues above expectations. Real government expenditures were below projected levels as well. The full employment surplus, which had risen through 1973, continued to increase through the third quarter contrary to intentions.

Measured in terms of short-term interest rates, monetary policy was relaxed somewhat in late 1973 and early 1974 during the uncertain oil embargo period. But once the embargo ended in March 1974, monetary policy turned sharply restrictive again. As the Council of Economic Advisers put it in its 1975 *Annual Report,* ''Real balances declined as a result of a monetary policy that was unwilling to accommodate economic expansion until the steepness of the price trend was reduced."

The administration adopted limited specific measures aimed at aiding adjustment as the economy worsened and it became apparent that substitution elasticities were lower than the council projections. They included differential price controls on "old" and "new" oil and natural gas and a windfall profits tax on oil companies. More traditional recession assistance measures such as extension of unemployment benefits and the renewal of the Public Employment Program (PEP) in the form of the Comprehensive Employment and Training Act (CETA) were also employed.

During the period of record high interest rates associated with the restrictive monetary policy, the thrift and housing industries suffered substantially. From a high of about a 2.4-million-unit annual rate at the end of 1972, housing starts plummeted to a 900,000-unit annual rate in the first quarter of 1975. A variety of subsidies designed to lessen the disproportionate effects of the restrictive monetary policy on housing and the thrift institutions was provided through the Federal Home Loan Bank Board, the Federal National Mortgage Association, and the Government National Mortgage Association.

With the exception of the special actions directed toward the energy price and supply problem, economic policy responded essentially as it had in earlier periods of inflation. Traditional policies to combat excess demand were employed: a very tight monetary policy combined with relative restrictive fiscal policy. Limited temporary assistance was provided for the thrift and housing industries as it had been during episodes of tight monetary policy during the 1960s.

The record high interest rates and very high inflation in 1973 and 1974 sharply increased the opportunity costs of holding financial assets subject to regulatory ceilings. Moreover, tax deductibility of interest payments and accelerating inflation provided incentives for dissaving and borrowing in anticipation of price increases, to take advantage of potential capital gains, and to obtain increased yields on nonregulated financial assets. These factors led to an observable break in the stability of previous patterns of financial behavior and the existing financial regulatory structure at the macroeconomic level.

By 1975, it was apparent that standard money demand functions had begun to overpredict money (M1) growth systematically, as discussed by Goldfeld (1976) and others. The money shortfall ultimately was attributed to much closer financial asset management, primarily in the corporate sector (see Porter, Simpson, and Mauskopf, 1979, and Tinsley and Garrett, 1978).

The Federal Reserve and administration economic officials were clearly aware of this development. The Council of Economic Advisers, for example, discussed the role of financial innovation in the apparent money demand "shift" in the 1975 *Economic Report of the President*. It was not so much a case of being surprised by the fact that the change occurred—experience was similar, although less pervasive, in periods of restriction in the previous decade—as it was an inability to do much about it under the circumstances. Inflation was far worse than expected, and interest rates had to rise much higher than anticipated so long as the objective continued to be to "reduce the steepness of the price trend" relatively quickly. Although the exact manner in which it occurred was a matter of some debate, the outcome was dictated by the monetary policy pursued. Legal restraints prevented the Federal Reserve from acting to remove or substantially relax the Regulation Q ceilings on regulated deposits, and the likely effects on the thrift industry would have made such a course unpalatable in any event.

At the time of the Penn Central failure in 1970, the Federal Reserve abolished rate ceilings on large shorter-term certificates of deposit. This action was taken to provide an avenue to commercial banks for acquisition of funds to be used to support business credit extension during the "liquidity crisis" of the period, during which the availability of funds through the commercial paper market was curtailed. As documented elsewhere in this volume by Eisenbeis, similar steps were taken by the Federal Reserve in 1973 for other categories of large certificates of deposit. In addition, the central bank responded weakly to the outflows from the principal-regulated deposit categories—demand deposits and small time and savings deposits—by raising Regulation Q ceilings modestly in mid-1973.

But, as interest rates increased sharply later in the year in response to tightening monetary policy, the Federal Reserve imposed marginal reserve requirements of up to 11% on these same recently deregulated certificates and on bank-related commercial paper in order to curtail the shift to these funding sources by banks as regulated deposits began to run off.

Private-sector responses to those financial regulations that were rendered inconsistent by macroeconomic conditions and monetary policy were quite evident in this episode, and they clearly complicated policy making. In addition to the liability management responses of the banks under reserve pressure, this episode involved the actions by asset holders that led to the money demand "shift" mentioned earlier. Further discussion of private-sector responses to policy actions and subsequent economic conditions is contained in the third section of this chapter.

During 1975, economic policy turned toward stimulating recovery of the economy. The Tax Reduction Act of 1975 provided for a rebate against

1974 personal income tax liabilities, a tax credit was allowed for purchases of newly constructed houses to aid the housing industry, and reductions in corporate taxes including an investment tax credit were adopted.

During the recovery period, the Federal Reserve experienced less difficulty in dealing with financial market asset and liability substitutions. Monetary aggregate growth targets that appeared to be low at the outset were announced for the year publicly. As the year progressed, however, any concern turned out to be groundless as the Federal Reserve altered the base against which growth of the aggregates was measured in order to permit higher actual growth without restrictive action. This phenomenon came to be called "base drift" and was a recurring pattern until 1979 in Federal Reserve operations. Consequently, the trend rate of growth of money increased substantially and interest rates fell back to the levels of 1972 and 1973.

Growth in real output turned positive during 1975, and the unemployment rate began to decline slowly. During 1975 and 1976, there seemed to be general satisfaction in Washington with the pace of recovery and the progress that had been made in reducing inflation. There did not appear to be any great concern that monetary growth was excessive or interest rates too low.

The performance of productivity was a matter of concern to the administration, however. The decline in the rate of growth of productivity was dated in the late 1960s by the Council of Economic Advisers in its 1977 *Annual Report*. The adequacy of saving and capital investment as a means to increase productivity and noninflationary real income growth became an issue in the mid-1970s. Nevertheless, other than general proposals to enhance the incentives for investment and the investment tax credit mentioned previously, no major specific programs resulted from these concerns. (For discussions of the adequacy of saving and investment see Federal Reserve Bank of Boston, 1982, Enzler et al., 1981, and Bosworth, 1983.)

However, the renewed discussions in the mid-1970s of the need for review of government regulation in a number of industries, including the financial sector, did lead to significant changes. The shift in sentiment toward deregulation as a means of increasing economic efficiency was clearly important for financial deregulation just as it was in the airline, trucking, rail, communications, and other industries. In part, the growth in support for deregulation accelerated after the 1973–1975 interval when the need to find ways to aid more rapid, efficient economic adjustment became obvious.

By the end of 1977, it was believed that the effects of the shocks of the early 1970s on the general price level had largely dissipated. But the problem of the inflation rate "ratchet" remained a concern. According to estimates by the Council of Economic Advisers, the underlying inflation rate was 1% in the early 1960s, 4 to 5% in the latter part of that decade, and 6 to 7% during 1977 and 1978.

In the language of the stabilization policy literature, the feeling grew that there was a "missing instruments" problem. Traditional monetary and fiscal policy had been used to reduce very high inflation while specific programs had been used to reduce somewhat the severity of the effects of broader macroeconomic policies on selected sectors. Nonetheless, concern increased that there were no readily available means to attack the problem of residual effects of shocks spilling over into the underlying rate of inflation—the "ratchet"—or to lessen the tendency for prices and wages to begin to rise before the economy reached satisfactory levels of employment and real growth.

Therefore, the Carter Administration proposed voluntary wage and price guidelines in 1977. Rather than supporting any of the existing incomes policies proposals directly, the administration also proposed a variant of an incomes policy in the form of real wage insurance to go hand in hand with the guidelines. The latter received very little attention and was never seriously considered.

At the beginning of 1978, expansion of the economy was expected to continue and policy concerns were focused on means to improve investment and reduce inflation over a longer time horizon. Monetary policy was not an area of major concern, and some signs of moderation in the money demand "shifts" which had continued through 1976 and 1977 were perceived.

The Federal Reserve did face another problem, however. In the wake of high interest rates and the depressing effect on earnings of the 1974–1975 recession, banks began to rebel against the non-interest-bearing reserve balances required for member banks of the Federal Reserve System. As interest rates began to rise again in the latter half of the 1970s, an increasing number of banks opted to leave the Federal Reserve System in order to avoid this "reserve tax," giving rise to the so-called membership problem.

As 1978 progressed, the performance of the economy deteriorated once again. The rate of inflation increased rapidly, depreciation of the dollar accelerated, and productivity fell sharply. Both monetary and fiscal policy turned restrictive as the year progressed.

Interest rates again rose, accompanied this time by the approval of the six-month money market certificate (MMC) for commercial banks and thrifts. In addition, these institutions were permitted to offer automatic transfer from saving (ATS) accounts. The adoption of these accounts represented further steps to protect housing and the regulated financial intermediaries from the effects of monetary policy on the deposits regulated under Regulation Q—particularly in view of the strong expansion of relatively unregulated money market mutual fund accounts (discussed further in the third section of this chapter).

There was explicit recognition that these efforts to protect housing and the liability structures of depository institutions were likely to cause interest rate swings to be larger than they otherwise would be in order to achieve the same amount of restrictive or expansive effect of monetary policy changes. Quantity (or "credit availability") effects had been lessened, particularly for housing finance, and a greater burden was placed on funds costs and more diffuse effects on economic activity.

As financial market practices continued to change, the Federal Reserve experienced growing problems in defining the monetary aggregates. Since monetary policy targets were expressed in terms of the monetary aggregates (as required by the Full Employment and Balanced Growth Act of 1978), the conduct of monetary policy was also complicated by the continuing market changes. During 1978, for example, the Federal Reserve adopted an ad hoc M1+ monetary aggregate to take account of the introduction of MMCs and ATS accounts. These problems finally led to a formal redefinition of the monetary aggregates in 1980. Nevertheless, in the redefinition M1 was temporarily divided into two parts denoted M1A and M1B, another reflection of further ongoing changes in financial markets.

During 1979 the combined effects of the second round of OPEC price increases and the restrictive monetary policy stance caused greater problems than expected. With a weakening economy and accelerating inflation came an increase in inflationary expectations and further downward pressure on the dollar.

Early in the year, the Federal Reserve found it difficult to establish an appropriate target for M1 because of the problems in estimating the likely effects of ATS and NOW accounts, as well as the continued growth of money market mutual funds and other changes in liquid asset demand. In July, a complex system of floating ceilings was adopted for various time deposits at commercial banks and thrift institutions (SSCs), principally to counter the rapid growth of nonregulated funds. Bank credit expanded rapidly and banks relied heavily on nondeposit sources of funds. After very slow growth early in the year, monetary expansion accelerated sharply in the middle two quarters of the year, accompanied by rapidly rising interest rates.

On October 6, 1979, the Federal Reserve changed its operating procedure and made further monetary policy changes. The change in operating procedure involved targeting reserve growth rather than setting a Federal funds rate band in order to achieve shorter-term monetary aggregate growth objectives. (For the details of the procedure, see Axilrod, 1982, or Meek, 1982.) In addition, marginal reserve requirements on total managed liabilities of banks were imposed, similar to the steps taken in 1973.

It was recognized that this change implied higher volatility of short-term interest rates, but it was believed that better control of the monetary aggregates would be a compensating benefit. The change also represented an attempt to enhance the credibility of the commitment of the Federal Reserve to achieve stated monetary aggregate targets and to pursue a noninflationary course. It seems probable that the major part of the credibility concern arose from the "base drift" experience of the mid- to late 1970s. The concern was also heightened somewhat by the rising influence of the monetarist–rational expectations views during the late 1970s. A principal argument of proponents of these views was that a reduction in the uncertainty associated with monetary policy would go a long way toward permitting normal market adjustments to fill the role of the "missing instruments."

In fact, however, the initial result was sharply higher volatility of both M1 growth and short-term interest rates in the months following the change. Figure 2.4 indicates the increased amplitude of the M1 growth rates, and Figure 2.6 shows the striking change in the variation of the

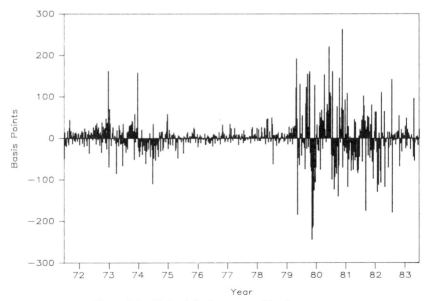

Figure 2.6.   Federal funds rate; weekly changes.

weekly Federal funds rate after the new procedure was adopted. Moreover, the increased variation was not simply an introduction phenomenon. Greater monetary growth variation, in part reflecting continuing change in financial markets and the behavior of interest rates, has persisted for three years. Short-term interest rate variability moderated somewhat after two years but remained about as high through 1983 as during the 1973–1974 period, the last period in which the Federal funds rate constraint was relaxed substantially as a major element of a dramatic antiinflation effort.

By almost any measure, monetary policy was erratic during 1980, swinging from sharp restriction early in the year to sharp expansion in the middle of the year and turning very restrictive again toward year end. This record was partly, perhaps predominantly, attributable to the dislocations brought on by the selective credit control program adopted in the spring.

The experience of 1979 and 1980 presented another example of the difficulty of preventing the combined effects of shocks and past policy from spilling over into the underlying inflation rate of future periods. Although the monetary policy operating procedures differed, the ratchet effect operated in much the same fashion in 1979 and 1980 as it did in 1973 and 1974. The Council of Economic Advisers estimated that the underlying inflation rate increased from 6 to 7% in 1977 and 1978 to 9 to 10% by the end of the 1980 recession. The subsequent cost of restraining inflation later proved to be similar as well.

The year 1980 also brought another episode of piecemeal chipping at the financial regulatory structure—at least insofar as Regulation Q ceilings on time and savings deposits were concerned. The Congress passed the Depository Institutions Deregulation and Monetary Control Act of 1980 with the intent to phase out all interest ceilings on these deposits over a six-year period. In addition, NOW accounts were authorized on a nationwide basis beginning in 1981, a transition schedule to uniform reserve requirements was provided, and asset powers of thrift institutions were broadened. Finally, financial institutions that offered transaction accounts but were not members of the Federal Reserve System were subjected to reserve requirements, thereby equalizing the "reserve tax" burden.

In one respect the Reagan Administration's approach to the problem of inflation in 1981 completed a full circle back to 1973 and 1974. As then, the new administration professed the belief that the workings of the market would permit progress against inflation along with adequate growth in real output and employment without the need for additional policy instruments—given appropriate monetary and fiscal policy.

Emphasis was placed on stable and credible policies, a reduced federal role in the economy, further regulatory relief, and incentives to save and invest. A longer-term perspective was adopted with a willingness to absorb short-term costs in order to achieve longer-term benefits. Indeed, misguided attempts to ameliorate shorter-term problems were blamed for the poor performance of the economy in previous years. Operationally, this meant that a recession was anticipated in 1981, but it was expected to be short-lived.

Once again, expectations were not realized: Inflation was reduced sharply only at the expense of a severe recession brought on largely by very restrictive monetary policy, and prices and wages were more "sticky" than expected. By early 1983, the annual report of the Council of Economic Advisers duplicated the swing that occurred in 1974 and 1975 in the assessment of the principal economic problem of the country. In its 1982 report, the principal problem was inflation; by 1983 the problem had become unemployment.

In response to the recession of 1981–1982, monetary policy eased dramatically in the last half of 1982, as did fiscal policy in accordance with the provisions of the tax reductions legislated during 1981. In the process of easing monetary policy, the Federal Reserve encountered a further problem in interpreting the degree of ease in monetary policy that existed. For reasons that remain imperfectly understood, the velocity of money (M1 and M2) declined sharply and unexpectedly, setting off another money demand "shift" discussion similar to the one that occurred in the mid-1970s (see studies in the Federal Reserve Bank of San Francisco compendium, 1984). To date, the sharp increase of money balances demanded relative to income has been attributed to declining interest rates, falling inflation, and further changes in liquid asset demand stemming from deregulation and continuing change in financial market practices.

In addition to the problem of interpreting the meaning of monetary aggregate behavior for economic activity caused by the velocity or money demand change, the Federal Reserve had to take into account the most recent major regulatory change affecting the monetary aggregates. Late in 1982, in accordance with the Garn-St Germain Depository Institutions Act of 1982, the Depository Institutions Deregulation Committee authorized banks and thrift institutions to issue money market deposit accounts (MMDA) and Super NOW accounts. These accounts were subject to minimum deposit size, but no interest rate ceilings, and they quickly became substitutes for money market mutual funds accounts as well as direct market instruments, as discussed in the next section.

Again, economic developments intervened to alter regulatory objectives. Instead of a gradual phase-out of Regulation Q ceilings by 1986, this legislation had the effect of greatly accelerating the deregulation schedule. Without the change in the original schedule brought about by 1982 legislation, the very rapid growth of the money market mutual funds would have continued, exceeding the approximately $230 billion level reached in late 1982.

CHANGING PATTERNS OF FINANCIAL INTERMEDIATION

The story that emerges from this review is that regardless of the policies employed, economic performance fell significantly short of goals. Economic policy makers attempted to achieve the mandates of the Employment Act of 1946 and the Full Employment and Balanced Growth Act of 1978 concerning employment, growth, and inflation, but they met with only limited success. On average, from 1973 to 1983 real output grew at a compound annual rate of approximately 2%, and total employment increased about 1.7% per year over the same period. But the implicit GNP deflator increased at a compound annual average rate of 7.4% over the 10-year period. As the review discloses, each of these averages masks significant unevenness of economic performance during the period. Perhaps Solow was close to the mark in his recent comment: "As for that part of inflation that stemmed from OPEC in 1974 and again in 1979, it may be that there was *no* practical way to avoid a bad outcome in the second half of the 1970s" (see Tobin, 1983, p. 280).

Given this record of economic performance, it comes as no surprise that patterns of financial intermediation underwent change over the past decade. The discussion to follow begins with a summary description of saving behavior in the economy, followed by a brief discussion of changing asset–liability behavior in the individual private sector and debt patterns in the business sector. Finally, the changes in the economic environment and in the behavior of the private net saving and borrowing sectors are related to changes in the relative positions of the major financial intermediaries.

Growth of real individual net worth and real disposable personal income during the past decade followed serpentine patterns around trends distinctly lower than the previous post–World War II experience. Downward pressure on real aggregate welfare was reflected in changing consumption–saving and asset–liability behavior patterns of the society.

As Friedman (1984) notes, the gross saving rate in the United States followed a rising trend after World War II, accompanied by an increasing capital consumption rate. Total net saving, however, declined after the mid-1970s as rising federal government dissaving reduced roughly trendless personal and corporate net saving rates, offset partially by rising state and local government saving. For each of these measures, saving rates are expressed as a percentage of gross national product.

On the basis of the more typical expression of personal saving as a percent of disposable personal income, Corrado and Steindel (1980) and Slifman (1981) analyzed the sharp reduction in the personal saving rate after the mid-1970s. The former also note the declining ratio of consumer net worth to disposable personal income over the 1970s. Consumers suffered losses on financial assets (principally corporate equities) while experiencing capital gains on tangible assets. The response to reductions or lower growth in income and net worth was a reduction in the personal saving rate accompanied by diversions of saving flows from financial assets to tangible assets. As noted earlier, tax provisions, financial regulation, and high inflation reinforced the incentives to make these changes.

Figure 2.7 portrays these trends in a somewhat different manner. The upper series shows the acquisition of financial assets inclusive of corporate equities as a percentage of disposable income. The lower two series indicate the behavior of changes in net debt and net tangible assets to disposable personal income, respectively.

Displayed in this way, the shifts to tangible assets and the sharp increase in debt—principally home mortgages—are quite clear. The increased proportion of financial assets to disposable income in the upper series resulted from larger increases in the acquisition of deposits and other credit market

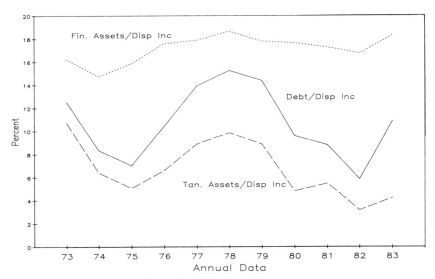

Figure 2.7. Asset and debt flows of individuals relative to disposable personal income. (*Source:* Shawmut Economics and Federal Reserve Board Flow of Funds.)

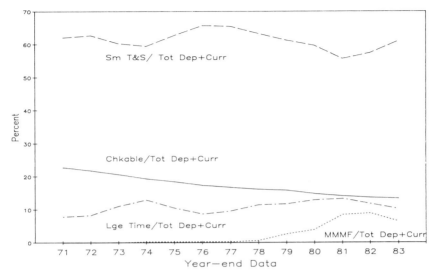

Figure 2.8.   Deposit type relative to total deposits and currency. (*Source:* Shawmut Economics and Federal Reserve Board Flow of Funds.)

instruments than the declines that occurred in direct acquisition of equities and bonds during the mid-1970s.

From their analyses of personal saving behavior, Corrado and Steindel (1980) and Slifman (1981) concluded that consumers may have maintained expenditures at the expense of saving on the assumption that the income and net worth experience of the 1970s was not permanent. By 1979, however, the combination of the accrued outstanding debt and the turn to restrictive economic policy combined sharply to reduce net debt and tangible asset acquisition. The pattern of all three series during the economic recovery beginning in 1983 parallels the experience of 1975.

Figures 2.8 and 2.9 contain information that relates more directly to the financial intermediaries by focusing on deposit behavior. The charts do not show the downward trend of total deposits relative to the nonequity financial assets of private domestic nonfinancial investors. Except for a recovery between 1975 and 1977, this percentage declined from about 71% in 1973 to about 69% in 1983. Over the period, deposit-issuing institutions as a group lost share to other issuers of credit instruments.

Figure 2.8 indicates the percentages of deposits by type within total deposits since 1971. Small time and savings deposits declined in the period preceding the recession of 1973–1975 as interest rates increased and large time deposits took a larger share of the total. When interest rates declined during the recovery of economic activity in 1975, this pattern was reversed.

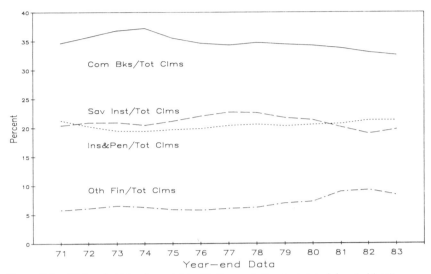

Figure 2.9. Claims held by financial institutions relative to total claims held. (*Source:* Shawmut Economics and Federal Reserve Board Flow of Funds.)

During this interval, banks relied heavily on increased issuance of certificates of deposit and the use of nondeposit sources of funds. The latter increased about $30 billion in two years.

As indicated, checkable deposits declined steadily as a percentage of total deposits throughout the period shown on the chart. Over the same period, direct acquisition of federal government securities by private domestic nonfinancial investors increased from about 11% of nonequity financial asset acquisition to over 14.5% of this total, exceeding the two-percentage-point decline in the share of total deposits to nonequity financial assets.

As interest rates increased from 1977 to 1980, small time and savings deposits turned down and large time deposits increased as a share of the total. Beginning in 1978 money market mutual funds became an important competitor in deposit markets, rising from less than 1% of total deposits to almost 9% by 1982 (and to more than 9% within the year). Liberalization of regulatory constraints did not stem the relative decline in small time and savings deposits, but the share of large time deposits continued to increase as interest rates moved higher in 1978 and 1979.

It was not until the 1981–1982 period that the combination of regulatory change and declining interest rates reversed the decline of small time and savings deposits and arrested the rapid growth in the share taken by the money market mutual funds. As the chart indicates, the turnaround was dramatic, demonstrating the degree of sensitivity to market returns that had developed over a decade of high inflation and interest rate volatility. The success in attracting share to these deposits was costly to the financial intermediaries, however, as offering rates considerably higher than comparable market interest rates were posted during the initial introduction of money market deposit accounts.

Figure 2.9 indicates how well each of the major financial intermediary classes fared in terms of claims held as a percentage of total financial institution claims. After 1974, the commercial bank share trended downward only gradually as regulated deposit losses were largely replaced by nonregulated deposits or nondeposit sources of funds. Perhaps surprisingly, given the difficulties of the thrift industry during this period (as described, for example, by Carron, 1982), the savings institutions maintained share fairly well. This was accomplished largely by relying on the issuance of large-denomination certificates of deposit and borrowings from the Federal Home Loan Bank System as deposits subject to Regulation Q declined.

In similar fashion, insurance companies and pension funds also avoided major share losses despite downward pressure on disposable personal income and increases in insurance policy loans during the period. Reductions in direct acquisition of longer-term claims by individuals did not extend

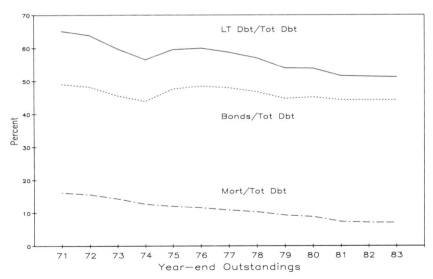

Figure 2.10. Nonfinancial corporate business: long-term debt relative to credit market debt. (*Source:* Shawmut Economics and Federal Reserve Board Flow of Funds.)

to the indirect acquisition of longer-term claims offered by these institutions.

Although marginal gains of other financial institutions became a major concern of the larger intermediaries during the decade, on average the share inroads were not large. Furthermore, institutions such as money market mutual funds in part simply became another layer of intermediation by providing deposits (shares) to the public and purchasing commercial bank CDs as earning assets. Nevertheless, the accelerating erosion of share to the "other" financial institutions after 1978 demonstrates that the expressed fears were not without foundation. In the absence of the regulatory changes undertaken after 1978, the erosion of share would have continued.

The sharp increase in net debt of individuals during the 1970s (discussed earlier) largely took the form of mortgages, with lesser relative increases in consumer credit. Slifman concluded that some portion of the proceeds from mortgage debt was used to support consumption—so-called liquefaction of a part of the capital gains on real estate in the mid-1970s.

Business debt patterns also changed during the past 10 years, as shown in Figures 2.10 and 2.11. From Figure 2.10 it is evident that the proportion of long-term to total debt continued the decline that began in the mid-

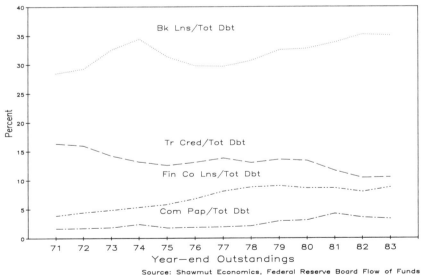

Figure 2.11. Nonfinancial corporate business: short-term debt relative to credit market debt. (*Source:* Shawmut Economics and Federal Reserve Board Flow of Funds.)

1960s. Attempts to restructure debt maturities are evident in the increase of the bond proportion in the mid-1970s and to a lesser extent in the maintenance of the bond ratio more recently. Mortgage debt has followed a steady downward trend over the period.

In addition to the declining relative importance of commercial mortgages, financial intermediaries were affected by changes in the composition of the rising share of short-term business credit market debt. From Figure 2.11 it can be seen that corporations turned to commercial loans at banks, and net trade credit, after adjustment of the figures for a reporting change that occurred in 1974, appears to have declined during the restrictive period in 1973–1974. During the recovery of the mid-1970s, dependence on bank loans declined, as is typical, but trade credit extensions were partly restored, and loans from finance companies became a larger share of total short-term credit market debt.

Late in the decade, dependence on bank loans increased typically as the cyclical peak approached and rose further as liquidity problems mounted in the early 1980s in an inhospitable equity and bond market environment. The share of commercial paper shows a typical cyclical pattern in the latter part of the period, while high interest rates and liquidity constraints adversely affected the maintenance of reliance on trade credit extensions in the early 1980s.

Changes in financial intermediation over the past decade might be summarized in the following manner. Consumers, faced with reduced growth in net worth and income, responded by reducing saving to maintain consumption levels. In part because of financial regulation, reduced saving flows were diverted toward tangible assets. Real estate was particularly attractive until the late 1970s, given tax provisions, the availability of fixed-rate loans in an inflationary environment, and the prospect of capital gains. Financial asset acquisition was diverted toward shorter-term liquid assets that paid market interest rates, particularly government securities and money market mutual funds. Consumers and businesses continued to support larger time deposits subject to less or no regulation.

Businesses took actions to economize non-interest-bearing cash assets, reduced needs for short-term credit where possible, and were generally forced by market conditions to continue to shorten the maturities of debt positions. Equity extensions were difficult despite rising corporate profits in the mid-1970s. Commercial banks were not the sole beneficiary of the increased relative demand for short-term credit as businesses sought other avenues of finance with significant increases in borrowing from finance companies (some of which were bank affiliated) and in commercial paper.

Traditional financial intermediaries lost share moderately to other issuers of credit instruments, particularly in terms of regulated deposits that formerly constituted "core deposits." Nevertheless, depository institutions were able to maintain shares of holdings of credit claims reasonably well by means of liability management to offset losses of regulated deposit funds. Insurance companies and pension funds benefited from the maintenance of contractual or institutionalized flows of funds to their institutions. Regulatory changes finally stemmed the growth of newer entrants to the consumer deposit market by the early 1980s.

Financial institutions shortened maturities of earning assets as interest rate volatility and inflation increased. Cost structures changed significantly as deregulation proceeded, and interest rate risk bearing appears to have shifted over the decade away from savers toward financial and nonfinancial businesses, as well as to obligors of variable-rate mortgages.

CONCLUDING COMMENTS

The economic conditions of the 1970s were tailor-made for major changes in the financial intermediation markets. High inflation and volatile interest rates provided strong incentives for development of alternative financial instruments and means of conducting transactions in order to evade the opportunity costs that resulted from existing regulations. Pressed by slower growth (even actual declines) of net worth, income, and cash flow, and facing further erosion of the real returns on financial assets as inflation worsened, businesses and consumers took new initiatives.

What seems remarkable is that the composition of the major financial intermediaries markets changed so little in view of the turmoil of the period and the somewhat helter-skelter fashion in which change in financial regulation occurred. Many have argued that the process should have proceeded more quickly in a more logical manner. Be that as it may, both financial institutions and financial regulators proved to be more flexible than might have been expected.

Despite the volatility of the economy, on average institutions and individuals responded rationally to the changes in costs, returns, and constraints with which they were confronted. Nevertheless, the ability to analyze and predict the dynamics of market behavior deteriorated during the decade—independent of the analytical approach employed. The consequent problems of understanding and predicting the timing, size, and form of economic changes with any degree of precision made public and private decisions far more difficult.

The question of whether these shifts have constituted a breakdown in the stability of financial market relationships is unresolved. The definition of like financial assets is based on the degree of substitutability for given economic purposes. The process of measurement will be possible only after sufficient time passes for new customary liquid asset demand patterns to evolve in the wake of the changes in financial markets that have already occurred. Since further regulatory changes are likely in the future, resolution is not likely in the near term. Thus, uncertainty concerning appropriate monetary aggregate targets for the conduct of monetary policy will persist as well.

From the perspective of early 1984, the prospects for achieving stable, noninflationary growth were clouded by the size of the federal deficit and the perceived difficulty of reducing future deficits. The need to reduce the deficit as the economy approaches full-capacity output and employment was apparent. Furthermore, given the behavior of inflation in 1977 and, to a lesser extent, 1980, the need to take steps to reduce the deficit was close at hand. The possibility of new external "shocks" given the world political environment adds an additional element of urgency to the quest for better balance between domestic monetary and fiscal policy.

Changes in regulation (especially the elimination of many Regulation Q ceilings) have lessened the quantity restrictions formerly available to the Federal Reserve in acting to restrain economic activity. Recent experience suggests that much larger interest rate increases are required to slow the growth of a rapidly expanding economy than was the case previously.

During the next few years, however, the Federal Reserve will have little latitude within which to raise interest rates without causing problems for international borrowers and for the thrift institutions. Effective easing of the debt problems of the less-developed countries will hinge on sustained economic growth and the avoidance of sharply higher interest rates. The thrift institutions barely returned to break-even earnings in 1983 (on average), and higher interest rates would quickly reverse this progress.

These considerations raise the possibility of the imposition of undesirable politically mandated changes in financial regulation and monetary policy if sustainable noninflationary growth cannot be achieved in the near future. Traditional means of combating inflation have been used twice in recent years, and in both cases inflation was not restrained without serious dislocations in the economy. Both mandatory and voluntary wage–price controls have also been attempted with the same ultimate result.

During the most recent antiinflationary episode, a number of proposals intended to avoid this outcome were actively discussed in Congress. These no doubt would surface again in the event of another inflationary surge. The proposals included targeting of GNP, real interest rates, or the price level by the Federal Reserve, and more explicit approval of annual monetary policy objectives by Congress. Other proposals that have been made or techniques that have been used in the past include the imposition of various portfolio control measures, capital controls on financial institutions, reinstitution of credit controls on consumers and businesses, and quantitative controls on international financing.

The prospects for successful implementation of such proposals in a crisis atmosphere are questionable. On balance, the substitution of such measures for the previous financial regulatory structure and monetary policy procedures would appear to be a poor trade-off. The possibility that this Pandora's box could be opened provides the final element of urgency to the search for ways to avoid an acceleration of inflation without interrupting economic growth.

REFERENCES

Axilrod, S. "Monetary Policy, Money Supply and the Federal Reserve's Operating Procedures." *Federal Reserve Bulletin*, 1982, *68* (1), pp. 13–24.

Blinder, A. "The Anatomy of Double-Digit Inflation in the 1970s." In R. Hall (Ed.), *Inflation: Causes and Consequences*. Chicago: University of Chicago Press (NBER), 1982, pp. 261–282.

Bosworth, B. "Capital Formation, Technology and Economic Policy." In Federal Reserve Bank of Kansas City, *Industrial Change and Public Policy*. Kansas City, 1983, pp. 231–265.

Bryant, R. *Money and Monetary Policy in Interdependent Nations*. Washington, D.C.: the Brookings Institution, 1980.

Carron, A. *The Plight of the Thrift Institution*. Washington, D.C.: the Brookings Institution, 1982.

Corrado, C., and Steindel, C. "Perspectives on Personal Saving." *Federal Reserve Bulletin*, 1980, *66* (8), pp. 613–625.

Eckstein, O. *Core Inflation*. Englewood Cliffs, N.J.: Prentice-Hall, 1980.

Enzler, J., Conrad, W., and Johnson, L. (Eds.), *Public Policy & Capital Formation*. Washington, D.C.: Board of Governors of the Federal Reserve System, 1981.

Federal Reserve Bank of Boston. *Saving and Government Policy*. Conference Series No. 25, Boston, 1982.

Federal Reserve Bank of Kansas City. *Industrial Change and Public Policy*. Symposium Series, Kansas City, 1983.

Federal Reserve Bank of San Francisco. *Monetary Targeting and Velocity Change*. Conference proceedings, San Francisco, 1984.

Friedman, B. "Implications of the Government Deficit for U. S. Capital Formation." In Federal Reserve Bank of Boston, *The Economics of Large Government Deficits*. Conference Series No. 27, Boston, 1984, pp. 23–95.

Goldfeld, S. "The Case of the Missing Money." In *Brookings Papers on Economic Activity*, No. 3. Washington, D.C.: the Brookings Institution, 1976, pp. 683–730.

Klein, L. "Identifying the Effects of Structural Change." In Federal Reserve Bank of Kansas City, *Industrial Change and Public Policy*. Kansas City, 1983, pp. 1–19.

Lawrence, R. "Changes in U. S. Industrial Structure: The Role of Global Forces, Secular Trends and Transitory Cycles." In Federal Reserve Bank of Kansas City, *Industrial Change and Public Policy*. Kansas City, 1983, pp. 29–77.

Lucas, R., Jr. "Econometric Policy Evaluation: A Critique." In K. Brunner and A. Meltzer (Eds.), *The Phillips Curve and Labor Markets*. North Holland: Carnegie-Rochester Conference Series on Public Policy (Vol. 1), 1976, pp. 19–46.

Lucas, R., Jr., and Sargent, T. *Rational Expectations and Econometric Practice*. Minneapolis: University of Minnesota Press, 1981.

Magaziner, I., and Reich, R. *Minding America's Business*. New York: Vintage Books, 1982.

Meek, P. *U. S. Monetary Policy and Financial Markets*. New York: Federal Reserve Bank of New York, 1982.

Porter, R., Simpson, T., and Mauskopf, E. "Financial Innovation and the Monetary Aggregates." In *Brookings Papers on Economic Activity*, No. 1. Washington, D.C.: the Brookings Institution, 1979, pp. 213–229.

Richardson, J. "International Trade Policies in a World of Industrial Change." In Federal Reserve Bank of Kansas City, *Industrial Change and Public Policy*. Kansas City, 1983, pp. 267–312.

Slifman, L. "A Dissection of Personal Saving Behavior." Working Paper No. 24. Washington, D.C.: Board of Governors of the Federal Reserve System, 1981.

Tinsley, P., and Garrett, B. "The Measurement of Money Demand." Unpublished manuscript. Washington, D.C.: Board of Governors of the Federal Reserve System, 1978.

Tobin, J. (Ed.). *Macroeconomics, Prices, and Quantities*. Washington, D.C.: the Brookings Institution, 1983.

United States. *Economic Report of the President*, together with the *Annual Report of the Council of Economic Advisers*. Washington, D.C.: United States Government Printing Office, 1981, pp. 29–88, 131–136.

Wachter, M., and Wascher, W. "Labor Market Policies in Response to Structural Changes in Labor Demand." In Federal Reserve Bank of Kansas City, *Industrial Change and Public Policy*. Kansas City, 1983, pp. 177–215.

2 Major Forces for Change Affecting Financial Intermediation

This section addresses the "whys" of changes in the processes of intermediation. That is, it deals more specifically with the major dynamics underlying general shifts in financing practices and institutions. Primary attention is devoted to two major issues: (1) the effects of interactions between economic conditions and regulation on patterns of financial activity, including a review of regulatory responses to these financial reactions; and (2) the changing role of technology in financial activity—including underlying technological change itself, organizational forms of innovation, and the feasibilities of new applications of existing technology. Here, as elsewhere in the book, the implications of lessons of the past for future financial activity are assessed.

3 Inflation and Regulation: The Effects on Financial Institutions and Structure

Robert A. Eisenbeis

The period since World War II with its persistent inflation and successive rounds of disintermediation spawned a series of economic "incentives" and "pressures" that have served as the driving forces in the process of financial innovation that has characterized our financial system.[1] These innovations have significantly altered not only the array of financial services available and the way they are provided to the public but also the portfolios and, hence, risk characteristics of financial institutions. These innovations include new instruments (such as CDs, NOW accounts, rising rate notes, financial futures, and variable-rate mortgages), new technological applications (such as ATMs, videotext, in-home banking, POS, and the use of computers to solve operations problems within financial institutions), new methods for supplying services through joint ventures and related financial arrangements (such as deposit sweep accounts, cash management accounts, and shared EFT networks); new institutional forms (such as bank holding companies, money market mutual funds, nonbank

Helpful comments on an earlier version of this chapter (see Eisenbeis, 1980) were received from Cynthia Glassman, Edward C. Ettin, Myron Kwast, John J. Mingo, John T. Rose, and Benjamin Wolkowitz. The author also benefited from numerous conversations with Edward J. Kane and, especially, Richard C. Aspinwall on this topic over the past several years.

banks, broker–bankers, and other financial congenerics) and, of course, the growth and development of new markets for the new instruments (such as the Federal funds/RP, commercial paper, financial futures, and the Eurocurrencies markets).

The key feature of many of these innovations is that they were generated in response to economic incentives as attempts to circumvent or to avoid statutory or regulatory constraints.[2] In many instances these constraints were imposed to restrict various terms under which financial services could be provided to the public and/or indirectly to redirect the flow of funds, particularly into mortgage credit. These restrictions are of several different types and include: (1) rate ceilings on time and savings deposits and demand deposits; (2) capital requirements; (3) reserve requirements; (4) tax laws; and (5) limits on geographical expansion and product diversification.

This chapter focuses on financial innovation and regulation as a "dialectic" process to highlight its implications for the financial structure.[3] It is important to understand this process to evaluate how institutions are evolving and how they might respond to reregulation and deregulation now in process. It will be established that, far from being an innocent bystander, regulation and regulatory response to change has played and will continue to play a critical role in providing stimuli for innovation to take place. It has and will continue to affect how financial organizations structure their activities and operations. It is also argued that regulation-induced innovation tends to lead to potential increases in financial instability. Finally, it is understood that many of the financial innovations that have been forthcoming were facilitated by technology (see Phillips' chapter in this volume and Kane, 1983). They were also in direct response to changes in consumer attitudes and alterations in consumer asset and debt positions, most notable of which was the growth of credit cards that has accompanied the significant increases in consumer debt in the last decade. These and other changes on the demand side which have affected the potential range of financial services may not always be explicitly mentioned in the following discussion but are covered in other chapters of this book.

THE PROCESS OF FINANCIAL INNOVATION AND THE ROLE OF REGULATION[4]

Commercial banks entered the post–World War II period flushed with liquidity. For example, in 1947 the banking system had an aggregate loan–deposit ratio of 26.4% and liquid assets ratio of 74.1% (see Table 3.1). S&Ls and mutual savings banks were small, unaggressive institutions that accepted savings deposits and made mortgage loans, and credit unions

Table 3.1.   Loan–Deposit and Liquid Asset Ratios for All Commercial
Banks (in percentages)

Date	Ratio of Loans to Total Deposits	Ratio of Cash Assets plus Treasury Securities to Total Deposits
12/21/47	26.4	74.1
12/30/50	33.7	65.9
12/31/55	43.0	56.4
12/31/60	51.2	49.2
12/31/65	60.7	36.2
12/31/70	65.2	32.3
12/31/74	73.4	24.4
12/31/75	69.5	27.7
12/31/76	71.0	28.5
12/31/77	71.3	28.0
6/30/78	73.5	26.9
12/31/82	76.0	22.2
12/31/83	75.4	24.4

SOURCE: Board of Governors of the Federal Reserve System, *Banking and Monetary Statistics 1941–1970, Federal Reserve Bulletin,* (various issues), and Federal Deposit Insurance Corporation, *Bank Operating Statistics.*

were a negligible part of the picture. These two major classes of institutions—thrifts and commercial banks—tended to operate in segmented markets. Commercial banks accepted demand deposits and provided payments services, made short-term business loans, and purchased Treasury obligations. Thrifts served as depositories for consumer savings that were channeled into mortgage loans.

With the conversion to a peace-time economy and the Federal Reserve Accord with the Treasury eliminating the policy of pegging government security rates, interest rates began to climb. Corporate treasurers began looking more carefully at their cash management techniques and began seeking new, higher-yielding assets (see Gaines, 1967). Throughout the 1950s, bank liquidity ratios declined significantly as commercial bank holdings of Treasury securities were run down to fund the growth of loans. For example, by 1955 banks had increased their average loan–deposits ratio 63% with liquidity ratios declining commensurately. Interest rate ceilings were in effect for commercial bank offering rates on time and savings deposits but were not significant constraints until 1956, at which time they were raised slightly.

The first key event to stimulate significant financial innovation was the 1959–1960 period of monetary restraint. Because of the inflationary pressures that resulted from the pent-up demand and high liquidity emerging from World War II and the subsequent financing of the Korean War, market rates pressed against and finally rose above Regulation Q ceilings. Large investors, and in particular corporate treasurers, recognized that there were more attractive investment alternatives to bank interest-bearing liabilities and/or holding funds in the form of demand deposits which earned no interest. Consequently, more and more attention was given to the development of corporate cash management techniques in an attempt to earn market rates on cash balances. The result was to reinforce the slowdown in the growth of deposits, particularly demand deposits, during the period as more sophisticated depositors (both corporations and individuals) sought higher returns. This coupled with reduced liquidity and high loan demand placed both commercial banks and thrift institutions in a liquidity and earnings squeeze.

Shortly after the pressures of this first round of disintermediation subsided, the negotiable CD was introduced by First National City Bank (now Citibank) in 1961. The CD promised to be a new instrument that would enable banks both to hold deposits and to attract new funds by segmenting the time deposit market and paying rates closer to market rates on only the more interest-sensitive deposits components.[5]

This innovation was the first of what proved to be a long series of financial innovations to avoid Regulation Q constraints that prohibited the payment of interest on demand deposits and specified maximum rates to be paid on time and savings deposits. It was also the first step in what became an increasingly tight circle in a dialectic process. Whenever interest rates rose above the ceiling rates, depository institutions innovated new deposit instruments and institutions or developed new sources of funds in order to pay market rates and to achieve their objectives for deposit growth. The regulatory response, often out of concern for housing and the stability of financial markets, was either to shut down the new process or to ratify the innovation by raising the relevent interest rate ceilings on close substitutes offered by commercial banks and thrifts.[6]

In each succeeding round, however, disintermediation became increasingly worse, for two reasons. First, depositors were on a steep learning curve. Each time interest rate ceilings became binding, a smaller differential between open market rates and offering rates on regulated deposits triggered greater disintermediation. Second, unregulated nonfinancial institutions also realized the potential of providing financial services and offered new, more attractive instruments in an attempt to take advantage of the widening of the spread between market rates and deposit ceilings.

The principal financial innovations are detailed in Table 3.2 and Table 3.3. (See p. 80) Where relevant, the regulatory responses are cataloged.

Table 3.2. Regulation Q–Related Financial Innovations and Regulatory Response

Date—Period	Innovation	Regulatory Response
1. Late 1950s—early 1960s	1. Development of liability management.	1. None.
2. January 1957		2. January 1, 1957, ceilings on nearly all accounts are raised 50 basis points.
3. 1961—early	3. Citicorp (FNCB) offers negotiable CDs.	3. Rate ceilings on selected categories of time and savings deposits are adjusted. a. January 1, 1962 b. July 17, 1963 c. November 24, 1964 d. December 6, 1965
4. September 1964	4. FNB of Boston announces sale of short-term promissory notes.	4. Note sales of issues with maturities less than two years by banks (including commercial paper) are subject to Regulations D and Q in 1966.
5. Mid-1960s (1965–1969)	5. Federal funds market developed.	5. a. July 1969, applied Regulations Q and D to Federal funds transactions except for exempt categories which included corporations. b. August 28, 1969, RPs subject to Regulations Q and D. c. February 12, 1970, narrows exempt categories excluding corporations.

(continued)

Table 3.2. *(Continued)*

Date—Period	Innovation	Regulatory Response
		d. April 13, 1979, public comment requested on proposal to apply 3% reserve requirement on all Federal funds borrowings from institutions not subject to reserve requirements.
6. Mid-1966	6. Development of Eurodollar market as source of funds.	6. a. "London" checks are subjected to reserve requirements July 31, 1969.
		b. October 16, 1969, a 10% marginal reserve requirement is applied.
		c. November 1969, marginal reserve requirement increased to 20%.
		d. June 21, 1973, marginal reserve requirement reduced to 8%.
		e. May 22, 1975, marginal reserve requirement dropped to 4%.
		f. August 24, 1978, reserve requirement dropped to zero.
7. 1966–1979		7. a. Regulation Q ceilings are lowered on selected categories of intermediate short-term commercial time deposits, July 20 and September 26, 1966.
		b. Regulation Q ceilings extended to S&Ls September 26, 1966.

(continued)

c. Regulation Q ceilings extended to mutual savings banks, October 1, 1966.

d. Ceilings on selected categories of deposits for commercial banks, mutual savings banks, and S&Ls are changed at least once in 1968–1970.

e. July 1973, multiple-maturity rates on negotiable CDs greater than $100,000 are suspended.

f. July 1, 1973, ceiling rates on $1,000 new-denomination four-year CDs are suspended. Subsequently, a limit of 5% of total time and savings deposits is imposed.

g. November 1, 1973, a 7.5% ceiling on four-year $1,000 minimum-denomination CDs is imposed.

h. 1974–1979, minor modifications in the rates are instituted at least once yearly.

8. a. August 28, 1969, applied Regulations Q and D to repurchase agreements with all nonbanks and on all assets but U.S. government and U.S. agency securities.

8. Early–mid-1969

8. Repurchase agreements and loan sales.

Table 3.2. *(Continued)*

Date—Period	Innovation	Regulatory Response
		b. April 13, 1979, public comment requested on proposal to apply 5% reserve requirement on RPs made with all but member banks.
9. Early–mid-1969	9. Small capital note sales.	9. June 1970, extended Regulations Q and D to debentures with less than seven years' maturity issued in amounts less than $500.
10. Mid-1969	10. Bank holding company and related commercial paper.	10. September 18, 1970, bank holding company and subsidiary sales of commercial paper subjected to 10% marginal reserve requirement under Regulation D when proceeds used to fund bank. Bank Holding Company Act amendments, December 13, 1970, extended effective coverage.
11. Mid-1969	11. Documented discount notes and ineligible acceptances.	11. None.
12. July 1973	12. Variable-rate "wild card" CD.	12. Ceilings reimposed, October, 1973.
13. July 24, 1974	13. Citicorp floating-rate notes.	13. Passage of S.3838, signed October 29, 1974, giving Board authority to define any BHC debt issue as a deposit except commercial paper sold to institutional investors and to impose Regulations Q and D.

14. July, 1977	14. Citicorp rising-rate notes.	14. Federal Reserve decides to monitor developments at this time.
15. June 1, 1978	15. Six-month money market CD authorized.	15. a. Money market CD with ceilings pegged to T-bill rate authorized for both banks and S&Ls. Differential permitted for S&Ls. b. March 15, 1979, compounding is prohibited and 1/4% differential permitted thrifts is eliminated whenever ceiling reaches 9%.
16. June 1, 1978	16. Eight-year fixed-ceiling certificates.	16. Authorized for S&Ls and banks.
17. May 30, 1979	17. Four-year floating rate certificates.	17. Effective July 1, 1979, bases ceiling of new certificate rate on four-year Treasury rate, raises savings deposit rate to 5-1/4%, and eliminates minimum denomination on all but 26-week money market certificate.
18. October 6, 1979		18. An 8% marginal reserve requirement is imposed on increases in managed liabilities in excess of $100 million or the average amount of managed liabilities held by a member bank, Edge corporation, or by a family of U.S. branches or agencies of a foreign bank. Liabilities include time deposits over $100,000 with maturities less than one year, Eurodollar borrowings, RPs against U.S. government and agency

(continued)

Table 3.2. *(Continued)*

Date—Period	Innovation	Regulatory Response
19. January 1, 1980	19. 2½-year certificates.	securities, and Federal funds borrowings from nonmember institutions (Federal funds borrowings from member banks, Edge corporations, U.S. agencies, or branches of foreign banks with worldwide assets in excess of \$1 billion are exempt).
		19. a. 2-½-year CD with ceilings pegged 50 basis points below similar rate on Treasury obligation for thrifts and 75 basis points below that rate for banks, rate determined three business days before first of month. CUs permitted to offer same rate as S&Ls and MSBs on share drafts over 90 days.
		b. Eliminated four-year floating-rate CD authorized May 30, 1979.
		c. Ceiling raised to 5-¾% on certificates maturing between 90 days and one year.

d. Eliminates differential on IRA/Keogh funds and governmental unit funds when placed in 26-week MMCs or new 2-½-year certificate.

20. Congress passes Monetary Control Act which provides for six-year phase-out of deposit rate ceilings under guidance of DIDC.

21. January 14, 1981, "Purchase Plus" disapproved by Federal Reserve Board.

22. FRB approves plan because bank maintains reserves against balances and because it is a bank plan and not one by a subsidiary of a bank holding company.

23. May, 1981, Federal Reserve Board rules plan violates Regulation Q.

24. May 12, 1981, Federal Reserve rules Regulations Q & D apply to the new account.

21. Citicorp introduces "Purchase Plus" plan paying 8% interest on credit balances of credit card.

22. FNB of Maryland introduces credit balance plan on credit card paying 5-¼%.

23. Western Savings Bank offers "Floating Rate" certificate with $10,000 minimum adjusted weekly.

24. Bank of California offers "Money Market Plus" account which transfers domestic deposits to London branch where higher than Regulation Q rates are paid.

25. Twelve Midwest banks announce formation of multistate money market fund that will pay money market rates and invest in member bank CDs.

20. March 1980
21. December 1980
22. January 14, 1981
23. March 1981
24. May 7, 1981
25. May 11, 1981

Table 3.2. *(Continued)*

Date—Period	Innovation	Regulatory Response
26. May 13, 1981	26. Merrill Lynch announces plan to purchase small bank CDs to help recycle small deposits.	
27. May 1981	27. Provident National Bank announces "Deposit Sweep Account" from which funds are transferred daily to a money market fund. A number of other banks subsequently announce similar plans for both consumers and corporate customers.	
28. June 1981	28. Bank of Utah and Bank of Ravenswood (Chicago) announce retail RP for consumers.	
29. June 30, 1981	29. Equitable Life Insurance becomes first insurance company to offer corporate cash management service.	
30. August 1981	30. Philadelphia banks gain attention for fierce rate competition in retail RPs in anticipation of all savers certificates.	
31. August 1981	31. Sears announces offering of money market mutual fund through its Dean Witter subsidiary.	
32. August 1981	32. Dreyfus offers sweep account in conjunction with Bank of New York.	

No.	Date	No.	Event	No.	Description
33.	October 1, 1981	33.	Banks and thrifts begin to offer all savers certificates which pay up to 70% of T-bill rate, and first $1,000 of interest income ($2,000 for couple) is tax free.	33.	Offered pursuant to federal legislation to stem disintermediation.
34.	December 1, 1981			34.	Ceilings are lifted on IRA and Keogh accounts.
35.	February 16, 1982	35.	ORBANCO offers $5,000-minimum denomination note of the BHC with one-day maturity.	35.	February 18, 1982, note is not allowed by Federal Reserve Board.
36.	March 9, 1982			36.	Union National Bank is ordered by OCC to stop its "Investor Account" (which swept funds from NOW accounts into large CDs).
37.	May 1, 1982			37.	DIDC eliminates deposit rate ceilings on time deposits with maturities in excess of 3½ years.
38.	September 1, 1982			38.	DIDC authorizes new seven-to-31-day-maturity nonnegotiable time deposit in minimum denominations of $20,000 whose rate is tied to T-bill rate (90 days). Thrifts may pay T-bill rate while banks pay 25 basis points less.
39.	October 1982			39.	Congress passes legislation which authorizes banks and thrifts to offer account to compete with money market mutual funds.
					a. Money Market Deposit Account is authorized effective December 14, 1982.

(continued)

Table 3.2. *(Continued)*

Date—Period	Innovation	Regulatory Response
		b. Super NOW account is authorized effective January 5, 1983.
40. November 17, 1982	40. Pittsburgh National offers small business sweep account.	
41. April 1, 1983		41. Rate ceilings on 2½–3½-year time deposits are removed as per schedule of DIDC.
42. October 1, 1983		42. Rate ceilings on all bank accounts except passbook savings accounts, NOW accounts, and time deposits in accounts less than $2,500 maturing between seven and 31 days are removed.

For the most part, the regulatory responses noted have been reactions to innovations and market pressures that were perceived to be having significant effects on depository financial institutions, market shares, and profitability. Regulatory changes were rarely made in anticipation of market changes. These responses to market innovations were generally of two types: those designed to deal with broad financial industry problems affecting deposit fund flows (such as disintermediation) and those designed to restore "competitive balance" between banks and thrift institutions. The imposition and changes in the levels of deposit rate ceilings and the development of new savings certificates reflect the former type of action, while the NOW account, telephone and automatic transfer activity, and actions affecting the differential ceilings applicable to commercial banks and thrifts reflect the latter.[7]

The general process being described, then, is a cycle with several parties—commercial banks, thrifts, unregulated (or less-regulated) competitors, and the regulators—all responding to economic pressures affecting the configuration of services to customers. The principal forces sustaining this dynamic process have been inflation, the rapid rise and volatility of interest rates, and the availability of technology needed for cost-efficient implementation. The persistence of the pressures stimulating innovation and the variety of institutional responses are quite striking. These forces and their consequences are analyzed in the balance of this section, which is divided into several parts. The first focuses on the general evolution of new instruments and markets as banking organizations attempted to pay rates competitive with open market rates. The second deals with a subset of innovations that have evolved as a means to pay interest on transactions balances. The remainder explore other types of regulations and the related innovations they stimulated.

Market Innovations and Regulation Q

Federal Funds and RPs.   The Federal funds market has existed since the early 1920s. However, it did not begin to expand until the early 1960s, following the decline of bank excess reserves, the run-up of interest rates, and the earnings and liquidity problems associated with 1959–1960 credit crunch. In the early postwar years, interest rates were relatively stable, and banks had ample security holdings and excess reserves to meet liquidity needs. By 1960, however, banks' cash assets and Treasury securities had declined to 49.2% of total deposits (compared with 74.1% in 1947). Furthermore, since much of their Treasury holdings were at low rates, sale of these securities to meet liquidity needs in 1959 and 1960 as market

Table 3.3 Payments System Innovations

Date—Period	Innovation	Regulatory Action or Response
1. July 28, 1970	1. Consumers Savings Bank asks Massachusetts Commissioner of Banks to permit NOWs.	1. Request denied September 28, 1970.
2. September 1970	2. Nonnegotiable preauthorized transfers for household-related expenditures for S&Ls.	2. FHLBB promulgates enabling regulations under authority contained in Housing Act of 1970.
3. May 2, 1972	3. NOWs are permitted in Massachusetts for state-chartered MSBs.	3. Massachusetts Supreme Court rules on May 2, 1972, that NOWs are legal.
4. September 1972	4. NOWs offered in New Hampshire by state-chartered MSBs.	4. None.
5. January 1, 1974	5. NOWs permitted by federal law for all depository institutions in Massachusetts and New Hampshire except credit unions.	5. Public Law 93-100, August 16, 1973.
6. January 1974	6. First Federal S&L, Lincoln, Neb., establishes Hinky Dinky EFT Terminal.	6. None.
7. Early 1974	7. Growth of money market mutual funds.	7. None.
8. 1974	8. Comptroller of Currency rules CBCTs are not branches.	8. Decision overturned by courts.
9. August 1974	9. CU share drafts experiment authorized.	9. Section 721.3 of Rules and Regulations of NCUA.
10. November 1974	10. Commercial banks are authorized to accept savings deposits from state and local governments.	

	Date	Event
11.	April 7, 1975	Member banks are authorized by Federal Reserve to offer telephone transfers from savings to checking account.
12.	April 11, 1975	FHLBB broadens the 1970 power of S&Ls to make preauthorized transfers for any purpose.
13.	September 2, 1975	Commercial banks are authorized to make preauthorized third-party transfers from savings accounts for any purpose.
14.	November 10, 1975	CBs are authorized to offer savings deposits to partnerships and corporations in accounts less than $150,000.
15.	February 27, 1976	NOW accounts for all of New England become effective.
16.	December 8, 1977	CUs are permitted expanded asset powers and permitted share drafts.
17.	October 1978	NOW accounts authorized for New York.
18.	November 6, 1978	CBs are authorized to make automatic transfers from savings to checking accounts.
19.	November 1978	FHLBB proposes nonnegotiable third-party-payment account through which paper transactions can be made.
20.	April 20, 1979	U.S. Court of Appeals for District of Columbia rules ATS, RSUs, and share drafts are illegal.

(continued)

Table 3.3. *(Continued)*

Date—Period	Innovation	Regulatory Action or Response
21. December 28, 1979	21. PL 96-161 authorizes NOWs in New Jersey.	
22. March 31, 1980	22. Monetary Control Act.	22. a. Extends NOW accounts nationwide. b. Expressly permits ATS, RSUs, and share drafts to banks, S&Ls, and credit unions, respectively.
23. January 20, 1981		23. FHLBB rules regulatory approval no longer needed to establish RSUs except on interstate basis.
24. April 3, 1981	24. Dean Witter begins new cash management account to compete with Merrill Lynch.	
25. Mid-1981	25. Numerous banks announce in-home banking experiments.	

26. Mid-1981

27. May 21, 1981

28. August 31, 1981

29. October 31, 1981

30. Early 1982

31. March 12, 1982

32. October 15, 1982

26. Numerous different bank groups announce shared interstate ATM networks.

27. AT&T unveils videotext network.

28. CHIPS announces same-day settlement.

29. SWIFT will begin charging debit and credit card transactions.

30. Numerous joint ventures in supplying in-home banking are announced.
    a. Knight Ridder—Southeast Bancorp.
    b. B of A—Times Mirror.

31. SWIFT and Interbank Association announce on-line systems to provide instant confirmation of overseas balances.

32. Bank Wire announces same-day settlement.

rates rose implied that large capital losses would be realized. As an alternative to selling assets, banks began to recognize that by applying "liability management" concepts they could simply purchase short-term funds through the issuance of deposits or through Federal funds borrowings to meet temporary liquidity requirements.[8] Repeated overnight recourse to the Federal funds market began to be regarded by many banks as permanent source of funds.

In reality, the Federal funds market owes its existence principally to four regulations: the prohibition of the payment of interest on demand deposits, Regulation D (requiring reserves to be held by member banks on deposits), borrowing and lending limits, and the limits on minimum maturity for time deposits. Moreover, since the 1959–1960 period federal intervention and regulation have significantly shaped this market. For example, in 1963 the Comptroller of the Currency paved the way for the growth of the market when he ruled that national bank Federal funds transactions were exempt from statutory borrowing and lending limits.[9] Similarly in 1964 the Federal Reserve ruled that the borrowing of interbank deposits was exempt from Regulations D and Q which had the effect of expanding the definition of Federal funds to include not only balances held at the Federal Reserve but also borrowings of interbank deposits. Bank participation in the Federal funds market was also given momentum by the Federal Reserve's switch in 1968 to lagged-reserve accounting. This provided additional incentive for banks to manage their reserve accounts to meet their required reserves.

The Federal funds market expanded significantly during the 1969 credit crunch. Participation broadened as the minimum size of the transaction dropped. In addition, banks began to evade the restrictions on the payment of interest on demand deposits in 1969 to channel funds for their corporate customers from their demand deposits into the funds market on an overnight basis for which interest was paid. On February 12, 1970, the Federal Reserve acted to stop the practice as being equivalent to paying interest on demand deposits because idle demand balances were being sold in the overnight market. Regulations D and Q were applied to all Federal funds transactions except for those among banks and a few exempt institutions. Paradoxically, while the Federal Reserve acted to exclude the flow of corporate and other funds into the market, at the same time it encouraged participation by other depository financial institutions and U.S. agencies. This was done by expanding the definition of a bank under Regulations D and Q (and hence, permissible suppliers of Federal funds) to include S&Ls, cooperative banks, mutual savings banks, the Export-Import Bank, Minibank Capital Corporation, Edge Act and Agreement corporations, and foreign banks. In addition, federal agencies and government securities dealers were exempt.[10]

Closely related to the growth of bank participation in the Federal funds market was the practice of obtaining immediately available funds through the sale of loans and securities under agreements to repurchase (known as RPs) at open market rates. This use of RPs was also viewed by the Federal Reserve as an avoidance of Regulation Q. On August 28, 1969, RPs were subject to Regulations D and Q whenever the purchaser was a nonbank or the sale involved assets other than U.S. Treasury or agency securities. As was the case with the Federal funds market, the potential use of RPs was expanded in 1970 through the interpretation of the definition of a bank under Regulations D and Q.

The net result of the 1969 and 1970 interpretations was that the Federal funds and RP markets grew in importance. Simpson (1979) indicates that as of June 30, 1978, banks obtained about 8.5% of their funds from these markets. Moreover, dependence upon these markets increases with bank size. Banks with over $1 billion in deposits borrowed about 14.3% of their funds from these sources; about one-fifth of these banks in this class relied upon these markets for between 20 and 40% of their funding. More recent data show that reliance on the Federal funds and RP market has persisted. As of 1982, banks attained about 8.7% (banks over $300 million borrowed about 11%) of their funds in this market.

Interestingly enough, thrift institutions and the Home Loan Bank System became significant suppliers of Federal funds to commercial banks in the late 1970s. By 1978, thrifts accounted for about 75% of the nonbank sources of Federal funds, mostly in the form of overnight, unsecured funds. The thrift industry supplied about 20% of all RP/Federal funds. One implication of this growth of the RP/Federal funds market is that it may have served to tie the thrift industry and banking organizations closer together and transmit thrift problems during periods of disintermediation to the banking sector. It is interesting to speculate on the extent to which the introduction of the money market certificate in 1978 forestalled a withdrawal of thrift industry funds from the Federal funds and RP market in 1979 and 1980 and avoided a bank liquidity problem.

In late April 1979, First Pennsylvania Corporation announced the offering of a "small saver" RP with a $1,000 minimum denomination and a one-year maturity whose rate was based on one-year Treasury obligations. This represented a clear attempt to provide the smaller saver with an attractive alternative outside of Regulation Q.

On October 6, 1979, as a result of the concern for credit expansion supported by heavy bank reliance on managed liabilities (including financing in the Federal funds/RP market) the Federal Reserve Board imposed an 8% marginal reserve requirement on increases in member-bank-managed liabilities in excess of $100 million, including Federal funds and RPs. Included in the definition of managed liabilities were time deposits

in excess of $100,000 maturing in less than one year, Eurodollar borrow-
ings, RPs against U.S. government and agency securities, and Federal
funds borrowings from nonmember institutions. Federal funds borrowings
from member banks, Edge corporations, U.S. agencies, or branches of
foreign banks with worldwide assets in excess of $1 billion were exempt.
The combination of the differentiation between exempt and nonexempt
lenders and the imposition of marginal reserve requirements led to a tiering
of the funds market. Funds from exempt lenders traded at about 25 basis
points more than those from nonexempt lenders. This was far less than
the 120 to 130 basis points that would be justified by the reserve requirement differential. Following enactment of the Depository Institutions Deregulation and Monetary Control Act (hereafter MCA), these marginal
reserve requirements were dropped.

Eurodollars.   In addition to increased dependence on the RP/Federal funds
market during tight money periods, banks developed other sources of
funds. In mid-1966, for example, banks were faced both with large runoffs
of CDs as market rates rose above the applicable ceilings and with large
loan demands as the result of heavy commitments. Those large money-
center banks with foreign branches began to borrow heavily in the Eurodollar market. Eurodollar borrowings were an attractive source of funds
since they were not subject to interest rate ceilings nor were they reservable. Subsequently (October 1969) a 10% marginal reserve requirement
was imposed on Eurodollar borrowings, and this was increased to 20% a
month later. The effect was to price U.S. banks out of the Eurodollar
market (except, of course, for offshore uses). Reserve requirements of
Eurodollar borrowings have subsequently been lowered three times.[11]

Commercial Paper.   As the result of pressures of disintermediation in
1969, the Eurodollar, Federal funds, and RP markets expanded as sources
of funds. It was also during this period that the first of the financial innovations having significant implications for the growth and expansion of
bank holding companies as funding vehicles also developed.
     Shut out of the Eurodollar and other markets and pressed for funds in
late 1969 and into 1970 as interest rate ceilings again became a significant
constraint, banks began to exploit the holding company organizational
form by issuing nonreservable commercial paper as a liability of the holding
company and downstreaming funds to subsidiary banks.[12]
     The sale of bank holding company commercial paper was a variation
of earlier bank experience with sales of promissory notes. Note sales first
received attention in 1964, when First National Bank of Boston announced
plans to offer a short-term promissory note. In 1966 such notes with ma-

turities less than two years were subjected to Regulations D and Q. Specifically exempted, however, were subordinated notes with maturities greater than two years. Thus, it was not surprising in 1969 that, when rates began to rise, some banks began to market small-denomination subordinated-capital notes and debentures with maturities in excess of two years. Predictably, the Federal Reserve extended Regulations D and Q in June 1970 to instruments with maturities less than seven years and amounts less than $500.[13]

There is little if any direct evidence to suggest that banks perceived the financing advantages of one-bank holding companies when the first wave of formations occurred. It is interesting to note, however, that the surge of interest in the one-bank holding company organizational form occurred over the last half of 1968 when the gap between Regulation Q ceilings and commercial paper rates widened to over 250 basis points. Between September 1 and December 31, 1968, seven banks with $14.1 billion in deposits formed one-bank holding companies and another 76 banks with deposits of $71.8 billion announced their intentions to form such companies.[14] This included 34 of the nation's 100 largest banks.

Over the last two and one-half quarters of 1969 and the first half of 1970, commercial paper issued by bank holding companies became a major source of funds to banks. Sales of bank-related commercial paper increased from about $1.9 billion in July of 1969 to a high of $7.8 billion a year later. The impact of this source of funds is particularly striking when it is recognized that banks lost over $13 billion in CDs between November 1968 and September 1969 and were able to recover nearly 20% through commercial paper sales over that period.

In the last week of June, 1970, Penn Central failed. This caused considerable concern on the part of the Federal Reserve about the viability of the commercial paper market. Total commercial paper outstanding declined by about $2.4 billion or 6% between June 24 (just prior to the failure) and July 1 (following the failure). Most of this decline ($2,253 million) was in nonbank-related outstandings. Of this amount, Timlen (1976) indicates that $1.25 billion or 55.5% of this decline was in the paper of Chrysler Financial and Commercial Credit, which were two captive finance companies. As the result of these disruptions, the Federal Reserve realized it could not shut banks out of all wholesale funding markets and temporarily suspended the ceilings on large CDs with maturities less than 90 days.[15] This action sought to make it easier for banks to obtain short-term funds, which in turn would facilitate bank lending to accommodate those firms no longer able to issue commercial paper.

Analysis of the available data (see Eisenbeis, 1980) suggests that the plan to substitute bank credit for commercial paper was substantially successful. About 90% of the borrowings frozen out of the commercial paper market were supplied by bank sources.

It is also interesting to note that issuing conditions in the paper market appeared to have stabilized within another week, albeit at a somewhat lower level of activity. Moreover, by the end of July, bank C&I loans (both total and short term) had declined below their pre–Penn Central failure levels while loans to nonbank financial institutions—principally personal and sales finance companies—had also stabilized, but at a higher level. Large CDs, on the other hand, continued their rapid growth as a result of the relaxation of the ceilings and more than doubled their pre-failure level by the end of the year.

Bank-related sales of commercial paper remained high over the summer of 1970 until Regulation D was amended to cover commercial paper sales by bank holding companies and their subsidiaries whenever the proceeds were used to supply funds to bank affiliates. The effect of this regulatory change was to price banking organizations out of the paper market. Interestingly, withdrawal of banking organizations from the commercial paper market had essentially no effect on the supply of funds to nonbank issuers, nor were more funds made available to nonbank issuers. Nonbank outstandings remained relatively stable over the period, but $1 billion or so lower than prior to the Penn Central failure.

Variable-Rate CDs and Note Issues.   During the first half of 1973, disintermediation pressures were again increasing. On May 16 interest rates ceilings were removed on all large CDs over $100,000. Ceilings were also removed on July 1 on four-year, $1,000-minimum-denomination CDs.[16] As a result, large CDs expanded rapidly. In an attempt to keep the funds of their smaller depositors, institutions also began to offer the small, four-year certificates at rates more than 200 basis points above the previously applicable ceilings. Some institutions developed variable-rate forms of this four-year instrument, with rates pegged to the short-term Treasury bill rate, the prime, and even the CPI. Alarmed at what appeared to be dangerously high offering rates and wishing to shut off what was mistakenly regarded to be a disastrous experiment, the Federal Reserve imposed a 7.5% ceiling rate as of November 1, 1973.

Closely related to the 1973 variable-rate CDs was the $800 million floating-rate note issue announced by Citicorp on July 24, 1974. These notes were long term (15-year maturity) and issued in minimum denominations of $1,000. The notes were negotiable, a secondary market was maintained, and they were redeemable every six months after a two-year holding period. The rates were pegged one percentage point above the Treasury bill rate, and initial offerings were 200 basis points above the comparable Regulation Q ceilings. Other similar note issues appeared over the next few months, with volume totaling nearly $1.5 billion. The note issues were imitated with varying success by a variety of financial institutions, including savings banks, S&Ls, and life insurance companies. They were also copied by nonfinancial firms such as Standard Oil of Indiana and Tennessee Steel Forge Corp. While terms varied somewhat, the essential features of these issues were that the notes were long term (six to 25 years) with a variable yield pegged to a short-term market rate (usually the three-month Treasury bill rate).

The issuance of these floating-rate notes generated great congressional concern over possible disintermediation and the threat to flows of funds into thrift institutions and housing. Congress acted promptly, passing S.3838 in October of 1974 giving the Federal Reserve Board authority to regulate nearly all BHC note issues and to subject them to Regulations D and Q. The congressional activity and interest in Citicorp's note issue caused Citicorp to scale down its intended note issue to $650 million. After passage of S.3838 with its threat of application of Regulations D and Q, no new issues were forthcoming. As might be expected, issues of floating-rate notes slacked off markedly as market rates declined after 1974.

Citicorp innovated a similar note issue in July 1977 when it began to test-market in four midwest states a five-year, $500-minimum-denomination, small-note issue. Although the notes were designed to be attractive to small savers, they did not generate much attention.

There were several subsequent deposit innovations for banks, S&Ls, and mutual savings banks, which are detailed in Table 3.2. These included the authorization of a new, longer-maturity, eight-year certificate and a nonnegotiable short-term money market CD that went into effect June 1, 1978.[17] These were followed by a no-minimum-denomination, two-and-one-half-year certificate whose rate was tied to the rate on two-and-one-half-year Treasury securities.

Pass-through Certificates. In addition to the development of new liabilities and liability management techniques in order to segment deposit markets and offer more attractive alternatives to money market instruments, attempts were made to increase the liquidity and attractiveness of longer-term, relatively illiquid assets, especially mortgages. Following the GNMA pass-through mortgage certificates, and mortgage-backed bonds issued by thrifts, banks also began to form pools of mortgages held in trust against which pass-through certificates or bonds are issued; the first was Bank of America.

The pass-through security is a more attractive instrument to investors than individual mortgages for several reasons. First, the securities may be issued in relatively small denominations and they appeal to a broader class of investors. Second, because of overcollateralization and low default rates, the securities are extremely safe. Third, because they may be rated by investment rating services, they are eligible (and thus more attractive) instruments for institutional investors, many of whom are limited to rated securities. Fourth, the maturity of the instrument is equal to the average maturity of the pool, which is substantially less than the 30 years or so for which most mortgages are made. Fifth, the yields are closer to open market yields. And last, the securities themselves are likely to be more liquid than mortgages, and secondary markets are likely to develop. These instruments are the precursor of what may be a broader involvement in asset sales by banks, again as a means to avoid Regulation D if the opportunity costs of holding reserves in non-interest-bearing form increase again.

Innovations by Nondepository Institutions. Depository financial institutions were not the only institutions to respond to disintermediation pressures. As interest rates rose in the 1970s and the differentials between Regulation Q ceilings and market rates widened, incentives were created for nonregulated nondepository financial institutions to offer and/or innovate financial instruments that were close (often superior) substitutes for those offered by banking organizations and that bore market rates. The small note issues by Sears and other firms mentioned earlier are but one example.

New organizational forms also came into existence. Money market mutual funds, for example, became an important way for small depositors to obtain rates higher than Regulation Q rates on their funds while also offering several advantages over traditional savings and time deposits. Money market mutual funds were more liquid than time deposits because they had no fixed maturity or withdrawal penalties. Second, rates fluctuated with market rates, and that was particularly important in the period of rising rates of late 1979 and early 1980. Some funds permitted drafts to be written that could be used for transactions purposes, and deposits in one closed-end investment fund sponsored by Merrill Lynch were also 100% insured by the FDIC.

In 1974, there were only six such funds with about $200 million in assets. By the end of September 1979, prior to passage of the Monetary Control Act of 1980, there were 68 funds totaling more than $36 billion. At the time of the Garn-St Germain Depository Institutions Act of 1982, non-institutional deposits in these funds approached $182 billion, or about 15% of bank and thrift small time and savings deposits. Even the subsequent authorization of the $2,500 minimum-deposit Super NOW account and the MMDA account mandated by the 1982 act (both of which were free of interest rate ceilings and grew to over $290 billion in just two short months, as of February 16, 1983) did not reduce the importance of money market mutual funds. Only about $10 billion of this growth was estimated to have come from the money funds.

Another equally important innovation by nondepository institutions was the development of the cash management account, first by Merrill Lynch and then widely imitated by other brokerage firms. This account combined a margin account at a brokerage firm, a captive money market mutual fund, a Visa debit card, and a bank servicing arrangement. The cash management account paid interest on funds placed in the special margin account by investing them in a captive money market mutual fund. At the same time payable through drafts or a Visa debit transaction could be made against funds in the account. Margin credit could be extended automatically when need to cover overdrafts. Variants and refinements of this basic service have subsequently been offered by numerous other brokerage firms.

Finally, the recent expansion of the money brokering activity of brokerage firms and other institutions has enabled both individuals and corporate customers to obtain high rates, risk free. The money brokers are placing funds as agents in federally insured deposit accounts across the country. Because of federal insurance, risk is of little concern to the depositor and so funds flow to the highest bidder, which in some instances has been risky and in danger of failure.[18]

The Responses of Consumers

Just as financial institutions were induced to avoid the implicit costs of rate ceilings, individuals were quick to perceive the advantages of searching among a broader range of financial instruments for market rates. During the 1969 credit crunch, for example, individuals turned to Treasury bills and other Treasury obligations for higher returns. These instruments were risk free and highly liquid, and the yield spreads more than compensated for any associated transaction costs. Again, however, regulatory action was taken, this time by the Treasury in February 1970 when minimum denominations were raised from $1,000 to $10,000. This action effectively provided a barrier to shifts of funds in smaller denominations from thrifts and banks into this market. Individuals soon, however, discovered that federal agency securities had lower minimum denominations than Treasury obligations and were virtually risk free.

The rapid consumer acceptance of alternatives—such as Treasury instruments, money market funds, and cash management accounts—to earn market rates during the 1970s and 1980s clearly indicated that when the opportunity costs to consumers resulting from regulatory constraints were sufficiently high (1) to overcome the inconvenience and costs associated with seeking out higher rate alternative, (2) to break down the resistance to dealing with nonlocal institutions, and (3) to compensate for holding a greater portion of their financial assets in insured forms, consumers readily shifted their funds into alternative investments.

The Consequences of Market Innovations to Avoid Reserve Requirements and Deposit Rate Ceilings.   Innovations triggered by Regulations Q and D have had several effects on the portfolios and organizational structure of depository institutions. First, banks were spurred to adopt the bank holding company form to exploit the additional financing capabilities of the organizations.[19] This was particularly true of the large money-center banks and others whose deposit sources of funds were likely to be more interest sensitive. By 1977, 71.8% of commercial bank deposits were in subsidiaries of bank holding companies, but only 14% of subsidy bank deposits (both foreign and domestic) were in banks other than the organizations' lead banks.[20] As of 1982 about 30% of the nation's banks were subsidiaries of bank holding companies, and these controlled about 75% of the banking resources.

Second, both banks and thrifts are relying more on relatively short-term, interest-sensitive sources of funds. For example, the sum of managed (wholesale) liabilities and ceiling-free retail deposits at commercial banks increased from 14.5% of assets in 1969 to about 40% by year-end 1982.

Third, Regulation Q pressures stimulated banking organizations to look for nondomestic sources of funds and in the process to expand their foreign operations. For example, the number of foreign branches of U.S. banks increased from 477 with assets of $55.1 billion in 1971 to over 738 with $247 billion in assets in 1977, accounting for about 25% of commercial bank assets. The number of Edge Act and Agreement corporations increased from 85 with $5.5 billion in assets in 1971 to 122 with more than $11.1 billion in assets in 1977. In November 1983 about $260 billion of the outstanding $463 billion in liabilities of U.S. foreign branches was owed to foreigners.

Finally, it has resulted in increased competition for funds from not only thrift institutions but also nonregulated firms.

Innovations to Pay Interest on Demand Deposits

As noted previously, the development of cash management techniques by businesses resulted in the evolution of instruments and markets to provide a rate of return on what otherwise might have been idle demand deposit balances. Hence, many of the innovations discussed above may be viewed, at least in part, as the means to pay explicit interest on demand deposits. This is particularly true of the developments in the Federal funds/ RP markets and in the short-term large CD markets (see Simpson, 1978). Financial institutions also evolved ways of paying implicit interest on demand deposits by providing free or subsidized services, convenience of location (through branching and installation of EFT terminals), gifts, "premiums," and other inducements to open accounts and increase balances, and by offering lower rates on loans.[21]

In periods of unusually high interest rates, the value of these implicit returns was swamped by what depositors could earn elsewhere. This led, of course, to innovations such as consumer sweep accounts, money market funds, EFT, and NOW accounts, which now provide for explicit interest on certain types of transactions balances, mostly for consumers.[22]

Federal regulators of financial institutions have played an important role in payment system innovations, in particular through the selective relaxation of inhibiting restrictions. As distinct from the regulatory responses to innovation discussed in the previous section, which were usually coordinated attempts by all the regulators to deal with broader financial industry problems such as disintermediation, action in the payments area has typically been more partisan. By and large, the actions have been designed to promote the interests of the public and one segment of the industry and/or to restore competitive balance.

Perhaps the single most dominant force generating innovations in the payments system area is again rooted in the prohibition of interest payments on demand deposits, in Regulation Q, and in the problems related to disintermediation. For example, the common interpretation of the "thrift institution" problem prior to the Monetary Control Act and Garn-St Germain Act related to the mismatching of the maturities of the institutions' assets and liabilities. Basically they borrowed short and lent long. The usual prescription to alleviate the associated problems as put forth by the Hunt Commission (1971) and other reform efforts was to expand the range of asset and liability powers for thrifts. Numerous payment system innovations were instituted as a means to correct the effects of disintermediation from thrifts by permitting them to offer various kinds of payments accounts to broaden their potential customer base.

The expansion of thrifts into the payments business followed three concurrent paths. These included the use of (1) checklike instruments, such as NOW drafts and NINOWS, (2) telephone and preauthorized transfers, and (3) electronic funds transfers. The first was initiated by a regulatory change and the others resulted from a combination of innovations by the institutions and subsequent changes in statutes and regulations.

In 1970 two events took place which resulted in expansion of thrift institutions in the payments area. In July of 1970 the Consumers Savings Bank in Massachusetts requested approval to offer a negotiable order of withdrawal (NOW) account as a means of attracting checking account customers. In September, the Massachusetts Commissioner of Banks denied the request and consumers took the issue to court. At about the same time, the FHLBB promulgated regulations enabling thrifts to offer preauthorized nonnegotiable transfers from a savings account for payment of certain household-related expenses, mainly mortgage payments. The movement of New England thrifts was given a significant boost by the May 1972 ruling of the Massachusetts Supreme Court that NOW accounts were legal. The accounts spread to New Hampshire. In an attempt to deal with the fact that state-chartered mutual savings banks had a competitive advantage over federal S&Ls and commercial banks, a federal law was passed permitting NOWs in Massachusetts and New Hampshire for all depository financial institutions except credit unions, effective January 1, 1974. Pressure to expand the "NOW account experiment" gained momentum. A share draft "experiment" was authorized in late 1974 permitting credit unions, which had no comparable transaction powers, to offer accounts on which drafts could be written. And NOW accounts were expanded by Congress to all of New England in 1976 and to New York in October of 1978. The NCUA granted share drafts to all federally chartered credit unions in 1977 along with expanded asset powers.

This pattern—where the introduction of a financial innovation in the payments area that bestowed a competitive advantage on one segment or class of financial institutions and in turn generated a subsequent regulatory or legislative response—appeared time and again. For example, in 1974 CBs were given telephone transfer powers from savings to checking accounts on April 7. Nine days later the FHLBB expanded the preauthorized transfer powers of S&Ls. Less than six months later commercial banks were granted equal powers. Finally, as part of the move to extend NOW accounts nationwide, commercial banks were given the authority, effective November 6, 1978, to transfer funds automatically from a customer's savings account to his or her checking account. In effect, this permitted a customer to earn interest on transaction balances held in a savings account that was tapped whenever the checking account balance fell below the level required to cover a check. In the extreme, the checking account could carry a zero balance. The FHLBB proposed a nonnegotiable paper-based transfer account through which automatic transfers could be made in an attempt to enable S&Ls to compete with banks.[23]

Unlike many other financial innovations, the spread of computers and the automation of deposit accounting played an important role in enabling the practical use of automatic and preauthorized transfers, both in facilitating circumvention of restrictions on the payment of interest on transaction balances and in reducing the costs of branching.

It was more probably the branching and operating efficiency considerations than interest on demand deposits, however, that spurred commercial banks to embark on EFT experiments during the late 1960s and early 1970s. Most states and federal law were silent on the question of whether automated teller machines (or other EFT terminals) would be construed to be branches. If they were branches under federal definitions, their deployment would be subject to the McFadden Act. If not, EFT devices promised a means for banks to expand geographically where they were not permitted to branch both intra- and interstate. There was a great deal of uncertainty for commercial banks surrounding the legal status of retail EFT machines.

In 1974 the Comptroller of the Currency brought the issue to a head, ruling that ATMs were not branches and hence could be deployed statewide by national banks in states without explicit statutes governing their deployment. The results were an acceleration of activity, particularly in unit banking states, and a host of court cases. The controlling decision is *Independent Bankers Association v. Smith,* where ATMs were found to be branches.[24]

While the initial motive for commercial banks in the deployment of ATMs was rooted in constraints on branching, there was a different factor for S&Ls in the early 1970s, since there was no McFadden Act or similar restraint on branching by federally chartered S&Ls. For thrifts, EFT terminals and more sophisticated systems permitted them to offer third-party-payment accounts and transfers without having to deal with paper checks and without the necessity for congressional reform. As such, they promised to allow thrifts to tap the personal checking account market and break the tied relationship between demand and savings accounts by offering payments services in connection with an interest bearing account. Thus, thrifts saw EFT as a means to enter a market on attractive terms to the customer by offering interest on transactions accounts. This advantage was partly removed by the Financial Institutions Regulation and Interest Rate Control Act of 1978, which eliminated the differential interest rate ceiling advantage between banks and thrifts on such accounts.[25]

Thrift entry into the payments system was resolved once and for all by the Monetary Control Act of 1980, which provided for the phase-out of deposit rate ceilings by 1986 and authorized nationwide NOW accounts for banks and thrifts.[26] The Garn-St Germain Depository Institutions Act of 1982 went even further and permitted thrifts to offer checking accounts and money market deposit accounts (MMDA) and super NOW accounts to compete with money market funds. Corporate customers remain the only depositors not able to receive explicit interest on transaction deposits.

The Monetary Control Act of 1980 also required the Federal Reserve to charge for services that previously had been provided to member banks without charge and stated that these prices should be sufficient to cover the Federal Reserve's costs. This move to explicit pricing, together with the elimination of deposit rate ceilings, has ushered in a new set of pricing and marketing problems for depository institutions. A premium is now placed on knowledge of operating costs as competition has become price oriented rather than service oriented. In addition, explicit Federal Reserve pricing has altered the correspondent banking business, shifting a larger proportion of check processing to the private sector. Finally, explicit pricing, together with the requirement that the Federal Reserve also charge for float, is reducing the economic incentives for making payments using paper checks and favoring electronic means.

The payment system innovations discussed above promise to affect the competitive balance among depository financial institutions in a number of ways. First, they completely blur the distinction between demand and savings accounts. As it becomes feasible to hold all funds in a savings account and effectively make payments either directly via EFT or through a third-party paper payment account, there is no practical difference between a checking and a savings account. Second, with complete ease and instantaneous transfer of funds from one account to another at different institutions, the element of convenience that tends to induce depositors to keep savings and demand deposits at the same institution is further reduced. Third, this blurring of the distinction among accounts raises into question the practicality of maintaining existing prohibitions on demand deposit interest. These new devices—and in particular automatic transfers—offer the payment of interest but are less efficient instruments in that they use more real resources than would simply paying interest on demand deposits. Fourth, many of these innovations, particularly EFT, increase competition geographically because institutions can offer services at more and more widely spread locations than before. Fifth, the changes in Federal Reserve pricing charges following the Monetary Control Act are changing the competitive balance in both the correspondent banking systems and payment services more generally. The move to explicit pricing, together with the elimination of deposit rate ceilings, has ushered in a new set of strategic and planning problems for depository institutions. For some this has meant unbundling and explicit pricing of services that had previously been priced implicitly. To others, the future is seen in offering a wide range of services in an attempt to become department stores of finance. Whether the future lies in diversification or specialization has yet to be determined. However, the absence of evidence on significant scope or scale economies suggests that the structural implications of these changes may not be as great as some have argued. Finally, as nonbank financial institutions (especially merchants) become more directly involved in the payments mechanism by offering funds transfer services and accounts, it will become increasingly more difficult to distinguish between those institutions that are and are not banks. The greater is this shift, the stronger will be the pressures to revise Glass-Steagall and the separation between banking and commerce.

Capital Restrictions

It has already been argued that deposit rate ceilings and reserve requirements have provided a significant inducement for banking organizations to resort to nondeposit sources of funding. Regulatory agency capital policy has tended to accommodate the increased leverage that resulted by treating certain long-term debt issues as capital.

At the bank level, for example, following a ruling by the Comptroller of the Currency redefining unimpaired surplus to include subordinated debt with a maturity of more than three years, the agencies began considering such debt as "capital" for the purposes of assessing capital adequacy. In 1970, the Federal Reserve Board amended Regulations D and Q to exempt from those regulations subordinated debt issues with a maturity in excess of seven years. In July 1976, the regulations were amended to provide even greater flexibility to issue subordinate debt. Criteria were also established under which such debt could be considered for the purposes of assessing capital adequacy.[27] These rulings have been clarified and modified slightly since.

Another consequence of the regulatory avoidance was to provide incentives for bank holding company formation. More importantly, these regulations also induced holding companies to spin banking activities out into other parts of the organization, and for parent companies to fund both bank and nonbank expansion, especially during tight money periods when interest rates were rising. As noted in a Federal Reserve Board staff study of the bank holding company movement, one of the main implications of the bank holding company form of organization was that it facilitated increased leverage (see Curry, 1978). Indeed, the thrust of early regulatory and supervisory policy, and in particular capital policy, was to reinforce and unintentionally to encourage the conduct of financing and certain activities in other parts of the organization rather than within bank subsidiaries.

Following the 1970 amendments to the Bank Holding Company Act of 1956, BHC regulatory policy was designed to compartmentalize BHCs into two segments—a regulated component consisting of the bank subsidiaries and the parent holding company with its nonbanking subsidiaries. The objective was to isolate and protect banks from risk taking and abuse and, thus, to limit deposit insurance risks flowing from the rest of the organization, which was permitted to compete and operate in a less regulated and relatively unsupervised manner. At the same time BHCs were expected to be "sources of strength" to their bank affiliates, and there was an attempt to permit any benefits from bank holding company affiliation to be downstreamed to bank subsidiaries. In particular, the issuing of debt at the parent level with the proceeds going to purchase equity of subsidiary banks—a practice known as double leveraging—was not only condoned but often encouraged as a means to improve the capital positioning of bank holding company bank subsidiaries. This double leveraging was permitted, since the financing capabilities of the parent were presumably being relied upon to inject equity into subsidiary banks. As long as bank affiliates were effectively isolated by laws and regulations, such as Section 23A of the Federal Reserve Act, it was believed that the corporate veil would not be pierced in the event of bankruptcy or other legal action, and no harm would befall subsidiary banks.[28]

Such a policy would be appropriate if it were truly possible to isolate BHC bank subsidiaries totally from the rest of the organization. The available evidence, however, indicates that BHCs tend to operate more as integrated firms with the parent company dictating the key aspects of the bank subsidiaries' operations, such as organizational structure, financial and managerial philosophy, and specific functions such as funds management, correspondent relationships, asset and liability management, capitalization, and budgets. Moreover, BHC nonbanking subsidiaries appear to be even more integrated and tightly controlled than their bank subsidiaries (see, e.g., Murray, 1978, Rose, 1978, and Whalen, 1982a, 1982b). Supervisory experience with Hamilton Bankshares, for example, illustrates the infeasibility of isolating banking subsidiaries from the rest of the organization.

This realization has been reflected in recent changes in the banking agencies' capital adequacy standards. Until 1981, no explicit numerical capital standards had been put forth for bank holding companies, and previous bank standards had fallen into disuse. In December of 1981, the Federal Reserve and Comptroller of the Currency published numerical guidelines for community and regional national and state member banks and for bank holding companies (coverage was extended to multinational banking companies in June of 1983). In addition to specifying ranges for capital and varying supervision according to those ranges, limits were imposed on the degree to which subordinated debt would count as capital. More important, the guidelines were applied to consolidated bank holding companies, thereby limiting the practice of double leverage to avoid capital adequacy regulation.

Tax Incentives for BHC Formation

Favorable tax treatment of the bank holding company form relative to commercial banks probably served as the single most important catalyst to the creation of most of the nation's bank holding companies. Of the more than 1,800 BHCs in existence today, about 80% are one-bank holding companies. Of these one-bank holding companies, Strover (1978) suggests that about 55% are single-subsidiary bank holding companies. Thus, geographic expansion and product diversification seem to have played relatively minor roles in many one-bank holding company formations. There are, however, several reasons why the bank holding company form might be preferable for tax purposes. These advantages stem from the fact that, if the BHC is properly structured, dividends received from subsidiaries are tax deductible, and a consolidated tax return may be filed for the entire organization.

The tax deductibility of dividends especially benefits those who purchased control of a bank through the use of debt, and it facilitates capital injections into subsidiary banks as compared with nonsubsidiary banks. In the former case, the typical procedure is for an individual or group of individuals to borrow money to purchase a bank. They then form a BHC which is given the bank stock and assumes the debt in return for stock in the BHC. Since dividends received from a bank by the BHC are tax deductible, the principal on the debt can be repaid out of dividend income. This dividend income is only taxed at the bank level. In addition, the BHC interest payments are a deductible expense, just as they are for individuals. In the case of individual ownership, dividends received would be taxed before the principal on the acquisition debt could be paid.

The ability to file a consolidated tax return also provides an advantage to the BHC form of ownership. Since the only source of BHC income is typically tax-deductible dividends from subsidiaries, the BHC usually starts with a zero-taxable-income base from which interest and other expenses are subtracted.[29] This results in negative taxable income for the parent. Filing a consolidated return allows the organization to offset positive taxable income in the rest of the organization. In addition, consolidation permits operating losses in some subsidiaries to offset operating gains in others for tax purposes.

There are two other dimensions of taxation that have provided incentives for banks to form holding companies and also to spin off permissible banking activities into subsidiaries. The first relates to the ability to avoid local taxes. Income generated within a bank is taxed by the state and perhaps municipalities in which the institution is headquartered or operates. Performing the same activity in a subsidiary of a BHC permits the organization in some instances to charter the subsidiary in a state with lower taxes, which then subjects the subsidiary only to "doing business" taxes in the original state. A vivid example of this type of tax avoidance is provided by the method Citicorp chose to market the rising-rate thrift notes it announced in July of 1977. The prospectus indicated that the notes were to be offered through a specially chartered, wholly owned subsidiary of Nationwide Financial Services Corporation (Citicorp's consumer finance company subsidiary). This subsidiary was organized to avoid subjecting the parent company to taxation in the states in which the notes were to be sold and to avoid the necessity of qualifying Citicorp to do business in those states. Additionally, it simplified meeting the technical SEC net capital rules to qualify as a broker–dealer. (This ability to avoid local taxes, combined with the efforts by some states to provide an attractive business climate, is likely to spell an end to the unitary tax proposals of California and other states.)

Federal tax law also provides an incentive for a holding company (and/or bank) to conduct foreign business through separately chartered subsidiaries rather than through foreign branches. The incentive stems from a provision in the present tax law permitting a subsidiary of a U.S. corporation also holding a foreign charter to retain abroad indefinitely any portion of its net income rather than upstreaming it in the form of dividends. Since only repatriated income is subject to U.S. tax, there is an incentive to conduct foreign business through separately chartered subsidiaries in low-tax countries. In contrast, income earned abroad through a foreign branch is treated as if it were earned domestically and is subject to U.S. tax (and perhaps foreign tax as well). This feature of the tax law helps to explain the growth of foreign subsidiary activities of the large U.S. money-center banks in Bermuda and the Cayman Islands, both of which are low-tax countries. It may also stimulate the proliferation of foreign operations in countries that would not be profitable except for the tax advantages that result.[30] For example, until March 16, 1978, banks were able to claim full foreign tax credits for a 25% tax that Brazil imposed on interest banks earned in the country. Brazilian authorities typically rebated 85% of the tax to the borrowers, but the bank still received a full tax credit on the paper transaction. The intent of the tax and rebate system was to stimulate investment in Brazil by reducing the interest cost on foreign loans; the borrower benefited because of the rebate and the lender got a tax savings.

Geographical and Product Diversification

In spite of the 1927 McFadden Act limitations on interstate branching, banking organizations have been very successful in establishing physical presences across state lines (see, e.g., Eisenbeis, 1980, Whitehead, 1983, Kane, 1981, Department of the Treasury, 1981, and Golembe Associates, 1979). Whitehead (1983), for example, shows that banking organizations now have over 7,800 offices outside their home state. Banks have employed loan production offices, Edge Act corporations, corporate calling officers, and EFT facilities to expand interstate.[31] Beginning in mid-1968 larger banks began to employ the bank holding company form of organization to facilitate the operation of nonbanking subsidiaries such as consumer finance companies, industrial banks, mortgage banking firms, and trust companies throughout the country.

Among the first of the nation's largest banking organizations to adopt the one-bank holding company form was Citicorp, in September 1968. The principal reasons cited for becoming a one-bank holding company related to the additional flexibility to expand geographically and to offer new services. In the proxy statement it was noted that:

> Some of the Bank's present departments or activities such as leasing, factoring or travel services could have greater growth potential if operated by First National City Corporation directly or through subsidiaries, because geographic expansion would be easier. . . .

> It is also expected that the new corporate structure can be used advantageously to move into other financially oriented activities either directly or through newly-formed subsidiaries, or by acquiring companies already established in such fields.[32]

There is little evidence to suggest that the early formations—those prior to 1969 and the expansion of the commercial paper market—were motivated by financing opportunities associated with the holding company form.

Clearly, however, geographical expansion has always been a prime motive to form multibank holding companies as a means to circumvent restrictive state branching laws. Savage (1978) indicates that the ability of bank holding companies to serve as a substitute for branching was of political concern even in the early 1900s.

Multibank holding company activity has been greatest in those states that have had the more restrictive branching laws—for example, Texas, Florida, Ohio, and Colorado—and/or where the device has been used as part of a transition plan for more liberalized branching, such as New York, Virginia, and New Jersey. About 75% of the multibank holding companies are in unit banking and limited branching states. Moreover, one-half of the multibank holding companies and 70% of the subsidiary banks in statewide branching states are in New York, New Jersey, and Virginia. These three states have liberalized their branching laws to permit statewide branching and were favorable to bank holding company expansion as a transitional device.

Just as banking organizations found ways to avoid interstate banking limitations, many customers found it profitable and attractive to incur the costs and inconvenience to deal with nonlocally based suppliers of financial services. Large corporate customers have long operated in the national and international markets, and the establishment of a relationship with a nonlocal financial institution also has meant that all or a portion of both loan and deposit balances flowed into the national market.

While the prohibitions on intra- and interstate banking have become progressively eroded by financial innovations, it is also noteworthy that, except for the largest customers, most of these innovations have affected lending activities. Until recently, the principal area that has remained less affected by these developments has been the retail deposit market. Significant developments have taken place, however, that are breaking down the insulation of retail deposit markets. For example, the Monetary Control Act of 1980 and the Garn-St Germain Depository Institutions Act of 1982 broadened the range of asset and liability powers of thrifts to enable them potentially to become full competitors with commercial banks for the retail consumer business. Increasingly, S&Ls have been permitted to expand nationwide as troubled S&Ls have been merged to form interstate networks, and it is likely that the Federal Home Loan Bank Board may permit unrestricted interstate expansion.[33] In addition, numerous unregulated suppliers have sprung up, offering close substitute services for those offered by commercial banks on an interstate basis. These firms have innovated ways both to take retail deposits across local markets and on an interstate basis and to offer a wide range of financial, investment, and insurance services not available to commercial banks.

The principal innovation that evolved to collect consumer deposits on an interstate basis was the money market mutual fund. At the time of the Garn-St Germain Depository Institutions Act of 1982, noninstitutional deposits in these funds approached $183 billion, or about 15% of bank and thrift small time and savings deposits.[34] The real importance of money market mutual funds, however, is that they served to break down the dependence of previously locally limited customers on local depository institutions for financial services.

As distinct from the supply- and delivery-oriented methods banks have developed to avoid restrictions on interstate banking, the growth of money market mutual funds has affected the structure of both the demand and supply of deposit funds. Clearly, these funds increased the number of alternative suppliers of deposit-type services offering near–money market rates. In addition, their growth and customer acceptance signaled fundamental changes in the nature of the demand for deposit and other financial services. Once customers are less dependent on local sources of supply for deposit service, the geographic market ceases to be local; and in this case it has become an interstate market with price and terms determined by broader market forces. Under these circumstances, any benefits that might have accrued previously to in-state banks from prohibitions on intra- or interstate banking—by protecting local deposit markets from actual entry or the threat of entry by out-of-state banks—are dissipated.

Four other recent interrelated financial innovations have served to bring existing interstate banking restrictions into question by increasing the competitive presence of nonlocal suppliers in consumer markets. The first is the joining together of independent firms to provide services that the participants could not legally or economically provide individually (Merrill Lynch's cash management account is the classic example) (see Eisenbeis, 1981a, 1981b). Not only do these services capitalize on the fact that consumers have learned that they can obtain financial services from nonlocal and nontraditional firms, but also some of these firms have extensive interstate presences that are being developed into additional consumer service centers.

The second of the four financial innovations was the creation of the broker–bankers. Recent combinations of Shearson–American Express, Bache–Prudential, and Sears–Dean Witter–Coldwell Banker, just to name a few, have resulted in a whole new class of financial service firms.[35] These firms are internalizing certain symbiotic financial arrangements to take advantage of potential synergistic or scope economies. The broker-bankers are also positioning themselves to offer a wide range of consumer and corporate financial, brokerage, and insurance services (see Murphy and Brunner, 1981). Thus, the potential competitive threat to banks of these less-regulated broker–bankers and other competitors spreads far beyond their immediate activities with money market mutual funds and cash management accounts.

The third financial innovation that heightens the interstate competitive threat to commercial banks has been the recent wave of acquisitions of nonbank banks. Brokerage firms, insurance companies, retailers, money market funds, and financial conglomerates have discovered that they can diversify into either the commercial banking or consumer banking business outside the present scope and jurisdiction of the Bank Holding Company Act or Glass-Steagall by acquiring insured commercial banks and divesting either the demand deposit or commercial loan business. Such an entity—although federally insured and regulated as a commercial bank—does not meet the technical legal definition of a bank for purposes of the Bank Holding Company Act. Therefore, it may be acquired by any nonbanking or nonfinancial firm and still not subject the acquiring firm to the restrictions of the Bank Holding Company Act or to regulation or supervision by the Federal Reserve.[36] Because of the potential for linking brokerage, commercial, and industrial activities with interstate deposit taking, the expansion of nonbank bank acquisitions should be perceived as a real competitive concern to banks under the present regulatory system.

The fourth innovation has been the recent expansion of activity by money brokers. Brokerage firms and other institutions are brokering insured deposits for customers, both individual and corporate, and placing them in federally insured accounts across the country. Because of federal insurance, risk is irrelevant to the depositor and so funds flow to the highest bidder.[37] The effect is to create a national market for insured deposits.

With respect to product diversification, the ability of banking organizations to expand into nonbanking activities was severely limited by the 1970 Amendments to the Bank Holding Company Act of 1956 when compared with the potential perceived by many during the 1968–1969 period. The requirement that the activity be "so closely related to banking or managing or controlling banks as to be a proper incident thereto" resulted in only a few activities being authorized by the Federal Reserve Board. As of February 1980, for example, only 22 activities (15 by rule making and seven by order) were approved by the Federal Reserve Board. All but two of these—underwriting credit life insurance and operating an industrial bank—were essentially permissible for national banks at the time the activity was approved.[38] Thus, it does not appear that the bank holding company movement, because of legislative and regulatory restrictions, has resulted in significant additional product diversification potential. In fact, it is a misnomer to call such activities "nonbanking" activities. They are really banking activities being conducted in separately financed departments or subsidiaries, often outside of Regulation Q, Regulation D, and McFadden Act restrictions.[39] That is, they permit the banking organization to conduct lending and other services outside of subsidiary banks that could just as well, except for certain regulatory constraints, be done by the banks directly.

The Federal Reserve Board has recently added five new permissible activities to the list as part of a complete revision of its Regulation Y and has sought public comment on a number of other activities. These proposals are part of what now appears to be a liberalizing of policy toward BHC expansion reflecting new competitive pressures in the marketplace.[40]

THE EFFECTS OF INNOVATION AND REGULATION ON BANKING ORGANIZATION STRUCTURE

The financial innovations and regulatory actions discussed above have had a number of significant effects on the structure and operations of banking organizations that have important implications for our financial system. First, it is clear that the bank holding company form has become the dominant organization form in banking. More than 70% of total domestic banking deposits are in bank subsidiaries of bank holding companies. Second, it appears that, over time, more and more banking activities are being conducted at the holding company level in an attempt to avoid regulation. For example, prior to the Monetary Control Act, parent holding companies began to pay an increasing role in the financing of both bank and nonbank activities through commercial paper, small note sales, and debt issues. This was presumably due to an attempt to avoid Regulations D and Q as well as to the accommodating capital policies of the regulators. In addition, there are increasing incentives to spin operations out of the bank, both to avoid federal and local taxes and to evade the prohibition of geographic expansion in restrictive state banking laws and the McFadden Act. Third, both banks and bank holding companies have become more highly leveraged and have also tended to rely more and more on short-term, interest-sensitive sources of funds. To this extent regulation has indirectly induced more risk taking. Fourth, in the 1970s, the combination of higher-yielding investment alternatives, accommodating tax laws, and Regulation Q ceilings has resulted in significant expansion of U.S. banks' foreign operations. Indeed, many of the major U.S. money-center banks are generating more of their earnings abroad than domestically. The recent problems with third world debt suggest that such expansion may not be risk reducing. Fifth, the process of financial innovation has resulted in a blurring of the distinctions among the liabilities of not only different types of depository financial institution but also nondepository institutions. Consequently, competition has been increased. Sixth, payment system innovations in the form of NOWs and automatic transfers make the prohibition of interest payments on demand deposits obsolete. Seventh, the requirements for explicit pricing by the Federal Reserve are altering the correspondent banking system and, together with the removal of Regulations Q ceilings, are changing the competitive climate in the pressure of payments services. Eighth, explicit pricing is also forcing many institutions to decide whether they must become diversified financial service centers or boutiques to survive in the future. Lastly, financial innovation has resulted in increased competition from merchants and other financial and nondepository institutions, creating a disparity resulting from the fact that these institutions are not regulated and raise issues concerning the efficacy of both interstate banking restrictions and Glass-Steagall.

Out of this morass of changes it is possible to identify a number of regulatory issues pertaining to all financial institutions. The regulatory issues resulting from financial innovation can be divided into several different categories:

1. *Structural Issues.* These focus on the type and number of financial and other institutions providing financial services.
2. *Payment System and Monetary Policy Issues.* These deal with potential changes in the way transaction services are provided and the implications for macroeconomic policy.
3. *Supervisory Issues.* These deal with the implications of financial innovations for safety and soundness regulation in the financial system.
4. *Consumer Issues.* These are concerned with the way that changes in the payments system (mainly EFT) affect the consumer. They are not considered in this chapter.[41]

Structural Issues

There are several ways that this process of financial innovation may affect the competitive structure and composition of the financial industry. Broadly speaking, there are (1) intraindustry effects, which refer to the impacts on competition among like types of financial institutions, such as commercial banks; (2) interindustry effects, for example, commercial bank–thrift competition; and (3) extraindustry impacts, which involve competition between depositing institutions and other firms providing financial services.

Intraindustry Effects. Financial innovation has broadened competition among commercial banks by expanding the effectual geographical representation of institutions and by expanding the kinds of services offered. The proliferation of loan production offices and the growth of bank holding companies have increased the representation of some of the larger organizations on an intrastate basis across banking markets. The expansion into "nonbanking" activities, notably mortgage banking and consumer finance, has facilitated interstate expansion.

Similarly, the deployment of ATMs is also a clear substitute for branching and is a way for more banks to come into direct competition with each other.[42] More generally, to the extent that ATMs reduce dependence upon the convenience of brick-and-mortar branch locations to generate funds, it should increase rivalry among institutions and broaden the extent of geographic banking markets.[43]

With respect to increased competition among banks for funds by offering new instruments, the principal effects have resulted from holding companies and their marketing of small notes as substitutes for small time and savings deposits, from the growth of the Federal funds/RP and commercial paper markets, and from the growth of large time certificates offered by banks. In the corporate area, the development of cash management techniques, lock boxes, and deposits scanning has increased the ability of larger correspondent banks to attract funds more quickly than would otherwise have been the case. These developments have played an important role in the relaxation of Douglas Amendment restrictions by many states on out-of-state bank holding company entry and the stimulation of interest in regional interstate banking compacts in New England and several other areas of the country (see Eisenbeis, 1984).

Interindustry Effects. The interindustry effects of financial innovation involve principally the blurring of the distinctions among the liabilities offered by banks and thrifts. Within the last few years, an expanded array of time instruments and the elimination of legal rate ceilings have heightened competition for consumer deposits. Furthermore, thrifts have expanded into transactions-related services, with preauthorized transfers, share drafts, NOW accounts, and demand deposits, which had previously been the sole domain of commercial banks. On the asset side they now enjoy, as a result of the Monetary Control Act of 1980 and Garn-St Germain, an array of commercial and consumer lending powers that potentially make them full competitors of commercial banks. The end result of this process has been a significant increase in the liabilities of other than commercial banks performing many of the functions of money. This has led to an increase, particularly in local consumer markets, in the effective number of competitors offering packages of services that are nearly perfect substitutes. Because of this increased substitutability, even perhaps marginal differences in powers may carry with them important competitive advantages (especially if scope economies exist). (The more liberal branching powers and broader range of activities for thrifts' service corporations are two important examples.) Therefore, one would expect a continued acceleration in efforts to liberalize and equalize the asset, liability, tax, and other important powers of all financial institutions to promote competitive equality.

Extraindustry Competition. In addition to the effects that the tendency toward homogenization of financial institutions has been having on market structure and competition, increased competition is resulting from the fact that nondepository and nonfinancial institutions are beginning to offer services directly substitutable for those provided by banks and thrifts. The breadth of financial services has expanded substantially in the last 15 years. Table 3.4 lists just a few of the financial services being offered by major U.S. corporations. These include a wide range of both retail and wholesale services including commercial finance, consumer and real estate lending, insurance leasing, investment and brokerage, business and personal services, and payments services.[44]

In short, it is becoming increasingly difficult to distinguish between depository and other institutions that provide financial services. Moreover, cost considerations may give traditional nonfinancial institutions a competitive edge, especially considering that they do not have the same regulatory burden as depository financial institutions. They are not subject to reserve or capital requirements, branching restrictions, interest rate ceilings, or other regulatory constraints that limit their flexibility and ability to meet competition, particularly during inflationary periods with rising interest rates. In the face of this erosion of the historic separation among banking, investment banking, and commerce, it is not surprising that reform and revision of Glass-Steagall and relaxation of the barriers separating banking and commerce have become major policy issues.

Payments System and Monetary Policy Issues

The regulatory issues related to payments system financial innovations are of two types. The first is concerned with the implications of these innovations for macro monetary policy formulation and implementation. The second focuses on the need for a continuing federal presence in the clearing and settlement of payments.

Monetary Policy Implications. The monetary policy implications of regulatory-induced financial innovation relate to the effects that such innovation has had on the behavior of the monetary aggregates and their linkages to economic activity. Effective formulation and implementation of monetary policy rely on relatively stable and predictable relationships among bank reserves, interest rates, the monetary aggregates, and economic activity.

It has been argued, however, that (1) the expansion of cash management techniques, (2) the growth of new (regulatory-induced) markets, such as the Federal funds/RP market, and (3) the blurring of the distinction among demand deposits and other types of financial liabilities at depository and

Table 3.4. Who Does What

	Commercial Bank	American Express	Merrill Lynch	Dreyfus	E. F. Hutton	Fidelity	Prudential	Aetna	American General	Equitable Life	Travelers	Household	Beneficial	Sears	Kroger	J. C. Penney	Gulf & Western	Loews	General Motors	Greyhound	Transamerica	AVCO	Parker Pen	Dana	American Can	Armco	National Steel	General Electric	Westinghouse	RCA	ITT	Control Data
Take money/pay interest	$	$	$	$	$	$	$	$	$	$	$	$	$	$	$$	$	$				$	$	$	$	$		$	$		$		$
Check writing	$	$	$	$	$	$	$	$	$	$	$	$	$	$	$	$	$	$	$	$	$	$	$	$	$	$	$	$	$	$	$	$
Loan	$	$	$	$	$	$	$	$	$	$	$	$	$	$	$	$	$			$	$	$	$	$	$	$	$	$	$	$	$	$
Mortgage	$	$	$	$	$		$	$	$	$	$	$	$	$	$	$	$			$	$	$	$	$	$	$	$	$	$	$	$	$
Credit card	$	$	$	$	$	$	$	$	$	$	$	$	$	$	$	$	$				$	$	$	$			$					
Interstate branches	$	$	$	$	$	$	$	$	$	$	$	$	$	$	$	$	$	$	$	$	$	$	$	$		$	$	$	$	$	$	$
Money market	$$	$	$	$$	$		$	$	$	$	$	$	$	$	$	$	$			$	$	$	$$	$		$	$					
Securities	$$	$	$	$	$		$	$	$	$	$	$	$	$	$	$	$			$	$	$	$	$			$					
Life insurance							$	$	$	$	$	$	$	$		$	$	$		$	$	$		$	$	$		$	$	$	$	$
Property insurance							$	$	$		$	$	$	$		$	$	$	$	$	$	$		$		$		$		$	$	$
Casualty insurance							$	$	$		$	$	$	$		$	$	$	$	$	$	$		$	$	$		$		$	$	$
Mortgage insurance							$				$		$	$			$			$	$	$		$								$
Real estate	$	$	$				$	$	$	$	$	$	$	$		$	$			$	$	$	$	$	$	$	$		$	$		$
Cash management account	$	$	$	$	$	$				$	$												$									
Travel agency/service											$						$			$	$											
Car rental																				$	$	$								$		$
Data processing (general)	$	$						$	$																			$	$	$	$	$
Telecommunications	$	$	$																												$	$
Owns/is buying S&L	$$	$$	$$	$$	$	$	$			$		$	$				$			$	$	$	$									$
Owns/is buying bank	$$	$	$$	$$		$	$		$		$	$	$			$				$	$	$	$	$	$		$		$		$	$

SOURCE: Reprinted with permission from *American Banker*, Aug. 19, 1983, p. 14.

NOTE: **$** = financial activity since fall 1981.

nondepository institutions have altered in as yet unknown ways previous underlying relationships.[45] That being the case, the predictability and stability of these relationships may have been affected as well.

The macro policy problems induced by innovation are likely to persist, at least in the short run, and they may accelerate, as the substitutability among bank and nonbank liabilities increases and different types of liabilities become acceptable as payments instruments. Within the past four or five years thrifts have become actual suppliers of payments services nationwide. Even more significant may be the effect of the automatic transfer service, which effectively eliminates the distinction between checking and savings accounts. Thus the formulation and implementation of monetary policy will continue to be complicated by financial innovation because of the functional evolution of the major categories of the monetary aggregates (see also Kalchbrenner's chapter in this volume).

The tendency of regulatory agencies to adopt regulatory changes in response to short-run problems has often elicited unintended responses by individual financial and nonfinancial institutions with unintended macro policy implications. Two examples illustrate this point.

First, in an attempt both to accommodate bank needs for liquidity and to stimulate the market for government securities, regulatory actions were taken that had the effect of fostering the growth and expansion of the Federal funds/RP market. The long-run macro policy effects of these changes have been important. The regulatory changes permitted selective avoidance of Regulations D and Q. They contributed to increased bank risk taking by encouraging a shortening of the liability structure of bank portfolios. They induced thrifts (S&Ls and mutual savings banks) and the FHLBB to supply overnight funds to banks, thereby subjecting the market to the threat of abrupt withdrawals should disintermediation again prove a problem for thrifts. Finally, they have accommodated a temporary shift of funds from corporate and other large depositors into the funds market, thus contributing to the prediction problems with M1 and related aggregates. The redefinition of the monetary aggregates (*Federal Reserve Bulletin,* February 1980) was the direct result of all the changes that have taken place in financial markets as the consequence of financial innovation.

Second, low reserve requirements (and sometimes none) on time and savings deposits, together with high requirements on demand balances and a high opportunity cost of holding non-interest-bearing demand balances, provided incentives for banks to develop methods to enable their depositors to hold temporarily idle demand balances in the form of time and savings deposits or nonreservable nondeposit liabilities.[46] This had the effect of further contributing to the blurring of the distinction between transaction balances and other liabilities and has exacerbated the problems of defining the monetary aggregates.[47]

Failure to consider the macro implications of changes in micro regulatory policies suggests a continuation of macro policy formulation problems in the future. For example, the process of financial innovation, and particularly EFT, raises the very real policy question of what is the optimal way to formulate and conduct monetary policy in a world in which the basic monetary aggregates and their relationship to real level of economic activity are suddenly altered in unknown ways. In a rapidly changing world such as we experienced during the 1970s, there is also a continual information problem on the monetary aggregates, particularly if they turn over rapidly or if there is shifting among different types of liabilities and into the liabilities of unregulated firms.

A related issue pertains to the general change in the composition of bank assets and liabilities as functions such as debt financing and consumer credit are shifted out of a bank into other parts of a bank holding company. Traditional methods of assessing and monitoring banking extensions of credit as well as liquidity may need to be revised to recognize the change in the financial structure of banking organizations.

Finally, the need to rationalize the structure of reserve requirements and to lower the cost of member bank reserves which led to the Monetary Control Act of 1980 is only a first step if banks and nonbanks continue to innovate nonreservable liabilities to serve the same function as reservable liabilities. This implies that even if all banks and thrift institutions were subject to mandatory (but not interest-earning) reserve burdens, there would still be an incentive for nonfinancial institutions to innovate competing instruments. This would generate the need to regulate these firms as well. The implication is that viable long-run solutions must reduce the earnings penalty for holding reserve balances and this implies the need to pay interest on reserves.

The Role of the Federal Reserve in Operating the Payments System.   The Federal Reserve has been an active participant in the payments process in clearing and settling transactions. By providing a service that has guaranteed acceptability of payments at par, a more efficient and accommodating system has evolved than the old, nonpar circuitous routing system that existed prior to the establishment of the Federal Reserve. At the heart of this system are two quasi monopolies—settlement, with its intendant reduction in the need for multiple correspondent balances for clearing and settlement purposes, and the transportation system to deliver the payments. The spread of payments services beyond banks and thrifts to other institutions means that a significant volume of payments operations continues to be conducted outside of the Federal Reserve System, despite the Monetary Control Act, with no access to Federal Reserve services, guarantees of payments, or access to the discount window. This may prove destabilizing if public confidence in these institutions is not maintained. Moreover, the loss of check volume by the Fed once it began mandatory pricing for services under the Monetary Control Act has begun to change the correspondent banking system and raises a question whether the Fed can become efficient enough to be an effective alternative in many areas of the country. The spread of technology and electronic payments raises another set of payments system issues with unknown risks. There are already uncertainties, for example, with respect to the risk potential faced by the clearinghouse members for the settlement of their sponsored (foreign and domestic) members in the CHIPS automated clearinghouse system in New York. In addition, the spread of EFT and the use of computers operating nationwide over existing communications lines can effectively eliminate or perhaps significantly reduce one or both of the monopoly elements in the present system, which gave rise to the Federal Reserve's role in the payments area.

The question, then, as new payments processes evolve, is whether there still is a valid rationale for a federal presence in the payments system.[48] If so, should the presence be as it currently exists or should it take some other form (see for example Wolkowitz, 1977, or Corrigan, 1981). Clearly, a federal presence may be most justified in those areas characterized by significant barriers to entry or economies of scale so as to constitute natural monopolies.[49] Evidence on costs and scale economies associated with EFT is scarce, but preliminary analysis suggests that there are aspects of a nationwide POS system that do constitute natural monopolies. These include the distribution network associated with the access cards and the settlement function. Mere identification, however, of potential areas where monopolies and hence anticompetitive behavior may exist does not provide much guidance as to what form a federal presence in EFT might take. The options run all the way from the establishment of a privately run public utility to public ownership.

Supervisory Issues. Under the heading of supervisory issues associated with financial innovation are lumped a number of different types of issues related to the way in which financial institutions are supervised and regulated. They hinge on the risk implications and equity considerations implicit in the financial innovative process.

The risk implications of regulation-induced financial innovation are quite varied. First, there are many factors that suggest that banks and thrifts have become increasingly more vulnerable to shocks and variations in domestic economic activity. The dependence upon shorter-term, more interest-sensitive managed liabilities subjects banking organizations to greater interest rate and liquidity risk over the cycle. Second, greater reliance upon foreign sources of funds and the growth of the foreign assets of U.S. banks indicate that the U.S. financial system is becoming more and more intertwined with that of the rest of the world. Political instability, such as the financial problems related to the crisis in Iran, higher correlations in the variation in levels of economic activity in other countries, exchange rate risk, and credit risk problems of Mexico, Brazil, Argentina, and third world countries suggest greater vulnerability of U.S. banking organizations to exogenous shocks.

One result of the perceived increased risks associated with foreign expansion has been increased attention given by the major money-center banks to diversifying their domestic loan portfolios. It is quite possible that, with virtually unrestricted access to funds in both the domestic and international money markets, the push for interstate banking may ultimately be driven by the desire for asset creation rather than the desire to tap cheap sources of funds. To the extent that this is true, then the expansion of the nonbanking subsidiaries of bank holding companies represents an important alternative in the event interstate banking barriers are slow to erode.

Third, the increased competition for funds due to the homogenization of financial liabilities, particularly increased competition with nonregulated institutions, implies greater pressures on earnings and less flexibility relative to other competitors in adjusting to changes in economic conditions. Fourth, especially through the use of the bank holding company form, leverage had been greatly increased in banking organizations. Until the recently revised capital standards, this suggested greater vulnerability to a deterioration in asset quality as well as other risks. Finally, many have expressed the concern that there are special risks that are associated with the automation of payments functions. It has been argued that the ease of transfer of funds in EFT systems may facilitate runs on institutions so that they may be more susceptible to failure. Moreover, some have suggested that the entire system may become more fragile if the velocity of circulation of money becomes unstable without bounds or if there is pyramiding of deposits outside the settlement facilities of the Federal Reserve.[50]

Another risk issue that has broad-reaching implications is related to the response of bank holding companies to capital and regulatory policies designed to segment them into regulated and less-regulated components. Such policies might be appropriate if bank subsidiaries operated as a collection of independently run firms and the parent holding company functioned as a passive investor. The evidence and discussion cited in the section on capital, however, suggested that bank holding companies tended to operate as integrated entities. In such circumstances, the very attempt to isolate the more heavily regulated subsidiary banks from the rest of the holding company only creates further economic incentives for the organization to attempt to circumvent banking regulations and to spin more and more activities out of subsidiary banks into less heavily regulated segments of the organization.[51]

This shifting of activities within a banking (or thrift) organization to avoid regulation raises special policy problems when a parent company or its nonbank affiliates issue uninsured liabilities that are close substitutes for federally insured liabilities of a bank (or thrift) subsidiary. As a greater and greater proportion of financial liabilities shifts from insured to uninsured status, the stabilizing benefits of deposit insurance may be lost, unless the government chooses implicitly to extend guarantees to such claims. In fact, this appears to be what has been done, at least where larger troubled or failed banking organizations have been involved.[52] With this extension of implicit guarantees to more than nominally insured liabilities, however, also goes the legitimate concern on the part of the regulators, and particularly the insurance agencies and the Federal Reserve in its capacity as the lender of last resort, for monitoring and limiting undue risk taking in the nonbank segments of the organization.

Indeed, the regulators have responded quite predictably to the shifting of certain funding and other activities to the nonbank components of an organization and to the realization that it is not possible to isolate a bank subsidiary from what goes on in the rest of the organization. In particular, they have extended bank-type supervision and regulation, on a selective basis, to formerly unregulated segments of holding companies. The objectives have been both to monitor risk taking and to facilitate monetary control. The application of Regulations D and Q to BHC commercial paper and short-term debt and the newly revised capital adequacy standards are clear examples.

The observations about firm behavior and the infeasibility of isolating risks to the insurance funds raise important policy issues concerning proposals to expand asset and liability powers of insured depository institutions. For example, one should question the feasibility of permitting nondepository institutions to enter the banking business by acquiring nonbank banks or through the issuance of liabilities that are functionally equivalent to insured liabilities.

The problem is further complicated by the fact that existing deposit insurance is priced in such a way that a subsidy is conveyed to insured institutions. Subsidies implicit in government guarantees also induce uninsured firms to attempt to innovate ways to enter the banking business and capture those subsidies.[53] Any subsidy carries with it an inherent competitive advantage, just as burdensome regulations carry inherent disadvantages. Thus, the concept of competitive equity as a criterion for reform is also not operative. Unless all firms have the same set of subsidies and regulatory burdens, then some firm will always be at a competitive advantage to others. Thus the real public policy issue concerns deciding which entities will be subsidized and on what basis, rather than ensuring competitive equity. This raises a whole set of competitive equity issues concerning what types of liabilities should be federally insured, if any; which institutions should be permitted to issue those liabilities, have access to the discount window, and thus obtain a federal subsidy; and what types of regulations and supervision should be instituted to protect the insurance agencies.[54]

A final risk problem relates to the appropriate regulatory policy if the homogenization of financial institutions and the breaking down of barriers to entry into previously segmented markets result in too many competitors in the industry. If this process implies increased competition and a large number of institutions being potentially forced out of business, then there is a need for a transition policy to control exit from the financial industry. The role of McFadden Act and Douglas Amendment restrictions in interstate banking becomes important in this respect. Clearly, merger, acquisition, and antitrust policy could significantly affect the future structure of the industry. Regulatory policies in this area should be directed at maintaining competition and at the same time providing for an orderly exit.

SUMMARY AND CONCLUSION

This chapter has examined the interactions between regulation and financial innovation. Particular emphasis was given to the impacts of regulation on innovation, on financial institutions and structure, and more generally, on the stability of banking organizations.

Many of the significant changes in financial instruments, portfolio composition, and banking structure have occurred in response to economic pressures that have encouraged financial innovation to avoid statutory or regulatory constraints. These constraints include rate ceilings on deposits, reserve requirements, tax laws, capital standards, and limits on geographical location and product diversification. The analysis also suggests that regulation has not always achieved its intended goals and sometimes has had significant unintended effects, particularly in increasing the riskiness of institutions.

Financial innovation and regulatory actions have had several important effects on financial structure. One of the first was that bank holding companies played an increasingly important role in the financing of both bank and nonbank activities through sales of commercial paper, small notes, and debt issues. This resulted from attempts to avoid Regulations D and Q (the most pervasive regulations in terms of their effects) as well as the accommodating capital policies of the regulators.

Both banks and their holding companies have become more highly leveraged and have also tended to rely more and more on short-term, interest-sensitive sources of funds. Moreover, in the past two decades, the combination of higher-yielding investment alternatives, accommodating tax laws, reserve requirements, and deposit rate ceilings spurred the expansion of U.S. banks' foreign operations. Many of the major U.S. money-center banks recently have generated more earnings abroad than domestically.

Domestically, there are increasing incentives to spin operations out of banks, both to avoid federal and local taxes and to avoid the prohibitions in restrictive state banking laws and the McFadden Act on geographic expansion and product restrictions in Glass-Steagall and the Bank Holding Company Act. As a result, it is clear that the bank holding company has become the dominant organization form in banking in the sense that more than 70% of total domestic banking deposits are in bank subsidiaries of bank holding companies. Moreover, an increasing proportion of banking activities is being conducted at the holding company level.

The process of financial innovation has also resulted in a blurring of the distinctions not only among the liabilities of different types of depository financial institutions but also between depository and nondepository institutions. While competition has increased, provisions for exit are little changed from circumstances during the era of widespread (and effective) protection.

Payments system innovations, particularly in the form of automatic transfers and remote services, have made the prohibition of interest payments on demand deposits functionally obsolete. Financial innovation has also reflected increased competition from merchants and other entities. This has created a competitive disparity in that such institutions are not regulated. Restrictions on the separation of banking and commerce are moving on the same track as demand deposit interest prohibitions.

Finally, as incentives for financial innovation multiply and distinctions among financial institutions lessen, rational expression of the priorities of regulation becomes an increasingly complex problem. Since regulation tends to reduce flexibility, those institutions subject to the most restrictive regulation undoubtedly will be competitively disadvantaged.

If the past is any guide, compelling evidence of shifts in market position will have to occur before regulatory solutions will be forthcoming.

NOTES

1. Silber (1975) identifies a number of factors that may provide opportunities and incentives for financial innovation, including (1) changes in the composition of surplus and deficit units in an economy, (2) technological progress, (3) changes in attitudes toward risk, and (4) response to regulation. Greenbaum and Haywood (1971) also identify innovation in response to structural changes brought about by changes in credit conditions over the cycle, especially when rates are rising. See also the series of articles in Greenbaum (1982).

2. See for example, Silber (1975), Kimbrel and Dill (1974), Meigs (1966), Greenbaum and Haywood (1971), Holland (1975), Chase and Mingo (1975), Kane (1977, 1981), or Eisenbeis (1980) for discussions.

3. See Kane (1981) for a development of this idea.

4. This section draws heavily on the work of DePamphilis (1974), Knight (1969, 1970a, 1970b, 1970c), McKelvey (1978), Simpson (1979), Simpson (1978), and Boltz (1978).

5. These first CDs offered rates above those available on non-interest-bearing demand deposits, but they were still subject to Regulation Q ceilings.

6. Up until 1966, the regulatory response of the Federal Reserve was simply to relax the constraint by raising the ceilings. This was done five times between January 1, 1957, and December 6, 1965 (see Table 3.3).

7. Share drafts, RSUs, and ATS services were struck down by the U.S. Court of Appeals in Wahington, D.C., in April 1979. The Monetary Control Act of 1980 extended NOW accounts to insured depositors' institutions nationwide and explicitly authorized credit union share drafts, RSUs, S&Ls, and ATS services for banks. The Garn-St Germain Act of 1982 further broadened the utilities powers of S&Ls by permitting them to offer transaction accounts in connection with their commercial-base accounts.

8. See Gaines (1967) for an excellent description of early innovations in bank liability management.

9. For a discussion of these points see Simpson (1979).

10. The latter were only exempt if the funds were lent for one day and had been derived from the proceeds of the sale of U.S. government securities. The purpose of tying RPs to U.S. securities was to broaden the market for these instruments.

11. In July of 1969, Regulation D was amended to eliminate certain technical or bookkeeping advantages associated with the use of London checks in repaying Eurodollar borrowings (see Knight, 1970a). On June 21, 1973, they were dropped to 8%, to 4% on May 22, 1975, and to zero on August 24, 1978. On October 6, 1979, Eurodollars were included in the definition of managed liabilities and subjected to the 8% marginal reserve requirement when applicable. Following the Monetary Control Act of 1980, all Euro-currency liabilities were subject to a 3% reserve requirement.

12. Commercial paper sales by banks were reservable.

13. Technical amendments were later made to exempt subordinated note issues with an *average* maturity in excess of seven years.

14. This compares with the $17.8 billion in deposits in the 684 companies existing prior to September 1, 1968 (U.S. Congress, 1969).

15. It is interesting to note that in the interest of avoiding potential disruptions to the commercial paper market in 1973, the Board approved BankAmerica Corporation's

acquisition of GAC Finance, Inc., on August 14, 1973, reversing its previous denial on July 27, 1973 (*Bulletin*, August 1973 and September 1973).

16. The suspension of ceilings on large CDs with maturities in excess of 90 days had been in effect since June 27, 1970.

17. A similar certificate was authorized, effective November 20, 1978, for federal credit unions.

18. Both the FDIC and Federal Home Loan Bank Board have limited federal deposit insurance coverage on brokered funds so as to discourage this practice.

19. This is probably a more inefficient form of financing than simply paying high rates on existing bank liabilities. Supportive evidence to this inference is found in the 1972–1973 experience when BHCs abandoned the commercial paper market when rate ceilings were eliminated on bank CDs over $100,000 in 1973.

20. The average of the ratio of non-lead bank to total subsidiary bank deposits was only 6%.

21. These are all analyzed and discussed in detail in Board of Governors (1977).

22. Legislation has been proposed to permit interest payments on corporate demand deposits.

23. Federal Home Loan Bank Board, 12 CRF Part 545.

24. 402 F. Supp. 207 (D. DC. 1975), 534 F. 2d. 921 (1976), *cert. denied*, 45 U.S.L.W. 3238 (October 5, 1976).

25. To the extent that S&Ls were not heavily involved in paper checks, electronics might still convey certain operating advantages over commercial banks.

26. An important catalyst for this legislation was a series of rulings by the U.S. Court of Appeals of D.C., which struck down (1) an NCUA ruling permitting share drafts for credit unions, (2) the regulations of the FHLBB permitting remote service units (RSUs), and (3) automatic transfer accounts for commercial banks. The court postponed the effective date of its ruling until January 1, 1980, so as to encourage congressional review of the issues. The resulting political pressures created a vehicle for financial reform legislation that led to the Monetary Control Act of 1980, which not only permitted nationwide NOW accounts and authorized the continuance of RSUs, share drafts, and automatic transfer accounts, but also provided for the phase-out of deposit rate ceilings, provided some asset and liability reform for thrifts, and extended Federal Reserve reserve requirements to all depository institutions offering transaction accounts. The Garn-St Germain Act of 1982 accelerated the phase-out of deposit rate ceilings.

27. *Federal Reserve Bulletin*, July 1976.

28. See Chase (1971) and Chase and Waage (1983) for a discussion of this view of BHC regulation and whether the corporate veil provides adequate protection.

29. This assumes, of course, that the parent company is not an operating company, in which case it would have other sources of income.

30. Citicorp was alleged to have engaged in significant intracorporate foreign exchange transactions so as to manipulate and reduce its tax liabilities.

31. There are now over 100 shared and proprietary EFT systems that allow customers to obtain cash by drawing down funds in an account across state lines. In addition, several bank- and non-bank-sponsored EFT systems now enable consumers to shop and arrange for a mortgage on a nationwide basis without even entering a depository institution (see LaGesse, 1984).

32. First National City Bank, proxy statement, September 17, 1968, p. 1.

33. No change in federal law would be required.

34. Even the subsequent authorization of the $2,500-minimum-deposit Super NOW account and the MMDA account, which were both free of interest rate ceilings, did not reduce the importance of money market mutual funds. To be sure, the phenomenal growth of these two new accounts to over $290 billion in just two short months (as of February 16, 1983) suggests that, ceteris paribus, consumers prefer insured to uninsured accounts. However, it was estimated that only $10 billion of this initial growth came from money market mutual funds.

35. For a detailed listing of such combinations see Rosenblum and Seigel (1982) and the Rosenblum and Pavel chapter in this volume. Sears has most recently announced its intention to use its Sears World Trade, Inc., subsidiary to market financial services worldwide.

36. Acquisition of more than 10% of such banks' stock must still be approved by the appropriate federal bank regulator under the Change in Bank Control Act. To date such approvals have been given by all three federal regulators. Recent changes in the Federal Reserve's Regulation Y broadening the definition of a bank may reduce somewhat nonbank bank expansion (see *Banking Expansion Reporter*, 1984). Of course such banks would still be prohibited from branching interstate, but interstate companies could be created. Fleet Financial, for example, has proposed to expand into Massachusetts and Connecticut.

37. Both the Federal Home Loan Bank Board and FDIC have limited federal deposit insurance coverage on brokered funds so as to discourage the activity and to limit the agencies' risk exposure.

38. Only two activities that were denied (real estate brokerage and travel agencies) were approved activities for national banks. The latter has since been ruled impermissible for national banks by the courts.

39. It may also be a misnomer to call them "banking" activities when nonbank firms are significant suppliers.

40. See *Federal Reserve Bulletin*, January 1984, p. 19.

41. Consumers appear to have been one of the prime beneficiaries of financial innovation, as they now are able to receive market rates on their savings funds as well as interest on transaction accounts.

42. For a review of the extent to which small and large banks have adopted EFT, see Walker (1979, 1976).

43. For a discussion, see Eisenbeis (1976) and Eisenbeis and Wolkowitz (1977).

44. For a detailed discussion see the chapter in this volume by Rosenblum and Pavel.

45. See Porter, Simpson, and Mauskopf (1978), and Tinsley, Garrett, and Friar (1978) for discussions of the development of the Federal funds and RP markets and cash management techniques and their implications for monetary policy and the definition of the aggregates.

46. The creation of corporate savings deposits helped accommodate the use of savings deposits as a temporary abode for idle transaction balances. The institution of lagged reserve accounting stimulated bank liability management and the growth of the Federal funds market as well.

47. An alternative representing the opposite extreme would be to restructure reserve requirements on time and savings deposits to be equal to or exceed those on demand deposits, to permit interest payments on demand deposits, and to remove deposit in-

surance on all time and savings deposits so as to create a greater distinction between transaction and precautionary balances.

48. For an excellent discussion of the monetary policy issues of EFT see Kane (1978).

49. For discussions see B. Wolkowitz (1977), Eisenbeis and Wolkowitz (1977), and National Commission on Electronic Fund Transfers (1977).

50. For discussion see NCEFT (1977).

51. The reason, of course, is that to the integrated firm total profits of the organization are being maximized and not necessarily the profits of individual subsidiaries. Thus, it matters little to the firm where a particular function is being conducted within the organization as long as its contributing to total firm profits is optimized.

52. The payout of Penn Square represented a change in philosophy. These issues received attention in the FDIC's (1983) report to the Congress on deposit insurance reform, and Chairman Isaac has argued for modification in the way failing banks are handled in purchase and assumption cases. This policy seems to have been reversed with Continental Illinois.

53. See Buser, Chen, and Kane (1981) and Karaken and Wallace (1978). Risk, however, is not a particularly useful criterion on which to base a decision on new activities for the insured entity. It is not the riskiness of the activity itself that is relevant, but rather whether (because of covariances) it reduces or increases the overall riskiness of the insured entity.

54. These issues become especially difficult in an electronic world where assets can be liquified instantaneously, and thus it is not obvious how the integrity of the payments system is maintained.

REFERENCES

Board of Governors of the Federal Reserve System. "The Impact of the Payment of Interest on Demand Deposits." Staff study, January 10, 1977.

Boltz, Paul W. "Commercial Banking under Coordinated Deposit Ceiling Rates at Banks and Thrift Institutions." Government Finance Section, Division of Research and Statistics, Board of Governors of the Federal Reserve System, July 14, 1978.

Buser, Stephen A., Chen, Andrew H., and Kane, Edward J. "Federal Deposit Insurance, Regulatory Policy, and Optimal Bank Capital." *Journal of Finance,* March 1981, *35* (1), pp. 51–60.

Chase, Samuel B., Jr. "The Bank Holding Company as a Device for Sheltering Banks from Risk." In *Proceedings of a Conference on Bank Structure and Competition.* Federal Reserve Bank of Chicago, October 1971.

Chase, Samuel B., Jr., and Waage, Donn L. "Corporate Separateness as a Tool of Banks Regulation." Washington, D.C.: Samuel B. Chase & Company, 1983.

Chase, Samuel B., Jr., and Mingo, John J. "The Regulation of Bank Holding Companies." *Journal of Finance,* May 1975, *30* (2), pp. 281–292.

Corrigan, E. Gerald. "The Payments Mechanism System: Emergency Changes and Challenges." In *Proceedings of a Conference on the Future of the U.S. Payments System.* Federal Reserve Bank of Atlanta, June 23–25, 1981.

Curry, Timothy J. "The Performance of Bank Holding Companies." In *The Bank Holding Company Movement to 1978: A Compendium.* Staff study, Board of Governors of the Federal Reserve System, September 1979.

DePamphilis, Donald M. *A Micro-Economic Econometric Analysis of the Short-Term Commercial Bank Adjustment Process.* Federal Reserve Bank of Boston Research Report No. 55, April 1974.

Eisenbeis, R. A. "The Competitive Implications Associated with the Use of Electronic Terminals." Paper prepared for the National Commission on Electronic Funds Transfers, Board of Governors of the Federal Reserve System, October 10, 1976.

Eisenbeis, R. A. "Economic and Policy Issues Surrounding Regional and National Approaches to Interstate Banking." Prepared for the New York State Bankers Association, February 18, 1984.

Eisenbeis, R. A. "Financial Innovation and the Role of Regulation: Implications for Banking Organization Structure and Regulation." Board of Governors of the Federal Reserve System, February 1980.

Eisenbeis, R. A. "Interstate Banking: Federal Perspectives and Prospects." In *Proceedings of a Conference in Bank Structure and Competition.* Federal Reserve Bank of Chicago, May 14, 1981a.

Eisenbeis, R. A. "Pressures for Interstate Banking." *Issues in Bank Regulation,* Summer 1981b, 5 (1), pp. 21–27.

Eisenbeis, R. A., and Wolkowitz, B. "Sharing and Access Issues in Electronic Funds Transfer System." Research Papers in Banking and Financial Economics, Financial Studies Section, Division of Research and Statistics, Board of Governors of the Federal Reserve System, September 1977.

Federal Deposit Insurance Corporation. "Deposit Insurance in a Changing Environment." A study of the current system of deposit insurance pursuant to Section 712 of the Garn-St Germain Depository Institutions Act of 1982, April 15, 1983.

Gaines, Tilford C. "Financial Innovations and the Efficiency of Federal Reserve Policy." In George Horwich (Ed.), *Monetary Process and Policy: A Symposium.* Homewood, Ill.: Richard D. Irwin, 1967.

Golembe Associates. "A Study of Interstate Banking by Bank Holding Companies." Prepared for the Association of Bank Holding Companies, May 25, 1979.

Greenbaum, S.I. (Ed.). "Proceedings of the Financial Innovation Conference, 22–24 April 1981." *Journal of Banking and Finance,* March 1982, 6 (1), pp. 1–143.

Greenbaum, S. I., and Haywood, C. F. "Secular Change in the Financial Services Industry." *Journal of Money, Credit and Banking,* May 1971, pp. 571–589.

Holland, Robert C. "Speculation on Future Innovation: Implications for Monetary Control." In William Silber (Ed.), *Financial Innovation.* Lexington, Mass.: D. C. Heath, 1975.

Hunt Commission. *Report of the President's Commission on Financial Structure and Regulation.* Washington, D.C.: U.S. Government Printing Office, December 1971.

Kane, Edward J. "Expanded Powers for Thrift Institutions: Superthrift vs. Superlobbyist." In *Proceedings of a Conference on Bank Structure and Competition.* Federal Reserve Bank of Chicago, 1976.

Kane, Edward J. "Good Intentions and Unintended Evil: The Case against Selective Credit Allocation." *Journal of Money, Credit, and Banking,* February 1977, pp. 55–69.

Kane, Edward J. "EFT and Monetary Policy." *Journal of Contemporary Business,* Spring 1978, pp. 29–50.

Kane, Edward J. "Accelerating Inflation, Technological Innovation, and the Decreasing Effectiveness of Banking Regulation." *Journal of Finance,* May 1981, 36 (2), pp. 355–367.

Kane, Edward J. "Technology and Regulatory Forces in the Desegmentation of Financial-Services Competition." Presented at the ASSA meetings, December 29, 1983.

Karaken, John H., and Wallace, Neil. "Deposit Insurance and Bank Regulation: A Partial-Equilibrium Exposition." *Journal of Business,* July 1978, *51,* pp. 413–438.

Kimbrel, M., and Dill, A. A. "Other Sources of Funds." In H. Prochnow and H. Prochnow, Jr. (Eds.), *The Changing World of Banking.* New York: Harper and Row, 1974.

Knight, Robert E. "An Alternative to Liquidity: Part I." Federal Reserve Bank of Kansas City, *Monthly Review,* December 1969, pp. 11–21.

Knight, Robert E. "An Alternative to Liquidity: Part II." Federal Reserve Bank of Kansas City, *Monthly Review,* February 1970a, pp. 11–22.

Knight, Robert E. "An Alternative to Liquidity: Part III." Federal Reserve Bank of Kansas City, *Monthly Review,* April 1970b, pp. 3–12.

Knight, Robert E. "An Alternative to Liquidity: Part IV." Federal Reserve Bank of Kansas City, *Monthly Review,* May 1970c, pp. 10–18.

LaGesse, David. "Mortgage Networks Arrange Loans on Computers." *American Banker,* January 23, 1984, pp. 1, 20, 22, 23.

McKelvey, Edward F. "Interest Rate Ceilings and Disintermediation." Study by the staff of the Board of Governors of the Federal Reserve System, Staff Economic Studies No. 99, April 1978.

Meigs, A. J. "Recent Innovations in the Functions of Banks." *American Economic Review,* May 1966, pp. 161–197.

Murphy, C. Westbrook, and Brunner, Thomas W. "Will Anyone Try to Block Amexco?" *American Banker,* April 13, 1981, p. 3.

Murray, William J. "Banking Holding Company Centralization Policies." Prepared for the Association of Registered Bank Holding Companies, Golembe Associates, Inc., February 1978.

National Commission on Electronic Fund Transfers. *EFT and the Public Interest.* Washington, D.C.: National Commission on Electronic Fund Transfers, 1977.

National Commission on Electronic Fund Transfers. "Electronic Funds Transfer and Monetary Policy: Compendium of Papers Prepared for the National Commission on Electronic Fund Transfers." IWD-33, January 1977.

Porter, Richard D., Simpson, Thomas D., and Mauskopf, Eileen. "Financial Innovation and the Monetary Aggregates." *Brookings Papers on Economic Activity,* 1979, *1,* pp. 213–229.

Rose, John T. "Bank Holding Companies as Operational Single Entities." In *The Bank Holding Company Movement to 1978: A Compendium.* Staff study, Board of Governors of the Federal Reserve System, September 1978.

Rosenblum, Harvey, and Siegel, Diane. "Competition in Financial Services: The Impact of Nonbank Entry." Federal Reserve Bank of Chicago, 1982.

Savage, Donald T. "A History of the Bank Holding Company Movement: 1900–1978." In *The Bank Holding Company Movement to 1978: A Compendium.* Staff study, Board of Governors of the Federal Reserve System, 1978.

Silber, William. "Towards a Theory of Financial Innovation." In William Silber (Ed.), *Financial Innovation.* Lexington, Mass.: D. C. Heath, 1975.

Simpson, Thomas D. "The Market for Federal Funds and Repurchase Agreements." Paper presented at the Southern Economic Association Meetings, Washington, D.C., November 10, 1978.

Strover, Roger. "The Single Subsidiary One-Bank Holding Company." Federal Reserve Bank of Chicago, *Proceedings of a Conference on Bank Structure and Competition,* 1978, pp. 141–156.

Timlen, Thomas M. "Commercial Paper—Penn Central and Others." In Edward I. Altman and Arnold W. Sametz (Eds.), *Financial Crisis: Institutions and Markets in a Fragile Environment.* New York: John Wiley & Sons, 1972.

Tinsley, P. A., Garrett, B., and Friar, M. E. "The Measurement of Money Demand." Special Studies Paper 133, Board of Governors of the Federal Reserve System, 1978.

U.S. Congress, House Committee on Banking and Currency. *The Growth of Unregistered Bank Holding Companies—Problem and Perspectives.* Staff report. Washington, D.C.: U.S. Government Printing Office, 1969.

U.S. Treasury Department. *Geographic Restrictions on Commercial Banking in the United States.* The Report of the President, Department of the Treasury, 1981.

Walker, David A. "An Analysis of EFTS Activity Levels, Costs, and Structure in the U.S." FDIC Working Paper No. 76–4, 1976.

Walker, David A. "An Analysis of Financial and Structural Characteristics of Banks with EFT Machines." FDIC Working Paper No. 79–1, October 13, 1979.

Whalen, Gary. "Multibank Holding Company Organizational Structure and Performance." Federal Reserve Bank of Cleveland, Working Paper No. 8201, March 1982a.

Whalen, Gary. Operational Policies of Multibank Holding Companies." Federal Reserve Bank of Cleveland, *Economic Review,* Winter 1981–1982b.

Whitehead, David D. "Interstate Banking: Taking Inventory." Federal Reserve Bank of Atlanta, *Economic Review,* May 1983.

Wolkowitz, B. "The Case for the Federal Reserve System Actively Participating in Electronic Funds Transfer." Research Papers in Banking and Financial Economics, Financial Studies Section, Division of Research and Statistics, Board of Governors of the Federal Reserve System, March 1977.

4 Changing Technology and Future Financial Activity

Almarin Phillips

INTRODUCTION

The scientific community and suppliers of computers, telecommunications, and information system hardware and software say that there is an abundance of available technology. This technology makes possible the production of new financial services and reductions in the costs of providing present services. Integrated circuits are predicted to grow from the present 64K and 256K capacities to over 1,000K by the end of the decade. These VLSICs will provide great reductions in the cost of memory and will also offer increasingly complex and efficient microprocessing and switching. "Smart" terminal devices associated with two-way, interactive information networks are said to be in their infancy and susceptible to rapid development. Digital PABX and other local network switching and transmission facilities are now being deployed. Security and privacy remain critical issues in systems development, but new technologies are emerging on these fronts as well.

There is more here than greater functional capability and lower costs. In addition to improved hardware and software for switching and computation, there are new techniques for network design and network management. Networks and subnetworks can be interconnected in horizontal and hierarchical arrangements, with specialized functions in some parts of a network and collections and rearrangements of these functions in others. In a generic sense, technology appears to provide means for efficiently hooking any kind of information in any form to anything else, with broad processing, storage, retrieval, and transmission alternatives through time and across large geographic areas. The use of technology for the provision of financial services will in large measure be shared and combined with its use in other telecommunications and data processing services.

A quick assessment—and probably a correct one—is that technology, narrowly defined, will not be an important impediment to the provision of new and lower-cost financial services. Such services are, after all, increasingly nothing more than new means of moving numbers about on a growing array of balance sheets of individuals, nonfinancial businesses, financial institutions, and governments. As seen by Dee W. Hock (1977), the "new world" will

> unlock a value reservoir to which [transactors] have never had access. . . . [A transactor] from anywhere in the world [will be] in full possession of all his assets, whether credit, deposit, investment, or equity . . . [and will be able] to exchange them for whatever [any other transactor wishes] to sell.

That such a world will quickly arise seems more than a fantasy. A good deal of it has been put in place, some before and some after Hock gazed into his crystal ball in 1977. An indication of the magnitude of growth in asset transacting appears in bank debits. In 1970, for example, the annual turnover rate for demand deposits of New York City banks was about 150. On average, each dollar in New York demand deposits was exchanged 150 times per year. By late 1983, that rate had reached more than 1,800. New York demand deposits were turning over nearly five times per day. This reflects nothing other than an acceleration in the rates at which various types of assets are being exchanged for one another. New markets have appeared, better information is available, transactions costs have fallen, the liquidity of many assets has increased and, of great importance, the increase in interest rates over the period has put a premium on efficient asset management.

The technologists indicate that there is no end in sight to what they can do. Further, it appears that institutional impediments for using technology are becoming less importance. The deposit institutions gained new operating freedoms in the Depository Institutions Deregulation and Monetary Control Act of 1980 and still more in the Garn-St Germain Depository Institutions Act of 1982. The Glass-Steagall Act's prohibitions on mixing investment banking and the taking of deposits remain the letter of the law, but the number of ways to circumvent the act grows almost daily. Similarly, the McFadden Act and Douglas Amendment constraints on interstate banking have become of considerably less relevance to imaginative financial entrepreneurs.

These developments raise important questions. Will the pace of innovations in financial services continue? Will there be a rapid demise of the older and, particularly, the smaller financial institutions? Will consolidations and disproportionate internal growth result in the evolution of a few national and international financial supermarkets? Is the end in sight for the locally owned and the specialized financial institutions?

These questions cannot be answered with certainty. There are reasons for believing, nonetheless, that the pace of innovation in financial services, while brisk, will be a good deal slower than that which appears to be technologically feasible. Additionally, there are reasons for believing that, while significant restructuring will occur, the few financial supermarkets that do arise will not cause the wholesale displacement of smaller institutions. In fact, the success of the supermarkets may depend on their effective use of smaller, local institutions.

One reason for holding that the rate of change will be moderate lies in the extent of deregulation that has now transpired. A number of notable service innovations—money market funds, a variety of "sweep balance" accounts, NOW accounts, and, to a degree, new markets for instruments such as commercial paper, Eurodollars, and repos—arose primarily as vehicles to circumvent regulations. With Regulation Q largely eliminated and with explicit payment of interest on some types of transactions deposits, the impetus for the growth in such services has abated.

Another reason for the moderation of change is related to technology. Major innovations typically rest not on a single, independent development but rather on the nearly simultaneous development of several interrelated strains of technology. The several strains, moreover, often reside in different scientific and technical disciplines. Innovation and the diffusion of innovation require a confluence of technologies, a confluence brought about by several firms whose primary production and marketing interests are not immediately and organizationally related.[1]

The innovative process is not uniquely dependent on technological feasibility. Technical feasibility is far from a sufficient cause for innovations. Introductions of new goods and services and of new means of production are as dependent on new organizational forms—on organizational innovations—as they are on narrowly defined technological innovations. Innovation occurs, that is, only when markets are structured and organized in such a fashion that those investing and participating in the new developments see reasonable probabilities of receiving benefits commensurate with their costs and risks. The *actual* innovations that do appear from what in perspective is a vast set of technologically *feasible* innovations are restricted to those for which there is an organizational structure that allows for the capturing of economic rewards.[2]

Organizational innovations are as important as the more obvious technological innovations precisely because they change the set of *actual* innovations for which rewards can be captured. To the extent that organizational structures do not coincide with those necessary to realize benefits from using feasible technological opportunities, the latter remain "near technologies"; they do not become "in-use" technologies.[3] Gradually— but only gradually—organizational innovations are arranged to accommodate the more apparent and the more potentially rewarding of the possible technological innovations. If the character of organizational innovation follows the patterns that now seem likely, the role of financial supermarkets will be a limited one and one that will depend on their being organizationally associated with other, smaller institutions.

A DIGRESSION ON MARKET ORGANIZATIONS

It is customary to think of an organization as, say, a business firm, a bank, an investment company, a trade association, the governing body of an art museum, a transportation authority, a church, a hospital. These clearly are organizations, but the term has far broader connotations.[4]

For present purposes:

1. An organization is a group of individuals (or a group of suborganizations) the members of which can communicate with one another. Intragroup communications often utilize a "coded language" best understood by members of the group.
2. The group has at least one shared goal, but the members are not interested in the shared goal(s) to the exclusion of other individual or subgroup goals.
3. The collective accomplishment of the shared goal(s) requires compromise and conflict resolution, with trade-offs between the achievement of the collective, shared goal(s) and other individual or subgroup goals.
4. For survivability, the organization must:
   a. provide perceptions to the members that the shared, collective goal(s) will be better achieved through concerted and coordinated group actions than it will through individual actions;
   b. provide perceptions that the gains achieved by the organization with respect to the shared, collective goal(s) compensate for the

compromises and trade-offs made with respect to other nonshared goals.

5. The organization must in some fashion collect contributions (including foregone individual goals) from and distribute rewards (benefits) to the members.

6. The organization provides rules (codes of conduct) with respect to intragroup relations and with respect to relations with nonmembers and other organizations.

7. The organization provides internal governance mechanisms, usually fashioned by a hierarchical power structure, and enforces (more or less) the group's rules and mediates or resolves intragroup conflicts.

8. The strength of members' identification with the group varies directly with the extent to which the group goals are congruent with individual goals and inversely with the extent to which the group goals conflict with the attainment of individual goals. Participation in group activities is directly related to the strength of this identification.

In the case of an ordinary business, the organization is formal and easily recognizable. It is formal in the sense of reasonably definable and measurable group goals, the need for coordinated activities to achieve the goals, defined functions of (contributions from) the employees, a defined system for distributing benefits (wages, salaries, profits, perquisites, etc.), established bylaws and work rules, internal enforcement mechanisms (fiat controls, incentive systems), and indeed, the "eager beaver" and the "drone" types of participants.

Many organizations are, however, less formal than a business. A car pool, for example, is an organization—an informal organization. So might be a joint venture among firms to develop the design and manufacturing method for a 1,024K VLSIC. So are the relationships defined by McDonald's hamburger franchises. A family is an organization. Different types of organizations are used for different purposes in different circumstances. Formality—in the sense of charters, incorporations, bylaws, and so forth—are not necessary for all collective purposes. Contracts, express agreements, tacit agreements, and just plain "working relationships" constitute the corpus of many important organizations.

An individual does not "belong" to one organization to the exclusion of all others. An officer of a bank trust department and an officer of the commercial department of the same bank are both members of the larger bank organization. Yet each is a member of a suborganization, the goals of which may in some respects be in conflict with the bank's. Each is probably also a member of a separate family organization, separate social and religious organizations, and perhaps different political organizations. Each of these other, simultaneous group identifications may, to a degree, cause goal conflicts that require resolution.

Goal achievement is accomplished through organizations and is multidimensional. The individual tends to identify more strongly with and to contribute more to organizations the goals of which are congruent with his or her own and with respect to which perceived rewards are at least equal to contributions. This balance—or lack of balance—between individuals' perceived rewards from and contributions to various organizations is paramount in the explanation of organizational change. New organizations *tend* to appear when existing organizations are incapable of capturing and distributing benefits that some of the individuals perceive to be realizable through organizational innovations. The innovations may take many forms. The focus here is on *interfirm* organizational change, not on *intrafirm* changes, but the latter are in many contexts extremely important.[5]

One obvious interfirm organizational change is to merge two or more organizations. Another is to "federate," with the creation of a supersidiary organization encompassing existing organizations. A holding company is an example of a formal supersidiary organization; an industry trade association is another, usually less formal example.

New organizations may be formed that intersect with only selected parts of existing organizations. A joint R&D venture is an illustration. Such limited interfirm organizations typically comprise individuals who perform like functions in each of the firms—an organization, say, of the trust or of the data processing officers of several banks. Clearly, too, the organizational change may have the purpose of replacing or terminating an existing organizational arrangement—dissolving a federation, a trade association, or any other interfirm organization that is perceived to be ineffective in balancing rewards and contributions.

In this context, changes in technology—narrowly construed—offer opportunities for new rewards. Sometimes the rewards are achievable through existing organizational structures, but often they are not. Old organizations must be changed or new organizations created for opportunities to be translated from "near" to "in-use" technologies.

ORGANIZATIONAL INNOVATIONS AND FINANCIAL SERVICES: A LOOK AT THE PAST

There are numerous illustrations of the interdependency of organizational and technological innovations in the history of financial services. Curiously, however, the organizational aspects of the changes are not typically emphasized. On examination it becomes clear that the service innovations and organizational innovations have developed in a highly interdependent way.

Checkable Deposits

Histories of the introduction and spread of checkable deposits emphasize that the innovation began in state banks in the post–Civil War period after the imposition of the tax on state bank note issues. While true, these histories are also far too simple.

An individual bank—unless it were a near-monopoly bank over a substantial group of customers—could not easily and profitably have introduced checkable deposits by itself. If all checks written by any of its depositors were redeposited by others of its depositors, the new instrument would have had few problems. To the extent, however, that the use of checks by the customers of one bank depended on the acceptability of the checks by customers of other banks and, in turn, payments to other banks for settlement, a more general use of checkable deposits was necessary. Thus, the value of the new service to one bank (and its customers) depended on other banks (and their customers) having a similar service. And mutual use required a new interfirm organization.

The initial new organization in the United States was the local bank clearinghouse, or some modification of the clearing associations used previously for clearing bank note issues. The whole idea of clearing is that all of the members of the association have items to be cleared or, in this case, that all of the banks have the new checkable deposits. Through the associations, the banks agreed on payment terms, settlement periods, the basic asset to be used to settle adverse balances, ways in which to handle fraudulently issued checks and checks against which there were insufficient deposits, holder-in-due-course procedures and, clearly, the basis on which the ownership and costs of the clearing functions were to be shared. Since customers used both national- and state-chartered banks, the former had to be included in the clearing arrangements even though they initially had less of an incentive to use checkable deposits. The clearinghouses were contractually arranged supersidiary joint ventures, vertically related to each of the participating banks. The diffusion of checking deposit banking depended on the new organizations.

The local clearinghouses proved to be an inefficient means for regional and national checking, as they had been for note issues. The clearinghouse worked well so long as all of the checks presented to a member bank were drawn on another member. Checks drawn on nonmember banks created problems. Nonmembers did not contribute to the costs of clearing these checks. This was true even if they were members of another clearinghouse.

The problem was at least partially resolved in three ways. First, the local associations gradually organized regional clearing associations. Second, for nonmembers with some regular volume of checks or with other relations with one of the members, a correspondent arrangement could be established. The member bank cleared for and on behalf of its corresponding nonmembers on the basis of contracts. The latter usually provided for the nonmembers' holding of correspondent balances with the member banks.

The third way to handle nonmember checks was to charge a fee. As checkable deposits spread, the fee was increasingly exacted by the receiving bank as a deduction from the face amount of the check. Checks from nonmembers were accepted at less than par. So-called nonpar banking yielded another problem, however. The spread in the use of checks as a means of payment was retarded. Payees tended to refuse payments by check when less than the bill amount due was credited to their accounts.

Historical accounts are again too simple or, at least, misleading. Nonpar banking may to some extent have been caused by the questionable credit of the issuing banks, but that probably was not the major reason. The major reason was that if the receiving bank credited its payee customers the face amount of checks drawn on distant banks at the time of presentation, that receiving bank would in effect have been extending credit pending collection from the payor's bank. The payee was unwilling to pay for this credit and so was the payee's bank. A larger, more comprehensive, national organization was needed to establish interfirm cost sharing if checks were to attain nationwide and general use.

No such organization arose for several decades, and the use of checks was restricted because of this fact. After the Federal Reserve System was established, it required all of its member banks to clear checks at par. The Fed also established its own means of extending credit so as to minimize the costs of par clearings. This was done through Federal Reserve float—the reserve account of the receiving bank was credited when checks were presented to a Federal Reserve Bank for clearing. The reserve account of the paying bank was debited only on its return to that bank by the same or another Federal Reserve Bank. No bank paid explicit interest for this Federal Reserve credit.

Actually, even the Federal Reserve System was for years unable fully to implement the cost sharing and interfirm payments needed for nationwide check use. Nonmember banks behaved like "free riders." These banks—several thousand in number through the 1930s—provided checking accounts for their customers, relying on par payments by other banks even while they selectively received checks on other banks at less than par. The nonpar banks received the benefits of the Federal Reserve's interfirm clearing subventions without contributing to the costs of the system.

It is clear that checkable deposits could hardly have been introduced in the absence of contemporaneous innovations in the functions of clearing associations. A new interfirm organization involving many banks was needed. Even had the larger banks made more extensive use of correspondent relations for check clearing within the set of banks covered by correspondent contracts, a clearing arrangement among the larger banks would have been necessary for system efficiency.

Note too that the attractiveness of checking was affected by other technological developments only remotely related to financial services. In particular, improved rail transportation and telegraph services were instrumental in extending the geographic area over which clearing could be efficiently performed. The period for which float had to be extended fell as transportation improved. The telegraph allowed for crude versions of electric funds transfer—thus also reducing float—and permitted the use of some check verification procedures.

MICR Encoded Checks

The development of MICR (magnetic ink character recognition) encoded checks represents more of a process innovation than a service innovation. The diffusion of MICR, nonetheless, makes clear several important points relating to the organizational innovations required for the use of new technologies.

MICR arose directly from an American Bankers Association task force, the Subcommittee on Mechanization of Check Handling, which was created in 1954. There would hardly have been such a committee, however, in the absence of fundamental innovations in data processing, and the latter were motivated by factors quite apart from financial services. That is, there were technological opportunities the major components of which existed for reasons exogenous to the burdens of manual check handling.

Use of these opportunities for electronic clearing obviously depended on the nearly ubiquitous introduction of a single system. While banks might be furnished MICR equipment from several manufacturers, the value of the equipment depended on its ability to read information from checks drawn on any bank. Standards were required before character recognition could be economically employed. These standards had to be compatible with manual sorting during the transition to electronic sorting. Further, the concomitant check-punching format had to be universally accepted so that MICR could be extended to the information systems within as well as among the participating banks. The R&D underlying MICR thus included interfirm organizations of equipment suppliers as well as the interfirm organizations of the financial institutions.

All banks did not have the computational capabilities required by MICR. Thus, as in the case of the clearinghouse, other organizational innovations became attractive. The correspondent system changed to include MICR check processing by host banks. Service bureaus for data processing operated by nonbank firms appeared. Some banks began proprietary joint ventures for MICR check handling and other computational services.

No single bank could profitably have introduced MICR. It required many banks. No single manufacturer of data processing equipment could profitably have developed a specific MICR technology without an organizational arrangement with many banks. The latter, to preserve competitive options, required the other equipment manufacturers not to be foreclosed. The interfirm organization was a complex one.

Bilateral Contracting and Financial Services

The use by a bank of services provided contractually by another firm has hardly been restricted to ordinary correspondent and data processing services. Loan participations are ad hoc interfirm organizations that permit a single bank to offer services to some customers that would otherwise be impossible or improvident. In the same way, national banks that were prohibited until 1913 from having their own trust departments entered into contracts with state-chartered banks so that they could indirectly provide those services. Even today the trust services of many smaller banks are made available in part or in full through interbank contracting. Similarly, the early restrictions on real estate lending by national banks could be partially overcome by informal contracting between a bank and a savings and loan assocation or a mutual savings bank. After the enactment of the Banking Act of 1933, many banks continued at least restricted securities brokerage services—"upon the order and for the sole account of customers"—with organizational arrangements effected with a security dealer. The more recent "sweep balance" accounts are modern versions of the same sort of interfirm organizations.

Interfirm correspondent relations, loan participations, trust services, and sweep balance services may often provide services more efficiently when organized through bilateral contracting than would a full merging of the affected businesses. So long as each of the parties is of sufficient size and scope in its general operations so that a full merger would not lower the costs of all of the services of the banks involved, the fact that the contracts are restricted to limited activities does not exact cost penalties. Bilateral and multilateral interfirm contracting works quite well if the activities covered by the contracting do not require one or the other of the parties to invest substantially in capital that is idiosyncratic to the transactions, if the costs and benefits of the transactions from the point of view of each of the transactors are identifiable and largely independent of other activities of each, and if there are not foregone cost reductions or increases in benefits due to failures to include other parties in the contracting.[6]

The Bank Card Innovation

The introduction of bank cards provides an excellent illustration of the need for more complex organizational innovations in order to implement technological opportunities. The basic idea, like that of the check, was simple; as with the check, however, broad usage was required to bring forth the efficiency characteristics of the new service.

The value to a card holder of having a card depends on the number of vendors of goods and services who will accept the card. If only an isolated merchant will take the card, there is little advantage in having one. The traveler would still have no good alternative to carrying cash or travelers checks. And the person who wanted consumer credit in making purchases would similarly gain little over other available credit sources.

On the other side, the value to vendors of accepting card payments depends, among other things, on the number of card holders who wish to use it at their locations. A large base of card holders promises higher sales, the avoidance of losses on credit the merchant would otherwise extend, reduced costs for credit investigations, immediate cash proceeds from sales to credit customers, reduced costs and loss from handling cash or checks, and improved internal control techniques.

If—as was not the case—a single bank were of sufficient size to operate its own card system, all aspects of pricing and system design could be internalized in that bank. When a card holder purchased anything through use of the card, the merchant could return the sales paper to the bank, where the card holder's account would show a credit extension or the debiting of a deposit account. The merchant's account at the same bank would be credited.

If there were only one bank, there would be no problems with respect to cost sharing or interbank clearings. There would, however, be a pricing problem. For the most part, the bank's potential card holders would be unwilling to pay much for the card itself or for card-based transactions. Cash, checks, and merchants' own revolving credit schemes would be good substitutes for many consumers for purchases from the merchants from whom most purchases were made.

Given the limited attractiveness of the card to purchasers, the merchants themselves would similarly be unwilling to pay much toward the operation of the system run by a simple bank. They would gain few customers, and some merchants might lose some of the profits from their own revolving credit plans. Thus, except for revenues that the bank could realize from consumer credit extensions, there would be few if any perceived benefits to any of the participants—the card holders, the merchants, and the bank— from the innovation. The bank card would not fly in the marketplace.

The interfirm organizational changes that took place to make bank cards popular are well known. The Visa and MasterCard organizations are the examples in this country. These interfirm organizations provide governance mechanisms necessary to make the bank card innovation a reality. The established regulations and bylaws of these card systems define functions and distribute costs and revenues in a manner such that card holders, card-issuing banks, merchant banks, and merchants all have incentives to participate.

What are these governance roles? First—and this is as essential for the cards as for checks—the card-issuing bank must accept the obligations generated by card holders as these obligations are presented for payment. The acceptance has to be in terms that are certain with respect to time and amount. Were this not true, merchant banks and, in turn, merchants would be less willing to accept cards. Second, and again as with checks and particularly MICR encoding, the participating banks have to agree on card, paper, and computational formats such that efficient data processing can occur on a systemwide basis. Thus, the initiation of processing at merchant's locations, even when performed manually, must be in a form readable by all issuing banks for the system to work. The processing of merchants' paper at merchant banks has also to be largely independent of the particular issuing bank for efficiency.

There is a third and very important governance function that the interfirm card organization has to perform. If only one bank were involved, all of the paper generated by customer–merchant transactions would be the so-called "on us" paper. For a transaction of $\$X$ between a merchant and a card holder, the former might receive $\$(X - a)$ and the latter might pay $\$(X + b)$, with $\$(a + b)$ being the bank's gross profit on the transaction. Nonetheless, no interbank clearings would be required. The merchants' and the card holders' accounts would "wash out" within the single bank.

When there are many banks in the system, the "washout" exists within the interbank organization, but it does not exist within the individual banks. There is still but one basic transaction for each piece of paper, but different banks are usually involved. A merchant has sold some good or service for a price of X, but the bank that has contractually agreed to pay the merchant some $(X - a)$ is not ordinarily the same as the bank to which the customer has agreed to pay some $(X + b)$.

Each of the participating institutions recognizes in a more or less defined way that there are costs associated with effecting a transaction. Each may see some other benefits from its offering the bank card service. Card-issuing banks and card holders contract bilaterally with respect to the b. Merchant banks and merchants contract bilaterally with respect to the a. Then somehow there must be a division of the sum of all the $(a + b)$s, the shares of which, together with the other perceived benefits, will make each of the participating banks willing to bear its costs. Since each must participate for the basic transactions between card holders and merchants to occur, the condition that incremental benefits be at least equal to the incremental costs exists for *each* bank, not just for the interfirm bank card organization as a whole. The interfirm governance mechanism designed to overcome this problem was the so-called interchange or issuer's reimbursement fee. Central clearing systems that employed this fee were set up, thus providing prompt and certain payments to merchant banks as well as a means for distributing the $(a + b)$s.

Conceptually, and ignoring prohibitive state and federal laws, mergers among banks are an alternative to the interfirm bank card organization. If that were chosen as the organizational mode, the governance provided now by interfirm bank card organizations would be done internal to the merged firm. The required scale of card operations was achieved by contracting rather than by a massive merging of banks. As a result, competition among banks and market forces has determined the a and b prices. The interfirm organizations were necessary for the bank card innovation and in this case created opportunities for increased competition in the services being rendered to merchants and to card holders.

ORGANIZATIONAL INNOVATIONS AND FINANCIAL SERVICES: A LOOK AT THE FUTURE

The organizational innovations that have been discussed are but a small fraction of those that have taken place in recent years. Others include automated clearinghouses (ACH), hundreds of automated teller machine (ATM) networks, a few point-of-sale (POS) networks combined with ATM networks, new domestic Bank Wire arrangements, and the SWIFT and CHIPS systems for international payments. All are interfirm organizations, with horizontal and vertical elements among the main participants and essentially vertical, bilateral contracting between the main participants and other institutions with which they "correspond." The several interfirm organizations intersect with one another—effecting transactions that involve more than one organization—through multiple organizational memberships by individual institutions and through the governance mechanisms of interorganizational organizations.

An Array of Possible Future Services

The present menu of technological opportunities goes well beyond anything now in place. Computer and communications technologies are expanding the timeliness, comprehensiveness, and reliability of information available to transactors. The same technologies are reducing transaction costs. Asset and liability management by households, nonfinancial businesses, and deposit and nondeposit financial institutions can be accomplished through electronic transactions among and within the historic organizational classes.

Only a very few of the technically feasible new services have thus far emerged. To emphasize this, consider the services that might be made available through videotex and teletext systems.[7] Sophisticated terminal devices at household and business locations would be capable of accessing:

Deposit financial institutions for transactions

Organized securities, commodities, and foreign exchange markets for transactions

Data banks of current and historic personal and general information

Data processing services, with sundry software–firmware packages and flexible user programmability

Account information from vendors of goods and services

Order and account servicing from vendors of goods and services

General information services such as common directory information, various schedules, news (local, regional, national, worldwide, with classifications by type), and weather

Word-processing systems with capabilities for transmission, receipt, editing, and output to varieties of "hard-copy" formats at different locations

Voice communications, both on line and stored

Audio and video entertainment services, both on line from network providers and through suppliers of stored, user-retrievable programs

User-owned and/or -controlled memory (storage) and processing facilities

Emergency and alarm services, both monitored and user controlled

Educational and social services

Behind such terminals there would exist transmission links. These links would for some sources be switched networks, capable of handling on-line, multiway interactive communication. For other services, one-way links would be adequate. Some services would require only voice-band channels; others broad-band channels. Digitization of analog signals would occur at the terminals.

For many of the services, the transmission links would switch to large numbers of service providers—the financial institutions, nonfinancial businesses, data bases, computer services, and the various information and entertainment services. In other cases, there would be switched networks between households and between financial and nonfinancial businesses. Some financial and nonfinancial businesses would provide state-of-the-art terminal devices for access by those without their own terminals as well as for use by persons away from their own terminals.

Economies of Scope and the Production of New Financial Services

While there has been no experience with so comprehensive a system, it is probable that system costs would reflect considerable economies of scope. That is, the costs of providing a number of the services through a single organization (although not necessarily a single firm) would be less than the costs of providing the services individually or in small sets with separate organizations. Thus, as was seen long ago by planners of "wired cities," local loops that carry a multiplicity of communications services are more efficient than are multiple systems of local loops, with each system dedicated to one or a few services. Scope economies in local loops would indicate that financial services would be provided on much the same facilities used for other services.

The same cost characteristic is likely to exist for modern versions of interexchange transmissions, whether by terrestrial fiber-optic links or by earth satellites. Costs on a given link tend to fall as the channel capacity and use density of the link increase. Furthermore, networking economies arise as an increasing number of nodes are interconnected with commonly controlled alternative routing capabilities. Again, the joining of financial and other services is suggested.

The extent to which scope economies will prevail in terminal and interexchange switching is not clear. Switching technologies appear to be moving toward the common handling of digitized signals, whether those are signals for voice, data, or video services. It seems probable that coding at the terminals by users—much like that in today's telephone network—will direct particular types of messages from one switch connecting many types of users onto more specialized subnetworks with switches and interexchange links designed for particularized message types. Some use-related switching may be done at the terminals, although switching further out in the network would likely be more efficient in most cases. Financial services generally and some specialized types of those services would, it appears, utilize unique subnetworks in the complex network of networks.

Terminal devices will also exhibit some scope economies. A single video display unit and/or a single hard-copy printer would be used over a wide range of services. Access to many data banks and to several processing/computer services would be joint, on common terminal equipment, as would that for entertainment, news services, and so on. Once more, specialized terminals for some financial services would be probable, but these would still interconnect for joint use of other parts of the global system.

The existence of scope economies does not necessarily preclude there being several competitive arrangements available to users. That is, the economies of scale, in contrast to economies of scope, need not be so extensive that only a single system could exist. Several purveyors, each offering a broad range of competitive services, could be formed. And it is possible also that the range of the scope economies would not be coextensive with the set of feasible services. Thus, there is no reason to assume that "natural monopoly" cost conditions would exist over all or even a large part of the full communications system. In fact, a very competitive situation is more likely in the provision of financial services.

Limitations on System Implementation

It is extremely unlikely that any system approaching that which is technically feasible will soon appear. The reason for this is obvious. Creating an organizational structure that would satisfactorily govern such a complex system is all but impossible.

The history of financial innovations suggests why. The introduction of checkable deposits depended on many banking institutions relatively simultaneously being hooked into the system. Too many checking transactions moved to outside institutions for a single bank to make checking a successful venture. The need for linking numerous financial institutions—and households and nonfinancial businesses—is even more important for the present electronic technologies.

The local or regional clearinghouse was an adequate interfirm organization to get checkable deposits into being. But in that case, there was a single type of instrument involved in the clearing. Beyond a bit of legal wording on the checks, each bank's checks could quite independently be prepared, issued, used by customers, and cleared with few worries about technical compatibility and the encoding of data into commonly readable language. Now the technology covers many transactors, many types of instruments, hierarchies of clearing functions, and settlements in several dimensions.

The clearinghouses had problems in arranging support for the functions that at once provided incentives for widespread participation and avoided free riders. These problems are far more acute with a full-fledged electronic payments system. And there is an added difficulty. Because of the economies of scope, the incremental cost of adding a service to an existing system will be low. Further, the sum of these incremental costs may be less than the full cost of the system even though the sum of the prices charged for the system's functions will be designed to cover costs. Thus, some services will of necessity be priced above incremental costs, leaving a system operator exposed to strategic, incremental cost pricing for the same services by another operator. This kind of exposure to the strategic and opportunistic behavior by others militates against investments in highly idiosyncratic, specialized capital.[8] Put another way, in the absence of a protective interfirm organization that reduces such exposure, the focus of investment will be on facilities that have relatively good alternative uses.

The history of MICR encoded checks tells a further story. Here the innovation required not only banks but also the participation of hardware and software manufacturers in the development process. In comparison with the number and diversity of participants needed to develop a system encompassing today's technological opportunities, the MICR development was indeed simple. Banks, other deposit institutions, securities and commodity dealers, insurance companies, and various retailers and service vendors would be involved. So too would computer and terminal manufacturers, common and private telecommunications carriers, software suppliers, and providers of data bank and related services.

Bilateral contracting between primary participants and others with whom they might deal would create an organizational milieu somewhat responsive to the system's scope requirements. Nonetheless, contracting is hazardous. The writing of comprehensive contingency provisions would be burdensome. Contract enforcement is both risky and costly. Opportunistic breach of contracts—particularly in an environment with unforeseen changes in technology and markets—is difficult to prevent. Again, investments in the idiosyncratic capital needed for the complete system would be deterred.

The development of bank cards illustrates another difficulty. The value of a card to a card holder depends on the number of merchants and other service providers who honor the card. At the same time, the value to merchants in accepting a card depends on the number of card holders who are likely to use the card for payment. This type of demand externality applies with added force in the complex services being discussed here. The value of each part of the system to each user of the system depends on the number of other users and the generality with which that part interconnects with other parts. Thus, what one party is willing to invest in facilities depends on what others are investing in complementary facilities. And what one user will pay to use the system depends on the amounts of its services being purchased by others.

These externalities lie behind the dilemma of appropriately sharing costs and benefits. On a broad scale, the technologies may promise benefits that far exceed costs. At the same time, there is no organization of sufficient scope to collect the attendant potential revenues and to compensate those incurring costs in a manner that assures efficient deployment of the technically feasible system. Significant organizational innovation is required before the technology can be used.

AN EVALUATION OF FUTURE FINANCIAL SERVICES

The organizational limitations are hardly so severe that significant new services will not appear. Some of the new technology is usable within the present interfirm organizational context, although even here a need for interfirm organizational change is typical.[9] The growing availability of discount brokerage services at banks is a simple example. These are often arranged as part of the correspondent relationship. Other aspects of the technical developments of new service offerings can be accommodated by interfirm organizational changes of a relatively modest sort. This has been seen, for example, in the networking of ATMs among banks and between banks and investment companies in money market funds and sweep balance services. It is to be anticipated that more such reorganizations will occur by contract. A single financial institution can become the outlet for virtually any existing service even though it produces few of them itself.

More formal reorganizations predicated on the creation of a governance mechanism running across the traditional service areas are also apparent. A number of so-called supermarket financial firms are being formed by merger. Much publicity has attended these consolidations. In the context of technical feasibility, however, none of these mergers goes far toward encompassing the full potential for the production and distribution of all financial services. It is, moreover, unlikely that any one or even the group of them will by themselves go far in this direction.

The supermarket organizations may be the leaders in service innovations. But as they innovate, the boundaries of an internally governed, single-firm organization will be quickly realized. They may produce and distribute the entire amounts of some of their services, but they will increasingly be forced into contracting modes for the production and distribution of others. Smaller institutions that reach customer groups otherwise unavailable to the large firm will be included. The supermarket firms, that is, will sell some services to and through other financial firms and buy some services from other financial and nonfinancial firms.[10]

Whether provided by a supermarket or more specialized firms, new financial service offerings will be severely circumscribed by developments outside of the finance area. The sweep of developments in computer technology is affected to only a minor extent by the needs of financial markets. The same is true of terminal equipment. Local, regional, national, and international telecommunications networks—digital local networks, new switching equipment, new network control devices, deployment of fiber optics, and so on—will for the most part be responsive to general demand and technology conditions of which financial services are a small part. Thus, the outer limits on the pace of innovation will in large measure be set by forces not at all unique to financial service needs. It is only at the margin where an added financial service has apparent incremental value adequate for the special adaptation of technologies that these services will dictate the directions of progress.

It is in the near-ubiquitous character of the basic technologies that one finds assurance that the financial supermarkets will not dominate the marketplace. What is occurring is a revolution in the creation, dissemination, and processing of information. Financial institutions are being affected by this revolution but are not terribly significant in shaping its overall directions. Since there are so many other actual or potential participants, the possibility of preemption of the technology by any firm or industry is extremely remote. Innovative entrepreneurial ventures can be launched not just by banks, other deposit institutions, and investment and brokerage firms, but also by insurance companies, bank card organizations, data processing firms, computer and terminal manufacturers, operators of communications networks, any large users of these networks, or some combinations of these.

Firms engaged in these activities can also enter one or more selected lines of financial services. This possibility is augmented if the firms are able to enter without major investments in specialized capital, and with more intensive application of facilities used in common for other nonfinancial services. Contracts and franchising with existing financial organizations round out the organizational structures needed for such entry. There may be a natural proclivity to price these selected service offerings at levels below those of integrated financial supermarkets—so long as incremental revenues exceed incremental cost. Here is a major element in the competitive environment of all of the innovators, large or small, multiproduct or specialized. The scope economies associated with the technologies produce numerous potential competitors, coming from various prior market bases.

At the same time, the financial institutions can potentially enter these nonfinancial lines of business. Existing regulations inhibit some such entry, whether de novo, by merger, or through joint ventures. Nonetheless, banks may be as inclined to engage in, say, data processing services, based on incremental costs, as are the data processing firms inclined to enter banking services. Thus the burden of erecting interfirm organizations for selective entry is relatively light even while that of broad entry over the range of technically feasible outputs is prohibitive.

The process of change will then be gradual even if the eventual revolution will be profound. Despite the gradualism, there will almost certainly be continued interorganizational consolidations. Efficiency gains will be one reason for mergers and joint ventures. In other cases, the process of change will itself force consolidations. Firms that make no effort to adapt to the new technologies will fail. So too will firms that move too fast—before the technology or markets are adequately defined—or that err in judgments of costs and revenues. Some interfirm organizational innovations will succeed, others will fail.[11]

CONCLUSIONS AND CONSIDERATIONS OF PUBLIC POLICY

Summary

The provision of financial services in the United States is one of the industries characterized by extensive interfirm organizational arrangements.[12] These arrangements have been required because of the nature of financial services—particularly transactions involving successive "holders in due course" of collection items—and because of the uniquely fragmented structure of U.S. institutions. Efficiency has necessitated the articulation of shared interfirm goals and the creation of interfirm mechanisms for the accomplishment of those goals. In a more concentrated structure, many (but not all) of the interfirm conventions found in the United States would be subsumed in intrafirm organizational arrangements.

The types of interfirm organizations that are needed to attain system efficiency depend on the technologies and market conditions underlying the provision of particular financial services. The organizations tend to change as technological opportunities and market forces converge in ways that make evident the inadequacies of an existing organizational structure. Thus, clearinghouses appeared concomitantly with checkable deposits, nationwide bank card systems were established to make possible card-based transactions, and regional and national ATM/POS organizations are now arising. Other interfirm arrangements are manifold, and include the many facets of correspondent relationships, loan participations, interbank deposits and, currently, the provision of new kinds of cash management, trust services, and securities offerings.

Creating the organizational settings in which new services can be efficiently produced (coproduced) and in which revenues and costs can be appropriately shared among the participants is often difficult. Further, the use of new technology is conditional on there being an organization such that the rewards to those participating in the innovation prospectively exceed the costs of participation. Many innovations that are in a narrow sense technologically feasible are economically infeasible because of the lack of an organization that can successfully internalize the costs and revenues associated with their introduction.

One way of internalizing costs and revenues and developing new governance mechanisms is to consolidate previously separate organizations. This has occurred and will continue to occur in the United States. Given the scope and scale of the operations required to employ many of the newly appearing technologies, it is very unlikely that consolidated "superfirms" will foreclose market opportunities. Product- and service-specific organizations among otherwise independent financial firms may be as efficient as a superfirm. And the superfirms themselves will in many cases have to include by contract other financial firms for the services they may provide.

As is always the case when there are fundamental technology changes, the structure of the financial service industries will change. Some existing firms and some existing interfirm organizations will succeed and others will fail. Some newly entering firms and some newly created interfirm organizations will succeed and others will fail. Neither failure nor success will be uniquely related to the size of the enterprise. Large firms and large systems as well as small firms and small systems will be exposed to the risks of failure.

Antitrust Concerns

The apparent, but limited, efficiency of interfirm organizations in accommodating the provision of new financial services does not mean that there are no policy problems associated with their formation and operations. At the same time that the organizations make possible the production and distribution of financial services that would not otherwise appear, their governance may at times extend to dimensions of conduct for which there is no social efficiency rationale. Clearinghouses, for example, were historically the locus for combinations in restraint of trade with respect to interest rates, banking hours, and other matters.

While interfirm agreements that have no purpose other than to restrain competition ought not be condoned, it is not always easy to distinguish those restraints on conduct that are essentially anticompetitive from those that are not. Moreover, the present status of antitrust law is such that legality of particular interfirm organizational arrangements cannot be determined with certitude prior to their initiation. Rules of an ATM network with respect to entry and access by nonmembers, for example, may seem reasonable to the organizers but quite unreasonable to others—and unreasonable to a regulator or a court. Similarly, interfirm cross-payments designed to share common costs or to allocate revenues could conceivably be regarded as per se violations of the Sherman Act, even when in fact they encourage competition and when without them the financial service would not be available.

It is perhaps true that the Department of Justice would not be likely to bring cases against interfirm organizational arrangements that yield net social benefits. Nonetheless, private suits do not have the merits of social benefits as their foundations. They are predicated on injury to an actual or potential competitor or class of competitors and may succeed on just these grounds. The probability of private litigants being awarded substantial damages may not now deter the formation of efficient interfirm arrangements, but it could become a deterrent.

There is a danger, too, that successful innovation will result in charges of monopolization and predation. The displaced producers of existing products often can point to particular aspects of the successful organization's conduct that appear monopolistic to them. The same is true of competitive, but unsuccessful, innovators. When entry is facilitated by prices based on the incremental costs of selective new product lines, these suits may succeed even when the practices yield socially beneficial consequences.

Monetary Policy

There is another policy matter that desperately requires attention. The introductions of new financial services over the past decade have already yielded a situation that hopelessly blurs the distinction between those liabilities of financial institutions that are essentially "money" and those that are not "money." The larger the array of assets that can be rapidly and efficiently exchanged for one another, the less distinct will be the advantage of any one of them as a medium of exchange. Monetary policy based on controls over the quantity or prices of any defined set of financial institution liabilities is—in an electronics age—apt to lead only to the increased use of another type of liability. That, in brief, is what led in recent years to the rapid increase in money market funds, repos, commercial paper, and Eurodollars.

As new technologies increasingly permit the exchange of any asset, by anyone, at any time, anywhere in the world, revisions in the fundamentals of central banking and monetary policy will be needed. These revisions are not impossible, but they, too, will require organizational changes that will not be easy to fashion.

NOTES

1. See Sterndl (1980) for a discussion innovation as a combination of several techniques.
2. The seminal work bearing on this point is Arrow (1962).
3. See de Solla Price (1980). This article discusses relations between science and technologies and uses the phrase "almost technologies" to describe things we know how to do but have not put into practice.
4. The following is based on Phillips (1962), March and Simon (1963), and Stinchcombe (1964).
5. For modern treatment of the view that internal firm organization is important, see Williamson (1975).
6. On the problems of using contracts rather than integration, see Williamson (1979) and Phillips (1980).
7. In popular usage, videotex involves the transmission of information from data banks over telephone lines and cable. Teletext transmissions are broadcast or utilized cable TV channels. These distinctions are not important for the present discussion. For background, see Woolfe (1980), Sigel (1980), and Martin (1978).
8. See Williamson (1979).
9. For discussion, see Macmillan (1982).
10. For a concurring view, see Gerstner (1983).
11. See Phillips (1971); Nelson and Winter (1978).
12. Other industries, of course, employ interfirm organizations. The financial services industry is unique only in degree. See Marti and Smiley as well as references in notes 4 and 6.

REFERENCES

Arrow, Kenneth. "Economic Welfare and the Allocation of Resources for Invention." In R. R. Nelson (Ed.), *The Rate and Direction of Inventive Activity*. National Bureau of Economic Research, Princeton: Princeton University Press, 1962.

de Solla Price, Derek. "A Theoretical Basis for Input-Output Analysis of National R&D Policies." In D. Sahal, *Research,Development and Technological Innovation.* Lexington, Mass.: Lexington Books, D. C. Heath, 1980.

Gerstner, Louis V., Jr. "Realities of Financial Services." *Financier,* March 1983, *7*(2), pp. 19–22.

Hock, Dee W. "Visa Head Says Public Will Never Go Cashless." *Computerworld,* November 28, 1977, p. 9.

Macmillan, Miller L. "Organizational Challenges to Banks in the 1980s." Speech to the American Bankers Association Personnel Conference, September 1982.

March, James G., and Simon, Herbert A. *Organizations.* New York: John Wiley & Sons, 1958.

Marti, P., and Smiley, R. H. "Co-operative Arrangements and the Organization of Industry." *Journal of Industrial Economics,* June 1983, *31*(4), pp. 437–452.

Martin, J. *The Wired Society.* Englewood Cliffs, N.J.: Prentice-Hall, 1978.

Nelson, Richard R., and Winter, Sidney G. "Forces Limiting and Generating Concentration under Schumpeterian Competition." *Bell Journal of Economics,* Autumn 1978, *9*(2), pp. 524–548.

Phillips, Almarin. *Market Structure, Organization and Performance.* Cambridge, Mass.: Harvard University Press, 1962.

——*Technology and Market Structure.* Lexington, Mass.: Lexington Books, D. C. Heath, 1971.

——"Organizational Factors in R&D and Technological Change: Market Failure Considerations." In D. Sahal (Ed.), *Research, Development and Technological Innovation.* Lexington, Mass: Lexington Books, D. C. Heath, 1980.

Sigel, E. (Ed.) *Videotext: The Coming Revolution.* White Plains, N.Y.: Knowledge Industry Publications, 1980.

Sterndl, Josef. "Technical Progress and Evolution." In D. Sahal (Ed.), *Research, Development and Technological Innovation.* Lexington, Mass: Lexington Books, D. C. Heath, 1980.

Stinchcombe, A. L. "Social Structure and Organizations." In J. G. March (Ed.), *Handbook of Organizations.* Chicago: Rand McNally, 1964.

Williamson, Oliver E. *Markets and Hierarchies: Analysis and Antitrust Implications.* New York: Free Press, 1975.

——"Transactions Cost Economics: The Governance of Contractual Relations." *Journal of Law and Economics,* October 1979, *22,* pp. 233–261.

Woolfe, R. *Videotext: The New Television-Telephone Information Services.* London: Hyden & Sons, Ltd., 1980.

3 Manifestations of Banking Change

The earlier sections relate to financial change in relatively broad terms. More detailed attention is now given to specific changes. The range of topics covers users of services (the treatment of consumer activity is contained in Richard L. Peterson's chapter in Part 4), banking institutions (in domestic and foreign markets), nonbank competitors, issues of capital, bank regulation, and regulatory and public policy questions.

Although this more specific treatment entails some increased recourse to institutional detail, the emphasis—as throughout this volume—is on analyzing and explaining *why* certain developments have taken place and under what conditions significant further changes can be expected.

5 Recent Developments in Business Financing

Robert A. Taggart, Jr.

INTRODUCTION: THE PLACE OF BUSINESS FINANCE IN THE U.S. FINANCIAL SYSTEM

The forces of inflation, economic instability, technological change, and regulation, which have altered the workings of the financial system generally, have had a strong effect on business financing as well. The purpose of this chapter is to describe recent developments in the financing of U.S. business corporations and to interpret them in the light of these forces for change. A partial view is afforded by examining recent trends in the traditional measures of business financing activity. To get a complete picture, however, it is also necessary to look at changing practices in business financial management, innovations in financing instruments, and the evolving competitive relationships among suppliers of business funds. Particular attention will be devoted to the changing role of the banking system in financing U.S. business.

Business Finance as a Means of Packaging Operating Returns

To interpret the developments in business financing, it is first necessary to understand the role of business finance within the overall financial system. A diagrammatic representation of the system, which omits the government and rest-of-the-world sectors for simplicity, is shown in Figure 5.1.

In the closed system depicted in Figure 5.1, the economy's ultimate assets are its tangible assets, and the ultimate wealth holders are households. That is, if we consolidated the balance sheets of the business, financial intermediary, and household sectors, canceling all offsetting fi-

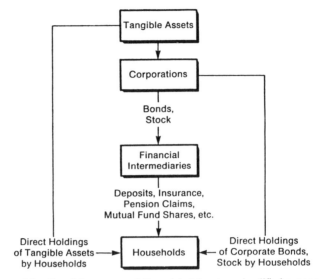

Figure 5.1.   Tangible assets and financial claims in a simplified economy.

nancial claims, we would be left with just tangible assets on the asset side of the balance sheet and household net worth on the liability side. However, this consolidation masks the role of the financial system in reconciling the portfolio desires of households with the characteristics of the tangible assets.

Households accumulate assets to smooth their own consumption streams and those of their heirs. To some extent, such tangible assets as houses and consumer durable goods serve this purpose by yielding flows of services and by acting as inflation hedges. In other respects, tangibles are less suitable as household savings vehicles. Tangible assets are rarely traded on organized markets and may not be easily convertible into cash. In addition, their pattern of returns may not coincide with households' desired consumption patterns. Tangible assets may provide riskier return patterns, for example, than most households desire, or may not yield sufficiently high payoffs under important contingencies such as death or illness.

The purpose of the financial system is to reconcile the desires of households with the return and liquidity characteristics of the tangible assets. This system may be broadly construed to include business corporations, securities markets, and financial institutions—that is, all of the intermediate links in the chain running from tangible assets to households. Corporations specialize in managing tangible assets and in packaging the return streams from these assets in the form of debt and equity securities. Households may prefer allocating some portion of their wealth to such securities because they require less management than the tangibles they represent, are easily traded on securities exchanges, and can be combined in varying proportions to transform and rearrange the tangible assets' return streams. Even the enhanced degree of portfolio opportunities represented in these securities may not be adequate to match households' desires, however, and this creates a role for financial institutions. Banks, insurance companies, pension funds, and mutual funds, for example, hold corporate securities and in turn issue their own claims with different liquidity characteristics and patterns of return. Some of these institutions lend to households as well, thus affording them further transformation opportunities.

Determinants of Business Financing

When viewed in the context of the financial system as a whole, the level and mix of business financing are ultimately determined by households' demands for asset characteristics, corporations' ability to satisfy these demands through the design and issuance of securities, and the strength of the competition that corporations face from other sectors in the capital markets. The choices open to corporations in this competition include the mix of debt, equity, and hybrid securities, the maturity structure of debt, and the level of liquid asset holdings.

On the demand side, households differ in their expectations and attitudes toward risk. Those who are more optimistic about corporate prospects or less risk averse might be more readily attracted to equity securities, while others might find debt securities better suited to their needs. More exotic hybrid securities can also be designed to appeal to particular segments of the investing public. Convertible bonds, for example, might attract investors who are basically optimistic about a company's prospects and wish to share in its potential gains but are at the same time averse to risk and desire some protection against losses. Corporations can further temper the risk inherent in their equity securities by increasing their holdings of liquid assets. Investors will also differ as to tax status, and securities can be designed to suit differing tax circumstances.

Finally, overall economic conditions will affect households' demands for asset characteristics. In times of inflation and instability, for example, corporations are likely to find investors more receptive to short-term debt than to fixed nominal claims such as long-term bonds.

On the supply side, corporations' need to issue securities is determined by their investment opportunities and ability to generate funds internally. To the extent that securities must be issued, the corporation faces a financial cost function. That is, the firm can issue securities that offer various financial services or return patterns to investors, but it faces varying costs in doing so. Some of these costs are explicit, such as underwriting fees and the costs of servicing the securities while they remain outstanding. Others are implicit, such as the cost of possible financial distress from excessive amounts of debt or the cost of resolving conflicts among different classes of security holders. The financial cost function is also affected by the government in a variety of ways. Certain types of tax-avoidance schemes between corporations and investors are restricted. For example, excessive accumulation of liquid assets might subject a corporation to a penalty tax, and business firms can issue tax-exempt bonds only under very limited circumstances. Nonfinancial corporations are also forbidden by federal and state regulation to issue certain kinds of securities. If it thought it could finance itself more cheaply by doing so, nothing in principle would keep a steel company, say, from issuing demand deposits or life insurance policies. Government regulation, however, would forbid the steel company from raising funds in these ways.

In general, then, the financing decisions of business firms have many characteristics in common with their production decisions. Firms examine both demand and cost conditions and strive to issue those securities that are worth more to investors than they cost the firms to "produce." As on the production side, firms' chances to profit from issuing securities are determined in large part by the extent of the competition they face in the capital market. Financial institutions, government units, and households all engage in activities that have the effect of transforming and repackaging the return streams from both real and financial assets. To this extent, they are in direct competition with the financing activities of business corporations, and the more intense this competition is, the smaller will be the opportunities for business corporations to profit from their financing choices.

With this background in mind, we turn now to a review of recent developments in business financing. The preceding discussion suggests that interpretation of these developments requires an awareness of the underlying factors that determine the supply and demand for corporate securities. Three such factors that have been emphasized throughout this volume are inflation, technological change, and government regulation. It will be argued in the following section that these forces have been primary agents in the changing patterns of business finance.

Since the late 1960s, inflation rates and interest rates have generally been higher than in preceding decades. Accelerating inflation has been accompanied by increased uncertainty over future economic conditions and thus asset prices and interest rates have been unusually volatile. In turn, rapidly fluctuating financial market conditions have affected both investors' portfolio needs and the ability of firms and financial institutions to serve these needs.

This period has also been characterized by rapid technological change, particularly in information processing and communications. These developments have encouraged the growing integration of different segments of the capital market. In particular, technological change has altered the financial cost function faced by business firms and their capital market competitors.

Finally, government regulation has been both an active and a changing force during this period. The regulatory system for financial institutions has been in a state of continual flux, as financing practices have changed rapidly, and as new competition has blurred institutional distinctions. If regulation is broadly construed to encompass the tax system, it has also had a substantial effect on the supply of corporate securities.

BUSINESS FINANCING DEVELOPMENTS AND THEIR INTERPRETATION

Traditional Measures of Business Financing Activity

Trends in business financing over the 1970s and early 1980s have been widely discussed using such traditional measures as funds flow proportions and balance sheet ratios. A typical set of these measures is shown in Table 5.1, in which various sources of funds for the nonfinancial nonfarm corporate sector are given as percentages of that sector's total yearly financing activity.

A wide range of observers—from the business press (*Business Week*, 1974), the financial community (Mains, 1980; Salomon Brothers, 1982), and the academic community (Minsky, 1977; Piper and Weinhold, 1982), have expressed concern over a perceived deterioration in these ratios in recent years. One worrisome trend has been the increased reliance business corporations have placed on external funds. Although the proportion of internal funds increased dramatically during the recession periods of 1975 and 1980–1982, it is apparent from Table 5.1 that there were recurring strings of years in the 1970s in which the relative availability of internal funds steadily declined.

Another trend attracting attention has been the increased use of debt financing relative to equity. Again in Table 5.1, while this pattern was sharply reversed in 1975, 1980, and 1982, debt usage has tended to rise during expansion phases of the business cycle. This trend is in large part the mirror image of the decline in the availability of internal funds, but it also reflects the relatively low levels of external equity issues.

Table 5.1. Yearly Funds Flows as Percentages of Total Sources of Funds to U.S. Nonfinancial Corporate Business

	1970	1971	1972	1973	1974	1975	1976	1977	1978	1979	1980	1981	1982
Total sources	100	100	100	100	100	100	100	100	100	100	100	100	100
Internal funds	57.1	53.7	56.1	47.7	45.1	76.3	63.7	62.4	55.7	54.5	59.2	65.6	76.2
External funds	42.9	46.3	43.9	52.3	54.9	23.7	36.3	37.6	44.3	45.5	40.8	34.4	23.8
Equity	5.5	8.9	7.2	4.1	2.2	6.3	5.0	1.1	-0.03	-2.3	3.9	-3.3	1.2
Total debt	37.4	37.4	36.7	48.2	52.8	17.4	31.4	36.5	44.3	47.8	36.9	37.6	22.6
Bank loans	5.7	3.1	8.2	15.4	16.3	-5.9	2.4	8.2	9.6	12.7	8.3	12.1	13.0
Commercial paper, acceptances, finance company loans	2.7	0.0	2.8	3.1	5.9	0.7	5.3	6.2	4.9	5.8	2.6	7.3	-1.0
Bonds and mortgages	25.7	23.2	10.2	6.7	11.7	18.3	13.1	12.4	10.1	9.7	13.4	9.8	12.5
Other debt	3.3	11.1	15.5	23.1	18.9	7.5	10.6	9.7	19.7	15.0	12.6	8.4	-1.9
Memorandum: Total short-term liabilities[a]	10.0	13.8	25.9	40.1	38.6	-2.5	16.1	22.7	31.7	34.6	19.5	21.8	7.4

SOURCE: Board of Governors of the Federal Reserve System, Flow of Funds Accounts.

[a]Includes loans, short-term paper, profit taxes payable, and trade debt.

A third trend has been the increased proportion of short-term debt, although this is difficult to measure precisely. Some unknown proportion of bank loans (included in Table 5.1 under short-term debt) actually represents term loans (i.e., loans with original maturities over one year). The Federal Trade Commission, for example, estimates that for U.S. manufacturing corporations, approximately 65% of bank debt at the end of 1981 had a maturity of more than one year (up from 48% in 1970). In view of the rise of floating rate debt, however, and shorter maturities for long-term debt, it seems undeniable that there has been some tendency toward shortening the average maturity of corporate debt. Again, the years 1975, 1980, and 1982 stand out as sharp exceptions to this general tendency.

Finally, there has been concern over declining liquidity in the nonfinancial corporate sector. Corporate liquidity is measured in Table 5.2 in terms of the ratios of liquid asset holdings to both total short-term liabilities and short-term credit market debt. The downward trend is more readily apparent in the latter ratio.

A better perspective on these recent trends can be gained by comparing them with both typical cyclical patterns in business financing and secular trends over the course of the twentieth century. It is not unusual, for example, for internal funds, short- and long-term debt usage, external equity issues, and liquid asset holdings to exhibit considerable swings over the course of the business cycle. In the early stages of a typical business cycle expansion, corporate profits rise sharply while dividend payments lag. Many corporations face the luxury of financing most of their investment needs internally, and some of these internal funds may even be used for such balance sheet rebuilding activities as paying down short-term debt and replenishing stocks of liquid assets. To the extent that external funds are needed, corporations often perceive such periods, when interest rates are typically relatively low and the stock market relatively buoyant, as good times to issue long-term debt or equity (see Marsh, 1982; Taggart, 1977). As the expansion accelerates and spending increases for plant and equipment and inventories, businesses begin to rely more heavily on debt financing and to draw on some of their liquid asset reserves. Once interest rates start to rise, there is also a tendency to emphasize shorter-term debt in the hope of postponing long-term financing until bond market conditions are more favorable. As the business cycle peaks and turns downward, short-term debt usage and corporate liquidity reach their high and low points, respectively, and as interest rates fall in the recession phase, companies begin to refinance some of their short-term borrowing with long-term debt.

Looking back at Tables 5.1 and 5.2, it is evident that recent business financing developments conform in most essential features to this typical

Table 5.2. Liquidity Ratios for U.S. Nonfinancial Corporate Business, 1970–1980

	1970	1971	1972	1973	1974	1975	1976	1977	1978	1979	1980
$\dfrac{\text{Liquid assets}^a}{\text{Short-term liabilities}^b}$	23.0	24.6	24.5	23.1	25.1	30.1	30.9	28.4	25.8	23.8	23.7
$\dfrac{\text{Liquid assets}^a}{\text{Loans and short-term paper}}$	53.9	59.4	58.9	54.5	46.0	56.6	59.1	53.0	48.9	45.2	44.3

SOURCE: Board of Governors of the Federal Reserve System, Flow of Funds Accounts.

[a] Liquid assets = currency, demand and time deposits, security repurchase agreements, foreign deposits, federal and municipal government securities, and commercial paper.

[b] Short-term liabilities = loans, short-term paper, profit taxes payable, and trade debt.

cyclical pattern. Internal funds declined for several years running, reaching low points in 1974 and 1979, but then rebounding sharply in 1975 and 1980–1982. Debt financing followed the opposite pattern, with peaks occurring in 1974 and 1979, followed by relatively steep reversals in 1975 and 1980. If there has been anything surprising in the general direction of these financing trends, it has been that businesses have been somewhat slow to start refunding their high levels of short-term debt, especially bank loans, and to begin rebuilding liquidity in the most recent recessionary period (see Gilbert, 1982). This may be at least partly attributable to a perception that real interest rates have remained at high levels.

Although the general direction of these trends has been in line with the usual cyclical pattern, the magnitude of the swings has been relatively large by historical standards. The concerns expressed by business analysts are highlighted better when these recent trends are compared with long-term patterns. It is apparent from the figures in Table 5.3, for example, that corporate debt usage has increased sharply in the post–World War II period, and it appears to have reached a historical peak in the 1960s and 1970s. A substantial portion of this increased debt has been accounted for by short-term liabilities, which also appear to have reached a historical peak in the most recent period. Conversely, the availability of internal funds has declined steadily over the postwar years and appears to be low at present relative to the rest of the twentieth century. Finally, as shown in Table 5.4, business holdings of liquid assets have declined substantially from their swollen levels at the end of World War II, and their ratio to total short-term liabilities is even low relative to those prevailing in the early part of the century.

In sum, concerns over the state of corporate financing activities seem to stem largely from the deterioration in funds flow and balance sheet ratios that took place in recent years. The availability of internal funds decreased, debt usage (in particular short-term debt) increased, and liquidity declined. For two reasons, however, fears over this perceived increase in financial risk may be somewhat exaggerated.

First, recent trends are often set against the backdrop of the post–World War II years, but as Tables 5.3 and 5.4 make clear, business corporations emerged from World War II with unusually low levels of financial risk. At least part of the postwar "deterioration" probably represents a return to more normal financing relationships.

Second, the period since 1970 has been one of unusually high inflation, and this may have caused some distortions in the traditional measures of financing activity. As vonFurstenberg and Malkiel (1977) have argued, inflation reduces the real value of already outstanding corporate debt and causes an inflation premium to be built into the interest rate on new debt.

Table 5.3. Funds Flows as Percentages of Total Sources of Funds to U.S. Nonfinancial Corporations: Selected Historical Periods

	1901–1912	1913–1922	1923–1929	1930–1939	1940–1945	1946–1959	1960–1969	1970–1982
Total sources	100	100	100	100	100	100	100	100
Internal funds	55	60	55	114	80	64	62	59
External funds	45	40	45	(Neg.)	20	36	38	41
Equity	14	11	19	19	5	5	2	5
Total debt	31	29	26	(Neg.)	15	30	36	36
Bonds and mortgages	23	12	22	(Neg.)	(Neg.)	14	15	14
Short-term debt	8	17	4	(Neg.)	20	16	21	22

SOURCE: Goldsmith (1958) and Board of Governors of the Federal Reserve System, Flow of Funds Accounts.

Table 5.4. Historical Liquidity Ratios for U.S. Nonfinancial Corporate Business, 1900–1980

	1900	1912	1922	1929	1933	1939	1945	1950	1960	1970	1980
$\dfrac{\text{Liquid assets}}{\text{Short-term liabilities}}$	29.9	32.2	30.0	31.1	29.7	45.2	82.2	68.0	41.7	23.0	23.7
$\dfrac{\text{Liquid assets}}{\text{Loans and short-term paper}}$	138.4	110.6	104.9	149.9	153.0	231.4	425.7	216.7	113.0	53.9	44.3

SOURCE: Goldsmith, Lipsey, and Mendelson (1963) and Board of Governors of the Federal Reserve System, Flow of Funds Accounts.

The first of these effects implies that since the real burden of old debt is reduced by inflation, firms can take on new debt with no increase in their overall real burden. Nominal measures of debt usage may therefore overstate the burden of this debt on firms. The second effect implies that corporations must repay sooner a portion of the real principal on new debt in order to compensate investors for expected inflation. But if a portion of interest paid is actually a return of real principal, nominal measures of corporate profits and internal funds may consequently be understated. At the same time, some of the borrowing done by corporations during inflationary periods should be thought of as a rolling over of this real principal rather than as net new borrowing.

Whether exaggerated or not, however, trends in the traditional ratios and the concomitant fears of business analysts reflect some fundamental changes in the business financing environment. These changes can be traced to inflation and economic instability and to the interaction of inflation with the corporate tax system.

In addition to the accounting biases, inflation and the tax system can have some real effects on internal funds availability. In an inflationary period, historical-cost depreciation deductions are insufficient to match the replacement cost of plant and equipment. Hence reported profits are artificially high, and the taxes paid on these phantom profits reduce internal funds relative to funds needed for investment. Likewise, to the extent that companies use FIFO accounting, the taxation of inventory profits reduces internal funds' availability.

Although there are similar accounting biases in measured debt proportions, the interaction of inflation and the tax system may also enhance real incentives to use debt financing. The inflation premium in interest rates is both tax deductible to corporations and taxable to investors. As expected inflation increases, therefore, the corporate tax advantage to debt increases, but at the same time so does the investor tax disadvantage, and corporations' net incentive to rely on larger proportions of debt financing depends on the relative magnitude of these two effects. If, as has been argued by Modigliani (1982), Gordon and Malkiel (1981), and others, the tax rate of the marginal investor in the bond markets is lower than the marginal corporate tax rate, the corporate tax advantage to debt would outweigh the investor tax disadvantage. Greater expected inflation would thus lead to higher corporate debt proportions.

The influence of inflation can also be found in the increased use of short-term debt and the decline in corporate liquidity. Particularly in the face of uncertainty over future inflation rates, investors have been increasingly reluctant to hold fixed nominal claims of long maturity. As a consequence, corporations have issued growing amounts of short-term debt, and even their long-term issues have been more in the five- to 15-year maturity range than in the 25-to-30-year range. In addition, inflation has made it more expensive for corporations to hold idle cash and bank deposits, and even interest-bearing liquid assets are made less attractive by the taxation of the inflation premium. It is not surprising, therefore, that corporations have economized on liquid asset holdings during the last 10 to 15 years.

While traditional measures of business financing activity contain serious biases, nevertheless, it is clear that inflation and taxation have had some real effects on that activity in recent years. Even if the shortage of internal funds has been exaggerated, the continual rolling over of real debt principal has necessitated more frequent trips to the capital market for corporations. The frequency of external fund raising has also been affected by the reliance on short-term debt and the decline in liquidity. Although the real burden of total corporate debt may not have increased significantly, corporations have been more exposed to interest rate fluctuations as they have had to raise external funds on a more frequent basis. It is in this sense that the risk of corporate financial positions has increased in the recent period.

New Developments in Financial Management Practice

While the traditional ratios give some indication of the changing financial environment, a more complete view is obtained from examining changes that have occurred in the practice of corporate financial management and in the competitive relationships among suppliers of business funds. The former set of changes is analyzed in this section, while the latter is detailed in the following section, The Changing Market for Business Financial Services.

In the past 10 to 15 years, the practice of financial management has undergone a striking transformation, marked by innovative terms on securities, the tapping of new funds sources, and increased attention to economizing on the cost of raising and managing funds. Inflation and economic instability have been initiating forces behind this transformation, but technological change and government regulation also have played strong roles.

New Debt Instruments and Loan Arrangements. In the face of inflation and economic instability, firms have striven to offer new financial instruments that better serve the changing portfolio needs of investors. A prime example is the inclusion of options on debt instruments that afford investors greater protection against changing credit market conditions. These new forms of debt include: extendible bonds, which give the holder the option to receive payment of principal at some initial date or else extend the maturity to one or more later dates (such bonds are typically callable by the company, protecting it somewhat against declines in future interest rates); bonds with warrants attached, enabling the holder to purchase additional debt with a similar coupon rate; and bonds with put options attached, enabling the holder to tender the bonds at par to the issuer on or after some specified date. In each of these cases the company offers some protection against future increases in interest rates by allowing the holder to cut losses early should rates rise. These innovations allow a shortening of the effective debt maturity, at the holder's option, and in this respect they accomplish much the same thing as another innovation—floating-rate debt, or, more simply, increased use of short-term debt. In each of these instances, the corporation absorbs the risk of future increases in interest rates, a risk it would have avoided under traditional long-term debt.

In much the same vein, corporations have offered lenders some degree of equity participation, allowing them to share in inflationary increases in asset values and thus protect the real values of their claims. Convertible bonds have been issued in growing amounts in the 1970s and 1980s, and equity participation clauses have become common in commercial mortgages. Among the more unusual equity participation debt instruments have been: the Sunshine Mining Company's 1980 issues of silver-indexed bonds, payable either at par or at the equivalent cash value of 50 ounces of silver; the Allegheny Beverage Corporation's 1980 debenture issue calling for premium interest payments if earnings exceed specified levels; and Oppenheimer and Company's 1981 debenture issue calling for additional interest depending on New York Stock Exchange trading volume.

The search for ways to overcome inflation-induced problems in the debt market may also account for the growing popularity of asset-based financing, the primary idea of which is somehow to separate the assets to be financed from the rest of the company's assets. As we have seen, traditional accounting ratios are subject to a variety of biases in the face of inflation, and accurate credit analysis is thereby made more difficult. To the extent that lenders can tie their claim to a specific segment of the company's assets, credit analysis is made easier.

To see how this works, consider a project financing arrangement that sets up a separate subsidiary upon which the lender has a prior claim. This technique is particularly prevalent in natural resource projects. In this case the subsidiary owns the rights to the entire output of a mine or an oil field, and the lender looks to this output to satisfy its claim. In addition, if the output is not sufficient to satisfy the corporation's contractual obligation to the lender, the arrangement may give the lender additional recourse to the corporation's other assets. (See Brealey and Myers, 1981 for a detailed description of one such project financing arrangement, associated with British Petroleum's development of its North Sea oil field in the early 1970s.)

Separating a project from the rest of the corporation in this way can reduce the lender's costs of oversight, thereby reducing the corporation's borrowing cost. Since the risk of the project is not commingled with other business or financial risks the company faces, it is more readily and cheaply analyzed, especially by lending institutions with expertise in that particular industry. This reduction in monitoring costs in turn allows the project to support more debt than it might if it were not organized as a separate entity.

Other asset-based financing techniques are similarly motivated, at least in part, by economy of loan administration in an inflationary environment. Although its growth may be largely attributable to tax factors, as discussed below, leasing shares some of the monitoring advantages of project finance. Likewise, accounts receivable financing allows some of the same economies of specialization in particular types of risk.

Changes in Methods for Raising Funds. In addition to changing investors' portfolio needs, the inflationary environment of recent years has increased the frequency with which corporations have visited the capital market. The reduced availability of internal funds and the shortening of effective debt maturities have necessitated these frequent visits, and in turn this has brought about changes in the way external funds are raised.

First, corporations have had greater incentives than ever to investigate all possible sources of funds and to tap new markets. A prime example is their increasing use of overseas financing. While U.S. multinational corporations have long made use of bank financing overseas, there has been a growing tendency to raise funds in the Eurobond market. This has been true even of utility companies and other firms having little or no overseas operations.

In part, this development can be attributed to the fact that domestic inflation has made U.S. corporations more accustomed to issuing the intermediate-maturity bonds that have long dominated the European markets. In addition, technological change and regulation have played a role in corporations' willingness to go further afield. Communications advances have increased the integration of world capital markets, and this has made the Eurobond market in particular larger, more liquid, and hence more attractive to U.S. corporations. From a regulatory standpoint, U.S. corporations also face fewer disclosure requirements in the Eurobond market than they do domestically.

A second consequence of firms' more frequent use of the capital markets is a tendency to engage in do-it-yourself financing. There is a point at which contact with the markets is sufficiently frequent and on a large enough scale to justify the maintenance of a finance staff that continuously performs duties that investment bankers or other intermediaries formerly handled for the company. Continual need for large amounts of short-term funds, for example, has induced finance companies and industrial or retailing companies with captive finance subsidiaries to take the lead in directly placing their own commercial paper. Some large companies have also begun arranging their own private debt placements with insurance companies. In a few cases underwriting services have even been bypassed on public securities issues. Exxon conducted two Dutch auctions of securities issues in the mid-1970s, in which interested investors were simply invited by the company to submit bids. In addition, dividend reinvestment plans, (by which investors receive new shares in lieu of cash dividend payments) as well as employee stock ownership plans have become significant sources of new equity for many companies. Such plans are often administered by commercial banks, but investment bankers' underwriting fees are avoided on the new shares.

A third consequence of the need to raise funds frequently in the face of increasingly volatile interest rates has been a greater emphasis on timing. Corporate financial officers have devoted more energy to finding "windows" in the market, or periods of relatively low rates when long-term debt securities can be floated advantageously. They have tried to streamline the securities issue process by organizing pricing committees of the board of directors, by feeding information about their companies to bond-rating agencies on a more frequent basis, and by pushing for regulatory changes that facilitate fast action on securities issues. (One of these, the shelf registration rule, will be discussed in more detail in the following section.) In addition, many financial officers maintain more frequent contact with bond market traders and in-house pension fund managers to keep abreast of market trends. Whether corporations have been able systematically to beat the market with their timing activities is an open question, but it seems clear they have been increasingly willing to make the attempt (see Osborne, 1981).

Economizing on Idle Cash and Taxes.   In addition to raising external funds in new ways, firms have utilized their internal financial resources more intensively by minimizing both excess cash and taxes. Increasingly, cash management practices have relied on computerized information systems and electronic funds transfer. Faster flows of information made possible by computers have enabled managers to forecast daily funds needs and cash balances with greater accuracy. It is now commonplace for a company's banks to feed information each night about that day's account activity—either directly to the company or to an independent data collection service. The financial manager is thus able to begin each day knowing his or her cash position exactly. Another common practice, known as controlled disbursement, enables managers to forecast daily cash outflows early in the day as well. Under this practice, a company writes checks on a bank that is small enough to have checks presented to it by the Federal Reserve for payment just once a day. If the bank is near a Federal Reserve regional check-processing center, this delivery of checks will be made early in the morning. The manager thus receives a report of funds needs early enough in the day that he or she can deposit funds to cover those needs and still have time to invest any excess funds in the money market. Together, these and other computer-aided cash management techniques have allowed corporations to be much more aggressive about minimizing idle cash.

Since these innovations in cash management would not have been possible without advances in communications and data processing, it might be argued that they have been caused by technological change. It should be noted, however, that much of the impetus for using and even developing new applications of technology in this area stems from inflation. Because it increases interest rates, inflation makes it more expensive to keep financial resources idle, and thus it has encouraged the use of techniques that speed the flow of transactions.

Corporations have also sought to tighten the management of tax payments. In cash management, for example, the preferred dividend rollover trading strategy has gained popularity, whereby corporations invest in preferred stock rather than the customary Treasury bills or commercial paper. The corporations then trade in and out of these preferred stock issues so as to receive as many dividends as possible during the year, and as long as each issue is held for at least 16 days these dividends qualify for the 85% corporate tax exclusion. Other corporations, particularly banks, have tried to take advantage of this new interest in preferred stocks by selling preferred issues with adjustable dividend rates to corporate investors.

Other financial transactions of a longer-term nature have been aimed at reducing the joint tax liability of the corporation and its investors. Leasing grew tremendously as a financing mechanism through the 1960s and 1970s, for example, with the advent of the investment tax credit. Leasing allows this credit and other tax savings to be allocated to those tax-paying entities that can use them to greatest advantage. This practice was furthered by the safe harbor leasing provisions of the Economic Recovery Tax Act of 1981.

Economizing on combined investor and corporate taxes also motivated, at least in part, the brief surge in corporate issues of deep discount (or original-issue discount) bonds in 1981 and 1982. By issuing bonds with below-market (sometimes zero) coupons, corporations save on cash outflows for coupon payments. At the same time, however, they are able to amortize for tax purposes these bonds' discount from par that results from their low coupon rate. In effect, corporations can receive a tax deduction for accrued interest without any immediate cash outflow. The disadvantage of these instruments to investors is that, in the United States, the amortization of the discount is also taxable income for them, but to the extent that the bonds can be sold to tax-exempt investors, a net tax saving is possible. For a brief period, until the Ministry of Finance effectively halted sales in March of 1982, many of these bonds were also sold to Japanese investors, for whom the discount is untaxed.

Somewhat more complex examples of financial innovations aimed at minimizing taxes are the debt–equity swap and the adjustable-rate convertible note. In a debt–equity swap, a corporation simply exchanges equity for some of its outstanding debt. Suppose that a company feels it has too much debt and would like to increase the equity component of its capital structure. Suppose further that some if its debt was originally issued at par but is now selling at a discount. The market price of the debt will reflect capital gains taxes that any current purchaser will have to pay on this discount when the bond is redeemed at par at maturity. If the company exchanges equity securities for this debt, however, the transaction is considered a non-taxable recapitalization. Thus the company can benefit essentially by taking a potential capital gain out of investors' hands and bringing it inside the company where it escapes taxation.

The adjustable-rate convertible note was first issued in a public offering by Borg-Warner in December of 1982. These notes have an interest rate that is pegged to the company's common stock dividend, and they are redeemable at maturity at 55% of par. For accounting purposes, the remaining 45% is treated as equity, and the net result of all these provisions is that the company has issued an equitylike instrument, while still claiming the tax advantages of debt.

Since all of these innovations are aimed at taking advantage of provisions in the tax code, their proximate cause could be interpreted as the broad system of government regulation of the economy. The evolutionary development of these innovations, in fact, reflects the working of what Kane (1977) has referred to as the "regulatory dialectic." This process consists of the sequential action and reaction of the different parties to the regulatory system as they variously strive to control each other or circumvent each other's control. In the area of taxation, the government sets the rules of the tax code in order to satisfy objectives concerning the government budget, wealth redistribution, and economic incentives. Corporations can then respond in one of two ways. First, they can design transactions to try to take advantage of tax loopholes. Original-issue discount bonds and debt-equity swaps are examples of this strategy. Alternatively, corporations can mount lobbying efforts aimed at changing the tax code to their benefit. The passage of the safe harbor leasing provisions, allowing corporations to trade formerly unusable tax credits, is one example of the latter strategy. Industrial revenue and pollution control bonds provide another example, whereby corporations have been allowed to borrow at the tax-exempt bond rate, for limited purposes, through state and local governments. These bond issues have surged in usage since the mid-1970s, with $14.7 billion worth, or 40% of total corporate bond issues for the year, being issued in 1982.

The process does not end, however, when corporations have either exploited loopholes or won advantageous tax rules for themselves. Corporations' success in these activities comes at the expense of other groups, such as household taxpayers, and reactions are often evoked from these groups that are translated into countervailing changes in the tax rules. For example, original-issue discount bonds were made less attractive in 1982 by a requirement that the discount be amortized on a compound rather than straight-line basis. Similarly, many of the more favorable safe harbor leasing provisions have been revoked, and the Internal Revenue Service has recently ruled that the "interest" on adjustable-rate convertible notes is not tax deductible to the issuing corporation. Consideration has also been devoted to imposing taxes on debt–equity swaps. Once the government has reacted in such ways, the whole process then begins anew, with corporations devising still other means for reducing their tax burdens.

It should also be noted that this series of adaptive responses has occurred in the context of the recent inflationary environment. Inflation decreases the real value of those corporate tax shields, such as depreciation, that are tied to the historical cost of assets. Thus it sparks a search for new tax shields. In this sense, there is a connection between inflation and the increased ingenuity of business in devising tax savings through financial transactions. Furthermore, inflation brings calls for tax reform, and this encourages businesses to increase their lobbying efforts to ensure that changes in the tax code will be favorable to them.

To summarize, recent years have been marked by increased aggressiveness in corporate financial management. Corporations have shown a willingness to absorb financial risks in order to tailor the terms of securities to investors' needs and to try to issue these securities at favorable times. They have shown an increased tendency to perform financial services themselves and to work their financial resources harder. While techno-logical change and regulation have played a role in intensifying the pace of financial activity, the inflation and economic instability of the 1960s and 1970s must be seen as fundamental causes of these developments. The changes in corporate financial management practice are also partly a reflection of and partly a cause of parallel changes that have taken place in the competitive relationships among traditional suppliers of business financial services.

The Changing Market for Business Financial Services

Commercial and investment bankers have traditionally been the primary suppliers of financial services to business, with commercial banks specializing in lending and deposits and investment banks handling public and private securities issues and advising on special transactions such as mergers. Over the last decade, however, these traditional roles have undergone a substantial and often painful transformation. Both classes of institutions have faced new competitive threats. This heightened competition has come from foreign counterparts, from other types of domestic financial institutions, and from one another. As a result, commercial and investment banks have been forced to change both the array of financial services offered to business and the pricing of these services.

The Response of Commercial Banks to New Competition. The changing competitive environment for commercial banks provides another illustration of the regulatory dialectic. U.S. commercial banks have long been subject to restrictions on geographical expansion, asset composition, and the ability to pay market rates to raise new funds. They have also borne certain regulatory "taxes" such as reserve requirements.

As the inflationary environment made these restrictions more expensive, there was growing incentive for nonbank institutions, not subject to the same regulations, to encroach on the commercial banks' territory. In effect, then, many of the competitive threats faced by banks in recent years have represented attempts to circumvent bank regulation.

For example, domestic banks have not only encountered foreign competition as they followed their multinational business customers abroad, but foreign banks have aggressively expanded into the U.S. market as well. By mid-1979, branches and agencies of foreign banks accounted for 11.6% of commercial and industrial loans made by banks in the United States (see Fry, 1979). In large part this is attributable to the fact that, until recently, U.S. branches of foreign banks faced considerably fewer regulatory constraints than domestic banks. An additional challenge posed by the foreign banks has been their ability, especially in the Eurocurrency markets, to offer corporations a full range of financial services, including investment banking services.

Domestically, insurance companies and finance companies have taken advantage of their freedom from geographical and other restrictions to expand their shares of the business loan market. As insurance companies have shortened their investment horizons with the onset of higher inflation rates and more volatile capital market conditions, they have increasingly come into competition with commercial banks for intermediate-term business credits. Finance companies have also encroached on the commercial banks' territory, as they have increased their business lending from one-third of total loans in the early 1960s to nearly half by the late 1970s (see Harris, 1979). Much of this growth in business lending has accompanied the growth in asset-based financing, as discussed in the previous section, and finance companies have been active in inventory and receivables financing as well as leasing. Even captive finance subsidiaries of nonfinancial corporations have expanded their activities to encompass lending to other businesses.

In another development of note, many corporations have bypassed the financial intermediary system altogether by turning to the commercial paper market for short-term credit. In this way they have avoided the implicit reserve requirement tax that is passed on to them in bank loan rates. Since 1974, approximately 500 new issuers have entered this market, bringing the total number of active issuers to nearly 1,200. During this time, outstanding paper of nonfinancial corporations has grown from $13.5 billion to approximately $60 billion (see Hurley, 1982). Business firms themselves have thus offered further competition to commercial banks by lining up their own funds in this market.

Commercial banks have responded to these threats in two ways. First, they have lobbied for changes in regulation that allow them to compete on a more equal footing with these new suppliers of business financial services. These changes range from additional restrictions placed on foreign banks, under the International Banking Act of 1978, to a loosening of the restrictions on domestic banks, such as lower reserve requirements and authorization for international banking facilities connected to domestic offices. On balance, as in the consumer financial services market, competitive incursions by less regulated institutions have tended to loosen commercial bank regulation.

This process does not always work in the banks' favor, of course, since other institutions have in some cases won greater freedom to compete with banks. Thrift institutions were empowered in late 1982 to allocate 10% of their assets to commercial lending and an additional 10% to leasing. It is not yet clear how much of a factor the thrifts will prove to be in these markets, but there are early indications that some of them are eager to gain a share of the business. Cooperative and franchising arrangements have constituted two forms of entry by new participants.

The second way in which banks have responded to increased competition is by altering the nature of the traditional customer relationship. Informal loan commitments, compensating balances, and processing of a company's checking transactions were the hallmarks of the traditional bank–customer relationship.

Inflation and competition, however, have forced changes in pricing methods, segments of the market that banks serve, and the types of services they offer. As inflation has made idle bank balances more costly and as competitive pressure from foreign banks, nonbank institutions, and the do-it-yourself financing option has strengthened the bargaining positions of corporate treasurers, firms have been able to obtain fee-based pricing of services instead of the traditional compensating balance arrangements. This has allowed the firms to pay for only those bank services that they wish to use. One other pricing development, however, has apparently come at the behest of the banks. This has been the move toward floating interest rates on loans, as banks and indeed financial institutions of all types found fixed-rate loans to be unacceptably risky in a volatile interest rate environment.

Competition from other institutions and the availability of the commercial paper market have also squeezed profit margins on loans to the best quality credit risks. This has in turn sparked a search for new segments of the business loan market, and hence competition to lend to middle- and smaller-sized firms has become more heated. Much of the movement by commercial banks into various forms of asset-based financing, in fact, has come in this market.

Banks have also tried to ease the strain that competition has imposed on their long-standing customer ties by devising new services to suit these customers' changing needs. As larger customers have turned to the commercial paper market, many banks have tried to carve out a role as lender of last resort by issuing standby lines of credit, for a fee, against customers' commercial paper issues. To some degree, this practice has enabled banks to circumvent regulation, since they incur contingent liabilities without affecting required reserves. The issuance of letters of credit to backstop other kinds of debt, such as industrial revenue bonds, has also become a flourishing business, and it is now estimated that bank letters of credit stand behind debt obligations of all kinds that total $65 billion, an increase from less than $30 billion at the end of 1979 (see Carrington, 1983). Commercial banks have even found their new competitors following them into this area, as some life insurance companies have also offered letters of credit.

Further expansion of services has come in transactions processing, where banks have long since ceased to confine themselves to clearing checks. Banks have even aided the decline of compensating balance arrangements by helping their customers to implement more sophisticated cash management systems. Here too, however, competitors have followed.

Other business financial services to which banks have turned include the arranging of private placements, merger and acquisition advising, the management of dividend reinvestment plans, and the underwriting of corporate commercial paper issues. U.S. commercial banks have also formed subsidiaries abroad to engage in securities underwriting of all kinds in foreign markets. This entire set of activities has brought the commercial banks squarely into competition with the investment banking industry and has materially blurred the separation between the two industries contemplated by the Glass-Steagall Act. Indeed, these competitive thrusts by commercial banks are symptomatic of parallel changes that have been taking place in the investment banking industry.

The Changing Nature of Investment Banking. Increased competition in investment banking has come not only from domestic commercial banks, but also from foreign merchant banks, from within the securities industry, and from business corporations themselves. As with commercial banks, this competition has put pressure on profit margins and altered traditional customer relationships. Investment banks have responded by increasing the range of services offered and by promoting the quality of their services, both to enhance profitability and to protect their customer relationships. As documented by Hayes (1979), investment banking firms have substantially increased their professional staffs over the past 10 to 15 years, and have thus strengthened their capability for merger and acquisition advising and other corporate finance consulting activities. These staffs have also been responsible for devising many of the innovative securities that corporations have issued in the 1970s and 1980s, as investment bankers have come to look upon new product design as a way of gaining entry to a corporation's securities business. In addition, investment bankers have opened new offices, both domestic and foreign, and have enlarged their trading departments in order to strengthen their capability for distributing securities to both institutional and retail customers.

A further instrument of competitive upheaval in the investment banking industry has been the Securities and Exchange Commission's Rule 415, or the shelf registration rule. Adopted in March 1982 on an experimental basis, this rule allows corporations to file one registration statement with the SEC, to cover securities issues that might take place any time within the next two years. Corporations are thus afforded much greater flexibility in timing their securities issues to coincide with "windows" in the market.

More important from the standpoint of competition in the securities industry, the corporation can list a number of potential investment bankers on the registration statement and need not settle on one or two to manage an issue. This encourages competitive bidding among the firms listed and has increased the incidence of "bought deals," in which one or a few investment bankers take on a whole issue without forming a syndicate or sounding out potential buyer interest in advance. These challenges to the traditional fixed-price syndicate system have thus accelerated the trend toward narrower underwriting profits. Rule 415 can be interpreted, in fact, as a regulatory manifestation of the forces for increased competition that have been altering the structure of the industry. Indeed, the more active search for ways to economize on financing costs and the chafing of institutional investors under the fixed-price system have set in motion forces for regulatory change.

Overall, the same forces at work on financial management practice in this section also have altered markets for business financial services. Volatile capital market conditions have been associated with increasingly aggressive competition and regulatory change. Traditional customer relationships, product lines, and pricing mechanisms have all been transformed as competition has forced financial institutions to aid the business sector's search for new sources of funds and more economical means of raising them.

THE OUTLOOK FOR FUTURE PATTERNS IN BUSINESS FINANCING

The key to future patterns of business financing is whether inflation and economic instability—primary forces in the past—will continue to characterize the economic environment. If inflation is brought under control and if a return is made to the more stable financing conditions of the early 1960s, the pace of further change will moderate—and some recent changes may be reversed. Internal funds will be more plentiful, and corporations will not have to resort to money and capital markets so frequently. In addition, the widely predicted demise of the long-term bond market will prove to be exaggerated as long-term investors, particularly institutions, resume their purchases of longer-maturity bonds. Concomitantly, there will probably be a retreat from the proliferation of innovative securities and a move toward greater proportions of "plain vanilla" bonds. Developments of this type would generally allow corporations to reduce the increased exposure to interest rate risk that they have built up since the 1970s.

Other developments, however, are likely to remain even if inflation subsides. Just as the energy crisis spurred the discovery of energy-saving measures that have remained in use, the economic environment of the past decade has induced lasting changes in the market for business financial services. Now that customer relationships have been forged and communications systems established, it is unlikely that the trend toward integration of world capital markets will see any reversal. Corporations will continue to raise funds on a global basis, and domestic financial institutions will face competition from their counterparts around the world. Similarly, it seems unlikely that the degree of competition faced domestically by both commercial and investment banks will ease. Other financial institutions have gained competitive footholds in areas traditionally dominated by bankers. Business corporations themselves have developed substantial internal expertise and will continue to manage many of their own financial transactions. Regardless of whether the future economic environment allows corporations to reduce their interest rate risk, the market for business financial services will remain intensely competitive for all participants.

REFERENCES

Brealey, R., and Myers, S. *Principles of Corporate Finance.* New York: McGraw-Hill, 1981.

Business Week, "The Debt Economy," special issue, October 12, 1974.

Carrington, T. "Bank Letters of Credit Proliferate, Creating Some New Safety Fears." *Wall Street Journal,* March 18, 1983, p. 29.

Clemente, H. A. "Innovative Financing." *Financial Executive,* April 1982, *50,* pp. 14–19.

Crane, D. B., and Hayes, S. L. III. "The New Competition in World Banking." *Harvard Business Review,* July–August 1982, *60,* pp. 88–94.

Friedman, B. M. "Postwar Changes in the American Financial Markets." In M. Feldstein (Ed.), *The American Economy in Transition.* Chicago: University of Chicago Press, 1980.

Fry, E. "New Measures of Commercial Bank Credit and Bank Nondeposit Funds." *Federal Reserve Bulletin,* 1979, *65,* pp. 707–715.

Gilbert, R. A. "The Puzzling Behavior of Business Loans in Current Recession." *Federal Reserve Bank of St. Louis Review,* November 1982, *64,* pp. 3–10.

Goldsmith, R. W. *Financial Intermediaries in the American Economy since 1900.* Princeton: Princeton University Press, 1958.

Goldsmith, R. W., Lipsey, R. E., and Mendelson, M. *Studies in the National Balance Sheet of the United States* (2 vols.). Princeton: Princeton University Press, 1963.

Gordon, R. H., and Malkiel, B. G. "Corporation Finance." In H. J. Aaron and J. A. Pechman (Eds.), *How Taxes Affect Economic Behavior.* Washington, D. C.: The Brookings Institution, 1981.

Harris, M. "Finance Companies as Business Lenders." *Federal Reserve Bank of New York Quarterly Review,* Summer 1979, *4,* pp. 35–39.

Hayes, S. L. III. "The Transformation of Investment Banking." *Harvard Business Review*, January–February 1979, *57*, pp. 153–170.

Hurley, E. M. "The Commercial Paper Market since the Mid-Seventies." *Federal Reserve Bulletin*, 1982, *68*, pp. 327–334.

Kane, E. J. "Good Intentions and Unintended Evil: The Case against Selective Credit Allocation." *Journal of Money, Credit and Banking*, 1977, *9*, pp. 55–69.

Mains, N. E. "Recent Corporate Financing Patterns." *Federal Reserve Bulletin*, 1980, *66*, pp. 683–690.

Marsh, P. "The Choice between Equity and Debt: An Empirical Study." *Journal of Finance*, 1982, *37*, pp. 121–144.

Minsky, H. P. "A Theory of Systemic Fragility." In E. I. Altman and A. W. Sametz (Eds.), *Financial Crises: Institutions and Markets in a Fragile Environment*. New York: John Wiley & Sons, 1977.

Mitchell, K. "Trends in Corporation Finance." *Federal Reserve Bank of Kansas City Economic Review*, March 1983, *68*, pp. 3–15.

Modigliani, F. "Debt, Dividend Policy, Taxes, Inflation and Market Valuation." *Journal of Finance*, 1982, *37*, pp. 255–273.

Osborn, N. "Playing the Window Game." *Institutional Investor*, April 1981, *15*, pp. 65–71.

Piper, T. R., and Weinhold, W. A. "How Much Debt Is Right for Your Firm?" *Harvard Business Review*, July–August 1982, *60*, pp. 106–114.

Salomon Brothers. *1983 Prospects for Financial Markets*. New York: Salomon Brothers, December 6, 1982.

Taggart, R. A. "A Model of Corporate Financing Decisions." *Journal of Finance*, 1977, *32*, pp. 1467–1484.

———. "Secular Patterns in the Financing of U.S. Corporations." In B. M. Friedman (Ed.), *Corporate Capital Structures in the United States*. Chicago: University of Chicago Press, forthcoming, 1984.

VonFurstenberg, G. M., and Malkiel, B. G. "Financial Analysis in an Inflationary Environment." *Journal of Finance*, 1977, *32*, pp. 575–588.

Wittebort, S. W. "The Frantic New Pace of Cash Management." *Institutional Investor*, June 1981, *15*, pp. 179–192.

6 Depository Financial Institutions

Donald T. Savage

INTRODUCTION

This chapter examines the provision of financial services by the traditional depository financial institutions, commercial banks and thrift institutions. Both the industrial structure of the various types of institutions and their current financial positions and problems are reviewed. In addition, the role of holding companies as owners of depository institutions will be described.

In recent years there has been a trend toward permitting thrift institutions to exercise more of the powers previously reserved to commercial banks. Until thrifts were permitted to offer checking accounts and related services—negotiable order of withdrawal accounts (NOW accounts) or credit union share drafts—the commercial banks were differentiated by their monopoly provision of third-party-payment instruments. They also had wider lending powers—encompassing loans to individuals, businesses, and governments—than the thrifts, which were limited mainly to consumer and mortgage loans.

Given the recent expansion of thrift institution powers, depository institutions are becoming more alike. If these trends continue, all institutions eventually will have the same deposit-taking and lending powers. However, all institutions may not exercise all powers to the same extent, and any deposit-gathering or lending specialization will be based on institutional

The views expressed in this chapter are those of the author and do not necessarily reflect the views of the Board of Governors of the Federal Reserve System or its staff.

choice, rather than on a compartmentalization of functions dictated by laws and regulations.

Innovations in the nondepository financial institution sector, such as the growth of money market mutual funds and the development of so-called financial supermarkets, have raised concerns relative to the prospects of the traditional institutions. While these new financial firms may lessen the role of depository institutions in the future, evidence does not yet suggest a deterioration of the relative role of depository institutions as financial intermediaries. Commercial bank profits do not appear to have declined below traditional levels, and the depository institutions' share of total credit market debt claims against nonfinancial sectors is higher than in 1956.[1]

The impact of the nondepository financial institutions on banks and thrifts will be noted in this chapter, although the main focus will be on the role of the depository institutions. A subsequent chapter will analyze the growing role of the so-called nonbank entities.

COMMERCIAL BANKS

An important distinguishing feature of American commercial banking is the dual banking system. Commercial banks may be chartered either under the statutes of the state in which they are to be located or by the Comptroller of the Currency under the National Bank Act. The chartering authority becomes the primary regulator of the organization, and the bank has those powers provided by the statutes under which it is chartered.

The First and Second Banks of the United States were organized under charters granted by the federal government. However, after the decision was made not to renew the charter of the Second Bank of the United States in 1836, bank chartering became a state function. Originally, state banks were individually chartered by the state legislatures, but gradually systems were devised allowing any group meeting certain standards to obtain a bank charter. While the establishment of a national banking system in the 1860s was intended to lead to a demise of state-chartered banks and the currency problems often attributed to the state banking system, the expected results did not occur and a dual system of chartering and regulation persisted.

The dual chartering system results in a multiplicity of bank regulatory agencies, one in each state as well as the federal agencies. In addition, the system creates the potential for inconsistencies within a state, as state banks may have different powers than their national bank competitors operating in that state. In some cases state laws govern aspects of national bank operations, while in other cases, national banks are not bound by laws and regulations governing state banks.

Beyond the agencies resulting from the dual chartering system, there are additional bank regulators. All national banks are required to obtain deposit insurance from the Federal Deposit Insurance Corporation (FDIC) and to be members of the Federal Reserve System (FRS). State banks may join the FDIC, and all but three states require their state banks to have FDIC insurance. State banks also may join the Federal Reserve System, but a majority of the smaller state banks have not become members. Finally, if a bank is owned by a holding company, the holding company is regulated by the Federal Reserve System, even though the subsidiary banks may be regulated by one or more of the other agencies.

A breakdown of the charter and membership classes of commercial banks is presented in Table 6.1. While 61% of all banks are state-chartered nonmember banks, 75% of total assets are held by national and state member banks.

Especially relative to other nations, the second distinguishing feature of the American commercial banking industry is the large number of banks. No other nation has so many banks. Several factors account for this phenomenon. First, entry into banking has been relatively easy during most of our history since the "free banking" era after the decision not to renew the charter of the Second Bank of the United States. It has been alleged that the dual banking system has resulted in some competition in bank chartering. When James J. Saxon was Comptroller of the Currency in the 1960s, the rate of state charter issuance increased as new national bank charters increased. Applicants rejected by one chartering authority can apply to the other authority. Therefore, some argue that an easing of standards on the national level may lead to a parallel easing of state standards. Otherwise, the federal–state balance would change.

Table 6.1. Numbers and Assets of Insured Commercial Banks by Charter Class, December 31, 1982.

	Number	Assets (in millions of dollars)
National banks	4,579	$1,069,984
State member banks	1,039	328,826
Insured nonmember state banks	8,818	462,389
Total	14,436	$1,861,199

SOURCE: *Federal Reserve Bulletin,* April 1983, pp. A74–A75.

Geographic limitations on bank expansion are a second factor accounting for the large number of banks. Except for a few "grandfathered" branches, no state allows banks from other states to operate branch offices in its territory. Because national banking law deferred to this restrictive system, the banking industry developed on a state-by-state basis. In many states, intrastate branch banking has also been severely limited. While some of these branching restrictions merely reflected territorial protection for existing banks, antibranching attitudes also originated from a traditional desire to avoid the concentration of financial resources into a small number of firms.

Finally, above a relatively small deposit size, the lack of substantial economies of scale in banking makes it possible for small banks to compete with much larger institutions. While many developments in banking and technology have led to forecasts of the demise of small banks, economies-of-scale studies, which are reviewed in a later chapter,[2] have not produced empirical evidence demonstrating a loss of competitive ability on the part of small banks. Thus, there have been no cost-based economic imperatives requiring the consolidation of the system into a few very large banks.

The size distribution of American banking organizations reflects the large number of banks and the restrictions on bank geographic expansion. As Table 6.2 indicates, 3.5% of banking organizations have assets below $5 million. Although only 0.5% of all banks hold assets in excess of $5 billion, these 56 banking organizations hold nearly 42% of total assets.

Table 6.2.   Asset-Size Distribution of U.S. Commercial Banking Organizations, December 31, 1982

Size Class (in millions of dollars)	Number of Organizations	Percentage of Total U.S. Commercial Bank Assets
$ 0–5	428	0.08
5–10	1,405	0.54
10–25	3,837	3.25
25–100	4,968	11.95
100–250	923	6.93
250–500	246	4.26
500–1,000	170	5.91
1,000–5,000	225	25.30
5,000+	56	41.78

SOURCE: *Report of Condition* files. Banks reporting zero deposits, such as nondeposit trust companies, are eliminated.

Table 6.3. Changes in Number of Commercial Banks and Banking Organizations in the United States, 1972–1982

Item	1972	1973	1974	1975	1976	1977	1978	1979	1980	1981	1982
Number of banks, beginning of period	13,786	13,930	14,174	14,459	14,631	14,672	14,704	14,712	14,708	14,836	14,880
New banks organized	265	344	405	275	190	200	180	237	266	267	373
Reopenings			1	3							
Mergers, consolidations, and absorptions											
Banks converted into branches	-106	-87	-105	-82	-128	-159	-154	-217	-117	-198	-289
Others	-10	-10	-13	-13	-13	-2	-16	-16	-18	-19	-10
Suspensions	-2	-3			-2					-1	
Voluntary liquidations	-2			-3				-2			
Other changes	-1		-3	-8	-6	-7	-2	-6	-3	-3	-6
Number of banks, end of period	13,930	14,174	14,459	14,631	14,672	14,704	14,712	14,708	14,836	14,880	14,960
Net increase or decrease	144	244	285	172	41	32	8	-4	128	44	80
Number of banking organizations, end of year[a]	n.a.[b]	12,606	12,619	12,663	12,682	12,717	12,719	12,785	12,572	12,343	12,138
Net increase or decrease	n.a.	n.a.	13	44	19	35	2	66	-213	-229	-205

SOURCE: *Annual Statistical Digest*, 1970–1979 and 1980 (Board of Governors of the Federal Reserve System, 1981).

[a] Companies that are subsidiaries of other bank holding companies are eliminated.

[b] n.a. = not available on basis of holding company group.

Many of the smallest banks are concentrated in the states prohibiting branching. Illinois and Texas each have over 1,000 banks; between them, these two states account for over 19% of the total number of U.S. commercial banks. Both are unit banking states; Texas has a well-developed multibank holding company system, while Illinois only recently allowed multibank holding companies. Even in the major statewide branching states, however, there are frequently substantial numbers of relatively small banks. In California, 7 organizations hold 80% of total domestic commercial banking assets, but there are 343 other organizations and 105 of these have assets of less than $20 million.

The result of all these factors has been to keep banking a deconcentrated industry on the national level. Even though there has been a high merger rate in recent years, new entry has been sufficient to keep the total number of banks on an upward trend, as is illustrated in Table 6.3. Although the number of banks increased steadily throughout the 1970s and into the 1980s, the number of independent banking organizations decreased by over 200 per year in the years 1980–1982 because of mergers and bank holding company acquisitions.

A consolidated balance sheet for the domestic offices of all insured commercial banks at the end of 1982 is presented in Table 6.4. Given the traditional heavy emphasis of commercial banks on demand deposits and related-payments accounts, the asset portfolio of the commercial banking system is heavily weighted toward short-term, highly liquid assets. Nearly 37% of total assets are cash and due from other banks, securities, and federal funds sold. The vast bulk of these assets can be converted into cash in order to meet outflows of demand deposits with little or no risk of capital loss. While some loans are longer term and relatively illiquid, the bulk of bank loans traditionally has been either short term or renegotiable on a regular basis.

The short-term nature of most commercial banking assets, while designed to preserve the institution's liquidity, also reduces interest rate risk exposure. The low average time to maturity of assets ensures that the yield on assets increases along with increases in the cost of deposits.

The balance sheet of the banking system also reflects the diversity of sources and uses of funds. All sectors of the economy hold a variety of types of demand, savings, and time deposits with the commercial banks. The banks, in turn, have their loan portfolios diversified over a range of loans to consumers, financial institutions, industry, and agriculture.

The progress toward interest rate deregulation is reflected by the fact that time deposits in excess of $100,000, six-month money market certificates, and all savers certificates comprised 40.7% of total commercial bank deposits as of the end of 1982. The interest rates payable on these

Table 6.4. Consolidated Report of Condition, Domestic Offices, All Insured Commercial Banks, December 31, 1982 (in millions of dollars)

Assets

Cash and due from depository institutions			$ 207,313	(11.1%)
Total securities			373,394	(20.1%)
U.S. Treasury	$ 117,782	(6.3%)		
U.S. government agencies	76,262	(4.1%)		
State and local governments	154,003	(8.3%)		
All other	25,348	(1.4%)		
Federal funds sold and securities repurchase agreements			102,807	(5.5%)
Total loans, gross	1,025,567	(55.1%)		
Real estate loans	298,162	(16.0%)		
Loans to financial institutions	73,220	(3.9%)		
Loans for purchasing or carrying securities	13,705	(0.7%)		
Agricultural loans	36,130	(1.9%)		
Commercial and industrial loans	379,566	(20.4%)		
Loans to individuals	191,618	(10.3%)		
All other loans	33,174	(1.8%)		
Unearned income on loans	18,512	(1.0%)		
Loan loss reserves	12,806	(0.7%)		
Total loans, net			994,260	(53.4%)
Other assets			183,397	(9.9%)
Total assets			$1,861,199	(100.0%)

Liabilities and Capital

Demand deposits	$ 369,933	(19.9%)
Time deposits	720,398	(38.7%)
Savings deposits	303,370	(16.3%)
Federal funds purchased and securities sold under repurchase agreements	178,849	(9.6%)
Other liabilities	153,467	(8.2%)
Subordinated notes and debentures	6,787	(0.4%)
Equity capital	128,390	(6.9%)
Total liabilities and equity	$1,861,199	(100.0%)

SOURCE: *Federal Reserve Bulletin,* April 1983, pp. A74–75.

deposits were established either by the market or by a ceiling rate based on market rates. In December 1982 and January 1983, the money market deposit account and the Super NOW account accelerated the transition to a freer market for deposits, and by June 1983, $367 billion and $22 billion, respectively, were invested in these accounts. Passbook savings accounts remained the only major source of nontransaction account funds paying a nonmarket-based interest rate.

The flexibility of the return on assets, the cost of funds in response to market interest rate changes, and the implied insulation from interest rate risk is reflected in the profit stability of commercial banking. Table 6.5 presents data on the return on assets and equity for 1977–1982, a period of high and variable interest rates. The rate of return on assets fluctuated within a range of only 0.09% over the six years, from a low of 0.71 to a high of 0.80.

The other interesting point illustrated by Table 6.5 is that the return on assets is, on average, higher for small banks than for large banks. In

Table 6.5.   The Profitability of Insured Commercial Banks, 1977–1982 (in percentages)

Type of Return and Size of Bank[a]	1977	1978	1979	1980	1981	1982
Return on assets[b]						
All banks	0.71	0.76	0.80	0.79	0.76	0.71
Less than $100 million	0.98	1.04	1.15	1.18	1.15	1.08
$100 million to $1 billion	0.82	0.90	0.96	0.96	0.91	0.85
$1 billion or more						
Money center	0.50	0.53	0.56	0.56	0.53	0.50
Others	0.62	0.68	0.72	0.66	0.68	0.63
Return on equity[c]						
All banks	11.8	12.9	13.9	13.7	13.2	12.2
Less than $100 million	12.4	13.2	14.1	14.2	13.6	12.7
$100 million to $1 billion	12.0	13.2	13.9	13.7	12.8	12.0
$1 billion or more						
Money center	11.4	12.8	14.0	14.4	13.4	12.3
Others	11.2	12.5	13.5	12.7	12.9	11.9

SOURCE: Barbara Negri Opper, "Profitability of Insured Commercial Banks in 1982," *Federal Reserve Bulletin,* July 1983, p. 498.

[a]Size categories are based on year-end fully consolidated assets.

[b]Net income as a percentage of the average of beginning- and end-of-year fully consolidated assets net of loan loss reserves.

[c]Net income as a percentage of the average of beginning- and end-of-year equity capital.

1982, for example, banks with assets of less than $100 million earned 1.08% on assets while money center banks with assets over $1 billion earned only 0.50% on assets. Because the larger banks are more highly leveraged, both large and small banks have nearly the same return on equity.

It is also interesting to note that a large portion of bank income is generated by the international business of the largest banking organizations. In 1981, net income attributable to international business was in excess of 16% of the net income of all U.S.-insured commercial banks. For the relatively few banks that have international business, this income source obviously would be a significant portion of their total earnings. The growth in foreign-source income reflects the rapid growth of overseas activity by American banks. Between 1970 and 1981, the assets of foreign subsidiaries of U.S. banks, bank holding companies, and Edge and Agreement corporations increased from $7 billion to more than $83 billion, and the assets of foreign branches of U.S. banks increased from $52.6 billion to $399.7 billion (Houpt and Martinson, 1982).

THE BANK HOLDING COMPANY FORM OF ORGANIZATION

The bank holding company has become an increasingly common form of organizational structure. As of the end of 1982, the 487 multibank holding companies held 45.8% of U.S. domestic commercial bank deposits, and the 3,802 one-bank holding companies held 33.7% of domestic deposits. The percentages of total domestic deposits held by holding companies in each state are presented in Table 6.6, as well as state branching law classifications and state three-firm concentration ratios. Multibank holding companies tend to be less important in those states permitting unlimited statewide branching. The largest numbers of one-bank holding companies are found in the states restricting both branching and multibank holding companies.

The bank holding company form of ownership of a bank or banks originated in the early twentieth century.[3] Bank ownership by a holding company is an outgrowth of the chain banking movement in which numerous banks were owned by one individual or a small group of individuals acting as a partnership. Bank holding companies, in the early years termed *group banks,* brought the corporate form of business ownership to the control of the stock of one or more banks. The early bank holding company movement was centered mainly in the upper midwestern states that prohibited branch banking. By organizing as a bank holding company, numerous unit banks in one or several states could be brought under common ownership.

Table 6.6.   Bank Holding Company Activity by State, December 31, 1982

State and Branch Banking Classification	Percentage of Domestic Deposits Held by:		1982 State Three-Firm Deposit Concentration Ratio
	One-Bank Holding Companies	Multibank Holding Companies	
Alabama (L)	17.7	48.1	41.4
Alaska (S)	36.6	8.2	58.7
Arizona (S)	68.5	26.9	82.8
Arkansas (L)	36.8	9.3	12.5
California (S)	80.3	13.3	56.2
Colorado (U)	19.2	69.9	41.1
Connecticut (S)	34.8	43.7	54.4
Delaware (S)	1.6	41.2	52.0
District of Columbia (S)	86.2	9.7	70.3
Florida (S)	12.0	70.8	30.8
Georgia (L)	9.5	65.2	42.4
Hawaii (S)	77.4	7.0	79.9
Idaho (S)	44.5	45.5	73.9
Illinois (U)	43.4	28.4	32.9
Indiana (L)	49.2	0.0	16.5
Iowa (L)	37.0	31.8	19.4
Kansas (U)	64.0	9.8	9.1
Kentucky (L)	36.5	10.3	24.0
Louisiana (L)	59.8	0.0	13.2
Maine (S)	8.7	62.8	48.0
Maryland (S)	13.5	67.9	43.5
Massachusetts (S)	7.6	80.1	48.8
Michigan (L)	6.9	74.5	39.6
Minnesota (L)	23.4	59.7	52.0
Mississippi (L)	47.7	0.0	25.5
Missouri (U)	11.9	70.6	30.6
Montana (U)	17.8	64.3	42.0
Nebraska (L)	71.8	8.1	19.0
Nevada (S)	33.1	52.3	84.5
New Hampshire (S)	11.5	39.3	37.2
New Jersey (S)	15.4	50.5	27.0
New Mexico (L)	20.2	49.2	43.2
New York (S)	21.0	75.4	39.0
North Carolina (S)	61.6	22.6	55.6
North Dakota (U)	31.0	43.4	37.8
Ohio (L)	12.5	65.6	25.3
Oklahoma (L)	77.3	1.2	20.4

Table 6.6.   *(Continued)*

State and Branch Banking Classification	Percentage of Domestic Deposits Held by:		1982 State Three-Firm Deposit Concentration Ratio
	One-Bank Holding Companies	Multibank Holding Companies	
Oregon (S)	4.5	87.4	76.4
Pennsylvania (L)	39.0	34.8	23.7
Rhode Island (S)	73.2	23.8	89.9
South Carolina (S)	54.9	0.0	46.3
South Dakota (S)	19.5	61.9	52.6
Tennessee (L)	16.1	47.7	29.3
Texas (U)	10.7	68.1	29.8
Utah (S)	33.0	55.7	62.3
Vermont (S)	27.3	25.7	46.0
Virginia (S)	36.6	45.3	37.4
Washington (S)	10.6	74.5	63.9
West Virginia (L)	12.3	0.6	8.4
Wisconsin (L)	12.0	49.7	27.3
Wyoming (U)	31.6	53.5	40.4
50 states plus District of Columbia	33.7	45.8	

SOURCE: Board of Governors of the Federal Reserve System.

NOTE: U = unit branching; L = limited branching; S = statewide branching.

There was considerable early opposition to bank holding companies, although there is little available evidence indicating any extensive abuses. The failure rate of the holding company banks in the 1930s was roughly half that of banks in general, but pressure for regulation continued, and the 1933 Banking Act imposed the first federal regulation on bank holding companies. The 1933 legislation was relatively weak and did not eliminate the pressure for more comprehensive regulation. After repeated attempts, Congress enacted further legislation in 1956.

The Bank Holding Company Act of 1956 provided the framework for the regulation of the holding company movement. A bank holding company was defined in the law so as to include only those organizations owning or controlling two or more banks. The law established the regulatory responsibilities for administering the law and vested those responsibilities with the Federal Reserve System.

The Federal Reserve System was empowered to regulate the formation of bank holding companies, the acquisition of banks by bank holding companies, and mergers of bank holding companies. While primary responsibility was assigned to the Federal Reserve, the states retained their regulatory powers over holding companies. Thus, the states could prohibit bank holding companies altogether, require state approval of bank holding company acquisitions of banks, or impose other constraints on bank holding companies.

The interstate expansion of bank holding companies was halted by the 1956 legislation. Under Section 3(d) of the act (the Douglas Amendment), bank holding companies were prohibited from acquiring banks in states other than their headquarters state unless the statutes of the state in which the bank to be acquired was located specifically permitted acquisitions by out-of-state holding companies. The small number of existing multistate holding companies were permitted to retain their out-of-state subsidiaries. The three largest of these were Western Bancorp (now First Interstate), First Bank System, and Northwest Bancorporation.

Little further interstate expansion occurred after 1956. Maine (1975) was the first state to permit general entry by out-of-state holding companies, but required reciprocal entry rights for Maine bank holding companies. In 1982, Alaska and New York enacted legislation permitting out-of-state entry; a new opportunity for the formation of interstate bank holding companies was thus provided. By July 1, 1983, Massachusetts, Connecticut, and Rhode Island had also enacted laws to allow reciprocal entry from other New England states. Delaware, Maryland, and South Dakota allow out-of-state holding companies to acquire special-purpose banks, and a small number of other states allow continued expansion by the bank holding companies that had entered the state before the passage of the 1956 act. Legislation in Delaware, South Dakota, and Maine was motivated by a desire to attract new capital into the state. The legislation in most of the other states appears to have been motivated by a desire to allow the state's banks to expand.

The 1956 legislation, as amended in 1966, provided a bank holding company regulatory structure in which applications to acquire banks were to be judged in terms of both banking factors and competitive factors. The banking factors were included to ensure that the acquisition of the bank by the holding company would not weaken the financial position of the bank. In its administration of the act, the Federal Reserve Board has insisted that the holding company be a source of strength to its subsidiary banks, especially in the area of providing the banks with adequate capital.

Beyond the financial and managerial factors on which the application was to be judged, the Board was required to assess the competitive impact of the proposed acquisition. The wording of the Sherman and Clayton Acts was included in the amended Bank Holding Company Act to provide standards for assessing the competitive impact of a proposed acquisition. Applications that would violate Clayton Act standards can be approved by the Federal Reserve if the anticompetitive effect is clearly outweighed by the positive effect of the transaction on the convenience and needs of the community served by the bank.

The 1956 holding company legislation provided for the regulation of multibank holding companies, but not one-bank holding companies. Beginning in 1968, however, a large number of major banks formed one-bank holding companies to engage in business activities that could not be engaged in by banks. Alarmed by the possibilities for the more extensive use of the holding company device to avoid the traditional separation of banking and commerce, Congress amended the Bank Holding Company Act of 1956 in 1970.

The 1970 Amendments expanded the coverage of the statute to provide for the regulation of one-bank holding companies. Controversy centered on the process for determining permissible nonbank activities. After considering various options, including statutory lists of permissible and impermissible activities, the Congress vested regulatory power with the Federal Reserve System.

Under the legislation enacted, bank holding companies were permitted to engage in those nonbank activities that the Federal Reserve Board found to be both closely related to banking and offering net public benefits. This two-step test restricted the range of possible nonbank activities by requiring that all activities be closely related to banking. Beyond this first limitation, the provision of the service must also promise net public benefits. Under the net public benefits test, the Board must find that the benefits of the proposed activity, such as increased public convenience, outweigh any likely adverse effects, such as decreased or unfair competition or conflicts of interest.

Under the authority of the 1970 Amendments, the Federal Reserve Board has approved 32 nonbank activities and denied 17 proposed activities, as listed in Table 6.7. Some of the activities were approved by regulation so that any holding company can engage in the activity without having to prove that it meets the "closely related test"; other activities were approved by order, and each bank holding company wishing to engage in the activity must file a separate application to engage in that activity. Nearly all of the activities approved by regulation are also permissible for national banks.

Table 6.7. Domestic Nonbank Activities Approved and Denied by the Board of Governors (as of February 1, 1984)

Activities Approved by Regulation

1. Extensions of credit
   Mortgage banking
   Finance companies: consumer, sales, and commercial
   Credit cards
   Factoring
2. Industrial bank, Morris Plan bank, industrial loan company
3. Servicing loans and other extensions of credit
4. Trust company
5. Investment or financial advising
6. Full-payout leasing of personal or real property
7. Investments in community welfare projects
8. Providing bookkeeping or data processing services
9. Acting as insurance agent or broker primarily in connection with credit extensions
10. Underwriting credit life and credit accident and health insurance related to consumer loans
11. Providing courier services
12. Management consulting to all depository institutions
13. Sale and issuance of money orders with a face value of not more than $1,000, and travelers checks, and retailing of savings bonds
14. Performing appraisals of real estate
15. Discount brokerage firm
16. Underwriting and dealing in certain federal, state, and municipal securities.
17. Acting as a futures commission merchant regarding foreign exchange, U.S. government securities, certain money market instruments, and options on those instruments.
18. Arranging equity financing with institutional lenders for commercial and industrial income-producing properties.
19. Offering informational, advisory, and transactional foreign exchange services.

Activities Approved by Order

1. Operating a "pool reserve plan" for loss reserves of banks for loans to small businesses
2. Operating a thrift institution in Rhode Island
3. Buying and selling gold and silver bullion and silver coin
4. Operating a guaranty savings bank in New Hampshire
5. Operating an Article XII New York investment company

Table 6.7. *(Continued)*

6. Acting as a futures commission merchant to cover gold and silver bullion and coins.
7. Retail check authorization and check guarantee
8. Providing consumer-oriented financial management courses
9. Executing unsolicited purchases and sales of securities as agent for the customer (limited securities brokerage)
10. Engaging in commercial banking activities through branches located in Nassau and Luxembourg of a limited-purpose Delaware bank
11. Operating a distressed S&L in the same state
12. Acquiring a distressed S&L in another state

Activities Denied by the Board
1. Insurance premium funding ("equity funding')—combined sales of mutual funds and insurance
2. Underwriting general life insurance not related to credit extension
3. Real estate brokerage
4. Land investment and development
5. Real estate syndication
6. General management consulting
7. Property management services generally
8. Armored car services
9. Sale of level-term credit life insurance
10. Underwriting mortgage guaranty insurance
11. Computer output microfilm services
12. Operating a travel agency
13. Operating a savings and loan association (except in certain states or unless the S&L is distressed)
14. Underwriting property and casualty insurance
15. Underwriting home loan life insurance
16. Real estate advisory activities
17. Offering investment notes with transactional features

Bank holding companies were allowed a 10-year period to divest those activities that were determined to be impermissible nonbank activities. Hardship exemptions could be granted by the board, and subsidiaries that had been acquired by the end of June 1968 did not have to be divested.

The one-bank holding company, in addition to being a method of performing activities within the holding company, but outside the bank, offers tax advantages to the owners of the bank. If the ownership of the organization is properly structured so that the holding company and subsidiary bank are eligible to file a consolidated income tax return, the holding company's principal and interest expense (resulting from servicing debt incurred in the acquisition of the bank) is offset against the income of the bank, and the tax liability of the consolidated organization is reduced.

In summary, the bank holding company has become a major form of bank ownership in the period since the Bank Holding Company Act of 1956. In many restrictive branching states, the multibank holding company allowed the formation of statewide banking systems. While a few states continue to prohibit multibank holding companies, the legislative trend has been toward greater freedom for bank expansion. In some states, the multibank holding company has been the transition vehicle between unit banking systems and statewide branching. As bank branching laws have been liberalized over time, the need for multibank holding companies has been reduced and there has been some consolidation of subsidiary banks into branching systems.

Future developments in the bank holding company movement center on the possible role of the holding company as the vehicle for product market and geographic market expansion by financial institutions. As noted above, recent statutory changes in a few states have permitted the acquisition of banks by out-of-state bank holding companies. The Carter Administration's 1981 study of geographic restrictions on bank expansion (Department of the Treasury, 1981) recommended interstate expansion by bank holding companies, rather than by interstate branching, and recent changes in the laws of several states permitting out-of-state bank holding company entry are steps in this direction. One part of the study's recommendations, allowing out-of-state bank holding companies to acquire large failing banks, was incorporated in the Garn-St Germain Act of 1982.

On the product market side, recent legislative proposals by the Treasury have recommended use of the holding company as a means for allowing banking organizations to expand into the provision of new financial services that are not necessarily closely related to banking as the current statute has been interpreted. Many consider product-line expansion to be necessary for banking organizations to remain competitive with nonbank financial conglomerates. Others, however, question the need for product expansion and cite potential problems relative to the risks of nonbank activities, the ability to isolate the bank from the problems of other subsidiaries, conflicts of interest, and the undue concentration of financial resources. Regardless of the outcome of the product-line debate, the holding company form of organization will be an increasingly important component of the financial industry.

THE THRIFT INDUSTRY

The institutions referred to as thrifts—savings and loan associations (S&Ls), mutual savings banks (MSBs), and credit unions (CUs)—have a number of common features. First, they were traditionally oriented toward consumer financial needs and they originated in an era in which the commercial banks were less consumer oriented than they are today. Although recent legislation has granted the S&Ls and MSBs some commercial lending powers, their customer base remains heavily concentrated in the consumer sector.

Second, their origins reflected self-help or eleemosynary concerns, rather than profit-making goals. The MSBs were organized to provide the working class with both a savings vehicle designed to encourage thrift and a source of small loans at reasonable rates. The credit unions and the S&Ls also had self-help motives. The goal of S&Ls was to provide a pool of funds from which the members of the association could borrow to finance home purchases. The credit union movement was a cooperative endeavor to provide a savings outlet and a source of small consumer loans.

The third original common characteristic of the thrifts was their mutual form of ownership. The members of credit unions and S&Ls were the owners, and operating profits were distributed to the members as dividends. Although savings banks and S&Ls can now be organized as, or converted to, stock corporations, all CUs, nearly all MSBs, and nearly three-quarters of the S&Ls still retain the mutual form of organization. Ultimate management responsibility for the mutual institutions is vested in a self-perpetuating board of directors (S&Ls) or trustees (MSBs), or, in the case of credit unions, in a board elected by the membership.

Fourth, all three types of institutions gained new powers as a result of the Depository Institutions Deregulation and Monetary Control Act of 1980 and the Garn-St Germain Act of 1982. The chronology of the new thrift powers is presented in Table 6.8. The changes have allowed the thrifts to provide third-party-payment services (mainly to consumers) and have permitted a greater degree of investment and loan diversification. These new powers are designed to widen the package of services the institutions can provide in order to help them compete with commercial banks and stabilize their earnings over the course of the interest rate cycle.

Fifth, all three types of thrifts now operate under dual chartering systems with regulation at either the state or federal level. Nearly all mutual savings banks have state charters because the federal chartering system is quite new. Most savings banks are mutual organizations, but can now be stock companies, and federal associations can switch between savings bank and savings and loan association charters. Nearly 40 S&Ls had cho-

Table 6.8. Changes in S&L Assets and Liability Powers Resulting from Recent Legislative Actions

Liability Powers

1. Nationwide NOW Accounts for:
   a. Individuals and not-for-profit organizations   DIDMCA-1980
   b. Governmental units   G-StG-1982
2. Federal S&Ls may offer demand deposits to persons or organizations that have established a "business, corporate, commercial or agricultural loan relationship with the association."   G-StG-1982
3. Authorizes new accounts to compete with money market mutual funds   G-StG-1982

   G-StG (11/15/81) indicated that effective 12/14/82 one account would have a $2,500 minimum balance, no interest rate ceiling, an option to guarantee a fixed rate for one month, limited check-writing facilities, and deposit insurance.

   A second account was authorized effective 1/5/83 identical to the 12/14/82 account but with unlimited transaction facilities. The account was subject to the reserve requirements on transaction accounts.
4. Authorizes establishment of remote service units   DIDMCA-1980

Asset Powers

1. Expands 20% limit of DIDMCA-1980 to 40% of assets that may be invested in commercial real estate loans   G-StG-1982
2. Up to 20% of assets may be invested in combination of commercial paper, debt securities, and consumer loans.   DIDMCA-1980
3. Expands limit in DIDMCA-1980 on consumer loans (including inventory and floor plan loans) from 20% to 40% of assets   G-StG-1982
4. May issue credit cards   DIDMCA-1980
5. May offer overdraft loans on any transaction account   G-StG-1982
6. Permits investment in time and savings deposits of other associations   G-StG-1982
7. Limited investment in state and local obligations of any one issuer to 10% of association's capital and surplus   G-StG-1982
8. May make commercial loans up to 5% of assets until December 31, 1983 and up to 10% thereafter. May be direct loans or participations   G-StG-1982

Table 6.8. *(Continued)*

9.	May invest in tangible personal property up to 10% of assets	G-StG-1982
10.	May make educational loans up to 5% of assets	G-StG-1982
11.	May make loans to small business investment corporations up to 1% of assets	G-StG-1982

SOURCE: Robert A. Eisenbeis, "New Investment Powers: Diversification or Specialization," in Federal Home Loan Bank of San Francisco, *Strategic Planning for Economic and Technological Change in the Financial Services Industry,* Proceedings of the Eighth Annual Conference, 1983.

sen to be federal SBs by April 1983. Most state-chartered mutual savings banks are insured by the FDIC, and federal savings banks can be insured by the Federal Savings and Loan Insurance Corporation. In some states, especially Massachusetts, there are state insurance plans also.

Savings and loan associations may be either federally chartered or state chartered, with federal chartering controlled by the Federal Home Loan Bank Board and insurance provided by the Federal Savings and Loan Insurance Corporation. Most state savings and loan associations are insured by FSLIC, although in a few states there are private insurance systems.

Credit unions are also under a dual federal and state regulatory system. The insuring agency for all federal CUs and most state CUs is the National Credit Union Share Insurance Fund. Credit unions can borrow from the Central Liquidity Fund that is open for membership by both federal and state credit unions.

Finally, all three types of institutions have suffered severe earnings problems to varying degrees because of high interest rates in recent years. The sources of these problems are discussed later in this section.

Mutual Savings Banks

The 414 mutual savings banks were located in only 16 states at the end of 1982, with their greatest concentration in the northeastern portion of the United States. All but about 25 operated branch offices. In the major savings bank states, however, their size frequently rivals that of the commercial banks. The total deposits of savings banks in Massachusetts, Connecticut, Maine, and New Hampshire exceed the total time and savings deposits of commercial banks in those states.

A condensed balance sheet of the mutual savings banking industry is presented in Table 6.9. Two points relative to the balance sheet are of

Table 6.9.   Assets and Liabilities of Mutual Savings Banks, December 31, 1982
(in millions of dollars)

	Assets	
Cash	$ 6,920	(4.0%)
U.S. government obligations	9,685	(5.6%)
State and local obligations	2,500	(1.4%)
Mortgage loans and securities	108,633	(62.4%)
Corporate bonds and stock	12,105	(12.6%)
Other loans	16,876	(9.7%)
Other assets	7,485	(4.3%)
Total assets	$174,204	(100.0%)
	Liabilities and Capital	
Savings deposits	$ 46,969	(27.0%)
Time deposits	105,766	(60.7%)
Other deposits	2,490	(1.4%)
Borrowings	7,159	(4.1%)
Other liabilities	2,583	(1.5%)
Total general reserve accounts	9,238	(5.3%)
Total liabilities and capital	$174,204	(100.0%)

SOURCE: *Annual Report of the President,* National Association of Mutual Savings Banks, May 1983, p. 5.

particular interest. First, the MSBs had over 62% of their assets invested in mortgage loans and mortgage-related securities. Second, 27% of their funds were obtained from traditional passbook savings deposits. This represents a tremendous decline from the 83% of funds obtained from savings deposits in 1970. The continued shifting of funds from low-cost savings deposits to higher-yielding time deposits will maintain pressure on MSBs' earnings.

Savings and Loan Associations

The nation's 3,833 S&Ls held $706 billion of assets at the end of 1982 and had an average asset size of $184 million. The average S&L is smaller than the average MSB but larger than the average commercial bank. However, only 126 S&Ls have reached an asset size in excess of $1 billion.

   The number of savings and loan associations has been declining steadily over the past two decades. While there were 6,320 S&Ls in 1960, the number declined to 3,833 in 1982. The long-term trend was accelerated by the merger of financially weak organizations into stronger firms.

   Of the 3,833 S&Ls, only 830 (21.7%) were stock associations, but the

Table 6.10. Assets and Liabilities of Savings and Loan Associations, December 31, 1982 (in millions of dollars)

Assets		
Mortgage loans outstanding	$482,234	(68.3%)
Cash and other liquid investments	70,179	(9.9%)
Insured mortgages and mortgage-backed securities	63,030	(8.9%)
Mobile home and home improvement loans	8,818	(1.3%)
Other loans	11,726	(1.7%)
Other investments	14,588	(2.1%)
All other assets	55,470	(7.9%)
Total assets	$706,045	(100.0%)
Liabilities and Capital		
Savings deposits	$566,189	(80.2%)
Earning regular rate or below	$ 95,912	(13.6%)
Earning in excess of regular rate	470,277	(66.6%)
Federal Home Loan Bank advances	63,861	(9.0%)
Other borrowed money	34,118	(4.8%)
Other liabilities	15,720	(2.2%)
Net worth	26,157	(3.7%)
Total liabilities and capital	$706,045	(100.0%)

SOURCE: *1983 Savings and Loan Source Book,* United States League of Savings Associations, p. 41.

stock associations held 31.1% of industry assets. The largest numbers of stock S&Ls were in Texas (208), California (125), and Ohio (76).

All but 490 S&Ls were insured by the Federal Savings and Loan Insurance Corporation, and the insured S&Ls held 98.1% of industry assets. Of the 3,343 federally insured institutions, 1,727 were federally chartered and 1,616 were chartered by the states.

The balance sheet of the savings and loan industry is condensed in Table 6.10. It reveals the heavy dependence of the thrifts on the mortgage market; over 77% of assets were invested in mortgages or mortgage-backed securities. This concentration of funds in one type of investment resulted from a combination of factors. First, most savings and loan associations were established for the sole purpose of aggregating savings from the associations' members in order to provide the members with mortgage loans. Only in relatively recent years have S&Ls dropped the direct association of deposits and mortgage loans. Second, the laws governing the investment powers of S&Ls were written to reflect their original purpose. Thus, until recent legislative changes, S&Ls' asset holdings were restricted primarily to mortgage-related investments. Finally, the tax laws encourage a concentration of assets in mortgage loans because if an S&L holds 82% (72% for mutual savings banks) of its funds in qualifying investments (mainly mortgages), it can deduct 40% of its income as a bad debt reserve in calculating its taxable income. This tax break from mortgage investments reduces the incentive to diversify assets. The Garn-St Germain Act also tied other privileges to maintaining a concentration of assets in mortgage related assets.

The second point revealed by the balance sheet is the conversion of deposits from those paying the regular rate (in most cases the passbook savings rate) to those yielding a higher market-determined rate. Clearly, this increase in the cost of funds has been a major factor in the earnings difficulties of the S&Ls.

Among the thrifts, the role of the holding company is much more limited than in the banking industry because only the stock savings and loans can be acquired by a holding company. In addition, thrift branching has been less restricted than bank branching. Therefore, there has been less need to use the holding company form of organization as a means of circumventing branching restrictions.

Savings and loan association holding companies are regulated by the Federal Home Loan Bank Board under authority of the 1967 Savings and Loan Holding Company Act. Most of the provisions of the S&L holding company legislation parallel the requirements of the bank holding company legislation, with one notable exception. A multiple-S&L holding company must restrict its non-S&L activities to those activities permitted by the Federal Home Loan Bank Board. A unitary-S&L holding company, however, has freedoms similar to that of one-bank holding companies prior to the 1970 amendments and can engage in any other business activity that does not pose a financial threat to the S&L.

Credit Unions

Credit unions are unique among the thrifts in that they are limited-membership organizations. Only those belonging to the "common bond" group can be members; for nearly 80% of credit unions, the common bond is employment by the same organization. Of the nation's 19,883 credit unions at the end of 1982, 11,412 were federally chartered and 8,471 were state chartered. The average-size credit union had assets of approximately $4.1 million; many of the largest credit unions serve the various military services, such as the Navy Federal Credit Union, which has branches at most major U.S. naval installations.

The assets of credit unions totaled over $82 billion at the end of 1982. Member loans constituted $51.4 billion of the assets with the bulk of the remaining assets invested in cash and liquid investments.

Table 6.11. Income of Depository Institutions, 1977–1982 (as pecentage of total assets)

	Insured Commercial Banks[a]	Savings and Loan Associations[b]	Mutual Savings Banks[c]
1977	0.71	0.79	0.55
1978	0.76	0.84	0.58
1979	0.80	0.68	0.46
1980	0.79	0.13	−0.12
1981	0.76	−0.74	−0.82
1982	0.71	−0.62	−0.74

[a]Federal Reserve *Bulletin*, July 1983, p. 498.
[b]*1983 Savings and Loan Source Book*, p. 40.
[c]*Annual Report of the President*, National Association of Mutual Savings Banks, May 1983, p. 6.

THE THRIFTS' EARNINGS PROBLEMS

Comparative earnings rates for commercial banks, mutual savings banks, and savings and loan associations are presented in Table 6.11. While bank earnings were relatively stable, the MSBs and S&Ls suffered severe losses beginning in 1979 and 1981.[4] The problems of the thrift industry stemmed from the mismatching of asset and liability maturities and the rise of interest rates. Assets had long maturities while a large percentage of liabilities were, in effect, subject to withdrawal on demand.

On the asset side of the thrift balance sheet, the largest proportion of funds was invested in fixed-rate long-term mortgages. As noted previously, thrifts were restricted by their historic purpose, limited investment powers, and tax considerations to concentrating on mortgage lending. Second, state usury ceilings, particularly in New York State, required lending at relatively low rates. Third, many regulations prohibited variable-rate mortgage loans that would have allowed for changes in asset yields as the cost of funds increased. Fourth, even where allowed, variable-rate mortgage lending was not popular with consumers and was accepted only as a last resort when no other financing was available. Finally, the rate of turnover of the mortgage portfolio declined as high interest rates decreased home sales and low-rate mortgages were assumed by subsequent home purchasers. Those assuming mortgages were often protected by legal barriers to the enforcement of "due-on-sale" clauses in the mortgage contracts. The net effect of these factors was a long lag between the rise in market interest rates and any significant increase in the return on mortgage portfolios.

On the liability side of the balance sheet, the thrifts funded their long-term mortgage holdings with short-term deposits. When the standard low-yielding passbook savings account was the "only game in town" for the average small saver, deposits were relatively stable. Financial innovation and the increasing sophistication of savers, however, put an end to that era. Beginning in the 1960s, disintermediation occurred when market interest rates rose above the low Regulation Q ceilings on passbook savings deposits, and depositors sought out higher-rate alternatives. The development of money market mutual funds was the final blow to the thrifts' supply of low-cost deposits. Even savers with as little as $1,000 could obtain a market rate of return on a relatively safe investment. The thrifts and their regulators then faced a choice between two unpleasant alternatives. If thrifts were not given the power to pay a competitive return on savings, funds would be withdrawn. To meet the outflows, low-interest-rate mortgages would have to be sold at large discounts from their face value and thrift capital accounts would quickly be exhausted. On the other hand, giving thrifts high-interest-rate deposit instruments would raise their cost of funds above their asset yields and cause operating losses. A third alternative, extending interest rate regulation to the money market funds, was rejected; by the time the scope of the problem was realized, so many people held money funds that there was extensive political opposition to lowering the yield.

As the earnings of the thrifts turned to losses and their capital evaporated, various active and passive regulatory measures were taken. Technical insolvencies (the inability to pay all liabilities by liquidating all assets) were ignored; otherwise nearly all thrifts would have been closed because of the drastic loss of market value of their fixed-rate assets. On the active policy side, mergers were arranged with stronger institutions acquiring weaker ones and by the creation of "phoenix" thrifts composed of two or more failed institutions combined with government assistance. Mergers were arranged on an interstate basis, and both bank holding companies and some nonthrift firms were allowed to acquire S&Ls. In order to minimize mergers and the amount of FSLIC financial aid required, S&L capital requirements were reduced, borrowings from the Federal Home Loan Banks increased, and a capital assistance program was begun under authorization of the Garn-St Germain Act of 1982.

To provide longer-run aid, regulatory limitations on variable-rate mortgages were reduced or eliminated and the Supreme Court removed barriers to the enforcement of due-on-sale clauses. The thrifts, along with the commercial banks, were given a variety of new deposit instruments, including the six-month money market certificate, the 30-month small saver certificate, the all saver certificate, and finally in late 1982 and early 1983, a money market deposit account with no interest rate ceiling and the Super NOW account. The gradual phase-out of Regulation Q ceilings, mandated by the Depository Institutions Deregulation and Monetary Control Act of 1980, will eventually provide free market competition for all deposits. The 1980 law and the subsequent Garn-St Germain Act of 1982 also expanded the lending and investment powers of the thrifts so that their excessive concentration in mortgages can be reduced over time.

Numerous long-term thrift problems remain, although the short-run crisis eased somewhat with the fall of interest rates in late 1982. First, consumers have accepted variable-rate mortgages only as a last resort. Many of those written when fixed-rate money was unavailable were refinanced into fixed-rate mortgages as interest rates declined. Second, little progress has been made in increasing the average maturity of thrift deposits. NOW accounts and money market deposit accounts do not provide funds to finance 30-year fixed-rate mortgages, although Individual Retirement Accounts (IRAs) and longer-term certificates do partially balance these short-term interest-sensitive deposits. Third, at least in the short run, thrifts have faced problems diversifying their loan portfolios. Few thrifts have developed expertise in the already highly competitive area of commercial lending. In order to gain a foothold in new lending areas, it is feared that they may either have to price loans unrealistically low or accept higher risks than banks are willing to accept. Both avenues have adverse implications for their financial position.

Finally, the possible transformation of the thrifts into commercial banks raises questions as to the future source of home mortgage financing. If housing continues to be a social priority, adequate financing is needed. It has not been established that other lenders can or will increase their lending to compensate for any decline in funds from the thrifts.

CONCLUSION

This chapter has presented the current status and some of the problems of domestic depository institutions. Because of the recent financial difficulties of the thrift industry, the trend appears to be toward greater homogenization of institutional functions.

Homogenization of functions, along with the introduction of new competitors in the financial services industry and the expected instability of interest rates, creates an uncertain environment for financial institutions.

Managers will have to pay increased attention to the management of interest rate risk and the careful pricing of services and deposits. In addition, deregulation offers opportunities for adopting new powers or new charters, and the advance of technology requires decisions in areas such as ATM deployment, home banking, and internal data processing requirements.

The old rules of the closely regulated environment are no longer applicable or risk minimizing, and the successful institution will have to plan its response to changes. Those who do not adapt to these changes will lose both income and market share to their more adaptive and innovative competitors.

NOTES

1. For data and analysis, see the appendix to the 1982 annual report of the Federal Reserve Bank of Minneapolis. The relative position of depository institutions is measured on a number of bases, all of which suggest that any substantial deterioration of their position is prospective rather than current.
2. See Chapter 24 of this volume, "Costs and Scale Economies in Financial Intermediation," by David Burras Humphrey.
3. The history of the bank holding company is traced in Savage, 1978, and Jessee and Seelig, 1977.
4. Those credit unions that held relatively large amounts of long-term fixed rate debt instruments also suffered earnings problems, but most credit unions suffered more from usury ceilings on loan rates that did not permit lending at rates sufficient to cover the increasing cost of funds.

REFERENCES

Federal Reserve Bank of Minneapolis, *Annual Report*. Minneapolis, 1982.

Department of the Treasury, *Geographic Restrictions on Commercial Banking in the United States: The Report to the President*. Washington, D.C., January 1981.

Houpt, James V., and Martinson, Michael G. "Foreign Subsidiaries of U.S. Banking Organizations." *Staff Studies* No. 120, Board of Governors of the Federal Reserve System, October 1982, pp. 3–4.

Jessee, Michael A., and Seelig, Steven A. *Bank Holding Companies and the Public Interest: An Economic Analysis*. Lexington, Mass.: Lexington Books, 1977.

Savage, Donald T. "A History of the Bank Holding Company Movement, 1900–78." In *The Bank Holding Company Movement to 1978: A Compendium*, a study by the staff of the Board of Governors of the Federal Reserve System, 1978.

7 Banking Services in Transition: The Effects of Nonbank Competitors

Harvey Rosenblum and
Christine Pavel

INTRODUCTION

Observers of the "revolution" in financial services often cite the rise of the "nonbank bank" as well as the banklike activities of such firms as American Express, Merrill Lynch, Prudential, and Sears. But most of the acquisitions of financial institutions and de novo expansion into financial activities of nonbanking-based firms involve extensions of interests and positions in financial services that, in many cases, go back several decades. Furthermore, the competitors in financial services include depository institutions—commercial banks, S&Ls, mutual savings banks, and credit unions—as well as the nonbank competitors mentioned above and many others such as General Motors, J.C. Penney, and General Electric.

This chapter examines the extent of competition provided to depository institutions (with special emphasis on commercial banks) by nonfinancial institutions, or at least those whose primary line of business activity has not involved the offering of federally insured deposits. The following sec-

The views expressed are those of the authors and do not necessarily represent those of the Federal Reserve Bank of Chicago or the Federal Reserve System. Helpful research assistance was provided by Toni Fitzgerald. This chapter is an update and extension of a previous monograph by Harvey Rosenblum and Diane Siegel, *Competition in Financial Services: The Impact of Nonbank Entry*, Staff Study 83-1, Federal Reserve Bank of Chicago.

Table 7.1. List of the 32 Companies Analyzed

Fifteen Industrial/Communication/Transportation-Based Companies

Associated First Capital (Gulf & Western)
Armco Financial Services
Borg-Warner Acceptance Corp.
Chrysler Financial Corp.
CIT Financial Corp. (RCA)
Commercial Credit Co. (Control Data)
Diamond Financial Holdings (Dana)
FN Financial Corporation (National Steel)
Ford Motor Credit Company
General Electric Credit Corp.
General Motors Acceptance Corp.
Greyhound Financial Group
IBM
ITT
Westinghouse Credit Corp.

Ten Diversified Financial Service Companies

American Express
Avco Financial Services
Baldwin-United Corp.
Beneficial Corp.
Walter E. Heller International
Household International
E.F. Hutton Group
Loews Corp.
Merrill Lynch
Transamerica

Four Insurance-Based Companies

Aetna Life & Casualty
American General Corp./Credithrift Financial
Equitable Life Assurance Society
Prudential (and Bache)

Three Retail-Based Companies

Montgomery Ward
J.C. Penney
Sears

tion gives a background on this subject, including reviews of the early research. The next section, Competition in Financial Services: 1981–1982, presents and analyzes the accounting data available on the extent of competition provided by 32 companies, most of whose main interest is not (or has not been) financial. Table 7.1 lists the companies analyzed. The financial activities of these 32 companies are compared with the nation's 15 largest bank holding companies and with the aggregate of all federally insured commercial banks in the United States. Important balance sheet and income data for these companies are given in the appendix to this chapter. The section on Implications of Nonbank Competition discusses the internal management and public policy implications. Finally, a summary and conclusions are presented.

In short, the results indicate that the sheer size and number of nonbank firms with substantial nationwide financial activities are impressive. Also, the erosion of the uniqueness of demand deposits together with the increased entry into many types of lending activities by nonbank firms has made obsolete the notion that commercial banking is a distinct line of commerce. Further, there appears to be considerable circumstantial evidence that the geographic market for many financial services is now national in scope, or will soon become so.

BACKGROUND

Although banks face many different types of competitors, they are the number one institutional lender to households and businesses. For many years, banks have had the largest share of the auto loan market as well as many other types of consumer loans. And the long-standing hegemony of banks in commercial lending is to be expected since commercial banks were chartered originally to meet the needs of business.

The preeminent market position of banks, however, is somewhat surprising when one recognizes the constraints under which they operate, particularly because many of their competitors, allegedly, are less constrained in a number of ways. Nonbank competitors, such as captive finance companies, are free to enter or exit virtually any geographic location. Further, many competitors can offer both financial and nonfinancial services and products that banks are prohibited from offering. For example, a business such as Sears can offer life insurance, money market funds, shirts, and hardware as well as retail credit at any of its more than 800 retail locations throughout the United States.[1] Apparently the ability to offer life insurance and money market funds in a department store setting, at least until 1982, did not confer a great competitive advantage upon a business enterprise; if it had, Sears would not have been alone among retailers in offering both products.[2]

In spite (and perhaps because) of the numerous regulatory disadvantages that banks face in comparison with their competitors, many segments of the banking business, including consumer lending, business lending, and deposit taking, have appeared attractive to a number of firms that do not have bank charters. As a result, these firms have entered financial services through de novo expansion and through acquisitions of existing financial concerns.

Industrial- and transportation-based companies, manufacturers, and retailers have acquired insurance companies, finance companies, and leasing operations. Also, because savings and loan associations and mutual savings banks have attained the ability to offer a wide range of consumer and business loans since 1980 by virtue of federal legislation contained in the Depository Institutions Deregulation and Monetary Control Act of 1980 (DIDMCA) and the Garn-St Germain Depository Institutions Act of 1982, they have become more attractive to nondepository firms as acquisition candidates than previously. And commercial banks, because of their unique position in the national (and the international) payments mechanism and their entrenched incumbent position as a profitable provider of a number of financial products, have also become attractive acquisition targets to J.C. Penney, Prudential, Dreyfus, and others who wish to extend or establish a delivery system for a wide range of financial products.

Although, as previously mentioned, nonbank competition in financial services is not a new phenomenon, the pace of nonbank entry has been accelerating. Most of the industrial and retailing giants that began to be significant financial services competitors nearly a decade ago have continued to expand their roles in financial activities. These companies have been joined by many others. Nonetheless, commercial banks have managed to hold onto their market share in the provision of most financial services, having gained in some product lines while retrenching in others.

Early Research Findings

About a decade ago Citicorp released a study detailing the competitive inroads made by unregulated firms into the financial services business. This monograph, authored by Cleveland Christophe (1974), provided an in-depth view of the relative importance of banks and nonfinancial firms in the extension of consumer credit. Some of the findings were startling to many bankers, as few had recognized the importance of the competition represented by firms such as Sears and General Electric whose primary activities were nonfinancial.

Most bankers, of course, were aware of competition from other depository institutions and from consumer finance companies. Yet Sears, a firm not generally regarded at that time as a banking competitor, had more active charge accounts as of 1972 than either Master Charge or National BankAmericard (the predecessors of MasterCard and Visa). Furthermore, Sears had credit card volume and receivables to match its greater number of accounts. Its $4.3 billion of credit card receivables at year-end 1972 were roughly 80% of the $5.3 billion of installment credit on *all* bank credit cards. Moreover, Sears earned more money after taxes in 1972 *on its financial service business* than did any bank or bank holding company in the country.

Sears's prominence in financial services should not have been surprising. Sears began to provide consumer credit in 1910 to support its retail operations, while most commercial banks concentrated their lending efforts on commercial customers until the post–World War II period. It is sometimes easy to forget that commercial banks are a "Johnny-come-lately" on the consumer lending scene.[3] Further, Allstate Insurance, Sears's insurance subsidiary, was formed in 1931 to sell auto insurance and long before 1972 had begun to offer a wide range of insurance products. By 1972, Sears was the largest retailer in the United States in the *Fortune* directory of the 50 largest retailing companies.

Though Sears and its two large national retailing rivals, Montgomery Ward and J.C. Penney, had combined consumer installment credit ($6.9 billion) that exceeded the amount outstanding at the nation's three largest bank holding companies (BankAmerica, Citicorp, and Chase Manhattan with $4.3 billion) by more than 50%, the retailers were overshadowed by the financing arms of three large manufacturers. Through General Motors Acceptance Corporation (GMAC), General Motors had $7.8 billion in consumer receivables at year-end 1972, more than the combined total of the three large retailers. The combination of GMAC, Ford Motor Credit Company (FMCC), and General Electric Credit Corporation (GECC) had more consumer receivables than the three retailers and three largest bank holding companies combined.

Again, the role of the manufacturers in consumer lending should not have been surprising. GMAC began making auto loans in 1919; GECC was formed in 1932; and FMCC was founded in 1959 (though Ford began making auto loans in 1928). GMAC and FMCC were largely captive finance companies in the true sense of the term; that is, they provided financing primarily to enable customers to purchase products manufactured by their parent companies or sold by their franchised distributors. GECC was a different story. Though it began as a marketing extension of General Electric's appliance division, largely financing dealer–distributor inventories and sales of General Electric products to consumers, GECC's customer orientation and profile began to change in the early 1960s when it began to extend its commercial lending and leasing business to finance products other than those made by General Electric. In 1965, GECC expanded its position in consumer financing by offering revolving charge plans to many retail dealers of electrical consumer goods. That same year, GECC began experimenting with direct consumer installment lending; by May 1972, it had expanded to 129 offices in 33 states.

In 1972, GECC accounted for less than 8% of General Electric's earnings; GMAC accounted for only 4.5% of General Motors's earnings; and FMCC, for just over 5% of Ford's net income. Although they were among the largest consumer installment lenders in the country, the income derived from consumer lending was still small relative to their parent manufacturers' primary businesses. Although these manufacturers became creditors as a byproduct of their primary manufacturing and marketing operations, their finance operations attained a size, status, and profitability that were the envy of many banks. Indeed, it could have been argued that these three companies were the prototypes of manufacturers-turned-bankers, a move followed in later years by the once-captive finance subsidiaries of such manufacturing giants as Westinghouse and Borg-Warner.

At the same time that many nonbanking firms were expanding their product lines into a wider range of lending activities, many banks began doing the same. During the late 1960s, many of the larger banks in the country formed one-bank holding companies for the purpose of expanding the range of products they could offer as well as the geographic locations at which these products could be sold. The range of products was circumscribed by the 1970 Amendments to the Bank Holding Company Act and the associated regulations issued by the Federal Reserve Board. Nevertheless, bank holding companies continued their vigorous expansion activity into a number of new geographic and product markets, both by establishing de novo affiliates and by acquiring going concerns. Indeed, in the first three full years (1972–1974) that applications could be processed under Section 4(c)(8) of the Bank Holding Company Act, the Federal Reserve approved 1,806 applications involving the acquisition or formation of nonbank companies, an average of 602 per year.

Beginning in 1974, however, a number of problems confronting the banking industry began to surface: large bank failures, massive loan losses, serious questions about capital adequacy, and "affiliated REIT" difficulties. Interest in expanding product lines and geographic markets quickly waned, due in part to increased regulatory pressure from the Federal Reserve Board's "go-slow" policy. This is reflected in the decline in the number of applications to engage in nonbanking activities approved by the Federal Reserve, down to 379 in 1975 and 384 in 1976.

During 1975–1977, the emphasis in banking returned to managing the fundamentals. And as banks retrenched from their aggressive geographic and product expansion posture, many financial product and service lines were left to the nonbank competitors. The ensuing technological changes and record-breaking interest rates provided customers additional impetus to turn to other firms that were in a position to provide financial products at locations and at terms that the customers desired.

Recent Findings

It was not until 1981, following the acquisition of several very large non-bank financial service companies by other financial and nonfinancial firms, that studies of the role of nonfinancial firms in the financial sector and the public's interest in these matters began to reemerge. The combinations that caught the public's eye were the acquisitions of Bache by Prudential, Shearson by American Express, Dean Witter Reynolds and Coldwell Banker by Sears, and Salomon Brothers by Phibro.

An article by Carol Loomis (1981) provided a detailed comparison of the financial activities of Citicorp with those provided by American Express, Merrill Lynch, Prudential, and Sears. According to the criteria used by Loomis, Citicorp (consolidated international) still held the edge in assets, deposits, commercial loans, and consumer loans but was second in revenue (behind Sears); it was last in money market funds (it had none while the other four companies had a total of $54.7 billion), and engaged in the second smallest number of financial activities (12), one more than Prudential but still behind Sears with 19, Merrill Lynch with 16, and American Express with 15. Among the financial activities were several prohibited for bank holding companies: real estate development, commercial and residential real estate brokerage, executive relocation services, and the underwriting of mortgage guarantee insurance, life insurance, and casualty insurance.[4]

More recently, William F. Ford (1982) questioned whether commercial banks need to fear competition from nonbank rivals. He argued that retailers like Sears, brokerage firms like Merrill Lynch, and insurance companies like Prudential are diversifying into new financial services because they have been doing poorly in many of their traditional product lines. He also argued that most medium and small banks need not fear Citicorp— probably the nation's most diversified banking organization with respect to product lines and geographic markets—since Citicorp's profitability in recent years has not matched that of a composite regional bank. Whether the performance records of giants like Sears, American Express, and Citicorp will improve in the future was left an open question, but the data cited by William F. Ford should provide some comfort to smaller firms.

COMPETITION IN FINANCIAL SERVICES: 1981–1982

Overview

To explore the prevailing degree of competition between banks and non-bank companies, the financial activities of 32 major U.S.-based companies (listed in Table 7.1) were analyzed and compared with the 15 largest bank holding companies as of year-end 1981 and 1982 by utilizing company annual reports and 10-K statements filed with the Securities and Exchange Commission.[5] Additional information was obtained from recent articles that have appeared in *American Banker, Wall Street Journal, Business Week, Fortune, Moody's Bank and Finance Manual,* and other current periodicals and publications believed to be reliable sources.

Companies were chosen on the basis of their being the most frequently mentioned nonbanking-based competitors of commercial banks. Several diversified financial service companies were also studied. Many other financial companies (in particular, many large insurance companies) were excluded because they have demonstrated little or no inclination to invade the turf of commercial banks during the last few years. Some nonfinancial companies that have begun to invade commercial banking product lines were likely omitted simply because they have maintained a low profile and were therefore not readily identified.

Many companies could easily become banklike entities if they were so inclined. That they have not done so to date does not mean that banks and other lenders are unaware of their potential to become a major force in commercial or consumer lending or both. Most strategic planners track developments at these companies (particularly data and information processing companies) despite the fact that the balance sheets of these potential entrants contain no deposits or loans.

In interpreting the data contained in this information base, the reader should keep in mind that accounting data have a number of shortcomings, particularly when used to make economic comparisons across different companies (see Benston, 1982). Moreover, many of the companies do not organize their accounting data into the same categories of assets and liabilities as those used by commercial banks. For example, unlike banks, some manufacturing-based lenders might include truck or tractor financing with auto loans. Or some foreign loans might be included with domestic loans in some categories but not in others. In such instances, estimates were made by company employees and/or by the authors in an effort to establish some consistency in the asset, liability, and income categories across companies.

No attempt was made in this chapter to delineate precisely the geographic areas served by nonbanking firms. It should be kept in mind in interpreting the financial statistics provided in this paper that the competitive influence or impact of the various nonbank companies is affected by the fact that they compete in many different geographic and/or product markets not served by many of the nation's commercial banks.

Profits from Financial Activities

In 1972, there were 10 companies whose earnings from financial lines of business were impressive. The financial earnings of these companies compared favorably with those of many of the largest banks and bank holding companies. These companies are shown in Table 7.2. During 1972 their net incomes from financial activities totaled $662.2 million, six times greater than a decade earlier. Indeed, in 1962, three of the 10 companies shown had virtually no earnings from financial activities, and four of the companies had financial earnings that averaged a mere $0.75 million. Within this group of 10, only General Motors and Sears would have been considered significant financiers in 1962.

Table 7.2.   Estimated Financial Service Earnings of Nonfinancial-Based Companies

	1962		1972		1982	
	Millions of Dollars	Percentage of Total Earnings	Millions of Dollars	Percentage of Total Earnings	Millions of Dollars	Percentage of Total Earnings
Borg-Warner	$0.5	1.5	$6.3	10.6	$37	21.5
Control Data	Nil	Nil	55.6	96.2	46	29.7
Ford Motor	0.4	Nil	44.1	5.1	229	n.a.[a]
General Electric	8.7	3.3	41.1	7.8	205	11.3
General Motors	40.9	2.8	96.4	4.5	688	71.4
Gulf & Western	Nil	Nil	29.3	42.1	89	53.4
ITT	1.2	2.9	160.2	33.6	350	51.7
Marcor	Nil	Nil	9.0	12.4	85	n.a.[b]
Sears[c]	50.4	21.6	209.0	34.0	580	89.2
Westinghouse	0.9	2.0	15.2	7.6	51	11.4
Total	$103.0		$666.2		$2,360	

SOURCE: 1962 and 1972 data from Christophe (1974), Table III, p. 10; 1981 data from company annual reports and 10-K forms.

[a]Ford Motor Company had a net loss of $658 million in 1982.

[b]Marcor's operating loss in 1982 was $75 million.

[c]Sears's financial service earnings are stated before allocation of corporate expenses to its business groups. In 1982, such expenses were $133 million.

By year-end 1981, these 10 companies had profits from financial ac-
tivities totaling $1.73 billion, more than 2.5 times the total in 1972 and a
considerably greater gain than could be accounted for by inflation alone.
Eight of the 10 companies showed an increase in the percentage of total
earnings attributable to their financial activities; only Control Data and
Gulf & Western showed a decline. Interestingly, the five largest New York
City bank holding companies—Citicorp, Chase Manhattan, Manufacturers
Hanover, Chemical, and Morgan—earned a similar total, $1.78 billion from
their *worldwide* activities during 1981.[6]

To ascertain whether 1981, the year the firms were studied intensively
by Rosenblum and Siegel (1983), was an unusual year in some way, the
evidence on penetration of financial services by nonbanking firms in 1982
was used for comparison. In 1982, the earnings of these 10 companies
from their financial activities totaled $2.36 billion, a 36% increase over
1981. Seven of the 10 companies experienced an increase in their volume
of financial service earnings. The nonfinancial earnings of these 10 companies combined grew faster between 1981 and 1982 than did their earnings
from financial services, as financial earnings amounted to 54% of total
earnings in 1982 compared with just over 58% in 1981. In contrast, the
nation's 15 largest bank holding companies had combined earnings of $3.15
billion in 1982, compared with $3.62 billion in 1981, a 13% decrease. As
a result, in 1982 it took the seven largest bank holding companies, ranked
by earnings, to equal the financial service earnings of the 10 companies
shown in Table 7.2.

The composition of earnings from financial services is different for
banks, bank holding companies, and nonbanking-based firms. For example, the financial service earnings of Sears were dominated by its insurance activities until 1982. The same is true for ITT following the acquisition of the Hartford Insurance Group in 1970. In 1982, the Coldwell
Banker and Dean Witter subsidiaries, each acquired on December 31,
1981, made significant contributions to Sears's earnings from financial
services. It should be noted, however, that banks and bank holding companies cannot engage in most of the financial activities engaged in by
Allstate, the Hartford Insurance Group, Coldwell Banker, or Dean Witter.
Thus the earnings figures shown in Tables 7.2 and 7.3 do not necessarily
signify competitive overlap or that nonbanking-based companies have been
taking business away from commercial banking firms.

Companies that had 1982 profits from financial activities exceeding $200
million are shown in Table 7.3. Results for 1981 are also shown. Nine of
the firms are bank holding companies, but of the top 11, only three are
bank holding companies. Moreover, the eight nonbanking-based companies had total 1982 earnings from financial services of $5.53 billion com-
pared with $3.10 billion for the nine bank holding companies.

Table 7.3. Earnings from Financial Activities, 1981 and
1982: Manufacturers, Retailers, Diversified Finance
Companies, Insurance-Based Companies, and Bank
Holding Companies (in millions of dollars)

Company	Earnings	
	1982	1981
Prudential	$2,014	$1,576
Citicorp	723	531
General Motors	688	365
Equitable Life Assurance	584	651
American Express	581	518
Sears[a]	580	385
BankAmerica Corp.	447	445
Aetna Life & Casualty	427	462
J.P. Morgan & Co.	394	375
ITT	350	387
Merrill Lynch	309	203
Chase Manhattan Corp.	307	412
Manufacturers Hanover Corp.	295	252
Chemical New York Corp.	241	215
Bankers Trust New York Corp.	239	188
Security Pacific Corp.	234	206
First Interstate Bancorp.	221	236

SOURCE: Company annual reports and 10-K forms.

[a]Sears's financial service earnings are stated before allocation of
corporate expenses to its business groups. In 1982 and 1981, such
expenses were $133 million and $103 million, respectively.

Nonbanking-Based Companies as Providers of Credit

If the manufacturing companies listed in Table 7.2 engaged solely in the financing of products manufactured by them, then one might suspect they did not compete vigorously with commercial banks. As shown in Table 7.4, several of the so-called captive finance companies provide credit, if not to all comers, then to a wide clientele involved in purchasing goods unrelated to their parents' products. This tendency to diversify the customer base has increased since 1972. It is clear that captive finance companies have the ability to evolve in ways not originally contemplated by the founding company. They can and oftentimes do take on a life of their own that is unrelated to their parents' operations. For example, financing of General Electric products accounted for less than 5% of GECC's financing volume in 1981 and an imperceptible proportion in 1982. Over 90% of Borg-Warner Acceptance Corporation's income and assets result

Table 7.4. Percentage of Financing in Conjunction with Sales of Parent's
Products

Company	1972	1981	1982
General Electric Credit Corp.	9	5	Virtually none
Borg-Warner Acceptance Corp.	n.a.	9	9
Westinghouse Credit Corp.	43[a]	Less than 1	Less than 1
Associates/G&W	2[b]	1	1
Commercial Credit/Control Data	8[b]	11	11

SOURCE: For 1972, Christophe (1974), except as noted. For 1981 and 1982, annual reports
and 10-K forms.

[a]Estimated from information in Christophe (1974), pp. 48–49. As of 1973, Westinghouse
stated in its 10-K form that the percentage of its parent's products financed was a "small
portion" of WCC's business.

[b]Data shown are for 1975, the earliest date available.

from financing other companies' products. Similarly, Westinghouse Credit
serves a diverse clientele. On the other hand, several of the finance companies included in this nonbanking-based sample are much more "captive." Included in this category are GMAC, Ford Motor Credit, and IBM
Credit.

Another way to look at the financial activities of the nonfinancial companies is to examine their total finance receivables. Table 7.5 ranks the
companies by financing volume. Although some of the receivables of
manufacturers such as General Motors and Ford are derived from foreign
countries, Table 7.5 assumes that all such receivables are generated by
domestic customers; consequently, the domestic receivables of bank
holding companies are used for comparison.

Table 7.5 illustrates that banks are not the only major lenders in the
United States. For example, in 1982, of the top 11 companies shown,
eight are bank holding companies, one is an insurance company and broker, and two are the finance subsidiaries of automobile manufacturers.
Of the next 11 companies, only five are bank holding companies. Of the
30 selected companies, 15 are bank holding companies and 15 are nonbanking-based firms; the former group had a total of $332.5 billion in re-
ceivables in 1982 while the latter group held $200.9 billion.

Perhaps the best way to examine the impact of nonbank entry upon
banks is to look at what has happened to competition in individual product
lines. Thus, the competitive thrusts made by 32 nonbank companies into
various segments of consumer and business credit and into the deposit
markets are examined below.

Table 7.5. Total Domestic Finance Receivables of 30 Selected Companies Having over $5 Billion in Receivables, 1981 and 1982 (in billions of dollars)

Company	Receivables	
	1982	1981
BankAmerica Corp.	$52.4	$52.0
Citicorp	49.8	40.6
General Motors	48.2	45.1
Manufacturers Hanover Corp.	26.7	23.1
Prudential/Bache/PruCapital	24.8	23.0
First Interstate Bancorp	23.7	21.3
Continental Illinois Corp.	23.5	23.7
Security Pacific Corp.	23.0	19.2
Chase Manhattan Corp.	21.8	21.2
Chemical New York Corp.	20.9	20.3
Ford Motor	17.6	19.5
Wells Fargo & Co.	17.0	16.1
First Chicago Corp.	15.4	14.5
Sears	14.8	13.8
Bankers Trust New York Corp.	14.5	13.0
Equitable Life Assurance	14.0	13.7
General Electric	13.1	11.1
Crocker National Corp.	12.9	12.7
J.P. Morgan & Co.	12.8	12.9
Aetna Life & Casualty	11.2	10.8
American Express	11.0	9.5
Merrill Lynch	10.9	5.1
Mellon National Corp.	9.4	8.1
Marine Midland Banks, Inc.	8.7	7.9
CIT Financial	7.3	7.2
Gulf & Western	6.1	5.9
National Steel	6.0	5.9
Walter E. Heller International	5.5	5.1
ITT	5.2	4.8
IBM	5.2	4.6

SOURCE: Company annual reports and 10-K forms.

Consumer Credit

At year-end 1972, the three largest bank holding companies held less consumer installment credit than the three largest nonfood retailers which, in turn, held less consumer installment credit than three large consumer durable goods manufacturers (see Figure 7.1(a)). As is apparent in Figure 7.1(b), these rankings have changed in a number of ways. Most notable is the dramatic gain made by bank holding companies, whether looked at on a worldwide or U.S.-only basis. Part of this gain was due to the ac-

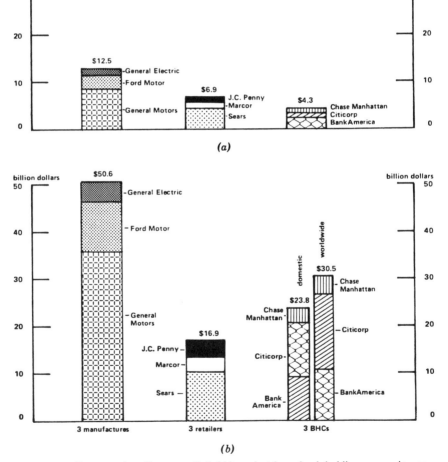

Figure 7.1. Consumer installment credit held by select large bank holding companies, retailers, and consumer durable goods manufacturers at year-end: (a) 1972; (b) 1982. *Source:* 1972 data from Christophe (1974); 1982 data from company annual reports and 10-K forms.

quisition of consumer finance companies by BankAmerica and Citicorp, but most of the increase is attributable to internal growth.

Over the 1972–1982 period, the consumer installment credit held by the three large retailers grew by a factor of 2.4; that held by the three bank holding companies grew by a factor of 7.1 (worldwide); and that held by the three manufacturers grew by a factor of 4.0. Clearly, the bank holding companies experienced the highest growth rate of the three groups.

Another way to examine the impact of nonbank competition in the market for consumer credit is to rank the companies according to their consumer credit outstanding. This is shown in Table 7.6 for the 15 largest lenders in consumer installment and revolving credit, a measure that excludes retail mortgage credit. Of the top 15 in this group in 1982, only five are bank holding companies; within the top eight firms, only two are bank holding companies. At year-end 1982 the top 10 nonbanking-based consumer installment lenders had $86.7 billion of such loans outstanding, just double that held by the 10 largest bank holding companies in this lending category.

Table 7.6. Top 15 Consumer Installment and
Revolving Credit Lenders, 1981 and 1982 (in millions
of dollars)[a]

Company	Installment and Revolving Credit	
	1982	1981
General Motors	35,623	31,077
Citicorp	11,213	9,556
Ford Motor	10,542	11,892
Sears	10,109	9,528
BankAmerica Corp.	9,506	9,703
Prudential/Bache/Prucapital	5,887	5,142
American Express	5,608	5,035
Merrill Lynch	4,778	4,725
First Interstate Bancorp	4,591	4,418
General Electric	4,459	2,792
Security Pacific Corp.	4,354	3,799
J.C. Penney	3,450	3,183
Montgomery Ward	3,291	3,623
Chase Manhattan Corp.	3,085	2,726
Equitable Life Assurance	2,911	2,692

SOURCE: Annual reports and 10-K forms.

[a]Data for bank holding companies are domestic loans; nonbank company data are worldwide.

Table 7.7. Domestic Automobile Loans Outstanding as of Year-End 1978–1982 (in millions of dollars)

	1982	1981	1980	1979	1978
General Motors Acceptance Corp.[a]	$ 33,520	$ 28,545	$ 20,298	$ 17,526	$ 13,519
Percentage of total	26%	23%	17%	15%	13%
Ford Motor Credit Co.[b]	$ 9,321	$ 10,450	$ 8,977	$ 7,678	$ 6,527
Percentage of total	7%	8%	8%	7%	6%
Chrysler Financial Corp.[c]	$ 1,665	$ 1,948	$ 1,742	$ 1,472	$ 1,728
Percentage of total	1%	2%	2%	1%	2%
Total of three auto finance companies	$ 44,506	$ 40,943	$ 31,017	$ 26,676	$ 21,774
Percentage of total	34%	32%	27%	23%	21%
Commercial banks	$ 58,851	$ 59,181	$ 61,536	$ 67,367	$ 60,510
Percentage of total	45%	47%	53%	58%	60%
Other	$ 26,870	$ 26,307	$ 24,285	$ 22,319	$ 19,363
Percentage of total	21%	21%	20%	19%	19%
Total auto loans outstanding	$130,227	$126,431	$116,838	$116,362	$101,647

SOURCE: *Federal Reserve Bulletin* and annual reports and 10-K forms.

[a]Includes small amount of financing of other General Motors products such as trucks and tractors.

[b]These domestic numbers are estimates. They also include a small amount of financing of Ford's other products.

[c]Includes Canadian and Mexican automotive receivables.

In the narrower field of auto loans, commercial banks have maintained their position as the leading lending group, but they have lost significant ground over the last few years to the captive finance affiliates of the auto manufacturers. As can be seen in Table 7.7, commercial banks as a group have the largest market share in the auto lending product line with 45% of the market at year-end 1982. This share had fallen by 15 percentage points from the peak reached only four years earlier in 1978. Over this same 1978–1982 period, the share of auto loans held by the captive finance companies of General Motors, Ford, and Chrysler had increased by 13 percentage points, to 34% of the market. GMAC alone in 1982 held $33.5 billion of auto loans, more than one-fourth of all auto loans outstanding and almost double its share of the total market just four years earlier.

By way of comparison, Bank of America was the largest auto lender among commercial banks with $2.1 billion of auto loans at year-end 1982, about 2.3 times the total of the second largest bank in auto loans but a mere one-sixteenth the total held by GMAC. It should be recognized that Bank of America's auto loans are confined almost totally to California, while GMAC lends throughout the United States. Nevertheless, GMAC's market position as measured by loans outstanding is enormous.

At year-end 1982, according to their domestic consolidated Call Reports, the top 25 commercial banks in auto loans had $10.5 billion of such loans on their books, and the top 100 banks had $18.1 billion. As mentioned above, GMAC alone held $33.5 billion, 1.6 times the amount held by the largest 100 commercial banking auto lenders. Ford Motor Credit held $9.3 billion, about the same as that held by the 19 largest commercial banking auto lenders.[7]

Auto Loans—Permanent or Temporary Shift in Market Share?

Shifts in market share of this order of magnitude over such a short time span are somewhat unusual. But a number of diverse yet concurrent forces account for these changes in market shares: a decrease in domestic car sales, liberalized bankruptcy laws, soaring cost of funds, and interest rate volatility. This combination of factors induced the captive finance affiliates of the auto manufacturers to offer low-cost auto credit, largely as a defensive measure to support their dealer networks.

Between 1978 and 1982, there was a sharp falloff in the number of cars to be financed. Thus the volume of potential business for all auto lenders declined dramatically during this four-year period. Domestic car sales, which totaled 9.2 million units in 1978, fell to 5.7 million units in 1982, a 38% decline. As would be expected, the volume of loans written fell simultaneously. As can be seen in Table 7.8, the total of net new automobile

Table 7.8. Automobile Credit by Holder (in billions of dollars)

	Amount Outstanding			Net Change during Year			New Loans		
	1978	1981	1982	1978	1981	1982	1978	1981	1982
Commercial banks[a]	$ 60.5	$ 58.1	$ 58.9	$10.9	$ -3.5	$0.8	$53.0	$41.6	$45.3
Finance companies	19.9	45.3	48.8	4.7	11.0	3.5	16.5	33.5	32.4
Credit unions	21.2	22.0	22.6	3.1	0.9	0.6	18.5	18.1	18.3
Total	$101.6	$125.4	$130.3	$18.7	$ 8.4	$4.9	$88.0	$93.2	$96.0

SOURCE: *Federal Reserve Bulletin*, April 1982 and April 1983, pp. A42–A43, and *Consumer Installment Credit*, G. 19, March 1983.

[a]Includes both indirect paper and direct loans.

credit extended (i.e., new loans written less paydowns and liquidations of old loans) fell from \$18.7 billion to \$4.9 billion between 1978 and 1982; furthermore, the volume of new business fell for each of the three major institutional auto lenders over this same period, with the greatest relative declines occurring at banks and credit unions, thus allowing finance companies to increase their share of the volume of net new lending.

Not all finance companies, however, increased their share. The finance company category in Table 7.8 includes three types of finance companies: (1) independent consumer finance companies such as Beneficial Finance, Avco Financial Services, and Household Finance; (2) consumer finance affiliates of bank holding companies; and (3) the auto captive finance companies (i.e., GMAC, Ford Motor Credit, and Chrysler Financial). Just as banks were decreasing their emphasis on auto lending, so too were independent and bank holding company-affiliated finance companies, thus abandoning this market to the auto captive finance companies who were forced, at least initially, to increase significantly the size and scope of their credit operations in order to support their already financially distressed dealer networks. As can be seen in Table 7.8, credit unions were also curtailing their auto-lending activity over the 1978–1982 period. But why were all those lenders that had some choice as to whether or not they remained in auto lending choosing to exit that business so quickly? The answer to this question is critical in assessing whether the shift in market shares is likely to be permanent or transitory.

Independent and bank-affiliated consumer finance companies had several reasons for their shift away from auto lending. Some of these same reasons apply to banks and credit unions. One factor that had an impact on all lenders was the liberalization of the nation's personal bankruptcy laws enacted in 1978. The ease of declaring bankruptcy had an especially heavy impact on independent and bank-affiliated finance companies because they typically dealt with a clientele at the middle to higher end of the credit-risk spectrum—that is, those with lower incomes who were forced out of the auto-buying market by the steeply rising prices of autos relative to income or those who were more likely to be included among the rising level of unemployed, and therefore more likely to have a need to declare personal bankruptcy.

Another important force behind this shift in market shares, and one that affected all lenders, was the soaring cost of funds. In many states, usury ceilings did not allow the increased cost of funds to be passed forward to borrowers. Consequently, independent finance companies tended to close offices in those states (such as Michigan and Arkansas) where binding usury ceilings made auto lending unprofitable. For example, in 1981 alone, Avco Financial, Household Finance, and the Associates closed a combined total of 1,050 offices. This cost squeeze also affected credit unions as their deposit rates were deregulated before their lending rates were allowed to rise.

The cost squeeze imposed by the high level of funding costs was not the only problem; equally important was the sharp rise in interest rate volatility, which increased uncertainty about funding costs (Rosenblum and Strongin, 1983). This can be seen in Figure 7.2(a),(b), and (c), which provide clear evidence that the level and volatility of rates hit modern-day records during the 1978–1982 period.

But a stronger force behind the changes in market shares was the combination of this interest rate volatility with an institutional framework that was unaccustomed to dealing with rate volatility and thus had no in-place mechanisms for shifting the associated risks to those who were willing and able to bear these risks. Virtually all auto loans made were fixed-rate loans, the majority of such loans having three- to four-year maturities. In addition, there is no secondary market where auto loan paper can be packaged, sold, or traded. Thus the originator of a fixed-rate auto loan is generally forced to hold that loan to maturity or sell the loan at a substantial discount due to lack of an efficient secondary market. If short-term interest rates (and thus the cost of funds) were reasonably predictable, fixed-rate auto lending could be a profitable activity even in the absence of a secondary market for auto loans. But with widely fluctuating interest rates, at times, fixed-rate auto loans could prove to be very unprofitable unless the lender could hedge its risks by locking in a cost of funds for the same duration as the auto loans being written. But this was difficult to do because deregulation of deposit rate ceilings, which began in June 1978 with the creation of the six-month money market certificate. In combination with an inverted yield curve that induced depositors to desire short-term deposits, deposit deregulation forced banks, credit unions, and S&Ls to place greater reliance on short-term sources of funds. The natural reaction was the increased desire, but not necessarily the ability, to engage in variable-rate lending wherever possible.

Lenders like GMAC and Ford Motor Credit, which enjoyed excellent access to national and international money and capital markets, were able to raise funds having a wide range of maturities and were able to sell innovative new instruments like long-term, zero-coupon bonds that allowed them to extend the weighted average maturity and duration of their liabilities to match the duration of their assets.[8] In so doing, GMAC and Ford Motor Credit could effectively immunize themselves against changes in interest rates while still offering fixed-rate auto loans, something that lenders subject to Regulation Q ceilings could not do. Many independent and bank holding company–affiliated finance companies had access to

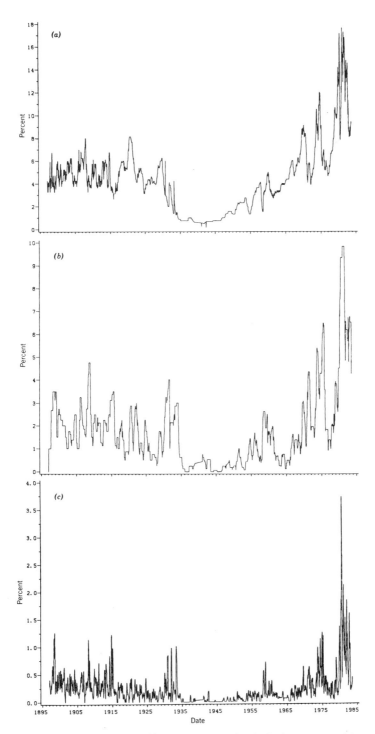

Figure 7.2. Level and volatility of interest rates: (*a*) level of prime commercial paper rate; (*b*) prime commercial paper rate—52-week range; (*c*) prime commercial paper rate—13-week standard deviation. *Source:* Rosenblum and Strongin, *Economic Perspectives*, January/ February 1983, pp. 14–15, as updated by the authors.

long-term capital markets, and a few of them did raise long-term funds in an effort to close the duration gap between their assets and liabilities. But most found it easier, and perhaps more profitable, to change their asset mix by deemphasizing auto lending and emphasizing second mortgage lending, which provided some preferential creditor status in the event of bankruptcy and had a significantly larger average size and maturity of loan, all of which reduced overhead noninterest expense.

Because the sale of autos is so dependent on credit, the auto captive finance companies had no alternative under these circumstances except to fill the developing vacuum caused by the strategic positioning of most lenders into other product lines. Thus the gain in market share by the captive auto finance companies appears to have been a reactive rather than a proactive move. This would suggest that the shift in market shares will be reversed as interest rates decline, interest rate volatility decreases, usury ceilings are relaxed or become nonbinding, and bankruptcy laws and their enforcement become less liberal. This could be the case, but there does not appear to be any inherent logical reason to expect that the stochastic process that determines shifts in market shares is (or should be) symmetrical.

The auto captive finance companies, at least according to their published income statements, have found auto lending to be a very profitable activity. Consequently, the auto companies and dealers have found that lending at seemingly below-market rates is an excellent marketing tool. If they have been able to achieve any economies of scale or economies of scope from their increased lending activities, then the captive auto finance companies may have become the low-cost producers of a fairly homogeneous product that is difficult to differentiate. If so, their increased market share may not be easily reversed.

Over the last several years, automobile-related credit has averaged between 37% and 38% of total consumer installment credit. Some of the same trends shown in auto lending are apparent for other consumer lending, as shown in Table 7.9. In 1978, commercial banks issued 55% of net new installment debt to households; finance companies accounted for only 22% of such debt. In 1981 these relative positions were reversed; commercial banks issued only 3% of the net new consumer installment debt that year while finance companies accounted for 72%.[9] Not all of this increased finance company share, however, was used to finance auto loans. Many noncaptive consumer finance companies have moved away from small, unsecured cash loans toward second mortgage loans; they held at least $13 billion of second mortgage debt at year-end 1981 (Luckett, 1982, p. 286). In 1982, commercial banks bounced back in new consumer lending, increasing their market share to 33% in spite of a poor showing in auto loans.

Table 7.9. Sources of Net New Consumer Installment Credit to Households

	1978		1981		1982	
	Billions of dollars	Percentage	Billions of dollars	Percentage	Billions of dollars	Percentage
Commercial banks	$23.6	55	$ 0.6	3	$ 4.4	33
S&Ls		[a]	1.7	9	2.3	18
Finance companies	9.4	22	13.1	72	4.5	34
Credit unions	6.7	16	1.9	11	1.3	10
Others[b]	3.4	7	0.9	5	0.6	5
Total	$43.1	100	$18.2	100	$13.1	100

SOURCE: *Federal Reserve Bulletin*, April 1982 and April 1983, p. A42–A43, and *Consumer Installment Credit* G.19, March 1983.

[a]Less than $0.5 billion or less than 0.5%.

[b]Includes mortgage pools, mutual savings banks, federal and related agencies, state and local governments, and other lenders. Amount of loans and percent of total are computed as a residual.

That there was a fundamental change in the competitive character of the market for consumer credit in recent years can be seen by examining the correlations of movements of changes in credit extended by various institutional lenders. Between 1945 and 1977, the correlation between the net annual changes in consumer installment credit at finance companies and commercial banks was 0.75; that is, increases in such loans at banks tended to be accompanied by increases at finance companies and vice versa. The correlation coefficient fell to 0.27 for the 1978–1982 period. The change in the correlation coefficient for net changes in auto loans was even more dramatic, falling from 0.68 during 1945–1977 to -0.52 during 1978–1982. The latter period clearly was not representative of the long-term trend.

The inference to be drawn from this discussion is that in consumer loan markets the share of *new* loans written by any single group of lenders can change dramatically as economic conditions change. Households apparently are willing to shift from one institutional supplier to another in response to noticeable differences in price or service. In a deregulated world, old habits may be short-lived.[10]

Credit Cards

As of 1972, Sears held a leading position over Master Charge and National BankAmericard in the credit card business. At that time Sears's 18.5 million active accounts were almost double that of its two bank card rivals, each of which had about 10 million active accounts. As can be seen in Table 7.10, Sears was also the leader in charge volume and account balances at that time.

As shown in Table 7.10, by 1981 Visa had become the undisputed leader in charge volume, an important measure of business activity in this product line because the income generated from merchants' discount fees is proportional to its charge volume. With U.S. charge volume of $29.3 billion during the June 1980–1981 period, Visa did nearly triple the volume of Sears; in 1972, Sears's volume was 43% greater than Visa's. Visa's and MasterCard's leading positions were augmented further in 1982.

As mentioned previously, Sears's lead in 1972 should have been expected; Sears began offering retail credit in 1910 while the two bank cards did not come into existence until the early 1960s. But since their inception, the bank cards have been very successful. Many retailers have begun accepting one or both bank cards in addition to their own proprietary cards. For example, J. C. Penney began accepting Visa in 1980 and MasterCard in 1981. Montgomery Ward now accepts both bank cards. Many of the smaller regional department store chains that formerly accepted only their own credit cards have begun to accept the two bank

Table 7.10.   Consumer Credit Card Programs of Major Card Issuers

	1972	1981	1982
Number of Active Accounts at Year-End (millions)			
Sears	18.5	24.5	24.8
MasterCard	10.3	22.1	n.a.
Visa	10.0	25.8	28.0
American Express	—	10.0	n.a.
Customer Charge Volume (billions of dollars)			
Sears	$ 6.3	$ 9.8	$10.5
MasterCard	5.9	26.1	30.7
Visa	4.4	29.3	35.3
American Express	—	n.a.	up 17%
Total Customer Account Balances at Year-End (billions of dollars)			
Sears	$ 4.3	$ 6.8	$ 7.1
MasterCard	2.8	12.3	n.a.
Visa	2.3	15.2	17.6
American Express	—	4.2	4.7

SOURCE: 1981 and 1982 company annual reports supplemented by telephone discussions. For 1981 and 1982, MasterCard and Visa data are U.S. only, while Sears and American Express data are worldwide. Data for 1972 are from Christophe (1974), Chart II, p. 6.

cards as well as American Express cards. In spite of this trend, General Electric Credit offers revolving credit programs to department stores whereby it issues private-label credit cards and services customer accounts. Indeed, in July 1983, General Electric Credit announced a plan to issue credit to finance the retail purchase of Apple computers. While not strictly a credit card transaction with the card being carried into the store in advance of the purchase, such sales of computer equipment at the retail level will nonetheless result in new consumer installment credit issued by a third-party, nonbanking-based company rather than a commercial bank.

The success of Visa and MasterCard vis-à-vis the Sears card does not necessarily imply a victory for banks over a nonbank competitor. The reason is simple; neither Visa nor MasterCard is a bank. They are cooperative organizations that license a product to their members. The original members were banks, but more recently other institutions have become members as well. According to Visa's 1981 annual report, during 1981

> 311 institutions joined Visa U.S.A. as proprietary members and another 571 joined as agent members. Many were thrift institutions—318 savings and loan associations, 28 mutual savings banks, and 98 credit unions—who [chose] Visa as the vehicle for exercising the new consumer payment powers granted to them by Congress.

Some of Visa's growth in the last few years is attributable to the popularity of Merrill Lynch's Cash Management Account, which includes a Visa card.[11]

An alternative way to interpret the data in Table 7.10 is to view Visa and MasterCard together as approximating a consolidated banking system in revolving installment credit. In this context the bank cards look even stronger. In 1972, the bank cards (taken together) were slightly more successful than the Sears card by all three measures—active accounts, charge volume, and account balances. By 1981, the banks had more than double the number of active accounts of Sears, more than five times the charge volume, and about four times the account balances. The same disparity was evident in 1982.

The latter interpretation of the success of bank cards has as much validity as the first interpretation. Very few banks issue their own proprietary cards, but more banks would issue such cards if they did not have a vested interest in Visa and MasterCard.

While it is true that on a consolidated basis, the banks have surpassed Sears, American Express, and other nonbank issuers of credit cards (such as department stores and petroleum companies), one should not lose sight of the fact that the two leading credit cards (as measured by customer account receivables) are Sears and American Express, whose combined credit card receivables are about equal to those of the 10 largest commercial banks in the credit card business. As can be seen in Table 7.11, the three largest bank credit card issuers together are about equal to Sears, and the volume of receivables falls off sharply as the number of included card issuers increases.

The small number of credit card issuers is suggestive of significant economies of scale in producing credit card services. The evolution of two major bank cards represents an efficient adaptation by the marketplace; banks generally produce products themselves when no significant economies of scale are present. When there are economies, banks purchase services or products from the Federal Reserve, large correspondents, or other suppliers who can produce the service or product more cheaply. Travelers checks, check clearing, and securities safekeeping are obvious

Table 7.11.   Leading Issuers of Credit Cards, 1982, Ranked by Customer Account Receivables (in billions of dollars)

Company	Receivables
Sears	$7.10
American Express	4.70
Citibank (South Dakota and Buffalo)[a]	3.28
Bank of America	2.77
First National Bank of Chicago	1.73
Chase Manhattan Bank	0.96
Continental Bank	0.74
Manufacturers Hanover Trust Co.	0.72
Wells Fargo Bank	0.48
Marine Midland Bank	0.47

SOURCE: For banks, domestic Call Reports, and for nonbank companies, annual reports.

[a]Citicorp, the parent of Citibank, has other credit-card-issuing subsidiaries that do not provide detailed information on credit card receivables for three heavily promoted credit cards: Diners Club, Carte Blanche, and the Choice Card.

examples. Charge cards appear to be similar in this respect. Indeed, many banks act as franchisees for the American Express (gold) card just as they do for travelers checks issued by American Express or by a few others.

Business Loans

Commercial banks are an important source of credit to all businesses, large and small. Banks have the largest share of outstanding commercial and industrial (C&I) loans in the United States. As can be seen in Table 7.12, the 15 largest bank holding companies held $155.5 billion of domestic C&I loans at year-end 1982, more than triple the total held by the 32 nonbank companies covered in Table 7.12. Nevertheless, the importance of nonbank lenders should not be underestimated. Funds that large firms raise from banks and from the money and capital markets are used to provide loans to many smaller businesses. For smaller businesses, trade credit is the most widely used source of credit, both in percentages of firms utilizing it as a credit source (Watro, 1982, Table 3) and in dollar volume (Eisemann, 1981, Table 2). Trade credit is admittedly an imperfect substitute for bank credit, since it cannot be used to pay other creditors or meet employee payrolls; nevertheless, its importance cannot be ignored.

Those firms that supply trade credit have alternatives to short-term bank credit; for example, nonfinancial firms had $48.0 billion of commercial

Table 7.12. Business Lending by Selected Nonbanking-Based Firms and Bank Holding Companies at Year-End 1981 and 1982 (in millions of dollars)

	Commercial and Industrial Loans		Commercial Mortgage Loans		Lease[a] Financing		Total Business Lending	
	1981	1982	1981	1982	1981	1982	1981	1982
15 Industrial/communications/transportation[b]	$ 39,365	$ 36,365	$ 1,768	$ 2,036	$14,417	$15,924	$ 55,550	$54,325
10 diversified financial[b]	3,602	4,705	3,054	3,451	1,581	1,419	8,237	9,575
4 insurance-based	399	827	35,506	36,419	892	737	36,797	37,983
3 retail-based	606	605	—	—	—	—	606	605
Total	$ 43,972	$ 42,502	$ 40,328	$ 41,906	$16,890	$18,080	$101,190	$102,488
15 largest BHCs								
Domestic	$141,582	$155,527	$ 19,481	$ 20,069	$14,279	$15,066	$175,342	$190,662
International	118,021	126,307	5,046	6,462	—	—	123,067	132,769
Total	$259,603	$281,834	$ 24,527	$ 26,531	$14,279	$15,066	$298,409	$323,431
Domestic offices, all insured commercial banks	$327,101	$379,566	$120,333[c]	$132,685[c]	$13,168	$13,738	$460,602	$525,989

SOURCE: Company annual reports and 10-K forms, and *Federal Reserve Bulletin*, April 1982, p. A76 and April 1983, p. A74.

[a]For nonbank companies and for BHCs, includes domestic and foreign lending and may include leasing to households and government entities.

[b]Financing by banking and savings and loan subsidiaries has been subtracted.

[c]Includes all real estate loans except those secured by residential property.

Table 7.13. Top 10 Commercial and Industrial Lenders
(in millions of dollars)[a]

	1982	1981
Citicorp	$18,627	$16,442
BankAmerica Corp.	17,580	16,187
Chemical New York Corp.	14,605	14,322
Continental Illinois Corp.	13,715	12,862
Manufacturers Hanover Corp.	12,961	9,866
Chase Manhattan Corp.	11,522	10,563
Security Pacific Corp.	10,051	9,866
General Motors	9,670	10,824
First Interstate Bancorp	9,259	10,464
Bankers Trust New York Corp.	8,766	6,549

SOURCE: Company annual reports and 10-K forms.

[a]Data for bank holding companies are domestic loans; data for General Motors are worldwide.

paper outstanding at year-end 1982. In addition, nonbank financial firms had $84.0 billion of commercial paper outstanding at that time; some (unknown) portion of this was used to provide credit to businesses.

Nonetheless, banks and bank holding companies still are the leaders in commercial lending. Among the top 10 commercial and industrial lenders, nine are bank holding companies. This can be seen in Table 7.13.

With respect to commercial mortgages, banks are an important source of funds, but so are insurance companies. In fact, in commercial mortgage lending, banks and bank holding companies are overshadowed by life insurance companies, but this is to be expected given the long-term nature of their liabilities. In 1982, the top 15 life insurance companies had roughly $88.0 billion in commercial mortgages, $62.2 billion more than the 15 largest bank holding companies and 67% of the commercial mortgages held by the domestic offices of all insured commercial banks. The four insurance companies covered in Table 7.12—Prudential, Aetna Life & Casualty, Equitable Life Assurance, and American General Corporation—had $36.4 billion of commercial mortgages outstanding at year-end 1982; this compares with $26.5 billion of worldwide commercial mortgages held by the 15 largest bank holding companies. Indeed, the three largest of these four insurance companies in commercial mortgage lending (i.e., Prudential, Aetna, and Equitable) had more commercial mortgage loans outstanding at year-end 1982 than the 21 largest banks in commercial mortgage lending, which includes four mutual savings banks (see Table 7.14).

Table 7.14. **Top Commercial Mortgage Lenders (in millions of dollars)**[a]

	Commercial Mortgage Loans	
	1982	1981
Bank Holding Companies		
BankAmerica Corp.	$ 4,402	$ 4,643
Continental Illinois Corp.	3,145	3,043
Citicorp	2,915	2,635
First Interstate Bancorp	2,472	n.a.
Wells Fargo & Co.	1,221	1,165
Total	$14,155	$11,486
Nonbank Companies		
Prudential	$14,675	$14,928
Aetna Life & Casualty	10,662	10,219
Equitable Life Assurance	9,399	9,357
American General Corp.	1,683	1,002
Transamerica Corp.	1,423	1,329
Total	$37,842	$36,835
Bank Holding Companies and Nonbanks		
Prudential	$14,675	$14,928
Aetna Life & Casualty	10,662	10,219
Equitable Life Assurance	9,399	9,357
BankAmerica Corp.	4,402	4,643
Continental Illinois Corp.	3,145	3,043
Citicorp	2,915	2,635
First Interstate Bancorp	2,472	n.a.
American General Corp.	1,683	1,002
Transamerica Corp.	1,423	1,329
Wells Fargo & Co.	1,221	1,165

SOURCE: Annual reports and 10-K forms.

[a]Data for bank holding companies are domestic loans; data for nonbank companies are worldwide.

Table 7.15. Top 10 Lessors (in millions of dollars)[a]

	1982	1981
General Electric	$4,188	$3,019
Manufacturers Hanover Corp.	3,882	3,601
General Motors	2,910	3,209
Greyhound	2,236	2,044
Ford Motor	2,059	2,088
BankAmerica Corp.	1,925	1,883
Citicorp	1,848	2,044
Security Pacific Corp.	1,465	1,195
Continental Illinois Corp.	1,172	1,123
Control Data	1,160	1,211

SOURCE: Annual reports and 10-K forms.
[a]All data shown are worldwide leases.

Commercial banks do not dominate in lease financing either. As shown in Table 7.12, with $15.9 billion of lease receivables, the 15 industrial-based companies engaged in more lease financing than the 15 largest bank holding companies, or for that matter, more than the nation's more than 14,000 insured commercial banks. Also, as shown in Table 7.15, four out of the five top lessors in 1982 were nonbank companies. However, eight of the top 15 lessors were bank holding companies.

Nonbank companies compete with banks in other ways as well. For example, Commercial Credit Corp. (a subsidiary of Control Data), Merrill Lynch, and ITT have become approved lenders for the Small Business Administration (SBA). This has increased the competition in lending to small businesses because, prior to January 1980, SBA lending was the sole province of commercial banks.

Perhaps the most important question is not whether nonbank companies have made significant inroads into various phases of commercial lending, but rather whether they are growing more rapidly in this area than banks. Since data on all nonbank lenders are not available, review was confined to the C&I lending of nine nonbanking companies for which data were readily available—ITT, Control Data, RCA, Borg-Warner Acceptance, Chrysler Financial, Ford Motor Credit, GMAC, Gulf & Western, and General Electric Credit. In 1975, these nine companies held $14.9 billion of C&I loans or about 8.5% of that held by all insured commercial banks and 23.5% of that held by the 15 largest banks ranked by C&I loans (see Table 7.16). In 1982, these nine companies held about 7.8% of the total C&I loans held by all insured commercial banks and 22.9% of that held by the 15 largest bank C&I lenders. While these comparisons are fairly

Table 7.16.   C&I Loan Comparison: Banks versus Nonbanks

	C&I Loans of Nine Nonbank Companies[a] as a Percentage of That Held by:		
	All Insured Commercial Banks	Top 15 Banks in C&I Lending[b]	Bank Subsidiaries of 15 Largest BHCs[c]
1975	8.5	23.5	23.7
1976	9.5	28.0	28.0
1981	9.6	28.4	28.6
1982	7.8	22.9	23.1

SOURCE: *Federal Reserve Bulletin* (various issues), annual reports, and domestic Call Reports.
[a]The nine nonbanking companies include ITT, Control Data, RCA, Borg-Warner Acceptance, Chrysler Financial, Ford Motor Credit, GMAC, Gulf & Western, and General Electric Credit.
[b]Ranked by C&I loans.
[c]Ranked by total assets.

rough in the way they were constructed, they do show that banks have probably neither gained nor lost a great deal of ground in C&I lending since the mid-1970s. Based on these rather sparse data, it appears that banks have held their own in C&I lending or at least that portion that flows through financial intermediaries. Given the volatile nature of interest rates, particularly during the 1979–1982 period, and the fact that many business loans are variable rate or repriced frequently, it is not surprising that banks have maintained their relative share of this type of lending.

Deposits

Substitutes for bank deposits have been around as long as there has been a reasonably efficient secondary market for government and private securities. Treasury bills, repurchase agreements with banks or government bond dealers, and large negotiable CDs are at least partial substitutes for bank deposits, including demand deposits. A comparatively recent substitute, money market mutual funds (MMFs), grew from only a few billion dollars in assets in 1975 to over $230 billion in assets by December 1982, just prior to the introduction of the money market deposit account permitted by the Garn-St Germain Depository Institutions Act of 1982.

Table 7.17 shows the MMF assets of those nonbank companies included in this study, ranked by total MMF assets as of December 1, 1982 and June 29, 1983. These 10 companies accounted for nearly 45% of all MMF assets at both dates. To the extent that MMFs provide a reasonably at-

Table 7.17. Money Market Fund Assets of Selected
Nonbank Institutions (in billions of dollars)

	Net Money Market Fund Assets	
Company	12/1/82	6/29/83
Merrill Lynch	$ 50.4	$ 33.6
Aetna Life & Casualty[a]	18.9	14.1
Shearson/American Express	15.5	11.7
Sears/Dean Witter	11.9	8.2
E. F. Hutton	7.7	8.1
Prudential/Bache	4.3	5.2
American General Corp.	0.4	0.3
Equitable Life Assurance	0.4	0.3
Transamerica Corp.	0.3	0.3
Ford Motor	n.a.	n.a.
Total	$109.8	$ 81.8
Total assets of all MMFs	$242.5	$178.2

SOURCE: *Donoghue's Money Fund Report,* December 6, 1982 and July 4, 1983.

[a]On November 1, 1982, Aetna acquired 87% of Federated Investors, an investment management services firm. Nearly all of Aetna's money fund assets are those of Federated Investors.

tractive substitute to commercial bank deposits, then the combination of these 10 companies, at year-end 1982, ranked in deposit size about halfway between BankAmerica and Citicorp, the nation's two largest bank holding companies in deposits. Merrill Lynch, with MMF assets of $50.4 billion as of December 1, 1982, was roughly comparable in size with Manufacturers Hanover and Chase Manhattan, which had worldwide deposits of $43.8 billion and $56.9 billion, respectively, at year-end 1982.

Only two of the 10 companies listed in Table 7.17, Sears and Ford, were among the companies studied by Christophe a decade ago. Sears itself had only about $0.5 billion of MMF assets in December 1982; the remaining $11 billion of its MMF assets were obtained through the acquisition of Dean Witter Reynolds in 1981. Ford's money market account is not an MMF by the usual standards, as it is only available to certain salaried employees of Ford and investments are used to purchase obligations of Ford Motor Credit.

In order to finance the loans extended to their customers, few of the nonbank companies rely to any significant extent upon deposits as a source of funds. (Even for the 10 companies shown in Table 7.17, MMFs are not a source of funds.) For the most part, their funds are raised in the money and capital markets at competitive rates. Consequently, the profit margins of most of these nonbank companies are not, and have never been, dependent upon Regulation Q. At year-end 1982, domestic offices of insured commercial banks had $303.4 billion in savings accounts subject to a Q-ceiling of 5.25%. Alex Pollock (1982) has estimated that roughly half of the 1980 profits of 31 of the 50 largest U.S. banks could be attributed to their ability to pay below-market rates on savings accounts. While estimates of this nature may overstate the importance of Regulation Q, particularly because the ability to offer deposits at Q-ceiling rates is not independent of having federal deposit insurance, the continued phase-out of Q-ceilings should enhance the market position in lending of the non-banking-based firms.[12]

In 1982 competition for deposits took other new forms. Alliances that would have been termed unholy not long ago are commonplace now. Merrill Lynch marketed, through its nationwide network of some 475 offices, all savers certificates for Bank of America, Crocker National Bank, and two S&Ls, one in Florida and another in Washington. Merrill Lynch, the same company that once had over $50 billion of MMF assets that purportedly compete with bank and thrift deposits, also maintains a secondary market for retail CDs issued by banks and S&Ls and has acted as a broker in the placement of retail CDs issued by many banks and thrifts, thus giving them a nationwide reach. Merrill Lynch is joined by several companies who compete directly with banks in some product lines. These include Sears/Dean Witter, Shearson/American Express, and E. F. Hutton. Together these four companies operate more than 1,300 offices throughout the United States. Even in rural locations where these companies have no physical office facilities, they are no farther than a newspaper, radio, TV, or magazine advertisement and a telephone call away. Thanks to Merrill Lynch, Sears/Dean Witter, and Bache, City Federal Savings and Loan of Elizabeth, New Jersey, now competes on a nationwide basis with Bank of America for retail CDs.

The importance of the cooperative affiliations between brokers and depository institutions represents one of the most significant reductions in entry barriers into the financial services business. No longer is deposit and loan growth of a de novo bank or S&L constrained by its ability to generate deposits from its local customers. To the extent that it has profitable lending opportunities, a new depository institution can engage in liability management through the sale of brokered, insured *retail* deposits by paying above the going market rate. The availability of federal deposit insurance should make depositors virtually indifferent to the identity of the institution they deal with. It is now conceivable that a de novo bank or S&L could develop a billion-dollar deposit base within a year or two of its opening. Furthermore, under current law the ability to own one (and only one) S&L is not constrained by the line of commerce engaged in by the parent company or one of its affiliates; thus, a nonbank firm can establish a de novo S&L or buy an existing one and gain a significant presence in financial services in a very short time by selling insured retail deposits on a national scale through brokers. Given the expanded range of lending powers granted to S&Ls by the Garn-St Germain Depository Institutions Act of 1982, a de novo S&L could, in a very short time, resemble a large, long-established commercial bank, especially if it were to receive outside capital infusions from a well-heeled parent.[13]

The market for funds in denominations greater than $100,000 has been national ever since Citibank devised the negotiable certificate of deposit in 1961. The same is true for the market for large repurchase agreements. Bank-related commercial paper, also sold in a national market, amounted to some $34.5 billion at year-end 1982. What was true a decade ago for wholesale deposit markets has now become true at the retail level—the market for deposits (and their close substitutes) is national in scope.

IMPLICATIONS OF NONBANK COMPETITION

The competitive inroads of nonbanking-based firms in providing selected financial services that compete both directly and indirectly with those offered by commercial banks provide a number of policy questions to those who must formulate appropriate public economic policies and to those managers of financial institutions who must formulate appropriate strategies to maintain the profitability of their companies. By quantifying the extent of these competitive inroads, this chapter has attempted to enhance understanding of the identity and nature of this competition. Managers of financial institutions must react not only to the competition but to the current and anticipated regulatory environment as well. Accordingly, appropriate public policy, in light of the information base developed in the preceding section, is discussed first.

Commercial Banking: No Longer a Separate Line of Commerce

In 1963 the U.S. Supreme Court ruled in *Philadelphia National Bank,* an antitrust case, that commercial banking was a distinct line of commerce. In the eyes of the Court, commercial banks' ability to offer business loans and demand deposits together with a cluster of other financial services sets them apart from other depository and nondepository financial institutions. The Supreme Court still has not changed its mind regarding the line of commerce in banking even though, in 1984, the uniqueness of commercial banking is open to question.

The demand deposit monopoly once enjoyed by commercial banks disappeared long ago. In 1972, mutual savings banks in New England innovated with NOW accounts, which spread, in a number of different forms, outside the northeast. By March 1980, Congress had no choice but to codify the (retail) NOW account nationwide when it passed the Depository Institutions Deregulation and Monetary Control Act (DIDMCA). More recently, Congress has permitted what amount to small-denomination, interest-bearing checking accounts for households and businesses, thus giving legal sanction to the sweep account that technology and high interest rates had already brought into existence. These new accounts (the money market deposit account and the Super NOW account) may be offered by all depository institutions. The only distinguishing feature between these two accounts is with respect to the frequency of debits; four or more checks written against one of these accounts make it a transaction account subject to reserve requirements.[13] Also, demand deposits and their generic equivalents are offered by a wide variety of institutions. Demand deposits have become a distinctly smaller source of funds for many banks. Essentially, the *uniqueness* of demand deposits and the uniqueness of commercial banks seem to have gone the way of the V-8 engine and the vacuum-tube radio.

Business loans have never been the sole province of commercial banks. As shown in the preceding section, banks have encountered increasing pressure from numerous nonbank lenders in meeting the credit needs of business. For many types of business loans other than short-term commercial and industrial loans, banks are not the dominant lender.

The combination of demand deposit powers and commercial lending powers does not seem to confer much advantage to banks. Mutual savings banks already have had such powers (though somewhat more restricted) since DIDMCA, and S&Ls obtained similar powers in October 1982. In recent years, competition has also increased in consumer lending and in taking deposits from households and other suppliers of funds. The entry of many nonfinancial firms into various segments of banking has heightened this competition.

Therefore, the record suggests that commercial banking is no longer a distinct line of commerce. The franchises that constituted the main value of a commercial bank charter in 1963 when *Philadelphia National Bank* was decided seem to be of substantially lesser value today.

Furthermore, barriers to entry into banking—legal and economic, perceived and real—seem to have diminished over the last decade. For example, one important barrier to entry that has been reduced in recent years is the information cost advantage of incumbent firms. Technological advances have made a national data base of household and business credit histories available to all interested parties at a reasonable cost. Also, competition in financial services can no longer be measured by the role of firms domiciled in a particular geographic area. Many economic entities have access to a wide range of suppliers for deposit and credit services, some of whom are hundreds or thousands of miles away. As a result, the number of potential entrants into any geographic market is very much greater than would have been thought a few years ago. Consequently, the opportunity to exercise market power seems to be more constrained.

The implication of the findings in this study is that the line of commerce that was once called commercial banking has evolved into a new line of commerce, the provision of financial intermediation services, a line of commerce that may be either narrower or broader than that embodied in commercial banking, depending on the context. Technological advances and long-overdue statutory and regulatory changes have blurred the distinctions between financial intermediation services offered at the wholesale and retail levels; among intermediation services offered to businesses, households, and government entities; among intermediation services offered by banks, S&Ls, and finance companies; and between intermediation services offered by old-line, traditional financial institutions (like banks and S&Ls) and the services offered by the finance arms of manufacturers like General Motors, General Electric, and ITT, retailers like Sears, and diversified financial conglomerates like American Express.[15] These companies are capable of exploiting profitable opportunities to provide financial services when traditional suppliers fail to meet the public's needs at a reasonable price. In the long run the low-cost producers will survive. The regulatory barriers that protected high-cost producers have begun to be removed; it is a matter of time before a Darwinian struggle determines the new order of species in financial intermediation.

Given the above analysis, the new Justice Department guidelines seem to be anachronistic with respect to their application to the banking industry today.[16] The market for many product lines seems to be national, and the existence of hundreds to thousands of competitors suggests an absence of significant scale economies, at least with present-day technology. (Exceptions are travelers checks and credit cards.) The number of potential new entrants is fairly large and seems to be increasing. Further, as shown in Table 7.18, the geographic scope of the financial activities of many of the larger bank holding companies covers a wide area and is almost as far-reaching as the geographic coverage of many nonbank companies.

Table 7.18. Geographic Locations of Major Financial Firms That Provide Credit, 1981

		Offices	
Banking Holding Companies	States	Nonbanking	Banking[a]
Citicorp	40 and D.C.	422	25
BankAmerica Corp.	40 and D.C.	360	38
Chase Manhattan Corp.	15 and D.C.	42	4
Manufacturers Hanover Corp.	32	471	28
Continental Illinois Corp.	14	20	28
Chemical New York Corp.	23	135	6
J.P. Morgan & Co.	6	7	5
First Interstate Bancorp	13	19	24
Security Pacific Corp.	39	427	7
Bankers Trust New York Corp.	4	2	8
First Chicago Corp.	27	23	14
Wells Fargo & Co.	16	52	6
Crocker National Corp.	6	15	5
Marine Midland Banks, Inc.	5	14	n.a.
Mellon National Corp.	13 and D.C.	151	11

Other Major Creditors	States	Offices[b]	
American Express	50	1,400 Plus	
American General's Credithrift Financial	24	524	
Avco Corp	47	694	
Beneficial Corp	36	1, 468	
Control Data's Commercial Credit	50	900	
Ford Motor Credit Co.	50	200	
General Electric Credit Corp.	50	480	
General Motors Acceptance Corp.	50	310	
G&W's Associates First Capital Corp.	50	670	
Household International	47	1,260	
ITT	31	590	
Merrill Lynch	50	475	
Sears	50	1,260	

SOURCE: Annual reports and 10-K forms.

[a]These figures are exclusive of banking branches in their home states but include offices of bank subsidiaries.

[b]Avco Financial closed 539 offices in 1981; Beneficial has closed 576 offices since 1980, stopped making loans in 12 states, and sold its operations in Alabama and Tennessee; Household International closed 271 consumer finance offices in 1981; and the Associates consolidated 240 domestic offices in 1981.

Managerial Implications

The most important findings from this study are the suggestions that commercial banking may no longer be a distinct line of commerce and that the combination of new entry with the repositioning of product and geographic mix by many of the larger (and smaller) incumbent firms has changed the underlying economics of production and distribution for the other firms in the industry. These findings are also the basis for the study's most fundamental managerial implication: Bank managers must realize that they are providers of financial services. In the environment of the future, the title "banker" may be a misnomer in that it connotes the purveyance of a range of products endemic to an earlier period. The range of financial services offered by "bankers" in the future may be wider or narrower than at present, and if the array of products remains unchanged, it will be largely due to fortuitous circumstances.

With this basic concept of the banking firm in mind, bank managers will then need to analyze their firms in light of each bank's internal strengths and weaknesses (e.g., its customer base, location, and financial and human resources) as well as external factors such as regulation, competition, and the macroeconomy. From this environmental assessment, a vision of the future organization must be developed; then a strategy can be devised to attain this goal.

Of course, there will be as many strategic "visions" as there are managers, but Bleeke and Goodrich (1981), after analyzing other industries that have undergone deregulation, offer some basic ideas about the possible strategies and types of firms that could develop in the financial services industry. Indeed, evidence suggests that this categorization of strategies has already begun to emerge.

The first type of firm is the national delivery company (NDC). It offers a complete line of differentiated products through a broad distribution network that has an integrated information system and uniform customer service requirements. An NDC emphasizes attractive service versus price trade-offs and is therefore very sensitive to the need for cost controls in order to compete with low-cost firms. In its marketing campaigns an NDC stresses image. Being an NDC, however, does not guarantee profitability. They are complex to manage and they must continuously walk a fine line between price and service. Examples of NDCs in the airlines and trucking industries are Delta Airlines and Consolidated Freightways, and examples of NDCs in the financial services industry are Citicorp, BankAmerica Corp., Manufacturers Hanover Corp., Merrill Lynch, American Express, and Sears.

The second type of firm to emerge is the low-cost, no-frills producer. A firm of this type offers one low-cost product line, or maybe a few related lines, that do not require much servicing. This provider of financial services aggressively discounts prices relative to conventional suppliers, eliminates or modifies old distribution systems, and emphasizes low cost in its advertisements. Following deregulation in the airline industry, for instance, a new tier of low-cost, no-frills providers of airline services on a narrow range of routes suddenly emerged. Many of these firms, such as People Express and Midway Airlines, have been profitable during a period when many of their larger NDC competitors were unprofitable. Because of their superior profit performance, the new no-frills airlines have been successful in attracting external sources of equity and debt capital (Subcommittee on Aviation, 1983). Examples of low-cost producers of financial services are money market funds, discount brokers, and Dreyfus, who intends to become a no-frills provider of consumer credit.

The third type of firm is the specialty firm. It offers specialized, high-quality products and services targeted at a particular group of customers. These firms depend on strong customer loyalty and emphasize information and quality service. In the airlines industry, for instance, many small, specialty carriers such as Air Wisconsin have found very profitable niches in serving small towns that were abandoned by the major carriers, and in the business terminal equipment market, firms such as Rolm and Northern Telecom have concentrated on the segment of the market that is willing to pay the price for a high level of service. A current example of a specialty financial services firm is J.P. Morgan & Co., which primarily serves corporations and governments. And many small and medium-size banks, especially those that consider themselves to be "full-service" banks, will probably emerge as specialty firms.

These banks have, as their greatest competitive strength, strong customer relationships that are primarily the result of tradition. They have always provided their customers with basic financial services such as loans and savings and transactions accounts. Arthur P. Soter (1983) terms this link the "primary relationship" and asserts that the number of these relationships "will largely determine the value of a [customer] franchise." These strong customer ties, however, may deteriorate as low-cost, no-frills providers of financial services enter the markets of the "full-service" banks. Consequently, for many of these banks, the future probably holds a more limited range of products, perhaps provided over a wider geographic area. One possible exception to the reduced product range is the offering of financial services that are not booked on the balance sheet and that can be sold through franchising relationships that add to fee income with little increase in overhead cost.

Because of its strong customer relationships, a small or medium-size bank could probably survive by exploiting its customer franchise and marketing the products of other financial services providers, including low-cost producers. For example, as of November 1983, over 1,000 banks and thrifts, many of them small, offer discount brokerage services through affiliations with such low-cost producers as Fidelity Brokerage Services and Quick & Reilly.

NDCs are using this supplier distribution scheme as well. Brokers are marketing, through their national distribution networks, the retail CDs of many banks and thrifts across the country. Also, Merrill Lynch began offering the MMDAs of 12 depository institutions as an option with its Cash Management Account. And Kroger, a large grocery store chain, is experimenting with financial centers in Ohio, Alabama, and Texas as joint ventures with an insurance concern and with depository institutions in these areas.

Regardless of the strategy that each provider of financial services adopts, however, all firms will need to take account of a few things to compete successfully in a broader and less regulated financial environment. (For examples of how some firms are responding to this changed environment, see Table 7.19.)

First, the financial services industry is now "customer driven," and product, price, and service are what matters to the customers. Changes in technology and consumer habits may make location a much less important factor in the future. Managers need to analyze their present as well as potential customer base and identify what products customers use and what related products they buy from competitors. Also, managers need to understand how customers view their firms and their competitors in terms of price, quality, and services.

Firms in the financial services industry will need to be more innovative than they were in the past. This requires gaining insight into customers' needs, whether those needs be for particular products, quality services, or faster and more convenient delivery systems. Often innovation will require segmenting the market in order to identify important customer/product segments and profitable, or potentially profitable, opportunities.

Second, with the existence of competitive pricing and the narrowing of profit margins, all firms will need to be more cost conscious. Firms will, therefore, need to develop information on costs and unbundle various product lines to understand their cost components and their relative profitability and to uncover unprofitable businesses and product lines that are destined to remain so. Further, some economies of scale may be attainable due to technological advances, and some reductions in overhead costs

Table 7.19.   Examples of How Some Firms Are Responding to the Changed Environment in the Financial Services Industry

1. Innovation

Products and Services:

In June 1981, Prudential Insurance Company introduced a stock fund that is available to the public and is designed to provide tax advantages for upper-income investors. It is distributed by Bache.

In March 1980, Merrill Lynch & Co. tested its Equity Access Account, which gives homeowners access to the equity in their homes through checks and debit cards. Now many banks, brokers, and consumer finance companies are offering such home equity loans.

First Interstate Bancorp, BankAmerica Corp., and Citicorp plan to buy state-chartered banks in South Dakota in order to enter the insurance business.

Century 21, a nationwide real estate brokerage firm, plans to establish subsidiaries for mortgage brokerage, property insurance, and the sale of real estate limited partnerships.

Security Pacific National Bank of Los Angeles plans a new fund, the Security Pacific Futures Fund.

Delivery Systems:

In July 1982, Sears opened financial service centers in eight stores and as of November 1983 operated 108 such financial centers. These centers offer insurance, real estate, and brokerage services, and in California, they offer Allstate Savings and Loan's products as well.

The Kroger Company is experimenting with financial centers in Ohio, Alabama, and Texas. These centers offer consumer banking and insurance products to customers at Kroger grocery stores.

First Nationwide Savings contracted with J. C. Penney to open and operate financial service centers that offer a full range of products at five Penney stores in Northern California.

Banc One leases space to agents of Nationwide Insurance in three Columbus, Ohio branches. The agents sell insurance products, mutual funds, and annuities.

2. Reduction in Costs

Sun Banks of Florida in Orlando acquired Flagship Banks of Miami and saved on data processing and back office operations through consolidation.

Westinghouse Credit Corporation restructured its Financial Service group so that representatives are closer to their customers. This helped Westinghouse Credit decrease its ratio of direct expenses to net receivables.

Citing insufficient business volume, Bank of Boston is phasing out the data processing service it provides to more than 100 correspondent banks.

Table 7.19. *(Continued)*

Bankers Trust is phasing out its less profitable retail operations to concentrate on the wholesale market.

3. Cross-Selling

In June 1981, Mutual Benefit Life Insurance Co. expanded into securities brokerage through Mutual Benefit Financial Co., an in-house broker–dealer. Mutual Benefit Life sells its new service through its 1,600 insurance agents nationwide.

American Express's insurance company, Fireman's Fund, offers an insurance and annuity plan through Shearson/American Express and Shearson/American Express offers insured money market deposit accounts through its branch system. Shearson directs the deposit to its affiliate, the Boston Safe Deposit and Trust Company.

Prudential-Bache Securities plans to begin offering home mortgage loans as well as MMDAs and retail CDs by mail to its brokerage customers through the securities firm's Georgia bank.

Travelers Corp. plans to offer a cash management service initially to its 10,000 independent insurance agents and later to business clients as well.

4. Legislative and Regulatory Responses

Twenty states have passed either full powers, reciprocal, emergency, or limited-purpose interstate banking legislation as of Mid 1984.

A bill was introduced in Congress to allow interstate banking in New England among states that permit the activity and to direct federal regulators to look favorably on its development.

In October 1982, Congress passed the Garn-St Germain Depository Institutions Act of 1982, which allows depository institutions, beginning in December 1982, to offer ceiling-free deposits directly competitive with money market mutual funds.

In April 1983, the Comptroller of the Currency declared a moratorium on bank charters to nonbanks, and the chairman of the Federal Reserve Board recommended a moratorium on bank–nonbank combinations.

SOURCE: Company annual report, various issues of *American Banker,* and other general business periodicals.

may now be possible because of the increased acceptance of automated teller machines and banking by phone and by mail.

Third, cross-selling is very important; a checking account customer is a potential customer for brokerage services, credit cards, loans, savings accounts, and so on. Cross-selling is especially important for NDCs and specialty firms because it not only increases business volume but also strengthens customer ties. There is a benefit to the consolidation of accounts, as witnessed by the success of asset management accounts. Customers purchasing all their financial services from one supplier are probably more reluctant to switch to a competitor than are customers having only one account with a single firm. As already mentioned, however, many small, regional suppliers may have to market the products of other suppliers in order to be able to offer their customers a complete line of products.

Fourth, in planning an appropriate response to inroads made by new and existing competitors, managers of financial institutions must be mindful of possible legislative and regulatory response that oftentimes in the not-so-distant past amounted to preservation of the status quo. Since the passage of DIDMCA, however, the regulatory response has become increasingly accommodative to experimentation.

In light of this, bank management must recognize that the regulatory rules have become increasingly flexible and the limits of the rules should constantly be tested. The present mood seems to be that all competitors should be given an opportunity to experiment and to succeed or fail, provided that failures are small, easily contained, and will not give rise to systemic failure. Such experiments or pilots with respect to new activities, new products, or new geographic markets (or some combination thereof) are likely to meet the above test if they are small relative to the size of the experimenting firm and its human and financial capital base. Under these circumstances, experiments that do not jeopardize the regulated firms are unlikely to cause systemic risk to the financial system and are, in turn, unlikely to encounter a negative regulatory or legislative response.

And finally, while drastic alterations of strategy may not be needed because a series of small adjustments have already been made in response to the changing competitive and regulatory environments, all banks will find it necessary continually to adjust their tactics and strategies in the future. The elimination of Regulation Q and the introduction of MMDA and Super NOW accounts mean that funding sources are changing for all depository institutions. The entry of nonbanks, many of whom already have a national distribution system, into the credit-supplying business (and to a lesser extent, the ''deposit'' business) will necessitate some repositioning of focus for all banks, large and small. And with nondeposit-based firms seeking a greater proportion of the financial services business, some incumbents must shrink in relative size by spinning off unprofitable and marginally profitable products.

To summarize, there exists no single strategy that is guaranteed to provide success in dealing with competition from nonbanking-based providers of financial services and/or other changes simultaneously taking place. It is probably easier to point out strategies that are unlikely to succeed because they were originally formulated for an external environment that has changed significantly than it is to identify a group of strategies that have a high likelihood for success irrespective of who tries to follow them.[17] But what a financial services manager can learn from these failed strategies is that the changed external environment—the formidable presence of nonbank competition and a somewhat more favorable regulatory environment—should at least be the starting point.

SUMMARY AND CONCLUSIONS

For many years, commercial banks have competed in some product lines with other depository institutions such as S&Ls, mutual savings banks, and credit unions. Recently, commercial banks have increasingly found themselves faced with heightened competition from manufacturers, retailers, insurance companies, and diversified financial concerns. Although many of these new competitors have been encroaching on banks' turf for nearly a decade, they have continually expanded their role in financial services, and they have been joined by many other companies. As a result, by 1982, these nonbank (even nonfinancial) firms have made significant inroads into banks' traditional lines of business.

Nonbanking-based firms have made remarkable gains in consumer lending, although banks have done quite well in the credit card sector. In 1982, the top 10 nonbank firms held twice the consumer installment receivables as those held by the top 10 bank holding companies in this area of lending. And in consumer installment lending, market shares have been very fluid, with the share of *new* loans made by any single supplier changing drastically with changes in the economy.

In auto lending, market shares have also been quite variable. Commercial banks are still the leading auto lender despite the significant loss of market share to the auto captive finance companies over the past five years. This shift is attributable to a decrease in car sales, liberalized bankruptcy laws, soaring cost of funds, and interest rate volatility. Although these factors motivated the captive finance companies of the auto manufacturers to offer below-market financing rates in an attempt to boost sluggish sales, these finance companies seem to have found auto lending to be profitable. They may have become the low-cost producers in this lending area.

While commercial banks have lost some market share in consumer lending, banks are still the primary provider of short-term loans to businesses. In long-term lending, however, commercial banks are not the leading institutional lender. Commercial mortgage lending is dominated by insurance companies, and leasing is dominated by manufacturing and leasing firms.

In the area of deposit taking, changes have taken place as well. In 1973, money market mutual funds emerged as a close substitute for bank deposits, and while not a big threat to banks when interest rates were relatively low, money market funds became very successful when rates rose, growing from only a few billion dollars in "deposits" in 1975 to over $230 billion by December 1982 when they reached their peak. Also, cooperative affiliations between brokers and depository institutions have developed. These affiliations could conceivably allow a de novo bank or S&L to develop a billion-dollar deposit base within a year or two of its opening.

These findings lead to one very important conclusion: Commercial banking may no longer be a distinct line of commerce. The significant presence of many nonbank firms in consumer lending, business lending, and deposit taking as well as the ability of S&Ls and mutual savings banks to offer a wide range of consumer and business loans have eroded the uniqueness of commercial banking. Thus, by 1984, commercial banking has evolved into a new line of commerce, the provision of financial intermediation services.

NOTES

1. In addition, Sears had 2,388 catalog outlets in the United States at year-end 1982.

2. More recently, J.C. Penney began offering retail financial services on an experimental basis in five of its stores in Northern California. This pilot program began in December 1982 and was conducted jointly with First Nationwide Savings Association, a subsidiary of National Steel.

3. In 1920, retailers and oil companies held almost four-fifths of consumer installment credit. At that time banks held just over 3%. By 1950, banks had become the largest consumer installment lender with just under 40% of the loans outstanding, well ahead of finance companies, which held about one-fourth and retailers and oil companies, which held one-fifth of consumer installment loans. For more detail, see Peterson (1983), Table 2.

4. Since the Loomis article appeared, Citicorp has acquired S&Ls in California, Florida, and Illinois.

5. More than 40 companies were actually analyzed, but accounting data concerning their financial activities were available on only 32 of them. Among the other firms studied were very recent entrants into financial services (Parker Pen, McMahan Valley Stores, and Krogers), potential competitors of commercial banks (Bradford National Corp., TRW, and Dun & Bradstreet), and two insurance companies that recently have expanded their range of financial services (John Hancock and Travelers).

6. Most of the financial activities of the 10 companies shown in Table 7.2 are carried on domestically; many of the larger bank holding companies, on the other hand, derive a significant portion of their business from foreign activities, although the portion of profits from retail foreign business is fairly small. Thus, the profits of nonbanking-based companies and those of the larger bank holding companies are difficult to compare directly.

7. The captive auto finance companies have a different profit orientation than their competitors. The use of a captive finance company gives auto manufacturers an added degree of pricing and marketing freedom not enjoyed by the competition. Indeed a captive finance company could, in theory, lose money on every loan it makes provided its parent made up for such losses in added sales volume at higher average prices.

8. No evidence is publicly available on the duration matching techniques utilized by GMAC or Ford Motor Credit. The weighted-average maturities of their assets and liabilities were computed for the years 1978–1982. In general, both companies tended to exhibit a weighted-average debt maturity between four and five years and a weighted-average receivables maturity of about two years, leaving a maturity (not a duration) mismatch of at least two years. It could be argued that portfolio immunization should take place for the consolidated company rather than an individual subsidiary. In any event, GMAC and Ford Motor Credit may not have taken advantage of their ability to immunize their portfolios. Their continued profitability throughout this period suggests that they were not impacted adversely by the interest rate movements that occurred.

9. The data are distorted somewhat by the fact that finance company subsidiaries of bank holding companies are included with finance companies. For example, in 1981, Citicorp held $9.6 billion of consumer installment loans, $2.2 billion or 23% of which were attributable to Citibank and Citibank (New York State); BankAmerica held $9.7 billion of consumer installment loans, $6.8 billion or 78% of which were attributable to Bank of America; and Mellon National Corp. held $0.9 billion of such loans, $.83 billion or 87% of which were attributable to Mellon Bank. Further complicating interpretation of the data is the tendency of some banks to sell consumer loans to their finance company affiliate, and vice versa. However, most bank holding companies reported no inter-affiliate transfers of assets in any year from 1976 to 1980 (Rose and Talley, 1983).

10. In this context it should be noted that the post-1978 period, in particular the three-year period from October 6, 1979 to October 1982, has provided an unusual testing ground. One desirable characteristic of a financial firm is that it be able to survive large economic shocks—be they interest rate or regulatory changes or the combined impact of the two. The least diversified firms, S&Ls, have not done well in this regard. More diversified firms, like banks, auto captive finance companies, and many diversified finance companies, have done somewhat better. Diversification of product lines is neither a necessary nor a sufficient condition for survival. Rosenblum (1981) has shown that with no expansion of product lines, even S&Ls could have taken steps to reduce the impact of interest rate changes on their net worth. Kane (1982) has shown how improperly priced FSLIC insurance induced S&Ls not to immunize themselves against interest rate risk. Eisenmenger has argued that the real risk is political risk of unpredictable, capricious changes in the legislative and regulatory environment (1981). It appears that firms with little opportunity to diversify out of unprofitable product lines have experienced greater difficulty over the last few years than those who are less constrained. Many of the manufacturers seem to have benefited from their presence in financial services and from their competition with banks and other lenders.

11. Some of the assessments of relative performance of Visa, Sears, and other credit cards may be overdrawn. Over the period of analysis, one could not use a Visa card in Sears nor could a Sears card have been used outside a Sears store. What is being observed is a derived demand for credit based on the relative demand for goods sold by Sears versus goods sold by merchants or other outlets that accepted Visa or MasterCard. Similarly, the American Express green card is perceived by many of its users as a "travel and entertainment" card rather than a credit card since the full amount of the purchase is due and payable when the customer receives his or her bill from American Express.

12. It could be argued that Regulation Q has hampered the ability of banks to raise funds and that removal of Q-ceilings will enhance their ability to compete for funds. However, all 15 of the bank holding companies shown in Table 7.5 have long had access to non-deposit funding sources not subject to Q-ceilings. It would seem that, at least for the larger bank holding companies, elimination of Q-ceilings would increase the cost of funds but not the access to funds.

    Offsetting this advantage to some extent is the probability that the phase-out of Q-ceilings will improve the ability of banks to immunize themselves against the earnings impacts of changes in interest rates. As shown in Rosenblum (1981), by limiting the menu of maturities and interest rates that can be paid on time and savings accounts, Regulation Q has been an important barrier to immunization by banks and S&Ls and has raised tremendously the interest rate risk exposure of these depository institutions over the last few years.

13. The FDIC and FSLIC, concerned with the safety and soundness implications of un-limited brokering activity, took actions to curtail deposit brokering in early 1984.

14. As of March 1983, noncorporate businesses as well as individuals are eligible to have money market deposit accounts; however, only individuals, certain nonprofit corpo-rations, and governmental units are eligible to have Super NOW accounts.

15. Commercial banking and investment banking are still, for the most part, separated by some Glass-Steagall provisions, but even these separations are breaking down as co-operative agency relationships eliminate the need for direct participation in underwriting.

16. For a brief description of the guidelines as applied to commercial banking, see Fortier and DiClemente (1983).

17. The literature on this subject matter is extensive. For a detailed analysis of old strategies that have outlived their usefulness, see Kramer (1983). Vojta (1983) provides a list of nine criteria or tactics that will be followed by the financial institution survivors. Horvitz (1982) dissects the many assumptions and assertions regarding the benefits of a number of strategies. The evolution of the public policy response is traced in Kaufman, Mote, and Rosenblum (1983). Many other articles (too numerous to mention) have been written on general strategy formulation and on the strategies followed by specific financial services companies.

REFERENCES

Benston, George. "Accounting Numbers and Economic Values." *Antitrust Bulletin*, Spring 1982, pp. 161–215.

Bleeke, Joel, and Goodrich, James. *Capitalizing on Opportunities Created by Deregulation of the Banking Industry*. Chicago: McKinsey & Company, Inc., September 1981.

Christophe, Cleveland A. *Competition in Financial Services*. New York: First National City Corporation, 1974.

Eisemann, Peter C. "Empirical Evidence on Sources of Business Finance." In *The Future of the Financial Services Industry*, conference proceedings, Federal Reserve Bank of Atlanta, June 1981, pp. 77–84.

Eisenmenger, Robert W. "The Experience of Canadian Thrift Institutions." In *The Future of the Thrift Industry*, Federal Reserve Bank of Boston, Conference Series No. 24, 1981, pp. 112–139.

Ford, William F. "Banking's New Competition: Myths and Realities." *Economic Review*, Federal Reserve Bank of Atlanta, January 1982, pp. 4–11.

Fortier, Diana A., and Di Clemente, John. "Justice's Merger Guidelines: Implications for 7th District Banking." *Economic Perspectives*, Federal Reserve Bank of Chicago, September/October 1983, pp. 14–23.

Horvitz, Paul M. "Deregulation and Financial Products and Services." *American Banker*, September 24, 1982, pp. 4–16.

Kane, Edward J. "S&Ls and Interest Rate Re-Regulation: The FSLIC as an In-Place Bailout Program." In *Proceedings of a Conference on Bank Structure and Competition*, Federal Reserve Bank of Chicago, 1982, pp. 283–308.

Kaufman, George G., Mote, Larry R., and Rosenblum, Harvey. "The Future of Commercial Banks in the Financial Services Industry." In George J. Benston (Ed.), *Financial Services: The Changing Institutions and Government Policy*. Englewood Cliffs, N.J.: Prentice-Hall, 1983.

Kramer, Orin. "Winning Strategies for Interstate Banking." *Fortune*, September 19, 1983, pp. 104–120.

Loomis, Carol J. "The Fight for Financial Turf." *Fortune*, December 28, 1981, pp. 54–65.

Luckett, Charles. "Recent Developments in the Mortgage and Consumer Credit Markets." *Federal Reserve Bulletin*, May 1982, pp. 281–290.

Peterson, Richard L. "Consumer Finance." In George J. Benston (Ed.), *Financial Services: The Changing Institutions and Government Policy*. Englewood Cliffs, N.J.: Prentice-Hall, 1983.

Pollock, Alex J. "The Future of Banking: A National Market and Its Implications." In *Proceedings of a Conference on Bank Structure and Competition*, Federal Reserve Bank of Chicago, 1982, pp. 31–36.

Rose, John T., and Talley, Samuel H. "Financial Transactions within Bank Holding Companies." *Staff Studies*, Board of Governors of the Federal Reserve System, May 1983, p. 8.

Rosenblum, Harvey. "Liability Strategies for Minimizing Interest Rate Risk." In *Managing Interest Rate Risk in the Thrift Industry*, Federal Home Loan Bank of San Francisco, proceedings of the Seventh Annual Conference, 1982, pp. 157–180.

Rosenblum, Harvey, and Siegel, Diane. *Competition in Financial Services: The Impact of Nonbank Entry*, Staff Study 83-1, Federal Reserve Bank of Chicago, May 1983.

Rosenblum, Harvey, and Strongin, Steven. "Interest Rate Volatility in Historical Perspective." *Economic Perspectives*, Federal Reserve Bank of Chicago, January/February 1983.

Soter, Arthur P. "Six Factors Will Play a Large Role in Banks' Survival." *American Banker*, August 25, 1983, pp. 4, 6, 8.

Subcommittee on Aviation, U.S. Congress House of Representatives. *Review of Airline Deregulation and Sunset of the Civil Aeronautics Board,* Hearing, 98 Cong. 1 Sess. Washington, D.C.: U.S. Government Printing Office, 1983.

United States v. Philadelphia National Bank, et al., 374 U.S. 321, 10 L ed 2d 915 (1963).

Vojta, George J. "New Competition and Its Implications for Banking." *The Magazine of Bank Administration,* July 1983, pp. 34–44.

Watro, Paul R. "Financial Services and Small Businesses." *Economic Commentary,* Federal Reserve Bank of Cleveland, January 11, 1982.

Table 1. Estimated Gross Finance Receivables and Selected Liabilities as of December 31, 1982:[a] Industrial-/Communication-/Transportation-Based Companies (in millions of dollars)

	General Motors Acceptance Corp.	Ford Motor Credit Company	General Electric Credit Corp.	CIT Financial Corp. (RCA)	Associates[b] First Capital (Gulf & Western)	FN Financial Corp. of California (National Steel)
Consumer Loans						
Mortgage	—	—	1,027	1,074	1,598	5,955
Installment, revolving credit	35,623	10,542	4,459	1,534	1,535	60
Total	35,623	10,542	5,486	2,608	3,133	6,015
Commercial Loans						
Commercial and industrial	9,670	4,890	2,386	4,054	2,667	—
Mortgage	—	102	1,059	—	—	—
Total	9,670	4,992	3,445	4,054	2,667	—
Loans to governments and financial institutions	—	—	—	—	—	—
Other loans	—	33	—	—	—	—
Lease financing	2,910	2,059	4,188	652	257	—
Total finance receivables	48,203	17,626	13,119	7,314	6,057	6,015
Selected Liabilities						
Deposits	—	—	—	—	—	4,458
Short-term debt	22,180	7,111	5,670	1,950	2,052	637
Long-term debt	17,876	5,963	3,239	2,360	2,496	1,691
After-Tax Net Income						
Finance subsidiary	688	229	205	129	66	7
Consolidated parent	963	(658)	1,817	223	169	(463)

(continued)

Table 1. *(Continued)*

	ITT Financial Corp.	Combined Insurance[c] and Finance Subsidiaries of ITT	Commercial[d] Credit Co. (Control Data)	Chrysler Financial Corp.	Borg-Warner Acceptance Corp.
Consumer Loans					
Mortgage	733	733	716	—	224
Installment, revolving credit	1,368	1,175	1,094	1,666	204
Total	2,101	1,908	1,810	1,666	428
Commercial Loans					
Commercial and industrial	2,689	1,769	1,301	1,419	1,573
Mortgage	193	193	—	—	—
Total	2,882	1,962	1,301	1,419	1,573
Loans to governments and financial institutions	—	—	—	—	—
Other loans	—	—	—	—	171
Lease financing	218	218	1,160	292	651
Total finance receivables	5,201	4,008	4,271	3,377	2,823
Selected Liabilities					
Deposits	—	38	749	—	—
Short-term debt	2,159	1,394	1,387	200	1,112
Long-term debt	1,707	1,382	1,382	2,376	874
After-Tax Net Income					
Finance subsidiary	350	72	46	52[e]	37
Consolidated parent	703	703	155	170	167

	Westinghouse Credit Corp.	Greyhound Financial Group Subsidiaries	IBM Credit Corp.	IBM Corp.	Diamond Financial Holdings (Dana Corp.)	Armco Financial Services
Consumer Loans						
Mortgage	—	—	—	—	557	—
Installment, revolving credit	63	—	—	—	23	—
Total	63	—	—	—	580	—
Commercial Loans						
Commercial and industrial	1,635	—	1,186	5,192	—	22
Mortgage	599	—	—	—	83	—
Total	2,234	—	1,186	5,192	83	22
Loans to governments and financial institutions	—	—	—	—	—	—
Other loans	—	—	—	—	31	—
Lease financing	323	2,236	82	—	65	532
Total finance receivables	2,620	2,236	1,268	5,192	759	554

(continued)

Table 1. *(Continued)*

	Westinghouse Credit Corp.	Greyhound Financial Group Subsidiaries	IBM Credit Corp.	IBM Corp.	Diamond Financial Holdings (Dana Corp.)	Armco Financial Services
Selected Liabilities						
Deposits	—	—	—	—	737	—
Short-term debt	938	150	352	529	50	464
Long-term debt	1,153	1,139	508	2,851	95	245
After-Tax Net Income						
Finance subsidiary	51	48	31	—	2	(5)
Consolidated parent	449	103	4,409	4,409	52	(345)

SOURCE: Company annual reports and 10-K forms.

[a]Commercial and industrial loans include construction lending; commercial mortgages exclude those purchased in the secondary markets; other loans include fedeal funds sold and securities purchased under resale agreements; and short-term debt includes the current portion of long-term borrowings.

[b]As of 7/31/82.

[c]Figures stated net of unearned income.

[d]International banking subsidiaries are not consolidated. As of December 31, 1982 they had net receivables of $429 million and deposits of $384 million.

[e]Includes an income support payment from Chrysler of $32 million.

Table 2. Estimated Gross Finance Receivables and Selected Liabilities as of December 31, 1982: Diversified Finance Companies (in millions of dollars)

	American[a] Express	Beneficial Corp.[b] & Unconsolidated Subsidiaries	Merrill[c] Lynch	Walter E.[d] Heller International	Household[e] International
Consumer Loans					
Mortgage	583	2,180	412	104	1,824
Installment, revolving credit	5,608	2,058	4,778	176	1,804
Total	6,191	4,238	5,190	280	3,628
Commercial Loans					
Commercial and industrial	2,057	16	615	3,302	650
Mortgage	213	96	n.a.	891	—
Total	2,270	112	615	4,193	650
Loans to governments and financial institutions	1,988	—	—	654	—
Other loans	512	—	5,095	—	—
Lease financing	72	245	—	329	355
Total finance receivables	11,033	4,595	10,900	5,456	4,633
Selected Liabilities					
Deposits	6,810	224	1,005	2,280	309
Short-term debt	3,757	705	10,225	2,500	1,403
Long-term debt	1,746	3,318	757	765	3,411
After-Tax Net Income					
Finance subsidiary	—				—
Consolidated parent	581	(31)	309	16	125

(continued)

Table 2. *(Continued)*

	E.F. Hutton Group	Transamerica Corp.	Avco[f] Financial Services	Baldwin-United	Lowes Corp.
Consumer Loans					
Mortgage	—	1,032	1,188	1,196	51
Installment, revolving credit	1,166	807	1,133	73	936
Total	1,166	1,839	2,321	1,269	987
Commercial Loans					
Commercial and industrial	144	905	220	531	—
Mortgage	—	1,423	256	461	459
Total	144	2,328	476	992	459

	E.F. Hutton Group	Transamerica Corp.	Avco[f] Financial Services	Baldwin-United	Lowes Corp.
Loans to governments and financial institutions	—	—	—	—	—
Other loans	2,674	—	—	—	—
Lease financing	534	n.a.	244	67	—
Total finance receivables	4,518	4,167	3,041	2,328	1,446
Selected Liabilities					
Deposits	—	—	86	1,153	—
Short-term debt	2,995	529	536	1,429	185
Long-term debt	352	2,185	1,947	637	715
After-Tax Net Income					
Finance subsidiary	—	—	80	—	90
Consolidated parent	81	186	72	66	216

SOURCE: Company annual reports and 10-K forms.

[a]American Express International Banking Corp. is consolidated. Its total loans were $4,474 million.

[b]Figures stated net of unearned income.

[c]Two international merchant banking subsidiaries are consolidated.

[d]American National Bank and Trust Co. of Chicago is consolidated. Its total loans outstanding were $1,519 million at year-end 1982.

[e]Valley National Bank is consolidated.

[f]As of 11/30/82.

Table 3. Estimated Gross Finance Receivables and Selected Liabilities as of December 31, 1982: Insurance-Based Companies (in millions of dollars)

	Prudential	Bache Group	PruCapital	Prudential + Bache Group + PruCapital	Equitable Life Assurance
Consumer Loans					
Mortgage	—	—	—	—	1,696
Installment, revolving credit	4,536	1,351	—	5,887	2,911
Total	4,536	1,351	—	5,887	4,607
Commercial Loans					
Commercial and industrial	—	—	799	799	—
Mortgage	14,675	—	—	14,675	9,399
Total	14,675	—	799	15,474	9,399
Loans to governments and financial institutions	—	—	—	—	—
Other loans	—	2,747	—	2,747	—
Lease financing	—	—	737	737	—
Total finance receivables	19,211	4,098	1,536	24,845	14,006
Selected Liabilities					
Deposits	—	—	—	—	—
Short-term debt	—	2,991	1,420	4,411	—
Long-term debt	135	50	185	—	414
After-Tax Net Income					
Finance subsidiary	—	(30)	25	(5)	—
Consolidated parent	2,014[a]			2,014[a]	584[a]

	Aetna Life & Casualty	American General Corp.	Credithrift Financial Inc.	American General + Credithrift Financial
Consumer Loans				
Mortgage	—	—	481	481
Installment, revolving credit	548	678	615	1,293
Total	548	678	1,096	1,774
Commercial Loans				
Commercial and industrial	28	—	—	—
Mortgage	10,662	1,683	—	1,683
Total	10,690	1,683	—	1,683
Loans to governments and financial institutions	—	—	—	—
Other loans	—	—	—	—
Lease financing	—	—	—	—
Total finance receivables	11,238	2,361	1,096	3,457
Selected Liabilities				
Deposits	—	—	265	265
Short-term debt	3	173	46	219
Long-term debt	414	774	661	1,435
After-Tax Net Income				
Finance subsidiary	—	—	24	24
Consolidated parent	427	163	163	163

(continued)

Table 4. Estimated Gross Finance Receivables and Seleted Liabilities as of December 31, 1982: Retail-Based Companies (in millions of dollars)

	Sears	Montgomery Ward Credit	J.C. Penney[a] Financial	J.C. Penney Financial[a] and J.C. Penney Co. Combined
Consumer Loans				
Mortgage	3,103	—	—	—
Installment, revolving credit	10,109	3,291	2,015	3,450
Total	13,212	3,291	2,015	3,450
Commercial Loans				
Commercial and industrial	603	—	2	—
Mortgage	—	—	—	—
Total	603	—	2	—
Loans to governments and financial institutions	—	—	—	—
Other loans	1,005	—	—	—
Lease financing	—	—	—	—
Total finance receivables	14,820	3,291	2,017	3,450
Selected Liabilities				
Deposits	2,461	—	—	—
Short-term debt	4,153	1,286	730	730
Long-term debt	6,488	1,118	718	2,102
After-Tax Net Income				
Finance subsidiary	—	85	50	—
Consolidated parent	861	(75)[b]	392	392

SOURCE: Company annual reports and 10-K forms.

[a]As of 1/29/83.

Table 5. Estimated Gross Finance Receivables and Selected Liabilities as of December 31, 1982: Banking Holding Companies (in millions of dollars)

	Citicorp		BankAmerica Corp.ᵃ		Chase Manhattan Corp.		Manufacturers Hanover Corp.	
	Worldwide	Domestic	Worldwide	Domestic	Worldwide	Domestic	Worldwide	Domestic
Consumer Loans								
Mortgage	10,996	9,261	10,901	10,901	1,237	1,237	1,195	1,195
Installment, revolving credit	16,302	11,213	10,484	9,506	3,745	3,085	2,326	2,285
Total	27,298	20,474	21,385	20,407	4,982	4,322	3,521	3,480
Commercial Loans								
Commercial and industrial	48,228	18,627	36,273	17,580	35,195	11,522	24,005	12,961
Mortgage	5,660	2,915	5,158	4,402	2,237	842	1,245	880
Total	53,888	21,542	41,431	21,982	37,432	12,364	25,250	13,841
Loan to governments and financial institutions	9,914	2,623	8,738	1,256	10,967	2,911	13,457	3,722
Other loans	3,292	3,292	6,962	6,784	2,787	1,981	1,778	1,778
Lease financingᵇ	1,848	1,848	1,925	1,925	237	237	3,882	3,882
Total finance receivables	96,240	49,779	80,441	52,354	56,405	21,815	47,888	26,703
Selected Liabilities								
Deposits	76,538		94,342		56,858		43,825	
Short-term debt	25,265		9,064		12,739		9,998	
Long-term debt	7,768		2,105		1,046		1,588	
After-Tax Net Income								
Finance subsidiary	—		—		—		—	
Consolidated parent	723		447		307		295	

(*continued*)

Table 5. *(Continued)*

	Continental Illinois Corp.		Chemical New York Corp.		J.P. Morgan & Company		First Interstate Bancorp	
	Worldwide	Domestic	Worldwide	Domestic	Worldwide	Domestic	Worldwide	Domestic
Consumer Loans								
Mortgage	866	866	1,068	1,068	73	73	2,311	2,311
Installment, revolving credit	1,344	1,337	2,152	2,149	198	141	4,591	4,591
Total	2,210	2,203	3,220	3,217	271	214	6,902	6,902
Commercial Loans								
Commercial and industrial	21,694	13,715	20,806	14,605	18,828	6,529	10,733	9,259
Mortgage	3,268	3,145	848	745	774	359	2,482	2,472
Total	24,962	16,860	21,654	15,350	19,602	6,888	13,215	11,731
Loan to governments and financial institutions	4,614	2,222	5,298	213	7,844	2,049	3,171	1,784
Other loans	1,518	1,202	1,119	928	3,418	3,351	2,126	2,121
Lease financing[b]	1,172	1,172	1,148	1,148	328	328	999	999
Total finance receivables	34,476	23,659	32,439	20,856	31,463	12,830	26,413	23,537
Selected Liabilities								
Deposits	28,175		27,998		37,910		30,542	
Short-term debt	9,949		13,232		11,237		5,098	
Long-term debt	1,272		601		683		898	
After-Tax Net Income								
Finance subsidiary	—		—		—		—	
Consolidated parent	78		241		394		221	

	Security Pacific Corp.		Bankers Trust New York Corp.		First Chicago Corp.		Wells Fargo & Co.	
	Worldwide	Domestic	Worldwide	Domestic	Worldwide	Domestic	Worldwide	Domestic
Consumer Loans								
Mortgage	4,912	4,912	294	294	820	820	4,319	4,319
Installment, revolving credit	4,389	4,354	187	181	1,936	1,900	1,724	1,724
Total	9,301	9,266	481	475	2,756	2,720	6,043	6,043
Commercial Loans								
Commercial and Industrial	12,052	10,051	13,073	8,766	11,476	7,694	8,422	7,436
Mortgage	905	647	565	536	863	641	1,221	1,211
Total	12,957	10,698	13,638	9,302	12,339	8,335	9,643	8,647
Loan to governments and financial institutions	3,226	624	5,986	1,159	5,214	1,638	2,302	513
Other loans	976	972	3,478	3,304	2,374	2,300	880	880
Lease financing[b]	1,465	1,465	296	296	362	362	920	920
Total finance receivables	27,925	23,025	23,879	14,536	23,045	15,355	19,788	17,003
Selected Liabilities								
Deposits	25,848		24,493		27,419		18,180	
Short-tert debt	4,742		10,489		3,988		2,698	
Long-term debt	1,241		440		311		1,267	
After-Tax Net Income								
Finance subsidiary	—		—		—		—	
Consolidated parent	234		239		137		139	

(continued)

Table 5. *(Continued)*

	Crocker National Corp.		Marine Midland Banks, Inc.		Mellon National Corp.ᵃ		Total Top 15 Bank Holding Companies	
	Worldwide	Domestic	Worldwide	Domestic	Worldwide	Domestic	Worldwide	Domestic
Consumer Loans								
Mortgage	3,384	3,384	653	653	1,011	1,011	44,040	42,305
Installment, revolving credit	1,095	1,095	2,143	2,127	907	907	53,523	46,595
Total	4,479	4,479	2,796	2,780	1,918	1,918	97,563	88,900
Commercial Loans								
Commercial and industrial	8,758	7,557	5,582	4,004	6,709	5,221	281,834	155,527
Mortgage	492	489	389	365	424	420	26,531	20,069
Total	9,250	8,046	5,971	4,369	7,133	5,641	308,365	175,596
Loan to governments and financial institutions	2,499	—	3,682	1,281	1,902	768	88,814	22,763
Other loans	132	129	255	190	917	858	32,012	30,070
Lease financingᵇ	206	206	80	80	198	198	15,066	15,066
Total finance receivables	16,566	12,860	12,784	8,700	12,068	9,383	541,820	332,395
Selected Liabilities								
Deposits	18,195		15,057		12,328		537,708	
Short-term debt	3,425		2,084		4,629		128,637	
Long-term debt	210		475		493		20,398	
After-Tax Net Income								
Finance subsidiary	—		—		—		—	
Consolidated parent	72		87		134		3,748	

SOURCE: Company annual reports and 10-K forms.

ᵃFigures stated net of unearned income.

ᵇTotal lease finance receivables are included under domestic receivables because of the difficulties involved in separating domestic from international

266

8 The Internationalization of U.S. Banking

Sydney J. Key

The international activities of U.S. banks have grown dramatically over the past two decades. During the past two years, however, the growth of these activities has slackened, partly as a result of the debt crisis in a number of developing countries and the slowdown in economic activity in the major industrial countries in 1982 and 1983. These developments, combined with the establishment of new capital adequacy guidelines by U.S. regulatory authorities, have caused U.S. banks to place more emphasis on their return on assets than on expansion of their balance sheets. In addition, partly because of concern about their international exposure, U.S. banks are exercising greater caution with regard to international expansion. Nevertheless, international activities will undoubtedly continue to play an important role in the activities of U.S. banks. One difference may be that a larger proportion of these activities will be conducted at offices in the United States, in part because of the ongoing deregulation of banking in the United States. This deregulation already has included the decontrol of interest rates and the introduction of international banking facilities.

The purpose of this chapter is to provide an overview of the international activities of U.S.-chartered banks. These activities include transactions

The author wishes to thank Richard A. Crowley, Frederick R. Dahl, Edward J. Green, James V. Houpt, Rodney H. Mills, Kathleen M. O'Day, Patrick M. Parkinson, Henry S. Terrell, and others for their comments and suggestions, and Lili B. L. Dung for her statistical assistance. The views expressed in this chapter are those of the author and should not be interpreted as representing the views of the Board of Governors of the Federal Reserve System or anyone else on its staff.

with foreign residents and trade financing transactions conducted at offices in the United States as well as transactions conducted at foreign offices.[1] The chapter first reviews the growth of the international activities of U.S. banks and discusses the reasons for their expansion. It then examines the present structure and scope of international activities of U.S. banks and concentrates on two major areas of activity: international lending and international money market activities. The chapter also includes a brief discussion of the profitability of the banks' international activities.

GROWTH OF INTERNATIONAL ACTIVITIES

History

The first surge in international activities of U.S. banks took place during and after World War I (see Board of Governors, 1914–1920, and Tamagna and Willis, 1956). It was made possible by provisions of the Federal Reserve Act, enacted in 1913, that allowed national banks to accept drafts and to establish foreign branches. Previously, some states had granted these powers to state-chartered banks, but there was no similar authority for national banks. A number of states also permitted the establishment of state-chartered international banking corporations that engaged exclusively in international activities; their growth led to a 1916 amendment to the Federal Reserve Act that permitted national banks to own such corporations, provided that they entered into an agreement with the Federal Reserve Board delineating their powers (hence the name Agreement corporations). A 1919 amendment to the act further facilitated the international activities of U.S. banks by permitting the establishment of federally chartered banking entities called Edge corporations for the purpose of engaging in international banking and financial activities.[2] By 1920, U.S. banks and their Edge and Agreement corporations had established 181 foreign branches, up from only 26 branches in 1913.

The high volume of activity associated with postwar reconstruction credits subsided in the early 1920s; subsequently, the extent of the international activities of U.S. banks closely paralleled movements in the volume of international trade (see Dahl, 1967). A sharp contraction in international lending and in the number of foreign offices occurred during the 1930s, and activity was further curtailed by the disruptions in banking and commerce associated with World War II. Sixteen of the 18 Edge and Agreement corporations that had been established between 1919 and 1929 were either liquidated or absorbed by other corporations or by banks. By

1945, U.S. banking institutions operated only 78 foreign branches (see Tamagna and Willis, 1956).

After World War II, the volume of foreign lending by U.S. banks increased, as did the number of foreign branches. However, growth was slow, paralleling the restoration of normal channels of trade. Moreover, throughout the 1950s, the international activities of U.S. banks consisted primarily of financing trade between the United States and foreign countries (see Dahl, 1967). By 1960, total claims on foreign residents on the books of banks in the United States amounted to less than $5 billion, compared with total assets of more than $250 billion. At that time, only nine U.S. banking organizations had foreign branches, and of those, only three had substantial foreign branch networks. In all, there were 139 foreign branches.

During the 1960s, the role of U.S. banks changed dramatically: Their international activities expanded well beyond traditional trade financing and foreign exchange activities, and they became a leading force in the development of multinational banking. A number of factors contributed to this change, as will be discussed in the following section. In the United States, the international departments of large money-center banks became a major part of the banks' operations. Abroad, U.S. banks opened ever-increasing numbers of offices. By 1970, 80 U.S. banking organizations operated 540 foreign branches in 66 countries. At first, U.S. banks' foreign offices were used primarily to service the foreign activities of U.S. multinational corporations and to establish a presence in international financial centers such as London. Over time, however, many of these offices began to engage in a wide range of commercial banking activities and to compete in local banking and financial markets in foreign countries.

As U.S. banks became more active internationally, they experienced increasing difficulties competing overseas with foreign banks that, in general, had broader financial powers. U.S. banks sought and received more flexibility through two amendments to the Federal Reserve Act (see Dahl, 1967). The first, adopted in 1962, broadened the powers of foreign branches of national banks by allowing them to exercise, in addition to the powers they already possessed, such powers as are usual in doing a banking business in the country in which they are located. The Federal Reserve Board was given authority to determine these additional powers, with the restriction that they were not to include engaging in a nonfinancial commercial business or the general business of underwriting.[3]

The second amendment, adopted in 1966, permitted national banks to hold stock directly in foreign banks; previously they had been able to do so only indirectly through their Edge or Agreement corporations or through bank holding companies. At the same time, the act was amended to remove strict collateral requirements on loans to foreign banking affiliates.

Another significant development in the legal framework for multinational operations occurred when, in the late 1960s, the Federal Reserve Board began to allow U.S. banks to establish shell branches, most of which were located in the Caribbean. The primary purpose was to enable regional U.S. banks that did not have foreign branches to participate in the Eurodollar market.

During the 1970s, as will be discussed in detail below, large U.S. banks continued to expand their international activities, and regional U.S. banks became increasingly active in international transactions. At the same time, ever-increasing numbers of foreign banks opened offices in the United States and began to compete more aggressively with U.S. banks in both international and domestic markets.

By the late 1970s, the size and growth of U.S. activities of foreign banks led to enactment of the International Banking Act of 1978 (see Key and Brundy, 1979). The primary purpose of that act was to provide a framework for the regulation of U.S. activities of foreign banks at the federal level. However, the act also directed the Federal Reserve Board to revise its regulations to permit expansion of the activities of Edge corporations. The aim was both to increase the ability of Edge corporations to finance U.S. trade and to provide U.S. banks with a more effective vehicle for competing with foreign banks both in the United States and abroad.[4]

The ability of U.S. banks to conduct international activities at their U.S. offices was further enhanced in 1981, when banking offices in the United States were allowed to establish international banking facilities (IBFs) (see Key, 1982 and 1984). IBFs are exempt from the Federal Reserve Board's reserve requirements and interest rate ceilings and from the insurance coverage and assessments imposed by the Federal Deposit Insurance Corporation. In addition, 10 states have encouraged banking institutions to establish IBFs by granting favorable tax treatment under state or local law for IBF operations. As a result, through their IBFs, banking offices located in the United States can conduct a loan and deposit business with foreign residents in a regulatory environment broadly similar to that of the Eurocurrency market without having to use an offshore facility. To date, for U.S.-chartered banks, the main effect has been to shift transactions that otherwise would have been booked at foreign branches, primarily those in the Caribbean, to IBFs at banks in the United States[5] (see Key, 1982 and 1984, and Terrell and Mills, 1983).

By December 1983, total claims on foreign residents at U.S. banks' domestic offices and IBFs amounted to about $210 billion, a figure more than 20 times as large as that for 1965.[6] (Excluding IBFs reduces the 1983 figure by about 40%.) In comparison, the 1983 level of total assets of banks in the United States was about five times as large as the 1965 level.

Overseas activities also increased substantially during this period. By December 1983, nearly 200 banking organizations operated 924 foreign branches. Total assets of these branches increased from $9 billion in 1965 to $466 billion in 1983. Total assets at foreign subsidiaries of U.S. banking institutions increased from about $3 billion to $86 billion over the same period. While activities conducted at Edge corporations also increased from 1965 to 1983, their growth has not been as dramatic as that of international activities conducted at other domestic and foreign offices (see Houpt, 1981).[7]

Incentives for Expansion

In the 1960s banks recognized international activities in general and the establishment of foreign offices in particular as a source of large potential profits. Moreover, the pursuit of these potential profits was not viewed as entailing increased risk of portfolio concentration, since at that time the risks involved in lending to one country were perceived as relatively independent of those involved in lending to another country.

A number of factors contributed to the perceived profit potential of international activities:

First, general economic conditions created a favorable environment. The emergence of the United States as the principal economic and financial power in the world economy, the rapid expansion of world trade and international capital flows, and the increasing interdependence of national economies were all important in the internationalization of U.S. banking.

Second, restrictions on geographic expansion and permissible activities of banks in the United States limited the potential for domestic growth.

Third, U.S. laws and regulations designed to carry out fiscal and monetary policy goals made foreign locations more profitable than domestic locations for many international banking transactions. Federal reserve requirements, interest rate ceilings, and minimum maturity requirements on time deposits at banks in the United States, as well as borrowing limits applicable to certain nondeposit liabilities at U.S. banking offices, enhanced the attractiveness of foreign branches. U.S. measures to reduce net capital outflows from the United States—the Interest Equalization Tax, the Voluntary Foreign Credit Restraint program, and the Foreign Direct Investment program, which were in effect from the mid-1960s through January 1974—provided additional incentives for U.S. banks to establish foreign branches and to expand the activities conducted at those branches.

Finally, tax considerations may have also been relevant. In particular, in some states, it may be advantageous under state and local tax laws for banks to book transactions at foreign branches. For Federal tax purposes, however, U.S. banks are taxed on the basis of their worldwide income and derive no apparent Federal tax advantage from booking transactions at an offshore branch. However, under certain circumstances, a U.S. Federal tax advantage in conducting transactions through foreign subsidiaries may be obtained from the combination of a low or zero foreign tax rate and the deferral of Federal taxes on the unremitted earnings of foreign subsidiaries.

PRESENT STRUCTURE AND SCOPE OF INTERNATIONAL ACTIVITIES

U.S. banks engage in a wide range of international activities. These include: servicing multinational corporations through extensions of credit and also cash management and other fee-based services; syndicating loans in Euromarkets; lending to local corporations in foreign countries; providing trade financing; providing correspondent banking services; conducting retail banking in foreign countries; participating in international money markets; and trading in Eurobonds and foreign exchange. Activities of foreign subsidiaries of U.S. banking organizations also include securities underwriting, equity finance, and some types of insurance underwriting, activities at present not generally permissible for banks in the United States.

This section will focus on two major areas of international activity of U.S. banks: international lending and international money market activities. However, the section will first review briefly the overall structure of the multinational operations of U.S. banks and give some indication of the range of their activities.

Organization

A U.S. banking organization may conduct its international activities through a variety of organizational forms: (1) the bank's head office in the United States and its IBF; (2) foreign branches; (3) foreign subsidiaries and joint ventures; (4) Edge and Agreement corporations located in the

Table 8.1. Structure of International Activities of Multinational U.S.-Chartered Banks, as of December 1983

	Number of Offices	Claims on Unrelated Parties (in billions of dollars)[e]	Share of Total Claims on Unrelated Parties (in percentages)[f]
Domestic offices including IBFs[a]	196	146	28.0
Foreign branches[b]	924	296	56.7
Shell branches	185	66	12.6
Other branches	739	230	44.1
Foreign subsidiaries[c]	1,025	68	13.1
Edge corporations[d]	203	11	2.2
Total	2,348	521	100.0

SOURCE: Board of Governors of the Federal Reserve System.

[a] Includes only multinational U.S.-chartered banks, that is, U.S.-chartered banks with foreign offices. U.S.-chartered banks owned by foreign banks are included in these data.

[b] Includes foreign branches of banking Edge and Agreement corporations, which had 11 foreign branches, mainly shell branches in the Caribbean, with total claims on unrelated parties of less than $1 billion. Excludes branches in territories and possessions of the United States. Figures for claims on unrelated parties are for shell branches with total assets of at least $50 million and for all other branches with total assets of at least $150 million.

[c] Includes majority-owned subsidiaries and non-majority-owned subsidiaries that are considered by the Federal Reserve Board to be controlled by U.S. banking organizations. December 1983 figures for claims on unrelated parties are estimated.

[d] Includes domestic offices (including IBFs) of banking Edge and Agreement corporations only.

[e] Figures for domestic offices (including IBFs) are for claims on unrelated *foreign* residents plus customers' liabilities on acceptances outstanding. All figures in this column include claims on foreign offices of other U.S. banks.

[f] Shares were computed using unrounded numbers.

United States; and (5) export trading companies (ETCs) located in the United States.

As Table 8.1 shows, foreign branches account for more than half of the international activities of multinational U.S. banks conducted at both domestic and foreign offices. Foreign branches of U.S. banks are engaged primarily in wholesale banking activities, although those located outside major financial centers usually conduct a local retail business as well. The bulk of foreign branch transactions is denominated in U.S. dollars; as of

December 1983, more than three-quarters of both their total assets and their total liabilities were dollar denominated. Most of the branch activity, in terms of both numbers of offices and assets, is accounted for by a small number of banks. As of December 1983, the nine largest U.S. banks accounted for about two-thirds of both the number of foreign branches and total branch claims on unrelated parties.

More than half of the U.S. banking institutions with foreign branches have only shell branches. These branches are located in foreign countries, but they do not engage in transactions with local residents and the business carried on their books is usually administered at the bank's offices in the United States. Although their importance has diminished since the introduction of IBFs, shell branches located in the Caribbean and other offshore centers accounted for more than one-fifth of claims on unrelated parties at foreign branches of U.S. banks as of December 1983.[8]

In terms of volume of activity, the United Kingdom is the single most important location for foreign branches of U.S. banks, primarily because the United Kingdom is the main center of Euromarket activity. As of December 1983, the 70 branches of U.S. banks located in the United Kingdom accounted for about one-third of claims on unrelated parties at all foreign branches of U.S. banks. Branches located in other western European countries accounted for an additional 12% of such claims, and branches located in Asia accounted for nearly 25%.

U.S. banking organizations also operate in foreign countries through subsidiaries, which are separately incorporated and capitalized foreign companies.[9] These subsidiaries engage in a wide range of banking and financial activities. As Table 8.1 shows, they accounted for about 13% of the international activities of U.S. banks as of December 1983. A small number of banks account for most of the activities of the subsidiaries. As of December 1982, only 29 U.S. banking organizations had foreign subsidiaries with assets of at least $50 million. The nine largest U.S. banking organizations accounted for about 70% of the number of subsidiaries and about 90% of their total claims on unrelated parties. As is the case for foreign branches, a large proportion of the activity of foreign subsidiaries is concentrated in the United Kingdom and offshore centers.

Many of the earliest subsidiaries were established as substitutes for branches where branches were (or still are) prohibited or where foreign tax or banking laws provide incentives to operate through a subsidiary rather than a branch (see Houpt and Martinson, 1982). These subsidiaries are engaged principally in making loans and taking deposits. Although the retail activities of some of these subsidiaries are significant and growing, their business is primarily wholesale; that is, their customers tend to be other banks, corporations, and governments.

As U.S. banks continued to expand their foreign operations in the 1970s, subsidiaries were established for special purposes. These include underwriting securities, engaging in retail financial operations, engaging in specialized finance and leasing transactions, and serving as tax-minimizing funding vehicles. The types of subsidiaries through which these activities are carried out include merchant banks, financing and leasing companies, and so-called tax haven subsidiaries (see Houpt and Martinson, 1982).

Merchant banks supplement the services offered by foreign branches by syndicating medium- and long-term loans to multinational corporations and to governmental organizations, providing investment and financial advice, and underwriting securities. Although branches may perform most of these activities, they may not generally underwrite securities.

Finance and leasing companies constitute another important category of foreign subsidiaries. Finance companies include both consumer finance companies, which concentrate on retail financial activities, and commercial finance companies, which are engaged primarily in business financing. Leasing companies include special-purpose companies that lease or charter a single piece of equipment, such as an oil tanker or an airplane, as well as companies that engage in a broad range of commercial leasing activities.

Tax haven subsidiaries have been established in countries where there are either no or very low taxes and where there are bank secrecy laws. The Bahamas and Cayman Islands are examples of such tax havens, which attract funds from individuals and companies seeking to take advantage of these features (see U.S. Department of the Treasury, 1984). Major U.S. banks have established trust companies in both locations to accommodate those kinds of foreign customers. U.S. banks also use tax haven and other offshore subsidiaries as vehicles for funding their domestic and foreign operations (see Houpt and Martinson, 1982). A specialized example is Netherlands Antilles finance subsidiaries (see U.S. House of Representatives, 1984).[10]

U.S. banking organizations also operate in foreign countries as participants in joint ventures.[11] The reasons for participation in joint ventures as well as their types of activities vary considerably. Consortium banks, one type of joint venture, typically involve four or five major shareholders. They have been used to bring together large money-center banks from different countries, to provide a vehicle for regional banks to participate in international markets, to enable international expertise of some banks to be combined with the industry expertise of others, or to bring together different types of banks such as commercial and merchant banks. Joint ventures involving two major shareholders, typically a large international bank and a local partner, have often been used to establish a presence in countries that prohibit branches and majority-owned subsidiaries of foreign banks.

Consortium banking, particularly in London, developed rapidly during the mid-1960s (see Blanden, 1981). Since at that time Euromarket banking was relatively new, sharing risk and pooling knowledge were attractive to many banks. However, as banks gained experience in Euromarket activities, they preferred their own operations. Moreover, problems arose in managing consortium banks because of different objectives and strategies among shareholders. As a result, in the last few years very few new consortium banks have been formed, and a number of existing ones have become wholly owned by one of the participants.

U.S. banking organizations may also establish certain types of subsidiaries in the United States for the purpose of conducting international business. Such subsidiaries include Edge corporations, which are chartered by the Federal Reserve Board to engage in international banking and financial activities and may be established in locations outside the state in which their owner operates (see Houpt, 1981).[12] Although there is no difference in their charter powers, in practice there are two types of Edge corporations. Nonbanking (or investment) Edge corporations do not take deposits from unaffiliated parties and are used primarily as holding companies for investments in foreign banks and nonbanks.[13] By contrast, banking Edge corporations engage in a broad range of banking activities in the United States, subject to the limitation that the activities involve a foreign customer or are related to an international transaction.[14] As Table 8.1 shows, U.S. offices of banking Edge corporations accounted for only about 2% of the international activities of multinational U.S. banks as of year-end 1983. Although Edge corporations may establish branches in foreign countries and IBFs at their U.S. offices, the volume of activities conducted at their IBFs and foreign branches is relatively small.

Under the Bank Export Services Act of 1982, bank holding companies, but not banks, are also permitted to own export trading companies (ETCs).[15] ETCs are corporations organized principally for the purpose of either exporting goods or services or providing services to facilitate the export of goods or services produced in the United States by unaffiliated parties. For example, through its ETC a U.S. banking organization may provide services it was not previously permitted to offer such as distribution, warehousing, insurance, and freight forwarding; most important, through its ETC a U.S. banking organization may take title to goods in trade.

By allowing banking organizations to invest in ETCs, the act departs from the long-standing policy of separation of banking and commerce in the United States. However, it does strictly limit the amount of a banking organization's investment in and extensions of credit to its ETCs. More-over, the banking organization must submit its proposal to invest in an ETC to the Federal Reserve Board for review. As of mid-1984, 28 U.S. bank holding companies had notified the Federal Reserve Board of their intention to invest. Most of these ETCs are still in the initial stages of operation, and it is not yet clear whether ETCs will play an important role in U.S. banks' international activities (see Dahl, 1984).

International Lending Activities

International lending by U.S. banks increased substantially during the 1970s, particularly lending to private and public borrowers in developing countries. In addition to their traditional role in trade- and project-related development financing, much of the banks' activity involved balance-of-payments financing that had previously been carried out primarily through loans from official creditors. After the first set of oil price increases in 1973 and 1974, U.S. banks played a major role in recycling dollars deposited by the surplus-earning oil-exporting countries to fund the deficits of both the net-capital-importing developing countries and the oil-importing developed countries.

From 1975 through 1981, banks from the United States and other major industrial countries financed about two-thirds of the total current account deficits and reserve accumulations of the developing countries (see Teeters and Terrell, 1983). The rapid growth in bank lending to these countries helped offset slower rates of growth of official bilateral aid and official contributions to multinational development banks. The role of the banks also helped to offset a decline in International Monetary Fund (IMF) resources relative to the dramatic increase in financing needs of a number of countries, which limited the ability of the IMF to offer temporary support to countries implementing adjustment programs.

The growth of bank lending to the developing countries began to slow considerably with the onset of the developing country debt crisis in 1982. At that time, several Latin American countries experienced severe problems in servicing the debt that they had amassed in their attempts, largely in the 1970s, to finance rapid economic growth. Since much of this debt was in the form of loans from U.S. and other foreign commercial banks that carried floating interest rates, difficulties arose when dollar interest rates increased sharply and the worldwide recession reduced the volume and price of exports from these countries.[16] U.S. banks accordingly faced the need to adjust the repayment terms on loans to some of these countries and became increasingly cautious in extending new credit to developing countries (see Glaessner, 1983, and Teeters and Terrell, 1983).

Table 8.2. Amounts Owed to U.S.-Chartered Banks by Foreign Borrowers, by Country of Borrower, as of December 1983

Country of Borrower	Amounts Owed to U.S. Banks (in billions of dollars)[a]	Share of Total Amount Owed (in percentages)[b]
G-10 countries[c]	164	45.7
Non-G-10 developed countries[d]	41	11.5
Eastern European countries	5	1.4
OPEC members	25	7.0
Non-oil exporting developing countries:	109	30.2
Latin America and Caribbean	72	19.8
Asia	33	9.3
Africa	4	1.1
Offshore banking centers	14	3.9
International and regional organizations	1	0.3
Total	359	100.0

SOURCE: Federal Financial Institutions Examination Council, *Statistical Release E.16,* May 24, 1984. Figures include all amounts owed to domestic and foreign offices of U.S.-chartered banks that have foreign offices, Edge and Agreement Corporations, or IBFs, and have total outstanding claims on foreign residents of more than $30 million. However, the figures do not include local lending in local currencies by foreign offices of U.S. banks.

[a] These amounts have been adjusted so that claims on borrowers in one country with a head office or guarantor in another country are reallocated from the first country to the second country.

[b] Shares were computed using unrounded numbers.

[c] Excluding the United States. G-10 (Group of Ten) countries are the 11 participants in the General Arrangements to Borrow of the International Monetary Fund; namely, Belgium-Luxembourg, Canada, France, Germany, Italy, Japan, the Netherlands, Sweden, Switzerland, the United Kingdom, and the United States. (Switzerland officially became a participant in 1984, but the countries are still referred to as the G-10.)

[d] Includes Australia, Austria, Denmark, Finland, Greece, Iceland, Ireland, New Zealand, Norway, Portugal, South Africa, Spain, and Turkey.

As of December 1983, non-oil-exporting developing countries accounted for 30% of the total amounts owed to U.S. banks by foreign borrowers (see Table 8.2). Lending to residents of G-10 countries other than the United States accounted for nearly half of the amounts owed to U.S. banks by foreign borrowers.[17] Lending by U.S. banks to borrowers in these countries and offshore centers also slowed in the latter half of 1982. This reflected in part the slowdown in lending by foreign banks to non-oil-exporting developing countries, since most of U.S. bank lending to borrowers in other G-10 countries and offshore centers represents claims on banks, which in turn lend some portion of the funds to other countries.

The increased participation of U.S. banks in international lending in the 1970s represented both increased activity by the largest U.S. banks, which have traditionally been the most active in international lending, and new activity by regional U.S. banks that had not previously participated in international lending on a large scale. The development of new techniques, in particular "rollover" pricing of loans and the syndicated Eurocurrency credit, made international lending more attractive for both groups of institutions.

Rollover pricing of loans allows relatively frequent adjustments of interest rates. For example, a bank may enter into a commitment to provide funds for perhaps as long as 10 or 12 years on the basis of an interest rate that is adjusted at regular intervals. A bank can therefore extend longer-term financing while at the same time minimizing its interest rate risk. However, because the interest rate risk is passed on to the borrowers, rollover pricing may increase the credit risk to the banks (see Pecchioli, 1983).

The syndicated Eurocurrency credit involves the development of a borrowing package and an information memorandum by a lead bank or group of banks and the participation by other, often smaller, banks in the credit without direct contact with the borrower. Syndication allows large amounts of credit to be raised for a single borrower on short notice and spreads the risk of loan losses among a number of banks. Responsibilities such as managing, underwriting, and various degrees of participation are divided among banks according to their respective lending powers and technical capabilities. Participation in a syndicate permits smaller banks to realize some of the economies of scale in the business development functions involved in international lending. By participating in loan syndications, regional U.S. banks have been able to expand their total lending activity at times of declining domestic loan demand.

U.S. banks have been active participants in the syndicated medium-term Eurocurrency credit market, which developed rapidly in the 1970s; by year-end 1983 total outstanding credits in that market amounted to an estimated $330 billion.[18] For the most part, these loans are priced on a rollover basis in terms of the London interbank offer rate (LIBOR); some are priced on the basis of the U.S. prime rate or U.S. CD rates. The bulk of syndicated Eurocredits are denominated in U.S. dollars, and maturities are most often between five and eight years, although occasionally final maturities have exceeded 10 years. Banks have used syndicated medium-term Eurocredits primarily to finance the balance-of-payments deficits of developing countries, although they have also been used for other purposes, such as project financing.

The international lending activity of U.S. banks can also be categorized by type of customer (see Table 8.3). Claims on foreign offices of foreign banks, discussed below, and business loans to foreign residents each accounted for more than one-third of the total; claims on foreign governments and official institutions accounted for an additional one-eighth. While syndicated loans play a major role in U.S. bank lending to nonbank foreign residents, other techniques for international lending, including longer-term lending in local currencies, ordinary short-term loans to corporations and official institutions, and trade financing, are also important.

Trade financing, as reflected in the volume of acceptance financing by U.S. banks, has increased dramatically over the past decade, primarily because of the increase in the volume of foreign trade, particularly oil imports. Bankers' acceptances are negotiable time drafts—typically with maturities of not more than six months—that are drawn to finance import,

Table 8.3. International Lending Activity of Multinational U.S.-Chartered Banks, as of December 1983

Category	Amount (in billions of dollars)	Share of Total (in percentages)[d]
Business loans to foreign residents	133	34.6
Claims on foreign governments and official institutions[a]	45	11.6
Claims on foreign offices of foreign banks[b]	141	36.6
Placements	94	24.3
Loans	47	12.3
Customers' liabilities on acceptances outstanding[c]	66	17.2
Total	385	100.0

SOURCE: *Federal Reserve Bulletin,* June, 1984, Table 4.20. Data include domestic and foreign offices of multinational U.S.-chartered banks, that is, U.S.-chartered banks with foreign offices.

[a] Includes loans to foreign governments and official institutions and balances with foreign central banks.

[b] Claims on foreign branches of U.S.-chartered banks are not included.

[c] Nearly three quarters of the customers' liabilities on acceptances outstanding shown in the table represent acceptances where the customer (the account party) is not a U.S. resident.

[d] Shares were computed using unrounded numbers.

export, storage, or shipment of goods and are termed "accepted" when a bank agrees to make payment at maturity (see Melton and Mahr, 1981).[19] As Table 8.3 shows, by year-end 1983, customers' liabilities on acceptances outstanding, an asset on the banks' balance sheets, amounted to $66 billion. Of this amount, about three-fifths was related to the trade of goods between foreign countries; U.S. exports and imports each accounted for about one-sixth; and the storage and shipment of goods accounted for the remaining portion of acceptances outstanding.[20]

International Money Market Activities

As discussed elsewhere in this book, since the mid-1960s asset–liability management has become an increasingly important part of bank operations, particularly in view of the volatility of interest rates and exchange rates in recent years. To the extent that most banks are following overall asset–liability management policies, their foreign and domestic money market activities have become increasingly integrated, with domestic and foreign sources of funding viewed as substitutes on the basis of relative costs. However, it should be noted that funding strategies vary widely among banks, depending on factors such as the organization of their international and multinational activities, the relative importance of their international business, the extent of their reliance on domestic deposits, and their access to domestic money markets (see Pecchioli, 1983).

By far the most important part of the international money market activities of U.S. banks is their participation in the international interbank market. Through redepositing, that market provides an efficient worldwide link between depositors and borrowers (see Ellis, 1981, and Pecchioli, 1983). For example, deposits of nonbanks in the Euromarket tend to be concentrated at large, well-established banks. Yet there are many banks that can fund their international lending activities only by relying on money market sources of funds. Because the interbank market enables banks to obtain large amounts of funds quickly, they are able to pursue active asset and liability management policies with less need for maintaining precautionary balances. The international interbank market is also important in the conduct of other banking activities such as foreign exchange.

U.S. banks supply funds to the international interbank market from their domestic and foreign offices through both placements and loans. Placements are generally for very short maturities, usually three to six months and almost always less than one year, and are typically made with banks chartered in one of the major industrial countries. By contrast, loans are most often made to banks chartered in less developed countries and can have maturities longer than a year; they are generally viewed as distinct from true interbank business (see Parkinson, 1982).[21] If placements alone are considered, U.S. banks in the aggregate have moved from a position of sizable net borrowers in the late 1970s to sizable net lenders in the early 1980s. In the second half of 1983, however, U.S. banks as a group reduced their net placements in the international interbank markets (see Table 8.4).

Different groups of U.S. banks participate in the international market for interbank placements in different ways (see Parkinson, 1982). The nine largest U.S. banks have generally regarded the international interbank market as one of several sources of funding for their worldwide operations as well as an outlet for short-term investments that cannot immediately be placed in higher-yielding loans. These banks are active on both sides of the market; in recent years, as a group, they have been net borrowers of funds.

By contrast, a group of about 100 U.S. regional banks have in the aggregate been net suppliers of funds. Most of those banks have participated primarily on the lending side of the market, and their aggregate gross placements increased substantially between 1979 and early 1983. The role of the regional U.S. banks in the international interbank market can be regarded as an extension of their role in domestic interbank markets where they have traditionally been net providers of funds to U.S. money-center banks.

The 15 banks just below the nine largest U.S. banks have tended to be in an intermediate position. These banks generally have a number of sizable foreign branches and have participated in international lending and in the international interbank market for a number of years, although to a more limited degree than the nine largest banks. As a group, these 15 banks shifted from being small net borrowers in the international interbank market in the late 1970s to net lenders in the early 1980s. Some banks in this intermediate group parallel the nine largest banks in the type and degree of participation in the international interbank market, while others are similar to the smaller regional banks (see Parkinson, 1982).

For both money-center banks and regional banks, the bulk of international interbank activity has been conducted through their foreign branches. This practice, together with global management of international funding, has contributed to the growth of cross-border claims on related banking offices.

Although the international money-market activities of U.S. banks are characterized by heavy use of the interbank market, other types of instruments—such as negotiable certificates of deposit (CDs) and floating-rate notes (FRNs)—are also important.

U.S. banks began to issue large-denomination negotiable CDs do-

Table 8.4. Net Placements with Foreign Offices of Foreign Banks by Multinational U.S.-Chartered Banks, 1979–1983 (in billions of dollars)

	Total[a]	9 largest U.S. banks[b]	Next 15 largest U.S. banks[b]	"Regional" U.S. banks[c]
December 1979	−22.3	−23.6	−0.6	1.8
June 1980	−16.8	−24.0	1.0	6.2
December 1980	−8.1	−20.4	2.8	9.4
June 1981	−2.5	−18.2	3.7	12.0
December 1981	3.8	−18.9	5.4	17.3
June 1982	18.2	−10.2	6.0	22.5
December 1982	18.3	−15.9	8.8	25.5
June 1983	27.8	−11.3	11.6	27.5
December 1983	9.1	−21.0	4.2	25.9

SOURCE: Federal Financial Institutions Examination Council, Quarterly Report of Condition (FFIEC 014). Figures include net placements with foreign offices of foreign banks by domestic and foreign offices of multinational U.S.-chartered banks, that is, U.S.-chartered banks with foreign offices. All figures are for last business day of month. A negative number indicates net borrowings from foreign offices of foreign banks.

U.S. bank placements with U.S. agencies and branches of foreign banks are not included in this table because they are usually considered part of the U.S. rather than the international interbank market; such extensions of credit do, however, represent exposure to the home country of the foreign bank. U.S. bank transactions in the international interbank market with foreign branches of other U.S. banks are excluded from the figures because, in theory, such transactions would sum to zero for U.S. banks in the aggregate.

[a] Details may not add to totals due to rounding.

[b] Banks in the groups "9 largest banks" and "next 15 largest banks" are based on consolidated worldwide assets as of June 1981.

[c] Figures in this column are for multinational U.S.-chartered banks other than the 24 largest U.S.-chartered banks.

mestically in the early 1960s, and since the late 1960s such CDs have been used in the Eurodollar market as well. Because negotiability gives them greater liquidity, CDs have a lower cost than non-negotiable time deposits of the same maturity and are therefore an attractive funding vehicle for banks. London is the major center for the issuance of Eurodollar CDs, and as of year-end 1983, London branches of U.S. banks had nearly $50 billion in outstanding CDs—almost half of the London market. This share is, however, somewhat lower than in previous years (see Hung, December 1983). Outstanding CDs at London branches of U.S. banks declined during 1983, in part because of the decontrol of interest rates in the United States, which led to some substitution of retail deposits at U.S. offices for the issuance of CDs by London branches in banks' worldwide funding activity.

In recent years, the FRN market has played an increasingly important role in international banking transactions. Although the volume of activity is still relatively modest, with $40 billion in FRNs outstanding as of year-end 1983 (see Parente, 1984), their use as a substitute both for interbank placements and for medium-term lending, notably to developed countries, has been increasing. FRNs are bonds that pay interest based on short-term rates, usually LIBOR; typically the rate is fixed for periods of six months. The major issuers of FRNs have been banks and governments, particularly governments that are among the most creditworthy medium-term syndicated loan customers. Banks, including some London branches of U.S. banks, are major investors in FRNs, although in the recent past the returns on these notes have been quite low relative to those on syndicated Eurocurrency loans to the same borrowers. FRNs have the advantage of an established secondary market, and banks appear to have placed a high premium on the perceived liquidity of FRNs relative to syndicated loans.

Several disadvantages to borrowers may be inhibiting the issuance of FRNs and may prevent FRNs from replacing the syndicated loan market. First, with FRNs all funds must be drawn immediately, whereas loan agreements may allow a lengthy period of time before the funds are drawn (for which a commitment fee is paid). Second, the length of the periods for which the FRN interest rate is fixed may not be changed; by contrast, at each successive rollover date a loan customer is usually able to choose the length of the next rollover period (typically one, three, or six months). Third, not all FRNs have a call feature and call dates may be some years in the future, whereas floating rate syndicated loans usually allow prepayment without penalty. In addition to these factors, both borrowers and banks value the direct relationship involved in a loan; this does not exist to the same extent for FRNs, which banks are likely to sell in the secondary market.

Profitability of International Activities

As international lending by U.S. banks increased rapidly in the 1970s, income associated with international activities accounted for over half of operating income at a number of the largest U.S. banks (see Hanley et al., 1983). Despite the importance of their international business, until recently few banks had the ability to assess systematically the profitability of this business in relation to their other activities (see Hakim, 1984). Moreover, short-term profits of their international business may have been a secondary consideration; instead, the major emphasis was on business development and long-term volume of assets. In part because no formal minimum capital ratios existed, banks could increase both their assets and their return on equity capital by increasing the volume of their marginally profitable loans. In the last few years, however, U.S. banks have increasingly focused on their return on assets. This trend was reinforced in mid-1983, when U.S. bank regulatory agencies adopted new capital adequacy guidelines for 17 large multinational U.S. banking organizations that established 5% as the minimum ratio of primary capital to total assets.[22] Prior to that time no explicit capital guidelines had been established for these banking organizations (see Comptroller of the Currency, 1984).

In order to assess the relative profitability of a U.S. bank's international business, it is necessary to have information by type of product, by type of customer, by maturity, and so forth. Although such information is used by large U.S. banks in their internal calculations, it is seldom publicly available. Data on overall spreads and net interest margins are often used as approximations, but they may be poor indicators of profitability both because of the conceptual difficulty of separating profitability and risk and because of the way in which the data are constructed.

Average spreads over LIBOR for medium-term Eurocurrency lending declined in the late 1970s as increasing numbers of banks participated in international lending. The usual explanation is that many of these banks were willing to accept low spreads in order to enter the international market and to establish customer relationships that would lead to additional, more profitable business. While this may be an accurate description of the banks' behavior, the narrowing of spreads that began in the late 1970s does not necessarily imply a proportionate reduction in profitability of overall international activities (see Pecchioli, 1983).

One reason is that published data on spreads usually refer only to medium-term syndicated loans, and to some extent the effect on profits of the narrowing of such spreads has been offset by the growth of other types of bank income. These include not only income from other types of credit such as trade financing but also earnings from fee-related business, correspondent banking services, investment banking, and other specialized activities such as factoring and leasing. For U.S. multinational banks, over the past five years, noninterest income attributable to international business has, on average, grown more rapidly than overall international income.

Another problem with the use of spreads over LIBOR for medium-term Eurocurrency lending as a measure of profitability is that they may not reflect the actual return on such loans, even if they were adjusted for associated fee income and special tax-related features. This is because a bank's marginal funding costs are likely to be lower than LIBOR; for example, bid rates on deposits in the international interbank market are usually set at levels about 1/8% below offer rates, yields on negotiable Eurodollar CDs can be substantially lower than LIBOR, and the cost of funds raised domestically through retail deposits can also be lower than LIBOR. Moreover, average funding costs may be lower than marginal costs (see Pecchioli, 1983).

Net interest margins, that is, interest revenue as a percentage of average earning assets, are also widely used as evidence of profitability. At the 10 largest U.S. banks, these margins have been consistently lower for international activities than for domestic activities (see Hanley et al., 1979–1983). However, no meaningful conclusion about relative profitability of banks' international business can be drawn from this comparison because of the basic difficulty of separating profits and risk premiums.

An economically reasonable definition of profitability of an asset would come from a model for the pricing of assets such as the capital asset pricing model or another financial asset model (see Van Horne, 1974). Such models imply that the profitability of a single asset or class of assets cannot be measured in isolation. Although riskier assets are likely to carry higher rates of return than other assets, riskier assets are not necessarily more profitable because they impose hedging costs that are borne elsewhere in the portfolio. Conversely, instruments with desirable risk characteristics may be highly profitable despite having relatively low rates of return. For example, floating-rate instruments, which until recently were used in international but not in domestic lending, have enabled banks to match closely their interest-sensitive assets and liabilities in an environment of considerable interest rate volatility, thereby shifting most of the interest rate risk to their customers. As a result, the small margin between lending rates on these assets and costs of funds is consistent with their achieving normal rates of profit for the bank.

In international lending, banks face country risk as well as credit risk, since asset quality is dependent on economic and political events in foreign countries. This is a particular problem at the present time with regard to the banks' exposure to developing countries. To date, reported losses of U.S. banks on international lending have been relatively smaller than those on their domestic lending. This reported difference is difficult to interpret, however, because the institutional features of default and rescheduling differ significantly between the two markets. Moreover, the evaluation of loan quality, which always involves judgment in assessing risks, is particularly difficult in the case of loans to sovereign borrowers.

CONCLUSION

The present caution, and in some cases reluctance, of U.S. banks regarding expansion of their international activities contrasts sharply with their attitudes in the 1960s and 1970s. This changed attitude is reflected in the fact that banks are already placing greater emphasis both domestically and internationally on enhancement of profits and reduction of risks rather than on expansion of their balance sheets. Toward this end, U.S. banks are making efforts to improve both asset and liability management, to strengthen capital positions, and to provide for possible loan losses. Tighter regulatory and supervisory controls for U.S. banks' international activities are reinforcing these trends.

Despite present difficulties, international banking is such a central feature of the international economy, and the United States plays such a major role in that economy, that U.S. banks will undoubtedly continue to be heavily involved in international finance. The goals of U.S. banks' future international expansion may differ from those in the past and there will undoubtedly be changes in techniques used to engage in international activities as U.S. banks adapt to changing circumstances. Nevertheless, international activities, although altered somewhat, can be expected to continue to grow.

NOTES

1. In addition, some transactions with domestic customers conducted at banking offices in the United States may also be related to the customers' foreign activities. However, such transactions cannot be distinguished from other transactions with domestic customers except in the case of Edge corporations (which may conduct transactions with domestic residents only if the purpose of the transaction is international) and trade financing that is included in customers' liabilities on acceptances outstanding.

2. The shortage of dollars available to foreign purchasers to pay for U.S. exports after World War I was a major reason for this amendment. Edge corporations were intended to enable groups to form specialized financing vehicles for U.S. exports and thereby gain independence from foreign financing sources. Although Agreement corporations

could be used for this purpose, it was felt that there would be greater confidence in federally chartered corporations.

3. As specified in the Federal Reserve Board's Regulation K, the additional powers include issuing guarantees, underwriting securities of the government of the country in which the branch is located, and acquiring shares in foreign central banks, development banks, or similar institutions of the country in which the branch is located.

4. One of the regulatory changes adopted by the Federal Reserve Board in implementing this congressional directive permitted interstate branches of Edge corporations. Previously, a bank could establish separate Edge corporations in more than one state. However, each Edge corporation must be separately capitalized with a minimum of $2 million, and the lending limit to a single customer for each Edge corporation engaged in banking is based on its own capital and surplus. By contrast, interstate branches of Edge corporations are consolidated with their parent Edge to determine capital requirements and lending limits. As a result, banks with multiple Edge corporations have, in general, converted them into networks of Edge branches.

5. By contrast, for U.S. agencies and branches of foreign banks, the primary effect has been to shift transactions that would otherwise have been on the U.S. books of the agency or branch to its IBF.

6. These figures are from the U.S. Treasury International Capital (TIC) reports, the only source of historical data available. The data have been adjusted to exclude custody holdings and to exclude U.S. agencies and branches of foreign banks. However, the figures are not comparable with the data in the tables in other sections of this chapter because of differences in definitions and coverage. For example, the TIC data include claims on U.S. banks' related foreign offices, and TIC reporters include all U.S. banks with claims on foreign residents above a small minimum amount.

7. Growth since 1980 appears particularly slow, primarily because the introduction of same-day interbank settlement procedures in 1981 substantially reduced assets of Edge corporations.

8. The Federal Reserve Board's limitations on IBF activities are more restrictive than those on activities of foreign branches of U.S. banks. However, for some U.S.-chartered banks, there may be tax advantages under state law in booking loans that are IBF eligible at an IBF rather than at a shell branch. This is because, in some instances, state tax authorities have attempted to treat shell branches differently than other foreign branches; in particular, they have attempted to attribute income of the shell branch to the domestic office of the bank, with the result that the income would become subject to state taxation. In such a situation, a bank may have an incentive to use an IBF instead of a shell branch in order to rely on specific statutory provisions granting tax relief to IBFs.

9. For bank regulatory purposes, a subsidiary is defined as a foreign company that a U.S. banking organization controls either through the bank itself, the bank holding company, or an Edge corporation. A U.S. bank may itself invest directly only in foreign banks; a bank holding company or an Edge corporation may invest in foreign banks and other foreign companies.

10. Provisions of Netherlands Antilles tax law, in combination with the provisions of its present tax treaty with the United States, have made the Antilles an attractive location for U.S. companies, including banks, to establish subsidiaries, especially for fund-raising purposes. As of this writing (summer 1984), the U.S.-Netherlands Antilles tax treaty is in the process of being renegotiated. More important, the Tax Reform Act of

1984 repealed the 30% withholding tax on portfolio interest paid to foreign residents and thus eliminated the major tax incentive for U.S. corporations to use Netherlands Antilles finance subsidiaries.

11. For bank regulatory purposes, a joint venture is defined as a company in which a U.S. banking organization has a significant but non-controlling ownership interest.

12. As noted earlier, Agreement corporations are state-chartered corporations that have entered into an agreement with the Federal Reserve Board to limit their powers to international banking and financial operations, that is, to the activities permitted to Edge corporations. There are only a few Agreement corporations in existence and their total assets are relatively small; they are included with Edge corporations in the tables in this chapter.

13. U.S. bank holding companies and Edge corporations may also establish state-chartered holding companies to conduct operations similar to those conducted by investment Edge corporations. In addition to serving as intermediaries through which investments in foreign companies are held, some of these companies lease fixed assets to foreign customers.

14. Under the Federal Reserve Board's Regulation K, Edge corporations engaged in banking are subject to limits on loans to individual borrowers in addition to minimum capitalization requirements.

15. An Edge corporation that is owned by a bank holding company may invest in an ETC, but an Edge corporation that is owned by a bank may not.

16. The International Lending Supervision Act of 1983 was enacted in response to widespread concern about the implications of this situation for U.S. banks. The act directs the U.S. bank regulatory agencies to consult with supervisory authorities of other countries regarding the adoption of effective and consistent international lending supervisory policies and practices. The act also directs the U.S. bank regulatory agencies to evaluate foreign country exposure and transfer risk and to establish procedures to ensure that these factors are taken into account in evaluating U.S. banks' capital adequacy; to collect foreign country exposure information from U.S. banks at least four times a year and to disclose to the public, on request, information regarding the banks' material exposure to foreign countries; and to establish minimum levels of capital for U.S. banking institutions. In addition, the act directs the federal bank regulators to require the maintenance of special reserves whenever the quality of an institution's assets has been impaired by a protracted inability of public or private foreign borrowers to make payments on their external indebtedness or where no definite prospects exist for the orderly restoration of debt service; and establishes requirements for accounting for fees by U.S. banking institutions in connection with their international loans (see Comptroller of the Currency, 1984).

17. G-10 (Group of Ten) countries are the 11 participants in the General Arrangements to Borrow of the International Monetary Fund; namely, Belgium-Luxembourg, Canada, France, Germany, Italy, Japan, the Netherlands, Sweden, Switzerland, the United Kingdom, and the United States. (Switzerland officially became a participant in 1984, but the countries are still referred to as the G-10.)

18. Unpublished estimate by the Bank of England. Estimate assumes that loans were repaid at maturity and does not include new credits advanced as part of rescheduling packages; the Bank of England estimates that adjustments for these factors would increase the outstanding credits to roughly $400 billion.

19. For a seller of goods, the major advantage in extending credit to a buyer through an acceptance is that the bank itself is obligated to make payment; this is particularly important in international trade where the parties involved may not be well known to each other or where the seller cannot readily ascertain the credit rating of the buyer. For a bank, acceptances have the advantage of an active secondary market; moreover, the sale by the bank of its own acceptance that it has discounted and which is eligible for discount by a Federal Reserve Bank is not subject to reserve requirements. However, there are limitations on the aggregate volume of eligible acceptances a bank may create.

20. Many of the U.S. banks' customers (account parties) are other banks; this is frequently the case when the activity being financed is third country trade. In this situation, a foreign bank often provides the original trade credit by accepting a draft drawn by an importer or exporter, which the foreign bank holds in its own portfolio. In turn, the foreign bank draws a draft on a U.S. bank using the original acceptance as collateral. The draft drawn on and accepted by the U.S. bank is known as an accommodation draft, or refinance bill. Such acceptances are eligible for discount if the underlying transaction meets the criteria for eligibility and appropriate documentation is maintained by the accepting U.S. bank.

21. In addition to placements and loans, a large portion of the acceptance financing provided by U.S. banks involves interbank extensions of credit (see note 20). Such acceptance activity still represents trade financing because of the nature of the underlying transaction.

22. As of this writing (summer 1984), the U.S. bank regulatory authorities had issued for public comment proposals that would establish 5½% as the minimum primary capital adequacy level for all U.S. banking organizations.

REFERENCES

Andrews, S. "The Bold New Look in Trade Financing." *Institutional Investor*, January 1984, pp. 231–238.

Blanden, M. "Joint Venture and Consortium Banking." *The Banker*, March 1981, pp. 93–99.

Board of Governors of the Federal Reserve System. *Annual Report*, 1914–1920.

Brimmer, A. F., and Dahl, F. R. "Growth of American International Banking: Implications for Public Policy." Paper presented at meeting of the American Economic Association, December 1974.

Comptroller of the Currency, Federal Deposit Insurance Corporation, and Board of Governors of the Federal Reserve System. "Report to Congress on Implementation of the International Lending Supervision Act of 1983." May 1984.

Dahl, F. R. "International Operations of U.S. Banks: Growth and Public Policy Implications." *Law and Contemporary Problems*, Winter 1967, *32* (1), 100–130.

Dahl, F. R. Statement before the Subcommittee on International Economic Policy and Trade of the Committee on Foreign Affairs, U.S. House of Representatives. June 20, 1984.

Ellis, J. G. "Eurobanks and the Inter-bank Market." *Bank of England Quarterly Bulletin*, September 1981, pp. 351–364.

Fleming, A. E., and Howson, S. K. "Conditions in the Syndicated Medium-term Eurocredit Market." *Bank of England Quarterly Bulletin*, September 1980, pp. 311–318.

Glaessner, T. C. "U.S. International Transactions in 1982." *Federal Reserve Bulletin,* April 1983, pp. 251–260.

Hakim, J. "International Banking Survey." *The Economist,* March 24, 1984.

Hanley, T. H., et al. "U.S. Multinational Banking: Semiannual Statistics." New York: Salomon Brothers Inc., 1979–1983.

Horst, T. "Taxation of International Income of Commercial Banks." In Hufbauer, G. C. (Ed.), *The International Framework for Money and Banking in the 1980s.* Washington, D.C.: The International Law Institute, Georgetown University Law Center, 1981.

Houpt, J. V. "Performance and Characteristics of Edge Corporations." Staff Study No. 110, Board of Governors of the Federal Reserve System, January 1981.

Houpt, J. V., and Martinson, M. G. "Foreign Subsidiaries of U.S. Banking Organizations." Staff Study No. 120, Board of Governors of the Federal Reserve System, October 1982.

Hung, T. Q. "The Changing Dollar CD Market." Salomon Brothers Inc., December 1983.

Hung, T. Q. "The Deceleration and Domestication of International Bank Lending and Funding." Salomon Brothers Inc., November 1983.

"International Banking Markets in 1980–81." *Bank of England Quarterly Bulletin,* March 1982, pp. 42–55.

"International Banking Markets in 1982." *Bank of England Quarterly Bulletin,* March 1983, pp. 43–60.

"International Banking Markets in 1983." *Bank of England Quarterly Bulletin,* March 1984, pp. 54–67.

Keller, J. S. "ETCs: The Perspective of the Federal Reserve Board." In Welt, L. G. B. (Ed.), *ETCs: New Methods for U.S. Exporting.* New York: American Management Association Management Briefing, 1984.

Key, S. J. "International Banking Facilities." *Federal Reserve Bulletin,* October 1982, pp. 565–577.

Key, S. J. "International Banking Facilities as a Free Economic Zone." *Aussenwirtschaft* (The Swiss Review of International Economic Relations). May 1984, pp. 57–74.

Key, S. J., and Brundy, J. M. "Implementation of the International Banking Act." *Federal Reserve Bulletin,* October 1979, pp. 785–796.

Melton, W. C., and Mahr, J. M. "Bankers' Acceptances." *Federal Reserve Bank of New York Quarterly Review,* Summer 1981, pp. 39–55.

Parente, G. M. "Anatomy of the Eurodollar Floating Rate Market." Salomon Brothers, Inc., March 1984.

Parkinson, P. M. "U.S. Banks' Participation in the International Interbank Market." Unpublished study paper, Board of Governors of the Federal Reserve System, September 1982.

Pecchioli, R. M. *The Internationalisation of Banking: The Policy Issues.* Paris: Organization for Economic Cooperation and Development, 1983.

"Recent Activities of Foreign Branches of U.S. Banks." *Federal Reserve Bulletin,* October 1972, pp. 855–865.

Tamagna, F. M., and Willis, P. B. "United States Banking Organizations Abroad." *Federal Reserve Bulletin,* December 1956, pp. 1284–1299.

Teeters, N. H., and Terrell, H. S. "The Role of Banks in the International Financial System." *Federal Reserve Bulletin,* September 1983, pp. 663–671.

Terrell, H. S., and Mills, R. H., Jr. "International Banking Facilities and the Eurodollar Market." Staff Study No. 124, Board of Governors of the Federal Reserve System, August 1983.

U.S. Department of the Treasury. *Tax Havens in the Caribbean Basin.* January 1984.

U.S. House of Representatives, Committee on Ways and Means, Staff of Joint Committee on Taxation. *Tax Treatment of Interest Paid to Foreign Investors.* April 1984.

U.S. Secretary of the Treasury and Board of Governors of the Federal Reserve System. "Report to Congress on Improving International Bank Capital Standards." May 1984.

U.S. Senate, Committee on Finance, Staff of Joint Committee on Taxation, *Taxation of Banks and Thrift Institutions.* March 1983.

Van Horne, J. C. *Financial Management and Policy* (3rd ed.). Englewood Cliffs, N.J.: Prentice-Hall, 1974.

Welt, L. G. B. (Ed.). *ETCs: New Methods for U.S. Exporting.* New York: American Management Association Management Briefing, 1984.

Williams, D. "Opportunities and Constraints in International Lending." *Finance and Development,* March 1983, pp. 24–27.

9 Capitalization Problems in Perspective

Reid Nagle and Bruce Petersen

Over the past 50 years, asset growth of insured depository institutions has outpaced the rate of growth of their capital. In turn, the resultant decline in capital–asset ratios has fueled the perception that risk in the financial system has increased. As discussed by several of the authors in this volume, a number of factors have contributed to the decline in capital ratios. Inflation resulted in a rapid growth in nominal banking resources. Regulatory policies unwittingly encouraged increased leverage, and the subsidies resulting from a mispriced deposit insurance system induced institutions to take on increased risk and substitute government guarantees for capital. Recently, however, the regulatory agencies have attempted to stabilize and even reverse the trend in capital ratios, and thrift institutions have begun to convert to stock form as one means to facilitate external capital formation. Moreover, numerous proposals have been made to place equity holders at greater risk as one means to reintroduce greater market discipline in capital formation policies of depository institutions. These recent reversals and reexamination of public policy toward the role of capital in insured depository institutions emphasize the increasingly important role of capital formation policies to managers of depository institutions.

This chapter briefly reviews the role and functions of capital in depository institutions and discusses regulatory policies toward capital. It concludes with a look at ways that depository institutions have recently attempted to tap equity markets in response to pressures to improve their capitalization.

PURPOSES OF CAPITAL

The purpose of capital for any institution (financial or nonfinancial) is twofold. First, together with earnings, capital is a firm's cushion against adversity. Corporations may from time to time experience losses resulting from specific problems like poor management and defalcation, or from business risks gone awry. Risk taking is a vital component of financial intermediation and is the chief contributor to the profitability of financial institutions. Mismatching the durations of assets and liabilities, thus exposing the firm to the risks of changing interest rates, is one common form of risk.[1] Making unsecured or undercollateralized loans is another. Regardless of the cause, when losses do occur, capital protects the firm from insolvency. Because capital funds need not be repaid they can absorb these losses. A firm can experience losses of up to 100% of its net worth, while meeting its obligations and continuing to operate.[2] Conversely, debt must be repaid and cannot absorb a firm's losses.

In addition to traditional equity, subordinated debt is considered capital by various regulators for purposes of assessing capital adequacy. This is largely due to its long-term nature and to its subordinated position to other liabilities. These qualities make subordinated debt desirable: the former because it helps reduce maturity matching problems and indirectly protects the institution against liquidity problems; the latter because it prioritizes the claims of the insuring agencies as well as depositors and creditors in a failure and assigns the greatest risk among creditors to a specified, generally better-informed group. These qualities notwithstanding, a firm cannot depend on subordinated debt for protection against losses. If a firm's capital is depleted and losses continue, it will default.[3]

The distinction, especially for thrifts, between pure capital and subordinated debt is clouded by the fact that financial institutions can and have continued to operate without default after their capital has been used up.[4] If a bank or thrift can continue to raise debt, it can use the proceeds raised at the margin to cover operating losses. This can be the result of either a conscious attempt to save the firm by its creditors or the unwitting behavior of insured depositors, whose primary concern is federal insurance rather than the health of the institution. If the institution can turn itself around and produce profits, it can survive. If, on the other hand, it continues to operate as before, its losses will increase and eventually it will fail.[5]

A second purpose of capital is as a funding source. Equity financing is a substitute for deposits and other forms of debt financing. The all-in cost of equity is its dilutive effect on earnings per share, the combination of earnings on the new funds, dividends paid to new shareholders, additional earnings made possible by leverage, and the division of profits among a greater number of shareholders. This cost of equity reflects the net cost or benefit to the firm (including existing shareholders) of an equity issue and suggests that a firm in maximizing its return on equity and earnings per share will consider a number of strategies, including expansion of its equity base and issuance of debt.

Financial and nonfinancial firms work to minimize the total cost of financing (the sum of the cost of debt and the cost of equity), but the underlying nature of their activities leads to different capital structures. This difference is reflected in the comparative net worth–assets ratios of financial and nonfinancial firms. Table 9.1 shows the equity–assets ratios for financial firms and nonfinancial firms from 1963 to 1979. The ratio for nonfinancial firms ranged from 39.72% to 53.97%, while the comparable range for financial firms was between 6.11% and 7.69%.

Thus, while nonfinancial firms use equity to finance a large portion of their balance sheet, the use of equity funding among financial institutions is small relative to the overall activity of the industry. This is not the result of differing rules or philosophies of financial and nonfinancial firms, since both types of firms attempt to minimize their total cost of funds. Financial institutions use a relatively small amount of equity in structuring their balance sheet because they have access to deposit funds at a cost lower than that of equity capital, whereas nonfinancial institutions have more limited access to debt financing. This reflects several factors. First, for depository institutions, the guarantee of the federal government in providing deposit insurance is a significant advantage in raising low-cost funds, due to the virtually risk-free return to the depositor. A second relative advantage of a financial institution in raising nonequity funding is the ability to manage funds for individuals and firms less capable of doing so independently. This is an advantage in tapping nonequity funding sources. A third reason for lower nonequity funding costs for financial firms is that creditors perceive the risk of a financial institution to be lower than that of nonfinancial institutions. *Standard and Poor's Rating Guide* (1979) observes that "for a number of reasons, banking companies in general are probably less likely to default on their debt than industrial companies; hence, they tend to be in the higher end of the rating spectrum." The "reasons" referred to, while not specifically identified, probably include the greater liquidity of assets of financial institutions. Paper is easier to sell than specialized buildings, equipment, and inventories. Another of these "reasons" is the simple fact that financial institutions have defaulted less frequently than nonfinancial institutions, and when

Table 9.1. Net Worth/Assets Ratios for Nonfinancial Industries and Financial Institutions

	Nonfinancial Firms[a]			Financial Firms		
	Net Worth (in millions of dollars)	Total Assets (in millions of dollars)	Ratio (in percentages)	Net Worth (in millions of dollars)	Total Assets (in millions of dollars)	Ratio (in percentages)
1963	$ 353,955	$ 655,821	53.97	$ 36,867	479,118	7.69
1964	373,480	701,659	53.23	36,810	523,119	7.04
1965	399,297	767,623	52.02	38,452	567,556	6.78
1966	422,995	837,059	50.53	39,569	595,811	6.64
1967	456,377	913,095	49.98	41,955	652,463	6.43
1968	488,305	1,012,707	48.22	44,475	715,197	6.22
1969	533,197	1,147,466	46.47	50,543	767,791	6.58
1970	555,931	1,233,553	45.07	55,605	854,153	6.51
1971	587,608	1,316,590	44.63	63,589	973,243	6.53
1972	640,151	1,446,631	44.25	71,860	1,144,351	6.28
1973	703,553	1,636,969	42.98	83,347	1,317,444	6.33
1974	762,588	1,839,815	41.45	88,987	1,457,453	6.11
1975	827,294	1,964,590	42.11	96,613	1,564,795	6.17
1976	910,026	2,171,140	41.91	108,098	1,717,671	6.29
1977	1,027,991	2,464,911	41.70	119,768	1,946,577	6.15
1978	1,129,217	2,765,055	40.84	135,762	2,221,087	6.11
1979	1,274,287	3,208,185	39.72	149,554	2,442,009	6.12

SOURCE: *Statistics of Income: Corporation Income Tax Returns, 1963–1979*, Department of the Treasury, Internal Revenue Service, Table 1.

[a]Finance, insurance, and real estate were subtracted from all industries to calculate a ratio for nonfinancial institutions.
[b]Banks and savings and loan associations were combined to calculate the ratio for finance as an industry. These ratios are for comparative purposes only. The assets reported include only domestic assets.

they have, the federal deposit insurance agencies have typically protected uninsured creditors and depositors with balances in excess of the insurance limit.

Creditors demand less capitalization for financial firms than for non-financial firms but are not indifferent to the capital structure of financial institutions. *Standard and Poor's Rating Guide* (1979), for example, considers profitability measures, liquidity measures, asset risk measures, and the balance of rate sensitivities of assets and liabilities along with capitalization in determining a rating for a financial institution's debt.

A level of capitalization considered excessively low by creditors will lead to a higher borrowing cost and possible exclusion from certain types of borrowings if ratings are unattainable. An excessively high level of capitalization will indicate a foregone opportunity for additional profit through additional leverage. In theory, the market will dictate the proper capital structure for a financial institution. An excessively low level of capital will cause creditors to charge more for funds, while maintenance of too much capital will impair earnings and drive the cost of capital up. Thus, the market optimizes the capital structure by dictating to the firm the level that minimizes the sum of the cost of debt (including deposits) and the cost of capital. In this regard, the role of federal deposit insurance and the policies toward resolving failures are critical. Policies that reduce risks to creditors at little or no cost imply that additional risks will be taken on to offset those absorbed by the government.

CAPITAL AND RISK SHARING

Financial institutions are clearly not risk free. Management abilities differ, competition varies according to geographic locations, national and regional economies go through business cycles that affect the fortunes of financial intermediaries, and other factors intervene that produce a wide variance in the performance of financial institutions. These factors generally translate into one of three major categories of risk confronting financial institutions: credit risk, interest rate risk, and liquidity (or maturity) risk. From a historical perspective, the failure of major financial institutions in the past half century can all be linked to one of these major forms of risk (see Table 9.2). Liquidity and credit risk dominated commercial bank failures of the 1930s while interest rate risk precipitated the thrift debacle of the 1980s. Clearly in both instances, some level of capital would have prevented these large numbers of failures. A bank may incur a credit loss when a loan goes into default and there is insufficient collateral available to cover principal and accrued interest. During the recession of the period

Table 9.2 20 Largest Depository Failures Based on Asset Size in Constant Dollars (1934–1983)

Rank	Name and Location of Institution	Year of Failure	Asset Size, Constant 1983 Dollars (in billions)	Asset Size, Current Dollars (in billions)	Cause
1	Franklin National Bank, N.Y.	1974	7.4	3.7	Losses in foreign exchange followed by major withdrawals
2	First Federal Savings and Loan Association, Chicago	1983	4.0	4.0	High interest rates
3	New York Bank for Savings	1982	3.5	3.4	High interest rates
4	Fidelity Savings of San Francisco	1982	3.0	2.9	High interest rates
5	First Federal Savings and Loan Association, Broward County	1981	2.9	2.6	High interest rates
6	United States National Bank, San Diego	1973	2.8	1.3	Loan losses associated with insider loans
7	West Side Federal Savings and Loan Association, N.Y.	1981	2.7	2.5	High interest rates
8	Suffolk County Federal Savings and Loan Association, N.Y.	1983	2.7	2.7	High interest rates
9	Greenwich Savings Bank, N.Y.	1981	2.7	2.5	High interest rates
10	Western Saving Fund Society, Haverford, Pa.	1982	2.2	2.1	High interest rates

11	Suburban Savings and Loan Association, Wayne, N.J.	1983	1.9	1.9	High interest rates
12	Biscayne Federal Savings and Loan Association, Miami, Fla.	1983	1.8	1.8	High interest rates
13	Union Dime Savings Bank	1981	1.5	1.4	High interest rates
14	County Federal Savings and Loan Association, Rockville Centre, N.Y.	1982	1.4	1.4	High interest rates
15	Northwest Federal Savings and Loan Association, Chicago	1982	1.4	1.3	High interest rates
16	First National Bank of Midland, Texas	1983	1.2	1.2	Energy-related loan losses, followed by major withdrawals
17	Franklin Society Federal Savings and Loan Association, N.Y.	1981	1.1	1.0	High interest rates
18	Banco Credito y Ahorro Ponceno, Ponce, Puerto Rico	1978	1.1	0.7	Loan losses
19	Western New York Savings Bank, Buffalo	1982	1.1	1.0	High interest rates
20	Farmers and Mechanics Savings Bank of Minneapolis	1982	1.0	1.0	High interest rates

NOTE: The FDIC does not consider the merger of Seafirst to be a failure.

1980–1982, the most visible signs of credit risk appeared in the delinquencies experienced by large commercial banks in the loans made to developing countries, and also in the problems encountered by banks with substantial portfolios of energy and energy-related loans.

Fluctuations in interest rates pose a risk to the economic net worth of a financial institution arising from a duration mismatch of assets and liabilities. The traditional thrift institution strategy of funding fixed-rate mortgages with rate-sensitive retail deposits is an example of maturity mismatching, which left the industry vulnerable to declining profitability during periods of disintermediation—1966, 1969–1970, and 1973–1974. It produced staggering industry losses in the period 1980–1982 as short-term interest rates rose relative to long-term rates over a sustained period of time. Table 9.3 displays the fortunes and misfortunes of the thrift industry over time in relation to short-term interest rates.

The most extreme form of liquidity risk was evidenced from 1929 to 1933, when the combination of the depression and absence of deposit insurance caused massive runs on banks. Institutions unable to develop alternative funding sources or liquidate assets without incurring substantial losses could not meet the demands that the run on deposits was creating, and many failed. From 1929 until the end of the Bank Holiday in 1933, 9,000 banks disappeared. Since the depression, the nature and scope of liquidity risks have changed. The advent of deposit insurance, the absence of severe economic depressions, and, until recently, the greater restriction on permitted activities of financial institutions have all served to reduce the possibility of illiquidity among depository institutions. In fact, Citicorp in a 1981 analysis of commercial bank capital requirements suggested that the growth of money market banking as evidenced by the development of the Federal funds, Eurodollar, and wholesale CD markets has further enhanced the ability of large institutions to manage liquidity. While this observation may be true for large, healthy institutions, the recent experience of entities hard hit by losses arising from energy and certain international loans suggests that institutions relying heavily on uninsured funding may be unable to retain these funds when serious financial problems develop.

For example, immediately prior to its acquisition by BankAmerica in July 1983, Seafirst was borrowing heavily from the Federal Reserve discount window, as a majority of banks that had previously agreed to a $1.5 billion safety net withdrew their support. Liquidity also became a major problem for First National Bank of Midland after it reported heavy losses on energy-related lending. Midland's deposit base shrank from $1.4 billion in December 1982 to $622 million less than one year later, immediately prior to its supervisory merger in October of 1983.

Table 9.3. Assets, Net Income, and Return on Average Assets for Insured Savings and Loan Associations Compared with the Average Prime Rate (1960–1983)

	Assets of Insured Savings & Loans (in millions of dollars)		Net Income of Insured Savings and Loans (in millions of dollars)	ROA (in percentages)	Prime Rate (in percentages)
	Average	Year-End			
1960	$ 63,345	$ 67,268	$ 548	0.87	4.82
1961	72,503	77,738	712	0.98	4.50
1962	83,534	89,330	817	0.98	4.50
1963	96,158	102,985	672	0.70	4.50
1964	108,819	114,653	788	0.72	4.50
1965	119,555	124,456	785	0.66	4.54
1966	126,671	128,885	609	0.48	5.63
1967	133,696	138,507	595	0.45	5.63
1968	143,130	147,753	846	0.59	6.28
1969	152,275	156,797	1,013	0.67	7.95
1970	163,668	170,538	925	0.57	7.91
1971	185,259	199,979	1,314	0.71	5.70
1972	218,088	236,196	1,687	0.77	5.25
1973	250,281	264,365	1,897	0.76	8.02
1974	275,974	287,583	1,483	0.54	10.81
1975	308,299	329,015	1,448	0.47	7.86
1976	355,343	381,671	2,250	0.63	6.84
1977	414,772	447,872	3,198	0.77	6.83
1978	479,313	510,754	3,918	0.82	9.06
1979	538,740	566,725	3,620	0.67	12.67
1980	591,020	615,314	784	0.13	15.27
1981	633,169	651,024	(4,632)	(0.73)	18.87
1982	681,694	712,364	(4,271)	(0.63)	14.86
1983	750,423	814,620	1,968	0.26	10.79

SOURCE: Federal Home Loan Bank Board, *Combined Financial Statements*, 1970 and 1983.

Other forms of risk, such as technological and exchange rate risk are becoming more important in their potential impact on the performance of depository institutions. Of these two classes of risk, technological risk will assume an increasing role in the operations of financial institutions, as the complexity and interrelationship of financial products and services require greater degrees of automation.

Regulatory Capital Requirements

Regulators take an active role in measuring and establishing standards for the capital adequacy of financial institutions. The justification for doing so is threefold: First, maintenance of capital adequacy provides a layer of protection that limits potential losses to the deposit insurance agencies; second, capital adequacy along with deposit insurance helps to control the externality arising from bank failures—namely, a loss of depositor confidence that can undermine and threaten healthy institutions; and third, capital standards serve to protect uninsured creditors that may not have complete information regarding the economic viability of an institution. For these reasons, capital adequacy has been an important regulatory objective over the past 70 years. The subjective nature of capital adequacy and the evolution of financial institutions over time have affected capital adequacy regulation in three ways:

Capital requirements have varied over time.
Capital requirements have varied according to type and size of institutions.
Capital requirements have varied among regulators.

Historically, bank capital requirements were a logical outgrowth of state requirements that state-chartered banks maintain specie reserves against note issues. Following passage of the National Banking Act of 1864, organizers of national banks were permitted, as part of a federal policy to finance the Civil War, to meet the minimum capital requirements by contributing holdings of public debt that the bank could then deposit with the Treasurer of the United States in return for U.S. notes.

The Comptroller of the Currency established a formal capital guideline of 10% of deposit liabilities in 1914. This became a generally accepted rule of thumb and was adopted for many state-chartered institutions as well. The standard lasted through the depression and the 9,000 bank failures in the 1930s. But the standard was revised during World War II as the acquisition of government debt expanded bank balance sheets faster than capital could grow. The Comptroller then promulgated a new standard based on risk assets (i.e., those assets other than cash, bank deposits, and government securities). Total capital was required to equal 5% or more of risk assets. Later this standard was modified to reflect different classes of assets, their respective risks, and the amount of capital required to be held against each asset classification.

This evolution of a quantitative standard of capital adequacy was followed in the late 1960s by a shift in emphasis to more qualitative and subjective determinations. In particular, the Comptroller announced that "henceforth, the capital position of banks will be analyzed and appraised in relation to the character of its management and its asset and deposit position as a going institution under normal conditions, with due allowance for a reasonable margin of safety, and with due regard to the bank's capacity to furnish the broadest service to the public. These factors which are necessarily imprecise, cannot be directly interpolated into any specific formula."

In the wake of concern about increases in the number and aggregate size of bank failures during 1980, the Federal Reserve, FDIC, and Comptroller of the Currency took steps to quantify and coordinate capital adequacy requirements. In December 1981, the Federal Reserve and Comptroller jointly advanced capital standards for regional and community banks, including bank holding companies. These standards were based on four principles:

1. Bank capital requirements should be based on size.
2. Secondary capital should include subordinated debt and limited-life preferred stock.
3. Large firms (the 17 multinational banks) should be subject to different (i.e., lower) capital requirements.
4. Conditional upon meeting minimum capital requirements, individual banks should continue to be evaluated on other, subjective criteria.

These capital standards set forth a minimum primary capital/assets ratio of 5%, where primary capital includes common and perpetual preferred stock and retained earnings. Secondary capital requirements were more rigorous, requiring a minimum of 5.5% for regional banks and 6% for community banks. In June 1983, the Federal Reserve and Comptroller amended the 1980 rules to include the 17 large multinational banking organizations, requiring them to maintain a primary capital ratio of at least 5%. In 1984 the minimum acceptable primary capital ratio (for "well-managed" banks) was set at 5.5% for banks in all size categories and for bank holding companies as well.

While banking regulators were tightening up on capital requirements, the Federal Home Loan Bank Board was relaxing capital adequacy tests for savings and loans. Beginning in 1970, required capital ratios for savings and loans were reduced several times, so that as of late 1983 minimum net worth was only 3% of a five-year moving average of liabilities. For rapidly growing institutions, the liability averaging technique permits a much lower current capital ratio—only 2% for an association growing 25% annually. Moreover, the FHLBB is more liberal in its definition of primary capital—it includes subordinated debt, limited-life preferred stock, and the excess of the appraised value over the book value of certain real estate.

Capital ratios of commercial banks and savings and loans have declined since 1970, as shown in Table 9.4. While it is true that savings and loan ratios have been consistently lower during this period, a more pronounced difference appeared by year-end 1982 as a result of the large losses experienced by thrifts in 1981 and 1982. There exists no empirical evidence to suggest that capital standards should be lower for thrifts than for commercial banks. In fact, recent experience suggests the opposite is true. Of the 20 largest depository institutions failing from 1934 to 1984, 17 have occurred since 1981 and of those, 16 were thrift institutions. The heavy losses incurred by thrifts as a result of interest rate volatility suggest a need for greater capital than for commercial banks.

Table 9.4. Capital Ratio of Commercial Banks and Savings and Loan Associations—Equity Capital Divided by Total Assets (1970–1982)

	Commercial Banks (in percentages)	Savings and Loan Associations (in percentages)
1970	6.8	7.0
1971	6.7	6.5
1972	6.4	6.2
1973	6.3	6.2
1974	5.6	6.2
1975	5.9	5.8
1976	6.1	5.6
1977	5.9	5.5
1978	5.8	5.5
1979	5.7	5.5
1980	5.8	5.3
1981	5.8	4.3
1982	5.9	3.7

SOURCE: Federal Deposit Insurance Corporation, *Annual Report,* various issues; and Federal Home Loan Bank Board, *Combined Financial Statement,* various issues.

Conflicting Interests in Capital Adequacy

Insured depositors, uninsured creditors, borrowers, regulators, and shareholders all have different objectives that affect their respective views about the capital adequacy of a financial institution. Insured depositors, those whose combined deposits in an institution total $100,000 or less, appear to have little concern about capital adequacy. The system of deposit insurance introduced in the 1930s has fulfilled its original purpose of instilling confidence in depositors, despite the fact that the actual resources of the deposit insurance agencies (FDIC and FSLIC) fall far short of what could potentially be required in a crisis.[6] During the period 1979–1982, as thrift industry losses mounted, many institutions on the brink of insolvency—and some that had actually reported negative net worth—continued to attract insured as well as uninsured deposits.

For uninsured creditors, capital adequacy of a financial institution involves a risk–reward trade-off. No creditor lends money with an expectation of losing it, yet lenders will accept greater risk for a high enough price. In most circumstances, the strongest financial institutions can borrow at a rate only slightly above that of Treasury securities, while those perceived as a credit risk must pay a significant premium.

Financial markets can effectively evaluate and price the risk of financial institutions provided there is access to timely and accurate financial information. A major difficulty in evaluating risk, and one regulators will encounter in pricing variable-rate deposit insurance, is that financial information as currently reported frequently does not present an accurate picture of an institution's economic condition. Historical value accounting distorts the true financial and economic condition of institutions during periods of interest rate volatility, and credit exposure is subject to considerable leeway in evaluation and reporting. In recent years, volatile interest rates, adjustment problems in the energy sector, and the financial plight of developing nations have combined to highlight the inadequacy of accounting and financial information available to the public.

Although borrowers have less at stake in the capital adequacy of depository institutions, they are affected in two ways: First, depository institutions have both legal and self-imposed loan-to-one-borrower limitations that are based on capital; and second, a borrower who requires continuous financing will be inconvenienced if a credit commitment to fund is not met because of lender failure. This latter situation can cause severe problems if the borrower is unable to secure replacement financing to complete a project.

Shareholders obviously have a major stake in the capital adequacy of a depository institution in which they invest. In general it is true that an institution that maintains a high relative level of capital has sacrificed shareholder return for safety. In such situations, return on equity and earnings per share will tend to be lower than would exist with a lower level of capital, while the safety and soundness of the institution will be enhanced. Conversely, institutions that consistently leverage their asset base at profitable spreads, driving their capital ratios down to the regulatory minimums, will ordinarily have a higher return on equity and earnings per share but will sacrifice the additional safety buffer maintained by more highly capitalized institutions.

The fact that shareholders have different investment objectives translates into a broad spectrum of capital strategies for financial institutions. The investor who purchases shares in Morgan Guaranty, a money-center institution with an equity–assets ratio of 4.6% and an annual asset growth of 13% from year-end 1977 through 1982, has different investment objectives than does a shareholder in Financial Corporation of America, a savings and loan holding company that seldom had a capital ratio above 3% and that grew at an annual rate of 58% over the same period.

These differences in capital strategies suggest that there exists no single optimum level of capital for shareholders, and that differences in capital ratios in many cases reflect differences in stockholder objectives. Not all financial institutions efficiently execute a capital strategy, however, and those that do not thus perform at a suboptimal level. Optimality refers to the efficient frontier of risk–reward combinations such that for every level of risk, profitability (as measured by earnings per share) is maximized, and for every level of profit, the level of risk is minimized.

To summarize the perspectives of the different players, it can generally be stated that unsecured creditors, uninsured depositors, the deposit insuring agencies, and, to a lesser extent, insured depositors and borrowers unambiguously prefer a higher level of capital. Evidence also suggests that unsecured creditors and uninsured depositors consider capital strength as a factor in negotiating credit terms. Stockholders in general favor additional, profitable leverage and seek an institution with a level of capital that places it at a desired position on the risk–reward frontier.

ALTERNATIVE SOURCES OF CAPITAL

Financial institutions can generate capital from sources internal or external to the organization. Internal capital formation refers to the additions to capital generated from earnings, less any dividends paid to shareholders. External capital formation includes all those forms of capital sold in the capital markets or privately placed that qualify under the regulatory, accounting, and economic definitions discussed earlier.

In recent years, inflationary pressures on nominal asset growth and increases in the perceived levels of risk of financial institutions have increased the need for capital. The average annual growth rate of 10.9% in GNP over the most recent complete business cycle (from January 1980 to July 1981) should have translated into a similar requirement for growth in financial intermediation, and one should have expected capital to have expanded by the same degree. At the same time, however, the rapid pace of financial deregulation expanded the risk–reward frontier for financial institutions;[7] the collapsing debt structure of developing countries substantially increased the credit exposure of money-center banks; and increased volatility of interest rates weakened a large number of financial institutions, particularly those within the thrift industry that had a duration mismatch between assets and liabilities. All of these events suggest capital should have expanded at a faster rate than GNP.

However, during this period of increased need for both absolute and relative levels of capital, the equity–assets ratio of commercial banks has continued to undergo a secular decline, from a ratio of 6.8% in 1970 to 5.9% 12 years later. If the growth of commercial banking continues at its present pace over the remainder of the eighties, there will be a requirement for an additional $157 billion of equity capital, assuming the current equity–assets ratio is maintained. Similarly, if the thrift industry is to restore its net worth ratio to 5% and grow at an annual rate of 8%, by 1990 it will require an increase in capital of $40.4 billion—an amount equal to 1.75 times its book net worth at year-end 1982. Where will this vast increase in capital come from?

An examination of the period from 1970 through 1982 indicates that the majority of bank equity capital growth was attributable to earnings retention. During this time, retained earnings accounted for $74 billion, or 81% of the $91 billion increase in net worth. Given the magnitude of future capital requirements in the eighties and the anticipated decline in financial institution profitability as a result of increased competition, it seems unlikely that retained earnings can continue to contribute as large a share of total capital growth. Increasingly, banks will need to utilize both traditional and innovative ways of accessing the capital markets to meet the shortfall.

Internal Sources of Capital

Within the financial services industry, a number of generalizations can be drawn that characterize the reliance on internally generated capital. Among commercial banks, it has been observed that large banks and banks situated in rapidly growing areas tend to rely less heavily on retained earnings as a source of capital expansion. The reasons for this difference relate primarily to economies in accessing the capital markets and investor perception of desirable geographic location.

While retained earnings have contributed the dominant share of equity growth for commercial banks, the thrift industry has had an even greater reliance upon retained earnings as a source of capital. In 1975, 79% of the assets of savings and loans were held by mutual organizations. That percentage decreased to 70% by year-end 1982 as the trend toward mutual-to-stock conversion accelerated, but the very existence of such a large base of mutual institutions resulted in an almost exclusive reliance on earnings retention as a means of capital augmentation. It was only in January of 1973 that the Federal Home Loan Bank Board authorized mutual institutions to include subordinated debt in the regulatory computation of net worth.[8] Later, in 1982, the Garn-St Germain Act included a provision for income capital certificates (ICCs) to be issued by the federal deposit insurance agencies to those institutions deemed viable but without sufficient net worth to meet regulatory requirements. This action expanded the alternatives available for mutual institutions to increase capital when retained earnings proved insufficient.

The wedge that separates retained earnings from net income is dividends. Shareholder-owned institutions, be they commercial banks or thrifts, distribute a share of profits to shareholders. Obviously, the greater the dividend, the smaller the amount of net income retained in the capital account. The decisions as to whether to pay a dividend, and how much, are complex and must be balanced against an institution's internal need for capital. The factors influencing these decisions include:

The Nature of the Financial Institution. Rapidly growing institutions need a greater rate of capital growth than do less rapidly growing institutions, and, as a result, they tend to distribute a smaller share of net income through dividends.

The Marginal Tax Rate of Investors. For most corporations, including financial institutions, dividends paid to individual shareholders are subject to double taxation—that is, net income is taxed at a corporate level and again at a personal level when it is distributed to shareholders. When tax-paying corporations are the dominant shareholders, the 46% marginal tax rate discourages a high level of dividend payout.

Impact of Dividends on Market Price of Stock. Managers of financial institutions, much as managers of other corporations, place a heavy emphasis on stock price performance, particularly when the managers have a large ownership position. Up to a point, payment of dividends tends to correlate positively with stock prices, thereby inducing managers to pursue a dividend policy that generates a desired price level while at the same time providing for capital adequacy.

Economic Return. Long-run economic returns of capital resources can differ greatly depending on where they are put to use. The degree of variation depends primarily on the investment opportunities belonging to the corporation and its shareholders. At one extreme, high dividend payments are justified when the shareholder has access to a higher after-tax return on investment than the dividend-paying corporation. At the other extreme, earnings retention will produce a greater economic return if the corporation has access to a higher after-tax rate of return than the shareholder. The desirability of dividends vis-à-vis earnings retention will frequently vary across industries as well as across firms, inasmuch as the investment opportunities and tax rates of corporations tend to correlate by industry. Among depository institutions, thrift institutions and, to a lesser extent, commercial banks currently have relatively low tax rates that allow them to invest at high after-tax yields, indicating a higher economic return than would accrue to most tax-paying shareholders and suggesting a lower dividend rate. Of course, there are exceptions, and institutions with a higher marginal tax rate and/or lower investment opportunity have an incentive to pay a higher dividend.

Once earnings and dividend distribution have been determined, capital adequacy and the need for external capital financing depend on the rate of asset growth as well as any changed risk perceptions. More important, the move by commercial bank regulators to assign strict quantitative measures of capital adequacy above industry averages, coupled with the capital needs of thrift institutions emerging from the interest rate debacle of the period 1979–1982, will increase the need for external capital financing in the future. The following section examines the methods available to financial institutions for securing external capital.

External Sources of Capital

Although external sources of capital have provided only about 20% of total bank capital generation in the past 10 years, external capital's importance in the future will increase along with growth and diversification of the financial services industry. The importance of external capital has become evident in the thrift industry, where, in 1983, 79 savings and loans and mutual savings banks converted from mutual to stock form, raising an aggregate of $2.7 billion in new equity capital, an amount equal to 450% of the total capital raised through thrift conversions through year-end 1982.

Capital can and does take many forms, provided it lives within the broad parameters discussed earlier that define permanent capital. Clearly the most basic forms of capital, common and perpetual preferred stock, meet the accounting and regulatory requirements for inclusion as equity capital. The variants of these two structures are many, and the section that follows examines some of the alternative means for raising capital, beginning with the most basic.

Common Stock.   This is the traditional form of equity financing, with investors taking the greatest risk in exchange for the opportunity to receive the potential rewards of ownership. Common shareholders stand last in line to be paid following liquidation. In exchange for the assumption of this risk, they enjoy the rights of ownership, and the benefits of appreciation and/or dividends. On the balance sheet, proceeds from common stock issuances go first into the common stock account, in an amount equal to the par value of the issue, with the excess channeled into the surplus account.

Perpetual Preferred Stock.   This form of stock has a higher claim on assets than does common stock in the event of liquidation. In return for this higher degree of safety, preferred shareholders generally accept a fixed dividend rate and forego any additional claim on profits. While the pure definition of capital precludes any predefined maturity on preferred stock, issuers frequently include a call provision in the issue that permits them to prepay the preferred stock after some elapsed period. Dividends on preferred stock possess the same advantages and disadvantages as dividends on common stock: (1) Dividends, unlike interest expense on debt, are not deductible for income tax purposes; (2) for individual investors, dividend payments are subject to double taxation—income is first taxed at the corporate level and then taxed a second time when dividends are paid to individual investors; and (3) for corporate investors, dividends received have an 85% dividend exclusion, reducing the marginal corporate income tax rate from 46 to 7%.[9]

Use of preferred stock by financial institutions began during the depression when the Reconstruction Finance Corporation used it to keep failing institutions afloat. This initial use created a misperception that linked preferred stock to an unhealthy financial condition. Largely because of this stigma and the double taxation of corporate income passed through to individuals in the form of dividends, preferred stock was never widely used as a form of capital financing. In fact, the rating agencies have frowned upon institutions showing too high a level of preferred financing on their balance sheets (i.e., in excess of 10 to 15% of total capital) and have viewed any excess as a negative factor in assigning a rating. Under appropriate business circumstances, there is no justification for this bias, and, indeed, it is becoming less and less a deterrent to issuing preferred stock. As perceptions have changed and as a greater number of financial institutions have become nontaxpayers, preferred stock issues have become more frequent and acceptable.

Convertible Preferred Stock.   This is preferred stock that is convertible into common stock at a predetermined exchange ratio. Because conversion is at the option of the investor, offering the possibility of appreciation, addition of a conversion feature enhances the value of a preferred stock issue and allows for a reduction in the required dividend rate. Typically, conversion premiums (the markup of the conversion price over the market price of the common stock at the day of issue) range from 10 to 30%, permitting a reduction in the dividend rate of 2 to 4%.

Another wrinkle in convertible preferred stock is the addition of an exchange feature (i.e., convertible exchangeable preferred stock) that permits the issuer to convert preferred stock into subordinated debt after a period of years. This feature is particularly attractive to financial institutions that know they will be nontaxpayers for several years but wish to have access to interest deductions later on when their tax pictures may have changed.

Adjustable-Rate Preferred Stock.   This is another relatively new vehicle utilized extensively by the commercial banking community during 1982 and 1983. It is nothing more than perpetual preferred stock with a floating rate based on the higher of three indices: three-month Treasury bill, five-year Treasury note, and 20-year Treasury bond. Its popularity arose from a number of convergent factors: (1) Large multinational banks faced increased capital requirements that drove them to the capital markets; (2) for nontaxpaying issuers, it was a relatively inexpensive means of acquiring funds, since the nominal payment to corporate taxpaying investors was below that of debt financing because of the dividends-received deduction; and (3) corporate investors viewed the adjustable-rate preferred stock as a near-tax-free alternative to commercial paper—even though the instrument itself was long term, the rate variability was perceived to offer principal protection in a volatile interest rate environment.

These forms of capital are the ones frequently used by financial institutions in recent years to secure additional capital. Numerous, less-popularized versions of capital financing exist that either have been employed infrequently or are on the drawing boards for future use. Among the former group, warrants, or the right to purchase stock in the future at a price specified today, have been sold in conjunction with common stock, preferred stock, and debt in order to raise the price of an offering, lower the required dividend yield, and secure the possibility of additional equity financing in the future. Leveraged preferred stock involves the private

Table 9.5. Capital Financing in the Banking Industry

	Dow Jones Industrial Average (year-end)	Equity Capital Financing (in millions of dollars)	Total Capital Financing (in millions of dollars)
1967	905.11	$ 36.4	$ 291.8
1968	943.75	82.0	424.6
1969	800.36	70.2	360.9
1970	838.92	103.4	229.5
1971	890.20	127.5	1,699.5
1972	1,020.02	221.8	2,636.8
1973	850.86	87.4	1,110.9
1974	616.24	45.5	1,340.0
1975	852.41	115.4	1,561.6
1976	1,004.65	349.3	2,481.2
1977	831.17	532.0	2,791.8
1978	905.01	576.3	1,618.7
1979	838.74	173.6	2,451.3
1980	963.99	543.1	1,509.4
1981	875.00	832.1	1,433.5
1982	1,046.54	2,283.3	5,506.1
1983	1,258.64	3,223.2	9,945.8

SOURCE: *Wall Street Journal,* various issues; Irving Trust Company.

placement of sinking fund preferred stock in a beneficial trust that is 75% financed by the equity investor who receives the full pass-through of interest expense and dividends. In the typical structure, the issuer is a nontaxpaying corporation, and the equity investor is a corporate taxpayer who makes full use of the deduction for interest expense and receives an 85% exclusion for dividends received.

Considered a form of quasi capital, subordinated debt is counted as a liability for accounting purposes, but, as mentioned before, it possesses the liquidation features of capital in that it is subordinated to the interests of unsecured creditors. Subordinated debt generally has a redemption feature or sinking fund and may or may not be convertible. Those issues that are convertible into common stock move one step closer to a strict definition of capital due to the possible conversion to permanent capital at a later date. As with convertible stock, addition of a conversion feature to subordinated debt serves to raise the price of the issue and reduce the required dividend.

Commercial bank equity financing (inclusive of subordinated debt) has

Table 9.6. Composition of Capital Financing: Commercial Banks (1967–1983)

	Dollar Composition of Capital Financing (in millions)				Percentage of Composition of Capital Financing		
Year	Capital Notes and Debentures	Preferred Stock	Common Stock	Total	Capital Notes and Debentures	Preferred Stock	Common Stock
1967	$ 255.4	$ 0	$ 36.4	$ 291.8	87.5%	0 %	12.5%
1968	342.8	0	82.0	424.6	80.7	0	19.3
1969	261.8	1.4	68.8	360.9	72.5	0.4	19.1
1970	126.1	0	103.4	229.5	54.9	0	45.1
1971	1,572.1	2.0	125.5	1,669.5	92.5	0.1	7.4
1972	2,415.1	6.8	215.0	2,636.8	91.6	0.3	8.2
1973	1,023.5	0	87.4	1,110.9	92.1	0	7.9
1974	1,294.6	10.0	35.5	1,340.0	96.6	0.7	2.6
1975	1,446.3	77.5	37.9	1,561.6	92.6	5.0	2.4
1976	2,132.0	0	349.3	2,481.2	85.9	0	14.1
1977	2,259.8	355.0	177.0	2,791.8	80.9	12.7	6.3
1978	1,065.6	147.8	428.5	1,618.7	65.8	9.1	26.5
1979	2,277.8	53.5	120.1	2,451.3	92.9	2.2	4.9
1980	966.3	343.9	199.2	1,509.4	64.0	22.8	13.2
1981	611.4	36.8	795.3	1,443.5	42.3	2.5	55.1
1982	3,223.1	1,910.0	373.0	5,506.1	58.5	34.7	6.8
1983:	6,722.6	2,504.9	718.3	9,945.8	67.6	25.2	7.2

SOURCE: Irving Trust Company.

demonstrated a cyclical behavior over the past 15 years with respect to both total financing and the composition of capital financing. Since 1967, there have been three periods of robust capital financing for the commercial banking industry: 1971–1972, 1976–1979, and 1982–1983. Not surprisingly, all three periods have occurred during economic recovery and have coincided with bullish stock markets (see Table 9.5).

More interesting is the movement in the composition of capital financing. Using the broad definitions of capital, one finds that subordinated debt (i.e., capital notes and debentures) has consistently dominated the yearly totals of financing, constituting 50% or more in all but one year— 1981. Preferred and common stock have performed more sporadically. In five of the 17 years surveyed, preferred stock financing exceeded that achieved through common stock issues—1975, 1977, 1980, 1982, and 1983 (see Table 9.6).

The success of preferred stock in recent years is largely attributable to three factors: (1) the increased acceptability of preferred stock as a form of capitalization among banks; (2) the lower tax rate of certain banks, eliminating the differential between the after-tax cost of preferred stock and debt; and (3) the introduction in 1982 of adjustable-rate preferred stock and its acceptance by corporations as a near-tax-free substitute for commercial paper.

Capitalization within the thrift industry is a newer phenomenon because of the industry's basis in mutuality. A few state-chartered stock institutions began in California during the 1960s, but it was not until 1974 that laws permitted federal institutions to convert freely from mutual to stock form. As Table 9.7 indicates, high interest rates in 1981 and 1982 effectively

Table 9.7. **Mutual-to-Stock Conversions in the Thrift Industry**

Year	Number of Conversions	Amount of Capital Raised (in millions of dollars)	Average Fed Funds Rate (in percentages)
1975	1	$ 1.3	6.15
1976	14	50.9	5.04
1977	14	29.6	5.54
1978	5	13.5	7.93
1979	16	114.4	11.19
1980	15	141.4	13.36
1981	37	126.6	16.38
1982	31	123.0	12.26
1983	79	2,732.5	9.07

NOTE: Excludes mutual savings banks converting to stock ownership while retaining FDIC coverage.

precluded conversions from taking place. Lower interest rates in late 1982 and early 1983 led to a rush of conversions that raised more conversion capital in the first nine months of 1983 than had been achieved in the previous seven years.

SUMMARY AND CONCLUSION

Over the years we have witnessed a secular decline in capital ratios of depository institutions at the same time that their perceived risk exposure has increased. Recently, however, the regulatory agencies have attempted both to quantify capital standards and to stabilize capital levels in depository institutions. If the agencies persist in maintaining strict capital standards in the face of historic growth rates of earnings and assets, then depository institutions will have greater need to access the capital markets than in the past. This increased need for capital carries with it several implications:

1. If the agencies continue to impose more stringent standards on small institutions than on large firms, the result will be increased incentives for consolidations to take advantage of the benefits of higher leverage permitted to larger firms.
2. Mutual thrift institutions will be forced to accelerate conversion to stock form because internal capital generation will not be sufficient to support anticipated growth. Furthermore, with capital ratios already at very low levels in these firms, their rate of capital growth will have to exceed their asset growth by far if they are to hope to be able to compete in the capital markets for funds. Alternatively, they may have to curtail their growth, or perhaps even shrink in sizes, in an effort to retrench.
3. Stock organizations will also face increased need to tap equity markets, and success at this suggests the need for slower growth and presumably wider spreads. If internal and external capital growth proves insufficient to support all the needs for depository institutions, then non-depository intermediaries and direct (unintermediated) funding will assume greater roles at their expense.

NOTES

1. Duration of an asset or liability is defined as the weighted life of a stream of cash flows, where the weights are the present value of each of the cash flows expressed as a per-

centage of the present value of the asset or liability. Conceptually, duration provides a proportional measure of the price volatility of a financial instrument in the face of a parallel shift in the yield curve.

2. At some point before 100% of a financial institution's net worth is exhausted, the various regulators may take some action to remedy the situation. A detailed discussion of regulatory capital adequacy standards for depository institutions follows.

3. This distinction is blurred in the savings and loan industry, where the regulators allow subordinated debt to be included in the definition of primary capital. This means that an institution will not be declared insolvent by its regulator even after its common, preferred, and retained earnings accounts have been depleted. The institution must, however, continue to meet its obligations to holders of the subordinated debt. Otherwise, it will be in default.

4. A recent example of such a firm is Suburban Savings and Loan of Wayne, New Jersey, which first reported negative net worth in June 1982 but was not closed until September 1983 when its GAAP net worth approached negative $200 million.

5. This is a concern expressed by the FDIC and FSLIC in the recent controversy over brokered deposits. The insurers believe that brokers may allow failing financial institutions to survive temporarily by raising on their behalf large amounts of deposits that they would not be able to attract on their own. The insurers further contend that this will allow the losses of these institutions to grow.

6. The adequacy of FSLIC insurance was tested during 1981 and 1982 when thrift institutions lost 26% of their beginning net worth and had an estimated mark-to-market net worth of negative $116 billion. During this period, FSLIC had only $6.4 billion of reserves and another $3 billion in credit lines with the Treasury. Should FSLIC have exhausted all its resources in assisting failing thrift institutions, there was no federal guarantee to make good on the remaining insured deposits at risk. For this reason, the U.S. Senate passed a Sense of the Senate resolution in 1982 that affirmed congressional intent that deposits in federally insured depository institutions are backed, up to the statutorily prescribed amount, by the full faith and credit of the United States.

7. It may well be that these increased options will increase exposure to "management risk" in the short term as institutions gear up to offer new services, but in the long term these new powers will lead to increased diversification and a consequent reduction in overall risk.

8. As of December 31, 1982, $59.2 million of subordinated debt had been raised by savings and loans, representing an increase of less than 0.3% in net worth as defined for accounting purposes.

9. There are very few hard and fast rules in packaging capital issues. For example, under "participating preferred stock" for financial institutions, the dividend rate is a function of an institution's profitability.

REFERENCES

Agenda for Reform: a Report on Deposit Insurance to the Congress from the Federal Home Loan Bank Board. Washington, D.C.: Federal Home Loan Bank Board, 1983.

Friedman, M., and Schwartz, A. *A Monetary History of the United States.* Princeton, N.J.: Princeton University Press, 1963.

Orgler, Y. E., and Wolkowitz, B. *Bank Capital.* New York: Van Nostrand Reinhold, 1976.

Standard and Poor's Ratings Guide. New York: McGraw-Hill, 1979.

10 Regulatory Objectives and Conflicts

Manferd O. Peterson

INTRODUCTION

The bank regulatory environment in the United States is characterized by a complex structure of federal and state agencies with multiple and sometimes conflicting objectives. The structure is most often described as confusing, overlapping, and inefficient—certainly not the system a rational creator would build from scratch. But building from scratch is not really a feasible option, and we are left with the more modest but still considerable tasks of understanding where we are and how we got here, and then making policy recommendations regarding some details of the structure.

This chapter starts from the premise that proposals to reform the regulatory structure should rest on an understanding of the social objectives of regulation. Understanding at minimum requires a taxonomy of objectives and an examination of the conflicts and complementarities among them. It is in most cases useful to identify two types of conflicts: conflicts inherent in the objectives and conflicts that arise in implementation. Conflicts of the first type are more fundamental in that resolution implies a choice among social goals, involving such general issues as the kind of society we should have and specifically the relative roles of government regulation and private markets. These fundamental inherent conflicts are unlikely to be eliminated or even resolved by changes in the way regulatory tasks are assigned among various agencies. However, analysis of the con-

The author wishes to thank Tom Zorn for helpful comments.

317

flicts of implementation will more likely lead to suggestions for bank and financial regulatory structure on which there would be widespread agreement. If agreement is valued, one would hope that most conflicts turn out to be conflicts in implementation rather than conflicts inherent in the objectives.

The difference between inherent goal conflicts and implementation problems is important, although not always easy to identify. For example, a competitive system implies that some firms will fail. Does competition then inherently conflict with the objectives of safety and soundness or does the conflict arise because in implementation we have taken safety and soundness to mean that no individual institution should fail? To presume that an inherent conflict exists involves a type of "fallacy of composition." The failure of an individual bank doesn't mean that the system is inherently more risky. In fact, just the opposite may hold.

While the dichotomy between inherent and implementation conflicts is important, we must keep in mind that there is no policy without implementation. Policy must be implemented by people and to be effective must constrain the behavior of people. In this process, incentives are created that may induce behavior quite different from that intended in the regulation.

There are at least three views of regulation that influence our methods of analysis and policy recommendations. The first is that regulation exists for the public good, usually to correct some alleged deficiency of the private marketplace. Explaining a particular regulation would begin with a claim, perhaps supported by evidence, of market failure, such as the existence of natural monopoly or externalities. This market failure is often taken as prima facie evidence in favor of government regulation. In this view of the world, for example, the Interstate Commerce Commission (ICC) is seen as a social response to the problem of natural monopoly in railroads.

While the stated purpose of ICC regulation may be the control of natural monopoly, it has been argued that the policies implemented have not always had this effect. The impetus for regulation and the effect of it may be quite different. The second view, the "capture" or "special interest" theory, sees regulation as implemented and operated for the benefit of politically powerful special interest groups, rather than for the public interest (Stigler, 1972). Even if regulation is implemented for the public good, regulatory agencies tend to become captured by the regulatees or by other special interests. According to this model, railroad regulation is best explained in terms of its benefits to the railroads themselves or to other special interests, such as particular classes of shippers.

A third view extends this analysis, recognizing that regulators and legislators are not passive dupes or agents of some special interest, but respond in purposeful ways to various incentives. Kane, in two important papers (1977, 1981) has analyzed bank regulation and innovation by market participants as a dialectical process that has accelerated in recent years because of inflation and technological change. Regulation imposed with (possibly) good intentions leads to regulatee avoidance and a consequent decreasing of the effectiveness of regulation and other, perhaps harmful, unintended effects. Political pressure and bureaucratic incentives lead to reregulation. "Just as regulation calls forth regulatee avoidance, circumvention activity generates political pressure for reregulation. This third stage in the original process becomes simultaneously the first stage in a fresh cycle of regulation and avoidance" (Kane, 1981, p. 363).

> For some time after a truly new class of regulations is adopted, its sponsoring coalition is apt to remain powerful enough to respond to circumvention by increasing penalties, by enforcing more extensive reporting requirements, and by insisting that important substitute activities be brought into the control network. The rising budgetary expense, social inconvenience, economic waste, and distributional inequity of a growing network of controls generates new coalitions that demand countervailing regulation on their behalf. [Kane, 1981, p. 363]

This insightful analysis is particularly useful in understanding the historical development of banking regulation and the current deregulation phase. However, the analysis also leaves us with some troubling questions. Are we doomed to a never-ending cycle of regulation, avoidance, and reregulation, with attendant social costs? If so, are swings in the cycle becoming larger or smaller, trending to more regulation or less? Can regulation accomplish any of its stated goals at acceptable benefit–cost ratios? And, most troubling from the point of view of a dispassionate academic, what is our role in this process? Can the results of scientific analysis influence the direction of policy, or are economists and other students of public policy relegated to the role of observer?[1] We will finesse this issue by making the weak assumption that the intellectual curiosity of the writer and that of the reader are sufficient for us to proceed without a definitive answer.

One further question requires more attention before we proceed. If regulation is best described as a dialectic process and if unintended results are often quite different from intended results, does it make sense to analyze stated policy objectives? The answer is yes. First, if the intended goals are in conflict, that is worth knowing. If one stated goal of government is to reduce crop production through acreage allotments and another goal is to increase crop production through genetic research, one need not identify unintended results to see that there is a problem. Second, careful analysis of the conflicts and complementarities among stated goals will help identify unintended results. Third, the existence of unintended results and incentives to avoid regulation does not always imply that stated policy goals are never achieved. For example, federally provided deposit insurance has achieved the goal of stopping bank runs. It may also have unintended results, but its stated goals are still worth analyzing.

A representative list of bank regulatory objectives would include the following:[2]

1. Competitive financial markets
2. Safety and soundness of financial institutions and markets
3. Fair treatment of customers
4. Avoidance of conflict of interest
5. Protection of investors, including avoidance of insider dealing and fraud
6. Allocative preferences, for example, housing and small business
7. Monetary policy objectives—price stability, growth, full employment

These objectives are presumably pursued by federal and state regulators through the imposition of various restrictions on banking structure, pricing, product lines, risk taking, and other banking practices. These restrictions and other laws are enforced by threat of criminal or civil penalties and by regulatory sanctions and moral suasion, and are supported by reporting and disclosure requirements, on-site examinations, customer-reported complaints, and prior applications for structural or product line changes. Monetary policy objectives are implemented by the Federal Reserve largely through open market operations, with reserve requirements, discount rates, and moral suasion playing lesser roles. The Federal Reserve, presumably in support of other goals (e.g., competition or safety and soundness, as well as its macroeconomic goals), has a key role in maintenance and operation of the payment system. It serves as a lender of last resort to individual banks and to the banking system, and it has broad regulatory authority over member banks and bank holding companies.

Goal and implementation conflicts can exist within agencies charged with pursuing multiple goals and between agencies charged with implementing the same or different goals. Conflicts among either goals or implementation strategies are likely to be resolved differently in the two cases. For example, the above-mentioned monetary policy and regulatory goals of the Federal Reserve System may at times conflict. Since monetary policy goals typically are given the highest priority within the Fed, conflicts with other goals tend to be resolved in favor of monetary policy. In contrast, when safety and soundness goals (as implemented by the bank regulatory agencies) conflict with the goal of protection of investors (as implemented by the Securities and Exchange Commission), then the conflict must be resolved externally. In this particular case, Congress has resolved the conflict largely in favor of greater disclosure. We will return to these two particular examples later. For now, suffice it to say that suggestions for regulatory reform should assess the circumstances under which conflicts are best resolved within a regulatory agency, keeping in mind that agencies with different mixes of goals may resolve the same conflict differently. By implication, this assessment would identify situations in which we would be better off externalizing the resolution of conflicts. Although the advantages of internal or external conflict resolution will not always be apparent, it is hoped that thinking about the issues in this way will lead to some principles for regulatory reform.

TRADITIONAL CONFLICTS

Safety and Soundness

From 1929 to the bank holiday in 1933, over 9,000 commercial banks in the United States ceased operations and the money supply fell by one-third. It is not surprising that the banking laws passed in the wake of this experience should have as a primary goal the safety and soundness of banking institutions. The shape of our regulatory apparatus and the conflicts that have existed over the past five decades stem mostly from the way this goal has been interpreted and implemented. There are basically three ways in which the goal of safety and soundness can be interpreted: protection of depositor accounts, protection of the system as a whole (particularly the money supply), or protection of individual institutions. It is because the agencies have chosen to implement the safety and soundness goals so as to protect individual institutions that conflicts have developed with other regulatory goals.

In the absence of deposit insurance, there may be no way to separate the three approaches. The failure of an individual institution may lead to runs on and failures of other institutions—institutions that were well run and sound. Protection of individual institutions would then be necessary to protect depositors of the given institution as well as of other institutions.

However, with depositors protected by government deposit insurance, the experience since 1934 indicates that failure of one bank does not lead to runs on other banks. Therefore, the advent of deposit insurance should then have freed regulators from the need to preserve individual institutions.

Yet, restrictions on entry, portfolios, and pricing came on the scene along with deposit insurance. Perhaps it was reasonable for the policy makers to err on the side of caution. After all, it was not clear that government provision of deposit insurance could do the job by itself. In fact, as will be discussed later, the existence of deposit insurance as it is currently constituted sets up incentives that require a regulatory response. Nevertheless, what emerged was a regulatory structure that encouraged "cartel banking," justified by the belief that unrestricted competition among financial institutions conflicts with the priority goal of safety and soundness. Indeed the fundamental issue in bank regulation continues to be the extent to which competition in banking is consistent or conflicts with other goals. Therefore, in what follows we will in most cases compare various other goals with the goal of competition.

Regulations took the form of (1) entry regulation, (2) rate ceilings, and (3) restrictions on permissible asset holdings, liability offerings, and activities of banks and bank holding companies.

Entry in banking is restricted by the rationing of bank charters and de novo branches, by state home office and branch office protection laws, and by limitations on interstate and intrastate branching and holding company formations. Entry restrictions were designed to prevent "over-banking" (a term we don't hear much any more). It was thought that whenever there are "too many" banks in a market for each to make adequate profits, the result would be excessive competition, unsound banking practices, and eventual failure of some banks. Unrestricted entry was also thought to lead to abuses and unsound practices to the extent that frivolous entry occurs, fraud is facilitated, and the fiduciary nature of banking is ignored. Evidence from the bank failures of the depression and from banking practices of the "wildcat" banking era was cited in support of this position.

Although protection of financial institutions was accorded priority, entry limits were not absolute, and other goals were considered. In an attempt to strike a balance between competition and safety and soundness, a "needs" criterion developed to determine whether a new bank or office was justified in a particular banking market. Entry was permitted on a case-by-case basis where existing banking services and alternatives could be shown to be inadequate, provided that entry could be accomplished with a reasonable probability of success and without causing undue harm to existing banks. The judgment of regulators was substituted for judgment of individuals willing to risk their own capital in a banking venture. To the extent that regulators were influenced or captured by existing banks, there would be pressure to deny new charters. However, even without undue influence by existing banks, bureaucrats would be expected to err on the side of excessive limits on entry. With failure of a bank considered by Congress and the public to be a failure of the regulator, the costs to regulators of permitting entry are apparent. The benefits to the public of greater competition are more widely dispersed and difficult to identify. In other words, the costs of denying entry that should have occurred— assuming some entry applications should have been approved and some denied—are foregone opportunities for which a bank regulator is unlikely to be held accountable. Thus, the intent of the 1930s legislation was consistent with the incentives of bureaucrats. Not surprisingly, the result was restricted entry. Peltzman (1965, p. 48) estimates that entry was reduced by 2,200 banks over the period 1936–1962.

Restrictions on entry of course attract substitutes and imitators. Entry restrictions could not isolate banks from the competition by nonbank depository institutions, finance companies, money market mutual funds, and others. Furthermore, commercial banks in specific markets were not protected from distant aggressive commercial banks intent on extending their geographic markets. The inevitable loopholes, in this case permitting loan production offices and offshore subsidiaries, along with the technological evolution in communications and data processing, have by now produced de facto nationwide banking. Entry restrictions were confronted with competition, and competition won, albeit with unnecessary costs to society.

Did these restrictions promote the safety and soundness of the banking system? Other things being equal, limits on entry mean there are fewer banks to fail, less competition, higher prices, and (perhaps) less risk. Other things were more or less equal for many years, and entry restrictions very likely contributed to safety of the banking system and a quiet life for bankers and regulators. However, it is difficult to be more specific about the impact of entry restrictions on safety and soundness since the introduction of other reforms at the same time, particularly deposit insurance, confounds the issue. But, in the longer run, as noted above, other things did not remain equal. Recent history has shown that a lack of failures does *not* imply that the system is strong. Many banks and other financial institutions nurtured in a world of cartel banking were not able to deal with impinging competition, changing technology, and inflation. Entry restrictions made the system as a whole less robust and less able to adapt to changing economic conditions. Artificially low failure rates contributed to a weakened financial system.

In addition to entry restrictions, ceilings were placed on rates banks could pay on time deposits, and banks were prohibited from paying interest on demand deposits. It was argued that excessive competition bid up the cost of funds to banks, led them to acquire more risky assets, and increased the probability of failure. Evidence suggests that payment of interest, particularly on demand deposits, did not significantly contribute to bank failures (Benston, 1964). Nor is there evidence that the payment of interest on deposits resulted in the acquisition of more risky assets. In particular it was argued that the large money-center banks offered higher rates on demand deposits of individuals and for interbank deposits and invested these funds in high-yielding loans to support speculation in the stock market. The alleged result was a flow of funds from rural areas to the money centers that contributed to the speculative stock market bubble and that spread the results across the nation when the bubble burst. Warburton (1966) was unable to document that money-center banks attracted significant funds from rural banks, or that conditions in particular industries or regions could explain the depression.

In 1966, rate ceilings were extended to thrift institutions with a differential rate advantage to protect thrifts from the competition of commercial banks and to assure thrifts low-cost deposits to keep mortgage rates down. Experience soon showed that rate ceilings could not provide protection against competition from open market instruments or from innovations to avoid the ceilings. Whenever market rates exceeded Reg Q ceilings, interest-sensitive funds flowed out of financial institutions into more attractive market alternatives.

The institutions themselves developed new instruments not subject to the regulations and engaged in nonprice forms of competition. Kane (1981, p. 359) states:

> During the last two decades, our "money stores" turned increasingly to barter. Bank windows become full of ads and displays promising tableware, working utensils, radios, TV sets, luggage, and even discount coupons redeemable at local department stores. Bank advertisement seldom mentioned anything as old-fashioned as differences in explicit interest.

Competition was suppressed for only a short time, although smaller and more rural institutions were probably sheltered longer. Overall, Reg Q led to money market mutual funds and left the traditional financial institutions ill-equipped to compete . In particular, institutions with heavy investments in branches, which were important in nonprice competition, have had difficulty adjusting to price competition.

Also, in the name of safety and soundness, permissible activities of banks have been limited. The central theme is that banking should be separate from commerce, and thus banks generally have been prohibited from holding common stock or other equity interests in business and from owning real estate except as used in the banking business or for a prudent time period if obtained in foreclosure. Until passage of the Depository Institutions Deregulation and Monetary Control Act of 1980 and the Garn-St Germain Depository Institutions Act of 1982, thrift institutions were restricted in their lending to businesses and consumers and in offering transaction services. With the passage of these acts, the most significant and controversial remaining limitations are provisions of the Glass-Steagall Act that prohibit banks from underwriting corporate stocks, bonds, and municipal revenue bonds, and from sponsoring and distributing mutual funds. These restrictions, which limit competition with investment bankers and brokers, are regarded not only as measures to reduce risk but also as measures to reduce concentration of power and prevent conflicts of interest. Benston (1983, p. 222) states:

> Presently, this prohibition is supported by reference to fears of banks controlling loan and equity sources of funds. But were banks allowed to offer customers funds packaged as securities as well as loans, this would hardly result in a concentration of power, as long as the customers have the alternative of obtaining funds and services from insurance companies, pension funds, investment companies, underwriters and others. Another frequently expressed fear concerns the possibility of banks abusing their fiduciary responsibilities. In particular, they might use information gathered in the course of lending to trade in a corporation's equities. Or they might attempt to "bail out" of a bad loan by selling equities to the public, the proceeds of which would be used to repay the bank.

Benston also rejects the latter argument since it applies as well to underwriters, "since they hold, buy and sell the corporate obligations," (p. 222) and also because these were not the arguments originally advanced for the Glass-Steagall Act. Whether these arguments were advanced for the original bill is irrelevant. Neither is potential abuse of fiduciary responsibility the key issue. The key issue is whether it is desirable to have institutions whose liabilities are insured by the government undertaking the risks involved in investment banking. A more careful cost–benefit analysis of the separation of commercial and investment banking is needed before a policy recommendation can be advanced. Meanwhile, the regulatory dialectic rolls on, with investment bankers and brokers moving into banking, and bankers moving into discount brokerage, syndication, and advisory services.

The Federal Reserve is specifically empowered under the 1970 amendments to the Bank Holding Company Act to regulate the permissible activities of bank holding companies. Under Section 4(c)(8) of the Act, these activities must "be so closely related to banking as to be a proper incident thereto." The Board is to weigh the benefits to the public such as convenience, increased competition, and efficiencies against possible adverse factors such as concentration of resources, anticompetitive behavior or unfair competition, conflicts of interest, and safety and soundness. Limits on nonbank activities are rationalized by claims that (1) these activities are more risky than those in which banks can engage directly, and (2) the health of the bank cannot be isolated from that of its subsidiaries. Ironically, a rationale for holding companies was in part to isolate banks from the risks associated with the nonbanking activities of the holding company while allowing the institution as a whole to expand.[3] Evidence indicates that under the existing holding company structure, this has not been the case.

The more fundamental issue is whether nonbank activities increase or decrease the risk of the overall organization. The answer is that it can go either way. Bank holding companies tend to be more diversified than independent banks even though they are constrained to activities closely related to banking. This effect would tend to reduce risk and would reduce risk more if wider diversification—activities not closely related to banking—were permitted. However, individual activities undertaken by holding companies may by themselves be more risky. This, along with the fact that the bank's assets may be used to satisfy claims against nonbank subsidiaries, works to increase the risk of bank failure.[4] Thus, there are two effects at work: the undertaking of individually more risky activities, increasing risk to the holding company and potential "claims" on the bank's assets, and the diversifying of activities serving to reduce risks. Which effect dominates is a difficult empirical question, the resolution of which requires an acceptable measure of risk. Overall, it can be concluded that restrictions on permissible activities have reduced competition and have had an ambiguous impact on bank safety.

In summary, entry restrictions, rate ceilings, and limits on permissible activities have worked to limit competition and to redirect competitive effort into socially unproductive activities, for example, regulation avoidance. Does this mean that safety and soundness goals inherently conflict with goals of competition? A more definitive answer will have to await our discussion of recent deregulation, but the conflicts discussed so far are clearly conflicts arising from implementation. In particular, it is the interpretation and implementation of the safety and soundness goal through policies designed to keep institutions from failing that causes the conflict. Moreover, the very policies designed to protect institutions have left institutions and the system as a whole vulnerable to the inevitable arrival of new competition. In a world with deposit insurance, preservation of individual financial institutions is neither necessary nor sufficient for safety and soundness of the system. In a competitive environment, only the strongest and most adaptable survive. Hence, they should be very safe.

Fair Treatment of Customers

Of more recent vintage are laws designed to assure that banks and other financial institutions treat customers fairly. Examples are the Fair Housing Act of 1968, the Equal Credit Opportunity Act of 1974, and the Community Reinvestment Act of 1977, which taken together prohibit banks and others from denying loans on the basis of race, color, religion, sex, national origin, age, receipt of public welfare benefits, or neighborhood. Other laws, including the Truth-in-Lending Act of 1968 and the Real Estate Settlement Procedures Act of 1974 (amended in 1976), are designed to provide borrowers with information necessary to make rational decisions.

The issue with these and other laws regulating credit practices is not so much whether they conflict with other regulatory goals as why they came about and whether they are needed. Kane (1981, p. 364) suggests that these laws were the political reregulatory response to nonprice credit allocation that had developed under the regime of deposit rate and usury law ceilings. The burden of rate ceilings

> fell particularly hard on the young, the old, and the poor, whose adaptive efficiency to financial change is inherently low. On the political front, the blatant discrimination against small savers and borrowers enhanced and legitimized by these regulatory actions generated consumerist political pressure to get even. Exploiting this pressure, public-interest lobbyists have called down upon banks a veritable plague of what we may call financial *fair-play regulation*.

This analysis of the regulatory dialectic suggests that the goal of fair play is not inconsistent with competitive financial markets. Rather, the lack of price competition occasioned by other regulation led to the perceived need for these laws. By implication, greater price competition would have mitigated the political pressure for them. Unfortunately, we cannot be at all confident that these laws will go away as financial markets become more competitive and we no longer remember why they were enacted.

There is a question whether the alleged unfair practices were a serious problem even in the environment that existed before passage of these laws. Benston (1983) cautions against the acceptance of anecdotal evidence gathered from half of a sample:

> Passage of the Equal Credit Opportunity Act was supported by testimony before the National Commission on Consumer Finance and before Congressional committees that described incidents of invidious discrimination in lending to women. However, any activity, including credit granting, is conducted with some error and insensitivity. When these occur to women, blacks, or other persons who have experienced invidious discrimination in other situations, the refusal of credit is likely to appear to have been delib-

erate and unfair. Since testimony by men and whites who were turned down for loans was not heard, it is not possible to know whether the lenders systematically practiced discrimination. [p. 238]

Studies by Chandler and Ewert (1976) and Peterson (1981) find no evidence of discrimination against women. Other studies (Benston, 1979) of discrimination based on neighborhood (redlining) or race generally find no evidence of invidious discrimination. It should be noted that these studies were testing for the existence of discrimination "on average." The law, of course, says it is illegal to discriminate even once and thus these studies do not show that there were no instances that would have violated the law. Rather, these studies indicate that the fair treatment laws have at best small benefits. They do, however, have substantial costs to the regulators (and taxpayers) and to the lending institutions (and their customers). Compliance examination is taking an increasingly larger share of bank examiners' time. The cost of examinations to the FDIC, Federal Reserve, and Comptroller of the Currency was $7.1 million in 1978 (see Rohner, 1980, p. 107). Additional substantial costs are also incurred by the bank. Smith (1977, p. 619) estimates that compliance costs of the Equal Credit Opportunity Act of 1974 were $127.5 million in recurring costs every year and $165.8 million in one-time implementation costs.

Allocative Preferences

It is only a slight exaggeration to say that federal policy toward housing is finance policy. Mortgage loan rates are subsidized for low-income families, the federal government guarantees mortgage loans, Reg Q and asset restrictions on S&Ls were intended to support housing, and other government policies are designed to divert funds to housing. Since these programs allocate funds by nonmarket means, they are fundamentally in conflict with the goals of a competitive financial system. Funds are allocated according to politically determined social goals, rather than according to the most productive uses signaled by the market.[5]

Again, the central question is not the conflict with other goals, but whether these programs have worked. Our previous analysis has shown that the protection afforded by Reg Q ceilings below market rates was temporary. Even in the short run, the resultant episodes of disintermediation were clearly disruptive to housing markets. Restrictions limiting nonmortgage lending (and the form of the mortgage contract) were detrimental to the long-run health of the thrift industry.

Whether these policies resulted in more mortgage loans and lower rates even in the short run is not a simple question. Consider a situation in which, on the margin, funds are being provided to the mortgage market by diversified (discretionary) lenders such as pension funds or life insurance companies. Since they have the option of investing in mortgages or bonds, they will be expected to switch back and forth depending upon rate differentials between mortgages and bonds. If the bond market participation of these lenders is large relative to their mortgage market participation, their supply of mortgage funds will be highly elastic in the relevant range. If demand intersects the supply curve in this range, mortgage rates will be determined by the differential of mortgage rates over bond rates required to induce diversified lenders to make mortgage loans. The volume of mortgage loans made is determined by demand. The activities of restricted lenders (S&Ls) are purely intramarginal and have no impact on mortgage rates or the equilibrium quantity of mortgage loans. Tuccilo, Van Order, and Villani (1982) estimate that in recent years demand for mortgage funds has been such that the above situation holds. In this case, portfolio policies designed to increase mortgage lending of restricted lenders will change the share of mortgage loans made by these lenders, but will not affect total mortgage lending or stimulate housing.

If restrictions on financial institutions have not unambiguously increased the flow of funds to mortgages, what about the other mortgage subsidy programs and their impact on housing? These programs in total most likely channel more funds to housing than would the market in the absence of subsidies. The *net* increase is, however, less than the gross increase, since government borrowing or taxing to support these programs "crowds out" some funds that would have gone to housing anyway. Furthermore, indirect subsidies are likely to be inefficient because of problems in measuring costs and benefits. But let us grant that government programs have increased the availability or lowered the cost of mortgage funds. Does this mean that housing is aided? No. Research has found no direct link between mortgages and housing demand. With subsidized mortgage rates, people have simply used more mortgage debt to finance other things they purchase. Down payments are reduced when houses are purchased, equity built up in houses can be realized by refinancing or second mortgages, and the proceeds can be used for a variety of purchases. Alan Meltzer (1974) has analyzed the long-run relationship between mortgage borrowing and investment in housing. In 1912 the value of housing as a percent of total assets of households was 25.2 and the value of mortgage debt as a percent of total debt was 47.8. By 1958 these ratios were 24.9 and 65.9 respectively. During this time housing had become a social priority and social allocation of credit was the means to that end. Yet, the impact was higher loan–value ratios but no change in household allocation of wealth to housing.

Monetary Policy

Responsibility for the conduct of monetary policy in this country rests with the Federal Reserve System. Although the Fed was established to provide an "elastic currency," it now allegedly attempts to influence the money supply, the volume of credit, or interest rates in a manner designed to achieve economic stability and growth, full employment, a favorable balance of payments, and an acceptable rate of inflation. In addition, there has at times been pressure on the Federal Reserve to support other government activities (e.g., fiscal operations of the Treasury, war financing, and reelection bids of government officials) and to support various social goals.

The analysis that follows will emphasize the conflicts between monetary policy and other regulatory goals, particularly the goal of safety and soundness, and not the internal conflicts of monetary policy. While in the short run there may be trade-offs between monetary policy goals, for instance, full employment versus stable prices, a good case can be made that in the long run monetary policy affects only the price level (Friedman, 1982). Given this, a further case can be made for a monetary rule increasing the money supply at a fixed preannounced rate per year, rather than a discretionary policy that attempts to fine-tune the economy. This policy clearly would not require a regulatory role for the central bank. However, since the wisdom of a monetary rule has not been seen by the Fed, the assumption made, at least initially, is that the Fed pursues what it believes to be countercyclical monetary policy. Conflict of this policy with other regulatory goals is then analyzed.

Monetary policy and other regulatory goals may conflict in at least three ways:

1. Safety and soundness goals, as implemented by the bank examination process, may conflict with countercyclical monetary policy.
2. Implementation of various goals may compete for the time and energy of policy makers.
3. Implementation of various functions by the same agency may involve conflicts of interest.

If the primary goal of monetary policy is economic stability and the primary goal of bank regulation is safety and soundness, it is not obvious that there is a conflict. "To the extent that monetary policy is successful in stabilizing economic activity, it should enhance the safety and soundness of the banking system. Conversely, a stable and sound banking system, with predictable response to Federal Reserve actions, should simplify the task of monetary policy" (Peterson, 1977, p. 27).

However it is possible that even if there is no inherent conflict in the goals, there may be conflicts in implementation. In particular, bank examination, in support of the safety and soundness goal, may cause banks to contract loans during downturns in the economy and expand during upturns.

> There are two versions of this argument. One states that examiners implicitly or explicitly change their asset evaluation standards over the business cycle. In times of recession, loan and security values are questioned more closely, stricter standards are applied, and more asset classifications result. In times of expanding business conditions, examiners are more easily satisfied, standards are relaxed, and fewer assets are classified. The second version of the argument states that even if examination standards do not change, the change in economic conditions will cause asset classifications to increase in recessions and decrease during expansions. The effect of the examination process will still be to intensify the business cycle. [Peterson, 1977, p. 27]

There is some indirect evidence on the potential for a procyclical impact of bank examination. Bank examiners are explicitly told to consider economic and monetary factors in evaluating banks' investment policies. The FDIC's *Manual of Examination Policies* states:

> An endeavor to predict with any degree of assurance the future course of economic events is futile. But it is quite possible for any intelligent observer to ascertain a few basic facts about the prevailing economic climate, such as whether business conditions are stagnant, expanding, or contracting—in short, whether times are prosperous or depressed. Study of graphic material will show whether money rates are relatively high or low and whether the financial structure of the economy is expanding or shrinking. Intelligent portfolio management will give consideration to these basic factors in formulating and executing investment policies. Undue preoccupation with these considerations, however, may be indicative of speculative tendencies which are unwholesome in banking. [FDIC, 1976, Section G, pp. 2–3]

Although instructions for evaluating loans omit similar explicit instructions to consider the phase of the business cycle, examiners are instructed to consider the probability of orderly repayment and the circumstances of the bank and its market area. If these considerations depend upon general business conditions, they may contribute to the procyclical nature of bank regulation.

There exists little direct evidence of conflict with monetary policy. Garlock and Gile (1935), Garlock (1941), and Hardy and Viner (1935), in studies of bank examination, found sharp increase in criticized loans from 1931 to 1932 and another increase in 1934. The 1931–1932 increase was attributed to a decline in loan quality, but the 1934 increase appeared due to increased rigor of examiner's classifications.

It should be noted, however, that during this critical period of the Great Depression, supervisory policy, to the extent that it was effective, reinforced rather than conflicted with monetary policy. Unfortunately, monetary tools were being employed in precisely the wrong direction, causing a depressed economy to contract further. [Peterson 1977, p. 27]

In fact, it may well be that the procyclical impact of bank examination has been swamped by the procyclical or at least destabilizing influence of monetary policy itself. The implementation of monetary policy, at least during the depression, was in conflict not only with the goal of safety and soundness but also with its own goal of economic stability.

If one looks beyond the examination process to other regulatory matters, other conflicts may arise. One is competing demands for the time and attention of the regulators. Governor Robertson (1966) has stated that Board members spend at least as much time on supervisory matters and merger and holding company applications as on issues of monetary policy. Governor Maisel (1973) disagrees with this division of time and suggests that the official duties do not impose unreasonable time demands on Board members. Maisel concedes that the Chairman may be under more time pressure than the other Board members.

In any event, since it is not clear that more time devoted to monetary policy would result in better monetary policy (those advocating a monetary rule would conclude the opposite), this issue is relatively unimportant. More important is the issue of whether or not bank supervision should be available as a tool of monetary policy. Here two opposite propositions regarding the proper location of supervisory and monetary authority have been advanced.

The first states that supervisory and monetary policy authority should not be located in the same agency, because a regulatory conflict of interest will result. The second states that authority for the two functions should be located in the same agency, and furthermore, that bank supervision should be available as a tool of monetary policy.

Proponents of the second proposition minimize the importance of conflicts of interest, or believe they should be resolved in favor of monetary policy goals. They further contend that examination data, day-to-day contact with banks, and supervisory powers are necessary for the implementation of monetary policy.

If one looks at macro or aggregate monetary policy, primarily open market operations, it is difficult to see how supervisory powers could be a help. There is no evidence that data from bank examinations have been used in formulating open market policy. The meager evidence that exists in the literature suggests that examination data are not very useful for monetary policy. If it is believed that bank examination conflicts significantly over the business cycle then, of course, examination standards could be altered to serve the purpose of monetary policy; but, this brings us face-to-face with the conflict-of-interest argument.

It can be argued quite persuasively that bank examination and other supervisory tools are ill suited for the implementation of macro-monetary policy. The two functions differ vastly in the information they generate and use, in the enforcement powers necessary to execute them, and in the degree to which they can or should be centralized.[6] Furthermore, it seems that supervisory tasks of detecting violation of laws and regulation, determining risks of individual institutions, attempting to predict problem banks, "working out" problems and regulating chartering, merger and branching activity are sufficiently difficult without attempting to adjust standards to reinforce monetary policy. Any attempt to do so would result in diminution of examination's usefulness for accomplishing its goals, since examination reports would lose comparability over time. The result would be suboptimal regulation of bank structure and a distraction from primary monetary policy concerns. [Peterson, 1977, p. 34]

Milton Friedman, in discussing the "membership problem" and the role of regulatory and monetary policy function, concludes:

Monetary theorists have demonstrated that the conduct of monetary policy does not require that the Federal Reserve System have any member banks. I have argued frequently that it would be desirable to separate the regulatory and monetary control activities of the Fed. The latter requires simply that the monetary authority have a monopoly on the printing press or its equivalent to control the total amount of high-powered or base money. Control over the base exerts about as much influence on non-member commercial banks as on member banks, on thrift institutions as on commercial banks, and so on in unending circle. [1982, p. 115]

A stronger case could be made for Fed supervisory powers if proper monetary policy actions include selective credit controls, nonprice rationing of discount window borrowing, or encouragement of individual bank support for Fed policies. Effective moral suasion requires discretionary supervisory authority. If these are not proper or desirable monetary actions, the case for Fed supervisory powers is weak.

The Fed also serves as lender of last resort to individual banks and to the system as a whole. The Fed can be viewed as the ultimate deposit insurer, providing in effect reinsurance or overline coverage for the FDIC. We later make the case that deposit insurance creates incentives for risk taking by insured institutions and hence the need for regulation, or insurance premium pricing to limit risk. Do not the same arguments apply to the Fed as a reinsurer? Or, more fundamentally, why not simply use the discount window as a "lender of first resort," in effect providing all deposit insurance through the creation of reserves as needed? The danger with this policy is overexpansion of the money supply and inflation. Separation of monetary policy and first-dollar insurance coverage of deposits permits the Fed to pursue an independent monetary policy within broad bounds without concern for failure of individual institutions. To combine these functions within the same agency would likely lead to less desirable insurance and risk incentives and less desirable monetary policy.

But what if the Fed remains in its reinsurance role as a lender of last resort? Does this imply the need for Fed supervisory authority over individual banks? I think not. What may be important is information that can be supplied by the primary supervisor. If that supervisor is also the insuring agency, there should be sufficient incentives to gather information useful for analyzing and controlling risk. It is this information that would be useful to the Fed in its role as lender of last resort.

DEREGULATION AND THE REMAINING FUNDAMENTAL CONFLICTS

Deregulation of the financial system in recent years has mitigated some of the conflicts discussed above. Regulation Q is on the way out. Entry barriers have been punctured by the extension of product and geographic markets and by less restrictive chartering policies. If in this new environment we have "too many" financial institutions, the goals of competition and safety and soundness would both be served by mergers or other consolidations of institutions.

While reduced regulation and greater reliance upon market forces are generally applauded by most economists, it is not a unanimous standing ovation. There are some fundamental issues yet to be resolved, the most important of which is the extent to which the marketplace can replace regulation. Simply appealing to our a priori preference for less regulation and more competition will not suffice.

Even those who are advocates of laissez faire in general recognize that banking with our basic institutional setting is different. Government regulation of banking, at some level perhaps considerably diminished from current levels, is justified because bank deposits constitute the largest share of our money supply and competitive market solutions without restrictions are likely to be indeterminate or unstable (see Volcker, 1983; Corrigan, 1983). Even with restrictions imposed by a central bank, market failures may result from information asymmetries and externalities in deposit markets, particularly because of the difficulty and cost to depositors of assessing bank risks and the externalities imposed on other banks and their depositors when failure of one bank leads to runs on other banks. If one assumes that fractional reserve banking and government-provided deposit insurance are here to stay, there are limits to the deregulation process.

BANK REGULATION AND DEPOSIT INSURANCE

Consider a system without deposit insurance in which banks issue deposits, payable on demand, that are claims on risky assets of the bank and that are used as money. Depositors in this world would have incentives to monitor the risk of banks. But this is likely to be difficult and costly for most, particularly small, depositors. Depositors who fear, correctly or incorrectly, that a bank is in difficulty are rational in withdrawing their funds quickly. A run on a bank may force it to liquidate assets at a loss, perhaps producing insolvency. History shows that runs can spread to other banks and lead to a general banking panic. The bank failures of the Great Depression contributed to the contraction of the money supply and the resulting macroeconomic instability. That problem was apparently solved by government deposit insurance. But, with government sharing the costs of bank failures and depositors relieved of the need to monitor banks, an incentive was created for banks to take excessive risk. Regulations on entry, portfolios, and pricing could be viewed as a reaction to or anticipation of incentive problems caused by deposit insurance, rather than alternative means of preventing bank runs.

The relationship between deposit insurance and regulation has been studied by many analysts. In particular, the equivalence of adequate capital and fair insurance premiums has been demonstrated by Sharpe (1978), Merton (1977 and 1978), and others. Buser, Chen, and Kane (1981) analyze regulation as implicit insurance premiums on institutions in addition to the flat-rate explicit premiums. A recent book, *Risk and Capital Adequacy in Commercial Banks,* edited by Sherman Maisel (1981), also advances the theory that deposit insurance creates incentives for risk taking and that regulations of various kinds have been employed to control these risks.

This is a plausible story, supported by rigorous theory, but is there any evidence that the predicted behavior actually takes place? Benston cites the following evidence:

U. S. history prior to the FDIC bears this out and also provides lessons that should be heeded. Deposit guarantee systems were established in New

York (1828), Vermont (1831), Indiana (1834), Ohio (1845) and Iowa (1858). The New York and Vermont systems were state run, the others were based on mutual agreements among participating banks. They operated successfully, largely because they empowered system officials to monitor operations of the participating banks and to control excessive risk-taking. Yet a second wave of deposit guarantee plans for state banks proved less successful. With one exception (Mississippi), the plans did not include effective supervision and they failed. These included the compulsory plans of Oklahoma (1908), Nebraska (1909), and South Dakota (1916) and the voluntary plans of Kansas (1909), Texas (1910), and Washington (1917). Since depositors were told that their money was safe there was a great incentive for unscrupulous operators to take excessive risks; the record shows greater failure rates of guaranteed banks than among similar non-guaranteed banks operating in the same areas. The Mississippi plan (1915), which included supervision and bank examinations, continued until 1930. Thus, effective supervision appears to be a necessary aspect of deposit insurance. [1983, pp. 8–9]

A popular policy prescription advanced in many of the above and other studies is that deposit insurance should be priced according to risk. Maisel states:

If charges were related to the risks they assumed, individual banks could have far greater freedom in deciding what were and were not logical loans. Our system of intermediation would improve. The amount of required regulation would fall. The straightjacket within which the system operates could be removed. [1981, p. 177]

Problems with this theoretically appealing approach are largely practical. Finer risk classes would have to be developed than are now used. Suppose, to take an admittedly extreme example, banks were placed into two risk classes, problem banks and normal banks. Given, say, about 250 problem banks and 14,000 normal banks, deposit insurance premiums assigned actuarially to banks in these classes would assign negligible premiums to 14,000 normal banks and nearly all the insurance bill to the 250 problem banks, "insuring" their failure. Also, if owners of bank stock are not fully diversified, owners' risk–return trade-offs would have to be known in setting optimal insurance premiums. This would be particularly the case if variable premiums were used not simply to cover actuarial costs but to affect risk taking. If variable premiums are used to induce a particular degree of risk taking, it is necessary to measure actual risk and to determine the optimal level of risk for the system as a whole. This is indeed a major problem.

Methods of estimating risk (Maisel, 1981) impose such large information costs on the insurance agency that, while regulation could be reduced, surveillance and related costs would not be. On-site examinations would likely continue, and more reports required. Even with increased information, proponents of risk-based insurance premiums have yet to show how to implement the proposal in anything but an arbitrary way.

This is too bad, since most of the recommendations to date have not been based on sound theoretical reasoning and suffer serious shortcomings. One prescription would be to keep deposit insurance as it is. Buser, Chen, and Kane (1981) have shown that when implicit premiums in the form of regulatory costs are included, total premiums are no longer fixed. The problem is that there is little reason to think these premiums are optimal. It is difficult to assess whether these total premiums are closer to optimal than could be achieved under an explicit variable premium plan. Also, given the regulatory changes underway, the status quo may not be possible, even if deemed desirable.

Some plans call for increasing deposit coverage to 100% coverage (at least of transactions accounts), while others are recommending lowering coverage to increase market discipline on banks. See, for example, Benston (1983b) and Flannery (1982). The problem with raising deposit coverage is that it has a tendency to increase bankers' incentives for risk taking, while lowering coverage increases the chances of runs on banks. Unfortunately, we have a poor idea of the nature and magnitude of the trade-offs involved, with some wanting the discipline of the market without the failures that discipline implies.

Other plans call for competition in the provision of deposit insurance, either by competition among government agencies or by turning all or some deposit insurance over to private companies. There is no reason, theoretical or empirical, to assume that having rivalry among three or four government agencies will be optimal or even desirable. Government oligopolies are unlikely to approximate the results of market competition. There are problems in the operating instructions given to agencies by Congress (e.g., the full-cost-coverage requirement in pricing of Fed services) and problems of assessing agency performance. In other words, questions of both constraints and objective function of agencies are grounds for skepticism.

Plans to privatize all or part of the insurance function deserve further study. One question that needs to be addressed is the extent to which economies of scale in surveillance and insurance activities would limit the number of firms. If a natural monopoly exists, this solution will have obvious drawbacks. Another issue is whether private companies would have credibility needed to instill confidence and prevent bank runs. The ultimate insurer against widespread catastrophic failure must still be the federal government with its power to tax and print money. This would imply at least some government reinsurance. But then there are the problems of pricing this insurance and the incentives created for risk taking by private deposit insurance companies. Perhaps these problems would be easier to solve than the current problems; but it is not obvious why.

Deposit insurance and deregulation present a fundamental conflict. Deposit insurance is necessary for stability, given our other institutional arrangements. It is successful in preventing runs on banks. However, it creates incentives for risk taking, and thus the need for regulation. How much regulation and what kind are difficult questions to answer.

Deregulation and Monetary Control

One provision of the Depository Institutions Deregulation and Monetary Control Act of 1980 extended reserve requirements to nonmember banks and other financial institutions offering transactions accounts. The Fed has long argued that universal reserve requirements are necessary for control of the money supply.[7] This act, however, and other legislation and financial innovation, have features that have made monetary control more difficult and may have contributed to macroeconomic instability. In particular, problems in defining the money supply and thus in achieving stable growth in money have caused some economists to oppose deregulation (see, e.g., Cagan, 1979; Pesek, 1982). Questions remain as to whether these problems are transitory or permanent and how serious they are.

Mayer (1982) summarizes the arguments and outlines the cost–benefit calculations that are necessary to resolve the issues. Costs of financial innovation are of two kinds: (1) problems in defining and measuring money and the demand for money during periods of financial innovation; and (2) "the possibility that a large real stock of money, or near money, or low transformation costs between money and other assets are destabilizing" (p. 29). The second point is called the "loose cargo" agreement. The first problem may be called the "scotch and soda" problem. Pesek explains it as follows:

> To use a metaphor, before 1980 demand deposits with an annual velocity (in F.R.S. terms, "turnover") of over 200 were akin to scotch. Time deposits with annual velocity of 3 were akin to soda. After 1980, each bank now markets its own—changeable—mix of scotch-and-soda, with the proportions unknown even to the bank since a great deal is left to the depositors' discretion. To aggregate the individual gallons marketed (into "the money") is an exercise in futility: the sum tells us nothing about the alcoholic (inflationary) content of the brew. We have ceased to know *what is*. [1982, p. 469]

Recent changes in the definitions of the money supply and instability in its various measures support the view that this is a problem, at least in transition.

The loose cargo argument, more subtle, but potentially more important since it could be "permanent," is this:

> With the public holding a large real stock of money or near money, it can readily accommodate an increased desire to spend. One person's increased liquidity is therefore another person's increased exposure to inflation. [Mayer, 1982, p. 29]

The impact on macroeconomic instability is not clear. The answer depends upon how innovations affect the demand for money and equilibrium in the money market and upon where shocks to the system come from. If shocks to the economy come largely from monetary policy itself, then innovations that reduce the link between monetary policy and economic activity are likely to be stabilizing. If, however, shocks to the system come from the real sector, these innovations are more likely to be destabilizing. Recent years have witnessed shocks from both sources, with oil and food price shocks vying with unstable monetary policy for first-place honors.

Mayer also considers the impact of deregulation and financial reform on the risk of financial crises. A priori, it could go either way. Increased real money or near money balances relative to liabilities should diminish the probability of financial crises. However, innovation has also increased the proportion of uninsured money (e.g., money market accounts) relative to insured money, thereby increasing the likelihood of financial crises. Mayer concludes that arguments against financial innovation and deregulation based on increased risk of financial crises are weak. More serious is the "transitory" problem of conducting monetary policy in a world of financial innovation and changing regulation. None of the policy alternatives for solving the money measurement problem is satisfactory, and we may be stuck with significant monetary problems during periods of financial innovation. These costs should certainly be considered in any cost–benefit analysis of regulatory reform and innovation.

A cost–benefit analysis assumes that we have some choice. May not the incentives for innovation be so strong that regulators are powerless to stop them, at least at acceptable levels of interference with individual liberty? A reasonable position is that some regulations are easier to enforce than others and that regulations needed for monetary control need not conflict with private maximizing behavior. Regulators should attempt to take account of the long-run incentive effects of regulation. Mayer states:

Trying to anticipate private sector avoidance may seem an obvious thing to do, but when the Board lowered the Regulation Q ceiling in 1966 it did so without any consideration of the avoidance techniques that this would stimulate. [1982, p. 33]

Of course, implementing "incentive-based" regulation is difficult. However, some conjectures about such a process can be advanced. First, an analysis of the regulations needed for monetary control would come up with a very short list. Most of the regulation in existence today is not needed for monetary control. Second, of the regulations deemed necessary, most could be made more compatible with private maximizing motives. For example, if reserve requirements are necessary for monetary control, payment of interest on those reserves would be one way to discourage innovation into nonreservable instruments.

Deregulation and Disclosure[8]

Substituting market discipline for regulation presumes that market participants can make informed judgments. Deregulation has thus rekindled a long-running debate over disclosure of bank data.

Historically, the debate has been among agencies with conflicting regulatory mandates. The Securities and Exchange Commission (SEC) has long maintained that publicly held banks should be subject to disclosure requirements similar to those of other corporations. The Federal Deposit Insurance Corporation (FDIC), the Federal Reserve System, and the Comptroller of the Currency have insisted that such disclosure may further weaken banks that are experiencing some degree of financial difficulty. These bank regulatory agencies, especially the FDIC, are, of course, primarily concerned with the stability and viability of the banking system. The SEC, on the other hand, is primarily concerned with the truthful disclosure of a publicly held company's financial condition.

In the jurisdictional dispute between the SEC and the bank regulatory agencies, the SEC currently has the upper hand. In 1974 Congress mandated that the bank regulatory agencies follow the disclosure requirements of the SEC. Although interagency disagreements still exist, the public debate now appears to be between the banking industry, opposing more disclosure, and the regulatory agencies, including the SEC, proposing more disclosure. While some protagonists may have publicly changed sides, the issues remain the same—namely the conflict between depositors', investors', and potential investors' right to know and concern over stability of and confidence in the banking system.

At first glance it may appear that there exists an irresolvable conflict between these two points of view. There is, however, a policy that, based on efficiency criteria, is preferable from both points of view. Such a policy has not been apparent because the arguments have been miscast as well as embedded in assumptions about the regulatory setting that are no longer valid. Specifically, arguments for greater disclosure have been presented largely as "consumer protection" measures, designed to protect investors and supported by appeal to equity and fairness. This appears to conflict with goals of safety and soundness because it ignores longer-run considerations, in particular the impact that disclosure will have on bankers' incentives.

Arguments against disclosure also give insufficient weight to changes in the regulatory environment. As so-called core deposits become less important, banks will be forced to bid for funds and pay, at least on uninsured deposits, rates commensurate with their risk. In this setting, banks will desire to signal to the markets that they are safe. Credible signaling (disclosure) may well be something that bankers should support.

Consider a simple hypothetical example in which there are only two classes of banks, safe banks and risky banks. If depositors and investors could distinguish between them, they would require a risk premium for investing in risky banks. Safe banks would have an incentive to signal to the market that they are indeed safe—that is, to disclose information to investors and depositors. The problem is that risky banks would also have an incentive to signal (falsely) that they are safe, disclosing information to make this appear to be the case. Absent a reason to believe the banks' pronouncement or ability to verify their data, depositors will be unable to distinguish between the two groups and some sort of average risk premium is likely to be required for all banks. If this is the case, risky banks will have a decided advantage over safe banks and the incentive will be for all banks to become risky. Prudence and conservatism are no longer rewarded, but rather are penalized in the marketplace.

This situation is clearly not in the best interests of the banking industry, the bank regulators, or the general public. In particular bankers should support disclosure that will lead to a signaling equilibrium in which safe banks can successfully identify themselves to the market. In abstract terms, for this signaling equilibrium to exist, two conditions must hold. First, signaling must be consistent with the interests of the signaler. Second, the signal must in some sense be true. In this case the first condition clearly holds; it is unambiguously in the interest of safe banks to signal that fact to the market. The problem of false signals is more complicated, since it will also pay the risky banks to signal that they are safe. One way truth will be revealed in equilibrium is if the cost of signaling is less for a safe bank than for a risky bank. Differential costs could be assured by imposing penalties if false signals are subsequently detected. The law in fact imposes such penalties for falsification of bank records. One may also induce truth telling by requiring some independent verification of the disclosure, and this provides a legitimate role for bank regulators in a deregulated banking environment. In fact, a safe bank, in order to make its signal credible, might even "contract" to submit to severe penalties should regulators subsequently discover that its signal was false. Note that this would use the regulator as a verification tool and also increase the cost of false signals. In this way not only would depositors and investors be informed but incentives for risk taking would be correct.

PRINCIPLES TO GUIDE REGULATORY REFORM

Regulatory reform can mean two things: (1) changing regulations; or (2) changing the structure of the regulatory agencies. The first is generally regarded as more fundamental or more important than the second. Analysis in this paper found existing regulatory conflicts to be those of implementation or interpretation rather than conflicts of fundamental objectives. It was also suggested that the resolution of conflicts among goals will differ if done internally or externally. Moreover, agencies with different mixes of goals will resolve the same conflicts differently. These findings, as well as more recent theories of regulation, suggest that the way regulation is implemented is at least as important as the regulatory intent. It is in implementation that unintended results occur, that information costs become critical, and that practical realities force imperfect choices among competing second-best solutions. Regulations (or regulatory goals) and their implementation (or regulatory structure) interact in ways not fully understood. As the regulatory dialectic unfolds, the agency structure and the way regulations are implemented will feed back on the regulations themselves in direct and indirect ways.

One guiding principle that is reconfirmed by our regulatory experience and supported by recent theories of regulation is that *people respond in purposeful ways to economic incentives*. Regulation sets up private incentives for innovation and regulatory avoidance. Regulators and legislators respond according to their special incentives. These incentives and the response costs involved must be considered in formulating and implementing regulation.

Regulatory policy should also recognize that the private market by its invisible hand under a wide range of circumstances directs private incentives to the public good. Although there are some well-known cases of market failures, even here there should be no presumption that regulation will do better. Private incentives will not go away but will be rechanneled by government regulation—often rechanneled to socially unproductive avoidance activity. The benefit of the doubt should be given to market forces.

With respect to organization of the regulatory agencies, one corollary principle emerges: Where goal or implementation conflicts exist, resolution of the conflict within an agency is likely to differ from resolution of conflicts among agencies. The struggle takes place in a different arena, with different players, different incentives and objectives. Conflicts among goals of different agencies are probably better resolved by Congress. An example is the conflict between investor protection goals of the SEC and safety and soundness goals of the FDIC. When a single agency is charged with implementing regulations having conflicting goals, there is less likely to be an explicit resolution. Agency officials will claim to be pursuing both goals according to congressional intents and it may be difficult for the outside observer to tell for some time whether and how the conflict has been resolved. If this sounds like an argument for assigning each agency only one goal, perhaps some form of functional regulation, and resolving all conflicts externally, it is not. No such universal principle emerges, although reasons for both methods of conflict resolution exist. Congress may well intend that some goals be given lower priority than others, yet be unwilling explicitly to say so. Assignment of these responsibilities to agencies with other clearly higher priority goals may accomplish this purpose.

This does not tell us that we should have one regulator or many, but rather that conflict resolution should be considered in any proposal for regulatory reform. With one regulator, goal conflicts will more likely be resolved internally. With more than one regulator, conflicts are more likely to be resolved externally, and Congress and the general public are more likely to be involved in implementation as well as fundamental goal decisions.

SUMMARY AND CONCLUSION

The analysis in this chapter has considered numerous historical conflicts in financial regulation and found most to be conflicts either of implementation or of interpretation, rather than fundamental conflicts of objectives. Furthermore, innovation and deregulation to date have already resolved many conflicts in favor of a larger role for the market. However, it seems reasonable to predict that two important institutional features of the present system will remain: government-provided deposit insurance and government-produced fiat money with a fractional reserve banking system. With these taken as given, it is clear that some regulation of financial institutions must remain. The precise form this regulation should take is difficult to know, but may well involve less regulation than currently exists.

Many important questions remain unanswered. What can regulation accomplish? If regulation is best described by some endogenous dialectic process, what discretion do we have in designing regulation? Against what standard is regulatory performance to be measured?

It is likely that these questions will not soon be answered. In the meantime, the dynamic processes of regulation, deregulation, and reregulation are likely to continue, driven by the private incentives that motivate special interest groups, voters, regulators, and legislators.

NOTES

1. It appears to me that Professor Kane has exhibited uncharacteristic and unjustified self-modesty by neglecting the role of economists, and in particular his own role, in the deregulation of interest rate ceilings. Were Congress to award a Medal of Honor for heroic action in the battle against Reg Q, Ed Kane would assuredly be the recipient.
2. See Aspinwall (1983) and Federal Register (1983). Benston (1983) includes avoidance of competition as a goal. While this may be the goal of some participants, we view avoidance of competition as a side effect of regulations designed to achieve other goals.
3. In fact, risk isolation has not likely been a motivating factor in holding company formation. Tax policy and the treatment of dividends, followed by avoidance of product and geographic restrictions, have been the most important factors (Eisenbeis, Chapter 3 of this volume).
4. For an excellent discussion of this issue see Black, Miller, and Posner (1978).
5. Housing programs have been chosen for purposes of illustration. The same analysis applies to programs to allocate credit to small business, education, agriculture, New York City, Chrysler Corporation, and other social priorities.
6. A further problem is that the timing of the examination data is not uniform since examinations are conducted at random intervals throughout the year.
7. For a dissenting view, see Friedman (1982).
8. Discussion in this section draws heavily on Peterson and Zorn (1983).

REFERENCES

Aspinwall, Richard C. "Banking Deregulation or Reregulation?" Proceedings of a Conference on Bank Structure and Competition, Federal Reserve Bank of Chicago, May 2–4, 1983, pp. 19–27.

Benston, George J. "Interest Payments on Demand Deposits and Bank Investment Behavior." *Journal of Political Economy,* October 1964, pp. 431–449.

Benston, George J. "Federal Regulation of Banking: Analysis and Policy Recommendations." *Journal of Bank Research,* Winter 1983a, pp. 216–244.

Benston, George J. "Mortgage Redlining Research: A Review and Critical Analysis." In *The Regulation of Financial Institutions*, Conference Series No. 21, October 1979, Federal Reserve Bank of Boston, pp. 144–195.

Benston, George J. "Deposit Insurance and Bank Failures." *Economic Review*, Federal Reserve Bank of Atlanta, March 1983, pp. 4–17.

Black, Fischer, Miller, Merton H., and Posner, Richard A. "An Approach to the Regulation of Bank Holding Companies." *Journal of Business*, July 1978, *51*, pp. 379–412.

Cagan, Phillip. "Economic Developments and the Erosion of Monetary Controls." In W. Fellner [Ed.], *Contemporary Economic Problems*. Washington: American Enterprise Institute, 1979, pp. 117–51.

Chandler, Gary G., and Ewert, David C. "Discrimination on the Basis of Sex under the Equal Credit Opportunity Act." Working Paper No. 8, Credit Research Center, Krannert Graduate School of Management, Purdue University, 1976.

Corrigan, Gerald E. "Statement to the U. S. House of Representatives." *Federal Reserve Bulletin*, July 1983, pp. 532–535.

Federal Deposit Insurance Corporation, *Manual of Examination Policy* (Rev. ed.). Washington: July 1, 1976.

Federal Register, 48, Monday, February 7, 1983.

Flannery, Mark J. "Deposit Insurance Creates a Need for Bank Regulation." *Business Review*, Federal Reserve Bank of Philadelphia, January/February 1982, pp. 17–27.

Friedman, Milton. "Monetary Policy: Theory and Practice." *Journal of Money Credit and Banking*. February 1982, *14*, pp. 98–118.

Garlock, Fred L. "Country Banking in Wisconsin during the Depression." U. S. Department of Agriculture, Technical Bulletin No. 777, July 1941.

Garlock, Fred L., and Gile, B. M. "Bank Failures in Arkansas." University of Arkansas, Agricultural Experimental Station, Bulletin No. 315, March 1935.

Hardy, Charles O., and Viner, Jacob. "Report of the Availability of Bank Credit in the Seventh Federal Reserve District." U. S. Government Printing Office, 1935.

Horvitz, Paul M. "Reorganization of the Financial Regulatory Agencies." *Journal of Bank Research*, Winter 1983, pp. 245–263.

Kane, Edward J. "Good Intentions and Unintended Evil: The Case Against Selective Credit Allocation." *Journal of Money, Credit and Banking*, February 1977, *9*, pp. 55–69.

Kane, Edward J. "Accelerating Inflation, Technological Innovation, and the Decreasing Effectiveness of Banking Regulation." *Journal of Finance*, May 1981, *36*, pp. 355–367.

Maisel, Sherman J. *Managing the Dollar*. New York: W. W. Norton & Co., 1973.

Maisel, Sherman J. (Ed.). *Risk and Capital Adequacy in Commercial Banks*. Chicago: University of Chicago Press, 1981.

Mayer, Thomas. "Financial Innovation—The Conflict between Micro and Macro Optimality." *American Economic Review*, May 1982, *72*, pp. 29–34.

Meltzer, Allan H. "Credit Availability and Economic Decisions: Some Evidence from the Mortgage and Housing Markets." *Journal of Finance*, June 1974, *14*(3), pp. 763–777.

Pesek, Boris P. "There is Another Bank Reform in the Wings." *Journal of Post Keynesian Economics*, Spring 1982, *IV*(3), pp. 468–473.

Peterson, Manferd O. "Conflicts between Monetary Policy and Bank Supervision." *Issues in Bank Regulation*, Autumn 1977, pp. 26–37.

Peterson, Manferd O., and Zorn, Tom. "Bank Disclosure and Incentives." Mimeograph, University of Nebraska—Lincoln, 1983.

Peterson, Richard L. "An Investigation of Sex Discrimination in Commercial Banks' Direct Consumer Lending." *The Bell Journal of Economics,* Autumn 1981, *12,* pp. 547–561.

Robertson, J. L. "Federal Regulation of Banking: A Plea for Unification." *Law and Contemporary Problems,* Autumn 1966, *31,* pp. 673–695.

Rohner, Ralph J. "Problems of Federalism in the Regulation of Consumer Financial Services Offered by Commercial Banks." In *State and Federal Regulation of Commercial Banks,* Leonard Lapidus et al., Federal Deposit Insurance Corporation, 1980, Vol. II, pp. 1–168.

Smith, James F. "The Equal Credit Opportunity Act of 1974: A Cost Benefit Analysis." *Journal of Finance,* May 1977, pp. 609–627.

Stigler, George J. "The Theory of Economic Regulation." *Bell Journal of Economics and Management,* Spring 1971, *2,* pp. 3–21.

Tuccillo, John, Van Order, Robert, and Villani, Kevin. "Homeownership Policies and Mortgage Markets, 1960 to 1980." *Housing Finance Review,* January 1982, *1,* pp. 1–21.

Volcker, Paul A. "Statement before the Committee on Banking, Housing and Urban Affairs, U. S. Senate." *Federal Reserve Bulletin,* May 1983, pp. 356–364.

Warburton, Clark. *Depression, Inflation and Monetary Policy.* Baltimore: Johns Hopkins Press, 1966.

11 Regulatory Attitudes toward Risk

Joseph F. Sinkey, Jr.

I think the industry as a whole has become overregulated by the way its supervisors set standards for a bank's capital and assets. We need to stop treating banks like public utilities and allow the market place by its own risk analysis to make a determination between the successful and the unsuccessful bank. No government official, regardless of how competent or well intentioned, can manage an individual bank or the industry as a whole as well as the collective efforts of bank stockholders, directors and officers. [p. 6]

> P. C. Jackson
> Member of the Board of Governors
> of the Federal Reserve System
> May 11, 1978

INTRODUCTION

Like Zeus, who made a habit of appearing in unusual disguises to unsuspecting maidens, bank regulators sometimes appear in unusual disguises. Sometimes they use words traditionally reserved for advocates of the free marketplace. To unsuspecting students of the banking industry, this Zeus-like behavior may have appeared puzzling or downright shocking in the 1970s. However, in the 1980s, the rethinking of regulatory attitudes toward risk is the rule rather than the exception. For example, on February 17, 1983, William M. Isaac, chairman of the Federal Deposit Insurance Corporation (FDIC), stated:

We would like to supplement our supervisory system by bringing market forces into play to a greater degree. We must gradually, and in a nondisruptive fashion, move away from the notion that all large-bank liabilities have a federal guarantee behind them.

When the FDIC established on July 5, 1982 (before Isaac's speech) a Deposit Insurance National Bank (DINB) to replace the failed Penn Square Bank of Oklahoma City, this notion was (unavoidably) conveyed to the marketplace. That is, since uninsured deposits were not given the full protection that a purchase-and-assumption transaction would have accorded them, the de facto expectation of 100% deposit insurance behind all the liabilities of "large" banks was punctured. Continental Illinois has, of course, changed all this.

This chapter focuses upon three major themes: (1) regulatory attitudes toward risk, (2) how the changes taking place in the banking system are affecting these attitudes, and (3) the implications and challenges of these changes for regulators and managers in the 1980s and beyond. The framework of the presentation is as follows. First, a brief historical perspective of the origins of risk regulation in U.S. banking is presented. This perspective is updated by considering deposit insurance and related reasons for limiting risk taking in banking. The changing nature of risks in banking, the problems of measuring and quantifying these risks, and the alternative methods for limiting risk taking occupy the bulk of the chapter. The presentation ends with a look at future directions and issues, followed by a summary and some conclusions.

HISTORICAL PERSPECTIVE: WHY LIMIT RISK TAKING IN BANKING?

Regulation means a principle, rule, or law designed to govern behavior. Thus, bank regulation is designed to govern bank behavior and to limit risk taking in banking. A lot of current bank regulation grew out of the financial and economic crisis of the 1930s, a period known as the Great Depression. In a crisis, frequently there is overreaction. The Great Depression was a crisis of enormous magnitude, and there was some overreaction. The Depository Institutions Deregulation and Monetary Control Act of 1980 (DIDMCA) and the Garn-St Germain Depository Institutions Act of 1982 are dismantling some of the shackles of that overreaction. The legislators of the 1930s, of course, had good intentions.

They did not want the banking crisis of the 1930s ever to be repeated. Sometimes, however, good intentions have unintended evils. Moreover, unintended evils tend to linger for a long time, as evidenced by the fact that it required almost five decades for the counter-events (e.g., DIDMCA).

The existence of bank regulation can be traced to some fundamental macroeconomic and microeconomic motives. First, on the macroeconomic level, the money supply is an important determinant of total economic activity—monetarists would say the *most* important. Alternative views of the macroeconomic transmission mechanism focus upon interest rates (the Keynesian approach) or the supply of bank credit as critical linkages. Although in today's economy commercial banks are not only the creator of money, they still are the most important single component of the money supply process. Thus, to protect the money supply and give the central bank some leverage to attempt to control bank reserves, interest rates, or credit, banks are regulated. The MC (monetary control) of DIDMCA is an example of this kind of *control* regulation. Ironically, as Milton Friedman (1962) has pointed out, a fractional reserve banking system is "inherently unstable." To counteract this tendency to self-destruct, a central bank (the Federal Reserve System) with lender-of-last-resort powers was created in 1913. One of the tasks of macroeconomic stabilization policy is to protect the money supply from rapid shrinkage via open market operations and access to the discount window, a task that was not accomplished in the 1930s. Since the Fed failed to prevent the financial crisis of the early 1930s, the U.S. Congress established the Federal Deposit Insurance Corporation in 1933 and imposed various restrictions on commercial banks (e.g., prohibition of interest payments on demand deposits and rate ceilings on savings and time deposits) to attempt to control "ruinous competition." By 1959, Friedman (1959) was saying that deposit insurance had made the banking system "panic-proof." By 1980, after a decade and a half of increasingly severe disintermediation, savers were avoiding many of the effects of deposit rate ceilings, and the thrift institutions were threatened with extinction because of the ceilings *and* product restrictions. As a result, the banking acts of 1980 and 1982 were aimed directly at dismantling the interest rate and product specialization restrictions imposed by the legislation of the 1930s and thereafter. Geographic restrictions, the other major class of bank regulation, are due to the McFadden Act of 1927 and the Douglas Amendment (1970) to the Bank Holding Company Act (1956). Major deregulation in this area is also likely to reflect the forces that eliminated most deposit rate ceilings.

The overall goal of bank regulation and deposit insurance is to maintain public confidence in the banking system. On the microeconomic level, the focus is upon limiting the risk exposure of *individual* banks and isolating bank failures to avoid a "domino effect" within the system. To do this, the banking authorities try to see that each individual bank is operated in a "safe-and-sound" manner. The main tool for the prompt detection of potential bank insolvency is the on-site bank examination. This kind of failure prevention regulation is manifested in such factors as capital and liquidity requirements, asset quality standards, and compliance with laws and regulations. The banking authorities use direct regulatory interference (e.g., cease-and-desist orders, removal of officers, required capital injections, etc.) to channel bank behavior away from undesired or improper courses. By pursuing the microeconomic goal of limited failure prevention, the banking authorities expect to maintain public confidence in the banking system.

In addition to maintaining the safety and stability of the financial system, bank regulation has attempted to promote competition, to provide consumer protection, and to encourage efficiency. Of course, the multidimensionality of this goal structure leads to conflicts and trade-offs. To date, the safety and soundness objective always has been favored by the banking authorities, as it should be. However, each of the other areas also has had its day—and its costs (e.g., the costs of compliance in the consumer protection area). At present, the promotion of competition and the efficiency of the financial marketplace is being highlighted. This focus has, in turn, created concern about the ability of the current deposit insurance and regulatory structures to function in a deregulated environment.

The Deposit Insurance and Lender-of-Last-Resort Functions

There will be a need for bank regulation as long as the banking authorities continue to provide the deposit insurance and lender-of-last-resort functions. These functions, as they are currently administered, encourage a bank to hold as risky a portfolio as regulations permit. Clearly, they create the wrong kinds of incentives. Risk-based pricing of the insurance and lender functions would be a step in the right direction. Thus, a major problem with today's financial system, but one that is being addressed (albeit slowly), is the need for *structural* reform of the regulatory and insurance systems. Although these frameworks have worked effectively for the past five decades, they have not kept pace with the revolution that has occurred in the financial services industry over the past few years. An environment characterized by price and interest rate volatility, major deregulation, intense competition, and extensive international financial activity requires a modern, fair, and flexible regulatory and insurance apparatus. Since the current system is antiquated, inequitable, and at times less than flexible, a major overhaul is needed. For the purposes of this chapter, the major areas of concern are the identification and measurement of risk and the mapping of this risk into an appropriate deposit insurance contract (i.e., one that is rationally priced). The current system of bank regulation and deposit insurance encourages risk taking and forces "safe-and-sound" managers to subsidize the "high rollers."

The SEC Effect, Disclosure, and Market Discipline

The banking authorities mainly are concerned with protecting the deposit insurance fund and promoting the safety and soundness of the banking system. Given these objectives, authorities have a tendency to portray a brighter picture of a troubled bank's financial condition than reality might dictate. By contrast, the Securities and Exchange Commission (SEC) is concerned that stockholders and would-be investors have full information (via disclosure) before making investment decisions. The failure of several large banks in the 1970s strengthened the demand for greater bank disclosure. The clash between "secrecy" and "disclosure" was inevitable. The fact that there is something called the "SEC effect" indicates who is winning most of the battles. At present, the banking agencies must adopt disclosure requirements "substantially similar" to the corresponding SEC regulations, or publish reasons for the differences (see Dince, 1979). Moreover, the Fed, FDIC, and Office of the Comptroller of the Currency (OCC) have established securities disclosure units (in effect "mini-SECs") within their own agencies. A bank or bank holding company (BHC) with 500 or more shareholders is subject to SEC disclosure standards. The basic bank disclosure issue relates to the amount of detail that should be supplied regarding the loan concentrations, loan loss reserves, and non-earning (or nonperforming) assets of major banks. Litigation in the case of First Pennsylvania Bank focused upon the disclosure issue as the shareholders claimed that they did not have enough information to judge the quality of the bank's loan portfolio. The fact that bank regulators have become more "user oriented" in terms of financial disclosure is a manifestation of the SEC effect and of their recognition (see Isaac, 1983; Volcker, 1983) that market discipline has an important role to play in constraining the risk exposure of major banks. If the marketplace is to perform this function effectively, it must have adequate and reliable information via disclosure. In its deposit insurance study, the FDIC (1983) considered disclosure proposals dealing with the measurement of interest rate risk, a narrative analysis of the bank's operating results and financial position, and the publication in the *Federal Register* of final statutory enforcement actions taken against banks.

THE FUNDAMENTALS OF RISK IN BANKING

Any financial decision involves three important factors: (1) money, (2) time, and (3) risk. The theory of finance is concerned with the problem of evaluating alternative future monetary flows or values. Since the future is in general uncertain, the problem becomes one of evaluating risky monetary flows or values over time. In banking, the risk factor is a multidimensional one that includes such elements as credit risk (also called asset or default risk), liquidity risk, operating risk, and fraud risk. In addition, the money and time factors have important risk considerations in banking. In the time domain, maturity or interest rate risk (also called investment risk) is critical because traditionally banks have tended to borrow short at variable interest rates and to lend long at fixed interest rates. During periods of rapid inflation this kind of maturity imbalance squeezes earnings and erodes a bank's capital base (e.g., the plight of thrift institutions during the 1970s and early 1980s).

In international banking, the money factor has a unique risk known as foreign exchange risk. This risk (also called currency risk or transfer risk) is primarily due to the fact that inflation rates and hence interest rates differ across countries. It is manifested under conditions in which a country is unable or unwilling to obtain enough foreign exchange to service its external indebtedness. International banking also complicates a bank's traditional risk analysis (with respect to the credit, liquidity, operational, and fraud elements of risk) because of the existence of sovereign (political) risk and country (economic) risk. The combination of sovereign risk, country risk, and foreign exchange risk can be referred to as foreign risk. Because of the economic and political instability in such countries as Mexico, Poland, Brazil, and Argentina, foreign risk is a major concern for the U.S. banking authorities and the international banking community. In terms of risk exposure, it is the greatest risk to the banking system. The concern, of course, is with the possibility of a default by a major country and the subsequent "domino effect" that this default could have on other debtor countries and the lending banks. In this context, foreign risk is simply a form of credit or default risk.

A Framework for Analyzing Bank Risk

A bank can be conceptualized as either a balance sheet or a deliverer of financial services. These two notions provide a convenient and logical foundation for constructing a framework for analyzing bank risk (see Figure 11.1).[1] Viewing a bank as a balance sheet, the notion of a portfolio and hence portfolio risk comes to mind. The three basic portfolio risks that a

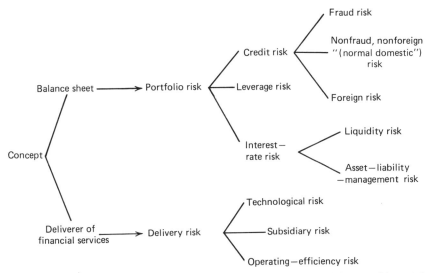

Figure 11.1. The notion or concept of a bank as a *balance sheet* and a *deliverer of financial services* suggests the following framework for analyzing bank risk.

bank faces are credit risk, interest rate risk, and leverage risk. Credit risk can be associated with three factors: (1) fraud risk (e.g., insider trans-actions), (2) foreign risk, and (3) nonfraud/nonforeign or "normal do-mestic" risk. Fraud-type risk has been an important cause of modern (i.e., since 1950) bank failure. This kind of risk frequently takes the form of concentration of credit to friends, relatives, and/or business associates of the bank's top managers, for instance, USNB of San Diego (1973) and United American Bank of Knoxville (1983). In addition, fraud-type risk usually is associated with bank directors who tend to function merely as "rubber-stamp bodies" and do not exercise proper oversight of the bank's activities. When these irregularities are discovered by bank examiners, they usually are so pervasive that they eventually lead to the bank's in-solvency.

The three largest bank failures in U.S. history (see Table 11.1)—Frank-lin National Bank of New York in 1974 with $1.45 billion in deposits, United States National Bank of San Diego in 1973 with $932 million in deposits, and United American Bank of Knoxville in 1983 with $794 million in deposits—were all plagued to varying degrees by insider or fraud-type transactions.

Although the fraud component of the credit risk has been a major cause of U.S. bank failure, it is not the source of portfolio risk that the banking authorities are *most* concerned about today. Fraud risk must take a back

Table 11.1.   The 10 Largest U.S. Commercial Bank Failures as of January 1, 1984

Bank	Year Closed	Total Deposits (in millions of dollars)
1. Franklin National Bank, New York	1974	$1,445
2. United States National Bank, San Diego	1973	932
3. United American Bank, Knoxville	1983	794
4. First National Bank of Midland, Texas	1983	622
5. Banco Credit y Ahorro Ponceno, Ponce, Puerto Rico	1978	608
6. Penn Square Bank, Oklahoma City	1982	465
7. The Hamilton National Bank of Chattanooga, Chattanooga	1976	336
8. American City Bank, Los Angeles	1983	267
9. City and County Bank of Knox County, Knoxville	1983	254
10. The Drover's National Bank of Chicago, Chicago	1978	197

SOURCE: FDIC *Annual Report,* various issues, and FDIC press releases.

seat to foreign risk and interest rate risk. The reasons for this are threefold. First, fraud-type risk tends to be deliberately masked and therefore more difficult to uncover. For example, to avoid the scrutiny of bank examiners, records have been hidden and adversely classified loans shuttled among banks under a single control. Nevertheless, fraud-type risk is the source of portfolio risk that the banking authorities have been best able to handle. Second, it is unlikely that fraud risk ever could be so pervasive as to jeopardize the integrity of the entire financial system. Of course, these reasons do not suggest that bank examiners should not look for fraud risk. In fact, although examiners claim that their inspections are not designed to uncover fraud, they seem to do a better job at it than many auditors (e.g., the UAB case). And third, in today's environment of interest rate volatility (which affects all banks) and foreign lending (which affects mainly multinational banks), interest rate risk and foreign risk are the two relevant concerns.[2] Unfortunately, these risks have not been the primary focus of traditional bank regulation and deposit insurance pricing, which helps explain why the system needs to be overhauled. However, what can bank examination do about the default risk of a Mexico or a Brazil? These concerns are a matter of U.S. foreign economic policy and are beyond the scope of bank asset quality monitoring. As preventive medicine, bank regulation and examination need to focus upon policies and procedures that limit concentration of credit, whether to LDCs, particular industries, or insiders. The measurement *and* pricing of foreign and interest rate risks are critical needs for an efficient regulatory and insurance system.

In our framework, it is useful to distinguish between bank-specific risks and systematic risks. By focusing upon the credit, liquidity, and capital adequacy risks of individual banks, regulation and deposit insurance have been geared to identifying bank-specific risks. In today's environment these risks still are important, but the systematic risks associated with interest rate volatility and technological change must be recognized and monitored also. In a portfolio context, systematic risk is risk that cannot be diversified away or eliminated. Thus, foreign risk can be viewed primarily as a systematic risk affecting the giant multinational banks, which account for the bulk of assets and deposits in the U.S. banking system. Systematic risks, which affect all banks or a relevant subset such as the multinationals, can lead to systemwide instability or failure. The task of preventing such a disaster falls upon macroeconomic stabilization policies for domestic crises and international monetary policies for worldwide crises. Deposit insurance and bank-specific regulations cannot provide protection against depression-type failures (see Gibson, 1972).

Leverage risk (capital adequacy) refers to the dollar amount of assets that a bank or BHC has pyramided on its capital base. This ratio of assets to capital is called the *equity multiplier* or EM for short. The reciprocal of EM is, of course, the familiar capital–asset ratio. The relationship between leverage and profitability as measured by the return-on-equity (ROE) model is

$$ROE = ROA \times EM \tag{1}$$

where ROA = return on assets. Depository institutions are highly leveraged organizations. The typical commercial bank has an EM of roughly 17, which when combined with an ROA of 0.8% generates 13.6% ROE. In contrast, the giant BHCs are more highly leveraged but less profitable in terms of ROA. However, the effects tend to be offsetting with respect to ROE. That is, the typical giant BHC has an ROA of 0.6% but an EM of 24 for a similar ROE of 14.4%. An ROE analysis by bank size for the year 1981 is presented in Table 11.2.

Since deposit insurance was instituted in 1933, banks have been substituting deposit insurance for bank capital (see Peltzman, 1970). In addition, BHCs have used the technique of double leverage (i.e., parent

Table 11.2.   Return-on-Equity Analysis by Bank Size, 1981

Asset Size	ROE	ROA	EM	Number of Banks
Less than $5 million	0.0766	0.0105	7.29	452
$5 million to $9.9 million	0.1003	0.0107	9.37	1,607
$10.0 million to $24.9 million	0.1228	0.0113	10.87	4,463
$25.0 million to $49.9 million	0.1316	0.0112	11.75	3,645
$50.0 million to $99.9 million	0.1360	0.0110	12.36	2,182
$100.0 million to $299.9 million	0.1295	0.0097	13.35	1,287
$300.0 million to $499.9 million	0.1138	0.0080	14.22	188
$500.0 million to $999.9 million	0.1365	0.0092	14.84	185
$1.0 billion to $4.9 billion	0.1232	0.0071	17.35	164
$5.0 billion or more	0.1382	0.0057	24.24	41
All banks	0.1308	0.0077	16.99	14,214

SOURCE: *1981 Statistics on Banking,* FDIC, Table 119, p. 80. The equity multiplier (EM) was derived as ROE/ROA and is only an approximation for group data.

company debt downstreamed as bank equity capital) to increase further their effective degree of leverage. Although bank capital serves as a cushion or buffer to absorb realized losses, the ability of banks to pass a major portion of their portfolio risk on to the deposit insurer encourages them to seek riskier assets and additional leverage. The ability of the banking authorities to control this process of "adverse selection" is important for maintaining public confidence in the banking system.

Focusing now on the lower half of Figure 11.1, the notion of a bank as a "deliverer of financial services" suggests the concept of "delivery risk," which can be separated into three components: (1) operating-efficiency risk, (2) subsidiary risk, and (3) technology risk. The operating efficiency component focuses upon the fundamental economic concept of cost minimization or, more colorfully, as the "run-'em-cheap" notion. The risk of inefficient bank operations is, of course, a reduced stream of earnings. Bank operating risks are becoming more complex and potentially more dangerous. For example, with the growth of franchising, networking, and purchased processing, the risks associated with the collapse of vendors and suppliers of services are increasing.

Regarding subsidiary risk, the dominant organizational form in U.S. banking is the bank holding company. With the growth of BHCs and subsidiary activities, the notion of subsidiary (and affiliate) risk becomes important and therefore is included as a major component of delivery risk. The inclusion of subsidiary risk as a component of the risk framework implies that it is not feasible to separate such risk taking from the overall riskiness of the bank or BHC. Within the holding company, areas of fundamental organizational change include: (1) geographic expansion, (2) product expansion, (3) charter conversions (mainly for thrifts), and (4) joint ventures (with both depository and nondepository firms).

The metamorphosis in financial services delivery and production (Kane, 1983b) is most evident in the technological area where new applications of electronics, robotics, and telecommunications are reshaping depository institutions. These changes present technological risks that need to be managed and monitored. Banks with excessive amounts of "brick and mortar" are especially prone to technological obsolescence and greater risk exposure.

In practice, the components of delivery risk (and change) do not separate as easily as Figure 11.1 depicts. For example, the expansion of bank product lines involves a combination of technological and organizational changes. To measure the efficiency of this expansion, economists have developed the concept of scope economics or economies of scope. Panzar and Willig (1981) define the existence of economies of scope as a situation "where it is less costly to combine two or more product lines in one firm than to produce them separately" (p. 268). The notion is an extension of the concept of economies of scale derived from the traditional economic theory of the *one-product* firm. The cost-reducing effects of producing and delivering a package of financial services are accounted for by the notion of scope economies. Failure to develop or take advantage of potential economies of scale *and* scope leads to higher costs, lower net earnings, and greater delivery risk (see Humphrey's chapter in this volume).

Off-Balance-Sheet Activities and Bank Risk

Off-balance-sheet activities are contingent claims or financial services that generate income and create portfolio risk. A contingent claim involves a commitment or guarantee to lend that does not create an item *on* the balance sheet. The most familiar forms of bank contingent claims include such traditional activities as loan commitments, lines of credit, letters of credit, and forward contracts in foreign exchanges. Futures contracts and lease agreements represent recent innovations in bank contingent claims. A catalog of various off-balance-sheet activities is presented in Table 11.3. The activities are divided into contingent claims and financial services (see Goldberg, Altman, and Furash, 1983). The distinction between the two categories is based upon the fact that the financial services group includes "less traditional activities" that create portfolio risks that are "not readily apparent" and that "typically are managed differently from contingent claim businesses where credit risk is more obvious" (p. 8).

In terms of Figure 11.1, off-balance-sheet activities create both portfolio

Table 11.3. Some Off-Balance-Sheet Activities

Contingent Claims	Financial Services

Bank loan commitments, including:
    Formal loan commitments
    Revolving credits
    Lines of credit to customers
    Fed funds and Eurodollar lines of
    credit
    Commercial paper backup lines
	Loan servicing, including:
	    Mortgage servicing
	    Student loan servicing

Standby letters of credit	Loan pass-throughs, including:
	    Mortgages (GNMA, FNMA)
	    Student loans (SLMA)
	    Corporate loans (construction
	    loans)

Commercial letters of credit and
bankers' acceptances
	Trust-related services, including:
	    Portfolio management
	    Investment advisory services
	    Securities processing

Futures and forward contracts
    Foreign exchange activities
    Financial futures
	Customer stock, bond, and money
	    market brokerage
	    Trust and estate management

Agreements to provide financial
support to bank affiliates or
subsidiaries
	Payment services, such as:
	    Network arrangements
	    Transaction processing

Loan participations
    Direct extension of funds
    Risk participations
	Overdraft banking
	    Credit/debit cards
	    ATMs, POS, home banking
	    Cash management

Merchant banking which has
elements of both contingent claims
and financial services such as
    Private placements
    Securities lending (repos)
    Equity participations
    Corporate finance consulting
    Foreign exchange advisory
    services
    Gold and other commodities
    trading
    Tax shelters
    Asset sales
	Bank-to-bank payments
	
	Insurance services, such as:
	    Credit life insurance
	    Selected other insurance
	
	Correspondent banking services,
	such as:
	    Credit services
	    Securities services
	    Trust services
	    International services
	    Payments services
	    Other banking services

Customer leasing which has some
elements of both contingent claims
and financial services including:
    Tax leasing
    Lease brokering or packaging
	Export trading company services,
	such as:
	    Export/import consulting
	    Insurance services

SOURCE: Goldberg, Altman, and Furash, 1983, Table 1, p. 9.

risk and delivery risk. The most important form of portfolio risk for off-balance-sheet activities is credit risk. Customer nonperformance means that bank credit is substituted for that of the customer. In addition, off-balance-sheet activities may create interest rate risk because of maturity (duration) mismatches and leverage risk because of overextended activities (e.g., loan commitments). With respect to delivery risk, the major concern is in the area of operating efficiency risk. That is, does the bank have the personnel, organizational structure, and controls to manage properly the off-balance-sheet business? To the extent that modern technology and bank affiliates or subsidiaries are involved in these activities, then the bank also is exposed to technological risk and subsidiary risk.

Regulated versus Unregulated Risks

Prior to the 1960s, inflation, regulation-induced innovation, technological change, and nonbank competition were not the major systematic forces that they have been over the past quarter of a century. As far back as the early 1900s, the banking authorities mainly were concerned about the credit and liquidity risks of individual banks. These risks were perceived to be the major causes of bank failure. The major part of current bank examination procedures still is rooted in this view, which focuses upon determining a bank's asset quality and its capital adequacy. Only recently have bank regulators begun to measure and to attempt to control three heretofore unregulated risks: interest rate risk, foreign risk, and technological risk. In the rapidly changing environment of the financial services industry, some *unregulated* (i.e., not yet administratively penalized) risks are likely to exist. Figure 11.2 portrays Kane's (1983c) view of these risks as a bomb whose burning fuse threatens international financial stability. For the moment at least, the current round of lower interest rates has had a dramatic effect in extinguishing Kane's fuse. However, in the long run, without the reregulation of thrift institutions' interest rate risk and banks' sovereign risk, another dose of inflation would be likely to reignite the fuse.

Kane (1983b) explains the existence of unregulated risks as due to the fact that avoidance lags are shorter than regulatory lags. The differential lags reflect differences in the adaptive capacities of the regulated institutions and the regulators in response to changes in technology, market forces, or banking practices. In effect, the regulators always seem to come up "a day late and a dollar short." In addition to the two unregulated risks mentioned above, many of the risks associated with off-balance-sheet activities are largely unregulated or just now coming under regulatory purview (e.g., loan commitments).

Since the major function of any insurer is risk management, the exist-

Figure 11.2. The time bomb of unregulated banking risks. *Source:* Kane, 1983c, Chapter 4, Figure 4.1.

ence of unregulated risks creates a special problem for deposit insurers known as *adverse selection.* An insurance arrangement in which the insuree has more information about risk than the insurer leads to adverse selection behavior. Critical information gaps currently exist with respect to interest rate risk, foreign risk, and the risks associated with off-balance-sheet activities. To manage risk effectively (i.e., to control risk exposure), deposit insurers must have information systems that measure all relevant forms of risk (see Figure 11.1).

The adverse selection problem can be contrasted with another problem that insurers face, namely, *moral hazard.* This term refers to changes in behavior when insurance is introduced. Moral hazard and adverse selection problems are exacerbated by uniform or flat-rate insurance policies. Thus, most rationally priced insurance contracts are not uniform; they contain deductibles, coinsurance, and other special features. Such tailor-made contracts provide preferred premiums for low-risk customers. This process of self-selection permits insurees to choose from a menu of insurance contracts. The track record indicates that "good risks" select low coverage and "bad risks" select high coverage. When there is no choice, the deposit insurance record indicates that the "high rollers" take on excessive risk and, as a result, they are subsidized by the more risk-averse managers.[3]

PROBLEMS OF MEASURING AND QUANTIFYING BANKING RISKS

There are three kinds of data available for identifying potential banking risks: (1) bank examination data, (2) financial statement or accounting data, and (3) market return data. Table 11.4 presents a catalog of information regarding these data. Only a few clarifying comments are needed. First, classified assets consist mainly of loans judged by examiners to be loss, doubtful, or substandard. Second, a stock's annual holding period return *(h)* consists of a capital gains yield plus a dividend yield, or in symbols,

$$h = P(P_1 - P_0)/P_0 + D_1/P_0 \qquad (2)$$

where P_1 = end of year price
P_0 = beginning of year price
D_1 = end of year dividend

The price appreciation or depreciation is, of course, determined by the magnitude of P_1 relative to P_0. Third, because bankers sometimes attempt to distort or "window-dress" their financial statements, market data may be more reliable. And fourth, if the objective of the early warning system is to serve as an aid in *scheduling* bank examinations, then the history of past examinations should provide important information.

The Record of Problem and Failed Banks

To place the problem of measuring and quantifying banking risks in perspective, consider the data presented in Table 11.5. Using a population base of 14,500 and the 1982 figures for FDIC problem and failed banks, the problem and failure rates were 2.34% and 0.23%, respectively. Over the 15-year period from 1968 to 1982, the average number of problem and failed banks has been 265.4 and 9.27, respectively. In contrast, the average number of business failures for the same period was roughly 11,000 per year for a failure rate of 0.42%, which is about seven times the de jure commercial bank failure rate.[4]

Why are there so few bank failures and problem banks? Professor Anthony Santomero of the Wharton School contends:[5]

I think that the internal desire to run an orderly institutional structure and the internal desire to maintain a profit growth is 90 percent of the reason we have very few bank failures. I think auditing is 6 percent and examination is 3 percent—and 1 percent is fraud. But the main factor is a viable management. [Dince, 1982, p. 2]

Table 11.4.   Data Available for Identifying Potential Banking Risks

	Bank Examination	Financial Statement	Market Return
Description	Classified assets and evaluation of bank policies, practices, and procedures	Report of condition and report of income and dividends (accounting data)	Holding-period return (i.e., (price change + dividends over purchase price)
Source	On-site bank examination	Reported by banks to banking agencies	Stock market trading
Frequency	Usually only once a year but more frequent for problem banks	Mainly quarterly but some weekly data for the largest banks. Current delays of 90–120 days in getting the data ready limit effectiveness	Daily for trading days
Availability	All banks	All banks	Only for banks with actively traded securities
Reliability	Good	Good	Excellent
Early warning potential	Past exams should be relevant	Good	Good/excellent
Current use	Heavy	Used but not very effectively	Not used

Let's call this "Santomero's 90–6–3–1 rule." It suggests that the vast majority of banks are examined needlessly. Is such criticism unfair? What if, without examination, 90% of the banks in good condition went bad? If you believe this scenario, General Sherman's march through Atlanta during the Civil War can be called an urban renewal plan. Competent managers are clearly the critical factor in maintaining a growing, dynamic, and safe-and-sound banking industry. While *most* bank managers are intelligent, well-trained, and honest, *some* are not; they have deficiencies in one or more of the critical areas. Thus, the important questions are: (1) how to control the bad guys; and (2) how to protect against errors in judgment by the good guys.

Table 11.5. Number of Problem and Failed Banks, 1968–1983

Year	FDIC Problem Banks	Failed Banks	Ratio of Failed to Problem (in percent)
1968	240	3	1.25
1969	216	9	4.17
1970	251	7	2.79
1971	239	6	2.51
1972	190	1	0.53
1973	155	6	3.88
1974	181	4	2.21
1975	347	13	3.75
1976	385	16	6.25
1977	368	6	1.63
1978	342	7	2.05
1979	287	10	3.48
1980	217[a]	10	4.61
1981	223	7	3.14
1982	340	34	10.00
1983	642	45	7.01

SOURCE: FDIC problem bank lists, news releases, and annual reports.

[a]FDIC classification procedures were revised slightly in 1980.

THE SINKEY PLAN OR "14,000–500 RULE"

This cleverly named plan is designed to provide the most efficient allocation of scarce examination resources.[6] It is grounded in the notion of the "real dual banking system," a distinction based upon the economic and political realities of the banking industry. That is, the 500 or so large banks control the bulk of the industry's balance sheet and therefore they present the greatest risk to the stability of the financial system (e.g., deposit insurance fund). The rest of the industry, the 14,000 or so "little" banks, does not present a serious threat to financial stability. In the aggregate, these institutions only control about $3 out of every $10 on deposit in U.S. banks. In the political arena, however, the rest of the industry, because of sheer numbers (i.e., "one bank, one vote"), has been a potent force.

Now, the idea of this plan is to concentrate scarce examination resources on the 500 largest banks (roughly all banks with assets over $300 million), which would capture the Penn Squares, UABs, First Penns, Franklins, and so on. The rest of the industry would *not* be ignored; it would simply get less attention. Computer early warning systems would play a crucial role in scheduling the frequency and intensity of on-site inspections for the other 14,000 members of the industry. Since the principal business of any examiner or insurer should be risk management, the "14,000–500 rule" is a reasonable approach to identifying and managing banking risks. Implementation of the plan, however, requires an information system that measures all relevant forms of risks, especially foreign and interest rate risks. Foreign risk, of course, affects only those banks doing multinational business—namely, the largest banks—whereas interest rate risk affects all banks. To date, the banking authorities have not succeeded in measuring adequately these two critical risks. They are, however, attempting to remedy the shortcomings. For example, the FDIC is now collecting information on interest rate mismatches in the new Call Reports. In addition, the FDIC (1983) has proposed a present-value framework to measure the effect of interest rate changes on a bank's earnings and capital. Such information would be used to determine a bank's risk class and associated deposit insurance rebate (if any) under the FDIC's proposed plan. Regarding foreign risk, the banking agencies have been working on a supervisory approach to foreign lending since 1978. The approach analyzes credit risk along traditional lines and attempts to incorporate this analysis with measures of country risk. The system monitors concentrations of credit in order to encourage diversification and to evaluate a bank's risk management policies and procedures. Given the current problems of banks with foreign borrowers, it is clear that a system that is basically classificatory does not insulate against loss—especially with severe economic weakness.

The data sources presented in Table 11.4 are those available for building an information system. However, an information or early warning system based upon market return data is available only for banks or BHCs with actively traded securities. The number of banks meeting this requirement is relatively small—certainly less than 500 and probably around 250. Thus, the "14,000–500 rule" is merely a convenient description using general figures. The important point is that those banks with actively traded securities are the largest ones, and they present the greatest potential risk to the financial system. The availability, timing, and reliability of the three data sets suggest that the market return data should be an important information source for evaluating overall bank risk exposure (e.g., see Pettway and Sinkey, 1980). Specific sources of risk exposure (e.g., foreign or interest rate) can be determined through analysis of financial statements or from on-site bank inspections.

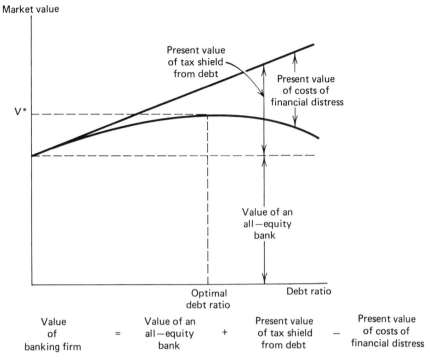

Figure 11.3. The value of the banking firm. *Source:* Sinkey, 1983, Figure 16.3, p. 476.

The Discipline of the Marketplace

At present, none of the banking agencies is seriously using market data to monitor the risk exposure of large banks or BHCs. However, the banking authorities are eager to have market forces play a greater role in this area. The way in which market forces operate to discipline banks can be seen from Figure 11.3. This figure shows the relationship between the market value of a bank and its debt ratio (i.e., financial leverage or, if you like, *capital adequacy*). It is assumed that the bank wants to maximize the market value of its debt plus equity. This objective is achieved at the optimal debt ratio (i.e., where the difference between the present value of the tax shield from debt and the present value of the costs of financial distress is maximized). The theory goes like this. As a bank increases its leverage, its market value increases, up to a point (the optimum), and then it declines. What happens is that the market penalizes banks for excessive leverage (i.e., "inadequate capital"). The discipline, which comes from existing or would-be equity shareholders and uninsured creditors, is manifested in the form of higher cost of funds (e.g., CDs) or inability to raise funds. Of course, if uninsured creditors come to expect a federal guarantee behind the debt of large banks (Isaac's point), the effectiveness of the market discipline will be reduced as risk is passed on to bank owners and the deposit insurance fund. Since owner–managers may be tempted to "bet the bank," minority shareholders have to protect themselves against such "high rollers." The FDIC attempts to protect the deposit insurance fund (and indirectly minority shareholders) through the use of regulations and on-site examinations.

As long as the notion of 100% deposit insurance for large banks exists, banks still may be able to generate funds if creditors view the situation as one of high return and no risk. For example, the FDIC (1983) is particularly concerned about brokers who place fully insured funds in banks at random without credit analysis or, worse yet, place them in known problem banks and collect higher fees. Bank capital traditionally has served as a buffer or cushion to absorb losses. With a federal guarantee of all bank debt, however, market requirements for capital are reduced. Moreover, since equity capital is not covered by the federal guarantee, high-risk banks may be able to raise debt but not equity.

Comptroller Conover has stated, "not all failures are bad and some were needed to maintain the discipline of the marketplace" (the New York Times, July 22, 1982, p. 34). Typically, it is assumed that uninsured creditors are financially sophisticated individuals (or institutions) who can monitor and protect themselves from adverse risk exposure. However, as the failure of Penn Square Bank demonstrated, this assumption does not hold for all members of the group. The credit unions and S&Ls who got caught with uninsured deposits in Penn Square testify to that fact. Moreover, even some of the giant banks (e.g., Continental Illinois, Chase Manhattan, and Seafirst), who were supposed to know better, got caught in the Penn Square debacle, although on the other side of the balance sheet through loan participations.

To help uninsured creditors, the FDIC is developing, as part of its insurance reform package, a disclosure form that would make it easier to assess a bank's financial condition. The FDIC hopes that uninsured creditors will force banks (via market discipline) to use the form. However, if the banks refuse, the FDIC has indicated that it will apply "insurance discipline" by recommending that uninsured depositors move their funds.

The Role of Accounting Data

Although market data can only be used for monitoring the performance of banks or BHCs with actively traded securities, accounting data are

Table 11.6. **Bank Performance Report Table of Contents**

Sections	Page Number
Summary Ratios	01
Income Information:	
Income Statement—Revenues and Expenses ($000)	02
Relative Income Statement and Margin Analysis	03
Noninterest Income and Expense Ratios	04
Balance Sheet Information:	
Balance Sheet—Assets Section ($000)	05
Balance Sheet—Liabilities and Capital ($000)	06
Balance Sheet—% Composed of Assets & Liabilities	07
Analysis of Loan Loss Reserve and Loan Mix	08
Analysis of Nonperforming Loans and Leases	8A
Sources and Uses of Funds	09
Margin Sensitivity Analysis	10
Liquidity and Investment Portfolio	11
Capital Analysis	12
Other Information:	
Summary Information for Bank in State	13
Peer Group Information	Appendix A
Bank and Bank Holding Company Information	
Certificate # Bank # Charter #	

SOURCE: Federal Financial Institutions Examination Council.

available for all banks. Since these data are supplied by the banks, how reliable and accurate are they? Applying "Santomero's rule" to this question, we have to conclude that at least 90% of the data are reported fairly and accurately. There are exceptions, of course, and that's why we have examinations, audits (internal and external), and regulations. How useful are these data in providing early warning signals about impending financial difficulties? The evidence is overwhelmingly favorable for both financial and nonfinancial firms (see Altman, Avery, Eisenbeis, & Sinkey, 1981; Sinkey, 1979). Despite compelling evidence, however, the banking agencies have yet to develop an efficient and useful packaging of accounting data for early warning purposes.[7] Taking the OCC's National Bank Surveillance System (NBSS) as an example, Dince (1983) quotes an OCC official as follows: "The system (NBSS) just doesn't do the job we expected it would. There is a serious time lag between when the statistics are received and when our peer-group ranking becomes effective. This delay weakens the early-warning system." Although both NBSS and the

Table 11.7. Bank Performance Report

	1982			1981			1980			1979		1978	
Summary Ratios	Bank	Peer 11	Per-cent	Bank	Peer 11	Per-cent	Bank	Peer 11	Per-cent	Bank	Peer 11	Bank	Peer 11
Average assets (in thousands of dollars)	93,775			87,703			81,976			81,418		73,747	
Net income (in thousands of dollars)	718			705			604			598		641	
Number of banks in peer group	659			654			645			607		554	
Earnings and Profitability													
Percent of average assets:													
Net interest income (TE)	4.18	5.28	18	4.51	5.23	30	4.34	5.15	22	4.20	4.95	4.49	4.72
+ Noninterest income	0.58	0.76	36	0.53	0.76	31	0.51	0.70	35	0.54	.64	0.45	0.59
− Overhead expense	3.02	3.87	24	3.07	3.71	30	3.02	3.55	34	2.84	3.40	2.77	3.25
− Provision for loan losses	0.21	.28	44	0.31	0.25	69	0.42	0.24	85	0.53	.23	0.41	0.23
= Pretax net operating income (TE)	1.53	1.84	33	1.65	2.00	35	1.42	2.05	20	1.37	1.98	1.74	1.83
Net operating income	0.76	1.00	29	0.85	1.06	33	0.73	1.08	20	0.73	1.05	0.87	0.96
Adjusted net operating income	0.70	1.05	23	0.96	1.12	39	0.75	1.13	19	0.90	1.12	0.95	1.03
Adjusted net income	0.75	0.94	33	0.86	0.95	40	0.75	1.02	24	0.83	1.02	0.91	0.94
Net income	0.77	0.99	32	0.80	1.02	31	0.74	1.06	21	0.73	1.04	0.87	0.95

Percent of average earning assets:													
Interest income (TE)	12.62	13.60	17	12.98	13.68	32	11.09	11.75	27	9.84	10.42	9.29	9.33
Interest expense	8.06	7.69	61	8.12	7.83	58	6.34	5.94	64	5.29	4.82	4.46	4.02
Net income (TE)	4.56	5.93	18	4.86	5.88	26	4.74	5.83	19	4.55	5.58	4.83	5.31
Loan loss history													
Net loan loss to average total loans	0.54	0.48	64	0.38	0.37	61	.75	0.36	87	0.64	0.30	0.56	0.30
Earn cover of net loan losses (X)	4.25	9.56	32	6.63	11.88	36	2.89	12.28	10	3.37	15.12	4.27	14.82
Loan loss reserve													
Loss reserve to net loan losses (X)	2.59	3.75	48	4.18	4.36	58	1.91	4.57	26	2.07	5.87	1.93	5.49
Loss reserve to total loans	1.30	1.04	79	1.66	1.03	93	1.41	1.02	86	1.31	0.99	1.07	0.93
Liquidity and rate sensitivity													
Volatile liability dependence	−22.01	−8.49	23	−21.90	−1.96	12	3.18	0.28	60	−2.88	3.14	1.85	3.77
Net loans to total assets	54.10	50.76	59	47.30	52.34	26	48.51	52.86	27	55.80	56.02	57.39	56.99
Net market rate position to assets	−16.59	−12.24	37	−15.09	−18.10	63	−24.38	−17.20	24	−12.03	−13.70	−4.62	−5.78
Capitalization													
Prime capital to total assets	7.67	8.16	44	7.51	8.24	35	7.03	8.11	24	7.18	7.95	6.90	7.85
Cash dividends to net income	40.25	32.70	66	42.98	29.94	75	37.58	28.48	70	17.73	28.18	30.11	28.90
Retained earnings to average equity	6.76	8.17	38	6.77	9.10	32	6.88	9.81	24	9.67	9.91	9.73	9.23
Growth rates													
Assets	3.07	11.87	15	1.17	10.30	11	8.85	10.00	46	7.39	10.46	10.07	10.88
Primary Capital	5.39	9.56	25	7.97	10.31	35	6.61	11.28	20	11.82	11.99	10.57	10.82
Total loans	17.45	8.20	80	−1.11	8.12	18	−5.28	4.32	14	4.67	9.07	6.76	15.81
Volatile liabilities	−24.76	11.37	19	−27.98	32.59	08	11.70	24.63	46	−3.40	23.34	109.09	50.34

Uniform Bank Performance Report employ peer-group frameworks, neither one of the systems uses statistical measures of dispersion to determine "outlier" banks. To illustrate the kinds of variables used in these reports, the contents of the 1982 Bank Performance Report are presented in Table 11.6. In Table 11.7, the summary ratios provided in the Bank Performance Report are presented. These data are for an unindentified bank that had average assets of $93.8 million and net income of $718,000 in 1982. The bank's peer group consists of 659 banks. The first stage of ROE analysis for the bank for 1982 is:

	ROE	ROA	EM
Bank	0.0992	0.0077	12.88
Peer group	0.1213	0.0099	12.25

The objective of the analysis is to determine why the bank consistently has had below-average profitability over the period 1978 to 1982 (see Figure 11.4 for an analytical framework).

The banking agencies are not alone when it comes to inconsistent and inefficient use of accounting data. Some accounting firms are just as bad (see Stricharchuk and Darlin, 1983). This evidence, along with the errors of the credit unions, the S&Ls, and the big banks in the Penn Square case, suggests that some market participants are not ready to dish out market discipline. Of course, once the notion of federal guarantee of all bank debt is displaced and the notion of caveat emptor reestablished, such behavior should be improved.

Performance Frameworks.   Figures 11.4 and 11.5 present two alternative frameworks for evaluating the performance and financial condition of depository institutions (see Sinkey, 1983, Chapters 7 and 17). Figure 11.4 presents the traditional du Pont analysis of ROA, a framework I call ROE *decomposition analysis*. Recall that equation (1) is ROE = ROA × EM. Now, ROA consists of a profit margin component (PM) and an asset utilization component (AU), that is,

$$ROA = PM \times AU \tag{3}$$

Substituting (3) into (1) produces:

$$ROE = PM \times AU \times EM \tag{4}$$

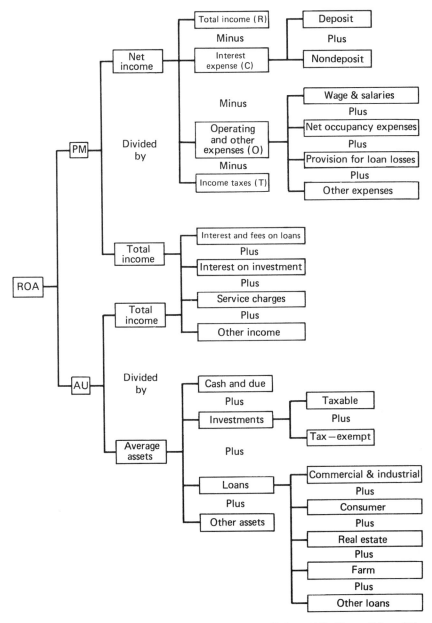

Figure 11.4. ROA Decomposition Analysis. *Source:* Sinkey, 1983, Figure 7.8, p. 213.

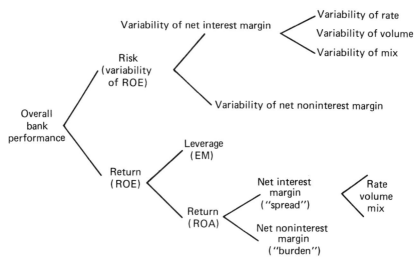

Figure 11.5. The performance forms of asset-liability management: net interest margin. Net interest margin ("spread") = net interest revenue/earnings assets, where net interest revenue = tax-equivalent interest revenue − interest expense. Net noninterest margin (net overhead or "burden") = (noninterest revenue − noninterest expense/earning assets). Earning assets = total assets − cash and due − fixed assets − other assets. *Source:* Sinkey, 1983, Figure 17.2, p. 486.

For the average commercial bank in 1982, equation (4), which is simply an identity, had the following values:

$$0.1318 = 0.0680 \times 0.1221 \times 15.88$$
$$= 0.0083 \times 15.88$$

Figure 11.4 shows how the PM and AU components can be decomposed into their constituent parts. The idea is to identify areas of strength or weakness using both time-series and cross-section analyses of the relevant ratios.

Figure 11.5 presents an alternative performance framework. Using an asset–liability management perspective, this approach focuses upon a bank's net interest margin. Again, a decomposition analysis is stressed as the risk–return components of overall bank performance are evaluated. Rate, volume, and mix are seen as the driving forces in this framework, where rate refers to interest rates (costs and returns), volume to the size of the balance sheet, and mix to the composition of the balance sheet. The planning, direction, and control of the levels, changes, and mixes of the various balance sheet accounts are the essence of asset–liability management.

The Bank Examination Process and Regulatory Interference

The on-site bank examination is the major tool used by the banking agencies for identifying potential bank insolvencies. Once these so-called problem banks are identified, they are subject to greater regulatory interference than nonproblem banks. Although regulatory interference may take many forms (e.g., cease-and-desist orders, removal of bank officers, etc.), it is chiefly reflected in capital regulation. Capital regulation typically entails an infusion of capital into the bank and/or restriction of the bank's expansion—through regulatory denials (on the basis of inadequate capital).

There is a need for regulatory interference to control bank risk exposure because of the existence of underpriced deposit insurance, especially with respect to unregulated risks. With bank risks mispriced (the nominal premium is a flat $\frac{1}{12}$ of 1%), insured institutions are faced with adverse incentives, which many of them eagerly pursue. As a result, high-risk banks are subsidized by low-risk banks. To keep the "high rollers" in line, a system of risk-sensitive implicit insurance premiums is employed (see Buser, Chen, and Kane, 1981). This regulatory interference mainly is manifested by penalties imposed through capital regulation. The focal point of this penal process is capital adequacy and capital ratios.

Capital Adequacy and Capital Ratios.   Most capital ratios, unadjusted for asset quality, show little or no association with groups of problem or failed banks. The current method of adjusting for adversely classified assets attaches a weight of 20% to the substandard *(S)* category, 50% to the doubtful *(D)* category, and 100% to the loss *(L)* category. Thus, the capital ratio that really counts is this weighted classification ratio (WCR) defined as:

$$\text{WCR} = (0.20S + 0.5D + L)/K \qquad (5)$$

where K = total capital accounts. In the Uniform Financial Institutions Rating System, equation (5) is the asset quality or the A component of a numerical scoring system called *CAMEL*. The acronym represents the following ratings: C = capital adequacy (e.g., the capital/asset ratio), A = asset quality, M = management rating, E = earnings rating (ROA), and L = liquidity rating (e.g., the ratio of liquid assets to total assets). Each category is assigned a score ranging from 1 (good) to 5 (bad) and then a composite rating is calculated by taking an unweighted average of the scores. The composite guidelines (with the actual scores in parentheses) are: 1 (1 to 1.4), 2 (1.5 to 2.4), 3 (2.5 to 3.4), 4 (3.5 to 4.4), and 5 (4.5 to 5). Banks with composite scores of 1, 2, or 3 are considered nonproblem banks whereas those with scores of 4 or 5 are considered problem banks by the FDIC (*Annual Report*, 1980, pp. 16–17).

Classified Assets and Problem Banks. Prior to the development of the *CAMEL* rating system and its *WCR*, the FDIC used two measures of capital adequacy called the net capital ratio (NCR) and adjusted capital ratio (ACR). Using previously defined symbols, the ratios are:

$$NCR = (K\text{-}S\text{-}D\text{-}L)/A \qquad (6)$$

and

$$ACR = (K\text{-}0.5D\text{-}L)/A \qquad (7)$$

where A = total assets.[8] In experiments replicating FDIC problem bank lists of the early 1970s, Sinkey (1979) showed that the NCR had 95.4% accuracy in reclassifying groups of problem and nonproblem banks. The NCR for the average problem bank was -2.3% (5.2) compared with 7.6% (3.0) for the average nonproblem bank (standard deviations are in parentheses). The classification rule (derived from a multiple discriminant analysis (MDA) quadratic equation) is: If NCR $\leq$ 2.74%, assign to the problem group. Since other experiments could not beat the NCR test for accuracy (e.g., the ACR accuracy rate was 73.2%), a de facto definition of a problem bank as one with a large volume of substandard loans relative to its capital was established. Note that the difference between NCR and ACR is all of the substandard category plus one-half of the doubtful (i.e., $S + 0.5D$). The WCR in the *CAMEL* system is a compromise between NCR and ACR that employs a more realistic set of weights for adversely classified bank assets.

Has the Bank Examination Process Really Changed?

Shortly after he took office on December 16, 1981, Comptroller Conover stated: "We're going to go right back to square one, and ask: What is an examination? Why do we do it? How should we do it? Who should we do it to? How often should we do it?" (Conover, 1982). Although the OCC's answers to these questions are still forthcoming, it is safe to say that the *CAMEL* system doesn't look much different from what examiners have been doing for the past 50 years. Moreover, what bank examiners are supposed to do sounds like the same old story. For example, according to the current OCC's *Examiner Handbook* (Sec. 1.1, p. 1), the functions of the bank examination process are:

1. To provide an objective evaluation of a bank's soundness
2. To permit the OCC to appraise the quality of management and directors
3. To identify those areas where corrective action is required to strengthen the bank, to improve the quality of its performance, and to enable it to comply with laws, rulings, and regulations

A chronology of what bank examiners do is presented in Table 11.8. The "new" examination process is supposed to be audit, review, and policy oriented. Will the modern record of 45 commercial bank failures in 1983, including the UAB fiasco, the third largest U.S. bank failure, lead to a substantial reform of the bank examination process? Given the history of regulatory lags, the prospects are dim, at least for this decade. Nevertheless, given the economic circumstances of the past few years, the bank failure record looks good. After all, only the failures are well publicized.

FUTURE DIRECTIONS AND ISSUES

Regulatory attitudes toward risk are changing. These changes are most evident in the area of deposit insurance, where substantial reforms are under consideration. For example, the FDIC is recommending that the current flat-rate premium be replaced by a variable-rate premium based on management quality.[9] In addition, reduced insurance coverage for large depositors, greater disclosure about banks' financial condition, and a merging of the FDIC and FSLIC are being proposed. The FDIC also has recommended the creation of a monolithic regulatory agency consisting of the Fed (except for its central bank function), the OCC, and the FHLBB.

The FDIC's plan for variable-rate pricing of *deposit insurance* would classify banks into three risk classes: high risk, medium risk, or normal. The insurance premium would, of course, be highest for the high-risk group and lowest for the normal group. The key parameters for determining a bank's risk class would be its capital adequacy, classified assets (problem loans), and interest rate risk (maturity mismatch). For example, the FDIC has suggested that a bank with very little capital (e.g., less than 3% of assets) or with a large volume of problem loans (note that the WCR, equation (5) above, should be crucial here) and a high degree of exposure to losses arising from interest rate volatility would be rated a high-risk bank. Until the FDIC develops an effective measure of *interest rate risk,* it is clear that the proposed rating system will be driven by the old regulatory standards of classified assets and capital adequacy.[10] Although these stan-

Table 11.8.   What Bank Examiners Do

When	What
1933 to 1974	Credit Review Asset appraisal Verification of items
1974—the watershed	Failure of Franklin National Bank of New York followed by the OCC's development (via Haskins & Sells) of NBSS
1974 to 1976	A transition period with double-digit bank failures in 1975 and 1976
Post-1976	The new examination process focuses upon sound audit procedures, managerial review practices, and director review of managerial policies.

dards have worked well in the past (i.e., almost all banks that have failed over the past three or four decades have been known as problem banks), will they continue to work in the environment of the 1980s?

Regarding the number of banks in each risk class, the FDIC has estimated the following distribution:

		Banks	
Risk Class	Proposed Premium Rebate	Percentage	Number
High	0	10	1,450
Medium	½	10	1,450
Normal	Full	80	11.600
		100	14,500

The FDIC is proposing to implement variable-rate pricing by varying the rebate according to risk class. Thus, "high-risk" banks would receive no rebate whereas "normal" banks would receive a full premium rebate. Given the most recent figure of 654 FDIC problem banks (see Table 11.5), the projection of 1,450 high-risk banks appears a bit strange. Since one would expect problem banks to be the highest-risk institutions, either the proposed high-risk class is somewhat indiscriminant, or there was subsequently a substantial deterioration in the banking system. Furthermore, given the *CAMEL* rating system of five risk classes, why wasn't a five-tier pricing scheme proposed? Ignoring the fine-tuning aspects, let us commend Chairman Isaac and the FDIC for their proposal to price deposit insurance on a risk basis. After all, it was only 50 years ago that this debate began.

Chairman Isaac has suggested that higher insurance premiums should encourage banks to behave more cautiously. During the energy crisis of the 1970s, energy conservation became popular. Will the 1980s witness a similar phenomenon in banking called "risk conservation?" If the added insurance costs price unregulated risks effectively, then banks should be encouraged to conserve on risk. Alternatively, what if banks regard the deposit insurance bill, like the electric bill, as just another cost of doing business? In this case, deposit insurance premiums would not substantially affect bank risk taking. Of course, as long as the risk is properly priced, the FDIC should not worry about whether or not its premium schedule affects bank behavior. Should automobile insurers expect high premiums to improve the driving habits of all high-risk drivers? No, that is one of the reasons there are traffic regulations. Similarly, variable-rate deposit insurance will not eliminate the need for bank regulation. To avoid potential conflicts of interest, the businesses of insurance and regulation, as in other industries, could be separate. One variation of this, optional excess deposit insurance, has been considered by the FDIC. Somewhat surprisingly, there was little interest by the private insurers, at least those surveyed by the FDIC, to provide this service.

SUMMARY AND CONCLUSIONS

Regulatory attitudes toward risk are changing. The forces of change, which are many and varied, include deregulation, competition, technology, financial innovation, inflation, interest rate volatility, and freedom of information (disclosure). As long as the banking authorities provide the deposit insurance and lender-of-last-resort functions, there will be a need for bank regulation. Although the regulatory structure has worked effectively for the past five decades, it has not kept pace with the recent revolution in the financial services industry. The major problem with the existing insurance and regulatory structure is that it encourages risk taking at the expense of more risk-averse individuals and institutions and then proceeds to bail out the high rollers, especially the large ones. The provision of regulatory financial assistance to Continental Illinois and First Pennsylvania is a clear illustration of this problem.

Although the principal business of any insurer is risk management, federal deposit insurers have had little experience in this functional area. They can be excused, however, because prior to the financial services revolution, there simply wasn't much risk to manage. In the good old days with the "3-6-3 rule" in operation (i.e., money in at 3%, out at 6%, and on the golf course by 3 P.M.), there was little need for bankers, regulators, or deposit insurers to worry about risk management. In addition, there was little need for uninsured creditors (at least at large banks) to worry about risk analysis because of the federal guarantee behind bank debt. In those days—and for the most part still today—the banking authorities searched for bank-specific risks such as fraud, incompetence, poor loan quality, illiquidity, and inadequate capital. Today, however, the issues are more complex and risk management is important to everyone. Before insurers, regulators, and managers can control their risk exposure, they must set up an information system that measures all relevant forms of risk, including the systematic risks associated with interest rate volatility and technological change. Given this information base, the next step is to estimate the market value of the bank's exposure to the various risks.

Modern risk analysis and management—whether conducted by a banker, regulator, or uninsured depositor—require reporting, analysis, simulations of effects of economic conditions, and knowledge of the principles and techniques of financial management. The dramatic changes in the financial services industry are forcing all interested parties, including bank regulators, to reassess policies in these critical areas.

NOTES

1. Each of the components of the risk framework (Figure 11.1), when realized (e.g., loan losses), produces a negative claim on bank reserves, earnings, and/or capital. Vojta (1973) describes a bank as facing six generic risks: credit, investment (interest rate), liquidity, operating, fraud, and fiduciary.

2. Flannery (1981) reports that for the period 1959 to 1978 15 money-center banks had effectively hedged their balance sheets against changes in interest rates. Contrary to "conventional wisdom," he found that the average large bank had an average liability maturity of 1.81 years compared to an average asset maturity of 1.26 years. Because of their maturity imbalance, interest rate risk is more relevant for thrift institutions than commercial banks. Moreover, one has to ask, as Kane (1983a) does, why do S&Ls and MSBs keep taking on interest volatility risk?

3. Jacobe (1983) addresses the question of whether or not deposit insurance is compatible with deregulation. Also see Bierwag and Kaufman (1983) and FDIC (1983).

4. Business failure data are compiled by Dun and Bradstreet. The real bank failure rate is unknown because de facto failures are absorbed through mergers without FDIC financial assistance, and therefore they never enter the de jure record. Over the recent past, the number of emergency mergers involving thrift institutions has far exceeded

that involving commercial banks. For example, from 1960 to 1981, the number of thrifts declined by 2,042 (from 6,835 to 4,795, with roughly 97% of the decline in S&Ls, which fell from 6,320 to 4,347).

5. See Dince, 1982, p. 16.

6. Sinkey (1977) presented a similar plan under the guise of "If I Were Banking Czar." The OCC's "Strategic Plan" (1981) provides a statement of its mission and how it is to be accomplished.

7. The early warning system developed by the Federal Reserve Bank of New York and applied to all member banks is the exception. However, since the Fed only examines about 1,000 banks, the benefits of the system are limited.

8. Some minor adjustments to equations (6) and (7) are excluded here (see Sinkey, 1979, pp. 51–55). The OCC reverses the definitions for NCR and ACR given in equations (6) and (7).

9. The FDIC reforms described in this section are from Conte (1983) (see FDIC, 1983, for the full study).

10. The FDIC's proposed weighting scheme for adversely classified assets has the following *absurd* form: $1.43S + 1.21D + 1.0L > K \rightarrow$ "high-risk" bank (see FDIC, 1983, p. II–12).

REFERENCES

Altman, Edward I., Avery, Robert, Eisenbeis, Robert A., and Sinkey, Joseph F., Jr. *Application of Classification Techniques in Business, Banking, and Finance*. Greenwich, Conn: JAI Press, Inc., 1981.

Bierwag, G. O., and Kaufman, George G. "A Proposal for Federal Deposit Insurance with Risk-Sensitive Premiums." Federal Reserve Bank of Chicago, Occasional Paper 83-3, March 16, 1983.

Buser, Stephen A., Chen, Andrew H., and Kane, Edward J. "Federal Deposit Insurance Regulatory Policy, and Optimal Bank Capital." *Journal of Finance*, March 1981, pp. 51–60.

Comptroller's Handbook of Examination Procedure. Comptroller of the Currency, Administrator of National Banks, Washington, D.C., 1976.

Conover, C. T. "New Changes Foreseen in National Bank Exams." *ABA Banking Journal*, March 1982, p. 151.

Conte, Christopher. "FDIC Chief Isaac Urges Overhaul of Rules and Insurance Covering Banks and S&Ls." *Wall Street Journal*, April 20, 1983, p. 3.

Dince, Robert R. "Deregulation and the Examiner: A Commentary on an Interview." *Issues in Bank Regulation*, summer 1983.

———. "Penn Square, Upstream Lending, and the Bank-Examination Dilemma." *Bankers Magazine*, November–December, 1982, pp. 15–18.

———. "The Regulators Have a New Point of View." *Fortune*, October 8, 1979, pp. 166–168.

Federal Deposit Insurance Corporation. *Deposit Insurance in a Changing Environment*. Washington, D.C.: FDIC, April 15, 1983.

Flannery, Mark J. "Market Interest Rates and Commercial Bank Profitability: An Empirical Investigation." *Journal of Finance*, December 1981, pp. 1085–1101.

Friedman, Milton. *A Program for Monetary Stability*. Bronx, N.Y.: Fordham University Press, 1959.

———. *Capitalism and Freedom*. Chicago: University of Chicago Press, 1962.

Gibson, William E. "Deposit Insurance in the U.S.: Evaluation and Reform." *Journal of Financial and Quantitative Analysis*, March 1972, pp. 1575–1594.

Goldberg, Ellen S., Altman, Edward I., and Furash, Edward E. *Off-Balance-Sheet Activities of Banks: Managing the Risk/Reward Trade-offs*. Philadelphia: Robert Morris Associates, 1983.

Isaac, William M. "International and Domestic Implications of U.S. Commercial Lending to Foreign Governments and Corporations. *FDIC News Release* (PR-13-83), Washington, D.C., February 17, 1983.

Jackson, P. C. "Address before the Alabama Bankers Association." Mobile, Alabama, May 11, 1978, Board of Governors of the Federal Reserve System, Washington, D.C.

Jacobe, Dennis. "Deposit Insurance: Compatible with Deregulation?" *Savings and Loan News*, April 1983, pp. 37–42.

Kane, Edward J. "The Role of Government in the Thrift Industry's Net Worth Crisis." In George J. Benston (Ed.), *Financial Services: The Changing Institutions and Government Policy*. Englewood Cliffs, N.J.: Prentice-Hall, 1983a.

———. "Metamorphosis in Financial Services Delivery and Production." In Federal Home Loan Bank of San Francisco, *Strategic Planning for Economic and Technological Change in the Financial Services Industry*, Proceedings of the Eighth Annual Conference, 1983b.

———. *The Gathering Crisis in Federal Deposit Insurance: Origins, Evolution, and Possible Reforms*. The Ohio State University, 1983c.

Panzar, John C., and Willig, Robert D. "Economies of Scope." *American Economic Review*, May 1981, pp. 268–272.

Peltzman, Sam. "Capital Investment in Commercial Banking and Its Relationship to Portfolio Regulation." *Journal of Political Economy*, 1970, pp. 1–26.

Pettway, Richard H., and Sinkey, Joseph F., Jr. "Establishing On-Site Bank Examination Priorities: An Early-Warning System Using Accounting and Market Information." *Journal of Finance*, March 1980, pp. 137–150.

Sinkey, Joseph F., Jr. *Commercial Bank Financial Management*. New York: Macmillan, 1983.

———. *Problem and Failed Institutions in the Commercial Banking Industry*. Greenwich, Conn.: JAI Press, Inc., 1979.

———. "Problem and Failed Banks, Bank Examinations, and Early-Warning Systems: A Summary." In Edward I. Altman and Arnold W. Sametz (Eds.), *Financial Crises*. New York: John Wiley & Sons, 1977, pp. 24–47.

"Strategic Plan of the Office of the Comptroller of the Currency." Washington, D.C.: The Department of the Treasury, 1981.

Stricharchuk, Gregory, and Darlin, Damon. "Ernst and Whinney's Audit of Bank That Failed Puzzles Investigators." *Wall Street Journal*, March 4, 1983, p. 25.

Vojta, George J. *Bank Capital Adequacy*. New York: Citicorp, 1973.

Volcker, Paul A. "Statement before the Committee on Banking, Finance and Urban Affairs." U.S. House of Representatives, February 2, 1983, Board of Governors of the Federal Reserve System, Washington, D.C.

12 Public Policy toward Bank Expansion

John D. Hawke, Jr.

There is a danger in addressing the topic of public policy toward bank expansion because the very title may suggest that there is a coherent and consistent national policy in this area. In fact, quite the contrary is the case. Expansion policy is reflected in a variety of federal and state laws, regulations, and regulatory pronouncements promulgated to serve many different supervisory, competitive, and political objectives. Policy is also reflected in judicial decisions in cases in which banks have sued regulators because of restrictive expansion decisions, as well as in cases in which competitors of banks—and even other government agencies—have sued banks and their regulators because of permissive expansion decisions.

Clearly, expansion policy cannot be understood outside the context in which it has evolved. Accordingly, the first section of this chapter will describe the sources of policy relating to the expansion of the banking activities of banking institutions. The second section will discuss in greater detail the evolution of bank merger and acquisition policy. Finally, the third section will address the special considerations involved in our policies relating to the interstate expansion of banking organizations.

THE SOURCES OF POLICY

Prior to the Civil War, commercial banks were created in the United States only under state authority—initially by individual legislative charters and later under "free banking" laws, which made charters easily available to entrepreneurs willing to put at risk the requisite initial capital. Our system

381

of national banks was created by the National Currency Act of 1863[1] and its successor law, the National Bank Act of 1864,[2] to assist in the financing of the Civil War and to bring some uniformity to the country's paper currency. Modeled on the state free banking laws,[3] these measures created the Office of the Comptroller of the Currency and provided for the issuance of a national bank charter to any group of five or more citizens who were willing to demonstrate a commitment to put up the minimum initial capitalization.[4]

While the National Bank Act seemed to imply that the Comptroller was to have little or no discretion in determining whether to issue a charter, the first Comptroller asserted a prerogative to withhold a charter if he believed there was no need for a new bank at the proposed location or if he concluded that the proposed managers of the bank might not be able to succeed (see Robertson, 1968). While Mr. McCulloch's successors reverted to a "free bank" philosophy for several decades (see Robertson, 1968), he gave birth to what remains today a significant element of bank expansion policy: the notion that in order to protect the solvency of existing banks, and to guard against the improvidence or optimism of entrepreneurs who might otherwise launch banks destined to fail, a bank regulator should first determine that the market can sustain an additional bank and that the applicant is sufficiently competent to be successful.

After our system of federal deposit insurance was created in the Banking Act of 1933,[5] Congress officially recognized the role of regulatory discretion in the chartering process. It required that the new Federal Deposit Insurance Corporation consider, before granting deposit insurance, the "financial history and condition of the bank, the adequacy of its capital structure, its future earnings prospects, the general character of its management, the convenience and needs of the community to be served by the bank, and whether or not its corporate powers are consistent" with the purposes of the act.[6]

Somewhat different concerns underlay federal policy toward the expansion of existing banks into new markets through branching. The National Bank Act was silent as to the authority of national banks to branch,[7] and in *First National Bank in St. Louis v. Missouri*,[8] the Supreme Court of the United States held that absent clear congressional authorization to branch, the states had the power to enforce state legislation prohibiting national banks from branching. National banking interests sought legislation to cure this shortcoming in their powers, and the ensuing debate resulted in a policy compromise in 1927 that endures to this day. In the McFadden Act, as amended by the Banking Act of 1933, Congress limited the branching rights of national banks to those explicitly authorized to state-chartered banks in the same states.[9] This policy choice, which struck a balance between those forces that wanted to prohibit national banks from branching at all and those that favored unlimited branching powers for national banks,[10] profoundly affected the structure of U.S. banking. It effectively prevented the development of nationwide banks, and while it did not limit the number of national banks that the Comptroller could charter within a state, it gave to each state the power to determine the extent to which such federally created entities could expand within a state.

Although the McFadden Act did not prevent either intrastate or interstate affiliations of separately chartered banks, the banking industry was slow to recognize the utility of the holding company format for accomplishing interstate expansion.[11] Some multibank holding companies were formed in states with restrictive branching laws, and a few organizations—most notably Transamerica Corporation, the holding company for the Bank of America—created multistate chains of banks, but by 1956 only some 11 multistate holding companies existed (see Whitehead, 1983).[12]

In that year Congress enacted the Bank Holding Company Act (BHCA), which, in section 3(d), the so-called Douglas Amendment, precluded future interstate acquisitions by bank holding companies except where the states chose to enact local laws expressly permitting entry by out-of-state bank holding companies.[13] Thus, once again, the expansion of banking organizations was limited by compromise—this time between single-state and nationwide operations. Furthermore, while the bank holding company format plainly provided a means of circumventing restrictive state branching laws within a state, Congress rejected the idea that intrastate expansion powers of bank holding companies should be linked to the branching powers conferred under state law.[14] Rather, it chose to leave to the states the determination whether and to what extent holding companies should be permitted to own multiple banks—and a number of states having limited branching laws imposed comparable limits on holding companies. Thus, the BHCA reflects a fundamental choice to delegate to the states the authority to determine whether and to what extent both intrastate and interstate bank expansion by bank holding companies should be permitted. In recent years an increasing number of states have relaxed their prohibitions against multibank holding companies, and as discussed in more detail below, many states have begun to experiment with the authority conferred upon them by the Douglas Amendment to permit out-of-state entry.

Finally, it should be noted that federal antitrust law has served as a source of expansion policy. Although the Federal Reserve's forays into the thicket of potential competition theory during the mid-1970s temporarily slowed the pace of geographic market extensions by bank holding companies, this theory has never received full blessing under the antitrust laws, which have been largely ineffectual in limiting bank expansion into new markets. However, conventional antitrust doctrine, as applied in a series of cases during the 1960s and 1970s, has significantly inhibited the growth of banking institutions through intramarket combinations.

BANK MERGER AND ACQUISITION POLICY

Historical Review

Throughout the first half of the twentieth century, it is fair to say, there was no national policy directed specifically at the expansion of the banking business of banking institutions through mergers and acquisitions. Indeed, many of the country's largest banks today are the product of extensive merger activity during this period in which there were virtually no federal controls.

Although section 7 of the Clayton Antitrust Act, as enacted in 1914,[15] prohibited stock acquisitions by any corporation engaged in commerce, where the effect "may be substantially to lessen competition, or to tend to create a monopoly," this statute was not an appreciable inhibitor of bank merger and acquisition activity. Because the Supreme Court had declared in 1850 that banks were not engaged "in commerce,"[16] the jurisidictional predicate of section 7 was viewed as unmet in the case of bank combinations. Moreover, section 7 addressed only stock acquisitions, and the predominant form of bank combinations was the acquisition of assets. The 1950 amendment to the Clayton Act—extending the scope of section 7 to include asset acquisitions—did little to affect bank merger activity, for the amendment specified that such acquisitions were included only in the case of corporations subject to the jurisdiction of the Federal Trade Commission.[17] Under section 11 of the Clayton Act, authority to enforce those sections of the act applicable to banks was vested in the Federal Reserve Board.

The Federal Reserve's effort to use its Clayton Act powers to prevent bank expansion involved an attack on Transamerica Corporation in 1952.[18] Transamerica, then the largest holding company in the United States, owned 645 banking offices accounting for 41% of the banks, 39% of the commercial bank deposits, and 50% of the commercial loans in the five-state area of California, Oregon, Washington, Nevada, and Arizona. The Federal Reserve Board, believing that these figures were sufficient to show a violation of the Clayton Act, invoked its section 7 and section 11 powers to enjoin Transamerica from acquiring stock in any additional banks and to order divestiture of existing holdings. When Transamerica appealed the

Federal Reserve Board's decision to the third circuit, that court emphatically rejected Transamerica's contention that banks lay outside the purview of section 7. The court said that while at the time of enactment Congress might not have contemplated specifically the application of section 7 to banks, the language of the statute was so clear and unambiguous that it left no room for doubt that its sweep included all corporations in commerce without exception.[19]

However, the court also found that the Federal Reserve Board's reliance on aggregate data showing the concentration of banking powers in the five-state area was misplaced. A violation of section 7 could not be predicated on a mere concentration of economic power, the court stated, however contrary to public policy that concentration might be. Rather it would have to be shown that Transamerica's acquisitions had substantially lessened competition in the area where the acquired banks competed.[20] Because this test was difficult, if not impossible, to meet in the context of a bank holding company's expansion into new markets, the Federal Reserve Board turned to Congress for assistance. It was in response to this initiative that Congress passed the BHCA in 1956.

As originally enacted, the BHCA applied only to companies controlling more than one bank, and, as noted earlier, the Douglas Amendment effectively precluded the creation of new interstate bank holding companies. The formation of new multibank holding companies, as well as the acquisition of additional banks by existing holding companies, required the prior approval of the Federal Reserve Board, and in passing upon such applications it was required to consider whether the effect of the acquisition "would be to expand the size or extent of the bank holding company system involved beyond limits consistent with adequate and sound banking, the public interest, and the preservation of competition in the field of banking."[21]

While the BHCA was a constraint on the expansion of holding companies through the acquisitions of additional bank subsidiaries, it did not reach expansion carried out through bank-to-bank mergers, which, still considered outside the scope of section 7 of the Clayton Act, proceeded unrestrained. The absorption of more than 1,300 banks through merger in the period from 1950 to 1958 gave rise to widespread concern, both among the public and in sectors of the banking industry, over the increasing concentration of banking power.[22] Debate focused on the question of how best to regulate bank merger activity: whether to do so by amending section 7 of the Clayton Act—the approach favored by the Justice Department and independent bankers—or by amending the Federal Deposit Insurance Act (FDIA), the means urged upon Congress by the federal banking agencies who sought to insulate bank merger activity from Justice Department enforcement (see U.S. Senate, 1959).[23]

Congress chose in 1960 to close this gap in the regulatory structure by enacting the Bank Merger Act (BMA) as an amendment to the FDIA.[24] Under the BMA, every bank merger involving a federally insured bank was subject to the approval of one of the three federal banking agencies, which were required to consider, as one of a number of factors to be given equal weight, the effect of the merger on competition. The original BMA did not set forth an explicit competitive standard, and, while it did require in every case—in the interests of obtaining "uniformity" in competitive evaluations—that the responsible banking agency solicit an "advisory" report on the competitive factors involved both from the other banking agencies and from the Justice Department, the act was understood by its proponents definitively to remove bank mergers from the ambit of the antitrust laws.[25]

Shortly after passage of the BMA, the development of national policy with respect to bank mergers was significantly affected by Supreme Court decisions in two government antitrust actions that challenged mergers approved by the Comptroller of the Currency. In *United States v. Philadelphia National Bank*,[26] the Department of Justice challenged, under section 7 of the Clayton Act and section 1 of the Sherman Act, the merger of two large banks headquartered in Philadelphia. While the Clayton Act standard of illegality was generally thought to be an easier test for the department to satisfy than that of the Sherman Act, since it had been held by the Supreme Court to reach even "incipient" anticompetitive effects,[27]—that is, not simply transactions that eliminated substantial existing competition, but also those that "may" have a substantial effect on competition—there was serious doubt, even at the department, that section 7 could be used in the context of bank mergers. For one thing, it was unclear whether the banking regulator's approval of a merger immunized the transaction from later antitrust attack; second, there was a question whether the Clayton Act's delegation to the Federal Reserve of the authority to enforce section 7 with respect to banks precluded Justice Department action; finally, there was an overriding question whether section 7, which spoke in terms of stock and asset acquisitions, even applied to statutory mergers, which did not fall easily into either category.

In the *Philadelphia* case, the Supreme Court resolved all of these questions in favor of the Department of Justice, thus greatly strengthening the department's hand in enforcing the antitrust laws against bank mergers. Moreover, the Supreme Court rejected the argument that allegedly procompetitive effects of a merger in one market could outweigh substantial anticompetitive effects in another. Finally, it held that in the assessment of anticompetitive effects, once the department proved that a merger would result in a combination controlling as much as 30% of a market, the burden shifted to the merging banks to establish that the merger would not significantly lessen competition.[28]

In a second case brought at about the same time as the *Philadelphia* case, *United States v. First National Bank and Trust Company of Lexington*,[29] the Supreme Court held that a bank merger could also be attacked under section 1 of the Sherman Act. Breathing new life into the old antitrust doctrine that a merger of substantial competitors constitutes an unreasonable combination in restraint of trade, the Supreme Court further strengthened the department's ability to interdict bank mergers.

The banking industry's experience with *Philadelphia* and *Lexington* and other contemporaneous cases[30]—as well as that of the Department of Justice—led to a legislative confrontation in 1966. On the one hand, industry proponents argued that bank mergers and acquisitions should not be subjected solely to an antitrust test, and that weight should be given to other benefits flowing from a merger. On the other, the department, having experienced great difficulty in the early 1960s in obtaining preliminary injunctions to prevent the consummation of mergers it had attacked in court, and fearful that arguments as to the difficulty of "unscrambling" mergers once consummated would make post consummation divestitures an inefficacious remedy, sought greater power to interdict mergers at their inception.

The results of this confrontation were reflected in amendments to both the BMA and the BHCA in 1966. Congress wrote into each statute a series of antitrust tests, mirroring almost verbatim the provisions of sections 1 and 2 of the Sherman Act and section 7 of the Clayton Act. It absolutely forbade the bank regulators from approving any transaction that would violate section 2—that is, that would constitute a monopolization of or attempt to monopolize a market. It further required them to deny any transactions that would violate section 1 or section 7 unless the agency found that such anticompetitive effects would be clearly outweighed in the public interest by the probable effect of the transaction in meeting the convenience and needs of the community to be served. Supporters of the amendment believed that this "balancing" test did not merely mitigate the antitrust standard but also effectively removed mergers approved by the agencies under the balancing test from the threat of attack by the Department of Justice.

Notwithstanding this mitigation of the antitrust standard, the Department of Justice emerged as the clear victor in the policy struggle. The amendments required that consummation of any merger or acquisition transaction approved by the regulators be delayed for 30 days in order to give the department an opportunity to sue. While the department was precluded from attacking a merger once the 30-day waiting period had expired (except on the basis of a complaint alleging monopolization under section 2 of the Sherman Act), the filing of a timely complaint would automatically stay consummation until the court ordered otherwise.

A series of Supreme Court decisions following the 1966 amendments further strengthened the Justice Department's hand. In *United States v. First City National Bank of Houston*,[31] the Supreme Court held that when the department files an antitrust case against a merger the issues are to be tried de novo by the court—including the application of the "balancing" test—and no presumptive weight is to be given to the bank regulator's decision. *First City* also held that the automatic stay should not be lifted unless the department's case can be said at the outset to be frivolous. A year later, in *United States v. Third National Bank in Nashville*,[32] the Supreme Court held that a merger that would otherwise violate section 7 could not be approved under the "balancing" test unless the merger represented the least anticompetitive means of achieving the public benefits claimed for the merger.

By the end of the 1960s the Department of Justice had a firm grip on bank merger and acquisition policy. The mere threat that the department would bring suit to enjoin a merger, thus bringing into play the automatic stay and the prospect of lengthy and expensive litigation, was sufficient to cause the abandonment of many merger transactions that would otherwise have been acceptable to the approving regulatory agency. The department's influence was felt particularly in horizontal merger proposals, where the antitrust laws had their strongest force. The department's influence in this regard may have waned in recent years because of the willingness of the banking agencies to approve transactions despite the department's opinion that an antitrust violation would result and because of the infrequency of litigation in such cases. A recent study calculated that in 39 cases, over a five-year period starting with 1979, in which the department rendered such opinions, the agencies approved 23 applications and denied 13 with three being withdrawn prior to agency decision. The department sued in only four cases, three of which it lost and one of which it settled on terms permitting the merger to be consummated (see Baxter and Shah, forthcoming). As intramarket combinations thus became more difficult, and as state laws began to relax structural constraints, banking organizations increasingly turned toward market extension acquisitions. As discussed below, the department had no success in its efforts to apply the antitrust laws to market extension acquisitions in the banking area, and while the Federal Reserve developed its own discretionary policies in this regard, those policies ultimately succumbed to court decisions limiting the Federal Reserve Board's discretion in this area.

The trend toward market extension acquisitions was given further impetus by the 1970 amendments to the BHCA, which brought one-bank holding companies under Federal Reserve regulation. With this enactment there was no longer any incentive for banking organizations to avoid the multibank holding company format, and holding company acquisitions proliferated, particularly in states in which the structural constraints on branching were more restrictive than those on multiple ownership of banks by holding companies.

The Legal Standards

The analytic process by which competitive policy is applied in bank expansion cases has two distinct steps. The first step involves the construction of the matrix within which the competitive effects of the combination will be measured—that is, the delineation of the relevant product and geographic markets. The second involves an assessment of the likely impact of the combination on competition within the markets so defined.

Product Market Definition. Section 7 of the Clayton Act proscribes mergers having certain specified effects on competition "in any line of commerce in any section of the country." When Congress embodied the Clayton Act standard in the BMA and the BHCA in 1966, it omitted the reference to "any line of commerce," thus raising a question as to the appropriate product market for bank merger analysis. In the *Philadelphia* case,[33] the Supreme Court was first called upon to consider this issue.

The problem that the Supreme Court faced was that commercial banks are comparable to department stores in the range of products they offer. While some bank products were unique—demand deposit accounts, for example, were then offered only by commercial banks—others, such as commercial and consumer loans and trust services, are offered not only by other types of financial institutions but by nonfinancial suppliers as well. If analysis were to focus on individual product lines, therefore, a particular merger might be seen as having a range of competitive impacts. While enforcement authorities might concentrate on the narrowest product line in order to show anticompetitive effects with respect to a product offered only by commercial banks, the merging institutions would be likely to focus on those product lines for which there were a variety of nonbank suppliers.

Recognizing the difficulties inherent in analyzing mergers on the basis of disaggregated product lines, the Supreme Court held in the *Philadelphia* case that the only relevant line of commerce in a bank merger is "commercial banking." Because banks alone can offer the "congeries" of products and services that they do, and because their ability to offer demand deposits gives them an edge in the offering of other products, the Supreme Court concluded that the product market should be constructed on the basis of commercial bank loans and deposits. The Supreme Court thus struck a pragmatic compromise, intended to assure that neither too many nor too few mergers would be reachable by the antitrust laws.

In the years after *Philadelphia*, it was frequently argued—by banks seeking to mitigate the effects of a bank merger—that thrift institutions should be included within the relevant product market.[34] In the cases that reached the Supreme Court during the 1970s, however, it held that the powers of thrifts had not yet expanded to the point where thrifts should be considered the functional equivalent of commercial banks.[35] The argument for inclusion of thrifts took on new force, however, after the enactment of the Depository Institutions Deregulation and Monetary Control Act of 1980,[36] which authorized transaction accounts for thrifts, and the Garn-St Germain Depository Institutions Act of 1982,[37] which gave federally chartered thrifts significantly expanded asset powers, including new commercial lending powers. Increasingly, the bank regulators and the Department of Justice were urged by applicants to include thrifts in the market calculus, and by the end of 1983 all of the agencies were willing to do so in one way or another (see Hawke, 1984, and Eisenbeis, 1982).

Despite *Philadelphia*, and notwithstanding the banking agencies' positions on thrifts, the Department of Justice nevertheless has continued to argue that bank mergers should be assessed in two distinct product markets—a "retail banking" market, comprising banking services offered to "individual" customers, including savings and time deposits, transaction accounts, and consumer and residential mortgage loans, and a "wholesale banking" market, including all services offered to commercial customers, such as demand deposits and commercial loans. While the department's two-market approach has not yet been tested in court, it has been advanced in the two most recent bank antitrust cases filed by the department—the *Virginia National Bankshares* case,[38] which was decided solely on the basis of geographic market, and the *Norwich* case,[39] which was resolved by a consent settlement.

The practical effect of including thrifts in the product market, of course, is to facilitate horizontal mergers of banks, and while the issue has generally been presented as a legal/factual argument as to whether thrifts are the competitive equivalent of banks, at least one observer has suggested that the question of product market definition, which may determine the legality of many mergers, really presents a policy choice—namely, is it desirable to have greater consolidation in the banking industry? (see Eisenbeis, 1982, p.24).

Geographic Market Definition.   In the *Philadelphia* case the Supreme
Court also addressed the "section of the country" question—that is, within
what geographic area the competitive effects of bank mergers should be
assessed. Again a compromise was necessary because of the variety of
services and products offered by banks. Clearly, the geographic area in
which large business customers might seek banking services could be regional or national, while the alternative sources of banking service for
some individual customers might be limited to their immediate neighborhood. In striking the compromise the Supreme Court noted that the appropriate inquiry is not where the parties to the merger do business or
even where they compete, but where, within the area of competitive overlap, the effect of the merger on competition will be "direct and immediate."
In the case of banking, delineating the market—the "geographic structure
of supplier–customer relations"—solely with reference to either the large
corporate customer or the individual customer would preclude finding that
a merger was anticompetitive, since in one case many suppliers other than
the parties to the merger would be included, while in the other, the parties
themselves would likely be found to be in different markets. The Supreme
Court avoided these "indefensible extremes" by drawing the market to
encompass the area where intermediate customers find it practical to do
their banking business.

Despite the Supreme Court's attempt to set out a standard for market
definition in bank merger cases, the *Philadelphia* decision has not been
a particularly useful model. In the first place, it rests on a certain circularity
of reasoning—how does one determine the "area of competitive overlap"
without making certain judgments as to the market? Second, the test is
of no use in market extension cases, where, by hypothesis, there is no
"competitive overlap." As a result, the banking agencies have continued
to apply their own techniques of geographic market definition, with varying
consequences for the implementation of competition policy. The Federal
Reserve has followed the practice of predefining markets in most metropolitan areas, generally by reference to Standard Metropolitan Statistical
Areas or Rand McNally Metro Areas, and without regard to where the
customers of the combining banks might actually be located. The OCC
and FDIC, by contrast, have typically defined markets primarily by reference to the service areas of the merging banks—that is, the areas from
which the banks draw some preponderance, generally 75%, of their deposits.

While the merits and demerits of these differing methodologies have
been widely debated, one consequence of the variance in approach has
been to cause applicants to structure transactions to come within the ju-

risdiction of the agency whose market-definition technique is most likely to result in an approval. Indeed, in some few instances, applicants denied by one agency on the basis of geographic market have refiled with a more favorable agency.[40] Thus, the variance has unquestionably had an impact on policy.

Assessment of Competitive Impact. Section 7 of the Clayton Act does not fix any market share levels of illegality; it simply proscribes those mergers whose effect may be substantially to lessen competition. How can the parties to a prospective merger judge in advance whether their transaction will pass muster under this test? In *Philadelphia* the Supreme Court said that a combination resulting in a 30% market share created a strong inference of anticompetitive effects, such that the burden to demonstrate the contrary should shift to the parties. But the *Philadelphia* rule was not useful in business planning, since the parties to a prospective merger could not be assured that, if sued, they would be successful in carrying this burden.

If the objective of competition policy is to discourage mergers whose effects would violate the law, while not inhibiting lawful mergers, whose effects may be beneficial, predictability should be important to the realization of that objective. Indeed, in *Philadelphia*, the Supreme Court commented that "unless businessmen can assess the legal consequences of a merger with some confidence, sound business planning is retarded."[41] Recognizing the need for a standard by which businesspeople might assess in advance the likelihood that a proposed business combination would avoid or survive antitrust attack, the Department of Justice first promulgated merger guidelines in 1968. The guides recognized two types of markets—highly concentrated and less highly concentrated—and established market share parameters for combining firms within each type of market. If the proposed combination fell within these parameters the parties could be confident that the department would not be likely to sue. Although the guidelines had no legal force, they provided a useful point of reference and undoubtedly contributed to predictability.

In 1982, the department revised the guidelines (see U.S. Department of Justice) to place more emphasis on market concentration, through the use of the so-called Herfindahl-Hirschman Index (HHI)—a measure of market concentration constructed by summing the squares of the market shares of each firm in the market (see the chapter in this volume by Arnold Heggestad). Markets with HHIs of 1800 or more were deemed "highly concentrated," and mergers in such markets that would increase the index by 50 to 100 points were subject to attack. In moderately concentrated markets—those with HHIs between 1000 and 1800—an HHI increase of

100 points was deemed tolerable, and any merger that resulted in an index of less than 1,000 was unlikely to be attacked, irrespective of the amount of increase in the HHI it caused.

Although the earlier Justice Department guidelines had not found great favor at the banking agencies, the revised guides, which appeared to be more accommodating to many mergers, have been heavily relied upon, particularly by the Federal Reserve, as a measure of permissibility. Moreover, the guidelines have been extremely useful as a planning device, since market shares can easily be calculated by using publicly available deposit data.

On the other hand, reliance on HHI calculations based on published deposit data is likely to overstate the competitive impact of a bank merger, for several reasons. First, since market shares are typically constructed on the basis of deposits booked at offices located within the defined geographic market, they cannot take account of deposits held at offices located outside the market by persons or businesses situated within the market. While it might be argued that this is a problem of proper geographic market definition, it is really a problem that derives from using depository data rather than depositor data to calculate market shares.

Second, deposit data are in effect used as a proxy for the entire product market—commercial banking. Thus, deposit data may not necessarily reflect competition for loans in the market—such as might result where banks having no deposit-taking offices in a market either establish loan production offices within the market or send calling officers into the market to solicit business.

Finally, where a large banking organization has only a small share of a local market, its competitive significance in the market is likely to be understated where sole reliance is placed on deposit shares. There is no necessary relationship between such an institution's local market share and its ability to compete vigorously in the market by bringing to bear its out-of-market resources. Thus, if the rationale for placing heavy reliance on measures of concentration is that highly concentrated markets are more susceptible to collusive or noncompetitive pricing, the rationale breaks down in nominally concentrated markets in which banks with substantial out-of-market resources have small local market shares.

These problems can be dealt with by more subjective techniques of competitive analysis—for example by "shading" market shares in some fashion where the facts so warrant. Indeed, the Federal Reserve has had a number of occasions to note that large banks with small local shares may have a disproportionately large effect on competition in the market.[42] Nonetheless, such subjective analysis does not attempt to quantify the effects of out-of-market competition. Thus, true competitive effects may frequently be overestimated, and predictability as to regulatory attitudes remains difficult to achieve.

Potential Competition. As banks sought to expand into new banking markets, antitrust enforcement authorities found that conventional methods of market analysis gave them little or no help in attacking such transactions. The doctrine of "potential competition" evolved as one possible means of reaching market extension mergers, but in fact the doctrine has proved virtually useless in the area of banking.

The "potential competition" theory is actually two quite distinct concepts. One—the "perceived" potential competition doctrine—looks to the present market impact that might result when a firm that is viewed by incumbent firms in a market as a likely potential entrant decides to enter the market by a large acquisition. In this situation, the theory posits, the resultant elimination of the effect that the perceived potential entrant might otherwise have in inhibiting collusive or oligopoly pricing in the market may be substantial enough to sustain a finding of Clayton Act illegality.

The second branch of potential competition—the "actual" or "probable future" potential competition theory—looks to future market effects. Here the notion is that a firm that is actually likely to enter a concentrated market should be forbidden to do so through the acquisition of a market leader, in order to induce it to enter on a small-scale basis—either de novo or through a "foothold" acquisition—and thus ultimately to become a competitor for the market leaders.

Although the Department of Justice attacked a number of mergers in whole or part on potential competition grounds,[43] it was never successful in obtaining a final judgment of illegality. In the only such case to reach the Supreme Court—*United States v. Marine Bancorporation*[44]—the court indicated that the web of regulatory constraints over bank expansion made it unlikely that any potential entrant could be perceived as so likely to enter a local market that it could affect pricing in the market. While the Supreme Court reserved judgment on the validity of the actual potential competition theory as a valid antitrust doctrine, it did not offer hope that this branch of the doctrine would prove useful to enforcement authorities.

During the mid-1970s, the Federal Reserve Board announced its own variant of the actual potential competition doctrine in a series of cases in Texas.[45] Under what came to be known as the Tyler Doctrine, the Board said that it would not allow the largest bank holding companies in Texas to expand into new markets through the acquisition of market leaders. Although the Board seemed to depart from this approach for a period thereafter,[46] it reverted to the concept in 1980 to deny a proposal by the fifth largest banking organization in Texas to expand into the El Paso and Waco markets by acquiring leading banks in each.[47] The Board's decision was challenged in court, and the resulting appellate decision overturning it effectively laid the potential competition doctrine to rest.

In *Mercantile Texas Corporation v. Board of Governors of the Federal Reserve System*,[48] the court laid down a set of demanding factual preconditions to a finding of illegality on potential competition grounds. It held not only that the target market must be shown to be significantly concentrated, but also that the proposed entrant must be shown to be likely to enter the market on a small-scale basis in the reasonably near future if denied entry through a large acquisition. The court furthermore required that in determining the likelihood of small-scale entry a factual analysis had to be made as to the expected profitability of that mode of entry and compared with the relative profitability of other uses of the applicant's resources.

Recognizing the practical difficulty of engaging in such analysis in every market extension case, the Federal Reserve Board issued proposed guidelines for identifying those cases warranting detailed factual investigation (see Board of Governors, 1982). Although the proposed guides are not a measure of illegality, but rather a device for "triggering" further fact-finding, they serve in effect to create a "safe harbor" for transactions that do not come within their purview, since, under the *Mercantile* rule, the Board cannot deny such a transaction without the detailed fact-finding specified by the court.

Although the proposed guides have never been promulgated in final form, the Federal Reserve Board has routinely—and rigidly—applied them as if they were final. Since the guidelines were proposed, it has not denied a single acquisition on potential competition grounds—indeed, it does not appear that it has found a case in which the guides have required more detailed fact-finding. In some few cases it has even approved transactions as to which the guides might have justified a more detailed inquiry.[49]

It thus seems a fair conclusion that there is no present vitality in the potential competition doctrine, in any of its variants, in the area of bank expansion.

The Role of Agency Discretion

While the Department of Justice has attained a significant position of influence in merger and acquisition policy, it can only bring its views to bear forcibly by asserting antitrust challenges against transactions that are approved by the banking agencies. It thus stands guard over the outer perimeter of competition policy. But are there narrower limits than those of the antitrust laws that might be enforced by the banking agencies?

There is, of course, a significant element of judgment and subjectivity involved in the application of antitrust standards, and to this extent it is entirely possible that the judgments of different enforcement authorities might differ in this regard. Indeed, virtually all of the leading court decisions reflect, at the least, a difference in judgment as between the Department of Justice and the Comptroller of the Currency.

There is no reason to believe that the banking agencies have enforced the antitrust laws more rigorously than the department—that is, that the agencies have denied mergers *on antitrust grounds* that would not have been attacked by the Justice Department. At least two of the agencies, the FDIC and the Federal Reserve, at one time asserted an authority, under the BMA and the BHCA, respectively, to deny mergers and acquisitions on competitive grounds even though an antitrust violation might not be present. However, as the result of a series of court decisions in which agency denial orders were challenged by disappointed applicants— *Washington Mutual* in 1973,[50] involving the FDIC, and *Mercantile Texas* in 1981 (see note 47) and *County National* in 1980,[51] involving the Federal Reserve—it has been clearly established that the banking agencies can apply no more demanding competitive test than that of the antitrust laws. Significantly, two of these cases—*Washington Mutual* and *Mercantile Texas*—involved market extension acquisitions as to which the agencies had attempted to apply their own variants of the potential competition doctrine.

With antitrust principles firmly established as a limitation on agency discretion to deny bank mergers and acquisitions, agency denials on competitive grounds, particularly at the Federal Reserve, have become rare.

The "Balancing" Test.   Although one principal objective of Congress in passing the 1966 amendments to the BMA and the BHCA was to allow approvals of transactions on "public interest" or "convenience and needs" grounds where antitrust violations might otherwise preclude approvals, this "balancing" test has not proved to be a significant exception to generally accepted competition policy.

There are several reasons for this: First, the "failing company" doctrine, which had existed in antitrust law even before the 1966 amendments, has been sufficient legal justification for all of those supervisory mergers involving banks closed by the regulators. Indeed, the Department of Justice has never brought suit to challenge a supervisory merger transaction— even though it may have conveyed a negative view of a transaction in its preapproval advice to the responsible banking agency. Second, in the *Nashville* case the Supreme Court engrafted on the "balancing test" the "alternative means" doctrine. Under this rule an otherwise anticompetitive merger may not be justified by a weighing of public benefits if there is a less anticompetitive means of achieving equivalent benefits. Thus, where a bank claims merely to be a "floundering" bank, needing an infusion of management strength or a capital infusion in order to regain competitive vigor, it has been forced, in effect, to look first to new markets and then to seek out the smallest feasible merger partner in its own market. As a result, very few case decisions have had to rely on the balancing test, and those that have have generally been in states in which structural constraints on expansion have limited the merging bank's choice of partners to those in its own market.[52]

INTERSTATE EXPANSION

Federal policy with respect to interstate expansion by banking organizations is riddled with the inconsistencies that one might expect would result when policy is shaped by populist dogma and local political concerns.

While Congress chose in the McFadden Act to limit the intrastate branching powers of all Federal Reserve member banks, state and national alike, to those permitted to nonmember banks, it absolutely prohibited domestic interstate branching. Yet when it passed the BHCA, which prohibits multistate bank acquisitions, it delegated to the states the authority to lift the interstate acquisitions bar so as to permit entry by out-of-state bank holding companies—undoubtedly in the belief that the states would be disinclined to do so. By contrast, federally chartered savings and loan association are not subject to any statutory constraints on branching, and but for the Federal Home Loan Bank Board's current policy of allowing interstate branching only as the result of supervisory mergers, federal S&Ls could branch nationwide. Yet except in the case of supervisory acquisitions, savings and loan holding companies are absolutely barred from multistate ownership of S&Ls.

To compound the anomaly, the BHCA imposes no geographic constraints on the ability of bank holding companies to expand interstate through nonbanking entities that offer many of the same products and services that are offered by banks, and savings and loan holding companies may engage in virtually any activity interstate so long as they do not own more than a single S&L. This anomaly has become even more pronounced as a result of the Federal Reserve Board's decision in the *U.S. Trust Company*[53] case, where it held that a bank holding company could acquire a "nonbank bank"—that is, an institution chartered as a commercial bank, but outside the BHCA definition of a "bank" because it does not both offer demand deposits and make commercial loans—under section 4 of the BHCA, to which the Douglas Amendment is inapplicable.

Congress, for its part, has assiduously avoided this political thicket, and when it has been forced to deal with issues of interstate banking it has done so most gingerly. In the Garn-St Germain Depository Institutions Act of 1982, after much prodding by the financial regulators, Congress made provision for interstate takeovers of failing banks having $500 million or more in assets. In doing so, however, it established a set of "priorities" to be applied by the FDIC that express a first preference for in-state acquirors, as well as a preference for acquirors from adjoining states over those more distant—apparently on the assumption that an invasion by neighbors would be less objectionable to local interests than a takeover by real strangers.

As indicated earlier, the states have shown increasing willingness to address interstate banking issues, and it now appears quite likely that an interstate banking structure will evolve principally through state action. As of mid-1984, 20 states[54] have passed legislation authorizing out-of-state bank holding companies to acquire in-state financial institutions. While three states—Alaska, Maine, and South Dakota—have elected to permit virtually unconditional entry,[55] others have done so on a limited or conditioned basis. Several states have permitted limited entry for special purposes, such as to take advantage of favorable local usury laws, and have required not only that the entrant achieve specified local employment levels, but also that it not operate competitively with local banks.[56] New York has permitted entry by holding companies in states allowing reciprocal entry to New York holding companies, and several states have permitted entry on a regional reciprocal basis.[57] Although some of these laws, in particular those limiting entry on both a regional and reciprocal basis, have precipitated legal challenges,[58] activity at the state level has probably relieved pressures on Congress to adopt legislation permitting interstate banking, and it seems unlikely that Congress will in the near future assert its authority to fashion a uniform national policy in this area.

In the context of state legislation, expansion policy has reflected a variety of local political and economic concerns. Some states, for example, have found it expedient to permit limited entry by out-of-state financial institutions under restrictions intended to protect local institutions from competition and to advance local economic development objectives. By allowing its banks to engage in all facets of the insurance business, so long as they do not attempt to compete to the detriment of local insurance interests, and by permitting any out-of-state bank holding company to acquire a single state-chartered bank in the state, South Dakota has attempted to provide a means of avoiding the BHCA's strict limits on bank holding company insurance activities, while attracting new enterprise to the state. States that have adopted regionally limited reciprocal entry laws have attempted to facilitate intraregion consolidation so that local institutions may be better prepared to cope with more permissive entry rules at later dates. Indeed, Rhode Island has provided that its regional limitation will expire two years after the reciprocal entry law takes effect.

The antitrust laws have had no perceptible impact on interstate expansion and, unless amended, are not likely to have such an impact in the future—largely because markets have been defined narrowly and because the potential competition theory has not been effective in reaching market extension acquisitions. While some states have imposed ''caps'' on the volume of banking assets or deposits that an institution may hold within a state, it seems unlikely, given its aversion to the subject, that Congress will adopt special competitive tests for interstate bank expansion.

While it appears to be a paradox that a national structure of interstate banking should evolve through a patchwork of state laws, often conflicting and inconsistent in approach, the political realities of banking make it seem inevitable. The unwillingness of Congress for more than 200 years to impose federal policy on the structure of banking reflects the fact that banking is inevitably entwined in local interests that carry significant political weight—and those interests vary from area to area. The process of state legislation has permitted these interests to be accomodated locally in a manner that would probably be impossible through uniform federal legislation, and it is principally for this reason that our historical approach of federal deference to the states on issues of banking structure is likely to endure.

NOTES

1. Act of February 25, 1863, 12 Stat. 665.
2. Act of June 3, 1864, 13 Stat. 99.
3. Prepared by Senator Sherman and Secretary of the Treasury Chase, the National Currency Act was modeled largely on New York and Massachusetts banking laws. See Board of Governors, 1941, p. 14.
4. The required minimum capitalization varied with the size of the town in which the bank was to be established. The National Currency Act provided generally for minimum capitalization of $50,000 but, in the case of towns with a population of more than 10,000, required a minimum capitalization of $100,000. 12 Stat. 665, § 6(3). The National Bank Act imposed a general requirement of $100,000, and a $200,000 capitalization for towns with populations of over 50,000, but permitted banks in towns with population of 6,000 persons or less to be established, with the special approval of the Secretary of the Treasury, with a capitalization of $50,000. 13 Stat. 99, § 7.
5. Act of June 16, 1933, c. 89 § 8, 48 Stat. 168.
6. 12 U.S.C. § 1816.

7. For a history of nineteenth-century attitudes toward branch banking, see U.S. Senate Committee on Banking, Housing and Urban Affairs, 1976.

8. 263 U.S. 640 (1924).

9. As enacted in 1927, the McFadden Act provided that national banks could branch within the limits of the city, town or village in which they were situated, if state law permitted state-chartered banks to establish such branches. Act of February 25, 1927, c. 191, § 7, 44 Stat. 1228. The Banking Act of 1933 extended branching rights statewide but again made those rights available to national banks only where available to similarly situated state-chartered banks. Act of June 16, 1933, c. 89 § 8, 48 Stat. 168, codified at 12. U.S.C. § 36(c).

10. The first version of the 1933 amendment to the McFadden Act, introduced by the chairman of the Senate Committee on Banking and Currency, would have permitted national banks to branch statewide irrespective of state law. S. 4412, 72d Congress, 1st Session, 1933.

11. As of December 31, 1939, there were only eight multistate holding companies, controlling 220 banks and 629 branches, and 33 intrastate holding companies, controlling 207 banks and 240 branches. See Board of Governors, 1941, p. 435, Table 19-2.

12. U.S. House of Representatives Report No. 609, 84th Congress, 1st Session, 1955, pp. 3–4.

13. Act of May 9, 1956, 70 Stat. 133, codified at 12 U.S.C. 1842(d).

14. Congress considered and rejected bills that would have permitted interstate acquisitions at the discretion of the Federal Reserve Board and that would have applied state branch banking laws to bank holding company acquisitions. S. Rep. No. 1095, 84th Congress 1st Session, 1956, pp. 10–11.

15. Act of October 15, 1914, c. 323, § 7; 38 Stat. 731.

16. *Nathan v. Louisiana*, 49 U.S. 73 (1850).

17. Act of December 29, 1950 (Cellar-Kefauver Antimerger Act), c. 1184, 64 Stat. 1125, codified at 15 U.S. § 18.

18. *Federal Reserve Bulletin*, 1952, p. 368.

19. *Transamerica Corp. v. Board of Governors of the Federal Reserve System*, 206 F.2d 163, 165 (3d Cir.), *cert. denied*, 346 U.S. 901 (1953).

20. *Transamerica Corp. v. Board of Governors of the Federal Reserve System*, 169-170.

21. Act of May 9, 1956, 70 Stat. 133, § 5(d).

22. U.S. Senate Report No. 196, 86th Congress, 1st Session, 1959, p. 10.

23. U.S. Senate Report No. 196, 86th Congress, 1st Session, 1959, pp. 25–29.

24. Act of May 13, 1960, 64 Stat. 892, codified as amended at 12 U.S.C. § 1828.

25. The relevant portions of the Senate debates on the Bank Merger Act of 1960 are contained in U.S. House of Representatives, 1965.

26. 374 U.S. 321 (1963).

27. *Brown Shoe Co. v. United States*, 370 U.S. 294 (1962).

28. The Supreme Court, in nonbanking contexts, has held horizontal mergers violative of the antitrust laws where the market share of the combined firm was as small as 7.5%, *United States v. Von's Grocery Co.*, 384 U.S. 270, 272-74 (1966), and 4.9%, *United States v. Pabst Brewing Co.*, 384 U.S. 546, 550–53 (1966).

29. 376 U.S. 665 (1964).

30. For example, *United States v. Manufacturers Hanover Trust Co.*, 240 F. Supp. 867 (S.D.N.Y. 1965); and *United States v. Crocker Anglo National Bank*, 277 F. Supp. 133 (N.D. Cal. 1967).

31. 386 U.S. 361 (1967).

32. 390 U.S. 171 (1968).

33. *United States v. Philadelphia National Bank*, 374 U.S. 321 (1963).

34. This argument was successful in at least two lower court cases: *United States v. First National Bank of Jackson*, 301 F. Supp. 1161 (S.D. Miss. 1969) (including thrifts, cotton exchanges as well as commercial banks); *United States v. Idaho First National Bank of Boise*, 315 F. Supp. 261 (D. Idaho 1970) (including thrifts, credit unions, life insurance and mortgage companies).

35. *United States v. Connecticut National Bank*, 418 U.S. 656 (1973) (reversing lower court decision expanding line of commerce to include mutual savings banks); *United States v. Marine Bancorporation*, 418 U.S. 602 (1974) (reversing lower court decision expanding line of commerce to include savings and loan associations and mutual savings banks).

36. 12 U.S.C. § 3501 *et seq.*

37. Pub. L. No. 97-320, 96 Stat. 1469.

38. *United States v. Virginia National Bankshares, Inc.*, No. 82-0083B (W.D. Va. June 21, 1982).

39. *United States v. National Bank and Trust Co. of Norwich*, No. 83-CV-537 (N.D.N.Y. filed May 6, 1983).

40. Toledo Trustcorp, Inc.'s acquisition of the National Bank of Defiance (NBD) is a case in point. In 1980, Toledo Trustcorp applied to the Federal Reserve Board for approval to acquire NBD, located some 21 miles from its own subsidiary bank, National Bank of Paulding (NBP). The Federal Reserve Board, initially defining NBD's relevant market as the better part of contiguous Defiance and Paulding counties, was prevailed upon to enlarge the relevant market to include parts of two additional neighboring counties, but nevertheless rejected Toledo Trustcorp's application on the grounds that the acquisition would eliminate substantial existing competition between NBD and NBP, reduce the number of competing banks, and increase the four-bank concentration ratio in an already highly concentrated markets. *Toledo Trustcorp. Inc., Federal Reserve Bulletin*, 1980, p. 426. NBP then applied to the OCC for approval to merge with NBD. The Comptroller, determining that NBD's service area consisted of Defiance County and thus that there was minimal overlap with NBP's service area—Paulding County— approved the merger. *Decision of the Comptroller of the Currency on the Application of National Bank of Paulding, Paulding, Ohio, to Merge with National Bank of Defiance, Defiance, Ohio, under the Charter of National Bank of Paulding and with the Title of Maumee Valley National Bank, December 12, 1980.*

41. 374 U.S. at 362.

42. See, for instance, *First Tennessee National Corp., Federal Reserve Bulletin*, 1983, p. 298; *Boatmen's Bancshares, Federal Reserve Bulletin*, 1983, p. 738.

43. See, for instance, *United States v. Deposit Guaranty National Bank of Jackson*, 373 F. Supp. 1230 (S.D. Miss. 1974); *United States v. United Virginia Bancshares, Inc.*, 347 F. Supp. 891 (E.D. Va. 1972); *United States v. First National Bancorp, Inc.*, 329 F. Supp. 1003 (D. Colo. 1971), *aff'd per curiam*, 410 U.S. 577 (1973); *United States v. Idaho First National Bank*, 315 F. Supp. 261 (D. Idaho 1970); *United States v. First*

National Bank of Maryland, 310 F. Supp. 157 (D. Md. 1970); *United States v. First National Bank of Jackson*, 301 F. Supp. 1161 (S.D. Miss. 1969); *United States v. Crocker -Anglo National Bank*, 277 F. Supp. 133 (N.D. Cal. 1967).

44.   418 U.S. 602 (1974).

45.   *First International Bancshares, Inc., Federal Reserve Bulletin*, 1974, p. 43; *First International Bancshares, Inc., Federal Reserve Bulletin*, 1974, p. 290; *First City Bancorporation, Federal Reserve Bulletin*, 1974, p. 450; *Texas Commerce Bancshares Inc., Federal Reserve Bulletin*, 1975, p. 109.

46.   *First City Bancorporation of Texas, Inc., Federal Reserve Bulletin*, 1978, p. 969; *Texas Commerce Bancshares, Inc., Federal Reserve Bulletin*, 1977, p. 500.

47.   *Mercantile Texas Corporation, Federal Reserve Bulletin*, 1980, p. 423. The author was counsel to Mercantile Texas Corporation in this case.

48.   638 F.2d 1255 (5th Cir. 1981).

49.   The Federal Reserve Board recently approved, over a strong dissent by Chairman Volcker invoking the potential competition doctrine, Omaha National Corporation's application to acquire 42.5% of, and then merge into itself, First National Lincoln Corporation, the fifth largest banking organization in Nebraska and parent of the largest commercial bank in Lincoln. Applicant, Nebraska's second largest bank, was one of only three companies that met the definition of a "probable future entrant" contained in the Federal Reserve Board's proposed market extension guidelines, which characterize acquisitions in other respects similar to that proposed by Omaha National as anticompetitive if there are fewer than six probable future entrants into the market in question. *Omaha National Corporation, Order Approving Acquisition and Merger of Bank Holding Companies*, Federal Reserve Board Order, April 24, 1984. See also Hawke, 1984.

50.   *Washington Mutual Savings Bank v. FDIC*, 482 F.2d 459 (9th Cir. 1973).

51.   *County National Bancorporation v. Board of Governors of the Federal Reserve System*, 654 F.2d 1253 (8th Cir. 1980).

52.   See, for example *Indiana Bancorp, Federal Reserve Bulletin*, 1983, p. 913.

53.   Federal Reserve Board Order, March 23, 1984.

54.   Alaska, Connecticut, Delaware, Florida, Georgia, Illinois, Iowa, Kentucky, Maine, Maryland, Massachusetts, Nebraska, New York, North Carolina, Oregon, Rhode Island, South Dakota, Utah, Virginia, and Washington.

55.   Alaska prohibits only the acquisition of a recently formed bank. South Dakota permits any out-of-state bank holding company to acquire a single state-chartered bank.

56.   Delaware, Maryland, Nebraska, and Virginia fall into this category.

57.   Connecticut, Georgia, Kentucky, Massachusetts, New York, North Carolina, Rhode Island, and Utah.

58.   The Iowa statute, permitting bank holding companies to acquire Iowa banks only if the prospective acquiror had owned at least two Iowa banks prior to the passage of the statute, was challenged unsuccessfully in *Iowa Independent Bankers v. Board of Governors of the Federal Reserve System*, 511 F.2d 1288 (D.C. Cir.), *cert. denied*, 423 U.S. 875 (1975). The constitutionality of the Connecticut, Rhode Island, and Massachusetts statutes authorizing entry by New England holding companies on a reciprocal basis is being litigated as of mid-1984.

REFERENCES

Baxter, Nevins D., and Shah, Shekhar. "Department of Justice Competitive Factors Reports as a Regulatory Tool." *Banking Law Journal*, forthcoming November-December, 1984 article.

Board of Governors of the Federal Reserve System. *Banking Studies*. 1941.

Board of Governors of the Federal Reserve System. "Statement of Policy on Bank Acquisitions." *Federal Register*, 1982, p. 9017.

Eisenbeis, Robert A. "Regulatory Agencies' Approaches to the 'Line of Commerce.' " Federal Reserve Bank of Atlanta, *Economic Review*, April 1982.

Hawke, John D., Jr. "Fed Smiles on Holding Company Expansion." *Legal Times*, January 16, 1984, p. 11.

Robertson, Ross. *The Comptroller and Bank Supervision*. Washington, D.C.: Office of the Comptroller of the Currency, 1968, pp. 59–61.

U.S. Department of Justice. "Merger Guidelines." *Trade Regulation Reporter*, Commerce Clearing House, par. 4500, p. 6881.

U.S. House of Representatives, 89th Congress, 1st Session. "To Amend the Bank Merger Act of 1960: Hearings on S. 1698 before the Subcommittee on Domestic Finance of the House Committee on Banking and Currency," 1965. p. 39.

U.S. Senate, 86th Congress, 1st Session. "Regulation of Bank Mergers: Hearings on S. 1062 before the Senate Committee on Banking and Currency," 1959, pp. 3–17.

U.S. Senate Committee on Banking, Housing, and Urban Affairs. "The Branch Banking Provisions of the McFadden Act as Amended: Their Rationale and Rationality, Compendium Relating to Branches by Financial Institutions." Committee Print, 1976, pp. 1-42.

Whitehead, David D. "Interstate Banking: Taking Inventory." Federal Reserve Bank of Atlanta, *Economic Review*, May 1983, p. 5.

4 Major Challenges to Effective Management

The rapid changes in financial services markets now in progress have reflected several interrelated forces. First, high and volatile interest rates have changed depositor and lender practices. Second, new applications of technology have improved the efficiency of funds transfers, access to cash (especially with the ATM), and the transmission and storage of financial information. Third, a number of burdensome banking restrictions—largely those applying to pricing, location of offices, and permissible product range—have encouraged unregulated or less regulated entities to take advantage of banks' constraints.

There have been a number of major consequences of these forces. First, a wide range of institutions have moved to "package" financial services, offering customers the convenience of centralized transaction services, investment outlets, credit, information and record keeping, and (in some cases) insurance and financial advice—all from one source. In doing so, many institutions have moved aggressively into new service lines.

Second, the shift of liability structures of depository institutions toward a materially greater reliance on market-rate deposits is pointing to a reconfiguration of many transaction practices. In the past, services often constituted implicit payments to customers for deposit balances. Numerous branches, "free" checks, and other services (provided free or below cost) are foremost examples. These are being supplanted. Explicit interest payments are being accompanied by explicit fees on many services. This evolving explicit fee system is furnishing new incentives for bank customers to curtail or eliminate costly forms of service. Over time, this is likely to mean less reliance on transactions employing paper documents. In turn, this may mean substantially less of a role for offices offering convenient locations. In short, this transformation process is at the heart of the so-called financial revolution.

Third, with the increased interest rate volatility of recent years there has been greater demand by lending institutions for more rate-sensitive assets. This preference has been reflected in lending terms on virtually all classes of credit. In this connection, there has been a rapid growth of interest in hedging techniques by which to protect against undesired exposure to interest rate risk.

The analyses of these forces contained in previous sections set the stage for treatment in this section of a wide range of major strategic issues facing banking management. The management of "normal" banking risks—including interest rate, credit, and foreign—in periods perceived as anything but normal is, of course, a primary component. This material covers questions of pricing, as well as portfolio composition. But there is more at stake. The broadening of product lines, planning regimes, merger and acquisition finance, and changing cost structures all have major bearings on the functioning of banking entities.

13 Managing Interest Rate Risk

Benjamin Wolkowitz

The sharp rise and increased volatility of interest rates in the late 1970s and early 1980s made interest rate risk management a pressing problem for lenders. Financial strategies that in a relatively stable interest rate environment produced a reasonable return on assets net of the cost of funds were not as effective when rates became higher and more volatile. This has led to a reconsideration of funding and investment strategies and, as a result, new instruments and techniques in an effort to maintain profitability in a changed economic environment.

Problems associated with the increased volatility and higher level of interest rates included outflows of funds resulting from the availability of higher rate alternatives. As a substitute for interest-regulated bank and thrift accounts, consumers increasingly took advantage of money market funds and Treasury bills, which usually paid rates in excess of federally mandated deposit ceilings. The phasing out of interest rate regulations and the creation of more market-related deposit vehicles provided a solution to the disintermediation problem. This solution resulted, however, in the cost of funds to depository institutions being more a function of market rates than it was before the phasing out of interest rate ceilings.

On the asset side, traditional management of interest rate risk exposure did not always prove adequate in the more volatile interest rate period. Timing the acquisition of assets, whether loans or government securities, became more critical. Moreover, efforts to pass interest rate risk on to borrowers by replacing fixed-rate with variable rate loans, although effective, has not been a complete solution. Consequently, lenders have

The assistance of Howard Lodge in improving the treatment of duration analysis is gratefully acknowledged.

407

had to expand the range of techniques and instruments utilized in the management of interest rate risk.

The purpose of this chapter is to analyze in detail how lenders can adjust their financial strategies to a volatile rate environment. The emphasis is on applications of financial futures to particular bank situations, although other methods of managing interest rate risk are also considered. The first section contains a brief review of the environment that has made interest rate volatility an issue. This is followed by a discussion of how interest rate risk affects a bank's balance sheet and an introduction to the available instruments and strategies applying to the management of exposure to interest rate risk. The focus is then narrowed to a discussion of financial futures with emphasis on applications; some attention is also given to debt options.

AN EMPIRICAL EXAMINATION OF INTEREST RATE BEHAVIOR

Figures 13.1 and 13.2 clearly illustrate why the recent behavior of interest rates has increased the difficulty of effectively managing interest rate risk. Not only did rate levels rise dramatically after the Federal Reserve's October 1979 announcement of new operating targets, but the volatility of rates also increased.[1] This pattern was true for short-term money market rates as well as long-term interest rates.

If the only change in interest rate behavior had been that rates had risen, then the management of rate risk would have been made more difficult only during the transition from low to high rates. Once the higher levels had been attained, investment managers could have shaped their strategies to these new levels. Unfortunately, at best such modifications would have had short-lived success, since interest rates not only rose to higher levels but also became more volatile. Consequently, investment managers had to adjust to an entirely new pattern of interest rate behavior.

While the amplitude of interest rate swings has diminished somewhat from the period of greatest volatility—and interest rate levels are lower (as of early 1984)—there can be little confidence that conditions will return to the stability of the 1960s. Indeed, mastery of the techniques of managing interest rate risk is a probable prerequisite to long-term financial survival.

EXPOSURE TO INTEREST RATE RISK—MANAGING THE GAP

Managing aggregate interest rate risk exposure in a bank is equivalent to managing the balance sheet gap. (For an excellent introduction, see Binder, 1980, 1980, and 1981.) This gap results from a mismatch in assets and

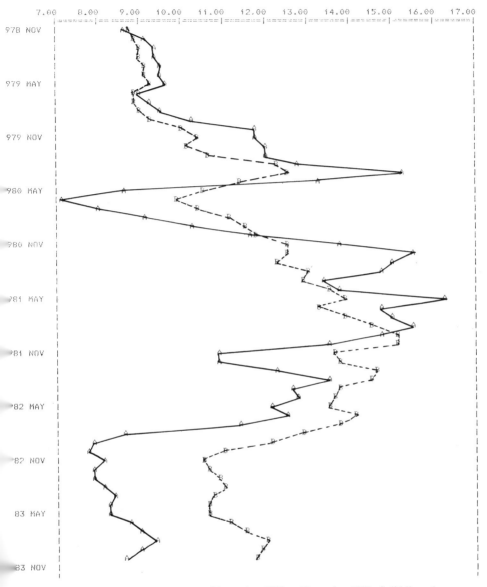

Figure 13.1. Level of interest rates, November 1978 to November 1983. Solid line: three-month U.S. Treasury bill; dashed line: 20-year U.S. Treasury bond.

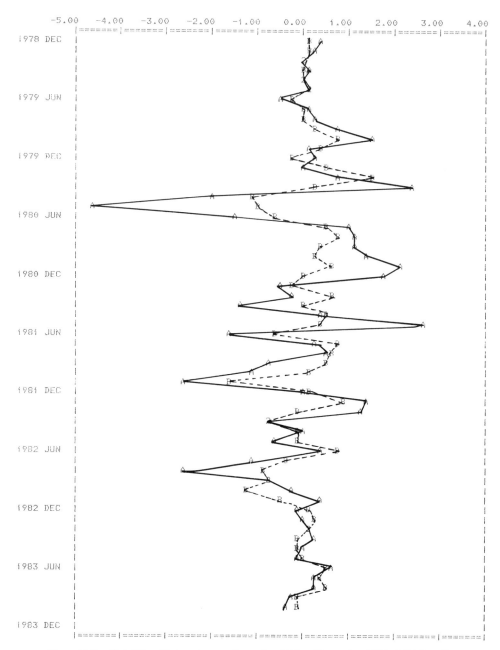

Figure 13.2. Volatility of interest rates, December 1978 to November 1983. Solid line: first-difference three-month U.S. Treasury bill; dashed line: first-difference 20-year U.S. Treasury bond.

liabilities, where the mismatch is expressed in terms of a maturity imbalance or some other measure reflecting sensitivity to interest rate changes. For example, where a bank funds long-term assets with relatively shorter-term liabilities, it is exposed to the risk of rising interest rates, since the liabilities will have to be renewed prior to the time when the assets will be repriced. The extent of this risk is directly related to how long it will take for the assets to be repriced after the liabilities are renewed. The greater this interval, the greater is the bank's exposure to changes in interest rates. Similarly, if the gap is reversed—that is, the liabilities are repriced less frequently than the assets—the bank is subject to the risk of falling interest rates.

A straightforward method of measuring the gap is to group the components of the balance sheet into designated maturity periods (e.g., one month, three months, six months, one year) according to when they reprice. For each period there may be a repricing gap on either the asset or the liability side (i.e., whether the dollar amount of assets to be repriced exceeds or falls short of corresponding liabilities). The difficulty with this procedure is that it represents a trade-off between tractability and accuracy. In particular, the ease of implementation depends on the number of designated periods. The fewer the periods, the easier is the procedure to implement. Alternatively, the accuracy of the procedure depends on selecting a sufficient number of periods so that the measured gap is not misleading. In the extreme, designating a large number of categories begins to approach a continuous and more accurate measure.

This method of calculating the gap has limitations resulting not only from the selection of categories, but also from the focus of the procedure. Interest rate risk affects a portfolio both when assets and liabilities reprice and—on a more continuous basis—as changes in interest rates affect a porfolio's valuation. Yet the repricing procedure ignores the impact of rates on the overall value of a portfolio. A more comprehensive measure of interest rate risk and its relation to the gap would relate interest rate changes to the overall valuation of the portfolio.

The first step in devising a comprehensive measure of portfolio exposure is to measure valuation. An effective and widely used method is present value, which as demonstrated by Equation 13.1 is the sum of the discounted stream of future payments where the discounting factor is an expression incorporating the current level of interest rates. This is a dollar measure of the value of a security, taking into account the security's maturity and schedule of payments.

$$\text{Present value} = \sum_{i=1}^{N} \frac{C_i}{(1 + r)^i} = \sum_{i=1}^{N} \text{PV}_i \qquad (13.1)$$

where C = scheduled payment of principal and interest
     r = yield to maturity on an annualized basis
     N = number of coupon periods

To illustrate the present-value calculation, consider a hypothetical security with two scheduled payments, the first equal to $10 and the second equal to $100. Assuming a current level of interest rates of 5%, the present value of the security would equal

$$\sum_{i=1}^{2} \mathrm{PV}_i = \frac{\$100}{(1.05)} + \frac{\$10}{(1.05)^2} = \$95.24 + \$9.07 = \$104.31$$

To measure how a portfolio is affected by interest rate changes requires calculating the elasticity of present value with respect to a change in interest rates. Such a measure provides a comprehensive reflection of how a portfolio's value is affected by a change in interest rates. This elasticity measure is equivalent to duration analysis, which is an interest rate risk measure that has been gaining attention because it represents the basis for an effective method of managing portfolio exposure to interest rate risk.[2]

In order to gain an understanding of what duration is actually measuring, it is instructive to consider precisely how a portfolio's present value is affected by a change in interest rates. In particular, interest rates and valuation are inversely related—that is, when rates rise, a security's value falls. A portfolio also generates a cash flow which is reinvested, and the value of this reinvestment is directly related to interest rates. The higher are interest rates, the greater is the reinvestment income. These two opposite effects will vary in magnitude. There will be one point, however, at which the relative magnitudes are such that the security attains a minimum value for a given change in interest rates. Duration measures that point in time at which these two effects result in minimum value for the security.

A numerical example is instructive. Technically, duration is calculated as a weighted average of future cash flows where the weights are proportional to the present value of the payments. Using the same symbols as in Equation 13.2, duration is calculated as[3]

$$\text{Duration} = \sum_{i=1}^{N} \left[\frac{\mathrm{PV}_i \times i}{\displaystyle\sum_{j=1}^{N} \mathrm{PV}_j} \right] \qquad (13.2)$$

To illustrate the implementation of this formula, consider the case discussed above of the security with two payments, the first $100 and the second $10. The present value of this security as calculated above is $104.31. The duration is then calculated from Equation 13.2 as

$$D = \frac{\$\ 95.24 \times 1}{\$104.31} + \frac{\$\ 9.07 \times 2}{\$104.31} = 1.08$$

Thus, although this security has a maturity of two years (assuming annual coupons), its duration is substantially shorter. As a measure of risk, this seems appropriate since this security pays down quickly, leaving relatively little of its value exposed to interest rate changes after the first coupon. By comparison, consider a hypothetical security with the same coupon payments which are paid in reverse order. Such a security would have a present value calculated as

$$\sum_{i=1}^{2} PV_i = \frac{\$\ 10}{(1.05)} + \frac{\$100}{(1.05)^2} = \$9.52 + \$90.70 = 100.22$$

The duration of this security is calculated as

$$D = \frac{\$9.52 \times 1}{\$100.22} + \frac{\$90.70 \times 2}{\$100.22} = 1.90$$

A comparison of these two securities indicates that although they have the identical maturity, the first security has a higher present value but a lower duration than the second security. Since the second security has most of its payback outstanding until its maturity, in contrast to the first security, it is more vulnerable to changes in interest rates. Consequently it has the higher duration.

To demonstrate how maturity and duration are related for actively traded securities, the duration of a number of government securities was calculated as of September 2, 1983. The date of the calculation is important because, as indicated above, duration is influenced by current interest rates and will change with changes in rates. The results of these calculations follow.

Treasury Issue	Coupon Rate	Maturity Date	Duration
2 years	10.625	8/1985	1.743
3 years	11.375	8/1986	2.444
4 years	10.500	6/1987	3.057

Treasury Issue	Coupon Rate	Maturity Date	Duration
5 years	11.750	11/1988	3.809
7 years	10.750	7/1990	4.691
10 years	11.875	9/1993	5.739
20 years	11.125	8/2003	7.573
30 years	12.000	8/2013	7.910

As these calculations illustrate, the longer the maturity of securities the less the difference in relative durations. That is, the difference in duration between a two- and a three-year security is greater than that between a 20- and a 30-year security. This is directly a function of the diminishing impact of coupon payments on present value, the further in the future are these payments.

The direct application of the duration measure to risk management derives from the recognition that two securities with the same duration have the same exposure to interest rate risk. Thus if a liability is used to finance an asset of equivalent duration, the value of the position would be unaffected by interest rate change. Generalizing, a duration-balanced portfolio is one in which the impact of interest rate changes will be offsetting. Such an interest-neutral portfolio is characterized as being immunized.

Immunizing a portfolio obviously reduces its exposure to interest rate risk, but immunization does entail a cost in terms of the expected return on the portfolio. Ensuring that a portfolio is neutral with regard to changes in interest rate risk guards against deterioration in the value of a portfolio while preventing any appreciation. Thus intentional mismatches have the potential to produce higher returns on a portfolio. Depending on interest rate expectations, bank management may decide to incur a gap using immunization strategies only to close those gaps viewed as undesirable in light of interest rate expectations.

Whether management achieves (by design) an immunized portfolio or one with exposure to interest rate risk is dependent upon the skills of the portfolio manager. As discussed in the next section, the management of interest rate risk exposure (as measured by overall portfolio exposure) depends on a number of decisions that go into the design and management of the components of the balance sheet.

MANAGING INTEREST RATE RISK

The effects of interest rate movements on overall profitability reflect the various subordinated actions that are aggregated in the balance sheet. To understand interest rate risk management more fully, it is useful to consider how interest rate risk influences investment and funding strategies.

Investment Portfolio Strategies

The two interest-rate-sensitive components of a bank's financial asset portfolio are, of course, investment securities and loans. The treatment of investment securities, such as government securities and money market instruments, is fundamentally no different for a depository institution than for any other investment manager having such instruments in portfolio. The primary concern is one of timing: acquiring an instrument at a relatively low price, that is, at a relatively high rate of return. The objective is to acquire a security with not only a high yield but also obviously a greater probability of appreciating rather than depreciating in value. Although bank accounting treatment may diminish the immediate importance of capital gains and losses for a bank portfolio manager, unrealized capital losses still curtail a bank's capacity to alter portfolio composition, since selling off depreciated assets results in the recogniton of such losses. Thus, portfolio managers are frequently challenged to improve the yield on an investment portfolio by acquiring higher-yield securities, but such actions are often effectively blocked by an inability to liquidate a current depreciated position. This is particularly true in a volatile and rising interest rate environment.

The upward spiral in interest rates that began in October 1979 had a devastating impact on the value of long-term fixed-rate loans that had been booked at substantially lower interest rates (perhaps the best example is fixed-rate conventional mortgages).[4] Moreover, to the extent these loans were funded with shorter-term liabilities, the net interest earnings on such loans were squeezed. Although the transition to a post-October 1979 environment is an extreme case, recent interest rate volatility has reduced the attractiveness of long-term fixed-rate loans.

A predictable response on the part of banks and thrifts to a more volatile interest rate environment was to promote redesigned loan agreements that shifted more of the interest rate risk onto borrowers. Such loans reprice periodically, rather than having a fixed rate for the entire term of the loan. Variable-rate loans began to appear in virtually all categories, except for the very shortest maturities. In particular, the mortgage market became a focus for the development of such instruments. In spite of the proliferation of such instruments, they did not replace wholly the conventional fixed-rate agreements.

The inability of lenders to replace fixed-rate with variable rate loans has largely reflected borrower resistance to such agreements and pricing problems. This appears to be particularly true of the mortgage market, where variable-rate mortgages often have not been priced attractively enough to induce borrowers to opt for such mortgages in lieu of fixed-rate mortgages. Although variable-rate loans are reasonably popular and constitute a rising share of total loans, they have not eliminated the exposure of loan portfolios to interest rate risk.

Liability Mangement

The impact of more volatile interest rates on the structure of liabilities has been somewhat different than that on assets. Whereas with the latter, there have been constraints on changes in composition and characteristics, depository institutions were literally driven to restructure their liabilities. When the level of market interest rates significantly exceeded the bank deposit rates mandated by Regulation Q, depositors abandoned bank instruments for near substitutes available elsewhere, principally Treasury bills and money market mutual funds.

In order to counteract this disintermediation, bankers and regulators were forced to abandon Regulation Q protection and move to the development of new deposits having more competitive features. These changes culminated in the phasing out of Regulation Q, the introduction of market-rate transaction deposits (e.g., super NOW accounts), the development of bank money market deposit accounts, and the issuance of other small-denomination certificates of deposit free from ceilings. Successfully countering disintermediation came at a cost, however, since these newer deregulated accounts paying market rates of interest reduced the proportion of non-interest-sensitive bank deposits.

Effectively adjusting the compostion of a bank or thrift liability structure predates the response to disintermediation described above. The potential for liability adjustments was significantly enhanced in the early 1960s with the development of active liability management. Prior to that time, banks (with the exception of money-center banks) were for the most part deposit-taking institutions in which the interest paid on deposits was generally subject to interest rate regulation. (Banks had some liabilities that were more market oriented, such as long-term subordinated debt, but this was generally viewed as a type of "near" capital and not actively managed in a manner that would make it a component of interest risk management.)

Certificates of deposit became just one of several instruments employed by banks to access the money markets. For example, the bankers' acceptance market also grew dramatically during the 1970s, in part in response to interest rate pressures imposed on U.S. banks (and in part because eligible acceptances are a reserve-free source of funds).[5] In addition, U.S. banks became extremely active participants in the vast Eurodollar deposit market, a largely interbank source of funds. These and other associated developments increased the scope of bank liabilities, enhancing the ability of banks to adjust to their liabilities in an effort to manage their interest rate exposure.

While banks may have an improved ability to manage exposure to interest rate risk, this has entailed having a greater proportion of liabilities paying market rates. In sum, although these changes in bank liabilities enhance liability management opportunities, they make such management dependent on decisions regarding not only the mix of instruments to be used but also the timing of their issuance and the method of their pricing.

Financial Futures

These changes in the composition and design of assets and liabilities required the adoption of complementary changes in interest rate risk management techniques. As the stakes in interest rate management grew, it was recognized that the evolving financial futures markets could expand the strategies available to bankers and portfolio managers generally.

Futures, or—as they are more traditionally called—commodity markets, developed in the United States immediately after the Civil War with the opening of the Chicago Board of Trade in 1868. The first contract designated a specified quantity of wheat of a particular grade as deliverable at a specified time in the future. A trade of such a contract required a buyer (or long) who agreed to accept delivery under the conditions of the contract from a seller (or short). This exchange activity formalized what had previously been conducted in a large forward market.[6] Contracting for the future delivery of wheat has become an important component of the financial activities supporting that agricultural market.

The development of an exchange-traded instrument was an improvement on the forward market because of the standardization of the terms of the contractual relationship. This avoided the problems of disputed contracts which had occurred in the forward market. The organization of the exchange also solved the credit or counterparty risk problem that was inherent to the forward market.[7] Moreover, because of the standardization of the terms of the contract and because of the activities of clearing corporations, futures contracts can be retraded continously prior to delivery and can be matched off so that delivery need not actually occur.[8]

Futures continued to be based on agricultural products until 1972. At that time the Chicago Mercantile Exchange opened a wholly owned subsidiary, the International Money Market (IMM), with the objective of trading futures contracts based on financial instruments. The first instruments were foreign currencies, which, after a slow start, have become an integral part of foreign exchange trading. Other exchanges followed the IMM, offering futures based on other financial instruments. Financial futures are available based on a variety of public and private debt instruments of varying maturities. The contracts on these instruments stipulate delivery on a quarterly basis (typically March, June, September, and December) and are traded for generally no more than 11 quarters in the future. (The appendix to this chapter contains an outline description of the actively traded contracts most likely to be of interest to those involved with asset liability management). Several examples illustrating the possible use of financial futures are discussed in the next section.

APPLYING FINANCIAL FUTURES TO THE MANAGEMENT OF INTEREST RATE RISK

The key to understanding the use of financial futures is appreciating that financial futures are a component of the securities market. Those factors that influence the cash component of the securities market are also likely to affect the futures component. Moreover, futures can be used as a surrogate for a cash instrument. In general, what can be accomplished with futures can be accomplished with cash and vice versa.[9]

Users of futures are typically hedgers or speculators. Hedgers presumably use futures as a risk reducing instrument, whereas speculators are presumed to take positions in futures reflecting their expectations of future interest rates. By regulation, banks are hedgers when they use futures, except for their dealer operations.[10]

The following example shows how financial futures can be used to hedge. Suppose in early June a bank calculated its gap over the next quarter and has identified a substantial repricing gap that will occur in mid-September. In particular, at that time a sizable amount of maturing CDs will be repriced with no offsetting asset adjustment.[11] Obviously, the bank is vulnerable to a rise in interest rates. Moreover, bank management is adverse to the effects of a rise of interest rates, which would put a squeeze on earnings. Consequently, management decides to hedge with financial futures.[12]

The details of this case are contained in Table 13.1. On June 8 (considering the cash market, or left side of the example), bank management recognizes it will be repricing $10 million of CDs on September 18. Current CD rates are 8.80%. Management expects those rates to rise and wishes to cover this exposure. (By September 18, cash market CD rates did rise to 9.30%. At this higher interest rate, bank liability costs rose $12,500, with no attendant increase in asset earnings—since assets did not reprice—thus reducing the bank's net income.)

Suppose on June 8 management had gone ahead with its financial futures hedge. The futures market on that day was quoting contracts at 9%, which

Table 13.1. Short—Pure Hedge

Cash Market	Futures Market

June 8
Anticipate repricing $10,000,000 of certificates of deposit in September. Current cash CD rate expressed on a discount basis is 8.80%—expect interest rates to increase.

June 8
Sells (short) 10 September CD futures at 9%.

	$10,000,000
Discount rate	× 0.09
Annual discount	$ 900,000
90 days	× 0.25
Actual discount	$ 225,000
Value of contracts	$ 9,775,000

September 18
Reprices $10,000,000 of 90-day certificates of deposit at 9.30% (discount basis).

September 18
Buys (long) 10 September CD futures contracts at 9.30%.

Cash Market		Futures Market	
Face Value of CDs	$10,000,000		$10,000,000
Discount rate	× 0.0930	Discount rate	× 0.0930
Annual discount	$ 930,000	Annual discount	$ 930,000
90 days	× 0.25	90 days	× 0.25
Actual discount	$ 232,500	Actual discount	$ 232,500
Value of CDs	$ 9,767,500	Value of contracts	$ 9,767,500
Interest expense June	$220,000	Short September	$ 9,775,000
Interest expense September	$232,500	Long September	−$ 9,767,500
Cost of increase	$ 12,500	Gain on hedge	$ 7,500

Discount paid without hedge	$ 232,500
Hedge gain	−$ 7,500
Effective discount paid (quarterly)	$ 225,000
Four quarters 360/90	× 4
Effective discount (annual)	$ 900,000
Effective discount rate with hedge	9.00%

although more than the cash market on June 8 was less than management's expectation for September. In other words, management would willingly accept the 9% rate because it believed it to be less than what CD rates would be when the repricing occurred. To secure the 9% rate, management sold futures contracts for September delivery—which was equivalent to arranging in June to sell or reprice CDs in September at 9%. On September 18 the futures price converged to the cash price (more on this later), and the contracts were bought back to end the futures transaction. Thus, the contracts were bought back for less than the price for which they were originally sold, resulting in a profit of $7,500.[13] This gain—when applied to the increased cost of the CDs of $12,500—resulted in a net increased cost of $5,000. Translated into rates, this means when the CDs were repriced in September (for 90 days) they cost (net of the futures gain) 9%, not the higher cash market price of 9.30%. This 9% was the originally contracted rate on CDs.

Omitted from this example are commissions and margin costs. Commissions are negotiable between the client and the broker, known as a futures commission merchant, or FCM. Margins are set by exchanges. FCMs can charge their clients higher than exchange minimum margins, but not lower margins. These margins represent a good-faith deposit and as such are very low relative to the par value of the contract (typically less than 5%). The margin paid at initiation of the futures position is called initial margin. If the value of a futures position deteriorates, the amount of the loss is charged against the initial margin. If the margin account is reduced below a level called maintenance margin (usually about 80% of initial margin), the client is required to add funds to restore the margin on account to the level of the initial margin. Alternatively, if the position appreciates the client may withdraw those funds in excess of the initial margin level.

The margin accounting procedure is conducted on a daily basis, based on the settlement (or closing) price on the futures contract. In the example discussed above, the position would have been valued (or marked to market) daily, ending in a profit of $7,500. In the interim period between June 8 and September 18, of course, there may have been some "losing" days when the client would have been called on to deposit additional funds— only to be followed by days when funds were then deposited into the client's account. As noted, the net outcome of these flows into and out of the margin account was the $7,500 gain.

The preceding example was of a short, or selling hedge, but long, or buying hedges also may be desirable. For instance, assume the example was reversed. That is, instead of being faced with a funding gap in a rising rate environment, an institution is faced with an asset gap in a declining rate environment. In particular, suppose management in reviewing its gap on June 8 observes that in mid-September it will have to roll over $10 million more of assets than liabilities. Thus, its earnings will be vulnerable to a decline of interest rates. Moreover, assume management actually expects interest rates to decline over the next quarter. Table 13.2 illustrates what would happen in this case.

Considering only the cash portion of Table 13.2 indicates that on June 8, when bank management was engaged in its gap review process, the cash market Treasury bill rate was 9%. Assume further that management anticipates reinvesting its maturing assets in Treasury Bills, so that their

Table 13.2. Long—Pure Hedge

Cash Market		Futures Market	
June 8		*June 8*	
Anticipate acquiring $10,000,000 of Treasury bills in September. Current cash Treasury bill rate expressed on a discount basis is 9%—expect interest rates to decline.		Buy (long) 10 September Treasury bill futures contracts at 8.75%.	
			$10,000,000
		Discount rate	× .0875
		Annual discount	$ 875,000
		90 days	× 0.25
		Actual discount	$ 218,750
		Value of contracts	$ 9,781,250
September 18		*September 18*	
Acquires $10,000,000 of 90-day Treasury bills at 8.50%.		Sells (short) 10 September Treasury bill futures contracts at 8.50%.	
Face Value of Treasury bills	$10,000,000		$10,000,000
Discount value	× 0.085	Discount rate	× 0.085
Annual discount	$ 850,000	Annual discount	$ 850,000
90 days	× 0.25	90 days	× 0.25
Actual discount	$ 212,500	Actual discount	$ 212,500
Value of Treasury bills	$ 9,787,500	Value of contracts	$ 9,787,500
Interest earnings June	$225,000	Short September	$ 9,787,500
Interest earnings September	$212,500	Long September	− $ 9,781,250
Cost of delay	$ 12,500	Gain on hedge	$ 6,250
	Discount earned without hedge	$ 212,500	
	Hedge gain	$ 6,250	
	Effective discount earned (quarterly)	$ 218,750	
	Four quarters 360/90	× 4	
	Effective discount (annual)	$ 875,000	
	Effective discount rate with hedge	8.75%	

concern is with expected bill rates. On September 18, when the projected gap materializes, management is indeed correct; Treasury bill rates have declined 50 basis points to 8.50%. This means that from June 8 to September 18 earnings on $10 million in 90-day Treasury bills fell by $12,500.

As part of the June 8 review, management could have elected to close the $10 million asset gap by hedging it in the futures market. Indeed, the futures markets reflected the same expectation regarding interest rates as did management. September futures contracts had a discount rate of

8.75%, 25 basis points lower than the cash market rate on that day. If management anticipated a greater-than-25-basis-point decline in rates (so that on September 18, an 8.75% 90-day Treasury bill would be appealing), the appropriate strategy would have been to buy the Treasury bills in the futures market for September delivery. This action would have effectively closed the impending asset gap.

Consulting the right-hand (i.e., futures market) side of Table 13.2 indicates how well this strategy would have worked. Buying contracts on June 8 meant acquiring $10 million par value in 90-day Treasury bills for delivery in September with an effective discount of 8.75%. By September 18, the cash market discount fell to 8.50% and the futures market converged to the cash market price. To close out the futures position required selling or shorting these contracts. Since the Treasury bill rate had fallen, the price of the contracts had risen so that the contracts were sold for more than they had cost. In particular, the futures position gained $6,250. When the futures gain was applied against the cash market discount available in September of 8.50%, it resulted in an effective discount rate of 8.75%. Thus, the use of futures had the effect of increasing the yield on the cash position.

This example also ignores commissions and margin costs. These two factors would have to be included in any deliberations regarding the advisability of engaging in a futures transaction. These examples share another important simplification. They assume that at the time a futures contract position is closed out, the price of the position has converged to the cash price. In fact, equality of cash and futures prices is the exception and only likely to be true at or very near to the delivery time on futures. The reason it is true when delivery approaches is because otherwise market participants could engage in a profitable, riskless arbitrage. In particular, suppose that at or near September 18, futures contracts for Treasury bills were at a lower price than the cash market. Were this the case, traders could go long in futures, take delivery of the Treasury bills, and then sell them in the cash market at a higher price. Alternatively, if the futures price were higher, the trader could short the contract and deliver in Treasury bills for a higher price than that at which they were acquired in the cash market. These arbitrage opportunities provide a discipline ensuring that the futures and cash prices will converge.

At other than delivery periods, cash and futures prices will typically not be equal. The difference between the cash and futures prices is an important concept known to futures analysts as the basis. Understanding the basis is crucial to using futures contracts unless transactions can always be structured so that they are closed out at the time of delivery on futures contracts.[14] The basis is generally a function of two factors: expectations and the cost of carry. The relationship between expectations and the cost of carry is in a sense represented by the yield curve. Thus, before discussing the basis it is necessary to have an understanding of the yield curve.

The yield curve depicts the relationship between maturity and yield. Yield curves can be drawn for any financial instruments, although the general reference yield curve in the money markets represents the relationship for Treasury securities. Such securities are a useful reference because they are actively traded, available in a wide range of maturities, and homogeneous in quality so that yield differences are solely a function of maturity. In concept, as well as in practice, a yield curve can assume any slope. A positively sloped yield curve, often referred to as a normal yield curve, indicates that longer-maturity securities have a higher yield than shorter-maturity securities. Inverted yield curves, indicating the opposite relationship between maturity and yield, and flat yield curves, indicating that yield is unaffected by maturity, also are observed from time to time.

The slope of the yield curve is a function of two influences: expectations and liquidity. Considering only the influence of expectations, a positively sloped yield curve demonstrates expectations of rising forward rates.[15] Assuming expectations regarding future interest rates are consistent with those demonstrated by the cash yield curve, the price of a contract guaranteeing future delivery should be at a discount to cash. That is, when forward rates exceed current cash rates, prices for future delivery should be less than current cash market prices. A symmetric line of reasoning supports why, in an environment of a downward sloping yield curve, the futures contract price should be at a premium to the spot price.[16]

An alternative way of explaining the relationship between current cash and futures prices is the cost of carry, which also relates to the yield curve. As an example of the cost of carry, consider the Treasury bond futures contract. Suppose, an institution is long (i.e., has bought) the March contract and is short (i.e., has sold) the June contract. When the March contract matures, the long can accept delivery of a Treasury bond. This bond could then be financed or carried for three months and delivered in fulfillment of an obligation under a futures contract when the June contract matures (commonly called "cash and carry"). The short-term financing cost will affect the relative price of futures and cash.

Yield curve relationships reflect the cost of carry, since the instrument being carried is earning a long-term interest rate while the financing cost is a short-term rate. When the yield curve is positively sloped (i.e., normal), so that the long-term rate exceeds the short-term rate, the instruments being carried are producing income net of the financing costs during the

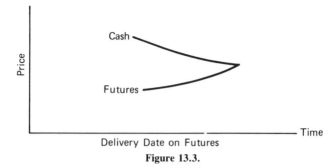

Delivery Date on Futures

Figure 13.3.

carry period. In such a case, the futures price should be at a discount to the cash price by the amount earned during the carry period. The seller of the contract is earning the difference between short- and long-term rates on the deliverable and therefore can afford to sell the instrument for future delivery at a discount to the current cash price. Similarly, buyers aware of the carry relationship would insist on a discount for futures relative to cash. Figure 13.3 illustrates the positive yield curve case. Note that as the delivery date of the futures contract approaches, the discount on futures declines, since the importance of the net income earned during the carry period diminishes as delivery approaches. That is, a futures contract near delivery is less affected by carry than a futures contract with a significant period of time remaining before delivery.

When the yield curve is inverted there is a net cost of carry, since short-term rates exceed long-term rates, and consequently the coupon earnings on the security being carried are less than the cost of financing the instrument. In such a case it is expected that futures would be at a premium to cash, since the seller of a futures contract who is financing the underlying cash instrument which is deliverable is losing money during the carry period. In addition, buyers would view the cash instrument as less expensive than futures. As a result the futures price converges to the cash price from above as illustrated in Figure 13.4.

Empirically, these yield curve relationships and the price differences between cash and futures follow the pattern described above. As Tables 13.1 and 13.2 demonstrated, and as is reflected by Figures 13.3 and 13.4, these concepts are not particularly important if the termination of the transaction is coordinated with the maturity of the futures contract. In every other case, however, futures and cash prices are likely to diverge, and therefore the basis will influence the outcome of a hedge. The impact of the basis can be demonstrated by another example.

Returning to the rationale for the examples in Table 13.1 and Table 13.2 consider a bank engaged in gap management. On September 14 this

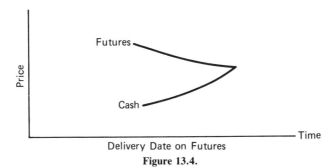

Figure 13.4.

bank identifies a significant liability gap of $10 million that will materialize in approximately one month. Management anticipates interest rates will rise in the interim period. The current cash market rate for CD's in September is 9.25%; however, by mid-September the rate has risen to 9.88%. As a consequence, the funding cost has increased from $231,250 to $247,000 or an increase of $15,750.

An offset in futures in September could have been acquired at a discount rate of 9.66%, indicating that the futures markets also anticipated an increase in interest rates. In October, when the hedge was closed out, the rate in futures was 10.43%. Since October is not a delivery month, December contracts were used. Because the hedge was closed out well in advance of delivery in futures, a divergence between cash and futures prices should be expected (as was explained above). Reviewing the outcome of the futures trade indicates that futures gained $17,000, which more than compensated for the $15,750 increased cost of funding. Adjusting the discount paid without a hedge ($247,000) by the $17,000 gain in futures results in an effective discount paid for the CDs of 9.20%. Not only is this below the initial rate on futures, but it is also below the initial rate on cash.

To understand why this occurred, consider the behavior of the basis. Converting to prices, on September 14 the cash market price was 90.75 (100.00-9.25) and the futures price was 90.34 (100.00 - 9.66). The basis was 0.41 (i.e., 90.75 - 90.34). On October 13, when the positions were unwound, the cash market price was 90.12 and the futures price was 89.66, resulting in a basis of 0.46. Thus, the basis had widened (become more positive), which means that the loss in cash was more than compensated for by a gain in futures. Another way of considering the same point is to compare what happened in the cash position, in terms of price, with what happened to the futures position (also in terms of price) over the same period. In particular, the cash price went from 90.75 to 90.12, a loss of 0.63, while futures went from 90.34 to 89.66, a gain of 0.68. This confirms

Table 13.3. Short—Pure Hedge

Cash Market		Futures Market	
September 14		*September 14*	
Anticipate issuing $10,000,000 of certificates of deposit in October. Current cash CD rate expressed on a discount basis is 9.25%—expect interest rates to increase.		Sells (short) 10 December CD futures contracts at 9.66%.	
			$10,000,000
		Discount rate	× .0966
		Annual discount	$ 966,000
		90 days	× 0.25
		Actual discount	$ 241,500
		Value of contracts	$ 9,758,500
October 13		*October 13*	
Issues $10,000,000 of 90-day certificates of deposit at 9.88% (discount basis).		Buys (long) 10 December CD futures contracts at 10.34%.	
Face Value of CDs	$10,000,000		$10,000,000
Discount rate	× 0.0988	Discount rate	× 0.1034
Annual discount	$ 988,000	Annual discount	$ 1,034,000
90 days	× 0.25	90 days	× 0.25
Actual discount	$ 247,000	Actual discount	$ 258,500
Value of CDs	$ 9,753,000	Value of contracts	$ 9,741,500
Interest expense September	$231,250	Short December	$ 9,758,500
Interest expense October	$247,000	Long December	−$ 9,741,500
Cost of increase	$ 15,750	Gain on hedge	$ 17,000
	Discount paid without hedge	$ 247,000	
	Hedge gain	−$ 17,000	
	Effective discount paid (quarterly)	$ 230,000	
	Four quarters 360/90	× 4	
	Effective discount (annual)	$ 920,000	
	Effective discount rate with hedge	9.20%	

what was determined by examining the basis: The cash loss was more than compensated for by the futures gain.

Thus, if the basis is zero when the hedge is unwound, the effective discount on the hedge will equal the rate available on futures when the position was initially established. Alternatively, if the basis widened over the course of the hedge, the futures position will more than compensate for the change in the value of the cash position, and the effective discount on the hedge will actually be below the rate initially contracted for in futures. Indeed, the effective discount may go below the initial cash market rate, as demonstrated in Table 13.3. This comparison suggests that a narrowing of the basis with a short hedge may result in a not entirely successful hedge. Such a case is considered next.

Suppose the preceding case is constructed with a slight alteration in interest rates. The motivation behind this example is identical to that of the preceding case, but interest rate details differ. In particular, assume on September 14 a bank expects a liability gap of $10 million will appear in the following month. Moreover, suppose management anticipates a rise of interest rates above the 9.65% level prevailing on September 14. The futures market on that day reflects the opposite expectation with a rate of 9.16%. Nevertheless, the hedge is executed and management turns out to have been correct in its expectations. When the CDs are repriced on October 13, rates have risen to 10.625%. As a result, the interest expense of issuing $10 million of 90-day CDs rose by $265,625. The interest rates in futures also rose during the period September 14 to October 13, but not as much as in cash. When the futures position was closed out, rates rose to 9.39% so that the gain in futures was only $5,750. Thus, the earnings on futures only partially compensated for the loss in the cash market. This outcome is reflected in the behavior of the basis.

The basis on September 14 was equal to the cash market price, 90.35, less the futures market price, 90.84, or -0.49. On October 13, the basis was equal to the cash market price of 89.375 less the futures price of 90.61, or -1.235. That is, the basis became smaller (i.e., less positive). Comparing the change in the cash position with the change in the futures position confirms that a narrowing in the basis with a short hedge means that the cash loss is not completely offset by the gain in futures. Thus, a narrowing of the basis reduces the success of a short hedge.

The implication of these cases is that unless the hedge is to be structured so that it will be unwound when the futures contract is in delivery—that is, when the futures price converges to the cash price—a futures hedge must be closely monitored. Otherwise, the outcome may be disappointing.

If the hedge was deteriorating—as shown in Table 13.4, where the basis narrowed—remedial action could be taken during the course of the hedge. In particular, if the hedge manager expected the basis to narrow (or if it had already begun to narrow and further narrowing was anticipated), additional futures contracts could be added so that the net result of the total hedge would be improved. Although basis risk can be a problem, it is generally more manageable than interest rate risk, as this example illustrates.

In the examples considered so far, basis risk always resulted from the timing of the transaction. For this reason, this type of basis is sometimes referred to as the temporal basis. One other characteristic of these examples is that there always exists a contract which has as its underlying

Table 13.4. Short—Pure Hedge

Cash Market	Futures Market

September 14
Anticipate repricing $10,000,000 of certificates of deposit in October. Current cash CD rate expressed on a discount basis is 9.65%—expect interest rates to increase.

September 14
Sells (short) 10 December CD futures contracts at 9.16%.

	$10,000,000
Discount rate	× .0916
Annual discount	$ 916,000
90 days	× 0.25
Actual discount	$ 229,000
Value of contracts	$ 9,771,500

October 13
Reprices $10,000,000 of 90-day certificates of deposit at 10.625%.

October 13
Buys (long) December 10 CD futures contracts at 9.39%.

Cash Market		Futures Market	
Face Value of CDs	$10,000,000		$10,000,000
Discount rate	× 0.10625	Discount rate	× 0.0939
Annual discount	$ 1,062,500	Annual discount	$ 939,000
90 days	× 0.25	90 days	× 0.25
Actual discount	$ 265,625	Actual discount	$ 234,750
Value of CDs	$ 9,734,375	Value of contracts	$ 9,765,250
Interest expense September	$241,250	Short December	$ 9,771,000
Interest expense October	$265,625	Long December	−$ 9,765,250
Cost of increase	$ 24,375	Gain on hedge	$ 5,750

Discount paid without hedge	$ 265,625
Hedge gain	−$ 5,750
Effective discount paid (quarterly)	$ 259,875
Four quarters 360/90	× 4
Effective discount (annual)	$1,039,500
Effective discount rate with hedge	10.395%

deliverable the cash instrument to be hedged. Of course, this need not always be the case, since there are a limited number of actively traded futures contracts. When a contract is used to hedge a different underlying instrument—for example, using Eurodollar futures contracts to hedge bankers acceptances—the hedge is referred to as a cross-hedge. Because two related but not identical instruments will usually have different prices, cross-hedges are vulnerable to another type of basis risk, known as the cross-hedge basis.

Minimizing the cross-hedge basis requires a careful selection of the contract to be used for hedging purposes. A typical approach is to calculate correlation coefficients over a reasonable period of time, usually encompassing one full interest rate cycle. The data used in calculating the correlation coefficient may be either price or interest rate data, quoted in a consistent manner and compiled in a way that reflects the design of the intended hedge. For example, if the cash instrument is marked to market daily and the objective is to hedge daily variation in the cash position, then the correlation coefficients should be based on daily data. If the objective is to hedge weekly variability, however, then weekly data should be used.

With longer-maturity instruments, duration analysis may well be superior to correlation analysis as a method of identifying the appropriate futures contract. In particular, duration-analysis-based comparisons of the instruments to be hedged and of the instruments for which there exist futures contracts should uncover the appropriate contract to be used so as to minimize cross-hedge basis. Duration analysis is also useful in constructing hedges for instruments having a maturity unlike that of any available futures contract.[17]

Regardless of the technique used to minimize the influence of the cross-hedge basis, it is important to understand how such basis risk affects the outcome of a hedge. For illustrative purposes, consider a bank holding company that, when applying gap analysis to its portfolio, determines that it has a funding gap in the foreseeable future. This gap is equal to a $10 million commercial paper position. Moreover, management is concerned about rising interest rates. Consequently, it seeks to hedge. Unfortunately, there is no commercial paper futures contract. After examining the available contracts, it is concluded that the hedge with the greatest likelihood of success entails the use of Treasury bill futures contracts.

On June 19, the cash commercial paper rate is 7.84%, which is a spread over the cash Treasury bill rate of 89 basis points. The futures market appears to be in agreement with management, since the June 19 quote for March[18] delivery on Treasury bill futures is 7.62%, 67 basis points higher than the current cash market rate. On December 11, when the commercial paper is issued, interest rates have indeed risen, with the commercial paper rate at 10.24%. This increases the cost of funding $10 million of 90-day commercial paper by $60,000 (see Table 13.5).

Unwinding the futures position indicates that the hedge was only partially successful. Futures reflected the rise in rates going from the initial 7.62% to 8.58%. Note also that futures expected the rise in rates to continue, since while March futures were 8.58%, cash Treasury bills were 8.09%. The gain on the hedge was $24,000, which—although it reduced the discount paid on the commercial paper from 10.24% without a hedge to 9.28% with the hedge—was still not sufficient to compensate fully for the additional interest expense.

Table 13.5. Short—Cross-Hedge

Cash Market	Futures Market
June 19	*June 19*
Anticipate selling $10,000,000 of commerical paper during December. The cash CP rate on June 19 is 7.84%. The cash 90-day T-bill rate on June 19 is 6.95%. (The CP/T-bill spread is 89 basis points.) Expect interest rates to increase.	Sells (short) 10 March T-bill futures contracts at 7.62%.

Discount rate	$10,000,000	
	×	0.0762
Annual discount	$	762,000
90 days	×	0.25
Actual discount	$	190,500
Value of contracts	$ 9,809,500	

Cash Market	Futures Market
December 1	*December 11*
Sell $10,000,000 of 90-day commercial paper. The cash CP rate on December 11 is 10.24%. The cash 90-day T-bill rate on December 11 is 8.09%. (The CP/T-bill spread is 215 basis points).	Buys (long) 90-day 10 March T-bill futures contracts at 8.58%.

Cash		Futures	
Face Value of CDs	$10,000,000		$10,000,000
Discount rate	× 0.1024	Discount rate	× 0.0858
Annual discount	$ 1,024,000	Annual discount	$ 858,000
90 days	× 0.25	90 days	× 0.25
Actual discount	$ 256,000	Actual discount	$ 214,500
Value of CDs	$ 9,744,000	Value of contracts	$ 9,785,500
Interest expense June	$196,000	Short March	$ 9,809,500
Interest expense December	$256,000	Long March	− $ 9,785,500
Cost of increase	$ 60,000	Gain on hedge	$ 24,000

Discount paid without hedge	$ 256,000
Hedge gain	− $ 24,000
Effective discount paid (quarterly)	$ 232,000
Four quarters 360/90	× 4
Effective discount (annual)	$ 928,000
Effective discount rate with hedge	9.28%

An examination of the basis should corroborate the outcome of the hedge. The cash futures basis on June 19 was -22 basis points. This was the difference between the cash commercial paper price of 92.16 and the futures price of 92.38. On December 11, this basis had narrowed (i.e., become more negative), equaling -166 basis points, the difference between the cash price of 89.76 and the futures price of 91.42. Thus, the basis had narrowed by 144 basis points. As in the previous case, a narrowing of the basis implies an outcome to a short hedge that is less than completely satisfactory.

Disaggregating the components of the basis illustrates the effect of the cross-hedge basis. Had this been a hedge of Treasury bills, the basis would have been the difference between the cash and futures price of Treasury bills over the two periods. In June this basis was 67 basis points; the cash price was 93.05 and the futures price was 92.38. On December 11, the basis had narrowed to 49 basis points. The cash price was 91.91 and the futures price was 91.42. Thus, of the total narrowing of 144 basis points, 18 basis points are attributable to the temporal basis. Most of the change in the basis must be due to a change in the cross hedge basis. Consider that on June 19 the difference between the cash commercial paper and the cash Treasury bill rate was 89 basis points (i.e., the price difference was -89 basis points). By December 11 the rate spread had changed to a substantial 215 basis points (i.e., the difference was -215 basis points). Thus, between the two dates, the cross-hedge basis had narrowed by 126 points.

The results of the above example can be generalized. Typically, the cross-hedge basis is more volatile than the temporal basis. This suggests that hedges not subject to cross-hedge basis are likely to be more successful—all else being equal. Careful monitoring of the hedge can overcome the inherently greater volatility of the basis in a cross-hedge. And even without any monitoring, the futures position is likely to provide at least partial compensation for a cash market loss.

Thus, the way in which the basis influences the outcome of a hedge depends on the nature of the hedge. For a short hedge, an increasing or widening basis is advantageous, since it means that the difference between the cash and futures prices diminished after the position was established. The futures contracts were bought (i.e., closed out) at a relatively lower cost than they were sold, so that futures more then compensated for the cash loss. With a long hedge, the futures contracts are initially bought and then sold. Since the objective is to have futures sell for more than they cost, a long hedge will be more successful the more futures rise relative to cash, which is equivalent to the basis decreasing or narrowing. In summary, an unchanged basis ensures that the effective discount with hedge will equal the initial discount on futures. If the basis changes, the outcome of the hedge is affected. The results of a short hedge will be improved if the basis widens and the results of a long hedge will be improved if the basis narrows.

Futures contracts can be used not only as a tool in managing exposure to interest rate risk, but also to create new products. A key example of such a product is a fixed-rate loan. Although fixed-rate loans were a fixture of bank product lines, as was noted earlier, when interest rates became more volatile in the 1970s and early 1980s banks and thrifts became reluctant to extend credit for prolonged periods at a fixed rate. As a consequence, many borrowers turned to other sources of credit since their own plans depended on obtaining credit at a fixed rate for longer periods than banks were willing to provide or at lower interest rates than banks were willing to offer for fixed-rate loans.

Futures contracts can be incorporated into lending programs in a way that enables a lender to satisfy an objective of minimizing exposure to interest rate risk while providing a borrower with a desirable product. An example demonstrates how futures can be used in the construction of a fixed-rate loan. In this case, a bank intends to make a one-year, $1 million loan. There are several ways in which this may be done. The bank may make a variable-rate loan which will be repriced quarterly at the then-prevailing prime rate. This would ensure the bank a reasonable return since the loan could be funded with 91-day CD's. Alternatively, the bank may issue a one-year CD and use the proceeds to fund a one-year, fixed-rate loan. Or the bank may make a one-year, fixed-rate loan funded with 91-day CDs. In the last alternative, the cost of funds may be left unhedged or hedged with financial futures.

The assumptions concerning rates in this example are simple, but they serve to underscore the effectiveness of applying futures in the construction of new products. Following the listing of hypothetical rates in Table 13.6 is the outcome of the first alternative, a variable-rate loan funded with 91-day CDs. The bank is able to retain a 200-basis-point spread over the one-year life of the loan—even with volatile interest rates. This spread equates to a $20,000 profit. The example also underscores why many borrowers have been hesitant to accept the terms of variable-rate loans. They are absorbing the interest rate risk exposure of the transaction, which in this case meant that an interest expense of $30,000 (at 12%) in the first quarter rose to $45,000 (18%) by the final quarter.

In the second alternative the bank offers a one-year, fixed-rate loan which is funded with a one-year CD, and the loan is priced at a 200-basis-point spread over the cost of funding. This alternative provides the bank with a $20,000 profit and the borrower with a fixed-rate loan at a lower rate (14%) than the average (15%) charged with the variable-rate alternative. Thus, it is a more desirable loan arrangement. Moreover, the bank's gap is unaffected by this transaction, since the assets and liabilities are paired off. In a volatile interest rate environment, however, one-year funding might not be as readily available as shorter-term funding. That is, short-term financing may either be more available or be available at more attractive spreads over long-term financing than is assumed in this case. Moreover, although this example demonstrates the different methods of structuring a one-year loan, the same principles are applicable for longer-term loans, except that for longer-term loans the differences in the availability and the cost of long-versus short-term funding are likely to be greater.

Suppose that a bank elects to rely on short-term funding, in this case 91-day CDs, and grants a one-year fixed-rate loan initially funded with such CDs. As a result, it is exposed to interest rate risk, since it will have to roll over the CD at prevailing rates in the future. Since management expects interest rates to rise, it offers the one-year loan at 14% in contrast to the 12% charged on shorter-term loans. Management is indeed correct and interest rates rise, unfortunately more rapidly and higher than anticipated. As a consequence, the spread on the loan rapidly deteriorates, falling to zero in the third quarter and resulting in a $5,000 loss in the fourth quarter. This example graphically illustrates why lenders have been reluctant to make long-term, fixed-rate loans funded by short-term instruments.

As an alternative, bank management could have relied on short-term financing for a longer-term loan by offsetting its interest rate exposure in the futures market. Two variants of such a hedge are described in Table 13.6, cases i and ii. In the first of these cases it is assumed that, contrary to management expectations, the futures markets anticipate stable interest rates and are currently at an 8% yield, the prevailing yield in the T-bill market.[19] This constant yield in futures provides an offset against rising rates in the cash market, however, resulting in a constant effective CD rate of 10%. This is a lower cost of funds than in the unhedged case. In fact, at this hedged cost of funds bank management could have met its objective of a 200-basis-point spread over costs and offered a one-year loan at the same cost at which competitors were offering a 91-day loan. Alternatively, bank management could have increased its spread and still offered a loan priced below the competition.

In actuality, however, cash market interest rates rose steadily over the period. In case ii, a more realistic one, the yield on futures also rises steadily but lags the increase in cash market rates. A hedge under such conditions still results in an improvement over an unhedged position. In this particular case, the average cost of funds over the period was 11.5%, lower than the 12.5% for the unhedged case. Thus, the bank by implementing a hedge had an additional 100 basis points to use to earn a higher spread and/or to price its loan more attractively than its competitors.

The results of these examples would not have been nearly as appealing if the CD/T-bill rate spread had widened. That is, if the cost of funding had risen more rapidly than the futures position had increased, the futures position would have failed to compensate fully for the increased cost associated with the cash position. This would be equivalent to the example of a short hedge in which the price basis narrowed (Table 13.3).

Ensuring the success of such products depends on careful management

Table 13.6. Hedging Bank Term Loans

Objective

Bank plans to make one-year term loan for $1 million.

Alternatives

1. Variable-rate loan with rate fixed at current prime rate at beginning of each quarter, funded with 91-day CDs.
2. One-year, fixed-rate loan, funded with one-year, fixed-rate CD.

Assume that the interest rates at the beginning of each quarter are as follows:

	January 1	March 1	June 1	September 1
Prime rate	12%	14%	16%	18%
CD rate	10%	12%	14%	16%
T-bill rate	8%	10%	12%	14%

Alternatives

1. Variable-rate loan, rate fixed at prime, funded with 91-day CDs.

	Q1	Q2	Q3	Q4
Loan receipts	$30,000 (12%)	$35,000 (14%)	$40,000 (16%)	$45,000 (18%)
CD costs	25,000 (10%)	30,000 (12%)	35,000 (14%)	40,000 (16%)
Profit	$ 5,000	$ 5,000	$ 5,000	$ 5,000

2. One-year, fixed-rate loan, funded with one-year, fixed-rate CD.
    Assumptions: 1.   One-year CD rate is 12%.
                   2.   Bank plans to make 200 basis points.

	Q1	Q2	Q3	Q4
Loan receipts	$35,000 (14%)	$35,000 (14%)	$35,000 (14%)	$35,000 (14%)
CD costs	30,000 (12%)	30,000 (12%)	30,000 (12%)	30,000 (12%)
Profit	$ 5,000	$ 5,000	$ 5,000	$ 5,000

3a. One-year, fixed-rate loan, funded with 91-day CDs—unhedged.

Assumption: Because bank anticipates increasing interest rates, it makes one-year term loan at 14% (versus 12% available bank rate for shorter-term loan).

	Q1	Q2	Q3	Q4
Loan receipts	$35,000 (14%)	$35,000 (14%)	$35,000 (14%)	$35,000 (14%)
CD costs	25,000 (10%)	30,000 (12%)	35,000 (14%)	40,000 (16%)
Profits	+ $10,000	+ $ 5,000	$0	− $ 5,000

3b. Hedging the transaction described in (3a).

Case i: Assume futures markets expect stable interest rates— January 1 T-bill rate is 8%.

		January Q1	March Q2	June Q3	September Q4
1.	T-bill futures	(8%)	8%	8%	8%
2.	Actual T-bill rate	8%	10%	12%	14%
3.	Profit (or loss) on futures	—	2%	4%	6%
4.	Actual CD rate	10%	12%	14%	16%
5.	Effective CD rate (4 − 3)	10%	10%	10%	10%

Case ii: Futures markets expect a rate rise, but less than what actually occurs. T-bill rates of 13%, 14% and 15% for March, June, and September respectively.

		January Q1	March Q2	June Q3	September Q4
1.	T-bill futures	8%	9%	10%	11%
2.	Actual T-bill rate	8%	10%	12%	14%

Table 13.6. *(Continued)*

		January Q1	March Q2	June Q3	September Q4
3.	Profit (or loss) on futures	—	1%	2%	3%
4.	Actual CD rate	10%	12%	14%	16%
5.	Effective CD rate (4 − 3)	10%	11%	12%	13%
					Average 11.5%

of the hedge and close monitoring of the basis. This section has demonstrated that hedging with futures can provide management with a successful way to managing interest rate risk. Moreover, futures when used in combination with cash instruments can provide products that are likely to be appealing to customers.

Futures as an Investment Alternative. The success of futures as a hedging instrument results from their close relationship to the underlying cash instrument. In effect, futures act as a surrogate for the cash instrument, enabling a banker to manage the risk inherent in a cash position by implementing an offset in futures. It follows that futures can also be used as a surrogate for cash for investment purposes.

Table 13.7 demonstrates how a futures position can be used profitably in lieu of a cash instrument to earn a higher yield. In this case the yield available on September 26, 1980, for a one-year U.S. Treasury bill was 11.35%. An alternative Treasury bill investment was to buy a three-month Treasury bill and then a strip of futures (i.e., the December 1980, March 1981, and June 1981 futures contracts). This latter combination of cash and futures positions would also have resulted in a one-year investment. As the example illustrates, this latter alternative would have provided a higher yield of 11.73%, or a 38-basis-point advantage over the one-year bill investment. Although commissions and margin may reduce somewhat the attractiveness of the futures-related alternative, this example demonstrates the usefulness of considering futures as an alternative to cash in applications other than hedging.

Options on Futures and Options on Debt Instruments. Another potentially useful risk management tool is options. Exchange-traded equity options

Table 13.7. Strip of Futures (prices as of September 26, 1980)

	Discount Yield
9/17/81 T-bill	11.35%
12/18/80 T-bill	10.80%
December 1980 T-bill futures (3/19/81 T-bill)	11.86%
March 1981 T-bill futures (6/18/81 T-bill)	12.07%
June 1981 T-bill futures (9/17/81 T-bill)	12.11%

Alternatives

1. Buy 9/17/81 T-bill—356-day investment.
2. Buy 12/18/80 T-bill and December 1980, March 1981, and June 1981 T-bill Futures Contracts.

Return on Alternative Investments

	Discount Yield		
1. Buy 9/17/1981 T-bill and hold to maturity.	11.35%		
		Price	Discount
2. a. Buy 12/18/1980 T-bill @ 10.80%		$975,000	$ 24,900
b. Buy December 1980 T-bill futures @ 11.86%		$970,021	$ 29,979
c. Buy March 1981 T-bill futures @ 12.07%		$969,490	$ 30,510
d. Buy June 1981 T-bill futures @ 12.11%		$969,389	$ 30,611
TOTAL			$116,000

Summary	Discount
(1)	11.35%
(2)	11.73%

NOTE: Commissions and margins are ignored in this example.

have been used successfully as a hedge against price risk in equity portfolios by both institutional and individual investors since their inception in 1973. Exchange-traded nonequity options based on both cash instruments and futures were introduced in 1982.

The introduction of nonequity options was delayed by a rather interesting and involved regulatory jurisdictional issue. From their inception, the regulation of equity options has been the responsibility of the Securities and Exchange Commission (SEC). The regulation of futures contracts was consolidated into one agency upon the formation of the Commodity Futures Trading Commission (CFTC) in 1975. With exchanges proposing options on cash instruments (i.e., debt options) and options on futures contracts (i.e., futures options), the issue of jurisdiction arose. What could have become a difficult issue was resolved by the chairmen of the SEC and CFTC with the issuance of the Johnson (chairman of the CFTC) Shad (chairman of the SEC) Agreement. Responsibility for the regulation of options on futures went to the CFTC and for the regulation of options on cash to the SEC[20]. This agreement opened the way for both CFTC- and SEC-regulated exchanges to propose a number of different options contracts.[21]

Options come in two varieties: puts and calls. A put is an agreement whereby the buyer of the put has the right (but not the obligation) to deliver a designated security to the seller (or writer) at a predetermined price called the exercise, or strike, price. A call is an agreement whereby the buyer has the right (but not the obligation) to require the seller, or writer, to deliver to the buyer a specified security at a predetermined price. For both types of options the seller receives a payment known as a premium.

Strategies vary, depending on whether puts or calls are being written. For institutional equity investors the most popular strategy appears to be *covered call* writing. In this strategy the investor has a portfolio in the underlying instrument, which could presumably be called away if the call options were exercised. The objective behind call writing is to provide protection against price declines, at least to the extent of the premiums.

The cost of reducing risk exposure by writing an option is the constraint it imposes on potential return. For example, if the price of a bond were to rise above the call price, the buyer of the call would be motivated to exercise the option, acquiring the bond at a lower-than-market price. As a result, the writer of the call would not realize the full extent of the price appreciation on the bond.

The potential impact that covered call writing can have on gains and losses associated with an investment is illustrated by an example. Suppose a three-month call was sold on a $100,000 Treasury bond and the market price of the bond was par. Also assume that the call premium had a value of 5 points and an exercise price of par. These characteristics of the call option and the underlying deliverable bond would lead to the following schedule of outcomes.

Bond Price at Expiration	P&L on Unhedged Bond	P&L on Hedged Position
125	25	5
120	20	5
115	15	5
110	10	5

Bond Price at Expiration	P&L on Unhedged Bond	P&L on Hedged Position
105	5	5
100	1	5
95	−5	0
90	−10	−5
85	−15	−10
80	−20	−15
75	−25	−20

These results when graphed illustrate the risk-return trade-offs of the strategy (see Figure 13.5). The straight line represents the profit and loss associated with the unhedged bank position while the dotted line illustrates the outcome when hedged. In order to gain a $5,000 cushion on the downside in this particular case, the investor gives up any gain above $105,000 in the price of the bond.

Another way of viewing options is in the context of a contingent asset or liability issuance by a bank. In a not-uncommon bank situation, a borrower (and in some cases a depositor) may have a contingent arrangement with a bank. For example, consider mortgage banking activities where a bank agrees to accept a portfolio of mortgages by a certain time at a predetermined price. If the agreed-upon price becomes relatively unattractive because market prices go up, the mortgage packager is likely to walk away from the deal (assuming it is legally possible). If market prices fall, however, the bank will have to accept the loans and pay a higher-than-market price. In such a case, the bank has in effect written an over-the-counter put. In order to hedge a contingent transaction, the bank should consider exchange options as an offset. In this particular case, the bank could buy a put. For the cost of the premium, the bank can offset the deterioration in the value of the contingent claim resulting from a rise in rates.

Exchange-traded nonequity options are currently in their developmental stage. The prognosis is bright given the number of potential applications, many of which are relevent to banking. This is an instrument that will merit increasing attention from anyone involved in the task of managing interest rate risk exposure.

SUMMARY AND CONCLUSION

The proliferation of new instruments generated by the recent behavior of interest rates has reflected efforts to avoid undesired interest rate risk. Of these, gap management has probably received the most attention. As

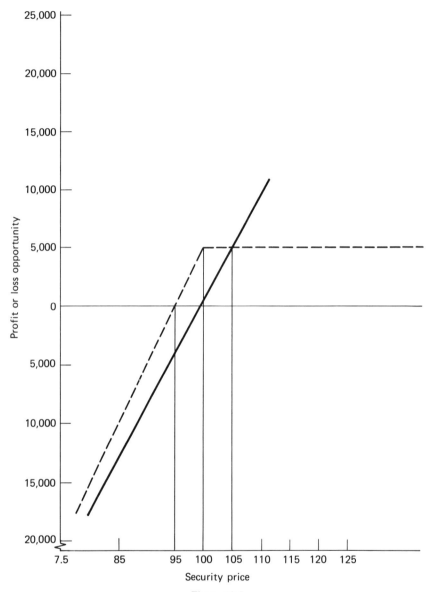

Figure 13.5.

this chapter has indicated, there are a number of methods for managing a gap, all of which are directed at the same objective: measuring a bank's exposure to interest rate risk.

As managers became more aware of interest rate risk issues and the problems associated with managing such risks, they naturally sought new tools to assist them. Financial futures have developed rapidly, providing banks and other investors with an instrument to facilitate hedging and other applications which require a surrogate for a cash position. Futures do not completely eradicate risk. Rather, they enable the user to substitute for interest rate risk the generally more manageable basis risk inherent in futures.

The next step in the progression of new risk management tools is options. Such instruments have been offered on an off-exchange basis for some time. In addition, equity options have been exchange traded since the early 1970s. Recently, however, exchanges have begun to offer options based on securities and on futures contracts. These instruments add another dimension to a manager's capacity to deal with interest rate risk.

This chapter has demonstrated how new strategies and new investment instruments can be used to manage interest rate risk. These instruments and procedures have rapidly become an established part of available techniques, and the use of these techniques is likely to grow.

REFERENCES

Asay, Michael, Gonzalez, Gisela A., and Wolkowitz, Benjamin. "Hedging a Bank Portfolio with Financial Futures." *Journal of Futures Markets,* Winter 1981, pp. 607–618.

Bierwag, Gerald, Kaufman, George, Schweitzer, Robert, and Toevs, Alden. "The Art of Risk Management in Bank Portfolios." *Journal of Portfolio Management*, Spring 1981, pp. 27–36.

Binder, Barrett F., "Asset/Liability Management. Part 1: Establishing a Function and Developing a Near Term Profit Plan; Part 2: Management and Control of Rate Sensitivity; Part 3: Funding and Capital Management." *The Magazine of Bank Administration*, November 1980, pp. 42–48, December 1980, pp. 31–35, January 1981, pp. 42–50.

NOTES

1. In October 1979 the Federal Reserve announced it would increase the emphasis on achieving targets for money growth, at the same time reducing the role of interest rate levels as policy objectives.

2. Mathematically the elasticity measure is $(d\mathrm{PV}/\mathrm{PV})/(dr/r)$ where PV = present value and r = interest rates. Duration can be expressed as $(d\mathrm{PV}/\mathrm{PV})/dr/(r + 1)$. The difference,

$r + 1$ rather than r in the denominator of the duration equation, is a quirk of the mathematical derivation and not a substantive difference. Modified duration, a variant on the traditional or Macauley (the developer of the duration measure) duration, is expressed as $(d\text{PV}/\text{PV})/dr$. All three expressions are measuring the identical effect and produce substantially the same results (see Bierwag et al., 1981).

3. Although Equation 13.2 may not resemble the elasticity of present value with respect to a change in interest, it is equivalent. The version in Equation 13.2 is used because it facilitates a comparison with Equation 13.1.

4. While valuation losses were not explicitly recognized under bank accounting procedures, they were certainly not ignored by bank management, analysts, or regulators.

5. The bankers' acceptance market predates CDs, but BAs as an active liability tool developed significantly only in the 1970s.

6. Forward agreements are less formal than futures in that the two parties involved agree to the future delivery of a specified commodity on a particular date, the specifics are negotiated by the two parties to the transaction, and the resulting agreement is not exchange traded or easily transferable. Thus, unlike futures contracts, forward commitments are not standardized, and since they are not exchange traded each party to a forward is subject to the credit risk of the counterparty.

7. In particular, each commodity exchange has a clearing corporation as an affiliated entity. After a trade is executed, the clearing corporation guarantees the viability of the contract. If a party to a contract fails, the clearing corporation honors the commitment. As a result, the identity of a counterparty to a trade is of no importance since the clearing corporation is in effect the counterparty to every trade.

8. Very few contracts result in an actual delivery; generally 5% or fewer of financial futures are delivered.

9. There are several exceptions to this statement, perhaps the most important being that any futures contract can be shorted, that is, sold for future delivery, but only a few cash instruments can be shorted.

10. In 1980, the Office of the Comptroller of the Currency, the Federal Reserve Board, and the Federal Deposit Insurance Corporation issued guidelines concerning the use of financial futures by bankers (a copy is contained in the appendix). The objective of these guidelines was to restrict bank use of futures to risk-reducing applications with the emphasis on the overall management of an institution's interest rate risk exposure. The guidelines also required that futures be marked to the market daily, which is inconsistent with generally accepted bank accounting practices for investments. As a result, the accounting industry has focused on the appropriate method for accounting for futures, and it is unlikely that current practices will remain unchanged. (For a discussion of the implications of the regulatory guidelines for bank income statements, see Asay, 1981.)

11. As noted in the section on managing interest rate risk, the repricing method of calculating the gap may not be the most accurate, but it is a commonly used effective management technique. Moreover, it is useful for heuristic purposes to assume a repricing gap is at issue.

12. This type of hedge belongs to a broad classification known as anticipatory hedges. Regulators have generally frowned on such hedges because in practice they have often been used to justify speculative positions. That is, one could claim to be hedging an anticipated action that in fact never occurs. Moreover, prior to the regulatory guidelines mentioned above there was motivation to claim that futures positions were really an-

ticipatory hedges, since such hedges enjoyed more favorable accounting treatment than speculative positions. The regulatory guidelines ended linking accounting treatment to the purpose of the application, thus ending the accounting motivation behind anticipatory hedges. Moreover, regulators became more attuned to the context in which futures were being used. Since the following examples are all in the context of overall gap management they would likely receive regulatory acceptance even though they are anticipatory by design.

13. This ignores commissions and margins, which are described below.

14. This is highly unlikely since futures generally go to delivery only quarterly, March, June, September, and December, and then only for certain days during those months.

15. To be precise, expectations of rising rates are reflected in a yield curve that not only is positively sloped but also has a slope that is increasing at an increasing rate.

16. Liquidity considerations impart an upward bias to the slope of the yield curve so that the slope cannot be entirely explained by expectations. In particular, longer-term securities have greater market risk and consequently are less liquid than short-term securities. Investors therefore demand higher returns the longer the maturity as compensation for the additional risk.

17. In particular, duration analysis can be used to determine the appropriate combination of long- and short-term futures contracts (e.g., Treasury bond and bill futures) to approximate (and thereby provide a hedge for) an intermediate-term Treasury note.

18. The March rather than December contract might be used because it would be expected to approximate more closely the cash commercial paper rate in December. If rates are expected to continue to rise, then in December the March futures rate will exceed the cash market Treasury bill rate. Since commercial paper is always quoted at a higher rate than Treasury bills, the March rather than December contract might be quoted at a rate that is closer to the December cash commercial paper rate.

19. A cross-hedge of CDs with T-bill futures under most circumstances is no longer needed since there exists a CD futures contract. The T-bill contract continues to be the more liquid contract, however. For heuristic purposes the choice of contracts is not particularly important.

APPENDIX 1: FINANCIAL FUTURES CONTRACT SPECIFICATIONS

Contract: *Domestic Certificate of Deposit Futures*
Exchange: *International Monetary Market (IMM)*

Summary Trading Details

Contract Size:	A domestic certificate of deposit in the amount of $1,000,000.
Contract Months:	March, June, September, December.
Last Trading Day:	The business day immediately preceding the last delivery day of the contract month.
Trading Hours:	7:30 A.M. to 2:00 P.M.–Chicago time (7:30 A.M. to 11:00 A.M. on last trading day).
Telerate Pages:	Price: 910 Volume/open Interest: 2188
Ticker Symbol:	DC + month code.

Margin Requirements (Exchange Minimums)

	Initial	Maintenance
Speculative/spot and nonspot months	$1,500	$1,200
Hedging/spot and nonspot months	$1,500	$1,200

Spreading

Intramarket spreads	$ 500	$ 300
Intermarket spreads versus 13 week T-bill	$ 500	$ 400
Intermarket spreads versus Eurodollar deposits	$ 500	$ 400

Pricing Details

Quotation:	In terms of the IMM index 100.00 minus the yield on an annual basis for a 360-day year (9.3% rate equals 90.70).
Min. Fluctuation:	One basis point (0.01) equal to $25.00 per contract.
Daily Range:	Normally 80 basis points ($2,000) per contract above and below the previous day's settlement price. There is no limit for trading in the spot month.

Whenever on two successive days any contract month closes at the normal daily limit in the same direction (not necessarily the same contract month on both days) an expanded daily limit schedule shall go into effect as follows:

(1) The third day's daily limit in all contract months shall be 150% of the normal daily limit.
(2) If any contract month closes at its expanded daily limit on the third day in the same direction, then the fourth day's expanded daily limit and each successive day thereafter shall be 200% of the normal daily limits, so long as any contract month closes at its expanded daily limit.
(3) The normal daily limit is reinstated the day following the failure of any one contract month to close at its expanded limit in the same direction.

Volume/Liquidity Information

Trading Volume:	1.56 million contracts in 1982.
Liquidity Assessment:	Good.
Comment:	Per FIA statistics the IMM's domestic CD contact was the twenty-first most actively traded futures contract in 1982, up from thirty-third most active in 1981. Among financial futures it was the eleventh most active contract in 1982.

Delivery Specifications

1. Timing

Delivery Months: March, June, September, December.

Delivery Dates: Any business day that is not a bank holiday in New York or Chicago beginning the fifteenth day of the contract month and ending the last business day of the contract month at the seller's option.

Notice Date of

Intention to Deliver: By 2:00 P.M. (Chicago time) one business day prior to delivery.

2. Deliverable Grade

Banks whose domestic certificates of deposit which will be accepted as deliverable grade will be listed by the IMM on the second business day preceding the fifteenth calendar day of each delivery month. Any domestic certificate of deposit of a bank included on the IMM's list and meeting the following conditions shall constitute a deliverable CD.

1. Having a fixed maturity value no less than $1,000,000 and not greater than $1,200,000.

2. Having no interest payments between the delivery date and maturity date.

3. Maturing not before the sixteenth of the month three months after the spot month nor after the last day of the month three months after the spot month.

4. Maturing on a business day that is not a banking holiday in either New York or Chicago.

5. Having no more than 185 days' accrued interest payable at maturity.

3. Settlement

The following formula is used to calculate the net invoice pricing for deliverable grade CDs as defined above:

$$\text{Dollar Value} = \text{maturity* value} \left[1 + (\text{yield**}) \frac{(\text{days to maturity})}{360} \right]$$

* Maturity value:
  a. for discount CDs equal to principal value.
  b. for add-on CDs equal to principal value plus interest payable at maturity.

** Yield: defined as the difference between 100.00 and the IMM index at settlement (expressed in decimals) on the day before delivery day.

4. Delivery Method

Delivery shall be made to a New York City bank registered with the exchange and a member of the Federal Reserve System, specified by the buyer's clearing member. All banks selected by the buyer and by the seller to effect delivery must be members of the Federal Reserve System.

The steps for physical delivery are as follows:

1. For each delivery day the clearing house instructs Irving Trust Co., New York (the agent), to receive and deliver CDs and to transact payment.

2. The seller through his bank shall deliver CDs to the agent for the account of IMM by 1:00 P.M. (New York time) on the delivery day.

3. The agent will authorize payment by wire transfer of federal funds to the seller's designated account, at the time certificates are received.

4. The agent will deliver CDs to the buyer's bank on a priority basis and not later than 2:15 P.M. on the delivery day.

5. The buyer's bank shall make payment by wire transfer of federal funds, per agent instructions, by the close of business on the delivery day.

445

Contract:	*Eurodollar Time Deposit*
Exchange:	*International Monetary Market (IMM)*

Summary Trading Details

Contract Size:	A Eurodollar time deposit having a principal value of $1,000,000.
Contract Months:	March, June, September, December.
Last Trading Day:	Trading ends at 3:30 P.M. (London time) on the second London bank business day immediately preceding the third Wednesday of the contract month.
Trading Hours:	7:30 A.M. to 2:00 P.M. Chicago time (7:30 A.M. to 9:30 A.M. last day of trading).
Telerate Pages:	Price: 910
	Volume/Open Interest: 2,188
Ticker Symbol:	ED + month code.

Margin Requirements (Exchange Minimums)

	Initial	Maintenance
Speculative/spot and nonspot months	$1,500	$1,200
Hedging/spot and nonspot months	$1,500	$1,200
Spreading		
Intramarket spreads	$ 500	$ 300
Intermarket spreads versus 13-week T-bill	$ 500	$ 400
Intermarket spreads versus certificates of deposit	$ 500	$ 400

Pricing Details

Quotation:	In terms of the IMM index 100.00 minus the yield on an annual basis for a 360-day year (a deposit rate of 8.23% equals 91.77).
Min. Fluctuation:	One basis point (0.01) equal to $25.00 per contract.
Daily Range:	Normally 100 basis points ($2,500) per contract above and below the previous day's settlement price. There is no limit for trading in the spot month.

Whenever on two successive days any contract month closes at the normal daily limit in the same direction (not necessarily the same contract month on both days) an expanded daily limit schedule shall go into effect as follows:
(1) The third day's daily limit in all contract months shall be 150% of the normal daily limit.
(2) If any contract month closes at its expanded daily limit on the third day in the same direction, then the fourth day's expanded daily limit and each successive day thereafter shall be 200% of the normal daily limits, so long as any contract month closes at its expanded daily limit.
(3) The normal daily limit is reinstated the day following the failure of any one contract month to close at its expanded limit in the same direction.

Volume/Liquidity Information

Trading Volume:	324,000 contracts in 1982.
Liquidity Assessment:	Fair to good.
Comment:	Per FIA statistics the IMM's Eurodollar time deposit futures contract was the forty-first most active futures contract traded in 1982 and the twenty-second most active financial contract traded. First quarter 1983 statistics indicate substantially expanded trading volumes over the same period in 1982. Currently at the IMM the Eurodollar contract is the third most actively traded interest rate futures contract.

Delivery Specifications

Special Note on Delivery against the Eurodollar Time Deposit Futures Contract

Delivery under the Eurodollar futures contract is by cash settlement only. Since nothing is actually received or delivered except a cash payment, many of the standard delivery conventions associated with other contracts do not apply.

1. *Timing*

   Delivery Months: March, June, September, December.
   Delivery Dates: Delivery takes place on the last day of trading in the contract month for all parties holding open positions at the close of trading.

2. *Settlement*

   On the last day of trading the clearing house shall determine the London Interbank Offered Rate (LIBOR) for three-month Eurodollar time deposit funds both at the time of termination of trading and at a randomly selected time within the last 90 minutes of trading. The final settlement price shall be 100 minus the arithmetic mean rounded to the nearest 1/100th of a percentage point of the LIBOR at these two times.

3. *"Delivery" Method*

   Clearing members holding open positions in Eurodollar time deposit futures contracts at the time of termination of trading in that contract shall make payment to or receive payment from the clearing house in accordance with normal variation margin procedure based on a settlement price equal to the final settlement price.

Contract: *13-Week Treasury Bill Futures*
Exchange: *International Monetary Market (IMM)*

Summary Trading Details

Contract Size: U.S. Treasury bills with $1,000,000 face value at maturity.

Contract Months: March, June, September, December.

Last Trading Day: The business day immediately preceding the first delivery day.

Trading Hours: 8:00 A.M. to 2:00 P.M.—Chicago time (8:00 A.M. to 10:00 A.M. last trading day).

Telerate Price: 910, 911
Pages: Volume/open interest 2,188

Ticker Symbol: TB + month code.

Margin Requirements (Exchange Minimums)

	Initial	Maintenance
Speculative/spot and nonspot months	$1,500	$1,200
Hedging/spot and nonspot months	$1,500	$1,200
Spreading		
Intramarket spreads	$ 500	$ 300
Intermarket spreads versus Eurodollar dep	$ 500	$ 400
Intermarket spreads versus certificates of deposit	$ 500	$ 400

Pricing Details

Quotation: In terms of the IMM index as 100.00 less T-bill yield or annualized discount rate (price of a bill yield of 6.75 = 93.25).

Min. Fluctuation: One basis point (.01) equal to $25.00 per contract.

Daily Range: Normally 60 basis points ($1,500) per contract above and below the previous day's settlement price. There is no limit on the last day of trading of a contract months.

Whenever on two successive days any contract month closes at the normal daily limit in the same direction (not necessarily the same contract month on both days) an expanded daily limit schedule shall go into effect as follows:

(1) The third day's daily limit in all contract months shall be 150% of the normal daily limit.

(2) If any contract month closes at its expanded daily limit on the third day in the same direction, then the fourth day's expanded daily limit and each successive day thereafter shall be 200% of the normal daily limits, so long as any contract month closes at its expanded daily limit.

(3) The normal daily limit is reinstated the day following the failure of any one contract month to close at its expanded limit in the same direction.

Volume/Liquidity Information

Trading Volume: 6.60 million contracts in 1982.

Liquidity Assessment: Excellent.

Comment: FIA statistics show that the IMM's 13-week T-bill contract was the fifth most active futures contract traded in both 1982 and 1981. Among financial future contracts traded it ranked third behind T-bonds (CBOT) and gold (COMEX).

Delivery Specifications

Timing

Delivery Months: March, June, September, December.

Delivery Dates: Beginning with the June 1983 contract, delivery shall be made on three successive business days. The first delivery day shall be the first day of the spot month on which a 13-week Treasury bill is issued and a one-year Treasury bill has 13 weeks remaining to maturity.

Notice of Intention to Delivery: Seller's delivery commitments are delivered to the exchange clearing house by 12:00 noon (Chicago time) on the last day of trading.

Deliverable Grade

At the seller's option U.S. Treasury bills maturing in 90, 91, or 92 days from the first delivery date may be delivered to satisfy his obligation. All bills delivered against a contract must bear uniform maturity dates.

Settlement

Payment is made on the basis of par value ($1,000,000) minus yield, as determined by the settlement price of the futures contract at the close of the last trading date, discounted from the final settlement date to maturity date on a 360-day year. Since U.S. Treasury bills with three different maturities are acceptable as deliverable grade a generalized formula may be used to calculate the value of the delivery amount:

$$\text{Dollar value} = \$1,000,000 - \frac{(\text{days to maturity} \times \text{T-bill discount} \times 1,000,000)}{360 \text{ days}}$$

$$\text{where T-bill discount} = (100.00 - \text{IMM index settlement price}) \times .01$$

Delivery Method

Delivery shall be made to a Chicago or New York bank registered with the exchange and a member of the Federal Reserve System as specified by the buyer's clearing member. All banks selected by buyer or seller to effect delivery must be members of the Federal Reserve System.

On delivery date seller delivers through his clearing member and the appropriate bank U.S. Treasury bills with face value at maturity of $1,000,000 for each contract. On delivery date the clearing member representing the buyer arranges a wire transfer of Federal funds for the net invoice price to the selling clearing member's bank upon receipt of the delivered bills.

Contract: *U.S. Treasury Bond Futures*
Exchange: *Chicago Board of Trade (CBOT)*

Summary Trading Details

Contract Size:	U.S. Treasury bonds with $100,000 face value at maturity.
Contract Months:	March, June, September, December.
Last Trading Day:	The business day prior to the last seven business days of the expiring contract month.
Trading Hours:	8:00 A.M. to 2:00 P.M. Chicago time (8:00 A.M. to 12:00 noon on the last day of trading)
Telerate Page:	Price: 912
	Volume/open interest: 2,178
Ticker Symbol:	US + month code.

Margin Requirements (Exchange Minimums)

	Initial	Maintenance
Speculative/spot and nonspot months	$1,500	$1,200
Hedging/spot and nonspot months	$1,200	$1,200

Spreading

Intramarket spreads 12 months or more apart	$ 200	$ 200
Intermarket spreads versus GNMA (CDR or CD)	$1,000	$1,000
Intermarket spreads versus Treasury notes	$1,000	$1,000

Margin requirements generally increase by a factor of 50% when expanded trading limits are in effect.

Pricing Details

Quotation:	As a percentage of par in 1/32's of a point, e.g., 75.06 equals 75 6/32.
Min. Fluctuation:	1/32 of a point equal to $31.25 per contract.
Daily Range:	The daily price limit is normally 64/32 ($2,000) per contract above and below the previous day's settlement price. There is no limit for trading in the current month (the ''spot'' month) after the 1st notice day for the contract.

If three or more contracts within a contract year (or all contracts in a contract year if there are less than three open contracts) close at limit up or down for one business day, then the limit would be raised to 150% of the normal limit for all contract months and remain there for three successive business days. These expanded limits will remain in place for successive three-day intervals as long as three contract months (or less as defined) continue to close at their expanded limits during each day the expanded limits are in effect.

Volume/Liquidity Information

Trading volume:	16.74 million contracts in 1982.
Liquidity Assessment:	Excellent.
Comment:	According to FIA statistics the CBOT's U.S. Treasury bond futures contract had the highest volume of trading of any futures contract of any type (agricultural, financial, precious metals, etc.) in both 1982 and 1981.

Delivery Specifications

1. *Timing*

   Delivery Months: March, June, September, December.
   Delivery Dates: Any business day during the delivery month at the option of the seller.
   Notice Date of Intention to Deliver: Notice of intention to deliver shall be given to the Board of Trade Clearing Corporation by 8:00 P.M. (Chicago time) on the second business day preceding delivery. If delivery is to be made on the last business day of the month, notice should be received by the clearing corporation by 2:00 P.M. (Chicago time) on the business day preceding delivery day.

2. *Deliverable Grade*

   U.S. Treasury bonds with a maturity or call date of at least 15 years from date of delivery. All bonds delivered against a contract must be of the same issue.

3. *Settlement*

   Settlement is based on delivery of U.S. Treasury bonds with a face value at maturity of $100,000, a coupon rate of 8%, and a maturity of 20 years. Deliverable grades differing from these specifications must be adjusted for the actual coupon and the time to maturity or call. This adjustment is made by obtaining the issue's conversion factor with bond tables prepared by the Financial Publishing Co. of Boston, Mass. To determine the amount to be invoiced by the seller to the buyer, multiply the futures settlement price (in decimals) times the contract size ($100,000) times the deliverable issue's conversion factor. To this figure one must add the accrued interest on the bond at the time of the delivery to arrive at the total invoice amount. The seller will deliver a $100,000 face amount (maturity value) of the deliverable grade bond to the buyer.

   The time to maturity for the above calculation is computed on complete three month increments from the first day of the delivery month.

4. *Delivery Method*

   Seller will notify his bank to transfer contract grade U.S. Treasury bonds by Federal Reserve book-entry wire transfer system to the buyer's account on a delivery versus payment basis (payment not made until bonds are delivered). Payment is then made in Federal funds to the seller's bank for his account.

448

Contract: *10-Year U.S. Treasury Note Futures*
Exchange: *Chicago Board of Trade (CBOT)*

Summary Trading Details

Contract Size:	U.S. Treasury notes with $100,000 face value at maturity.
Contract Months:	March, June, September, December.
Last Trading Day:	The business day prior to the last seven business days of the expiring contract month.
Trading Hours:	8:00 A.M. to 2:00 P.M. Chicago time (8:00 A.M. to 12:00 noon on last trading day).
Telerate Pages:	Price: 905 Volume/open interest: 2,176
Ticker Symbol:	TY + month code.

Margin Requirements (Exchange Minimums)

	Initial	Maintenance
Speculative/spot and nonspot months	$1,500	$1,200
Hedging/spot and nonspot months	$1,200	$1,200

Spreading

Intramarket spreads 12 months or more apart	$ 200	$ 200
Intermarket spreads versus Treasury bonds	$1,000	$1,000
Intermarket spreads versus GNMA (CD or CDR)	$1,000	$1,000

Margin requirements generally increase by a factor of 50% when expanded trading limits are in effect.

Pricing Details

Quotation:	As a percentage of par in 32nds of a point, e.g., 83.16 equals 83 16/32.
Min. Fluctuation:	1/32 of a point equal to $31.25 per contract.
Daily Range:	The daily price limit is normally 64/32 ($2,000) per contract above and below the previous day's settlement price. There is no limit for trading in the current month (the 'spot' month) after the first notice day for the contract.

If three or more contracts within a contract year (or all contracts in a contract year if there are less than three open contracts) close at limit up or down for one business day then the limit would be raised to 150% of the normal limit for all contract months and remain there for three successive business days. These expanded limits will remain in place for successive three-day intervals as long as three contract months (or less as defined) continue to close at their expanded limits during each day the expanded limits are in effect.

Volume/Liquidity Information

Trading Volume:	881,000 contracts in 1982.
Liquidity Assessment:	Fair.
Comment:	The CBOT's 10-year Treasury note futures contract began trading in 1982. During its first year it ranked twenty-eighth among all futures contracts in trading volume and sixteenth among financial futures contracts.

Delivery Specifications

1. Timing

Delivery Months:	March, June, September, December.
Delivery Dates:	Any business day of option of the seller.
Notice Date of Intention to Deliver:	Notice of intention to deliver shall be given to the Board of Trade Clearing Corporation by 8:00 P.M. (Chicago time) on the second business day preceding delivery. If delivery is to be made on the last business day of the month notice should be received by the clearing corporation by 2:00 P.M. (Chicago time) on the business day preceding delivery day.

2. Deliverable Grade

U.S. Treasury notes and noncallable U.S. Treasury bonds which have an actual maturity of not less than 6½ years and not more than 10 years are deliverable against the contract. All instruments delivered against a contract must be of the same issue.

3. Settlement

The mechanism for determining invoice pricing for the 10-year U.S. Treasury note future is identical to that used for U.S. Treasury bond futures except that the conversion factors for the note futures are different due to the differences in maturities of the deliverable grades against the two contracts.

Settlement is based on delivery of U.S. Treasury instruments with a face value at maturity of $100,000, a coupon rate of 8%, and a maturity of 6½ to 10 years. Deliverable grades differing from the hypothetical 8% coupon and with varying maturities within the acceptable range must be adjusted. This adjustment to the invoice price is made by obtaining an appropriate conversion factor for the issue from bond tables prepared by the Financial Publishing Co. of Boston, Mass. To determine the amount to be invoiced by the seller to the buyer, multiply the futures settlement price (in decimals) times the contract size ($100,000) times the deliverable issue's conversion factor. To this figure one must add the accrued interest on the note at the time of delivery to arrive at the total invoice amount. The seller will deliver a $100,000 face amount (maturity value) of the deliverable grade bond or note to the buyer.

The time to maturity for the above calculation is computed on complete three-month increments from the first day of the delivery month.

4. Delivery Method

The seller through his or her clearing member must have the securities in acceptable delivery form (to his or her bank) by 10:00 A.M. (Chicago time) on delivery day. He or she then notifies his or her bank to transfer the securities by Federal Reserve book-entry wire transfer system to the long clearing member's account. Once the securities have been transferred then the long clearing member will notify his or her bank to remit federal funds to the account of the short clearing member by 12:00 noon (Chicago time) on delivery day.

Contract: *GNMA Collateralized Depository Receipt Futures*
Exchange: *Chicago Board of Trade (CBOT)*

Summary Trading Details

Contract Size:	Underlying GNMA certificates with $100,000 principal amount.
Contract Months:	March, June, September, December.
Last Trading Day:	The business day prior to the last seven business days of the expiring contract month.
Trading Hours:	8:00 A.M. to 2:00 P.M. Chicago time (8:00 A.M. to 12:00 noon on last trading day).
Telerate Pages:	Price: 906 Volume/open interest: 2,177
Ticker Symbol:	M + month code.

Margin Requirements (Exchange Minimums)

	Initial	Maintenance
Speculative/spot and nonspot months	$1,500	$1,200
Hedging/spot and nonspot months:	$1,200	$1,200

Spreading

Intramarket spreads 12 months or more apart	$ 200	$ 200
Intermarket spreads versus Treasury Bond	$1,000	$1,000
Intermarket spreads versus Treasury notes	$1,000	$1,000

Margin requirements generally increase by a factor of 50% when expanded trading limits are in effect.

Pricing Details

Quotation:	As a percentage of par in 32nds of a point, e.g., 64.10 equals 64 10/32.
Min. Fluctuation:	1/32 of a point equal to $31.25 per contract.
Daily Range:	The daily price limit is normally 64/ ($2,000) per contract above and below the previous day's settlement price. There is no limit for trading in the current month (the 'spot' month) after the first notice day for the contract.
	If three or more contracts within a contract year (or all contracts in a contract year if there are less than three open contracts) close at limit up or down for one business day then the limit would be raised to 150% of the normal limit for all contact months and remain there for three successive business days. These expanded limits will remain in place for successive three-day intervals as long as three contract months (or less as defined) continue to close at their expanded limits during each day the expanded limits are in effect.

Volume/Liquidity Information

Trading Volume:	2.06 million contracts in 1982.
Liquidity Assessment:	Good.
Comment:	Per FIA statistics the CBOT's GNMA-CDR contract ranked sixteenth in volume among all futures contracts traded in 1982 and eighth among financial futures. This is down slightly from the activity experienced in 1981.

Delivery Specifications

Special Note Concerning Delivery on the GNMA-CDR Contract

The settlement vehicle for a buyer taking delivery and a seller effecting delivery on the GNMA-CDR contract is a collateralized depository receipt (CDR). Physically a CDR is a document signed by an exchange-authorized depository bank which verifies that the seller of the CDR or "GNMA originator" has placed with that depository bank GNMA securities equal to a minimum principal balance of $100,000 at the hypothetical 8% coupon. The originator of the CDR is required to maintain an amount of GNMAs equal to the starting balance at the depository institution for as long as the CDR remains outstanding. The holder of the CDR may hold the instrument in perpetuity and will continue to receive monthly income from the mortgages underlying the depository receipt.

Subsequent to settlement of the futures contract by delivery of the CDR, the holder of the CDR can request for delivery of the actual GNMA securities supporting his depository receipt. This is done by a request to the depository bank which in turn notifies the originator to prepare the securities for delivery.

This write-up will outline the delivery procedure for delivery of the CDR by the futures-short to the futures-long and is meant as simply an introduction to the mechanics of delivery on a GNMA-CDR contract. There are many technical factors that must be assessed in making or taking delivery against this contract.

1. *Timing*

Delivery Months:	March, June, September, December.
Delivery Dates:	Any business day during the delivery month at the option of the seller.
Notice Date of Intention to Deliver:	Notice shall be given to the Board of Trade Clearing Corporation by 8:00 P.M. (Chicago time) on the second business day prior to delivery day.

2. *Deliverable Grade*

In discussing deliverable grade for this contract we will focus on the GNMA securities underlying the CDR, the instrument that is actually delivered.

GNMA securities qualifying as "deliverable grade" are mortgage-backed certificates guaranteed for the timely payment of principal and interest by the Government National Mortgage Association and commonly known as modified pass-through certificates. Standard delivery grade is based on a stated coupon of 8% and a 30-year mortgage prepaid after 12 years.

GNMAs with coupons other than 8% can be delivered (at the long's option) and the amount to be delivered is determined in accordance with yield tables prepared by the Financial Publishing Co. of Boston. Mass.. to achieve equivalence with the standard 8% issues.

All GNMAs underlying the delivered CDR must be of the same issue.

3. *Settlement*

Unlike the factor settlement used for T-bond contracts. the futures buyer (long) taking delivery of a CDR will always pay the principal amount as reflected in the settlement price (subject to two adjustments explained below). For example. if the settlement price of the CDR contract is 75 10/32 the long will pay $75,312.50 in principal (subject to adjustments) to the short *regardless* of which coupon GNMAs are used by the originator (short) to support the CDR.

In determining the invoice amount to be paid there are two adjustments which must be made to the settlement price:

a. Accrued interest:

Interest accrued on the CDR shall be charged to the buyer by the seller from the first day of the delivery month to date of delivery of the CDR.

b. The tail:

Because the CDR contract states that $100,000 principal amount of 8% GNMAs or its equivalent must be delivered to support the CDR and because GNMAs themselves can only be issued in $25,000 pieces with $5,000 increments, the designers of the CDR contract permit the short a variance of 2½% on either side of the exact principal amount of GNMAs required. This 2½% variance, or tail, is settled in cash *on a par basis* between the buyer and seller. Because the tail is settled at par and not on a factor basis as per the principal, the short has the advantage of using the 2½% overage or underage to his or her financial advantage in making deliveries against the contract.

4. *Delivery Method*

Seller will deliver CDR in specified format that conforms to all exchange rules and requirements through his or her clearing corporation member to the buyer through his or her clearing corporation members.

Payment is made in same-day funds (1) by a check drawn on and certified by a Chicago bank or (2) by a cashier's check issued by a Chicago bank. Buyers obligated to accept delivery must take delivery and make payment before 1:00 P.M. (Chicago time) on delivery date in the absence of any Exchange ruling effecting this contract.

APPENDIX 2: FEDERAL RESERVE BOARD GUIDELINES APPLICABLE TO BANK USE OF FUTURES, FORWARDS AND STANDBYS

Acting pursuant to its supervisory authority over State member banks contained in Section 9 (12 U.S.C. § 321, *et seq.*) and Section 11 (12 U.S.C. § 248) of the Federal Reserve Act and the Financial Institutions Supervisory Act of 1966 (12 U.S.C. §1818(b)) and related provisions of law, the Board of Governors has amended its previously published policy statement which, as revised, is hereinafter set forth in its entirety.

Statement of Policy Concerning Forward Contracts and Futures Contracts

The following is a Board policy statement relating to State member bank participation in the futures and forward contract markets to purchase and sell U.S. government and agency securities. Information contained below is applicable specifically to commercial banking activities. An additional statement of policy applicable to trust department activities of State member banks may be issued at a later time.

The staff of the Treasury Department and the Board of Governors of the Federal Reserve System recently completed a study of the markets for Treasury futures. In part, the study notes that there is evidence that financial futures can be used by banks effectively to hedge portions of their portfolios against interest rate risk. However, the study also cautions that improper use of interest rate futures contracts will increase interest rate risk—rather than decrease such risk. In addition, various participants have advised that certain salespersons are attempting to suggest inappropriate futures transactions for banks, such as taking futures positions to speculate on future interest rate movements. Furthermore, some banks and other financial institutions have recently issued standby contracts (giving the contra party the option to deliver securities to the bank at a predetermined price) that were extremely large given their ability to absorb interest rate risk. In so doing, these institutions have been exposed to potentially large losses that could (and sometimes did) significantly affect their financial condition.

Banks that engage in futures, forward and standby contract activities should only do so in accordance with safe and sound banking practices with levels of activity reasonably related to the bank's business needs and capacity to fulfill its obligations under these contracts. In managing their assets and liabilities, banks should evaluate the interest rate risk exposure resulting from their overall activities to insure that the positions they take in futures, forward and standby contract markets will reduce their risk exposure; and policy objectives should be formulated in light of the bank's entire asset and liability mix. The following are minimal guidelines to be followed by banks authorized under State law to participate in these markets.

1. Prior to engaging in these transactions, a bank should obtain an opinion of counsel or its State banking authority concerning the legality of its activities under State law.

2. The board of directors should consider any plan to engage in these activities and should endorse specific written policies in authorizing these activities. Policy objectives must be specific enough to outline permissible contract strategies and their relationship to other banking activities, and record keeping systems must be sufficiently detailed to permit internal auditors and examiners to determine whether operating personnel have acted in accordance with authorized objectives. Bank personnel are expected to be able to describe and document in detail how the positions they have taken in futures, forward and standby contracts contribute to the attainment of the bank's stated objectives.

3. The board of directors should establish limitations applicable to futures, forward and standby contract positions; and the board of directors, a duly authorized committee thereof, or the bank's internal auditors should review periodically (at least monthly) contract positions to ascertain conformance with such limits.

4. The bank should maintain general ledger memorandum accounts or commitment registers to adequately identify and control all commitments to make or take delivery of securities. Such registers and supporting journals should at a minimum include:
   (a) the type and amount of each contract,
   (b) the maturity date of each contract,
   (c) the current market price and cost of each contract, and
   (d) the amount of money held in margin accounts.

5. With the exception of contracts described in item 6, all open positions should be reviewed and market values determined at least monthly (or more often, depending on volume and magnitude of positions), regardless of whether the bank is required to deposit margin in connection with a given contract.[1] All futures and forward contracts

---

1. Underlying security commitments relating to open futures and forward contracts should not be reported on the balance sheet. Margin deposits and any unrealized losses (and in certain instances, unrealized gains) are usually the only entries to be recorded on the books. See "General Instructions" to the Reports of Condition and Income for additional details.

should be valued on the basis of either market or the lower of cost or market, at the option of the bank.[2] Standby contracts should be valued on the basis of the lower of cost or market.[3] Market basis for forward and standby contracts should be based on the market value of the underlying security, except where publicly quoted forward contract price quotations are available. All losses resulting from monthly contract value determination should be recognized as a current expense item; those banks that value contracts on a market basis would recognize gains as a current income item. In the event the above described futures and forward contracts result in the acquisition of securities, such securities should be recorded on a basis consistent with that applied to the contracts (either market or lower of cost or market). Acquisition of securities arising from standby contracts should be recorded on the basis of lower of adjusted cost (see item 7(c)) or market.

6. Futures or forward contracts associated with *bona fide* hedging of mortgage banking operations, i.e., the origination and purchase of mortgage loans for resale to investors or the issuance of mortgage-backed securities, may be accounted for in accordance with generally accepted accounting principles applicable to such activity.

7. Fee income received by a bank in connection with a standby contract should be deferred at initiation of the contract and accounted for as follows:

    a. upon expiration of an unexercised contract the deferred amount should be reported as income;

    b. upon a negotiated settlement of the contract prior to maturity, the deferred amount should be accounted for as an adjustment to the expense of such settlement, and the net amount should be transferred to the income account; or

    c. upon exercise of the contract, the deferred amount should be accounted for as an adjustment to the basis of the acquired securities. Such adjusted cost basis should be compared to market value of securities acquired. See item 5.

8. Bank financial reports should disclose in an explanatory note any futures, forward and standby contract activity that materially affects the bank's financial condition.

2. Futures and forward contracts executed for trading account purposes should be valued on a basis consistent with other trading positions.
3. Losses on standby contracts need be computed only in the case of the party committed to purchase under the contract, and only where the market value of the security is below the contract price adjusted for deferred fee income.

9. To insure that banks minimize credit risk associated with forward and standby contract activity, banks should implement a system for monitoring credit risk exposure associated with various customers and dealers with whom operating personnel are authorized to transact business.

10. To assure adherence to bank policy and prevent unauthorized trading and other abuses, banks should establish other internal controls including periodic reports to management, segregation of duties, and internal audit programs.

The issuance of long-term standby contracts, i.e., those for 150 days or more, which give the other party to the contract the option to deliver securities to the bank will ordinarily be viewed as an inappropriate practice. In almost all instances where standby contracts specified settlement in excess of 150 days, supervisory authorities have found that such contracts were related not to the investment or business needs of the institution, but primarily to the earning of fee income or to speculating on future interest rate movements. Accordingly, the Board concludes that State member banks should not issue standby contracts specifying delivery in excess of 150 days, unless special circumstances warrant.

The Board intends to monitor closely State member bank transactions in futures, forward and standby contracts to ensure that any such activity is conducted in accordance with safe and sound banking practices. In light of that continuing review, it may be found desirable to establish position limits applicable to State member banks. Supervisory action in individual cases under the Financial Institutions Supervisory Act (12 U.S.C. §1818 (b)) may also be instituted if necessary.

By order of the Board of Governors of the Federal Reserve System, March 12, 1980.

(signed) Theodore E. Allsion

Theodore E. Allison
Secretary of the Board

(SEAL)

The FDIC and the Office of the Comptroller of the Currency issued substantively the same statement although they differ somewhat in format.

14 A Portfolio View of Loan Selection and Pricing

Mark J. Flannery

Good credit analysis is widely recognized as a crucial determinant of success in banking. Most such analysis is conducted at the level of an individual customer, where the decision is made to extend or not to extend a line of credit, or at the level of an individual loan, where the decision is made to accept or reject an applicant offering to pay a particular loan rate (given the other loan terms). All banks are familiar with loan exposure limits to individual borrowers, whether imposed by regulators or the policy of senior bank management. However, some banks have gotten themselves into serious trouble by failing to extend their assessment of credit risk exposure to *sets* of borrowers whose repayment capabilities are closely related to one another. The extent to which individual loans in a bank's portfolio are subject to shared risks of default is a second dimension of the credit risk problem that is less frequently addressed. While it is commonplace to observe that sufficiently diversifying the loan portfolio can reduce a bank's overall exposure to credit risk, identifying and assembling a truly diversified set of loans can be quite difficult in practice. Even firms that have been reasonably well diversified in the past may confront a substantially different investment environment as deregulation changes prod-

This paper was completed while the author was Research Advisor at the Federal Reserve Bank of Philadelphia. The views expressed here are not necessarily those of the Federal Reserve Bank of Philadelphia.

uct offerings and shifts historical alignments between customers and financial service providers. Fortunately, much of the investment literature on portfolio selection can be applied to a discussion of bank credit risk exposure. If a bank is viewed as a collection of assets and liabilities, the terms on which another asset (loan) should be added to the portfolio must reflect the effect of that new asset on shareholder returns. This, in turn, requires that management evaluate the interrelationships between the new loan's return and the return (cost) of other bank assets (liabilities).

The institutional characteristics of banking make it difficult to apply standard portfolio tools directly to the lending decision. This chapter bridges the gap between banking institutions and portfolio theory by providing a conceptual guide to portfolio issues in bank lending. The basic principles discussed here apply to all depository intermediaries (commercial banks and thrift institutions alike), regardless of size or geographic location. The first section of the chapter, "Making Bank Decisions under Uncertainty," briefly considers a banking firm's planning objectives in a world of uncertainty. The principle of risk reduction through diversification is described in the next section ("Portfolio Theory's Diversification Principle"), with special emphasis on loan contracts. The third section explicitly applies portfolio theory to loan selection and pricing, presenting several examples of common factors that affect loan defaults. The section on "Implementation" discusses application of these concepts in the context of bank management. The final section offers a brief conclusion.

MAKING BANK DECISIONS UNDER UNCERTAINTY

Any firm must have a rule or objective that guides its activities. Economists have traditionally (though not always) begun with an assumption that firms seek to maximize their profits. When risk is considered, however, the profit stream becomes two-dimensional. Profits can be characterized in terms of their *expected value* (i.e., their average level) or their *variance* (predictability). In well-functioning financial markets, securities with greater risk also tend to have higher expected returns. The objective function for a firm operating under uncertainty must therefore specify how shareholders feel about more (or less) risk[1] versus more (or less) expected profits. Banking (and other) firms are generally thought to behave in a *risk-averse* fashion. That is, the bank will expose itself to greater profit variability only if the expected returns are higher as well. In this view, the firm's objective is to maximize a utility function that values higher expected returns while preferring to avoid uncertainty in the return stream.[2] Risk aversion has an important effect on the way a bank prices loans. Suppose the bank can invest in either a perfectly safe Treasury bill or a customer loan that might not be repaid in full. A risk-averse banker will lend only if the net loan return (after expected defaults and other costs) exceeds the Treasury bill rate.[3]

Economic theory recognizes other firm objectives besides risk-averse utility maximization,[4] but risk aversion seems to be a reasonably accurate characterization of most banking behavior for several reasons. First, many bank managers exert substantial influence over firm behavior. The manager shares in extraordinarily high profits only to a limited extent, while poor profits (or firm failure) can cost managers dearly in terms of job security and future employment opportunities. As a result, managers may avoid very risky situations even when the expected return to shareholders is sufficient to compensate them for the risk. Second, many banks are owned by a small group of investors, each of whom has a substantial portion of his or her wealth in the bank's stock. The owners of poorly diversified portfolios prefer (at least to some extent) to avoid significant uncertainty about their primary asset's earnings. Third, bank regulators seek to avoid bank failures, and therefore view fluctuating profits with concern. The associated regulatory pressure and restrictions can importantly affect bank decisions. Finally, the existence of sizable bankruptcy costs will induce banks to avoid extreme risk positions that might cause firm failure. Because debtors bear the bankruptcy costs in a failed firm, riskier firms must pay higher interest rates on their debt (including uninsured deposits). These higher borrowing costs will discourage bankers from undertaking risks that do not offer correspondingly high expected returns.

The fact that banks trade off risk and expected return in evaluating various investments has important implications for loan selection and pricing. Developing these implications, however, requires a preliminary discussion of how an *individual* asset's riskiness differs from the riskiness of a *portfolio* of assets.

PORTFOLIO THEORY'S DIVERSIFICATION PRINCIPLE

A profitable loan contract rate must compensate the bank for two distinct types of costs. First, the loan rate must cover the time value of the funds advanced. This time value—the *pure rate of interest*—is generally the largest portion of a loan rate and is relatively easy to measure. The current market interest rate on a 91-day Treasury bill, for example, corresponds (after adjustment for state and local taxation) to the riskless time value of money on a 91-day loan. Second, the loan rate should also include a premium over the pure rate of interest to compensate for the possibility that full repayment may not occur. Setting this premium appropriately requires a sophisticated assessment of the borrower's financial future.

The loan rate premium can be further subdivided into a *default premium* and a *risk premium*. The default premium covers the lender's expected loss on the loan. Naturally, no lender should grant a loan he or she anticipates will not be repaid in full, but neither can the loan officer be entirely certain of repayment. The usual type of bank credit analysis is largely directed toward inferring the likelihood that a particular borrower will be unable to repay in full. Suppose, for example, that borrowers are known to repay either the full contract amount or zero. (Partial or late repayments and extraordinary collection costs are easily included in this type of analysis.) If the assessed probability of default is say, 2%, the lender would charge a rate approximately 2% above the pure time value of money.[5] This default premium can be assigned by examining a borrower's characteristics in isolation, without reference to other bank assets or liabilities (see, for example, Edward I. Altman's chapter in this volume).

The loan rate premium's second component compensates the lender for *uncertainty* about how much of the loan will be repaid. Such a risk premium—in excess of the expected loss—is needed to induce risk-averse lenders to make risky loans rather than concentrating exclusively on riskless Treasury bills. Two distinct factors determine the appropriate risk premium. The first is a lender's degree of risk aversion: The more reluctant is a lender to bear default risk, the higher will this premium have to be. Secondly, the lender's required risk premium is affected by the composition of other assets in the loan portfolio. Unlike the default premium, an appropriate risk premium cannot be assigned to an asset independent of what other assets are held by the lender. Rather, modern portfolio theory in any of its various forms[6] clearly indicates that a security's "risk" can only be assessed *in conjuction with* the other assets held in the same portfolio.

A simple example will clarify this concept. Consider two assets (A and B) available for purchase, each of which has a great deal of variation (dispersion) in its future value. Suppose there are two possible (equiprobable) future states of the world, and the assets will be worth the following amounts in each state:

Asset	State 1	State 2
A	$8	$4
B	$0	$6

Individually, A and B each appears quite risky. But a *portfolio* comprising 60% of A and 40% of B will have the same value—$4.80—regardless of which state of the world occurs.[7] In combination, these asset risks cancel one another leaving a riskless portfolio. This dramatic result occurs because A and B have *negatively correlated* values: When A is worth a lot, B is worth less and vice versa. (Positive correlation naturally indicates that two asset values tend to move together, rather than inversely as with A and B. *Covariance* is a statistical concept closely related to correlation.) While such perfect predictability of aggregate returns is rarely attainable, the diversification principle—that a portfolio has more stable returns than any individual asset in it—is quite generally valid. A direct implication of this observation is that one cannot judge the riskiness of any asset without evaluating how it relates to other assets that are available for purchase at the same time.[8]

Bank loan returns have a rigid upper bound—because one can never collect more than 100% of the stipulated contract amount—so the possibility of default is what generates credit risk in bank lending. A loan is risky if the lender is uncertain about the extent of repayment. (If it were *known* beyond question that a group of loans would generate 2% defaults, there would be no risk as defined here.) The diversification principle indicates that a loan portfolio's actual losses can be predicted more accurately the larger the number of separate loans in the portfolio.[9] In the extreme, a portfolio comprising a single loan would (ex post) either repay in full or pay nothing. The dispersion (risk) of this repayment flow may be quite large. At the other extreme, the "law of large numbers" guarantees that as the same aggregate dollar volume is lent to an ever larger number of independent borrowers, actual defaults become ever closer to their mathematical expectation.[10]

It is important to emphasize that the principle of diversification cannot reduce the portfolio's *average* default rate, but only the *variability* of actual loan losses (and thus the variability of bank profits). Consider, for example, an experiment in which a "fair" coin is flipped repeatedly. In any sequence, the expected (average) number of "heads" is one-half the number of tosses. In a short sequence—say five tosses—a run of heads (or of tails) is not terribly unlikely. That is, there is some significant probability that the actual number of "heads" will be substantially different from the expected number. Probability theory asserts, however, that as the number of tosses gets large the actual number of heads is ever more likely to be near the expected number, which remains 50% of total tosses no matter how long the sequence. Similarly, diversification does not change a bank's expected default rate, though actual defaults can be more accurately predicted in a portfolio composed of a larger number of independent borrowers.

LOAN COVARIANCES AND LOAN PRICING

Because bank shareholders are willing to trade off some expected profits in order to avoid uncertainty (and vice versa), the diversification principle has an important implication for loan pricing. Consider two loans with the same default probability. One, however, is likely to default when the rest of the loan portfolio is experiencing relatively low losses (negative correlation with other assets). The other will tend to default when the rest of the loan portfolio is also experiencing difficulty (positive correlation). The bank should charge the first borrower a lower loan rate, because adding that loan to the existing portfolio will leave the bank with lower overall risk. In short, a bank cannot set appropriate risk premiums without evaluating the covariance of an applicant's possible defaults with that of other assets in the portfolio.

Two practical considerations substantially complicate the direct application of portfolio theory to bank loan selection and pricing decisions. First, portfolio theory generally assumes that investors are "price takers," which means that the market somehow sets a price (interest rate) for each security and individual investors then choose how much of each asset to purchase at the going price. This view of asset acquisition is not applicable to bank loans, which do not trade in a market where prices are readily observed. Rather, bank credit analysis serves a pivotal role that is absent from standard portfolio investment models. The bank must examine each applicant's financial characteristics to infer the likely default probability and covariances, then choose a particular loan rate at which it is willing to lend. Naturally, this rate should compensate bank shareholders for the risks associated with the loan under review.

Second, most theories of portfolio selection assume that each potential asset's payoffs are fixed and known to lenders. In reality, however, bankers need not purchase securities whose characteristics are immutably fixed. A large component of the "art" in banking involves structuring a loan deal in the way that best satisfies the customer and the bank simultaneously. The maturity, rate, seniority, and collateral associated with a transaction may affect the loan's risk characteristics, as will the range of restrictive covenants specified, and, perhaps later, the banker's skill in promptly identifying problem loans and efficiently effecting repayment or renegotiation. Furthermore, an applicant's default probabilities cannot be determined without costly analysis, and not all potential lenders can evaluate the same applicant at equal cost. This suggests that, if credit information is costly to obtain and evaluate, specialization in a relatively few types of loans or within a relatively confined geographic area may be desirable. The specialized lender may distinguish more accurately applicants' default probabilities, for example, or may be able to draft more effective restrictive covenants. Collateral may be easier for a specialized firm to evaluate and control. Accurate information may be more readily obtained locally than it is across a greater distance. In short, unlike most portfolio models, a bank's credit analysis and bargaining skills affect the risk–return characteristics of the loans in its portfolio.

Even though bank loans do not neatly fit the usual model of optimal portfolio selection, the basic insights can (and should) be observed in lending. In particular, the portfolio theoretic viewpoint requires that credit analysis produce information about an applicant's default probability and the interrelationships between and among various borrowing customers. Loan default covariances are present whenever loan repayments are influenced by one or more common forces. Part of senior management's responsibility, therefore, is to identify such common risk elements and adjust the loan portfolio's composition and/or pricing to reflect the risk effect on total bank profits.

Covariances among Bank Assets

The most obvious source of a less than fully diversified portfolio is the heavy concentration of loans in a single sector: oil firms, construction, autos, steel, electronics, and so on. Because firms in the same industry share important common determinants of profitability, loan defaults will not be independent of one another. Just as an insurance company could not credibly "insure" exclusively houses located along the San Andreas fault, neither should a bank lend exclusively to firms in the same industry. It is often important to think of a "sector" in geographic terms as well as in line-of-commerce terms. The butcher, baker, and candlestick maker in a company town all suffer when the plant closes. Similarly, the recent loss experiences of banks with portfolio concentrations in the Pacific Northwest, industrial Midwest, or LDCs share a broad exposure to one event that affected a number of otherwise "different" types of borrower.

More subtle types of default covariance arise when firms in "different" industries respond similarly to the same exogenous events. (In fact, some such firms should be thought of as being in the *same* industrial sector for some purposes.) At one level, virtually all firms' fortunes move together, as reflected by business cycles in employment, prices, and GNP. The issue, therefore, is one of degree: Which types of firms are *especially* likely to default under similar circumstances? The difficulty with assessing this question is that many common influences on firms are neither simple *nor necessarily stable through time*. It is easy, for example, to infer that loans to plywood manufacturers and housing contractors will be positively correlated even though they operate in different (SIC code) industries. A similar connection is apparent between auto makers and manufacturers of sheet steel. Slightly more subtle reasoning leads to the inference that airlines and producer durables manufacturers may be correlated by virtue of their common, relatively extreme sensitivity to GNP fluctuations. One difficulty for bank management is that some interrelationships are not apparent until after they develop. For example, how many analysts would have specified (prior to 1982) a sizable covariance between domestic oil firms and Mexico? Yet hindsight indicates that a shared susceptibility to falling crude oil prices has made these two loan "sectors" behave quite similarly.

The preceding discussion suggests that concentrating the loan portfolio in similar industries should be avoided. An offsetting consideration, however, is that specialization may enable a lender to produce more attractive loan securities via better information availability or evaluation. Lenders are thus torn between a desire to reduce risk through diversification and the perceived benefits of concentrating management expertise in a few areas. The portfolio diversification principle indicates that the higher expected loan returns accruing from specialization are generally accompanied by greater credit risk in the portfolio. Management must ensure that loan contract rates include a sufficient premium to compensate shareholders for the riskiness of a specialized bank's earnings.[11]

Without a crystal ball, loan covariance analysis is not easy. Quite the contrary. This chapter cannot provide an exhaustive list of common factors to scrutinize but only seeks to acquaint bank managers with the broad implications of portfolio theory for this area of bank decision making. Before shared susceptibilities can be inferred, the set of possible (likely) adverse events must first be identified and defined. Toward this end, several specific examples are offered for discussion.

Interest Rates. During the 1970s, bankers sought to shed interest rate risk exposure by passing it along to borrowers via variable-rate loans. However, subsequent experiences have indicated that not all customers can bear interest rate uncertainty equally well. In fact, floating-rate loan provisions may importantly affect a bank's credit risk exposure (see Anthony M. Santomero's chapter in this volume). Some customers will be less likely to repay when market rates are very high. This set of firms includes producers of housing, autos, and other durables, along with their related sectors (plywood, sheet steel). Mortgage loan defaults also rise with interest rates, as lower house prices reduce owners' equity (at least under some circumstances). Some analysts further contend that recent LDC defaults and reschedulings would have been less widespread had the rates on their LIBOR-related loans not ballooned in the early 1980s relative to their export earnings.

Exchange Rates.   In an open economy, exchange rate movements affect many dimensions of economic activity, at least in the short run. The most direct effects are felt by domestic importers and exporters. Foreign borrowers also may experience difficulty repaying their dollar-denominated debts as the dollar strengthens (and vice versa). On the domestic front, many firms compete with foreign suppliers whose dollar prices vary with the exchange rate. California vintners and domestic manufacturers of consumer electronics and autos, for example, find themselves exposed to more severe price competition as the dollar strengthens.

Commodity Prices.   Many groups of commodity prices tend to move with one another and thereby affect different types of borrowers. A bumper crop in wheat, for example, will tend to depress other grain prices as well, with general effects on farm defaults or reschedulings. (At the same time, grain storage should increase, improving the quality of loans to grain elevators.) A fall in the price of oil tends to depress coal, gas, and wood prices as well. Generally lower energy costs will hurt vendors of home insulation, wood stoves, and down comforters, while helping large automobile sales and motel chains.

Major Local Events.   Many types of local (business and consumer) loans will be similarly affected by a major plant closing or the construction of a new highway nearby. The success of a proposed industrial park can affect the prospects of many loans beyond those to the park's developers.

Covariances between Bank Assets and Liabilities

Asset selection is often discussed independent of the way those assets are financed. However, many banks should also consider the relation between their asset returns and the cost or availability of various types of deposit funds. Several dimensions of this issue are briefly considered here.

One type of asset–liability covariance concerns the impact of market interest rate changes on liability costs and loan returns. With the demise of Regulation Q, an ever larger proportion of outstanding deposits has become rate sensitive. A change in market rates can therefore affect total interest costs quite promptly for banks of all sizes. To minimize the effect of unanticipated interest rate changes on profits, bankers practice various forms of gap management. By adjusting asset and liability maturities (durations) to complement one another, a bank can control its exposure to interest rate risk (see Benjamin Wolkowitz' chapter in this volume). Unfortunately, these calculations often fail to consider the fact that some borrowers' loan defaults will be correlated with the level of market interest rates. Interest rate risk management techniques based on an assumption that loan defaults are unrelated to interest rates will therefore fail to produce the shareholders' desired net risk exposure.[12]

A second liability characteristic that should be reflected in loan pricing concerns the availability of retail deposits, drawn from a relatively limited geographic area. A regional recession can generate substantial deposit withdrawals at the same time local loans are subject to unusually high default rates. The bank would then be forced to seek liquidity from unusual sources—city correspondents, debt markets, or the Fed—just when its asset portfolio appears weakest. This possibility should lead the bank to hold a relatively large, short-term (i.e., liquid) bond portfolio. To keep the loan–deposit ratio down, the bank will charge borrowers a relatively high risk premium in recognition of the covariance between deposit availability and credit quality.

A further consideration for banks heavily dependent on local retail deposits is that their efforts to hedge—or to bet on—interest rate movements must be undertaken largely via loan pricing.[13] A small bank wishing to lengthen its asset maturity relative to liabilities cannot shorten its portfolio of (nonexistent) negotiable CDs, but must induce borrowers to take more (longer) fixed-rate loans. This must be accomplished by adjusting the risk premiums on long- versus short-term loans to reflect the degree of interest rate risk perceived in each type, given the bank's rate forecast. Obviously, the asset maturity adjustment can extend beyond the corporate loan portfolio, as the bank revises other loan rates to encourage or discourage consumer installment loans, mortgages, lease financing, and so on.

Finally, multidimensional customer relationships—the fact that a customer tends to deal repeatedly with a bank as both borrower and depositor—can have an important influence on loan pricing for two reasons. First, customers vary in the amount and variety of bank services they purchase, and hence in the profitability of their overall relationships to the bank. In order to preserve (or initiate) profitable relationships, banks may set loan rates different from those implied by the preceding analysis, though diversification considerations will continue to have an important effect on loan selection and pricing. Secondly, covariance analysis should be extended to recognize the intertemporal dimensions of customer relationships. A new customer will have deposit flows and loan demands that are correlated with one another, and with the corresponding flows of other bank customers. A firm whose credit needs are positively related to those of other customers is less valuable than one whose loan demands are countercyclical. Deposit flows are much the same: A customer whose deposit balances are less correlated with other sources of funds will be more valuable to the bank. These correlations should be recognized in customer profitability analyses. The loan and deposit rates offered to individual customers should reflect their correlations with the bank's other customers' liquidity and financing needs.

IMPLEMENTATION

The preceding sections discuss some conceptual issues that should be applied to loan pricing decisions throughout the bank. Loan terms should reflect the borrower's contribution to the bank's overall risk, which is prominently determined by the extent to which individual assets and liabilities react to the same external events.[14] Three interrelated steps are required to monitor and control the institution's overall loan risk exposure. First, management must enumerate the systematic risks to be considered in assembling the loan portfolio. One bank, for example, may find the possibility of a regional recession very important, while another worries more about the effect of exchange rate changes on its borrowers. This stage of the analysis is tricky, largely because there is no systematic way to ensure that the bank has not ignored an important possibility. Statistical and economic analyses surely have important roles to play, but so do common sense and long banking experience. The basic point is that, explicitly or implicitly, any bank loan represents a bet on the economy's future course. By explicitly identifying the relevant risks and their probabilities, the bank will be in a far better position to assess its overall exposure and to price risk appropriately.

Second, a reporting system with a manageable number of appropriate loan categories must be designed and installed. An optimal system will require a substantial amount of preliminary analysis to determine how loans should be grouped or categorized. Potential borrowers can then be sorted into a set of categories that captures the bulk of shared reactions to external shocks. (While "Commercial and Industrial Loans" will surely prove too broad a category, a very specific one such as "Loans to Retail Hardware Stores with Annual Sales Under $1 Million" will be too numerous to allow practical management oversight.) Initial design of the loan categories would probably evaluate historical loan experiences (at one or more banks) using statistical techniques to infer past relations among loan types. The adequacy of existing loan categories must also be reviewed periodically, as the bank revises its assessment of relevant lending risks.

Finally, management must assign different risk premiums to loan types that are believed to pose different risk exposures. Simply "meeting the competition" on all loan deals amounts to accepting *other* banks' (implicit or explicit) risk assessments. A more activist stance on loan pricing requires the bank to project the possible magnitudes of the shocks relevant to each loan category, translate these shocks into a range of effects on total profits, and set loan terms that generate sufficiently high expected profits to compensate for the implied risks. Risk adjustments on various loan types can be implemented several ways.

1. Internal transfer prices can be varied to reflect the correlations of various loan categories with other bank assets.
2. For loans that are most highly correlated with the rest of the portfolio, contract terms can be structured to include collateral, restrictive covenants, shorter maturities, or other features that reduce the covariance.
3. A dollar limit on certain loan categories (or individual loan sizes) can be imposed.

Regardless of the specifics, overall risk management requires a basic focus on default covariances and identifiable risk exposures. Management's role is to define the set of relevant events, identify shared exposures, and assure that loan rates reflect the net effect on total bank profits. These decisions cannot be relegated to the lending officer level, but must involve senior management (in much the same way interest rate risk is managed via a high-level asset–liability committee). Only managers with a bankwide perspective on risk exposure are in a position to apply the principles discussed here.

CONCLUSION

When discussing the issue of bank credit risk, the tendency is to narrow one's focus to individual loan transactions. This perspective can result in a loan portfolio of individually sound credits that complement one another terribly. Because high default covariances have potentially devastating effects on bank profitability, adequate loan portfolio diversification requires active supervision and planning by senior management. The difficulty of this problem is recognized in a recent Federal Deposit Insurance Corporation (FDIC) report:

> One area where meaningful information is particularly scarce is loan diversification. A bank with a well-diversified loan portfolio is insulated from one source of serious problems. Unfortunately, credit diversification, as

important as it is, is difficult to evaluate. The examination process compiles information on concentrations of credit but the definition varies on what constitutes a concentration. Most of the banks that failed due to loan problems were not well diversified, yet relatively few were cited for credit concentrations. [FDIC, 1983, p. II–13]

The forecasts and risk assessments required of bank management are difficult to undertake, and do not always lend themselves to cut-and-dried statistical analysis. It is nevertheless far preferable to attempt an explicit analysis of bank risk exposure than unwittingly to undertake portfolio risks for which the bank is inadequately compensated.

NOTES

1. Throughout this chapter, risk is discussed as if the banker can assess the probability that untoward events will occur. However, there may be some external developments that the bank fears, but for which it has no reasonable assessment of probability. In the terminology of Frank Knight, this is the distinction between *risk* and *uncertainty*, two terms that are used here interchangeably. While Knightian uncertainty may be an important consideration for some bank investment problems, the methods discussed here require that managers be able to quantify (at least approximately) the probability of various events.

2. If managers work entirely in the interest of firm owners, this utility function would reflect solely the owners' preferences. Alternatively, managers may have some discretion to pursue their own interests (see Jensen & Meckling, 1976), which would lead them to maximize a utility function that combines the preferences of owners and managers. For further discussion of such utility functions, see Chapter 7 of Fama (1976).

3. Firms can differ in the extent of their risk aversion, which means that different banks might require different amounts of expected profit to bear the same risk.

4. One prominent alternative to risk-averse utility maximization is the hypothesis that shareholders instruct management to maximize the *market value* of the firm's equity. Finance theory specifies that, under certain conditions, firms are nothing more than corporate veils that pass earnings through to their owners who, in turn, hold widely diversified equity portfolios. Owners assess the bank's profit flow relative to their returns from other securities. Instead of focusing on profit variances, market value maximization specifies that shareholders are concerned only with the covariance between a firm's earnings and those of other firms in the economy.

5. More precisely, the final contract should call for repayment of $[(1+i)/(1-d)]$ dollars for each dollar lent (where i is the time value of money and d is the probability of default), to account for the lost interest income associated with default. Thus, if the riskless interest rate is 10% and the default probability on a one-year loan is 2%, the bank should charge a 12.24% rate on the loan. If the probability of default on a three-month loan is 2%, the annualized loan rate must be 19.67%.

6. The basic tenets of portfolio theory can be derived in the context of (at least) three separate analytic frameworks: the capital asset pricing model (see Chapter 8 of Fama,

1976), state preference (see Chapter 5 of Copeland and Weston, 1980), or arbitrage pricing theory (see Ross, 1976).

7. These proportions were obtained by picking a portfolio share (w) for asset A that equates the portfolio's value in both future states: $8w + 0(1-w) = 4w + 6(1 - w)$. If A and B are not negatively correlated, a riskless portfolio return cannot be guaranteed unless one or more of the assets can be sold short. For further discussion of portfolio diversification, see Chapter 7 of Fama (1976) or Chapter 5 of Sharpe (1978).

8. In a multiperiod setting, each security's return characteristics should also be compared with the properties of other assets that are expected to be available for purchase in the future (see Merton, 1973).

9. This statement holds unless various borrowers' defaults are perfectly positively correlated with one another.

10. In other words, the variance of losses goes to zero as the number of borrowers becomes infinite. If borrower defaults are positively correlated, an increase in the number of loans still leads to less uncertainty about default losses, though the uncertainty (variance) remains positive. Other things the same, smaller covariances among borrower defaults lead to more predictable overall loan losses.

11. Another type of loan specialization frequently occurs in smaller banks that only lend in a limited geographic area. To some extent this concentration occurs because the bank chartering agency requires attention to the local community's banking needs. In addition, many small institutions cannot justify the fixed costs of gathering information from a larger geographic area. A judicious acquisition of participations in correspondents' loan portfolios would circumvent the latter difficulty, but many banks will be unable to make large investments of this type and simultaneously serve the community's credit needs. Such banks are simply constrained to hold a poorly diversified portfolio, and management must charge loan premiums that compensate shareholders for the associated risk.

12. Many factors in addition to the current balance sheet can contribute to the interest rate sensitivity of bank profits. Rate-related default risk is perhaps the most important of these.

13. Futures positions or the maturity of marketable securities can also be adjusted, though this is a relatively small proportion of total assets for most banks.

14. Bennett (1984) provides another view on how these loan pricing principles can be implemented.

REFERENCES

Bennett, Paul. "Applying Portfolio Theory to Global Bank Lending." Forthcoming article in *Journal of Banking and Finance*.

Copeland, Thomas E., and Weston, J. Fred. *Financial Theory and Corporate Policy*. Reading, Mass: Addison-Wesley Publishing Company, 1980.

Fama, Eugene F. *Foundations of Finance*. New York: Basic Books, 1976.

Federal Deposit Insurance Corporation. *Deposit Insurance in a Changing Environment*. Washington, D.C.: April 15, 1983.

Jensen, Michael C., and Meckling, William H. "Theory of the Firm: Managerial Behavior, Agency Costs and Ownership Structure." *Journal of Financial Economics*, 1976, pp. 305–360.

Merton, Robert C. "An Intertemporal Capital Asset Pricing Model." *Econometrica*, September 1973, pp. 867–887.

Ross, Stephen. "The Arbitrage Theory of Capital Asset Pricing." *Journal of Economic Theory*, December 1976, pp. 341–360.

Sharpe, William F. *Investments*. Englewood Cliffs, N.J.: Prentice-Hall, 1978.

15 Managing the Commercial Lending Process

Edward I. Altman

The banking industry has become increasingly dynamic and complex in recent years, and it is no longer possible to control and evaluate the financial performance of an individual bank simply by analyzing its lending policies and loan portfolio. Despite the proliferation of banking services, however, the basic commercial and industrial lending process is still the lifeblood of commercial banking. In 1983, U.S. bank loans outstanding to business exceeded $1 trillion, with loans accounting for over 55% of U.S. bank total assets. With rare exceptions, the quality and profitability of a bank's loan portfolio still affect its success or, increasingly, its failure. In almost every case of a recent large bank failure in the United States, the cause was an unsound loan portfolio. In other words, errors were made by the bank's management in evaluating the risk of the loan portfolio relative to its expected return, or there were abuses of what should be an objective credit assessment process, for instance, inside dealings and loans made without adherence to prudent lending practices.

The importance of sound lending policies and effective credit analysis techniques is underscored by the sobering reality that in the fall of 1983, amid a seemingly robust economic expansion, the number of commercial banks in deep financial distress reached almost 600, or 4% of the nation's banks. Indeed, in 1983, a postwar record of 48 commercial banks in the United States failed, six more than the previous record in 1982. The primary reason for this record number of problem banks and bank failures, according to the FDIC, was that an increasing number of bank customers

473

were unable to repay loans. The previous high was 2.6% in the aftermath of the 1973–1975 recession. Indeed, the number of problem banks on the Comptroller of Currency list was even greater than that on the FDIC list. While the banking system typically suffers problems after recessions, the extent of these problems necessitates a careful review of the credit practices of banks, and this review should encompass both the actual loans made and the so-called "off-balance-sheet" commitments of commercial banks.

In this chapter, we will concentrate on the credit-granting and loan portfolio process. Of increasing importance, however, is the implicit risk exposure created by contingent liabilities and other off-balance-sheet activities of banks. Contingent claims, such as standby and performance letters of credit and commercial paper backup lines, are especially important in assessing the total customer relationship of individual banks. In 1981, noninterest income of the major commercial banks approximated 30% of total revenues. The figure was just 22% in 1979. These noninterest income items included trading account and foreign exchange profits, trust fees, service charges on deposits, fees and commissions on loans, letters of credit, and acceptances and business service fees. (For a discussion of off-balance-sheet activities of banks, see Goldberg, Altman, and Furash [1983].) Only the fees and commissions on loans are directly associated with the lending portfolio. Many of the other items, however, involve the credit process and risk assessment and as such qualify as related to the general subject of this chapter. Therefore, keep in mind that the various concepts and techniques of the lending process also are applicable to the nonlending activities of banks, and therefore the total credit exposure of banks must be considered in the discussion of lending policies.

Although the responsibility for avoiding unrealized returns on loans is initially with the individual lending officer and sometimes an appropriate credit committee, the risk–return trade-offs of the entire portfolio and its eventual performance are the overall responsibility of top management. A clearly defined set of lending objectives, policies, and procedures, with an organizational design created to achieve these goals and effectively control operations, is critical.

When assessing this chapter, the reader should not be misled by the emphasis put on the accept–reject decision and the relatively brief discussions of the various intangibles, which in reality are an important part of the complex bank–customer relationship. Since banks are essentially dealing in money and a common standard of performance is the amount of loans made and the receipt of interest and principal repayments, it is common to all but ignore the manner in which these loans are generated, that is, the sales-generating structure of banks. Putting a loan on the books is not simply a function of customer needs and available funds. An efficient process for satisfying those needs through an efficient customer management process is critical to this highly competitive market. Increasingly, major banks are being organized around an account manager, usually a lending officer, who has the knowledge and ability to call on other bank specialists to assist in account generation and maintenance.

The purpose of this chapter is to explore the organizational concepts and the procedures that are consistent with a successful lending process. This process is a series of activities involving the principals, lenders (banks) and borrowers (customers), whose association extends from the original loan request to the successful (or not) repayment. Most analysts of bank activities would agree that this process is an interdependent one, but the exact interactions of the various stages are rarely articulated in a rigorous and comprehensive manner. (For excellent descriptive presentations of the various individual steps of the lending process, the reader is referred to two recent banking texts, Sinkey, 1983, and Hempel, Coleman, and Simonson, 1983.)

This chapter is organized in the following way. We will present a description of the commercial lending process as an integrated system. Where appropriate, specific details will be provided. More in-depth analysis will be presented on several of the crucial concepts and procedures: namely the assessment of the various risks involved in lending, particularly credit risk, the loan review and charge-off process, and some recent thoughts on overall loan portfolio strategy and issues.

THE LENDING PROCESS

The commercial lending process has rarely been studied in its entirety. Cohen, Gilmore, and Singer (1966) did attempt a general analysis of the process, concentrating on the successful repayment situation. Figure 15.1 represents a conceptualization of the lending process. Some original thoughts on this process come from Altman (1980). The events involving decisions by commercial banks are boxed, while the "bullet" items are customer–applicant related. We have also noted several types of specific analyses performed by bankers in order to reach their decisions. As a subset of the broader process of managing the customer relationship, the lending process essentially involves five nonindependent steps: (1) application for a loan; (2) credit evaluation; (3) the accept–reject decision and the structuring of the loan; (4) internal auditing and loan review; and (5) repayment performance. We emphasize the interrelated nature of this process. For example, the terms of a loan influence default risk while the eventual repayment experience could influence future accept–reject decisions. If the repayment experience is unsuccessful, charge-off and

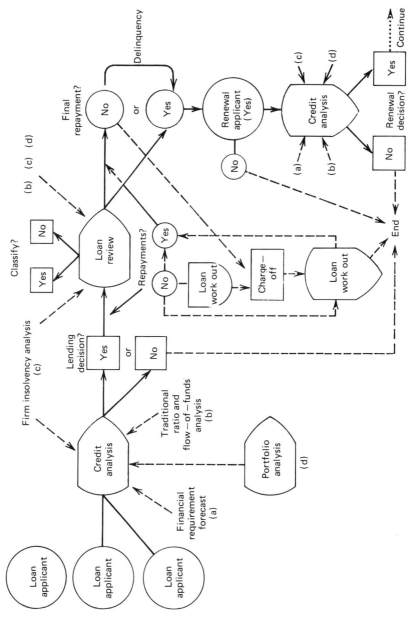

Figure 15.1. Commercial lending process.

476

workout procedures ensue; if successful, a loan renewal application is often forthcoming. Overviewing this process is the assumption of a set of lending policies from top management and an implicit, if not explicit, loan portfolio strategy.

The Loan Organization Structure

Implicit in the lending process is an organization of individuals that has many common features for banks in general but will vary with each bank's size and type of lending emphasized as well as the nature of its customers. For example, an officer of a relatively small bank may perform all of the work involved with loan solicitations, credit analysis, loan structuring, continuous customer contact and loan review, and possibly even collection. In larger banks, these functions are usually handled by different departments and individuals. Figure 15.2 indicates a typical loan organization structure of a large bank.

Loan Divisions, Lending Limit Authority, and Committees. The bank's overall lending policies should be articulated clearly by top management with the sanction of its board of directors. In the case of smaller institutions, the bank's primary trade area is usually defined, as well as other areas in which to concentrate its capital and resources. For large money-center banks and regional institutions, geographical constraints are usually not imposed in the commercial lending function. Consumer lending is, however, usually constrained geographically. The person responsible for the implementation of the lending strategy and the review process should be articulated in the loan policy. A target loan-to-asset or loan-to-deposit ratio as well as other targets, for instance, lending limits, will be specified, and approvals of loans by the appropriate lending committees are noted in Figure 15.2.

Lending officers, essentially a bank's sales force, are usually organized geographically, for example, local, state, national, and international, and/ or by type of industry of customers, for example, manufacturing, mining, agriculture, retail, transport, public utilities, construction, and services. Where the geographical division is large enough, a number of different industrial groups can be serviced individually. The concept of lending officer diversification is based upon individual specialization and superior service for customers.

We stress the importance of an organized customer relationship with an identifiable individual having primary responsibility for specific customer contact. The term *lending officer* has gradually been replaced in many banks as the customer relationship goes beyond loans and could

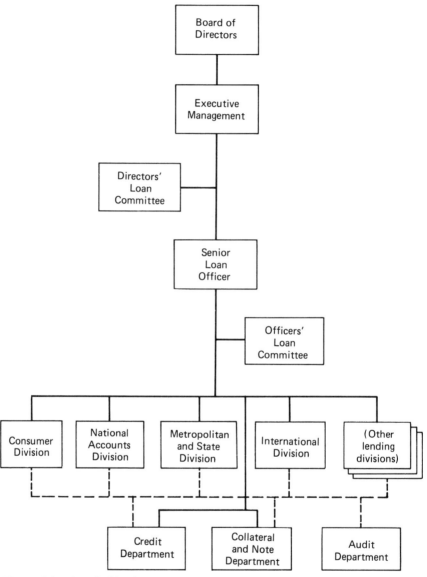

Figure 15.2. A typical bank's organizational structure for the lending function. (Dashed line: support function.) *Source:* Hempel (1983).

include leasing analysis, insurance advice, letters of credit, security guarantees, export activities, cash management counseling and processing,
investment-banking-related services, and other off-balance-sheet activities
for the bank. These other services and the noninterest income generated
are extremely important to the bank and can justify an otherwise non-
profitable interest rate spread on the loan. Such terms as *calling officers,*
account managers, and *relationship managers* have replaced the more
restrictive term to highlight these expanded services. This means that the
contact person must be familiar with both the availability and details of
other services and the persons in the bank who are specialists. Corporate
treasurers, however, oftentimes do not want to be bothered with seeing
a string of specialists from the same bank and will be skeptical if the contact
person is unfamiliar with bank services.

Another relatively new phenomenon emerging as the customer market
has become more competitive and the number of problem banks has
swelled to record levels is a reverse type of credit analysis whereby the
banks themselves are scrutinized as to their vulnerability to financial distress. Large, powerful firms especially will try to avoid banks where there
is a nontrivial probability that bank funding will be interrupted, or where
there is a possibility that an associate bank will get into financial trouble
due to its poor lending portfolio. Indeed, the new dynamics of bank–customer relationships have had a profound impact on the lending market,
and many banks claim that they are now in an unfavorable position as
price takers with respect to interest-rate-competitive pricing.

Depending on the size of the bank, again, individual officers are given
authority to commit funds to customers. For example, a regional bank
had the following guidelines (Sinkey, 1983):

1. The chairman of the board and president have authority to commit
   up to the legal limit of the bank. This authority is to be used sparingly,
   and the directors' loan committee is to be kept advised of any unusual
   or large commitments.
2. Executive vice-presidents may approve new loans up to $500,000.
3. Senior vice-presidents may approve new loans up to $250,000.
4. Vice-presidents may approve new loans up to $100,000.
5. Assistant vice-presidents may approve new loans up to $25,000.
6. Assistant cashiers may approve new loans up to $15,000.
7. Branch managers may approve new loans up to $15,000.
8. Assistant branch managers may approve new loans up to $10,000.
9. Other lending personnel may approve new loans up to $5,000.

Lending authority for individuals at the various levels of the bank will increase as the bank's size increases and as individual loan amounts are a smaller proportion of the bank's total loan portfolio. For example, a senior vice-president at a large New York City bank might approve loans up to $10 million, as compared to $250,000 at the regional bank. It is also likely that differential lending authorities for individuals at the same level might vary depending upon the lending division and the amount of funds committed to that division.

Committees for the review of major loan proposals and loan problems are common at many banks. Figure 15.2 identifies two of those committees, the directors' committee and the officers' committee. The former will usually review major loans approved by the latter group. The officers' committee, which might be called the loan policy committee, is usually the major review group, meeting quite frequently, for example, on a weekly basis, even for the largest banks. Individual lending officers make proposals to this committee, and this is one means for senior management to evaluate and control the performance of lending personnel.

Usually, the size of a loan request will determine whether it is submitted to an officers' lending committee for approval. In general, the larger the bank, the greater the loan request must be before it is discussed at the highest management levels. For example, at one of the very largest banks in the world, a loan request must exceed $80 million before it goes to the senior lending committee. On the other hand, a not-so-large money-center bank with assets greater than $8 billion requires this procedure for loans in excess of just $5 million. Some major banks, however, do not require committee *approval* on new loans but rely instead on a prescribed series of officer signatories. Committee *review* will follow in most cases.

The organizational structure will dictate the relevant players in the game at the initial stage of Figure 15.1 (loan application request). This chapter will not attempt to discuss the various marketing strategies of banks, including price considerations.

Credit Analysis

The next stage of the lending process involves the evaluation of an individual loan applicant's ability to repay the amount of the loan requested, whether a single disbursement is specified, or, in the case of a line of credit, an entire amount to be committed is the relevant figure. Here again, a distinction should be made between the loan amount actually being "taken down" or utilized and the entire line. The difference between an outright loan and a line, of course, is that the latter is a contingent liability of the bank. As such, it obviously deserves the same degree of emphasis as the amount of the loan.

While the dollar amount of the loan is quite important in guiding the repayment assessment process, it is strongly advocated that a more general solvency analysis on the applicant be part of the credit analysis stage. In this way, the bank can also evaluate whether the customer will be a continuing one or not. The short- and long-term credit assessment processes are interrelated with many of the same variables analyzed, for instance, pro forma cash flow analysis. Before discussing lending risk in general, and repayment risk in particular, the importance of financial requirement forecasting, indicated by (a) in Figure 15.1, is worthy of mention.

The following discussion will deal with the financial and cash flow implications of project forecasting. In the context of total "relationship management," however, the lending officer should also look beyond specific projects into the firm's strategic plans.

Forecasting Financial Requirements.   The amount of the loan request will almost always originate with the customer. The bank lending officer should not, however, accept the request as valid. A financial projection of sources and uses of funds should be undertaken jointly with the assistance and cooperation of the applicant. Is the loan request sufficient to meet the specified needs of the applicant? Will the short-term needs, for instance, for six to 12 months, result in further funding requirements? A loan that is too small can result in a problem situation just as can one that is too large. In the former case, an undercapitalized venture might stifle growth and profit objectives, while the latter might create a difficult interest burden for the customer. The loan officer should become familiar with the seasonal activity of the applicant and commence forecasting with a short-term cash flow budget. Surplus or deficit periodic results, for instance, monthly, should be assessed in advance so that adequate funds can be provided or interim investment vehicles planned. Whether short- or long-term forecasting is involved, the key variable to forecast and to analyze relative to other firm accounts is the firm's revenues. Collection and payable terms are factored in to forecast the timing of flows. The overall cash budget can usually be accomplished without pro forma balance sheet and income statement generation. Short-run estimates of sales coupled with receivable and payable policies, compared with experience, and other known outflow schedules should provide the raw data necessary for projections up to six to 12 months.

Longer-term forecasts involve more elaborate sources and uses of funds analysis. Again, sales projections are key, and statistical extrapolation, for instance, linear regression, of sales versus the appropriate balance sheet accounts, for instance, receivables, inventories, fixed assets, accounts payable, and taxes payable, will provide estimates of these items for various future dates. Differences between current balance sheet accounts and the projected future amounts will indicate uses (increase in assets and decreases in liabilities) and sources (decreases in assets and increases in liabilities). After retained profits are added in as a source of funds, the residual between uses and sources is the amount of external funds necessary to finance the operations of the firm. This is a crude estimate of the funds needed, and the analyst is cautioned to test the approach by comparing the historical reliability of the technique in accurately forecasting sources and uses for the firm in question. In essence, the historical stability of the relationships between sales and the various accounts should be verified before reasonable confidence in projections can be allowed. One process, then, for forecasting total *external financing* is:

$$
\begin{aligned}
\text{External} \\
\text{financing} \\
\text{necessary}
\end{aligned}
=
\left(\frac{\text{assets}}{\text{sales}} \times \begin{array}{l}\text{expected change}\\ \text{in sales}\end{array} \right)
-
\left(\frac{\text{liabilities}}{\text{sales}} \times \begin{array}{l}\text{expected}\\ \text{change}\\ \text{in sales}\end{array} \right)
$$

$$
- \left(\frac{\text{profit}}{\text{margin}} \times \begin{array}{l}\text{expected}\\ \text{sales}\end{array} \times \left(1 - \begin{array}{l}\text{dividend}\\ \text{payout}\\ \text{ratio}\end{array} \right) \right)
$$

Assuming a positive relationship between change in assets and change in sales, and also change in appropriate liabilities, the first two terms on the right-hand side are uses and sources of funds respectively. The third term indicates funds provided from profits on sales after taxes and dividends.

Many large banks engage in extensive simulations of repayment and other measures of firm performance under alternative interest rate, general economic, inflation, and key variable assumptions. Similar scenario-type analyses are performed by the customer firms themselves if resources and sophistication exist. Banks should, however, have the capability to perform these operations, too.

After the appropriate financing needs are established, we move to the other techniques involved with credit analysis; namely, traditional ratio and pro forma statement analysis and generic firm insolvency analysis. Implicit in the lending decision is some overall notion of combining the various loans of the bank into a coherent and clearly defined portfolio strategy. The discussion of loan portfolio strategy and procedures is deferred until the end of the lending process discussion. Note, however, that the portfolio composition properties of the loan portfolio should be evaluated at several stages.

Risk Assessment.   There are at least a half-dozen different types of risks associated with the commercial lending function of banks. The most important of the risk categories are:

1. Credit or repayment risk
2. Investment or interest rate risk
3. Portfolio contribution risk
4. Operations risk
5. Fraud risk
6. Syndication risk

One might think that liquidity or marketability risk is also relevant. But, since banks usually do not make loans in anticipation of liquidating the credit prior to the loans' maturity, the concern with the liquidity risk of the credit is not particularly important. The lending market in the United States is essentially a primary market only, and little secondary market activity is apparent. Banks do not rely on loans to meet their liquidity needs, and the Federal Reserve does not recognize those assets as primary reserves.

Operations risk refers to the administration of loans and the risk that poor operating procedures will jeopardize the eventual timely receipt of interest and principal payment or the priority status given a loan default. While the subject of operating efficiencies goes beyond the scope of this chapter, one cannot overestimate the importance of an effective monitoring of loans on a continuous basis. Receipts must be collected on time and particular attention must be given to effective communication among the loan officers, pricing staff, review staff, and collection personnel. The effectiveness of a dynamic lending organization can be reduced if, for example, the bank is not organized well to move quickly in case of loan irregularities. One large New York bank lost over $5 million recently due to the clearing of a check from a customer who had declared bankruptcy.

Fraud risk refers to the honesty of bank employees and the effectiveness of discouraging illegal insider transactions. Clear and precise loan policies coupled with unencumbered internal audit procedures are effective means to discourage fraud risk. Many of the major bank failures have resulted from operating and fraud-related activities associated with problem loan situations.

Syndication risk arises when the loan is part of a larger financing activity involving a number of lending institutions. When multiple banks are involved, the borrower's credit risk should be evaluated in conjunction with the creditworthiness of the participating banks. With the likely "shakeout" in the financial services industry coming in the wake of deregulation, the number of syndicated deals resulting in problems due to lender risk is likely to increase.

Credit Risk Assessment.   The reader has no doubt heard of the famous five C's of credit management related to the likelihood that a potential or existing borrower will successfully meet the scheduled interest and principal payments. These include:

1. Capacity (ability to repay)
2. Character (willingness to repay)
3. Capital (wealth of borrower)
4. Collateral (security, if necessary)
5. Conditions (external, economic)

We will concentrate on the first of these items since the others are relatively straightforward and involve a descriptive discussion of the issues. For example, the survival (so far) of Pan American World Airways but the bankruptcy of Braniff International Corp. can be attributed partially to the wealth differential between these two unprofitable carriers. Pan Am was able to derive over $1 billion from the sale of two of its nonairline assets (hotel and real estate) while Braniff did not have this wealth reserve. The discussion on creditworthiness and the capacity to repay centers on three related ingredients:

1. Traditional financial ratio and flow-of-funds analysis (indicated as (b) in Figure 15.1)
2. Cash flow issues (a subset of 1. above)
3. Generic solvency and bankruptcy prediction analysis

As indicated in Figure 15.1, these techniques are utilized in the credit analysis process and assist the decision maker in making the accept–reject decision and later on in the loan review function.

Traditional Financial Analysis.

Financial Data and Ratios.   All banking institutions include in their fundamental credit analysis a comprehensive examination of the loan applicant's status with respect to historical performance measures. By far, the most common technique utilized is a comparative and trend analysis of financial ratios reflecting a firm's liquidity, profitability, debt usage and capacity, activity, and a number of other performance categories. The raw data are assembled from information provided by the applicant and possibly outside references. In addition, secondary financial data are available from statistical information sources and from large computerized data bases.

Most banks use spreadsheets for recording an applicant's financial information. These sheets are comprehensive listings of financial statement data as well as some of the basic ratios. The data are conveniently formatted to meet the needs of the analytical procedures and are increasingly used as the first step in a computerized data storage and analytical system. Typically, bank trainees are assigned the task of working up these spreadsheets and doing the fundamental data calculations, providing ratios and possibly initial reports on the relative health of the applicant. As computerized spreadsheets become more popular, the range of ratios and analytical procedures performed on the raw data widens, as do the complexity and sophistication of analysis (see discussion below on failure prediction models). Personal computer availability enables the lending officer or credit department to access and analyze data instantaneously. "What-if" scenarios are no longer the sole province of planning and management science departments of banks.

Traditional ratio analysis involves the calculation of measures indicating the ability of an applicant to meet its short-term obligations (liquidity), its ability to utilize assets effectively (profitability), the relative contribution of owners versus creditors to the financing of those assets (leverage), and the turnover of certain assets in a normal accounting reporting period relative to the sales-generating ability of the firm (activity). An interesting anomaly exists with respect to ratios. While analysts, and particularly academics, criticize the conceptual basis of ratio analysis and question its information content, ratios pervade all aspects of the business environment and are perhaps utilized more than any other financial technique in the performance assessment of corporations all over the world. Hence, ratios are studied in classrooms, and applied in the credit, investment, merger, business strategy, auditing, legal, and many other arenas. There must be something to this technique, which transforms data reported in balance sheets, income statements, and flow-of-funds reports and is used to compare individual entities to other firms, usually in the same industrial sector, or to assess over time what a measure of performance has been indicating.

While there are some who question the ability of ratios to provide useful credit information, we believe that ratios do reveal a great amount of information for assessing the repayment ability of applicants and therefore should be used in the accept–reject decision. The questions, however, involve the following characteristics of ratio analysis. It is a univariate, one-ratio-at-a-time type of analysis. Interpretation is subjective, indications may be ambiguous or even misleading, and, perhaps most important, there is no "bottom line" to the result. With respect to credit analysis, there is no way that traditional ratio analysis can provide an unambiguous, objective answer to the question of whether or not to extend credit to an applicant.

The univariate or sequential nature of ratio analysis implies that each measure is analyzed individually and an assessment is made as to the applicant's strength or weakness. Then, the next ratio is examined. The relative importance of each measure either is not assessed or is a function of the analyst's subjective evaluation of that ratio's worth. The same ratio can therefore be assessed differently by one analyst compared to another. It is not unusual for one ratio to indicate a positive condition, another to show a neutral trend, and a third to point in a negative direction. The ambiguity problem is clear, and we lack the ability to provide an overall objective assessment of the applicant's ability to repay in a timely manner. Even assuming that univariate ratio analysis is useful, the varying importance of different ratios for different industry/size categories is rarely articulated in the credit policy guidelines.

The Loan Officers Experiment.   A study by Libby (1975) examined the question of whether accounting ratios provide useful information to loan officers trying to predict business failures. Using a subset of ratios from Beaver's (1967) classic univariate ratio article on business failure prediction, Libby found that five ratios provided sufficient information for failure analysis and were more manageable than the original 14 variables. The five ratios represented different dimensions of firm operations, including:

1.   Cash position: cash/total assets
2.   Liquidity: current assets/current liabilities
3.   Profitability: net income/total assets
4.   Asset balance: current assets/total assets
5.   Activity: current assets/sales

The usefulness of the information was judged based on the accuracy of the loan officers' predictions.

Forty-three commercial loan officers participated in Libby's experiment. Each loan officer was given 70 ratio data sets of five ratios each. To set the a priori probabilities, they were told that one-half of the firms experienced failure within three years of the statement date. The loan officers were instructed to work independently and to complete the cases within one week.

Libby found that the loan officers' predictive accuracy was superior to random assignment (i.e., fail–nonfail) and concluded that the ratio information was utilized correctly by the loan officers. On the basis of other tests, Libby concluded that: (1) there was no significant difference between the mean predictive accuracy of the small and of the large bank representatives; (2) there were no significant correlations between predictive accuracy and loan officer characteristics, such as age and experience; (3) there were no differences in short-term, test–retest reliability among user subgroups; and (4) there was a relatively uniform interpretation of the accounting data across bankers.

Critique.   Libby concluded that his reduced set of accounting ratios permits bankers with diverse backgrounds to make accurate predictions of business failures. While his experiment was interesting and useful (indeed, several similar studies have subsequently been performed), one can question the fact that the loan officers were told beforehand that one-half of the firms being analyzed failed. This type of information is, of course, not available to analysts. Indeed, Casey (1980) found that loan officers who were not informed about failure frequencies could only correctly predict 27% of a sample of bankrupt firms. Nonbankrupt accuracy was much better, however. My own experiments with loan officers, graduate business students, and credit analysts is that knowledgeable people do process ratio information fairly well in assessing failure propensities, but not as well as statistical models constructed for the explicit purpose of business failure classification. We also find that knowledge of the prior probability of failure does enhance the predictive accuracy.

In our opinion, the problem with traditional ratio analysis is not the lack of useful information, but that the technique has been unattractively "dressed" and presented in a nondynamic fashion. An enhancement of the traditional methodology is a procedure for utilizing the information content of ratios in a clear, unambiguous, and directly relevant manner. Before proceeding to such methods, it should be noted that one particular concept has received a great deal of attention of late from the credit community: operating cash flow analysis.

Cash Flow Analysis.   There is nothing new about the relevance of cash flows for assessing repayment probabilities. Interest and principal are paid from cash. An elegant balance sheet does not repay the loan, but cash does. Beaver (1967) found that of all the ratios he examined with respect to business failure prediction, the cash flow/long-term debt ratio performed best and had the highest and longest early warning interval prior to failure. Altman's studies confirm the usefulness of cash flows although he consistently (1968, 1977, 1983) finds that basic profitability measures, for instance, return before interest and taxes on assets, slightly outperform similar cash flow variables in bankruptcy prediction.

Defining Cash Flows. Most analysts utilizing large data bases have defined *cash flows* in the old, security-analyst manner. They add to after-tax profits noncash expenses, chiefly depreciation and amortization. A more precise and more useful cash flow figure concentrates on operations and specifically imputes working capital items, such as changes in accounts receivable, inventories, and payables. The suggested cash flow figure involves working capital provided by continuing operations plus or minus changes in noncash working capital accounts (except for short-term indebtedness, e.g., seasonal bank loans, nontrade notes payable, and current portion of long-term debt). This concept of operating cash flow is consistent with that favored by the FASB. The FASB is presently considering rules to permit publicly traded firms to expand and restructure disclosure of operating cash flow data and to permit the user (e.g., bank credit analyst) better to assess the amount, timing, and uncertainty of future cash flows. A survey commissioned by the Financial Accounting Federation (Harris, 1980) found that cash flow was rated by corporate and government executives as the single most important item on published financial statements. Most credit agencies and the popular business press of late, for instance, Green (1981), look toward operating cash flows as providing a better assessment of credit strength than earnings analysis. And, perhaps most important, operating cash flows are not affected by different accounting reporting practices such as inventory profits.

In an informative recent article, Casey and Bartczak (1983) assess the ability of operating cash flow data to discriminate between bankrupt and nonbankrupt firms. The results of an experiment by Casey and Bartczak do *not* confirm the recent claims for the additional information value of operating cash flows. They found that classification accuracy of a multivariate model that did *not* contain operating cash flow data was significantly greater than the accuracy of operating cash flow variables alone and that classification accuracy was not improved when the operating cash flow ratio was added to an existing multivariate model of bankruptcy assessment. The problems with cash flow data were particularly evident in the classification of nonbankrupt firms. Indeed, as reported in other studies, Casey and Bartczak found that profitability variables tend to have the greatest individual discriminatory power and also outperform cash flow variables, on a univariate basis. As will be shown, cumulative profitability measures (e.g., retained earnings) have consistently been amongst the best predictors of distress. In summary, Casey and Bartczak do not find support for what many policy makers are advocating, namely, the restructured presentation of data to facilitate operating cash flow analysis and the expected enhancement of early warnings of financial distress.

It is not suggested, however, that banks and other credit institutions abandon operating cash flow analysis. Indeed, it can be a very informative indicator. What is apparent is that operating cash flows are only one of a number of important factors likely to indicate a firm's creditworthiness and that multiratio techniques (similar to the Z-score and *Zeta*® procedures, taken up next) are more effective and conceptually appropriate.

Economic Profits and Cash Flows.   A final word on cash flows is appropriate. Even if one holds to the more classic definition of cash flow involving reported profits plus noncash expenses, one should also consider the concept of economic profits and cash flows. The latter is defined as:

$$\text{Reported profits} + \text{depreciation} \pm \begin{array}{c} \text{capital} \\ \text{consumption} \\ \text{adjustment} \end{array} = \begin{array}{c} \text{economic} \\ \text{cash} \\ \text{flows} \end{array}$$

The capital consumption adjustment (CCA) reflects the difference between book depreciation and economic depreciation. The accounting depreciation schedule, based since 1981 on the Accelerated Cost Recovery System's depreciation guidelines, includes accelerated or straight-line procedures. Economic depreciation reflects the replacement costs of assets and is directly affected by inflation. From 1973 to 1982, the CCA was negative for U.S. nonfinancial corporations and presented an even bleaker picture for those firms needing to replace worn-out assets. With the advent of more liberal depreciation schedules in 1982 and a dramatic drop in replacement costs in 1983, the CCA turned positive for the first time in a decade. While the sign (positive or negative) of the change in CCA is important, the aggregate level of real cash flows is most indicative of cash flows and debt repayment capacity and potential. This analysis can, of course, be brought down to the individual-firm level, especially with the expanded footnotes on replacement costs now required of many firms.

Z-Score and *Zeta* Models of Bankruptcy.   It is undeniable that the large firm is no longer invulnerable to financial distress. Table 15.1 lists 48 firms with liabilities greater than $120 million just prior to their bankruptcy petition. The concern amongst bankers for improved credit techniques and

Table 15.1. Largest United States Bankruptcies in Terms of Dollar Liabilities as of October 1983[ab]

Company Name	Total Liabilities (in millions of dollars)	Bankruptcy Petition Date	Filed under
Penn Central Transportation Co.	3,300	June 1970	Section 77
Wickes	2,000	April 1982	Chapter 11
Itel Corp.	1,700	January 1981	Chapter 11
Baldwin–United Corp.	1,600	September 1983	Chapter 11
GHR Energy Corp.[c]	1,200	January 1983	Chapter 11
Manville Corp.	1,116	August 1982	Chapter 11
Braniff Airlines	1,100	May 1982	Chapter 11
W. T. Grant	1,000	October 1975	Chapter XI
Seatrain Lines	785	February 1981	Chapter 11
Coral Petroleum[c]	682	June 1983	Chapter XI
Continental Airlines[d]	650	September 1983	Chapter 11
Continental Mortgage Investors	607	March 1976	Chapter XI
United Merchants & Manufacturing	552	July 1977	Chapter XI
AM International	510	April 1982	Chapter 11
OPM Leasing[c]	505	March 1981	Chapter 11
Saxon Industries	461	April 1982	Chapter 11
Commonwealth Oil Refining Co.	421	March 1978	Chapter XI
W. Judd Kassuba	420	December 1973	Chapter XI
Erie Lackawanna Railroad	404	June 1972	Section 77
White Motor Corp.	399	September 1980	Chapter 11
Investors Funding Corp.	379	October 1974	Chapter XI
Sambo's Restaurants	370	November 1981	Chapter 11
Amarex	348	December 1982	Chapter 11
Food Fair Corp.	347	October 1978	Chapter XI
Great American Mortgage & Trust	326	March 1977	Chapter XI
McLouth Steel	323	December 1981	Chapter 11
U.S. Financial Services	300	July 1973	Chapter XI
Chase Manhattan Mortgage & Realty Trust	290	February 1979	Chapter XI
Daylin, Inc.	250	February 1975	Chapter XI
Guardian Mortgage Investors	247	March 1978	Chapter XI
Revere Copper & Brass	237	October 1982	Chapter 11
Chicago, Rock Island & Pacific	221	March 1975	Section 77
Wilson Foods	200	May 1983	Chapter 11
Equity Funding Corp. of America	200	April 1973	Chapter X
Interstate Stores, Inc.	190	May 1974	Chapter XI
Fidelity Mortgage Investors	187	January 1975	Chapter XI
KDT Industries	185	August 1982	Chapter 11

Table 15.1. (*Continued*)

Company Name	Total Liabilities (in millions of dollars)	Bankruptcy Petition Date	Filed under
HRT Industries	183	November 1982	Chapter 11
Omega, Alpha Corp.	175	September 1974	Chapter X
Lionel Corp.	165	February 1982	Chapter 11
Reading Railroad	158	November 1971	Section 77
Boston & Main Railroad	148	December 1975	Section 77
Westgate-California	144	February 1974	Chapter X
Colwell Mortgage & Trust	142	February 1978	Chapter XI
Phoenix Steel Corp.	137	August 1983	Chapter 11
Pacific Far East Lines	132	January 1978	Chapter XI
Allied Supermarkets	124	November 1978	Chapter XI
Penn-Dixie Industries	122	April 1980	Chapter 11

[a] Does not include commercial banking entities.
[b] Compiled by E. I. Altman.
[c] Privately held firm.
[d] Subsidiary of Texas Air Corp. Estimate of long-term debt only.

reduced loan charge-offs is further heightened by the postdepression record level of business failures in the United States in 1982–1983. An increasingly common, although by no means pervasive, procedure found in bank credit and loan review departments is a set of techniques generally referred to as *Z*-score models.

Caveat: One thing should be made perfectly clear at this point. The techniques described below should not be construed as potential substitutes for traditional credit and loan review procedures. The *Z*-score tool is exactly that, another tool of analysis to help confirm or not the more subjective traditional techniques and to provide a rapid means for loan portfolio review so as to help allocate scarce resources to those situations requiring more in-depth time and analysis. There may be other benefits, such as criteria for pricing and inputs for portfolio decisions, as Bennett (1984) advocates.

Z-Score Analysis. *Z*-score analysis (Altman, 1968, 1983) is an attempt to bridge the gap between traditional financial ratio analysis and objective, statistical multivariate techniques. For example, discriminant analysis, utilizing multiple ratio measurements, can be performed to find a set of variables and to assign objective weightings to them so that the result, in the form of a single overall indicator (Z), best discriminates between the original groupings of data points. (In this case and also in the *Zeta* (1977) model the groups are represented by bankrupt and nonbankrupt firms.) The original 1968 model, built solely for publicly traded manufacturers, is

$$Z = 1.2X_1 + 1.4X_2 + 3.3X_3 + 0.6X_4 + 1.0X_5$$

where X_1 = working capital/total assets

X_2 = retained earnings/total assets

X_3 = earnings before interest and taxes/ total assets

X_4 = market value of equity/book value of total liabilities

X_5 = sales/total assets

The classification rule recommended after observing results is for

$Z < 1.81$: assign to bankrupt group

$Z \geqslant 2.99$: assign to nonbankrupt group

$Z > 1.81$ but < 2.99: assign to gray zone

These classification rules are not derived directly from the computerized model but are selected as practical guides for decision-making purposes when computerized discriminant programs are not available. (See Eisenbeis, 1977 for a relevant discussion.)

Misclassifications fell in the gray zone for the original sample of bankrupt firms. Since 1968, the model has retained its fairly high accuracy of classifying about 85% of the actual bankrupt firms as bankrupt, approximately one year prior to failure. The average score of U.S. manufacturers has fallen as the average firm's profitability is lower and leverage higher. Still, the 1.81 score is a fairly good indicator of financial distress. Approximately 4 to 5% of U.S. manufacturers had Z-scores below 1.81 in 1983. A score below 1.81, however, is certainly no guarantee that a firm will fail, as witnessed by the evolution of financial distress of two of the giant manufacturers in the United States: Chrysler Corporation and International Harvester Corporation. The Z-score trend of those two firms is shown in Figure 15.3. Note that Chrysler's score in 1980 (at the time of the government bailout) was definitely in the bankrupt zone but still considerably higher than the late 1983 situation at International Harvester. Note also the subsequent recovery of Chrysler and its movement out of the depths of the bankrupt zone. Harvester is still suffering, but with the

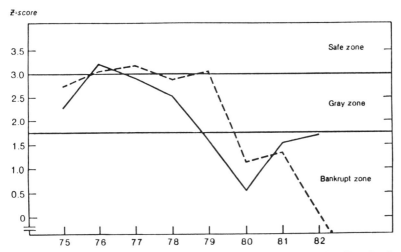

Figure 15.3. Z-score analysis: International Harvester Corporation (with Chrysler Corp. comparison). (Solid line: Chrysler; dashed line: International Harvester.)

help of a patient and forgiving set of creditors, it may also eventually recover.

Figure 15.4 shows the demise, and the prediction thereof, of two large recent bankruptcies: McLouth Steel and Penn Dixie Industries. In both cases the early warning was clearly evident although McLouth's movement into the bankrupt zone was fairly close to its 1981 petition date. The Z-score model cannot, however, indicate precisely the time of the possible failure since bankruptcy is essentially a legal and behavioral event, more so than an economic phenomenon. A firm might be economically insolvent and yet still remain a "going concern," operating outside the bankruptcy courts.

One problem with the original Z-score is its direct relevance to publicly traded firms only; that is, the fourth variable requires the market value of equity (number of shares outstanding of equity and preferred times the current share price). Modification of the Z-score model for privately held firms can be accomplished by substituting the book value of equity for the market value and reestimating the weights. This new model is described in Altman (1983). The accuracy of this model is somewhat less than that of the original but still respectable.

Zeta® **Analysis.** A second-generation model, designed for purposes similar to those of the Z-score, was constructed in 1977 (Altman, Haldeman, and Narayanan, 1977). It improves upon the Z-score in that it is based on a more up-to-date sample, includes the latest accounting reporting

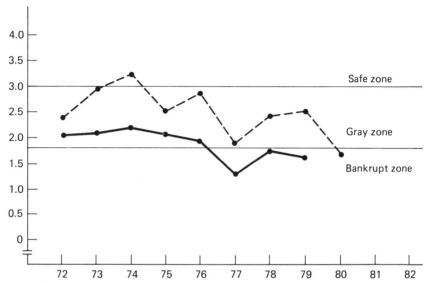

Figure 15.4. *Z*-score trend analysis: Penn Dixie Industries and McLouth Steel. (Solid line: Penn Dixie; dashed line: McLouth.)

changes (such as lease capitalization), is applicable to a broader range of companies, including manufacturers, retailers, wholesalers, airlines, and some service firms, and is more accurate, especially for long-term predictions. This newer model is also based on a discriminant analysis methodology and includes seven variables. Scott (1981), in his assessment of a number of empirical failure models, finds that *Zeta*® most closely resembles a conceptually valid failure specification.

Bank Usage of Z and Zeta®.   A number of banks have used (and are continuing to use) *Z*-score type models in their credit analysis. The demonstrated utility of these models in banks so far is more evident in loan review compared with the accept–reject credit evaluation (see Figure 15.1). Still, a number of bankers, for example, Bettinger (1980), advocate using *Z*-score-type models at the loan origination stage. It is fair to say that with acceptance in the literature (e.g., Brigham, 1982; Van Horne, 1983; Weston and Brigham, 1982; Sinkey, 1983) and by an increasing number of practitioners, these models are well tested for meeting the needs of the individual users. More work needs to be done on the private-firm application and on quarterly updates.

These models and others like them (e.g., Deakin, 1973; Chesser, 1974; Orgler, 1975; Wilcox, 1976; Ohlson, 1980; Kaplan, 1980) do not take into consideration the specific customer relationships that are important in commercial banking. Classification models can be used to complement the rest of the loan evaluation process (indicated as [c] in Figure 14.1). It should also be remembered that models like Z and $Zeta^{®}$ were designed specifically for bankruptcy prediction rather than for creditworthiness assessment. Others, like Orgler (1975), utilized loan data from those loans already accepted to construct similar models to be used in loan review.

Interest Rate Risk.   The lending decision and the specific loan structure parts (next section) must be coordinated with the bank's own financing sources and costs. One of the primary characteristics of sources of funds to banks is the volatile nature of their cost. Bank borrowing sources, primarily certificates of deposit or federal funds, are very short-term sources and are now virtually unregulated. Most of the loans made are either (1) short term, for instance, for working capital and seasonal needs, at fixed rates, or (2) longer term, that is, term loans, lines of credit, or revolving credit forms, and the interest rate charged is variable, usually based on a fixed premium above the prime rate. In both of these cases, there is little interest rate risk since the period in which the cost of funds to banks can rise close to or above the interest rate being received on loans is short.

Interest rate risks are certainly associated with long-term fixed-income loans such as real estate mortgages. Some corporate loans are also still being written at fixed rates. While commercial banks tend to avoid heavy concentration in such loans, mortgages are the lifeblood of mutual savings banks and savings and loan associations. During the early 1980s, when interest rates skyrocketed and the cost of money to financial institutions was commensurately high, or funds were unavailable due to competitive disadvantages, a large number of S&Ls and savings banks failed or were merged into stronger institutions. The savings industry was aided by legislation that permitted them to raise funds from individuals at money market rates and by the drop in interest rates. Commercial banks, with one or two exceptions, did not suffer during the high-interest-rate period because they were able to pass along those high rates to their customers. If commercial banks continue to avoid heavy concentration in long-term fixed-rate loans, the interest rate risk in bank lending portfolios is quite small. And, as variable-rate lending expands and interest rate risk is shifted to the borrower, one can expect firms to argue for lower interest rates. In other words, both the risk and the return on commercial lending are being reduced, although it is difficult to assess whether the two reductions balance out. The implications of recent trends for credit assessment, loan review, and customer relationships will be interesting to track.

Another reason that interest rate risk is not likely to pose problems for loan administration is the ability to hedge the fixed-rate loan portfolio in the futures market. A typical hedge could involve selling short financial futures to protect the lender against a rise in interest rates after a term loan has been made at a fixed rate or a long-term mortgage has been granted. If interest rates do in fact rise, the price of financial futures would drop and the resultant gain for the lender–hedger would help offset the "loss" involved with a fixed-rate loan.

Structuring the Loan

Once the decision to make the loan has been made, the specific terms must be set, including:

1. Term, price, and schedule of repayments of the loan
2. Compensating balances; commitment fee, if any
3. Collateral requirements, if any
4. Loan covenants

Pricing.   Details on pricing of loans and contingent bank liabilities go beyond the scope of this chapter, but a few general comments are warranted. The traditional thinking is to price a loan based on its risk characteristics, with the more creditworthy customers being charged the lower rate. This "prime" rate should, of course, still cover the bank's own cost of funds (e.g., its weighted-average cost of capital), its cost of administering the credit, and an acceptable profit margin. Increasingly, loan pricing is tied to the LIBOR (London Interbank Offered Rate) as representing the cost of funds for banks. (For a good discussion of customer profitability analysis, see Sinkey, 1983.) In recent years, some banks have begun to explore a type of portfolio approach to lending with the risk of an individual loan based on both traditional criteria and the particular loan's "contribution" to the overall loan portfolio's risk. We will return to this concept.

A straight credit-scoring approach does not consider unique customer relationships and characteristics, such as new-product development, the size of the firm, its average balances, the frequency of borrowing, and the historical relationship with the bank. These are very important considerations and could influence the credit decision in a manner that differs from the credit scoring results. Size alone, however, should not dictate credit decisions and pricing. No longer is the large firm invulnerable to distress. This lesson was learned the hard way recently as enormous oil and gas drilling and supply firms defaulted on huge amounts of short-term credit from banks, not to mention the over one dozen large firm failures (liabilities over $150 million) in 1981–1983.

Compensating Balances.   This is simply the practice of requiring customers to keep a certain percentage of their loan outstanding in a non-interest-earning demand deposit. These idle balances permit the bank to realize a higher return on its funds and commitments and ensure a buffer in times of emergency—both for the customer and for the bank. The latter will oftentimes attempt to set off the balances against an outstanding loan in times of default and bankruptcy, although the conditions when setoffs are permitted are restricted under the new Bankruptcy Code (see Altman, 1983).

Compensating balances are a phenomenon found primarily in American banking. Recently, bank customers, particularly the larger and more powerful firms, have negotiated loans with reduced (e.g., 5%–10%) compensating balances or, in the case of long-term revolving credit agreements, zero balances. It is likely that balances will continue to disappear as competition for prime customers intensifies and as banking becomes even more deregulated. If margins on loans diminish due to variable-rate lending and balances also are increasingly less common, then the trend toward more off-balance-sheet activities and noninterest revenues will be encouraged as banks adjust to lower profit levels. These trends are dangerous if top management underestimates the risk characteristics of such activities and does not treat contingent claims on the bank as important. Indeed, one can make the case for contingent liabilities being even more risky than regular loans since the priority status is less clear in a default situation.

Collateral Requirements.   Loans may be collateralized or unsecured, with the latter the more common for *short-term* commercial and industrial loans in the United States. This is a fairly unique feature in U.S. banking since most lending abroad requires collateral or third-party support. Aggressive U.S. banks have continued to lend on an uncollateralized basis abroad. Most *long-term* loans and many loans from small banks, however, are secured. In a secured loan, the customer grants the right to sell the collateral and apply the proceeds to the loan if the borrower cannot repay. This agreement is part of the written structure of the loan.

One of the principal types of assets used as security on loans is *real property*, which involves formal title search, property appraisal, and tax status. In all cases, title insurance is bought to protect the bank against defects not disclosed in the title search. Other types of collateral include both personal and business assets. Personal assets commonly used are:

1. Marketable securities: corporate, federal, and municipal bonds, preferred and common stocks
2. Mutual funds and cash surrender value of life insurance
3. Savings accounts in the bank and at other banks
4. Residences, automobiles, boats, and so on

Business property used as collateral includes:

1. Equipment, crops, inventory
2. Accounts receivable
3. Warehouse receipts for commodities
4. Commercial real estate

Each bank will determine the percentage of each of those assets that can be used as collateral; for instance, 90% of the value of high-grade corporate bonds, federal agency and municipal bonds, 90% of life insurance cash value, 75% of the value of common stocks listed on major stock exchanges, and 80% of assigned accounts receivable.

Loan Covenants.   In addition to demanding collateral on loans, banks attempt to protect themselves against deterioration of the customer's ability to repay interest and principal by writing restrictive features into the loan agreement. The longer the maturity of the credit, the more likely that extensive convenants will be pursued by the bank. *Affirmative covenants* stipulate responsibilities of the customer to submit financial statements, maintain adequate insurance, pay interest and principal as scheduled, and inform the bank of major activities of the firm. *Negative covenants* require certain performance criteria of the firm and can prohibit borrower activities. The former might include certain threshholds with respect to liquidity or leverage ratios while the latter might prohibit the purchase of major assets or the payment of preferred or cash dividends if certain other covenants, for example, ratios, are not met. The monitoring of loan covenants and other activities of corporate customers has become more prominent of late with the introduction into the corporate financial literature of the concept of agency costs. These are the costs involved with conflicts of divergent interests of the major parties involved with managing and financing a firm's operations. The principal parties are the managers (owners' agents), the owners, and the various types of creditors including banks. (See Jensen and Meckling, 1976 for a classic work in this area.)

Loan Review, Classification, Charge-offs, and Workout

The next set of stages in the credit process involves actual or predicted problems with the timely repayment of interest and principal on outstanding loans. The nature of taking risks on loans invariably means that some proportion of the loan portfolio will become delinquent and will possibly be charged off against reserves set up each period for that possibility. The loan review function is a critical process in reducing these losses and in the general monitoring of the quality of the entire loan portfolio. Experienced loan review personnel should, and often do, get involved in the workout and recovery activity. In Figure 15.1, these two functions are separated, indicating that loan workout steps can follow or come before the charge-off of loans as uncollectible in the normal collection phase. There is still the real possibility that all or a proportion of the amount actually charged off will eventually be recovered. The *charge-off* and recovery experience of U.S. banks will be pursued at a later point. It should be noted, however, that some banks channel problem loans to their workout personnel (experienced workout and review specialists, legal personnel, and staff) before a loan is charged off, in anticipation of a loan restructuring that can avoid the actual charge-off. Strategies to reduce risk exposures should also commence as early as possible once the loan is considered a likely charge-off.

Each year, Robert Morris Associates (the trade association of commercial lending officers) surveys loan losses. Bank responses are classified by bank size, location of bank, and whether the loan was domestic or international. One of the primary statistics published is the amount of loans charged off in that year compared to total loans outstanding or total equity of banks. In addition, results of recoveries on charged-off loans compared to loan losses are recorded. It is possible to derive even more comprehensive statistics from the Federal Reserve System based on results from its member banks. In recent years, the amount of net loan losses as a percentage of bank equity capital has ranged from about 2.5% to over 5.0%. Of course, banks that have failed can experience loan losses in excess of equity in extreme cases, or certainly the losses can reduce equity capital to such an unacceptable level that the FDIC will step in and close the bank in one way or another. See Orgler and Wolkowitz (1976) for a discussion of bank capital adequacy.

Loan review consists of a periodic audit of the outstanding loan portfolio. In addition to the objective of reducing loan losses, review procedures seek to detect actual or problem loans as early as possible, to document stated loan policy and ensure that it is being followed, and to inform bank management about the overall condition of loans and the credit quality of individual lending units.

Loan workout specialists spend time with troubled customers to determine whether, when, and how much of the loan is collectible, and, it is hoped, to work out a restructuring to avoid charge-offs. As such, a specific breed of lending officer is warranted, someone who has the patience and negotiating skills necessary to work through difficult and frustrating situations. With the recent increase in business failures, particularly those of large size, the role of the loan review and workout specialists has grown tremendously, and the value added of these people has become potentially quite significant.

The Importance of Early Warning of Problem Credits. The procedures for loan review and workout should be articulated in the overall loan policy of the bank. As indicated in Figure 15.1, a number of the same procedures used in the original accept–reject decision are also applicable to the review process. Indeed, the generic solvency assessment, for instance, Z-score analysis, is more likely to be embraced in loan review than earlier in the lending process. Since most banks are unable to review all credits on a short-interval basis, one of the critical aspects of a loan review function, particularly at a major bank, is the efficient allocation of its scarce resources (personnel) to the most critical areas. Hence, a rapid, accurate early warning device is vital to this phase. (See Hoffman and Fisher, 1980 for a typical bank credit grading system, including the frequency with which loans are reviewed based on the repayment outlook.) Firms that display financial profiles similar to past problem credits should get immediate attention.

Bankers desire as early warning as possible in order either to work with the customer so as to improve a deteriorating situation or to reduce the risk exposure of the bank. A minimum of two years is often cited as sufficient time to provide for risk reduction action. In certain instances, however, it is possible to work with a firm and turn a failing situation around even at the eleventh hour. The case of GTI Corporation, reported in Altman (1983, Chapter 6), illustrates how one firm used the Z-score model in an interactive manner in order to manage itself back to financial health. One could argue that it is the responsibility of professionals like bank officers and accounting audit personnel to work with troubled customers. It is to their advantage as well.

The responsible loan officer should take immediate corrective action once a problem loan is detected. A restructured loan agreement, often with a change of restrictive clauses, inclusion of third-party support on collateral, and a new repayment schedule, is often forthcoming. This should be attempted if there is a reasonable chance to work out of a difficult situation. More frequent reports and closer monitoring of the performance of problem firms are warranted. Additional collateral might be called for if the existing security is insufficient. Third-party guarantees or endorsements could be added to reduce the bank's risk. Particular attention should be paid to the detection of fraud on the part of the firm or its agents. Proof of fraud in a formal bankruptcy might raise the priority status of the bank.

Problem Credit Classification.   A related phase in the problem credit area is the formal classification of a loan into certain categories reflecting the seriousness of the situation. Classification can be made from in-bank examinations by the relevant state or federal regulatory authorities based on visits to the bank and assessment of credit quality and/or internal reviews by bank personnel. The goal of regulatory examinations is to evaluate the liquidity and solvency of a bank, the quality of its assets, the sufficiency of internal controls, the soundness of management policies, and, probably most important, the adequacy of the bank's capital base.

The primary focus of in-bank examination is on credit quality and control procedures. While some of the steps of the examination process are mechanical and can be handled by inexperienced personnel, others require a sophistication of analysis that implies an experienced, hard-nosed assessment of repayment prospects. Tests must be made of the borrower's potential earnings, cash flow, and willingness to repay. Loans that involve various types of concerns are "scheduled" for closer scrutiny. These might involve an excess concentration in one industry, for example, oil and gas drilling and supply, or one type of loan, for example, high-technology enterprises. Loans that lack appropriate legal or technical documentation might also be scheduled. While some may question the competency of bank examiners to perform their difficult tasks, Spong and Hoenig (1979) report that examiners are fairly successful in evaluating and classifying problem loans.

To the extent that examiner classifications are concentrated in a particular type of loan or loans to specific industries or locations, bank lending policy might be influenced. On the other hand, a portfolio approach might "allow" problem loans in certain areas. Loans that are adversely scheduled present significant repayment risks and are grouped by examiners into at least three primary classifications:

1. *Substandard Loans.*   In these cases, deficiencies, unless corrected, are likely to result in some loss or delinquency. This implies a correctable situation and is the "best" of the scheduled classifications. It is in this area that an effective early warning system could provide sufficient time for turnaround.

2. *Doubtful Loans.*   These are similar to substandard loans except the deterioration has been continued and there is a high probability of substantial loss. While loans usually go through the substandard stage of classification before becoming doubtful, the reality of many situations is that a firm's problems are detected too late for effective corrective action and the doubtful stage sets in very quickly after the initial scheduling.

3. *Loss Loans.*   These are considered uncollectible, either in part or in their entirety, and are charged off and sent to workout for possible recovery.

Loans in the doubtful and loss stage are deducted from bank capital by examiners in assessing capital adequacy. While no specific guidelines exist for closing a bank based on capital adequacy, there have recently been proposals to require banks to have a minimum of 5.5% of total assets in unencumbered bank capital. We have observed such minimum standard proposals from time to time, especially when the nation is experiencing a rash of bank failures.

Loan Charge-offs.   Banks establish loan loss reserves in anticipation of charge-offs. Usually these reserves are more than sufficient to cover the calender-year charge-offs. A typical reserve against losses is 1% of net outstanding loans. Net loans are the bank's total gross loans minus the allowance for possible loan losses and minus unearned income on existing loans.

Banks often establish guidelines for acceptable charge-offs against various types of loans. An actual situation involving guidelines is provided by Sinkey (1983) as:

Revolving credit	0.50 to 0.75% of borrowings
Installment credit	0.50 to 0.60% of outstandings
Loan and discount	0.15 to 0.25% of outstandings
Mortgage loans	0.10 to 0.15% of outstandings

It is difficult to say what should be acceptable charge-offs without knowledge of the risk–return trade-off strategy of the bank. The greater the risk taken by banks, the higher should be the anticipated problem credits.

One of the comparative statistics used in banking is to calculate the annual recovery from charged-off loans as a percentage of that year's charge-offs. This is an indication of the percentage of loans charged off that are recouped by workout efforts. This is an incomplete and possibly misleading statistic and does a disservice to the efforts of workout officers.

In addition, it perhaps presents a distorted picture of bank effectiveness in the total "recovery" process, particularly if we compare recovery performance across the spectrum of bank size classifications.

First, we can review some statistics on loan recovery experience that are available and are presumably being assessed by industry analysts and bankers. Altman (1980) calculated the following recovery statistic for over 5,000 member banks of the Federal Reserve System:

Loan losses recovered/total loan losses charged off

Figure 15.5 shows the *median* ratio, stratified by bank asset size for the period 1969–1976. The median for all banks was approximately 28%, ranging from 34% in 1972 to 25% in 1974. From Figure 15.5 we can clearly observe that small banks recover a far greater percentage of charged-off loans than do their larger counterparts. For example, the median recovery ratio was 32% for banks with over $6 billion in assets. The relationship between bank asset size and recovery is consistently inverse. One might conclude from these results that small banks are more effective in their recovery operation than are larger banks. Why larger banks appear to recover less on charged-off loans than do their smaller counterparts is

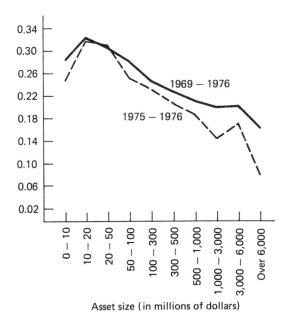

Figure 15.5. Median recovery (loan loss recoveries/losses) by bank asset size, 1969–1976 (coincident losses and recoveries).

difficult to know or ascertain. Indeed, even within specific asset size classes, the charge-off policy can vary tremendously. Some banks "ride" with a problem loan longer while others write off loans at an early indication of trouble. On the other hand, the individual bank's policy with respect to "reducing its exposure" when problems emerge also could explain differential recovery experience. Since larger banks typically make larger-sized loans and often are part of a lending consortium, it may be more difficult to extricate an individual bank once the loan is clearly in default. We will return to this large-versus-small-bank discrepancy.

The traditional way to measure recovery is to include only those amounts recovered by the bank *after* the loan is charged off. But the "recovery" function should start long before the official charge-off date. Bank trade statistics ignore the pre-charge-off experience and thereby report only a part of the story and performance of banks. What would be more revealing are statistics that also include the degree that banks reduce their risk exposure once the problem loan is detected. In other words, we are interested in what happens at both the pre-charge-off collection phase and the post-charge-off recovery effort. For example, a loan of $1 million that is reduced by $200,000 once the loan is identified as a problem and before it is charged off, with an additional $200,000 recovered after the charge-off, results in a loss to the bank of 60%, rather than the traditional calculation of 75%:

	Traditional Calculation	Suggested Calculation
Loan balance	$1,000,000	$1,000,000
Amount collected prior to charge-off	200,000	200,000
Amount charged-off	800,000	800,000
Amount recovered after charge-off	200,000	200,000
Loss	600,000	600,000
Percent loss	$\frac{600,000}{800,000} = 75\%$	$\frac{600,000}{1,000,000} = 60\%$
Percent "recovered"	25%	40%

If we ignore loan recovery administration costs and managerial and capital opportunity costs, we can use the loss statistics as an indication of the so-called Type I lending error cost. This is the cost to the bank of making a loan that will not result in a 100% recovery of the interest and principal. Of course, an individual bank should not ignore administrative expenses and opportunity costs incurred in the performance of its workout operation. These less tangible but potentially sizable opportunity costs are almost impossible to measure externally, and for our analysis we will merely note their existence.

We have utilized large data bases for assessing recovery experience at the bank level, but unfortunately data bases of *individual* loans do not exist. We had no choice but to complete our investigation on a loan-by-loan basis, sending out a short questionnaire to bank representatives in the New York, Southeastern, and Northern California regions of the United States. In all, we sent out over 400 questionnaires and we received back 55 responses of which 49 were usable. Each bank was asked to select up to three charged-off loans for each of the years 1975, 1976, and 1977, and to provide us with: (1) the loan balance 12 months prior to charge-off; (2) the balance charged off; and (3) the amount recovered after charge-off. We recognize that there may be a selection bias since we leave the choice of the bad loan up to the reporting bank. In all, we received usable data on 377 loans.

The following statistics from this 377-loan sample were examined:

1. Loan balance at 12 months prior to charge-off minus the amount charged off (amount collected) as a percentage of the loan balance.
2. Amount recovered after charge-off as a percentage of loan balance 12 months prior. This is designated as the recovery percentage.
3. Total recovery = (1) + (2)
4. Traditional recovery statistic = amount recovered after charge-off as a percentage of the charged-off amount.

The traditional recovery statistic was 25.7% based on an average of the recovery ratios for the 377 loans. This is comparable to our previous finding for a much larger sample.

For the entire sample, the average "collected" prior to charge-off was 16.5% while the average recovered after charge-off was 21.1%. Therefore, the average total recovery rate was 37.6%, and the revised loss rate is slightly over 62%. This is less than the 72% rate for all banks measured the traditional way. This differential is particularly striking for banks of certain sizes.

Table 15.2 lists the results stratified by loan size. Loan size is used as a proxy for bank size. To return to the "mystery" discussed earlier, namely, why small banks consistently outperform large banks in the re-

Table 15.2. Average Collection and Recovery Experience by Loan Size, Charged-off Loan Sample

Loan Size (in thousands of dollars)	Number	Collection	Recovery	Collection and Recovery
$ 0–10	128	8.9%	23.5%	32.4%
10–50	105	12.3	23.2	35.5
50–100	49	11.7	22.8	34.5
100–200	35	24.1	20.7	44.8
200–1,000	44	37.8	11.4	49.2
>1,000	16	45.3	10.7	56.0
	377			

covery function, we now see that when we include collection prior to charge-off, as well as the recovery, large banks do much better and in fact dominate smaller-bank total recovery. One possible reason for this is that larger banks "collect" more aggressively prior to charge-off and there is less available for recovery once the loan is written off. Smaller banks, on the other hand, do not pursue the accounts, which they probably know quite well, until there is no doubt that the loan should be charged off. At this point, they are fairly effective.

Cutoff Score Analysis.   The results from this study can be quite useful in defining and measuring the costs to commercial banks of extending credit. Combined with the cost of *not* making a good loan (essentially an opportunity cost concept), and specifying appropriate prior probabilities, these inputs can be quite useful in setting appropriate cutoff scores on commercial credit scoring models of the type discussed earlier. Details of this analysis are found in Altman (1980). If the results from the bank's loan charge-off and recovery experience are assessed correctly by bank management, they can be helpful in revising cutoff score criteria for acceptable loans earlier in the credit process. This indicates one way that the process can be more interdependent and managed as an entire process.

Final Repayment and Loan Renewal

As the individual loans approach maturity, two fundamental events become paramount to the principals. First is whether the final repayment, which might include a large "balloon"-type payment, will be paid in a timely manner; second is whether the customer will then, or in the near future, submit a loan renewal application. See Figure 15.1 again for these final stages. Another type of renewal request is to extend a line of credit or a revolving credit beyond the termination date of the initial agreement. If the final repayment is not accompanied by a renewal request, then this is one more way that the lending process between principals comes to an end.

If the renewal request is forthcoming, then it is up to the bank once again to evaluate the credit using the same techniques as for the earlier request. At this point, however, far more information is known about the applicant, including its payment history. Still, nothing should be taken for granted with respect to the customer's ability to repay in the future. Conditions change for the bank as well, and a particular loan might no longer be of a type being pursued by the bank for portfolio considerations. In most cases, however, the loan renewal will be evaluated favorably since repeat business is critical to a bank's ability to grow with confidence. All of this ties in with our earlier discussions of a total customer relationship.

PORTFOLIO STRATEGY OF LOANS

Earlier in this chapter we noted the importance of a clearly defined portfolio strategy for the commercial loan portfolio. This is indicated by (d) in Figure 15.1 relating to the overall credit analysis and review function for each loan. All bankers realize that the careful trade-off between default risk and return on the loan portfolio is the essence of sound loan management and is critical to avoid widely fluctuating performance. The concern in the mid-1970s and again in the early 1980s about concentration of assets (loans) in such sectors as real estate, retailing, shipping (1970s) and energy-related firms, some financial institutions, and developing and Eastern European countries (1980s) demonstrates the need to avoid investments in areas where a general decline could cause massive loan losses to lending institutions.

Most banks attempt to balance their loan portfolios and the tradeoff between risk and return by spreading loans over various industries with differing risk characteristics. In this regard, larger banks can have a distinct advantage over smaller ones since they are able to diversify by sector, geographic location, and domestically versus internationally to a greater extent. Still, some conceptual simulation work has indicated that even small numbers of loans can effectively reduce a bank's overall exposure to risk (Brealey, Hodges, and Selby, 1981). Strategic planning and portfolio management departments can be found in almost every money-center bank, and their charge is often to investigate the bank's overall risk exposure in various areas and also to do research on the means to diversify the assets of the bank more effectively. It is generally agreed that planning a bank's loan portfolio is a long-run objective although the bank must be responsive to the day-to-day loan requests of loan officers who themselves are primarily concerned with the repayment probabilities of that individual applicant. Therefore, the bank's loan portfolio strategy must necessarily be a top-management policy decision that is clearly articulated to those responsible for implementation. But, outside of limits on size of loans that specific individuals can make and some specific guidelines about exposures in various sectors and countries, there has not been a great deal written or observed about how banks should go about diversifying their loan portfolios.

Surprisingly little has been written in the theoretical and applied banking literature about how theories of asset portfolio management can be extended to international commercial banking. Since most large banks are struggling with these issues at the present time, we can probably expect a fairly significant increase in published works on this subject and perhaps some breakthroughs. Recent discussions by Mason (1969), Goodman (1981), Rush (1982), and Bennett (1984) are good examples of attempts made to extend asset management principles, which have been so eagerly embraced by the securities industry, to the bank lending area. Bennett's work is particularly interesting and potentially of substantial pragmatic impact in this area. In this volume, Flannery discusses the issues involved in assessing the risk–return trade-offs of bank loan portfolios. Combining the Flannery discussion with some of the suggestions of Bennett would be an excellent starting point for bank planners and senior management staff.

REFERENCES

Altman, E. "Commercial Bank Lending: Process, Credit Scoring and Costs of Errors in Lending," *Journal of Financial & Quantitative Analysis,* November 1980, pp. 813–832.

Altman, E. *Corporate Financial Distress: A Complete Guide to Predicting, Avoiding and Dealing with Bankruptcy.* New York: John Wiley & Sons, Inc., 1983.

Altman, E. "Financial Ratios, Discriminant Analysis and the Prediction of Corporate Bankruptcy." *Journal of Finance,* September 1968, pp. 589–619.

Altman, E, and McGough, T. "Evaluation of a Company as a Going Concern." *Journal of Accountancy,* December 1974, pp. 50–57.

Altman, E., Haldeman, R., and Narayanan, P. "ZETA Analysis: A New Model to Identify Bankruptcy Risk of Corporations." *Journal of Banking and Finance,* June 1977, pp. 29–54.

Beaver, W. "Financial Ratios as Predictors of Failure." In *Empirical Research in Accounting: Selected Studies*, 1966, supplement to Vol. 4, *Journal of Accounting Research*, pp. 71–111.

Bennett, P. "Applying Portfolio Theory to Global Bank Lending." *Journal of Banking & Finance*, forthcoming.

Bettinger, C. "Bankruptcy Prediction as a Tool for Commercial Lenders." *Journal of Commercial Bank Lending*, July 1981, pp. 18–27.

Brealey, R. A., Hodges, S. D., and Selby, M. J. P. "The Risk of Bank Loan Portfolios." Paper presented at the 16th Annual Conference of the Western Finance Association in Jackson Hole, June 1981 (London Business School).

Casey, C. J. "The Usefulness of Accounting Ratios for Subjects' Predictions of Corporate Failure: Replication and Extensions." *Journal of Accounting Research*, (Autumn 1980), pp. 603–613.

Casey, C. J., and Bartczak, N. "Using Operating Cash Flow Data: To Predict Financial Distress." *Journal of Accounting Research*. forthcoming.

Chesser, N., "Predicting Loan Noncompliance." *Journal of Commercial Bank Lending*, August 1974, pp. 28–51.

Deakin, E. "A Discriminant Analysis of Predictors of Business Failure." *Journal of Accounting Research*, Spring 1972, *10* (1), pp. 167–179.

Durand, D. *Risk Elements in Consumer Installment Financing*. New York: National Bureau of Economic Research, 1941.

Eisenbeis, Robert A. "Pitfalls in the Application of Discriminant Analysis in Business, Finance, and Economics," *Journal of Finance*, 1977, *32*, pp. 887–893.

Goodman, L. "Bank Lending to Non-OPEC LDC's: Are Risks Diversifiable?". Federal Reserve Bank of New York, *Quarterly Review*, Summer 1981, pp. 10–20.

Gombola, M. J., and Ketz, J. E. "A Note on Cash Flow and Classification Patterns of Financial Ratios." *Accounting Review*, January 1983, pp. 105–114.

Hempel, G., Coleman, A., and Simonson, D. *Bank Management: Texts and Cases*. New York: John Wiley & Sons, Inc., 1983.

Hoffman, M., and Fischer, G. *Credit Department Mangement*. Philadelphia: Robert Morris Associates, 1980.

Jensen, M., and Meckling, W. "Theory of the Firm: Managerial Behavior, Agency Costs and Ownership Structure." *Journal of Financial Economics*, March 1976, pp. 305–360.

Libby, R. "The Use of Simulated Decision Makers in Information Evaluation." *Accounting Review*, July 1975, pp. 475–489.

Mason, J. *Financial Management of Commercial Banks*. Boston: Warren, Gorham & Lamont, 1979.

Ohlson, J. A. "Financial Ratios and Probabilistic Prediction of Bankruptcy." *Journal of Accounting Research*, Spring 1980, pp. 109–131.

Orgler, Y. E. *Analytical Methods in Loan Evaluation*. Lexington, Mass.: Lexington Books, 1975.

Orgler, Y. E., and Wolkowitz, B. *Bank Capital*. New York: Van Nostrand Reinhold, 1976.

Rush, D. "Commercial Bank Loan Portfolios: Risk and Realized Return." Working paper, Univ. of Colorado, 1977.

Scott, J. "The Probability of Bankruptcy, A Comparison of Empirical Predictions and Theoretical Models." *Journal of Banking and Finance*, 1981, *5*, (4) pp. 317–344.

Sharpe, W. *Investments* (2nd ed.). Englewood Cliffs, N.J.: Prentice-Hall, Inc., 1982.

Sinkey, J. *Commercial Bank Financial Management.* New York: Macmillan Publishing Co., 1983.

Spong, K., and Hoenig, T. "Bank Examination Classifications and Loan Risk." *Economic Review,* Federal Reserve Bank of Kansas City, June 1979, pp. 15–25.

Walter, I. "Country Risk, Portfolio Decisions and Regulation in International Bank Lending." *Journal of Banking & Finance,* March 1981, 5 (1), pp. 3–5.

Wilcox, J. "The Gambler's Ruin Approach to Business Risk." *Sloan Management Review,* March 1976, pp. 33–46.

16 International Risk Management

Robert L. Slighton

One of the most striking changes in the nature of U.S. banking over the past several decades has been its increased internationalization. The claims of U.S. banks against foreigners have increased more rapidly than claims against U.S. entities. Foreign branches of U.S.-chartered banks have grown at a greater rate than their parents. And the rate of growth of bank assets and liabilities denominated in currencies other than the dollar has outpaced that of their dollar assets and liabilities. These changes in the United States simply mirror similar changes in the structure of foreign banking systems. The capital markets of the various national economies have become dramatically interdependent.

This rapid internationalization of banking has complicated the task of risk management enormously. The increased share of assets and liabilities denominated in currencies other than the dollar implies greater potential costs of a failure to manage foreign exchange risk—the risk of changes in future earnings resulting from changes in the foreign exchange value of the dollar. The increased share of assets held in the form of claims against foreigners has created a need for a more careful examination of country risk—the risk of events that would prejudice the orderly service of a major fraction of claims against borrowers domiciled in a given country.

In principle, the increased internationalization of banking need not increase its riskiness. The greater opportunities for portfolio diversification

The views expressed in this paper are the author's own and are not intended to represent those of the Chase Manhattan Bank.

511

resulting from the internationalization of a bank's activities imply the possibility of an actual reduction of risk. In fact, however, the events of the past few years suggest that the changes in bank asset and liability portfolios associated with internationalization have resulted in a significant increase in the uncertainty as to future bank earnings. The radical political restructuring of Iran in 1979, the interruption of normal Polish debt service in 1981, the Mexican payments crisis of 1982, and the subsequent spread of debt service problems across most of the countries of Latin America and much of Africa have altered perceptions as to the relative risks and rewards to international banking in a fundamental way. As a result, the market value of the equity shares of banks heavily involved in international lending has fallen relative to the stock prices of banks with little foreign exposure. The regulatory authorities have adopted more stringent oversight procedures with respect to international lending. And bank senior managements have given unambiguous signals as to the need to reduce the share of asset portfolios accounted for by loans to countries whose debt service capabilities have deteriorated—typically by stronger relative growth of other classes of loans.

There is thus a clear demand from all interested parties—stockholders, regulators, and bank management—that international risks, particularly country risks, be carefully managed. In considering how this overriding objective may be accomplished, three questions appear to be of particular importance. How have banks attempted to control country risk? Why, in spite of these controls, did the present debt problem develop? And what lessons can be drawn from this experience that should be of value in designing better control measures in the future?

HOW HAVE BANKS MANAGED COUNTRY RISK?

Managing country risk involves two distinct tasks. The first is assessing the magnitude of the risks incurred in increasing exposure in a given country. The second is translating those assessments into a set of constraints on a bank's asset portfolio.

Assessing Country Risk

In principle, assessing country risk can be described as the estimation of a probability function $P(z_i)$, where z_i is a given percentage impairment of the present value of the portfolio of claims against a given country and $P(z_i)$ is the probability that the degree of impairment will occur. In practice, however, the assessment is not presented as a probability function but rather as single-valued risk index or premium that reflects both the characteristics of the probability function and the risk preferences of the assessor.

Although more or less straightforward conceptually, in practice this assessment is extraordinarily difficult. One obvious problem is the sheer complexity of what must be analyzed. Country risk is not the risk of a particular event. It is not the risk of rescheduling—or debt denial—but the risk of impairment of the value of a large fraction of claims against entities that can be considered domiciled in a given country. It is the risk of one or more of a large set of events over a long period of time that would have a significant impact on the debt service capabilities of most borrowers in that country—or borrowers physically located in other countries whose economic circumstances are critically dependent on events in the country in question. It encompasses *transfer* risk—the risk that debtors may not be able to acquire foreign exchange to satisfy their foreign payments obligations—and *catastrophic* risk—the risk of total impairment of asset values arising from the physical destruction of war or civil disorder or political decisions to repudiate debt. It encompasses *sovereign* risk—the risk that a government or government agency may not service foreign debt per contract—and *private-sector* risk—the risk of political or economic events affecting the entire economy that would impair the ability of a large fraction of all private entities to acquire the domestic currency required to service foreign debt.

A second major problem in assessing country risk is that our understanding of many of the various processes leading to debt service difficulties is extremely sketchy. The economic process that most commonly leads to debt service problems—excess money growth and maintenance of an overvalued exchange rate—is well understood. But there is much less knowledge as to the political dynamics behind the decisions to implement such policies—or the political response to a debt service problem once it develops. We may speak of a subjective probability of such events, but the significance of these numbers is highly questionable. Strictly speaking we are not facing risks, which can be numerically assessed and insured against, but uncertainties.

A third basic problem is that the probability of debt service difficulties for any given country is not simply a function of events specific to that country. There are two aspects to this problem. The first is that changes in the external economic environment common to all countries—for example, a change in the price of oil or a relatively synchronized economic downturn in the major industrialized countries—imply a significant correlation among the demands for foreign borrowing of the individual countries. The second is that under certain circumstances the willingness of foreign lenders to supply credits to a given country will be closely related to their willingness to lend to other countries or groups of countries. In short, the risk of asset impairment in any given country cannot always be assessed independently of the risk of asset impairment in other countries.

Faced with these intrinsic difficulties, the banks have responded in various ways to the operational problem of risk assessment. The most common approach has been the adoption of some sort of alphanumeric scoring system, either devised by the individual bank or adopted from some external source, with the various countries assigned a particular letter or numerical grade. These scores may be single-dimensional or multidimensional, but in all cases, either explicitly or implicitly, they map into a set of single-valued risk premiums.

The basis for these scoring systems differs widely among banks, however. At least three distinct approaches can be identified. The first is the so-called checklist system, where the score

$$y = a_1 x_1 + \ldots a_n x_n$$

is defined in terms of a broad set of social, political, and economic variables commonly thought to be related to the probability of debt difficulties. The obvious problem with such a system is that while its scores are not exactly "theory free," the weights $a_1 \ldots a_n$ are essentially arbitrary. That is, they reflect hypotheses about the relationship between the known facts $x_1 \ldots x_n$ and the potential extent of asset impairment that have not been empirically tested.

A second approach is the estimation of the likelihood of future debt service difficulties on the basis of statistical analysis of the relationship between past defaults and various economic parameters. Statistical methods, such as logit and discriminant analysis, can be used to generate forecasts of whether a country will be able to service its debt and estimates of the probabilities that contractual debt service will be maintained. While the empirical basis of these systems is clearly a virtue, they suffer from several defects. First, the estimated coefficients relating the probability of debt default to the values of the independent variables are not robust, being relatively sensitive to the sample period from which they are estimated. For example, debt service ratios (ratios of interest payments on term foreign debt plus amortization of that debt to export receipts) that typically resulted in debt default in the 1950s and 1960s did not do so in the 1974–1981 period. Second, some of the key independent (predictive) variables are themselves highly uncertain. And third, these estimators

presume that debt service difficulties can be described in binary forms—
that is, a country either defaults or it doesn't. *Default* is a concept that
may have a precise meaning to a lawyer but not to an economist or a
financial analyst. A default may involve little if any impairment of asset
values or it may signal a possible major loss. In this context, statistical
estimators are highly instructive in indicating which variables are important
to monitor in assessing short-term "liquidity" risks—the most significant
being the ratios of total foreign interest payments or debt service to exports, the proportion of short-term debt to total debt, the ratio of international reserves to imports, and the rate of growth of foreign claims by
banks. They appear to be of much more limited value, however, in assessing the longer-term capabilities of a country in servicing existing debt.

A third basis for alphanumeric scoring, which may be combined with
the second, can be called the "informed judgmental" approach. It is judgmental in that the risk scores are not driven by formally estimated relationships between debt service events and a set of prespecified variables—
but informed in that judgments as to the likelihood of debt impairment
reflect detailed analysis of relatively likely scenarios as to the future evolution of a country's balance of payments. These in turn derive from
analysis of relatively likely changes in the external economic environment,
the evolution of economic policy in the country, and lender attitudes. This
basis for risk assessment can be thought of as the "brute force" technique.
That is, it involves the direct comparison of detailed projections of the
future foreign borrowing requirements implied by alternative assumptions
as to domestic policy and the external environment with estimates of the
supply of foreign loans likely to be forthcoming (on a voluntary basis)
under those assumptions. The major potential defects of this approach
are its relative lack of transparency and the large volume of skilled resources required to develop the underlying scenarios. Its major advantages
are that it encourages the participation of analysts of differentiated skills—
economists, political analysts, and bankers—and that it lends itself to the
analysis of the sensitivity of risk assessments to key assumptions as to
both the external and domestic environment.

Translating Country Risk Assessments into a Country Risk Management System

There would appear to be less difference in the procedures by which banks
use country risk assessments in managing country risk than the techniques
employed in assessing that risk. Banks generally manage country risk by
setting individual country limits—maximum acceptable levels of claims
against entities whose debt service capabilities are tied in an important

way to events in a given country. These limits are ordinarily set by a country risk committee whose membership includes both individuals whose incentives are primarily oriented to growth and individuals whose primary incentive is the maintenance of quality. The economists and political analysts responsible for individual country risk assessments serve as the committee's secretariat.

Three features of this country limit system are worth noting. First, the distribution by country of a bank's loan portfolio is mainly determined directly by administrative decision rather than indirectly through a centrally determined set of risk adjustments or discounts to the nominal return on loans to different countries (price guidelines). That is, there is typically no *explicit* attempt to ensure that risk-adjusted rates of return are equated at the margin for all countries. While many banks employ country pricing guidelines, and these guidelines are certainly influenced by risk assessments, the fact that country risk control procedures focus on maximum exposure limits rather than minimum returns over the cost of funds implies that these pricing guidelines are also heavily influenced by other factors, such as the degree of competitive pressure from other lenders.

This feature of most country risk management systems derives in large part from the nature of country risk assessments themselves. First, they are necessarily highly judgmental. Even when expressed in quantitative terms, these assessments are understood as ordinal rather than cardinal estimates of the degree of perceived risk. Second, there is generally a mismatch between the time horizon over which detailed risk assessment is attempted and the time horizon of business planning.

A further reason that direct (as opposed to indirect) control procedures are employed is the difficulty banks typically have in defining the nominal return on any given asset. With an important part of the total return to loans deriving from collateral sources—for example, income from foreign exchange trading services—and with much of this collateral income booked in internal profit centers other than the country profit center booking the asset, most banks do not have internal accounting systems that provide a reliable measure of the total return to an increase in exposure to any given country.

A second important feature of the country risk management systems employed by banks is their focus on individual country limits rather than the overall structure of the loan portfolio. While this is changing, current portfolios reflect lending decisions essentially made on a country-by-country basis. Primary attention has been paid to factors that are risks to one country only rather than to sets of countries or to the entire portfolio. There has been relatively little systematic effort to apply the techniques of modern portfolio analysis, in which the focus is not on how risky an individual asset is but rather on how much that asset contributes to the riskiness of the overall portfolio.

This past focus on individual country risks has reflected both the limited data base from which the covariances of individual country risks could be estimated and the implicit assumption by the banks that the major industrialized countries would follow economic policies that would prevent severe systemic stresses. The experience of the past few years has both invalidated that assumption and provided much more complete information as to the extent of the covariance of the debt service capability of individual countries. Risk management procedures are adjusting accordingly.

A third feature of the country risk management systems employed by banks is that they take on many of the characteristics of an adversary proceeding. This is an inevitable consequence of the judgmental character of country risk assessments. With its limited information base, a country risk management system cannot be accepted as a meaningful, permanent element in a bank's decision-making process unless each of the major interest groups of the bank—in particular the loan producers and the credit analysts—is directly involved. A system entrusted to "unbiased" technicians—individuals whose organizational incentives would appear to be oriented neither to growth nor to asset quality per se—is extremely susceptible to rejection by line management.

There may have been considerable differences among banks in the relative strength of the various parties to this adversary process, however. While many banks have made a strong effort to achieve an appropriate balance of bargaining power, in some cases the design of the country limit decision process may have favored those elements whose incentives were weighted more to growth than to portfolio composition. If so, this bias is changing. The emergence of widespread debt service difficulties has shifted decision making power over country limits to those elements of the banks whose essential focus is asset quality. There is a risk that this shift will go too far.

What Went Wrong?

In spite of relatively elaborate control procedures—and the expenditure of significant resources in their implementation—an unanticipatedly high fraction of the foreign assets of the international banks is now in negotiation. Some 35 countries have been forced to request a rescheduling of foreign debt. For a few borrowers the maintenance of scheduled interest payments has become difficult, and there is a growing doubt in these countries whether existing debt can be serviced on a long-term basis without a more thoroughgoing revision of original terms than hitherto contemplated. Clearly, something went wrong.

The key to an understanding of why the banks' expectations as to the debt-service capabilities of the developing countries were not fulfilled lies in the differences between the policy responses of the major industrialized nations to the oil price increases of 1973–1974 and those of 1979–1980, and the consequent differences in the adjustment paths of the global economy. While the first of these shocks was followed by a major downturn in the level of global economic activity, the prevalence of moderately re-flationary fiscal–monetary policies in the industrialized countries led to a relatively quick recovery. The adoption of accommodative monetary policies in the United States during the subsequent period of expansion encouraged a shift of asset preferences from financial to real assets. Commodity prices boomed, and inflation-adjusted dollar interest rates became negative. Indexes of debt service burden in the developing countries, which burgeoned in the period of initial adjustment, receded to manageable levels by 1979.

The rapid growth of global liquidity attendant on this adjustment left the industrialized economies, particularly that of the United States, in a vulnerable position, however. The second oil price shock of 1979–1980 thus led to an extremely rapid burst of inflation that sharply narrowed the options open to the industrialized nations in devising a policy response to that shock. In most of the OECD nations deflationary rather than re-flationary policies were adopted. With inflationary expectations—formed by nearly two decades of experience with largely accommodative monetary policy—slow to adjust, monetary authorities in the industrialized countries moved to an increasingly stringent stance. The consequences were an unprecedented rise in interest rates, a collapse of commodity prices, and a downturn of the global economy of a magnitude and persistence unknown since the 1930s.

While the general nature of this policy response to the second oil price shock—and its consequences for the debt service capabilities of the developing countries—was understood, the magnitude was not. Underlying the banks' projections of the performance of the world economy was the implicit assumption that deflationary policies would be eased if they threatened to produce a global recession. This presumption proved incorrect. As a result, the systematic risk of international lending—non-diversifiable risk—was greatly underestimated.

This forecasting error was compounded by the tendency of country risk management systems to focus on country-specific risks rather than overall portfolio risk. As long as total systemic stresses were moderate, this fault in risk management strategy was not costly. In these circumstances there was limited interdependence among the payments difficulties of individual developing countries, and a simple strategy of diversifying exposure across these countries was not greatly inadequate. What the banks failed to consider sufficiently was that the extent of the positive covariance among individual country risks was likely to increase dramatically in times of severe systemic stress—a prolonged global recession. The claim that there is no such thing as "developing country" risk, only individual country risk, was largely true in the circumstances of the late 1970s. Given the persistently deflationary policy response to the second oil price shock in the industrialized countries, this claim became essentially false in the early 1980s. But by then it was too late to effect a major reduction in the proportion of total bank portfolios accounted for by claims against these nations.

This failure to perceive the potential extent of positive covariance among the debt service difficulties of individual countries derived in large part from the focus of analysts on the covariance of balance-of-payments deficits—the demand for foreign borrowing. The possibility of large potential covariance between the supply of funds was given much less attention. Yet it was the sudden cessation of the market's willingness to lend to Latin America rather than a surge in Latin American demand for foreign loans, that was the major factor precipitating the present international debt problem. What the analysts in the major banks tended to ignore was the significance to the total supply of international funds of smaller financial institutions whose capability of assessing individual country risks is limited or nil. These institutions withdrew from the international loan market on an areawide basis, if not completely. As a result, the covariance between *market* judgments of the risks of any pair of countries turned out to be markedly higher than the covariance of the country risk judgments of the analysts in the major banks.

The failure to develop more complete information systems on developments in individual countries—or the possible undue weight in the country risk management process given to those elements of the banks most committed to growth—appears to have been of much less consequence to the banks' present international loan problems. What mainly went wrong was that the country risk management systems in place were highly vulnerable to an underestimate of the stresses on the global economy likely to result from the adoption of highly deflationary monetary policies. The banks underestimated those stresses—as did the architects of the policies that produced them.

THE FUTURE EVOLUTION OF COUNTRY RISK MANAGEMENT SYSTEMS

The shortcomings of the country risk management systems in place at the time the debt problem erupted are now widely recognized, and major changes in these systems are being implemented. While these changes vary somewhat from bank to bank, there are a number of common threads to the response.

One type of response is the search for credit instruments that would allow greater flexibility in debt or portfolio management than conventional adjustable-rate loan agreements. Two distinct objectives are being sought here—the enhanced marketability of debt and more flexible management by borrowers of interest rate risk. The limited marketability of conventional loans has proved to be a major barrier in resolving the present debt problem. While an interbank loan swaps market has emerged, transactions costs are high, and the similarity of the portfolios of the major banks limits the depth of the market. To enhance the marketability of their assets, banks are thus showing increased interest in instruments such as floating-rate notes.

The banks are also exploring means of reducing interest rate risk to borrowers. While conventional floating-rate instruments largely shift interest rate risk from lenders to borrowers, the banks have achieved very little if the borrower is unable to absorb this risk. Credit risk has simply been substituted for interest rate risk. In recognition of this difficulty, considerable attention is being given to credit instruments such as flexible-maturity loans, where changes in interest rates are reflected in changes in the value of loan principal (and hence the amortization stream) rather than current debt service payments.

More germane to the present discussion, however, are the changes being implemented in the procedures whereby portfolio risk is assessed and this assessment is translated into controls over asset composition. This type of response appears to be taking three forms: the development of improved country information systems; an increased focus on the risk characteristics of the asset portfolio as a whole as opposed to individual country limits; and the adoption of a markedly more conservative (risk-averse) posture in translating country risk assessments into country exposure limits.

While information gaps or lags are probably not a very important explanation of the failure of country risk management systems to prevent the present debt problem, the banks' information systems were deficient in some respects, and steps have been taken to correct these deficiencies. The objective here has been both to obtain more comprehensive information as to a country's economic performance and debt position and to reduce the time lags as to the availability of this information. For the major banks the primary difficulty has been incomplete debt information, particularly with respect to debt to nonbanks (mainly suppliers' credits and private placements through merchant banks) and military debt. Time lags as to the availability of data on short-term bank debt have also been somewhat troublesome, resulting in some tendency to underestimate total debt service obligations of a number of major borrowers. The smaller banks have been faced with the additional problems of very high costs of information relative to their scale of foreign lending. The resolution of these difficulties is being sought both through a more intense effort by the major banks to collect comprehensive debt information on a timely basis and a more efficient system of disseminating information to the smaller banks. The latter objective is being pursued through the Institute of International Finance, an institution supported by banks engaged in international lending whose membership fees are dependent on the size of the member banks. The institute maintains a comprehensive data bank to which member banks have electronic access and has initiated a series of country studies available to its membership.

A second important trend in bank country risk management procedures is an increased focus on the risk characteristics of the portfolio as a whole rather than the risks of exposures to individual countries. This reflects the banks' increased awareness of the relatively high positive covariance of the debt service problems of heavily indebted countries in circumstances of major systemic stress. In operational terms this change has been implemented by the adoption of exposure limits on various groups of countries that supplement individual country limits and to which the country limits must conform. These group limits may be defined for the developing economies as a whole, developing economies that are significant importers of energy, countries significantly dependent on oil exports, countries significantly dependent on commodity exports, or various regional groupings such as Latin America or eastern Europe. While the adoption of country group limits is a significant step forward in controlling total portfolio risk, such a change falls well short of those procedures suggested by modern portfolio management theory. To go further, a more systematic analysis of the interrelationships among the debt service problems of individual countries is needed, and—more important—the banks must develop more adequate internal accounting systems to track the total return attributable to country assets.

The third major change in bank management of country risk is the apparent tendency to adopt markedly more conservative postures in translating country risk assessments into exposure limits. The return to traditional lending practices—the provision of trade finance and the funding of well-defined projects—as opposed to overt balance-of-payments lending is one aspect of this change. More meaningful from the point of view of country risk management, bank judgments as to permissible exposure in any given country or groups of countries are reflecting a significantly reduced willingness to accept risk. Management reaction to prospective changes in indicators of debt service difficulty (such as the debt service ratio) is quicker, and there is much greater sensitivity to given absolute levels of such indicators. Evidence of possible debt service delays that in the past would have resulted in a decision to refrain from any increase in country exposure is now more likely to result in a determined effort to reduce exposure.

These tendencies have become particularly pronounced for those banks whose involvement in foreign lending has been relatively limited. Many such institutions have simply withdrawn from the market, in effect abandoning their effort to minimize the extent of the possible impairment of existing assets. The larger banks, with their focus on maintaining long-term credit relationships, have reacted far less precipitously. But even the largest institutions have adopted overall portfolio goals that will constrain foreign loan growth to rates well below the experience of the pre-1982 period. For these institutions the major factor limiting the growth of foreign exposure will be the growth of bank capital, for the objective of reducing existing exposure–capital ratios for major foreign borrowers or groups of borrowers has become nearly universal.

It was necessary that bank country risk management procedures be tightened. With the advantage of hindsight it is clear that the buildup of bank claims against a number of borrowing countries in the 1980–1982 period was excessive. The danger is that this reaction will go too far— that the risk management systems of the past that tended to underestimate country risk will evolve into systems that are prone to exaggerate those risks. Satisfactory resolution of the present debt problem of the developing countries cannot be achieved without the continued provision of foreign credit in significant amounts. The shift in the willingness of individual banks to increase their foreign exposure has become so pronounced as to raise the question of whether the required total flow of international lending will be forthcoming. If not, the current evolution of bank country risk management systems may turn out to have been more a cause of increased portfolio risk than a means of reducing it.

17 A Framework for Strategic Planning

Jerry E. Pohlman

The function of financial intermediation is to enhance the efficient accommodation of the financial needs of borrowers and lenders. Since the requirements of these two classes are not the same with respect to the amount, maturity, and location of funds, the role of an intermediary (generally speaking) is to transform the needs of one group into those of the other. While the fundamental concept of intermediation is straightforward, several factors, both internal and external to the intermediary, give rise to complexities and, in recent years, to significant problems in performing the intermediation role.

An intermediary is faced with three kinds of risk: credit risk, liquidity risk, and interest rate risk. The last arises from the maturity or repricing mismatch of the firm's assets and liabilities and, of course, has been extremely punishing for thrift institutions since the early 1980s.[1]

In one sense, all risks can be reduced to liquidity risk, since in the final analysis it is the lack of liquid funds with which to meet current obligations that most often results in the demise of an institution. For analytical purposes, however, it is useful to segregate the three forms of risk facing intermediaries.

Maturity mismatching—specifically, borrowing short and lending long—combined with a volatile interest rate climate beginning in the late 1970s to produce widespread losses for thrifts. Indeed, interest rate risk currently

The author gratefully acknowledges the editorial and analytical contributions of John D'Andrea, senior vice president and economist at American Savings.

constitutes the greatest of the risks facing savings institutions and therefore is the primary focus of this analysis.

Reflecting a favorable regulatory climate and relatively stable economic conditions, thrifts were able to grow and prosper during most of the post-war period without being overly concerned with the maturity mismatch they were incurring. Passbook savings were utilized to fund 30-year, fixed-rate loans. With relatively small rate variability and a positively sloped yield curve year after year, the practice was both profitable and straight-forward. The perceived risks were small from the perspectives of regulators as well as practitioners.

The actual risk of the maturity mismatch, however, proved to be sub-stantial, as the inflationary pressures of the 1970s and changes in Federal Reserve operating procedures produced high and volatile interest rates late in the decade and into the 1980s. Short-term liabilities first left the institutions due to binding Regulation Q interest rate ceilings, and S&Ls had to replace these liabilities with market-rate borrowings and Federal Home Loan advances. As the pace of financial innovations (and subse-quent demise of Regulation Q) quickened in the early 1980s, thrift insti-tutions were able to attract funds, but at costs typically far above the yields of the fixed-rate loans that comprised the bulk of their assets. Be-cause of shifts in the term structure, the cost of liabilities reflected *current* economic conditions due to their generally short-term nature, while most assets, in the form of long-term mortgages, reflected *past* economic con-ditions.

Strategic planning and asset–liability management provide the frame-work for restructuring thrift balance sheets to prevent a recurrence of the trauma and turmoil of the late 1970s and early 1980s. At best, this re-structuring will take several years, and for some firms it will prove im-possible. Indeed, if interest rates replay their pattern of that earlier period, the number of casualties will be quite large.

EFFECTS OF DEREGULATION

The course of financial deregulation that began in the late 1970s provided financial intermediaries—and particularly the specialized thrift institu-tions—with powers needed to compete with less-regulated sources of fi-nancial services. (Edward Kane's chapter in this volume analyzes the process of regulatory change.) This move was consistent with a broader political consensus that the consumer would be the ultimate beneficiary of a less-regulated economy. Competition (rather than government direc-tives) was to be utilized in allocating resources, with the expected result being lower costs and more efficient techniques of processing and delivery. In large part, this has been the result in sectors such as trucking, airlines, and stock brokerage, which have experienced deregulation. While the consumer is the ultimate winner in this process, difficult adjustments face the firms and industries experiencing sweeping regulatory change.

On the liability side of the balance sheet, Regulation Q was largely dismantled, giving savings institutions the power to offer competitive rates to savers in order to attract and keep funds. On the asset side, the thrust of deregulation has been to authorize shorter-term loans for consumers and businesses and to foster the development of adjustable-rate mortgages (ARMs) in order to reduce the maturity mismatch that had resulted from earlier funding practices.

Savings institutions are now endeavoring to implement these powers. *Setting out plans on how to restructure and then implementing these plans are the central strategic challenges facing these institutions.* And, while the environment of the mid-1980s so far has been less hostile for thrifts than that of the late 1970s and early 1980s, a number of serious problems remain. High interest rates continue to exert heavy pressure on profit margins, while strong competition from commercial banks and nondepository financial institutions hampers the ability of savings institutions to make the transition easily.

Finally, in addition to competitive and economic pressures, the increasing feasibility of technological change is forcing financial intermediaries to review intensively all processing and delivery systems. The use of electronic facilities, which for years was touted as the wave of the future, is rapidly gaining consumer acceptance and is reshaping the configuration of the financial services industry. Thus, as firms examine their processing and delivery systems (i.e., back office *and* front office), they must evaluate not only the traditional "brick and mortar" but also the cashless and checkless types of financial transactions that increasingly make up the financial marketplace. In essence, as Edward Kane points out in his chapter, technological risk itself has become a major element of the business risks faced by financial institutions.

THE PORTFOLIO APPROACH

The income statement and the risk exposure of a financial intermediary are functions of its balance sheet, and *any attempt to alter materially either risk exposure or income generation must be done through a restructuring of the firm's asset and liability configuration.* While marginal adjustments to both the income stream and risk exposure can be made in the short run, significantly altering the balance sheet to increase profits and reduce risk exposure is a long-term proposition.

To illustrate the nature of the structural imbalances, key financial measures of commercial bank and S&L performance are depicted in this chapter and then utilized to explore the opportunities and implications of efforts aimed at restructuring. The analysis first examines where savings institutions are currently positioned and the nature of their portfolio mismatch and profitability problems. Next there is a review of the general dimensions of portfolio restructuring. Finally, strategies aimed at moving institutions to more desired positions are identified.

TRACKING PERFORMANCE AND HIGHLIGHTING PROBLEMS

The variables that will be described have been shown to capture much of the financial performance of financial intermediaries. They are useful from a time-trend perspective as well as for comparisons of the cross-sectional performance of different entities, such as savings institutions with commercial banks. In addition, the performance of a particular firm in comparison with peer group firms can be examined along with a firm's current position in relation to its desired position.

Measures of Financial Performance

Eight performance measures are presented below.

1. *ROE (Return on Equity) = After-Tax Profits/Average Equity.* ROE measures the overall returns to the firm or industry and allows for interindustry as well as intraindustry comparisons. Rates of return above "normal" will attract new entrants into the industry, while below-normal returns will promote an exodus. From a management standpoint, calculating the rate of return on invested capital for various components of the firm is important for allocating capital to its most productive use.

    Various measures of both profits and equity are often utilized in financial analysis, making it necessary to be explicit and consistent concerning the terms. For the purposes of this analysis, after-tax profit, including gains or losses on the sale of securities, is utilized in the numerator of the ratio, and total equity capital (common stock, surplus, and undivided profits) comprises the denominator. In the case of mutual organizations the denominator is simply net worth.

2. *ROA (Return on Assets) = After-Tax Profits/Average Assets.* ROA reflects how well the institution is utilizing its entire asset base and

is a traditional measure of financial intermediary performance. ROA, combined with a measure of the leverage the firm is utilizing, produces the return on equity discussed above. At thrift institutions, assets, which are primarily mortgage loans, mature and/or are repriced only slowly. Thus, changes in ROA largely reflect changes in costs brought about by more rapidly changing liability components.

3. *PM (Profit Margin) = After-Tax Profits/Total Operating Income.* In the absence of barriers to entry (or exit), profit margins illustrate the degree of competitive pressure the firm or industry is facing and the degree of success in meeting this competition. When margins shrink, management can attempt to stave off the consequences by shifting to assets that generate greater income, but this can seldom be done quickly, especially where mortgage portfolios mature much more slowly than commercial loan portfolios.

4. *EM (Equity Multiplier) = Average Assets/Average Equity.* The equity multiplier measures the degree to which an institution is leveraged. The greater assets are relative to equity capital, the more leveraged is a firm. Return on assets (ROA) and the equity multiplier produce the total return on an institution's equity (ROE).

5. *AU (Asset Utilization) = Operating Income/Average Assets.* Asset utilization measures the amount of income the firm is able to generate from its asset base. Since the profit margin measures the amount of profit per unit of income, the two measures together (profit margin and asset utilization) determine the firm's total return on assets.

6. *NII (Net Interest Income) = Interest Income − Interest Expense.* Net interest income describes what is happening to the "spread" side of business. By omitting considerations of operating costs, extraordinary income, the sale of assets, and other income and loss factors, NII provides an accurate picture of the impact of interest rate movements on the firm or industry. If the firm or industry were perfectly hedged, changes in interest rates would affect interest costs and revenues equally, and NII would remain constant.

NII is especially important for asset–liability analysis where the primary focus is on interest rate risk. While broader measures of profitability, such as ROE, are more relevant for measuring the total performance of the firm, NII more adequately handles the measure of interest rate exposure. (It is usually employed on a tax-equivalent basis.)

7. *NIIR (Net Interest Income Ratio) = Net Interest Income/Average Assets.* This measure of performance standardizes NII by the size of the institution, thereby making interfirm and time-series comparisons for the same firm more meaningful.

8. *MR (Maturity Ratio or Measure of Interest Rate Sensitivity).* Measurement of interest rate risk exposure is of paramount importance for thrift institutions and underlies their recent attempts at portfolio restructuring. It therefore warrants more in-depth explanation.

Interest rate risk arises from a mismatch of assets and liabilities within a repricing interval. Measurement of this portfolio imbalance for depository institutions, however, is complicated because of the nature of the assets and liabilities on their balance sheets.[2]

The first step, then, in measuring interest rate risk is to group assets and liabilities into repricing intervals and then to weight the relative volumes of assets and liabilities in each interval so as to derive an overall index of rate exposure. A number of different methods have been proposed to calculate this exposure, and these are discussed later in the chapter. The measure used for illustrative purposes in this chapter is a maturity ratio, which measures the weighted amounts of liabilities to assets where the weights are expressed as the average effective maturities of each repricing interval. (See Table 17.1 and the discussion of Table 17.4 for details of this ratio.)

Converting this measure into a percentage, a "matched book" between assets and liabilities within repricing intervals implies a ratio of 100%. A ratio below 100% implies that long-term assets are effectively being funded with shorter-term liabilities, thereby exposing an institution to rising interest rates. A ratio above 100% implies that an institution is exposed to declines in interest rates.

A Historical Comparison of Bank and S&L Performance

The tables on the following pages track the historical performance of banks and S&Ls in order to determine the source of past problems. The key measures of performance discussed above are examined and broken into their component parts. Tracking these financial measures suggests ways of improving performance by altering the business mix through active asset and liability management. The terms discussed previously are summarized below in Table 17.1.[3]

The first step in tracking performance is an examination of ROE and its ROA and EM (equity multiplier) components. As Figure 17.1 demonstrates, return on equity at commercial banks has generally been more stable and higher than at S&Ls. This has been especially true since the late 1970s, when returns at S&Ls dropped from an ROE of 14.9% in 1978 to −15.6% in 1982.

Return on assets (Figure 17.2) tells a similar story, as S&Ls plunged from a 0.84% ROA in 1978 to a −0.74% ROA in 1981. Over the same

Table 17.1. Measures of Financial Performance

1. Return on equity:	ROE	=	NI/E
		=	ROA × EM
		=	PM × AU × EM
2. Return on assets:	ROA	=	NI/A
		=	PM × AU
3. Profit margin:	PM	=	NI/OI
4. Equity multiplier:	EM	=	A/E
5. Asset utilization:	AU	=	OI/A
6. Net interest income ratio:	NIIR	=	NII/A
7. Asset growth:	AG	=	% change in assets
8. Maturity ratio:	MR	=	$\dfrac{\Sigma w(i) \times l(i)}{\Sigma w(i) \times a(i)}$

where NI = net income
E = equity
A = assets
OI = operating income
NII = net interest income
$l(i)$ = liabilities in repricing interval i
$a(i)$ = assets in repricing interval i
$w(i)$ = average maturities

NOTE: Figures 17.1 through 17.7 show these measures of financial performance for commercial banks and S&Ls from 1970 through 1982. Data are from: *1983 Savings and Loan Source Book,* U.S. League of Savings Institutions, Chicago, Ill., 1983; *Statistics on Banking,* FDIC, Washington, D.C., 1982, 1983.

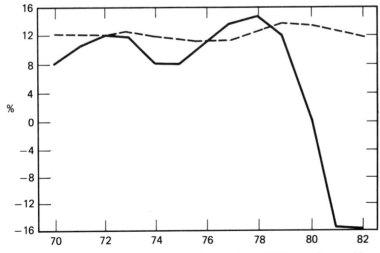

Figure 17.1. Return on equity. Dashed line: banks; solid line: savings and loans.

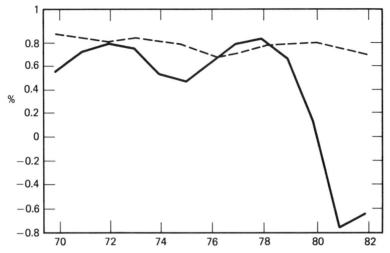

Figure 17.2. Return on assets. Dashed line: banks; solid line: savings and loans.

period, commercial banks, chiefly because of their greater reliance on shorter-term assets, experienced only a slight erosion of ROA, from 0.81% in 1979 to 0.71% in 1982. (For more details see the chapter by Donald Savage in this volume.)

As shown in Figure 17.3, S&Ls became increasingly leveraged during the 1970s as they attempted to increase their profitability in the face of declining profit margins (Figure 17.4) and ROA.

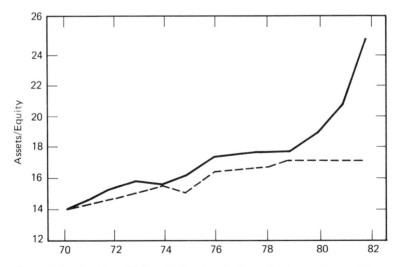

Figure 17.3. Equity multiplier. Dashed line: banks; solid line: savings and loans.

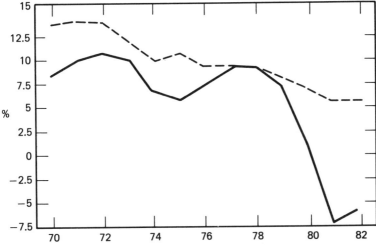

Figure 17.4.   Profit margin. Dashed line: banks; solid line: savings and loans.

A closer look at the components of ROA reveals what was happening to banks and S&Ls as a result of their different portfolio structures. In the case of commercial banks, downward pressure on profit margins from increasing competition was largely offset by greater asset utilization over the period (Figure 17.5) to produce a relatively stable ROA over the 13-year period. In the case of S&Ls, the sharp dip in profit margins could not be offset by the upward trend in asset utilization, and ROA tumbled.

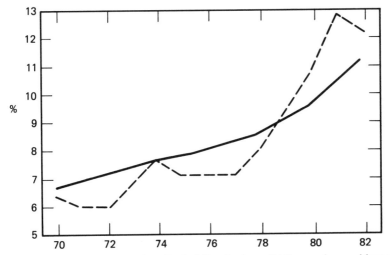

Figure 17.5.   Asset utilization. Dashed line: banks; solid line: savings and loans.

NII isolates the impact of interest rate movements on the institution's income stream and is therefore useful for analyzing the rate exposure of the firm. Figure 17.6, which depicts the net interest income ratio (NIIR) at banks and S&Ls in conjunction with interest rate trends, illustrates the vulnerability of S&Ls to rate movements. When interest rates began their steep ascent in the late 1970s, NIIR at S&Ls plummeted—from 1.4% in 1978 to −1.6% in 1982. This experience highlights the great exposure of S&Ls to interest rate risk. By contrast, commercial banks experienced a very stable NIIR over the period of sharply rising rates because of the virtual match between interest-sensitive assets and liabilities.

Figure 17.7 illustrates clearly the reason for the higher degree of rate sensitivity at S&Ls than that at commercial banks. S&Ls have had a maturity ratio (MR) of less than 20% over the 1970–1982 period, indicating extreme exposure to upward rate movements. This ratio has been declining even further in recent years as regulatory changes and consumer preferences have induced greater utilization of short-term liabilities.

On the other hand, commercial banks have a MR in excess of 100%, indicating that their assets reprice even faster than their liabilities. This extreme difference in portfolio mix explains the sharp difference in the response of net interest income to movements in rates and thus goes far in explaining the very large differences in ROE trends between banks and S&Ls over the past five years.

The above observations on past performance suggest several strategic planning options for improving future performance. All financial inter-

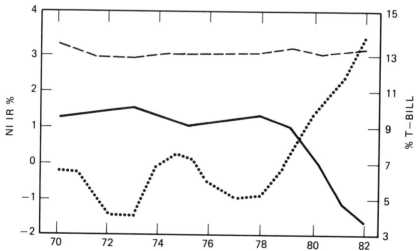

Figure 17.6. Net interest income ratio and three-month T-bill. Dashed line: banks; solid line: savings and loans; dotted line: three month T-bill.

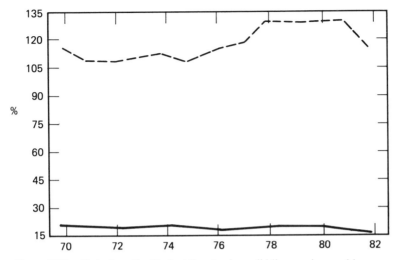

Figure 17.7.   Maturity ratio. Dashed line: banks; solid line: savings and loans.

mediaries are dependent to a large extent on spread income (NII) as a major source of earnings. Institutions having long-term assets funded by short-term liabilities will suffer an erosion of profits in a rising interest rate environment. A central long-term goal of strategic planning for a thrift institution should be to set out ways to restructure the portfolio so as to be able to weather rises of interest rates. While this includes greater reliance on maturity or duration analysis, it also covers the entire range of financial services and product diversification now available to thrifts. (A treatment of specific techniques for dealing with mismatching is contained in Benjamin Wolkowitz's chapter in this volume.)

The business restructuring necessarily implies an examination of alternative mixes between short-term and long-term investments and funding. For example, a thrift might consider offering more consumer loans, so as to shorten asset repricing intervals, and longer-term CDs, to lengthen liability repricing intervals. These various alternatives are the subject of the following section.

A CLOSER LOOK AT THRIFTS—THE OPTIONS

As we have shown, S&Ls have a great deal of interest rate exposure. Consequently, the primary restructuring under way at most thrifts is to reduce the degree of exposure while at the same time repairing depleted profitability. Unfortunately, these goals often conflict, and management must choose between immediate profits and a reduction in rate exposure.

This is because in a normal interest rate environment, where the yield curve is upward sloping, more short-run profits can be generated by borrowing short and lending long than through attempts to match the effective maturities of assets and liabilities. The borrow short, lend long strategy increases rather than decreases interest rate exposure. It was, of course, the cause of the severe profit beating S&Ls took recently. Because of these differing objectives—which reflect different management expectations of future interest rates as well as different propensities to accept risks—actual strategies vary widely among institutions even though problems are similar. Thus, there is no "right" strategy, only ones that are consistent with objectives.

Intermediaries can alter their portfolio mix (hence, future earnings) through two general means. First, there are the longer-term strategic options of choosing which businesses to be in and the overall directions of the firm. In an economic sense, all of the factors of production are variable in this longer-term view. In the shorter term, however, many factors are fixed, and alternatives are limited. The short term is viewed here as one year or less, and this aspect is the essence of asset-liability management. Long-term (or strategic) options thrifts face and short-term asset–liability positioning are examined in turn.

Strategic Alternatives

The Garn-St Germain Depository Institutions Act of 1982 significantly increased the powers of savings institutions. Thrifts can now enter a wide range of business activities that were formerly closed to them, thus giving management a much greater range of strategic options. Primary among these is the ability to make commercial loans, invest directly in real estate, offer trust and stock brokerage services, and in some cases provide real estate brokerage services. In addition, S&Ls can now write many different types of adjustable-rate mortgages (ARMs). Although this does not represent a new line of business, it is a significant factor in making the asset portfolio more responsive to interest rate changes.

On the liability side, deregulation is virtually complete and thrifts are able to offer deposits across the maturity spectrum at virtually whatever rates they choose. In addition to short-term asset–liability considerations, this has important longer-term strategic implications. The rates institutions choose to pay will depend, in large part, on their asset deployment alternatives. Those who are relatively more aggressive in asset generation will be able to pay higher rates on the liability side than less risk-prone or growth-oriented competitors.

The considerations that must go into the development of a corporate strategic plan are, in broad terms, three in number: (1) assessment of where the company currently stands; (2) development of a "sense" —either broad or specific—of where management wants the company to be positioned in the future; and (3) development of specific action plans to accomplish the move from (1) to (2).

An analysis of where the firm is currently positioned involves an examination of current competitive strengths with respect to both asset and liability deployment. Where is the firm doing a good job relative to its competition and where is it weak? For example, a firm might have a relatively strong position in the production of fixed-rate mortgages and be relatively weak in the production of adjustable-rate loans. Should it change this emphasis and, if so, by how much? Does it have the talent to make commercial loans or consumer loans? Should it develop these talents? Management must be somewhat brutal in assessing its capabilities in a broad range of areas or it will be unable to produce realistic plans for dealing with the future.

Concurrent with the assessment of where it stands, management should draw up a statement or "vision" of where it wants to be in the future. This must be more specific than simply "being competitive," "remaining in our peer group," or "providing quality services at competitive prices." Such platitudes will do little to direct the company and provide few, if any, specific action plans. Instead, management should focus on questions that will lead to the formation of specific objectives. Three areas are of particular importance:

1. *The Extent of Rate Exposure.* How much of a portfolio should be reasonably matched by year X? This will depend upon a mixture of management's propensity for risk, its assessment of the future economic and financial environment, the strength of its current net worth position (firms with stronger net worth can afford to take greater risks, other things being equal), and its assessment of the firm's current strengths and weaknesses.

2. *The Question of Size.* How much growth is desirable and how aggressively is management willing to pursue it? Altering the portfolio mix must be done through a combination of growth and repositioning, and any reasonable plan will contain elements of both. The growth element, while very important, is seldom addressed specifically. In many respects, it is a somewhat subjective factor dependent upon management's perception of its own capabilities and its desire to develop and instill throughout the organization the type of aggressive spirit that is necessary. Controlled growth does not "just occur" but must be planned for and directed if management wants to guide its own destiny and not simply be propelled by overall economic currents.

3. *The Extent of Diversity.* How much is management willing to explore new areas and how much does it desire to stay close to its traditional business lines? This is important for guiding both the growth and the restructuring process, but it is something that management often fails to consider explicitly. For example, suppose that an S&L wants to reduce significantly its interest rate exposure over a two-year period and that it is willing to grow and restructure aggressively in order to do so. Two strategies (among many others) suggest themselves: First, the firm could switch its mortgage production from fixed-rate instruments to adjustable-rate instruments. Second, the firm could aggressively pursue commercial lending, an area that may be outside its present areas of competence, in order to develop shorter-term assets as well as lessen its dependency upon real estate markets. Choosing the first course implies the development of new loan strategies, marketing programs, and labor commitments in an area closely related to the current business. Choosing the latter entails virtually a new kind of business. Management must recognize, however, that "we will try everything and see what works" is tantamount to having no plan. Also, such an approach will absorb sizable amounts of both financial and management resources.

After answering the questions of where the institution is currently positioned and where it wants to be, management is in a position to draw up specific action plans on how to proceed. Unfortunately, for many firms this final step is embarked upon without the development of satisfactory answers to the first two elements. Therefore, the results are disjointed, incomplete, and, more often than not, ignored.

Action plans focus on allocating scarce resources. If the company has chosen to undertake new endeavors, it must recognize that this will require a significant allocation of resources, generally apart from established areas of the company and (not insignificantly) their processing and delivery capabilities.

The heart of this element of the planning process is internal consistency: To make sure that all divisional plans and objectives fit into a cohesive whole that will support the corporate objectives for growth and restructuring. Budgets, labor needs, training, marketing, and capital allocations must all mesh in order to focus the entire company on the attainment of its corporate objectives.

Strategic Restructuring at a Hypothetical S&L

Given these considerations in the context of the previous analysis, consider how a hypothetical thrift institution might analyze its current position and

develop plans for altering its structure. Table 17.2 presents a highly simplified balance sheet for such a thrift. The company is almost solely a
mortgage lender: 82% of its assets are mortgage loans with an estimated
average maturity of 10 years. Deposits make up the bulk of liabilities,
with FHLB advances and $350 million of mortgage-backed bonds con-
stituting a relatively small share. The association is highly exposed to
rising interest rates, as reflected in its maturity ratio of 18%.

After examining its current market position, management strengths and
weaknesses, and financial vulnerability, management decides to embark
upon a three-year program to accomplish the following:

1. Grow to at least $7 billion of earning assets
2. Increase the maturity ratio to 50% in order to reduce interest rate
   exposure
3. Earn sufficient margins of profit to keep the net worth ratio above
   4%
4. Diversify into other areas

After considering its market position and management strengths, the
firm decides to enter commercial lending as a means of generating short-
term assets to provide better balance for its mortgage portfolio. It then

Table 17.2. Hypothetical Thrift Balance Sheet (in millions of dollars)

Present Position		Assumed Average Effective Maturity
Assets		
Cash and Federal funds	$ 200	1 month
Mortgage loans receivable	4,000	10 years
Securities	500	12 months
Real estate and other assets	200	n.a.
	$4,900	
Liabilities and Equity		
Deposits	$3,900	13 months
FHLB advances	400	20 months
Mortgage-backed bonds	350	7 years
Equity	250	n.a.
	$4,900	

NOTE: Maturity ratio = 18%; net worth ratio = 5.4%.

engages in developing a number of simulations in order to estimate the feasibility of reaching its goals and the paths it will have to follow.

Management first considers the practicalities of generating a commercial lending business from a base of zero and decides that producing $1 billion of commercial loans over the three-year period would be an achievable goal. In effect, such a target would make the firm's commercial lending comparable (relative to size) to that of many commercial banks. To grow faster than this in a new area would be highly unrealistic from an organizational standpoint and would entail exposure to unacceptable credit risk. In addition, the firm's growth is constrained by its goal of keeping its net worth ratio above 4% of assets.

Table 17.3 shows the financial impact of adding $1 billion of commercial loans with an average repricing interval of one month. The firm now faces the practical trade-off of increasing profits or reducing interest rate risk. The funding of these commercial loans with liabilities of equivalent maturity would do little to move the firm toward its new goal of a maturity ratio of 50%. Consequently, management decides to mismatch the new commercial loans by funding them with longer, one-year liabilities. As Table 17.3 illustrates, the counterparts to the $1 billion of commercial loans are $960 million of one-year deposits and (over the period) an increase of $40 million in stockholders' equity. The equity assumption is predicated on a 2% net interest margin on the commercial loans as they are booked, and the balance of equity contribution ($13 million) is from other continuing operations.

This simple illustration shows the difficulty of restructuring even in a fairly rapid growth scenario. By moving into commercial lending, the firm has increased its assets by 20% in the three-year period, deliberately mismatching in order to reduce interest rate risk, and yet its maturity ratio has increased to only 20% while the net worth ratio has fallen to 4.9%. Clearly, the firm will not meet its objectives under these circumstances.

Our hypothetical thrift next turns to a consideration of how it can restructure its mortgage portfolio in order to help achieve its goals. Management estimates that $900 million of its current loan portfolio will roll off during the three-year period. It decides to attempt to replace these with adjustable-rate mortgages having a one-month pricing interval. Also, it believes it can originate another $1.1 billion of ARM loans (for a total of $2 billion) over the three-year interval. In addition, the firm increases its securities portfolio in an attempt to shorten the average asset life.

Phase II (Table 17.3) shows the position of the firm at the end of three years after following this strategy. Many of the goals have been achieved. Fixed-rate loans, at $3.1 billion, fall to 42% of total assets from over 80% at the outset. Adjustable-rate mortgages now account for nearly 40% of

Table 17.3. Altering the Balance Sheet (in millions of dollars)

Phase I: Commercial Lending (Changes in Balance Sheet)

Assets		Assumed Average Effective Maturity
Commercial Loans	$1,000	1 month
Liabilities		
Deposit growth	960	1 year
Equity growth	40	n.a.
	$1,000	
	Maturity ratio = 20%	
	(Total portfolio, after Phase I)	

Phase II: Commercial Lending plus Mortgage Portfolio Restructuring (balance sheet at end of 3 years)

Assets		Assumed Average Effective Maturity
Cash and Federal funds	$ 200	1 month
Mortgage Loans		
Fixed rate	3,100	7 years
Adjustable rate	2,000	1 month
Commercial loans	1,000	1 month
Securities	800	1 year
Real estate and other assets	300	n.a.
	$7,400	
Liabilities		**Average Maturity**
Deposits	$5,970	14 months
Mortgage-backed bonds	650	8 years
FHLB advances	490	18 months
Stockholder' equity	290	n.a.
	$7,400	

NOTE: Net worth ratio = 4.1%; maturity ratio = 57%.

the mortgage portfolio. Commercial loans have increased to 14% of the company's total assets, making this a major component of the restructured firm. In this example, the thrift has achieved its growth primarily through deposits but also through a $90 million increase in FHLB advances and an estimated $40 million increase in stockholders' equity. In addition, the firm now estimates that its fixed-rate mortgage portfolio has dropped to an average maturity of seven years, thereby aiding in the move to shorten asset life.

This highly simplified example shows the process of achieving goals in the three major areas discussed above: (1) the extent of rate exposure; (2) the question of size; and (3) the extent of diversity. It also points out that the achievement of these goals will not be easy. It was necessary to do several iterations of the process in order to bring the maturity ratio above 50%. It should be noted that accomplishing this required management to fund short-term assets with longer-term liabilities, thereby generating added pressures on already thin profit margins (assuming a positive yield curve). Thus, although it is technically possible to extend the maturity ratio, in practice management probably would opt for the increased profits from shorter-term funding, thereby curtailing the improvement in the maturity ratio. This example also illustrates, of course, the close connection between considerations of longer-term business mix and short-term asset-liability management.

Shifting the Focus

One element in the planning process deserves special attention. This is the movement from a *product*-oriented process to a *market*-oriented focus. Having been closely controlled for most of their history, savings institutions had relatively few products to offer. In the current, less-regulated environment, however, these intermediaries can now offer a host of different products to a much broader market. The marketing implications are similar to those that general retailers have faced for many years, and financial institutions would do well to examine the strategic planning tools that these highly competitive firms have developed.

Primary among the techniques that retailers utilize is the concept of market-driven positioning. This involves carefully examining the markets the firm wants to serve in an attempt to discern the types of products those participants want, rather than attempting to force existing products into the market. For example, the institution should determine whether it wants to appeal to a wide market range or to a so-called up-scale segment. In addition, the firm should decide whether it wants to have a very broad product line (a "financial supermarket") or concentrate on a particular niche in the market. The answers to these questions will do much to determine the kinds of products on which the institution should concentrate.

In sum, by explicitly considering the degree of risk exposure it is willing to take, the amount of growth it seeks, the extent of diversification it desires, and profitability objectives, an institution can more clearly and effectively formulate its longer-term business strategies. One (or more) of these decision criteria generally will act to constrain the range of alternatives that are realistic for an institution. Indeed, even the highly simplified assumptions used here suggest a fairly limited number of options for specialized savings institutions.

SHORT-TERM POSITIONING: ASSET-LIABILITY OR "GAP" MANAGEMENT

In the context discussed above, shifts of asset and liability positions are undertaken over an extended period of time by varying business mix and overall growth. Asset-liability management has the same general objective of portfolio distribution but the timing is shorter and the alternatives are more limited.

In the short run, intermediaries have a choice of where to raise funds on the maturity spectrum. This directly illustrates the conflict between profits and risk reduction. By moving further out on the yield curve for liabilities, institutions may reduce their interest rate exposure, but in a normal yield curve environment this conflicts with profit maximization since short-term funds cost less than longer-term funds.

The chief asset–liability management tool discussed here is the "economic audit" resulting from an economic and financial modeling process that links the performance of an individual financial intermediary with overall economic activity. Once the linkages are identified, alternative simulations can be made to assess profitability under different economic conditions and different policy guidelines.

As this discussion suggests, the process of financial intermediation is one of profit maximization subject to risk constraints. There is almost always a positive correlation between increased risk and increased (expected) profits. Attempts to boost profits will generally entail accepting more risk. With the benefit of hindsight, it is now clear that thrift institutions accepted too much rate risk in the past. Figures 17.1 through 17.7 illustrate the extent of this miscalculation by managers and regulators alike.

It has become fashionable to talk of developing a "matched book" between asset and liability maturities (or repricing intervals). Such an approach would eliminate profits as well as risk, however, since an essential element of intermediation is to transform maturities from lenders to borrowers in the face of an upward sloping yield curve. With interest rate spreads at depository institutions already under new competitive pressures, running a completely matched book would not be likely to generate sufficient income to survive, let alone prosper and grow.

In this light, it is essential for financial intermediaries to take interest rate risks by deliberately mismatching the repricing intervals of assets and liabilities. The key to managing interest rate exposure is to know how much of it is being taken and be prepared for contingencies should rates move contrary to expectations. This entails measuring not only "base" earnings but also the effects on earnings of different environments and strategies. Once these measures are developed, the risks and rewards of various strategies can be analyzed within the parameters of the assumed economic environment, the risk propensity of management, and earnings goals.

While the time horizon can be as short as one week or one month in analyzing rate exposure, it can also be viewed in a longer-term perspective and—on that basis—fits into the framework of strategic planning discussed earlier.

Measuring Risk

Methods of varying degrees of sophistication have been proposed to characterize asset and liability portfolios and the extent to which they represent exposure to interest rate risk. Salomon Brothers, for example, publishes a summary ratio of interest-sensitive assets to liabilities. That ratio relates the relative volume of assets to be repriced within one year (including fixed-rate instruments maturing within one year and all variable-rate instruments) to the volume of liabilities to be repriced in the same period.

Such a measure, however, may provide a misleading picture of interest rate risk exposure if rates swing widely within one year and either assets or liabilities are concentrated at differing maturities within the one-year category. Another problem with the use of simple ratios of this type is that they do not take into account the fact that longer-term assets provide cash flows in the form of periodic repayments which must then be reinvested. Since these cash flows are subject to reinvestment risk, their yields are affected by interest rate risk as well.

To deal with this problem, methods have been developed to capture the fact that different financial assets and liabilities have both different cash flow characteristics and different maturities. The most common of these measures is based on the concept of duration, which is discussed in depth in the chapter by Wolkowitz.

The method used here to illustrate the management of interest rate risk exposure is based on the maturity ratio described previously. The method is to group assets and liabilities into repricing intervals, usually one to three months in length. Then the dollar volume of funds within each category is weighted by the average maturity of that category and aggregated over the n repricing intervals.[4] For example,[5]

$$\text{Maturity ratio} = \frac{\sum\limits_{i=1}^{n} \begin{array}{c}\text{average maturity} \\ \text{of category } (i)\end{array} \times \begin{array}{c}\text{dollar amount in} \\ \text{liability category } (i)\end{array}}{\sum\limits_{i=1}^{n} \begin{array}{c}\text{average maturity} \\ \text{of category } (i)\end{array} \times \begin{array}{c}\text{dollar amount in} \\ \text{asset category } (i)\end{array}}$$

To illustrate, consider a portfolio that is divided into two repricing intervals of one month or less and two to three months. The computations in a "matched book" case and a liability-sensitive case are demonstrated in Table 17.4. It can readily be seen that liabilities or assets in longer maturity categories get larger weights and will increase the numerator or denominator respectively. The effect can be dramatic when, for example, mortgages with maturities of 360 months (and comparable weights) are added to a portfolio.

As mentioned earlier, developing the maturity ratio first involves constructing the gap position of the institution. This means arranging assets and liabilities by their maturity or, more precisely, by the frequency of their repricing interval. It is important that these intervals represent the *effective* repricing interval, and not the contractual interval. This is especially important when analyzing assets, since prepayment assumptions concerning the mortgage portfolio must be made. These assumptions will vary depending upon the coupon rate of the mortgages, since high-rate mortgages have a much higher prepayment rate than lower coupons, giving them a much shorter effective life. Once the gap position of the institution has been determined, the maturity ratio, as discussed above, can be estimated.

Simulating the Risk–Reward Trade-Off

The institution is now in a position to analyze *both* profitability and risk given different management policies and alternative economic environ-

Table 17.4. Maturity Ratio Computations

	Assets	Liabilities	Weight	Maturity Ratio
Matched book				
0–1 month	5	5	0.5	$\frac{0.5 \times 5 + 2.5 \times 7}{0.5 \times 5 + 2.5 \times 7} = \frac{20.0}{20.0} = 100\%$
2–3 months	7	7	2.5	
Short book				
0–1 month	2	5	0.5	$\frac{0.5 \times 5 + 2.5 \times 7}{0.5 \times 2 + 2.5 \times 10} = \frac{20.0}{26.0} = 77\%$
2–3 months	10	7	2.5	

ments. As illustration, consider a simple case of four alternative management strategies for a thrift in conjunction with two alternative economic environments. The alternatives are as follows: case 1, $1 billion in fixed-rate loan production; case 2, $1 billion of new loan production in ARMs (adjustable-rate mortgages); case 3, increased loan production ($1.5 billion), all in ARMs; and case 4, increased loan production ($1.5 billion), with $1 billion in ARMS and $0.5 billion in fixed-rate mortgages.

These alternative strategies are used to demonstrate the impact on the maturity ratio (rate risk) and profitability of growth strategies and restructuring strategies. Using a simulation model, these strategies were first analyzed in a moderate interest rate environment (cases A-1 through A-4) and then, in cases B-1 to B-4, in a rising rate environment. (Moderate environment: Short and long rates rise 30 basis points per year, with a constant differential of 500 basis points between yields on three-month Treasury bills and 30-year fixed-rate mortgages. Rising environment: Short rates rise 200 basis points per year and the differential narrows to 200 basis points by the final year.)

While the model produces results for a wide range of financial variables, we look here only at the impact on net interest income (NII), a measure of profitability, and the maturity ratio (MR), a measure of interest rate risk. The hypothetical association that was constructed for this analysis has $5 billion in assets in the base year, net interest income of $68 million, a net worth ratio of 3.6%, and a maturity ratio of 11.8%, an indication of severe exposure to rising interest rates.

Figures 17.8 and 17.9 summarize the impact on risk and profits of the various strategies and illustrate in graphic format the trade-off between risk and reward. For example, of the policies examined, case 4, a combination of growth and restructuring, produces the greatest net interest income in the stable rate environment. However, with the emphasis on fixed-rate mortgages, this policy option does not improve the maturity ratio as much as the increased emphasis on ARMs (case 2), thereby leaving the association more exposed to interest rate risk. (See Figure 17.9).

This becomes clear in the high-rate environment where the lower maturity ratio of case 4 (fixed-rate production) cuts net interest income to less than that of case 3 (ARMs). Management may decide on a strategy that maximizes *neither* income nor risk protection but produces a better combination of the two. For example, case 3 does not optimize profits but does reduce risk, thereby giving the firm a degree of protection as it pursues a growth strategy in order to emphasize earnings.

Although highly simplified, this example of asset–liability modeling points out how the process can be used to explore the implications of a wide range of management and economic alternatives. In addition to the

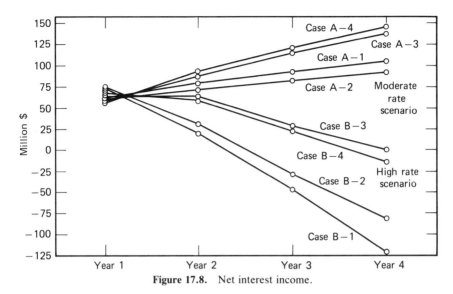

Figure 17.8. Net interest income.

fixed-rate–variable-rate loan options cited here, the analysis should include alternative funding strategies of liabilities with different repricing intervals in conjunction with the alternative asset strategies. These modeling procedures, combined with various interest rate scenarios, can identify the risk–reward trade-offs of various policies and contribute to the development of both short- and long-run strategies.

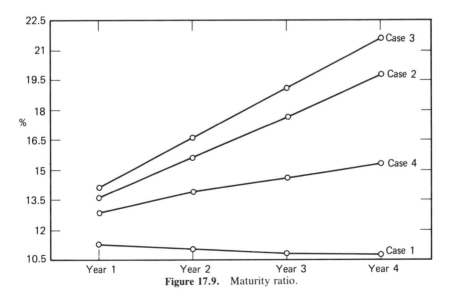

Figure 17.9. Maturity ratio.

As with longer-term business strategies, it should be apparent that there is no "best" asset–liability strategy. The appropriate course of action depends on management's interest rate outlook, its propensity for risk, its ability to manage risk, and available resources. The modeling process can be employed to determine a level at which further risk will not be incurred in the search for higher profits.

EXECUTING THE PLANS: OPERATIONAL CONSIDERATIONS

From a strategy as well as an asset–liability standpoint, portfolio restructuring requires constant monitoring of plan versus performance, as well as the ability to reformulate strategies as conditions change. For example, weekly or semiweekly meetings of the asset–liability management committee should be held in order to oversee an institution's position and make necessary adjustments.

On a longer-term basis, monthly monitoring meetings are useful for comparing division performance with the business plans. By meeting this frequently, problems can be identified before they force alterations in the plans of other divisions or in the overall corporate plan.

Finally, on an annual or semiannual basis, the overall goals and objectives of the institution should be reexamined. If management's philosophy or business judgment has changed, even marginally, from what prevailed at the time a plan was originally conceived, the corporate plan will cease to be an effective driving force within the company. The corporate plan should always be an accurate reflection of senior management's overall "vision" of the future. If the vision and the plan deviate, the planning document will become increasingly irrelevant. If they remain in harmony, strategic planning can be a powerful tool for restructuring the company and preparing it for the future.

SUMMARY AND CONCLUSIONS

In performing the role of intermediation, savings institutions are faced with underwriting, liquidity, and interest rate risk. The last mentioned, arising from the differing maturity desires of borrowers and lenders, has been shown to be the most deadly in the volatile rate environment of recent years. The most important aspects of strategic planning at savings institutions are the development and implementation of plans to restructure portfolios in such a way as to insulate them partially from interest rate risk while maintaining a viable level of profitability.

Attempts to alter either risk exposure or income generation must be made through a restructuring of the firm's asset and liability configuration. This restructuring must take place with regard to strategic options (such as what lines of business to be in) as well as short-term asset–liability management decisions (such as choosing the maturity of funding sources). In both cases quantitative analyses of options and their impacts, in different economic scenarios, are essential in developing a sound and viable strategic plan.

Once a plan has been developed, performance must be monitored regularly. Weekly asset–liability committee meetings can be used to control asset and liability maturity mixes by adjusting rates, for example, in order to stay within the guidelines called for by the plan. Finally, the plan must be reviewed and, if necessary, revised to ensure that it remains consistent with the current vision of senior management. Properly implemented strategic planning will ensure the viability of savings institutions even in hostile economic environments and will allow them to enjoy greater prosperity in more favorable climates.

NOTES

1. *Thrift institution* is a broader term than *S&L,* since it includes mutual savings banks and credit unions, where problems are similar. Unless otherwise noted, the terms *S&L, thrift instituton,* and *savings institution* are used interchangeably throughout this chapter. Indeed, in some circumstances generalizations are also applicable to retail-oriented commercial banks.
2. Some instruments are fixed term with periodic repayment streams, such as mortgages and bonds; some are discount instruments, such as Treasury bills and negotiable CDs; some have variable rates and are repriced as market rates change, such as prime- and LIBOR-based loans and variable-rate mortgages; and some have uncertain maturities, such as demand and savings deposits.
3. For a further discussion of the decomposition of earnings at financial institutions, see Sinkey, 1983.
4. It is important to note that, with the greater use of variable-rate assets and liabilities, the repricing periods of the instruments are of greater importance for measuring interest rate risk exposure than the nominal maturities. (Actual maturities are more important for measuring the degree of liquidity risk.)
5. For an example of the calculation and use of such a ratio, see Table 17.4. Needless to say, there remains the problem of specifying the maturities for weighting purposes of both variable-rate assets and liabilities, as well as liabilities payable upon demand, such as demand and savings deposits.

REFERENCES

Sinkey, Joseph F., Jr. *Commercial Bank Financial Management.* New York: Macmillan, 1983.

18 Pricing Consumer Loans and Deposits

Richard L. Peterson

Pricing consumer loans is, in some ways, more complicated than pricing commercial loans. Average costs of providing consumer loans vary greatly with loan size, and consumer protection regulations provide consumers with repayment options that are not available to business borrowers. Thus, both the impact of loan size and the value of consumers' repayment options must be taken into account explicitly when developing a pricing strategy for consumer loans.

The pricing of consumer deposits has become much more complicated in recent years, with the virtual elimination of ceiling regulations. Since banks now have to pay more explicit interest to attract funds, they will have to levy charges to cover the costs of those services that were previously part of depositors' returns. A possible exception to full-cost pricing can occur, however, if appropriate marketing techniques are used to induce high-tax-bracket depositors to substitute the receipt of free services for explicit interest. If high-tax-bracket depositors can be induced to make such a substitution, it can be shown that both they and the bank can gain.

Consumer loan and deposit pricing schemes can also be affected by competitive pressures, the ability to sell related products, and a host of other factors. Nonetheless, the essential elements in any pricing strategy are that a bank should know its costs and decide what competitive posture it wishes to assume in each market that it serves.

This chapter first considers the demand for and costs of consumer loans. It notes that costs of credit origination and collection materially affect loan pricing strategies. Pricing strategies for consumer loans ideally will call for different prices on loans of different sizes, loans with different maturities, and loans with different prepayment options and penalties. Pricing strategies also will differ for direct loans, indirect loans, credit card credit, and overdraft and variable-rate loans. Each is considered in turn. The chapter next considers factors that affect the pricing of consumer deposits and explains several strategies that may help a bank increase the profitability of its deposit services. Finally, the pricing of joint products is considered.

PRICING CONSUMER CREDIT—OVERVIEW

The Demand for Consumer Credit

The Federal Reserve has periodically surveyed consumers to determine the composition of their asset and liability holdings and their use of financial services. These surveys are useful for showing the types of financial services demanded by consumers and the characteristics of service users.

Table 18.1 summarizes results of two major Federal Reserve surveys, one in 1970 and one in 1977, that investigated the incidence of consumer credit and credit card use. The surveys indicate that the peak incidence of consumer credit use is by people between 25 and 34, with the 35-to-44-years-old and under-25 groups not far behind. Credit cards were used by somewhat older customers, with the 35-to-44-years-old group using cards most intensively, and the 45-to-54-years-old group using cards next most frequently. Further, the percentage of respondents using credit cards is higher than the percentage using installment credit in every age bracket over 35 and for every income group over $10,000.

The data presented in Table 18.1 are consistent with two hypotheses. First, installment credit use follows the distribution predicted by the "life cycle hypothesis" of consumer behavior. Second, credit card use strongly appeals to older, more established consumers, who value the transactional convenience provided by the card. Such customers may use bank cards even though they have little desire to use their credit features per se. Meanwhile, younger credit users may have difficulty obtaining credit cards.

The "life cycle hypothesis" of consumer behavior was first developed by Modigliani and Brumberg (1954). It indicates that there will be stages during individuals' lives when they engage in either heavy borrowing or saving in order to smooth their consumption patterns over their life cycle. When they are young, they borrow heavily to obtain consumption levels consistent with the income they expect to earn in the future. When they are middle-aged, they repay debt and accumulate savings to provide for retirement. When they retire, income drops, but dissaving allows a higher

Table 18.1. Percentage of Families Using Consumer Installment Credit and Credit Card Debt, 1970 and 1977

	With Installment Debt[a]		Using Credit Cards	
	1970	1977	1970	1977
All Families	49	53.5	50	59.8
Age of Family Head (years)				
Under 25	59	65.1	42	38.7
25–34	67	68.9	61	64.6
35–44	63	67.6	57	72.4
45–54	56	58.0	60	68.4
55–64	36	44.4	46	61.1
65–74	14	17.8	37	48.7
75 and over	6	5.1	20	33.5
Family Income (dollars)				
Less than 3,000	19	20.3	n.a.	22.2
3,000–4,999	31	30.8	n.a.	23.8
5,000–7,499	52	41.0	n.a.	33.3
7,500–9,999	61	55.7	n.a.	48.9
10,000–14,999	65	58.1	n.a.	62.6
15,000–19,999	49[b]	65.8	n.a.	72.8
20,000–24,999	n.a.	68.3	n.a.	82.1
25,000 and more	n.a.	58.3	n.a.	90.2

SOURCE: Federal Reserve *1977 Consumer Credit Survey.*

NOTE: Parts may not add to totals due to rounding.

[a] Excluding home mortgages and credit cards.

[b] $15,000 and more in 1970.

level of consumption than would otherwise be possible. This is illustrated by Figure 18.1, where income first is below consumption levels and then rises over time until retirement, at which point income again falls below consumption. In essence, borrowing and saving adjustments permit an individual to maintain relatively stable consumption in the face of widely fluctuating income levels.

The evidence provided by the Federal Reserve is consistent with the notion that consumers will demand consumer credit up to some point in their late thirties or early forties, when they are more likely to start re-paying their debts and accumulating savings. Such consumers are likely

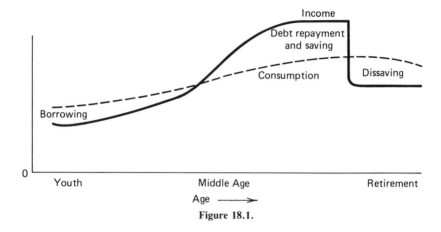

Figure 18.1.

to have occasional credit needs, however, and may value the credit line features of credit cards as well as the transactional convenience they can obtain from such cards. In addition, the data suggest that because cards provide transactional convenience, they are particularly highly valued by the highest-income customers. These facts have important implications for the pricing of joint services.

Costs of Consumer Credit

The demand for consumer credit from a given bank depends on the age composition of its clientele, as well as on its competitors' success in attracting the bank's actual and potential customers. The pricing of consumer credit, then, depends to a great extent on a bank's market position and competitive environment. However, pricing strategies also depend critically on the costs of providing consumer credit. The most comprehensive source of cost data is that provided by the Federal Reserve System in its annual *Functional Cost Analysis* reports.

Table 18.2 summarizes cost data for installment lending that were obtained from 780 banks in the Federal Reserve's 1978 and 1981 *Functional Cost Analysis* reports. Data for 1982 are similar to those provided for 1981, but, due to changes in the report, are far less comprehensive. Thus, 1982 data are reviewed in the text but not in Table 18.2. The data presented in Table 18.2 show there are very substantial costs associated with consumer lending. The *average* cost to originate a loan was approximately $80 in 1981 and 1982. Loan origination costs averaged slightly more for larger banks and slightly less for smaller banks. Smaller banks seemingly knew their customers better and therefore rejected a lower percentage of their credit applicants (and low rejection percentages reduce screening

Table 18.2. Costs of Installment Lending

Reported In:	1978	1981	1978	1981	1978	1981	1978	1981
By:	379 Banks, Each with Deposits under $50 Million	251 Banks, Each with Deposits under $50 Million	316 Banks, Each with Deposits between $50 and $200 Million	274 Banks, Each with Deposits between $50 and $200 Million	85 Banks, Each with Deposits over $200 Million	58 Banks, Each with Deposits over $200 Million	All Respondents (average)	
Dollar Costs per Loan								
Cost to acquire a loan (per loan)	$40.65	$56.19	$46.18	$72.24	$52.33	$ 97.54	$47.84	$78.41
Cost to collect a loan (per payment)	$ 2.15	$ 4.66	$ 2.65	$ 4.30	$ 3.72	$ 5.17	$ 3.06	$ 4.71
Loan loss rate (five-year average—based on average-size loan)	$10.39	$16.59	$ 9.93	$15.95	$13.99	$ 21.28	n.a.	n.a.

(continued p. 554)

553

Table 18.2 *(Continued)*

Reported In:	1978	1981	1978	1981	1978	1981	1978	1981
By:	379 Banks, Each with Deposits under $50 Million	251 Banks, Each with Deposits under $50 Million	316 Banks, Each with Deposits between $50 and $200 Million	274 Banks, Each with Deposits between $50 and $200 Million	85 Banks, Each with Deposits over $200 Million	58 Banks, Each with Deposits over $200 Million	All Respondents (average)	

Income and Expenses as Percent of Installment Credit Outstanding

	1978	1981	1978	1981	1978	1981	1978	1981
Interest and discount	11.299%	14.717%	11.060%	14.304%	11.374%	14.334%	n.a.	n.a.
− cost of making loans	1.519	1.400	1.331	1.546	1.276	1.477	n.a.	n.a.
− cost of collecting	1.101	2.007	1.295	1.826	1.646	1.827	n.a.	n.a.
Total cost	2.620	3.407	2.626	3.372	2.922	3.304	n.a.	n.a.
= Net earnings	8.679	11.310	8.434	10.932	8.452	11.030	n.a.	n.a.
− loss rate (five-year average)/$100	0.466	0.624	0.399	0.558	0.536	0.649	n.a.	n.a.
= earnings net of costs and losses	8.233%	10.686%	8.035%	10.374%	7.916%	10.381%	n.a.	n.a.

Credit Characteristics

	1978	1981	1978	1981	1978	1981	1978	1981
Average size loan	$2,229	$2,658	$2,488	$2,858	$2,611	$3,279	n.a.	n.a.
Average turnover (12 × number outstanding/ originations per year)	15.44/mo.	19.76/mo.	17.72/mo.	22.18/mo.	19.53/mo.	26.30/mo.	n.a.	n.a.
Percent accepted	85.29%	80.04%	80.38%	78.16%	61.30%	79.61%	n.a.	n.a.

SOURCE: *Functional Cost Analysis: 1978 and 1981 Average Banks*, Board of Governors of the Federal Reserve System, Washington, D.C.

costs per accepted loan). Loan origination costs are defined to include employees' and officers' salaries, computer expenses, and all occupancy, phone, and marketing expenses involved in obtaining credit applicants, processing, documenting, and approving loan applications, and placing new loans on the books.

In addition to costs of credit application, banks incurred substantial expenses for recording payments on good loans and collecting delinquent or defaulted debts. Collection expenses averaged approximately $5 per payment collected in 1981 and 1982.

The third major expense incurred by respondent banks was for loan losses. To some extent loan losses can be reduced if extra loan origination (screening and credit investigation) and loan collection expenses are incurred. Based on five-year-average loss rates and average-size loans ($2,859 to $3,316 in 1982), loan losses in 1982 were expected to average about $20 per loan—albeit, they might vary greatly from year to year.

When installment lending costs are calculated as a percentage of loan balances outstanding, costs of loan orgination average close to 1.5% of balances outstanding and costs of loan maintenance, collection, and liquidation average nearly 2%. Consequently, total costs of loan origination and collection reduce net earnings on consumer loans by more than 3% (3.36% at large banks in 1982 and 3.63% at small banks). When loan losses (equal to approximately 0.6% of outstanding loan balances) are included, it is clear that costs associated with making and servicing consumer loans are at least 4% to 4¼% of outstanding average loan balances. This means that a bank must earn at least 4% more than its costs of funds on its consumer lending just to break even. To the extent that either losses or costs of making and collecting consumer loans have risen since 1982, a bank may have to earn an even larger spread to make consumer lending profitable today.

Realized Rates of Return on Consumer Lending

The discussion above shows that the costs associated with consumer lending substantially reduce the realized rate of return on such lending below the contract rate. However, this reduction is not a flat 4% per loan. Instead, the reduction in the realized rate of return varies substantially with loan size and actual maturity. This is illustrated in Figure 18.2.

Figure 18.2 plots the contractual rates of return (APR) that must be charged on consumer loans of different sizes and maturities if it costs $50 to make a loan and $2.50, on average, to collect each monthly payment, and a lender wants to earn a 12% net rate of return (before losses). The data presented in Figure 18.2 show it may be necessary to charge extremely

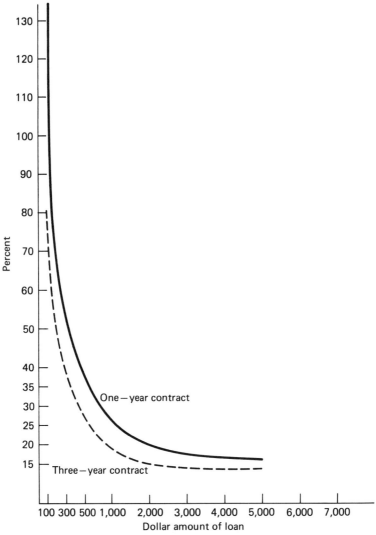

Figure 18.2. Contractual rate of return (APR) to generate a 12% return net of operating costs.

high contract interest rates to make small loans generate a respectable rate of return after costs. For instance, contractual rates of 138.9% on a $100 one-year loan and 40.52% on a $500 one-year installment loan would have to be charged if a bank were to net 12% after costs (but before losses) on those loans. In contrast, if costs remained the same, it would only be necessary to charge 13.48% on a one-year $10,000 loan and 12.87% on a three-year $10,000 to net a 12% return.

Contract Rates (APR) Required to Generate a 12% Return Net
of Operating Costs (assuming a $50 cost of loan origination and
$2.50/mo. collection costs)

Amount of Loan	One-Year Installment Loan	Three-Year Installment Loan
$ 100	138.90%	81.31%
$ 300	58.42%	38.23%
$ 500	40.52%	28.32%
$ 1,000	26.54%	20.41%
$ 2,000	19.34%	16.28%
$ 5,000	14.96%	13.73%
$10,000	13.48%	12.87%

Because business loans are typically much larger in size, banks do not
need to be quite so conscious of the impacts that loan origination and
collection costs have on the required "spread" over their costs of funds
as they do in the case of consumer lending. Because of these cost considerations, a number of factors must be taken into account—including
loan size, loan maturity, and prepayment possibilities—when consumer
loan pricing strategies are developed.

PRICING CONSUMER INSTALLMENT LOANS

Pricing strategies for consumer loans involve decisions to vary loan rates
or credit availability depending on loan size or maturity. Pricing strategies
can also involve decisions to vary fees and nonrate credit terms. The manner in which pricing strategies can profitably be varied is discussed below.

Price Taking and Price Setting

Price Taking.   The demand for bank products at any particular bank is
constrained by the size of the relevant market and competitors' behavior.
For instance, in the Federal funds market most banks are price takers in
the sense that they can buy all the funds they desire if they pay the going
market rate. However, if they offer less than the market rate, they may
attract no funds at all. This is illustrated in Figure 18.3 (*a*). The demand
for a bank's money market liabilities is horizontal over the relevant range.
That is, it can sell as much as it wishes at the present market price, P_O,
and, in most cases, the cost of selling one more dollar of money market
liabilities equals the cost of the last dollar sold, P_O. If a bank is a price
taker, its actions have very little influence on the market price—it basically
must "take" the price set in the marketplace by the interaction of all
buyers and sellers of a service (credit). It then sets its output so that the

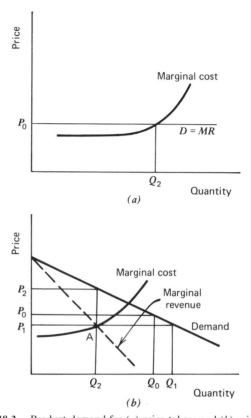

Figure 18.3. Product demand for (a) price takers and (b) price setters.

marginal (extra) revenues it receives from producing another service at least equal its marginal (extra) costs of producing. In the credit market, its marginal (extra) costs incorporate costs of personnel, funds, computer time, and so forth, required to make and finance an additional loan and put it on the books. Marginal costs tend to rise because more expensive sources of funds must be tapped, less experienced personnel must be used, computer files must be provided, and so on as more loans are made.

Price Setting. In the case of consumer credit markets, and, to a lesser extent, consumer deposit markets, most banks have price-setting capabilities. A price-setting bank is one that faces a down-sloping demand curve. In such a case, a bank will be able to attract at least a few customers (possibly because of loyalty, locational convenience, or customer ignorance of or inability to use market alternatives) even if it charges a relatively high price. By setting a lower price, however, it will be able to attract customers from a wider market area (including other institutions). The lower it sets its price, the greater the quantity demanded of its product. (The demand curve is illustrated in Figure 18.3(b).) If a bank lowers its price from P_O to P_1, the quantity of its product demanded will increase from Q_O to Q_1. Since the price cut will reduce its revenues on all products sold, the additional ("marginal") revenue it gains from attracting more customers will equal $P_1 \times Q_1$ (the new revenue earned) minus $P_O \times Q_O$ (the revenues previously earned). Since P_1 is less than P_O, the additional revenues will be substantially less than the revenue obtained on the additional product sold, $(Q_1 - Q_O) \times P_1$. Thus, the marginal revenue earned when a price setter cuts prices will be far less than the product price. Hence, when the marginal revenue curve for a price setter is plotted in Figure 18.3(b), it lies substantially below the demand curve. In contrast, for a price taker, the marginal revenue equals the product price.

The marginal revenue concept is extremely important for price setters to consider, since they can increase profits only if their incremental revenues from cutting prices and expanding sales equal or exceed their incremental costs (including marketing costs) associated with expanding output levels. Thus, in Figure 18.3(b), if a bank's marginal costs of funds were increasing as shown, possibly because it had to pay more to obtain liabilities as it borrowed more heavily, it would maximize profits by producing at point A. Any expansion beyond point A would not pay, as its marginal revenues (once price cuts were taken into account) would be less than its incremental costs. In such a situation, a price setter would set price P_2 and provide quantity Q_2 of its product.

A price taker would behave similarly. However, it would not mark its price up over its marginal costs. Thus, as shown in Figure 18.3(b), it would produce quantity Q_2, which it would sell at price P_O. Note that the price charged by a price setter will ordinarily be higher than that charged by a price taker if they have the same costs of production. Furthermore, the price setter must be very concerned with the effect a price change will have on the total demand for its product, while a price taker need not be so concerned.

Price Discrimination.   Price setters can enhance their profits if they have the power to segregate their markets and charge different prices for similar products in each case. For instance, a bank might find that the demand for its long-term, low-down-payment consumer loans was relatively insensitive to price (because borrowers who wanted such loans were more likely to be strapped for cash and thus were less sensitive to loan rates than to payment terms). At the same time, it might find that its short-term, high-down-payment loans were very sensitive to rates (as its higher-

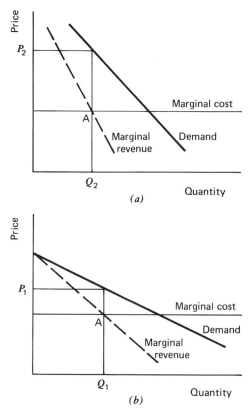

Figure 18.4. Demand for consumer loans: (a) low-payment loans; (b) high-payment loans.

income, wealthier borrowers were more able and willing to shop elsewhere to obtain lower rates). In that case, it might face two different markets for credit, as shown in Figure 18.4. Figure 18.4(a) shows the rate-insensitive demand for low-down-payment loans and Figure 18.4(b) shows the rate-sensitive demand for high-down-payment loans.

In order to maximize profits, the bank would want to set rates so the quantity demanded for each kind of loan would occur where the marginal cost of providing the credit exactly equaled the marginal revenues obtained on its loans. Note that because very few additional customers are attracted by cutting the price on low-payment loans (Figure 18.4(a)), the marginal revenue curve declines steeply. It intersects the marginal cost curve at A, where Q_2 amount of such loans is demanded and a price of P_2 is charged. Due to the insensitivity of demand to price cuts, P_2 is far higher than the rate (P_1) that must be charged in the rate-sensitive market for high-payment loans. Even though the marginal cost is the same in both markets, the rate charged is much lower in the rate-sensitive market.

Implications.   A key implication of the preceding analysis is that a bank must base its pricing strategies on a consideration of the extent to which it can be a pricesetter in the markets it serves. A bank must consider the impact that a price cut will have on both the quantity demanded of its product and its marginal revenues. It will increase its profits if its marginal revenues at least equal its marginal costs of expanding output. Furthermore, a bank can enhance its profits if it can devise a way to segment its markets so it can charge higher prices in markets that are not particularly price sensitive.

These are very general principles of pricing, based on economic theory. However, pricing strategies are also affected by a host of more practical problems—which are now considered.

Effect of Loan Size

As shown in Figure 18.2, the contractual rate of return required on a consumer loan to generate a 12% net rate of return is much higher for smaller loans. For that reason many states have legal rate ceilings that permit very high rates to be charged on very small loans. Also, for that reason, many banks (not wanting to be known as high-rate lenders) refuse to make very small loans. Some refuse to make loans for less than $1,000, $2,000, or even higher limits—requiring instead that potential borrowers either charge small amounts of credit on revolving credit lines or go elsewhere to meet their credit needs. Some exceptions to loan size limits do occur, of course. For instance, "good" prior borrowers probably can be qualified for a loan at low incremental costs. Thus, the making of small loans to accommodate good customers may be profitable (since costs of loan origination and collection are low) even when the value of their good will is not explicitly taken into account. As a general rule, however, a bank will either want to charge substantially more for smaller loans or not make them at all.

Effect of Loan Maturity on Pricing

The cost analysis in Figure 18.2 also shows that required contractual rates of return are lower, for every loan size, for loans with longer maturities. This is because the costs of loan origination can be recouped from a greater amount of finance charges when a loan is repaid over a longer rather than a shorter period. As a result, this suggests that a bank can afford to charge lower rates on longer-maturity loans than on short-maturity loans.

However, most loan pricing practices involve the charging of higher rather than lower contractual rates on longer-maturity loans. There are several reasons for this. First, borrowers who need longer-maturity loans may be riskier credit applicants who are expected to generate larger losses—both because they presently are more strapped for funds and therefore need a lower monthly payment and because adverse events may affect them over a longer rather than a shorter period of time. (Thus, higher rates must be charged to generate equal returns *net of expected losses*.) Nonetheless, it is unlikely that the difference in possible losses is sufficient to compensate for the increased rates often charged on longer-maturity loans. Second, borrowers who need longer-term loans to minimize their payments may be less rate-sensitive borrowers. Thus, from the analysis presented earlier (see Figure 18.4(*a*)), it may be possible for the bank to charge higher rates on loans sought by such borrowers. Third, consumer loans frequently are prepaid. Consequently, contractual maturities are irrelevant when it comes to calculating probable net rates of return on consumer loans. Only actual maturities count. Fourth, a financial institution may have "liquidity preference" in that it will require a premium rate if it is to extend consumer credit for a longer period of time—since it will be taking interest rate risk if it funds that credit with short-maturity liabilities—and also will incur risk if it funds the credit with (possibly higher-cost) longer-maturity liabilities and the loan is prepaid. Finally, a bank may desire a higher "inflation-risk" premium if it is to extend credit for a longer period of time and costs of funds are expected to rise with inflation.

Effect of Prepayments on Pricing Decisions

The data presented in Table 18.2 suggest that prepayments on consumer loans are frequent. While most consumer loans have initial maturities of three years or more, in 1981 actual maturities ranged from less than 20 months at small banks to only slightly more than two years at large banks. Clearly, many consumer loans are prepaid well ahead of schedule. This means that commercial banks incur higher costs, as a percentage of receivables outstanding, than would otherwise be the case. This can be seen graphically in Figure 18.2. If a $2,000 loan were repaid in one year rather than in three years, the required rate of return needed to net a 12% rate of return would rise by three full percentage points. Clearly, there is a danger that the loan would be underpriced if the possibility of prepayment were not taken into account.

Prepayment poses another problem for banks, and that is interest rate risk. If a bank hedges its consumer loan portfolio by issuing liabilities with similar average maturities, a sharp drop in interest rates could generate unexpectedly high prepayments and leave the bank with high-cost liabilities and a dearth of high-return assets.

Prepayment Penalties and the Rule of 78's.   The solution to the potential prepayment of consumer loans is to recognize that it exists and price it accordingly. Either explicit prepayment penalties can be imposed or, where they are not possible, de facto prepayment penalties can be collected by making less than proportionate interest rebates (such as the rule of 78's) for debts repaid early. Because incorporating penalties in rebates has, at most, a limited effect, banks may wish to consider other ways to impose de facto prepayment penalties. This can be done by charging nonrefundable loan origination fees.

Loan Origination Fees as De Facto Prepayment Penalties.   Loan origination fees can be imposed in many forms (e.g., credit investigation fees; application fees; filing fees; recording fees). If they are required as a condition of obtaining the loan, under Regulation Z they must be included in the schedule of finance charges and added into the annual percentage rate (APR) calculation. While origination fees and "points" are included in the APR, they need not be rebated if a prepayment occurs. Thus, if such fees are sufficient to cover origination costs, interest can be accrued based on a simple interest rate that is sufficient to cover costs of funds and collection costs (the APR will be higher, of course) and no loss will be incurred if a prepayment occurs. Even if origination fees are less than origination costs, they still will reduce the adverse effect that potential prepayments have on earnings. These effects occur because the use of origination fees, de facto, increases the realized rate of return on consumer loans that are repaid early.

Effect of Credit Insurance on Loan Pricing

A special form of extra charge that can be assessed on consumer loans is credit insurance. If credit insurance is required as a condition for obtaining the loan, under Regulation Z its cost must be added into finance charge and APR calculations. However, studies have shown that the vast majority of consumers (roughly 90%) desire credit insurance to protect them or their survivors in the event of their disability or death. Thus, if given the option, most consumers elect to take out credit insurance to cover their loan. If consumers freely elect to buy credit insurance, as most do, then it need not be added into the cost of the loan.

Credit insurance provides an important supplemental source of revenues for consumer lenders. Because most borrowers are relatively young, they have a low probability of dying over the term of their loan. Further, because the installment loan balance declines over time, the average credit insurance coverage will be less than the initial amount. As a result, credit insurance appears to be cheap, and most consumers consider it to be a good buy. Consequently, since premiums are high relative to the insurance risk, credit insurance usually is highly profitable—not only because the premiums are attractive, but also because it helps reduce losses on what would otherwise be problem loans.

Because it is profitable, lenders often can supplement their loan revenues substantially by offering borrowers credit insurance. Indeed, the 1978 *Functional Cost Analysis* report indicated that credit insurance provided extra revenues equal to 0.25% of large banks' credit outstanding, 0.40% of medium-sized banks' credit outstanding, and 0.58% of small banks' installment credit outstanding. Since the report subtracted insurance revenues from costs, in the absence of credit insurance revenues, requisite spreads on bank installment loans would have had to be at least 0.25% to 0.60% higher (spreads would have had to average nearly 4% at all banks) to generate the same net return after costs and losses.

Effects of Other Loan Terms on Pricing

Net revenues on consumer loans also can be affected by changing nonrate terms required on consumer loans. Loan maturities and monthly payments, down payments or collateral requirements, and delinquency and late fees can all be changed to alter the probability of default or chance of loss on a loan.

Down Payment and Collateral Requirements. Consumers are less likely to default on secured loans; thus, second mortgage loans have far lower default rates than consumer loans in general. In addition, secured creditors fare far better than unsecured creditors under the 1978 Bankruptcy Reform Act if a consumer files for bankruptcy. Furthermore, the better the security (the higher the down payment on an auto loan, for instance), the smaller the likelihood of default. Thus, lenders can reduce their risks of credit loss by raising down payment and collateral requirements.

Because defaults reduce net earnings, a bank can enhance its earnings by altering loan terms. However, the enhancement need not go one way. For instance, raising down payment requirements may reduce losses but it may also reduce the demand for auto credit and average loan sizes (thereby raising overhead costs per dollar of credit extended). In such a situation, reduced down payment requirements, even if they lead to somewhat greater losses, may enhance profits if they allow a bank to make more large loans at more favorable rates. In short, the effects of nonrate terms on loan losses, loan demand, loan rates, and loan costs all must be considered.

In many cases it will be desirable to offer different rates on loans with different down payment and collateral requirements, rather than uniform rates on all loans. If the incremental rate earned from taking more risk on loans with reduced down payment or collateral requirements exceeds the extra losses expected on those loans, a bank may wish to adopt a multiple price policy. Under a multiple price policy, loans with lower down payments or less collateral will carry higher rates than other loans, all else being equal.

Loan Maturity and Payment Requirements. Arguments similar to those relating to collateral can be made with respect to monthly payment requirements. Monthly payment requirements can be reduced by increasing the maturity of loans. However, over a longer period of time more adverse events can happen to a customer. Also, as payment terms are extended, the borrower's equity will build up more slowly in goods financed with the credit—particularly if those goods depreciate at a rapid rate. This is illustrated in Table 18.3.

Table 18.3 assumes that a $10,000 car is purchased on credit. The car is assumed to depreciate at 28% per year. Financing for the car can involve either a three-year loan or a four-year loan at 15%. Note that if the financing is with a three-year loan, by the end of one year, the buyer's equity in the car, $7,200, exceeds the remaining balance of the debt—and the equity continues to grow over time. This reduces the probability of loan default. However, if the financing is with a four-year loan, at the end of one year, the borrower's net equity is a negative $828. At the end of two years, the borrower's net equity is still a negative $556. Indeed, it is midway through the third year before the value of the car exceeds the remaining principal due on the four-year loan. Since default risk remains high as long as the balance of the debt exceeds the market value of the automobile, the four-year loan exposes the lender to considerably more default risk than the three-year loan.

Table 18.3. Comparison of Collateral Values and Loan Balances

	Value of car	Balance of Three-Year Loan	Balance of Four-Year Loan
Initially	$10,000	$10,000	$10,000
After one year	7,200	7,149.46	8,028
After two years	5,184	3,840.68	5,740
After three years	3,732.48	0.00	3,083

NOTE: A 15% auto loan rate and a 28%-per-year depreciation rate are assumed. Monthly payments are $346.65 on the three-year loan and $278.31 on the four-year loan.

While low-payment, long-maturity loans are riskier, banks may still want to make them. First, because they allow consumers to reduce monthly payment budget constraints, they are often more popular with borrowers. The greater demand for such loans may allow the lender to charge higher rates. Second, even if higher rates are not charged, the analysis presented in Figure 18.2 shows that longer-maturity loans can generate higher net rates of return even if the same rate is charged as on shorter-maturity loans. Third, those who are most likely to be interested in low-payment, long-maturity loans are younger customers whose incomes have not risen to their life-cycle peaks. Such customers may be good banking customers in the future for a wide variety of services. Offering long-maturity loans that appeal to younger people may be an effective way to attract good new customers—particularly if loan qualifications standards ensure that such loans will have a low expected rate of default.

Late Payment Fees.   Late payment penalties can also be altered to vary default risk. Typically, such charges are limited by state law. It is advisable, however, for a bank to assess the maximum charge that the law allows and clearly inform the customer that it will do so. Late fees usually do not generate sufficient revenues to cover both interest and the costs of curing delinquent debts. Thus, they should not be used as a revenue source but rather as a well-publicized sanction. Their use should encourage customers to pay their debts regularly and promptly. In this way they can reduce collection costs and potential losses by putting the bank at the head of the line when a cash-short consumer decides which debts to pay.

If late fees are high enough, they can also be used as a marketing device to induce consumers to participate in automatic payment plans. Automatic monthly charges of loan payments to customers' accounts can reduce delinquencies and administrative costs. Consumers can also be encouraged to adopt automatic payroll deductions, a practice that has helped reduce credit unions' costs and delinquencies.

PRICING CREDIT CARD CREDIT

There are several dimensions to credit card pricing. Card issuing banks can levy finance charges and a variety of fees on consumers and advertisers. Other banks can assess merchant discounts or interchange fees in return for processing and clearing credit card charge slips. Because costs of processing credit card charges and maintaining credit card accounts are large, a variety of charges have evolved.

Table 18.4. Credit Card Costs and Revenues (as percentage of receivables outstanding)

Reported in:	1978	1982	1978	1982	1978	1982
By:	33 Banks, Each with under $50 Million in Deposits	15 Banks, Each with under $50 Million in Deposits	93 Banks, Each with Deposits between $50 and $200 Million	63 Banks, Each with Deposits between $50 and $200 Million	55 Banks, Each with Deposits over $200 Million	60 Banks, Each with Deposits over $200 Million
Credit card expenses (percentage of receivables)	14.28%	17.19%	13.14%	12.54%	9.32%	10.75%
Net losses (five-year-average percentage of receivables)	1.44%	2.02%	1.41%	1.45%	1.72%	1.95%
Total costs and losses	15.72%	19.21%	14.55%	13.99%	11.04%	12.90%
Percentage of revenues from						
merchant discounts	35.1%	35.6%	30.7%	23.0%	24.1%	23.5%
net interchange fee	2.9%	2.3%	2.1%	3.1%	2.2%	−0.2%
interest and cash advance charges	61.4%	54.4%	66.3%	63.9%	72.8%	66.8%
Other income	0.6%	7.7%	0.9%	10.0%	0.8%	9.9%
Total revenues (percentage of receivables)	19.97%	24.52%	20.30%	22.87%	19.22%	24.87%
Returns (revenues less expenses) before cost of funds	4.25%	2.44%	5.75%	8.88%	8.18%	9.97%

SOURCE: *Functional Cost Analysis: 1978 and 1981 Average Banks*, Board of Governors of the Federal Reserve System, Washington, D.C.

567

Credit Card Costs and Revenues

Costs.   Table 18.4 summarizes data on credit card costs compiled by the Federal Reserve's *Functional Cost Analysis* for 1978 and 1982. Those data indicate that costs of processing credit card accounts in 1982 ranged from 10% of average receivables outstanding at large banks to over 17% at small banks. In addition, losses on credit card accounts are substantially higher on credit card credit than on consumer installment credit. The additional losses are due in part to fraud losses, which are much more important for credit card than installment credit accounts, and in part to the fact that credit investigations are not updated each time a customer borrows. In total, losses accounted for between 1.5% and 2% of average credit card receivables outstanding.

Revenues.   Revenues on credit card accounts are relatively high. Most credit card accounts charge an APR of 18% or more. Further, because banks can reinvest monthly interest payments, interest of 1.5% per month (18% APR) generates an annual return of $(1.015)^{12}$ or 19.56%. Nonetheless, most credit card issuers do not earn the full potential interest; many grant a "free period." A free period allows customers to avoid finance charges if they promptly pay their bills in full. Approximately one-third of all card holders pay their bills in full during this period, and finance charge revenues are correspondingly reduced.

The free period reduced the realized rate of return on bank portfolios of 18% APR accounts to approximately 13% in 1978. Furthermore, even in 1982, small and medium-size banks earned only a 13% to 14% rate of return on credit card receivables from finance charges, per se. Moreover, large banks, which often charge rates higher than 1.5% per month, still netted only a 16.6% return from finance charges in 1982.

Banks have tried to supplement their credit card interest revenues with a variety of other fees. The most important supplementary source of income has consisted of revenues earned from merchant discounts. When a merchant presents credit card receipts to a bank for payment, the merchant is paid less than the face value of the slips. The difference represents the prearranged merchant discount. Merchant discounts can vary from slightly over 1% to 6% or more. The size of the discount depends on the standing of the merchant, the average size of each charge, and the total volume of the merchant's business. Merchant discounts account for one-quarter of the revenues of the largest banks and over one-third of the revenues of smaller banks. They provide a greater portion of revenues for smaller banks because many small banks serve as agents for card-issuing banks and hold either none or only a portion of the receivables generated by their customers.

Additional revenues also are generated by card-processing banks in the form of monthly or annual fees charged to card holders or interchange fees paid to banks that help clear credit card receivables. In addition, advertising fees are paid to card-issuing banks by firms that include statement stuffer ads in credit card bills. Furthermore, card-issuing banks can earn revenues by selling customer mailing lists. Table 18.4 indicates, however, that card holder fees, interchange fees, and supplementary revenue sources only added a few percentage points to total revenues earned by credit card banks in 1978. However, in the wake of the credit control actions in 1980 and the period of record high interest rates, many banks began to charge annual or monthly fees to card holders. Thus, by 1982 "other income" plus "net interchange fees" contributed 10% to 13% of banks' total credit card revenues.

Pricing Credit Card Services

Consumer credit card services have several different attributes. Potentially, each attribute can be separately priced. The services produced by credit cards include:

1. Provision of a credit line
2. Provision of credit itself
3. Provision of transactions-related clearing services
4. In some cases, provision of "float"

Traditionally, services provided by credit cards have been primarily priced with a single charge—the finance charge. The finance charge has several limitations, however. First, it is often restricted by law. As a result, revenues are restricted and, when costs of funds rise, credit card operations may quickly become unprofitable. Second, the finance charge traditionally has not been applied in the first billing period for previously paid-up accounts. This free period reduces finance charge revenues and provides an incentive for consumers to use their credit cards to obtain free "float." (Some credit unions even suggest their members obtain loans, at lower rates, to pay off their new credit card debts after Christmas before they will have exhausted their free period.) The third problem with relying solely on finance charge revenues is that consumers have no incentive to minimize their use of scarce resources other than credit (once the free period is exhausted); consumers may make unlimited small transactions at no extra cost and run up large amounts of "float" so long as they pay their bills promptly.

The solution to present pricing (and profit) problems is to develop a broader range of pricing schemes, including the following:

1. Annual fees
2. Variable finance rates
3. Transactions charges
4. The pricing of "float"

Each of these charges can be associated with the provision of specific services. Many programs along these lines have already been implemented.

Annual and Monthly Fees.   Many issuers have already adopted annual fees for credit card users, and most consumers have already shown that they are willing to pay annual fees to retain their bank credit card lines. The possession of such a line lets them charge rental cars and hotel rooms and order merchandise by phone. Often, none of these services would be as readily available to people without credit lines. Furthermore, bank card credit lines can provide funds in case of an emergency. Thus, most credit card users willingly pay annual or monthly fees to retain at least one readily accepted bank credit card.

Variable Finance Rates.   Variable finance rates allow issuers to alter their revenues as market interest rates change. This eliminates possible earnings squeezes caused by rising costs of funds in a fixed-rate environment. However, variable rates can be constrained by state rate ceilings to move in a narrow range. If such rate ceilings are set too low, revenues cannot adjust fully when costs of funds rise, and issuers will still be vulnerable to interest rate risk on their credit card receivables. In addition, because of regulation (including the requirement that consumers be given advance notice of pending rate changes), variable-rate plans can be costly or cumbersome to administer. Consequently, the use of variable finance rates is feasible only if rate ceilings are either high or very flexible.

Transactions Charges.   Explicit transactions fees for credit card use may be highly desirable. Different fees can be assessed for cash advances, local and remote ATM usage, and retail purchases. One advantage of the use of explicit fees is that they would eliminate many frivolous small transactions, since consumers would have to pay for the resources required to process each transaction. Another advantage is that such fees could provide a supplementary source of revenues.

Transactions charges are commonly used for cash advances on credit card lines. Cash advance fees cover transaction costs associated with providing cash credit to consumers at remote locations. However, explicit transactions fees for retail purchases have not been widely implemented. Transactions fees are implicit in merchant discounts, but they are only explicitly passed on to the consumer if the merchant also offers a discount for cash purchases.

Float.   This is provided free to consumers whenever "free periods" are available for the settlement of credit card outstanding balances. Float can be priced very easily, however, by eliminating the free period. Nonetheless, competition from retailers and other financial institutions may limit an issuer's ability to eliminate the free period, except where state rate ceilings are low.

Pricing Business-Related Transactions

Due to the diverse sources of revenues on credit card plans, most issuers have many options available to obtain revenues from business-related services. These include merchant discounts, advertising revenues, and mailing list revenues.

Merchant discounts can be higher if competition for merchant business is limited. This was often the case when only one local bank serviced credit card slips from Visa and another one serviced credit card slips for the Interbank System. However, competition for merchant business has sharpened since local banks have been able to join both card systems. Thus, in recent years competition for merchant business has held down merchant discounts. As a result, in many markets, leeway for upward price adjustments may be severely constrained by market forces. Possible exceptions can exist, however, where state rate ceilings are restrictive—so there is greater reliance on merchant revenues to ensure that card business will be profitable—or where there is relatively little competition for merchant business.

National advertisers have a variety of marketing options, and their influence may limit pricing options such that a local entity may find itself a price taker, not a price setter. However, the sale of advertising space or mailing lists may have a greater potential for profit if the potential advertiser has a special reason for wanting to buy an institution's credit card mailing list. For example, access to names of creditworthy up-scale consumers in specific geographic areas may have great value to particular advertisers. Upward adjustments in advertising or mailing list prices may be possible in such cases.

PRICING REVOLVING CREDIT

Bank revolving credit lines have both advantages and disadvantages relative to conventional installment credit. Because full loan origination costs are incurred only once, when the line of credit is established, it generally is cheaper for a bank to provide revolving credit than to make a series of small loans to the same customer. However, credit data on revolving credit lines still must be kept current, lest major changes in customer creditworthiness go unnoticed by the bank and lead to credit losses. Also, the ready availability of revolving credit in general and the use of overdraft credit lines in particular can allow customers to hold lower deposit balances than would otherwise be the case.

Pricing strategies for revolving credit lines include the following:

1. Price revolving credit lower than small loans and make it more readily available. It costs less to extend revolving credit than to make small loans of equal size. Thus, $1,000 revolving credit lines can be profitable when $1,000 direct loans are not. Nonetheless, rates must be kept sufficiently high to cover costs. Consequently, estimated revolving credit account origination costs must be allocated to *expected* borrowings in order to ensure that all costs will be covered. If an account is expected to be used only once, a higher rate should be charged. Similarly, lower rates can be charged for repeat usage.

2. Since credit information needs to be kept current, an annual (or monthly) credit line maintenance fee should be charged or renewal fees should be charged when credit is reactivated. Annual fees are already charged by some institutions for granting customers the right to have overdraft privileges on their checking accounts. Also, annual maintenance fees are implicit in "special customer" accounts that charge a monthly fee and, in turn, provide safety deposit boxes, "free" checking, overdraft privileges, and so forth.

3. High monthly fees should be assessed on checking accounts with low balances. This will provide an incentive for consumers to maintain their deposit balances even if they have revolving credit lines available.

PRICING INDIRECT CREDIT

Indirect credit consists of consumer installment credit contracts originated by retailers and purchased by a bank or thrift. Thus, the credit is ultimately extended by the depository institution. However, to determine its return on a contract, a bank (for example) must consider not only the terms of the contract per se but also the value of the dealer relationship and guarantees. In particular, the bank can adjust the terms of the contract de facto by refusing to accept contracts without specific terms (adequate down payments or maximum maturities). A bank also can buy low-rate contracts only at a substantial discount (or in return for some other consideration). Further, the bank can impose conditions on the retailer that enhance the profitability of the contract. For instance, retailers can be required to absorb either all or a portion of the credit losses on contracts they originate (the bank obtains "full or partial recourse" in the event of default). Also, retailers can be required to "repurchase" delinquent contracts or to keep a non-interest-bearing deposit (loss-reserve) against which losses are to be charged. All these practices reduce risk and increase the lender's net returns. In addition, of course, the lender may profit from other aspects of the retailer's business.

The pricing of indirect credit can become quite complicated, since the value of dealer guarantees against loss and extra interest earned on dealer reserve balances must be taken into account in addition to interest returns on each loan. The multiplicity of terms provides a potential, however, for price setting rather than price taking.

One particularly interesting difference between direct and indirect installment credit is that the lender need not be as concerned with the terms of the credit per se. Provided that the dealer accepts liability for losses, and that either the dealer is of good standing or dealer reserves are adequate, liberalization of down payments or payment terms may have little effect on lender risk. Furthermore, if contractual rates are inadequate, the discounting of the purchase price of the contract can produce the desired rate of return.

When purchasing indirect credit, lenders obviously must be concerned about whether the dealer is able to meet its commitments. In addition to the commitments to absorb all (or part of) defaults, dealers frequently make commitments to repurchase paper on which the customer has stopped paying because of a grievance with the dealer. Federal regulations allow customers to withhold payment on a debt even if the debt has been sold to a third party if a dealer does not honor a warranty or other commitment. This breakdown of the holder-in-due-course rule puts a lender at risk unless it has a repurchase agreement with the dealer.

Because dealers have better information about the effects of credit terms on the demand for their product or service, they should be given some leeway in setting nonrate credit terms—provided that beyond some point of risk they bear the ultimate default risk. A lender can adjust for excessive credit risk in interest rate or dealer guarantees and for inadequate rates of return by buying indirect installment credit contracts at a discount.

Also, a lender may be able to enhance its overall profit by altering dealer "reserve" or compensating balance requirements.

If a lender cannot obtain a satisfactory dealer guarantee against default risk on credit contracts, the contract purchase price must be reduced, contracts must carry higher rates, or contracts originated with risky credit terms or risky borrowers must be rejected. Where the lender bears substantial default risk, it will want to play an active role in screening credit customers and setting credit terms in order to manage that risk. That role will entail conflict with the dealer, however, for the dealer will recognize that it could sell more goods if the lender were willing to accept riskier contracts.

In sum, a lender's bargaining power in establishing indirect credit terms and dealer risk assumption conditions depends upon: (1) the competitiveness of the market for dealer business; (2) the profitability of dealer accounts; and (3) the nature of consumer demand for credit. As a result, indirect pricing decisions are very complicated. However, pricing decisions can be simplified if the dealer agrees to absorb losses on credit contracts— and, in turn, is allowed great leeway in establishing terms on consumer loans. Then, a lender will need only to: (1) establish buying prices for indirect credit contracts with different terms sufficient to generate a profit; and (2) take steps to ensure that the dealer will honor its "repurchase" or "recourse" agreements.

VARIABLE-RATE CREDIT

In recent years, a number of banks and thrifts have experimented with variable-rate consumer credit plans. Such plans are popular because they reduce lenders' interest rate risk (although they may increase credit risk). Rather than get locked into low-rate loans of several years' duration, lenders are able to adjust rates of return on their consumer loan portfolios on a monthly basis. Also, the use of variable rates should help stabilize loan repayment streams—as consumers do not have the incentive either to repay quickly loans with high rates after market rates fall or to hold low-rate loans until final maturity if market rates rise.

There are several drawbacks, however, to variable-rate lending. First, it is only feasible for institutions that are fully computerized (or have access to computer service) and thus have the capability to recalculate rates, interest, and balances due on a monthly basis. Second, it eliminates all possible prepayment penalties, however small, that may be obtained by using the rule of 78's to compute interest rebates. Third, it may be unpopular with consumers. Many consumers are wary about assuming the interest rate risks that lenders may wish to avoid. As a result, borrowers may insist that potential rate fluctuations be capped, that all adjustments in rates be passed on through changes in maturities (or final payments), or that rate concessions be granted on variable-rate loans. Therefore, in deciding whether to offer variable-rate loans, lenders must determine whether the interest rate concessions and costs they incur in making such loans are worth the reduction in interest rate risk and possible stabilization of cash flows that can result. The more a lender values a reduction of interest rate risk, the more it should be willing to discount the rates it charges on variable-rate loans from the rates it charges on similar types of fixed-rate loans.

Revolving credit is probably the most fruitful area for variable-rate lending, since finance charges are routinely calculated on a monthly basis. Furthermore, variable rates reduce consumer incentives to draw more heavily on their credit lines when market rates (and lenders' costs of funding) are rising. However, regulatory restraints may require expensive advance notice of rate changes, and state rate ceilings may limit rate adjustments. If so, the costs of variable-rate plans may increase and some of the risk-reduction advantages of variable-rate lending will be lost.

PRICING CONSUMER DEPOSITS

The primary reason for paying interest on deposits is to obtain funds. Strategies for pricing deposits must aim at obtaining needed deposits at the least net cost. The net cost of obtaining deposits includes interest outlays plus expenses incurred in servicing depositors' accounts—less fees earned from service charges on depositors' accounts. Pricing strategies differ greatly for certificates and for checkable deposits.

Pricing Nonpersonal Certificates of Deposit

For some types of deposits, such as nonpersonal jumbo CDs, service costs and service charges are relatively small. Thus, the primary cost of obtaining such deposits is the interest rate paid on them. However, the interest forgone on reserves required to back them and FDIC insurance charges must also be taken into account. Consequently, the cost of obtaining funds by selling large CDs at rate r equals (r + deposit insurance premium + deposit service costs)/(1 − reserve requirement).

One advantage of selling CDs, especially long-term CDs or long-term savings certificates, is that it stabilizes the bank's costs of funds. This is illustrated in Figures 18.5 and 18.6.

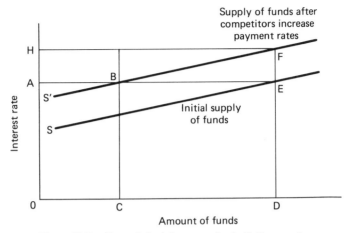

Figure 18.5. Cost of obtaining more funds if all rates change.

Figure 18.5 shows that if the bank's competitors increase their payment rates on deposits, the bank can obtain fewer funds by offering a lower interest rate—as shown on line S' BF. The bank then has a choice. It can continue to pay rate A and only attract an amount of deposits equal to OC rather than to OD. Alternatively, it can raise its payment rate to H and continue to attract the same amount of deposits (OD) as before. If it chooses to retain its rate, its total interest payment will equal the area OABC, with an average payment rate of A. If it chooses to raise its rate on all deposits, its total interest payments will equal the area OHFD, with an average payment rate of H. It should be noted, however, that the average payout rate will rise to H only after all CDs paying rate A have matured and been rolled over into CDs paying rate H.

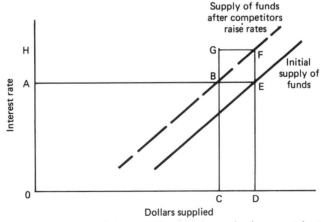

Figure 18.6. Cost of obtaining more funds by increasing incremental rates paid.

Because banks are basically price takers in the large CD market, the supply of funds in that market, SE, will be nearly horizontal. Thus, if they do not match market rates, they will sell very few CDs. As a result, they will generally have to match their competitors' rates in the large CD market.

Consumer Certificates of Deposit

In the consumer deposit market, in contrast with the CD market, the supply of funds, SE, is likely to have a steeper slope. In that case, the issuance of consumer certificates of deposit (which, incidentally, are not subject to reserve requirements) allows banks another option. That is illustrated in Figure 18.6. In Figure 18.6, it is assumed that competitors raise their rates, as before. Instead of raising rates on all deposits, however, the bank (or thrift) observes that a large portion of its depositors are content to receive rate A. Thus, it pays rate A to attract OC of deposits and offers certificates of deposit paying rate H to retain an additional CD of deposits. It still obtains a total of OD in deposits but pays an average rate only slightly higher than A (geometrically, the average rate equals the area OABGFD divided by OD). That is, the issuance of consumer certificates of deposit allows a bank to obtain more funds by varying only its *marginal* payout rate. Often its average payout rate will not be greatly affected. Consequently, if a bank feels competitive pressure, it may well want to offer higher-rate certificates of deposit rather than alter its basic NOW account, passbook savings, or MMDA payout rates. This approach holds average payout rates down because it does not raise interest rates to customers that do not actively seek to obtain higher interest.

The Maturity of Certificates of Deposit

Lengthening the maturity of certificates of deposit can have beneficial effects when interest rates, in general, are rising. For instance, even though market interest rates rise from A to H, in the short run, as shown in Figure 18.6, if only CD worth of certificates of deposit mature, the average cost of funds will not rise quickly. Even if new certificates pay rate H, the average rate paid will only equal area OABGFD divided by amount OD. Only after all certificates mature will an institution have to pay an average rate of H on its deposits.

Lengthening the average maturity of deposits may also be important if such action is undertaken to achieve better balance of the maturities of assets and liabilities (see chapters by Wolkowitz and Pohlman in this volume). Because many loans have rates that are reset at infrequent intervals, funding duration is of considerable importance. That banks have substituted money market deposit accounts (on which rates typically are adjusted weekly, or even daily) for large certificates of deposit (with maturities of 90 to 270 days) in their liability structure poses a threat that, in the short run, liability costs may rise more quickly than their rates of return on earning assets. This shift increases banks' interest rate risk unless steps are taken to offset it.

Pricing Super NOW and MMDA Accounts

Background. As of mid-1984, the entire spectrum of consumer deposits (with some exceptions) was free from interest rate ceilings. Except for the short-lived "wild card" certificate experiment in 1973, it marked the first time in nearly 50 years that consumer deposits were not subject to rate ceilings. These changes give banks and thrifts substantial pricing flexibility well in advance of the scheduled elimination of deposit rate ceilings in 1986.

Pricing schemes for Super NOW and MMDA accounts have been the focus of much interest. These programs have multiple characteristics. Surveys by the *American Banker* (1983) and the Federal Reserve Bank of Atlanta (1983) have shown a wide variety of interest rates, checking fees, and account maintenance fees. In addition, some institutions use "stepped" rate structures, while other use flat rates, and some vary their fees with the size of the account balance or frequency of use. Finally, pricing schemes vary both in the frequency with which institutions adjust rates and in the willingness to guarantee rates over some future period.

Rates paid on Super NOW accounts vary widely. The *American Banker* (1983) reported that initial rates across the country varied from 6.7% to 12%. Further, even though the rates offered in early promotions were not maintained, an Atlanta Fed survey in April 1983 showed that rates offered by banks in the Sixth Federal Reserve District ranged widely from 6% to 8.75% on Super NOW accounts and from 6% to 9.25% on MMDA accounts. Finally, a survey of New York bank rates on personal MMDAs in mid-April 1983 showed that offering rates also varied substantially— from 8.5% to 9.5%. Clearly, even in single markets, substantial variance exists in pricing strategies.

In addition to the range of rates, there has been substantial variability in the frequency with which rates are adjusted. The *American Banker* survey showed that a majority of the banks adjusted rates weekly, while most of the rest adjusted them daily. Only 11% adjusted rates monthly. The Atlanta Fed survey found similar results, with 75% of the banks adjusting rates weekly, 11% adjusting rates monthly, and 8% adjusting rates daily.

The Atlanta Fed survey also showed that fees and charges varied widely. For instance, 56% of the banks charged no monthly fees on Super NOW accounts, 27% charged flat fees, and 17% varied the fee with the balance. Also, 46% of the banks charged no fees for checking, while 29% charged flat fees and 25% charged fees that varied either with the balance in the account (9%) or with the number of checks written (16%).

Pricing Strategies for Super NOW Accounts. Given the substantial variance in the rates and terms associated with Super NOW accounts, institutions have a great deal of latitude in their pricing strategies. Within relatively wide limits, they can be price setters rather than strictly price takers. For instance, a bank may choose to design one variant of a Super NOW account for rate-sensitive customers, charging full fees for account usage, but consistently offering competitive rates. It may also wish to offer another type of account for fee-sensitive customers, either charging no fees or crediting against fees the value of balances—in either case paying below-market rates.

Given some degree of price-setting ability on consumer deposit accounts, there are three general approaches to strategies, including pricing to save taxes, split-rate pricing, and pricing to encourage balance maintenance.

Pricing to Save Taxes. What is often ignored in establishing pricing policy is that consumers should be concerned with after-tax returns on their deposits. Because of that fact, it may not be necessary to pay the highest rate possible to attract and retain depositors' funds. Instead, by offering free services in lieu of interest, both a bank (or thrift) and its depositor can save.

In particular, a customer's return on deposits can be expressed as R

> *where* $R = (1 - t_j) \times r \times D - F$
> R = after-tax net return
> t_j = customer j's marginal tax rate
> r = the rate of interest paid on bank deposits
> D = the amount of deposits
> F = fees paid to the bank for checking privileges and account maintenance (all fees are assumed to be non-deductible for tax purposes)

Assuming that an individual is in the 50% tax bracket, and maintains a $4,000 average balance, that individual would earn the same after-tax net return on deposits if (1) the bank paid 9% interest and levied a $5 monthly fee or (2) the bank paid 6% interest and levied no fee. Thus, the high-bracket depositor would be better off with any rate over 6% and no fee. However, the bank would have a total cash outlay of $25 per month in the first case and only $20 per month in the second. Thus, the bank would be well advised to market deposit accounts that offered no fees and lower rates to high-bracket depositors.

If this example were modified to apply to customers in the 25% tax bracket with a $4,000 balance, it is clear such customers would be better off with any rate over 7½% and no fee in preference to a rate of 9% and a $5 fee. However, the bank would have a cash outlay of $25 per month if it paid a 7½% rate on a $4,000 balance and received no fee. Thus, on balance it would not gain by trying to induce relatively low-bracket depositors to accept a lower interest rate in lieu of fees.

The attractiveness of terms will, of course, vary with the average balance held by the depositor and the size of the initial balance. Nonetheless, these examples show that both an institution and its high-bracket depositors may gain from accounts that offer free services and lower deposit rates. Finally, it should be emphasized that, before this strategy can work, institutions must convince the depositor that in this era of deregulated rates charges must *ordinarily* be levied to cover operating costs. Only then will depositors be willing to accept lower rates in order to avoid account maintenance charges.

Split-Rate Pricing. Split-rate pricing schemes are widely used, notably by credit unions. They provide a way that *average* payout rates can be reduced on deposit accounts without at the same time reducing depositors' *incremental* incentives to save. They work by paying one rate on a portion of the deposit balance, 5¼% on the first $2,500, for instance, and successively higher rates on incremental balances—such as 7% on that portion of the balance between $2,500 and $5,000 and 7½% on that portion of the balance over $5,000. Under this pricing strategy, the average rate paid on a $5,000 balance is 6⅛%, while the average rate paid on a $10,000 balance is 6¹³/₁₆%. However, at the same time, the consumer earns extra interest at the rate of 7½% *for every additional dollar* deposited above $5,000.

Split-rate pricing schemes allow financial institutions to compete intensively by raising rates for incremental (marginal) deposits while not increasing their average costs of funds to the same extent. A similar approach was illustrated for certificates of deposit in Figure 18.6.

Pricing to Encourage Balance Maintenance. There are two powerful incentives to encourage customers to hold larger average-size accounts. First, evidence suggests that many costs (postage, mailing, computer expense) vary little with account size. Thus, the fixed costs associated with carrying an account can be covered more easily in larger accounts—as the interest rate spread earned on balances in larger accounts will more fully cover the fixed costs associated with account maintenance. For instance, if a bank earns a 3% spread between its average return on assets and its interest payout on a $4,000 account, it will generate $10 a month to cover the servicing costs associated with the account. However, if the account has an average balance of only $500, it will only earn $1.25 per month to cover account servicing costs.

The second reason larger accounts entail a benefit is that they are less likely to be overdrawn, thereby triggering personal handling of the account, insufficient funds charges, and a potential loss of customer good will.

NSF Charges.   Banks can induce their customers to increase their average account holdings in several ways. One way is to levy steep charges for handling checks on accounts with insufficient funds. Steep charges, if they are well publicized, can encourage customers to keep larger account balances or to pay a fee to obtain an automatic overdraft credit line so they can avoid such charges. (Many banks charge $10 per return item, and some charge as much as $25. Others charge up to $50 yearly for credit line privileges.)

Low-Balance Charges.   Banks also can encourage customers to keep higher average balances by charging increasingly steep monthly fees as balances decline. Fees can be increased from $1, $2, or $3 per month to $5, $10, $15, or even $20 per month as balances decline. In addition, by basing monthly fees on *minimum* balances (rather than average balances) over the accounting period, customers will have a greater incentive to maintain larger balances.

Scaled Interest Rates.   As noted earlier, split-rate accounts can be structured so customers have an incentive to accumulate balances in their accounts. In addition, many banks offer *tiered* accounts, in which the average rate paid on an entire balance increases as average balance size increases. For instance, a customer might earn 5¼% if the account has balances below $2,500, 7% interest if the account has balances between $2,500 and $5,000, and 8½% interest if the account has balances over $5,000.

Both tiered and split-rate accounts can be used to encourage customers to hold larger average balances. Large accounts usually are more profitable, as they allow more earnings to be retained by the bank (from the spread between earnings on assets and interest payments) once costs of servicing the account are covered. In the April 1983 Atlanta Fed survey previously cited, however, more than 90% of the banks offered flat rates rather than tiered rates on their Super NOW and MMDA accounts. This is an area where more experimentation with alternative pricing schemes is likely in the future.

PRICING JOINT PRODUCTS

Institutions typically offer a variety of products to their customers—and the range is growing. The profitability of the customer relationship depends on the total revenues earned on all services provided less total costs associated with providing those services. This fact must be kept in mind when joint product pricing decisions are made. Joint product pricing is frequently used for consumer deposit and credit pricing decisions and is also used in joint product "package" pricing. Each will be discussed in turn.

Pricing Credit and Deposits

The way that consumer credit and deposits are jointly priced most frequently is by offering credit rate discounts to depositors. For instance, depositors may routinely receive a ¼% discount on their loan rates. At other times they may receive other loan concessions not available to nondepositors. Furthermore, at times banks have offered substantial rate discounts—ranging up to 3% for borrowers that have multiple accounts with a bank—in order to encourage one-stop banking.

The rationale for giving loan-rate (or credit availability) preference to depositors has been to promote deposit growth. Obviously, it is wise to promote deposit growth only if such growth is profitable after all expenses, including marketing expenses, are taken into account. If the objective is to promote deposit growth, special loan-rate concessions should be viewed as deposit marketing expenses. If an institution does not count the rate giveup as a deposit marketing expense, it may: (1) underestimate earnings on its loan portfolio; (2) underestimate its deposit-related costs; and (3) fail to consider explicitly whether some other deposit marketing approach might be more cost effective for promoting deposit growth.

If it is decided to encourage deposit growth through consumer loan-rate policies, rate giveups may be most effective if offered: (1) only to new depositors (although present depositors would need to be mollified); or (2) only to depositors that have maintained their deposits for more than one year (in order to encourage loyalty); or (3) only to those who agree to repay their loans via automatic deductions from their deposits or via payroll deduction plans (in order to encourage borrowers to keep their deposits with the institution and to channel their funds directly to it). Of the three options, the third may be most effective in obtaining and maintaining deposits—as it requires that the customer establish and maintain a deposit relationship during the duration of the loan. In addition, such an approach is likely to cut loan delinquencies and is cheaper and easier to administer. Thus, there is justification for lower rates on loans paid by automatic debiting of customer deposit accounts or payroll deductions; the justification comes from potential cost savings as well as deposit marketing advantages.

Finally, in seeking to price loans to attract deposits, an institution should be concerned with the stage of the life cycle of potential customers. Young individuals just entering their high-debt years are not likely to be as sensitive to small interest rate differentials as older borrowers. By contrast, older borrowers with IRAs or other accumulated savings may be potentially larger suppliers of funds (deposits). Thus, any depositor-related loan-rate reductions might work best in attracting depositors if they were tied to the maintenance of IRA or savings accounts, or if they were preferentially granted to new homeowners who temporarily have high borrowing needs. These considerations suggest that, once possible loan-rate reductions are recognized as a deposit marketing tool, they may be targeted toward specific classes of customers.

Credit and Service Packages

Special loan rates or credit availability provisions can be linked to more than deposits. For instance, many institutions offer consumers various combinations of "free checking," preferred installment loan rates, credit or debit cards, safety deposit boxes, insurance, travel discounts, brokerage discounts, travelers checks, money orders, or other financial services all for a single monthly fee. Pricing strategies for such accounts should be similar to those for linked credit and demand deposits. In either case, the total usage of services must be projected to be profitable, and marketing strategies should enhance total bank profitability.

Unfortunately, whenever multiple services are offered for a single fee, frequent users of priced services are most likely to be attracted to such a plan. Thus, people who keep small balances and heavily use credit cards, ATMs, or checks are most likely to be attracted to one-price-per-month plans. Also, for tax reasons, high-income depositors are more likely to avoid plans for which they must pay explicit fees if they can obtain free services by holding high deposit balances instead. Consequently, it may be desirable for banks to offer free or low-cost service packages to holders of large balances.

High-income people might be more willing to buy service packages by forgoing interest on large balances than by paying a steep monthly fee.

Furthermore, once acquainted with the potential tax savings (similar to the "free checking" case), it may prove less costly to lure high-income depositors by offering free (or cheap) services in return for large balances rather than by offering high interest rates on those deposits. Such services might be particularly appealing if they included waiver of annual credit card or debit card fees—since older, higher-income people (who presumably have more wealth to place on deposit) are the largest users of credit cards.

CONCLUDING OBSERVATIONS

This paper considers problems banks and thrift institutions may encounter in pricing their consumer financial products. It points out a number of considerations, some obvious and some not so well known, that can have an important influence on pricing decisions.

The pricing of consumer loans was considered in detail. Survey evidence was presented to show that the demand for credit varies over consumers' life cycles. Installment credit usage is higher by moderate-income people under 45, while people over 45 borrow less frequently and presumably save more. In contrast with installment credit, however, credit cards are utilized (seemingly for transaction convenience) by somewhat older and richer consumers. These considerations can be important in planning banks' market positioning and (joint) product pricing strategies.

Banks that have price-setting power can alter their loan rates and prices to vary the demand for their product. Nonetheless, the major consideration in pricing consumer loans is to establish prices so that extra revenues will cover all costs associated with making an additional loan. This is not always easy to accomplish, since the costs of making a consumer loan typically are large relative to potential finance charge revenues. In the absence of up-front fees, required rates may be very high on small or short-term loans. Thus, institutions must either charge very high rates on small loans, refuse to make them, switch potential borrowers to revolving credit plans, or cover their up-front loan origination costs by charging loan origination, credit investigation, or application fees.

To earn the same net return, a lender can afford to charge lower rates on longer-maturity loans than on short-maturity loans. However, the demand for long-maturity loans may be such that it is desirable to "price discriminate" and charge higher rates on such loans. Frequently, young people, who are heavy users of credit, have high time preference and are willing to pay higher rates so they can obtain either longer-maturity loans with low monthly payments or low-down-payment loans.

Consumer installment loans can be prepaid long before they are due.

When prepayments occur, lenders earn far lower rates of return than expected (as overhead costs must be written off against a smaller volume of finance charges). Consequently, institutions may wish to levy prepayment penalties on consumer loans. However, prepayment penalties are illegal in many states, and the use of the rule of 78's to calculate interest rebates imposes only small penalties on short-maturity loans. Nonetheless, rates of return on prepaid consumer loans can be increased by charging loan origination fees of various types. Rates of return on consumer credit can also be augmented by the sale of credit insurance. Most consumers are willing to buy such insurance, and it is usually quite profitable.

Banks and thrifts can adjust their rates of return on credit card credit through charges to merchants (merchant discounts), the sale of advertising or mailing list services, and the provision of credit card clearing services. Because many give a "free" period for credit card credit repayment, they must seek to augment their revenues in various ways. Annual fees, transactions fees, rate adjustments, and shortening the free period can all be used to increase net earnings from credit card plans. The use of explicit fees can also ration consumers' use of credit card services. For instance, transaction fees can limit card use for small transactions, and elimination of the free period can eliminate customers' use of credit card float.

Revolving credit can often be provided at lower cost than equivalently sized small loans—since multiple use of a credit line spreads credit origination costs over a larger volume of business. However, either annual fees or credit renewal fees may be needed to cover the costs of updating credit evaluations and providing "standby" revolving credit services to customers. Credit lines provide a service to customers, but they are not costless. Consequently, customers should be willing to pay for credit line maintenance.

Indirect credit is more complicated than direct consumer credit because the profitability of the dealer relationship must also be considered. If the dealer agrees to cover all risks, and the dealer's credit standing or reserve balance is sound, the dealer may be given great leeway in pricing the consumer credit contract. If the dealer does not assume the risk of loss, the lender obviously will want to play a greater role in establishing credit terms and qualifying credit customers. In either case, a lender ultimately can maintain the profitability of its indirect credit purchases by varying the discount or premium it pays for credit contracts of different quality and with different rates and terms.

Variable-rate credit reduces interest rate risk to lenders and may reduce fluctuations in prepayments on consumer credit contracts. However, such a program may increase credit risk to the extent borrowers' debt service obligation is increased.

The pricing of consumer deposits involves a number of issues. Institutions are usually price takers in the negotiable CD market. However, evidence suggests that they have considerable price-setting power in the consumer deposit markets. As a result, there are a wide variety of rate and price structures on consumer accounts, even in the same city.

Both institutions and their customers can come out ahead if depositors in high tax brackets sacrifice some interest return to obtain free checking services on their MMDA and Super NOW accounts. However, consumers will not be willing to make such sacrifices unless first convinced that, in the new deregulated environment, checking services ordinarily must be explicitly priced.

Institutions potentially can improve profits and simultaneously maintain customer incentives to hold large balances if they adopt split-rate pricing schemes in which rates paid on deposits increase only on the highest portion of the deposit as balances increase. At present, however, few institutions use split-rate or tiered-rate schemes.

Another way to enhance revenues from deposit accounts is to adopt price structures designed to encourage high-balance maintenance. High-balance accounts are often more profitable because they allow greater profits to be earned from favorable interest rate spreads while account maintenance costs vary little with the size of the account. Maintaining higher balances can be encouraged (and low-balance accounts made more profitable) by assessing substantial fees on low-balance accounts. This approach is particularly effective if fees are based on minimum rather than average balances. Also, assessing high charges on return items can encourage maintenance of higher balances, since consumers will have greater incentives to avoid inadvertent overdrafts.

Joint product pricing can be profitable if it provides marketing advantages. Rate or fee reductions on one product can be used to increase demand for other products in a joint product pricing scheme. Thus, preferential loan rates can be used as an incentive to encourage customers to transfer deposits, maintain higher balances, or utilize automatic loan payment and/or payroll deduction plans. Rate concessions for automatic loan payment and payroll deduction plans can be cost justified for computerized entities and, in addition, can generate a more reliable form of business. However, any loan-rate concessions given to attract customers to such plans should be counted as a deposit marketing expense, not as reduced loan revenues. Such an accounting treatment will ensure that deposit marketing expenses are efficiently allocated and that the full value of credit activities is not understated.

Other joint product pricing schemes are possible. In particular, customers can be offered one-fee plans that provide them with a wide variety of bank services. However, there is a danger in offering one-price plans in that they will be most attractive to potentially heavy service users.

Also, high-tax-bracket customers may prefer plans that offer packages of free services in exchange for the maintenance of high balances at relatively low rates.

Overall, consumer loans and deposits can be priced along many dimensions. Institutions may take one of two general tacks: a variety of pricing schemes that will appeal to a wide range of customers, or focused programs that will have the greatest appeal at the least cost to the bank to that class of customer the institution chooses to serve.

REFERENCES

American Banker. "A Sample of Super NOW Plans." January 12, 1983, p. 2.

Board of Governors of the Federal Reserve System. *Functional Cost Analysis* (annual publication).

Dunham, Constance. "Unraveling the Complexity of NOW Account Pricing." *New England Economic Review*, Federal Reserve Bank of Boston, May–June 1983, pp. 30–45.

Dunham, Constance. "Commercial Bank Costs and Correspondent Banking." *New England Economic Review*, Federal Reserve Bank of Boston, September–October 1981, pp. 22–36.

Durkin, Thomas, and Elliehausen, G. *1977 Consumer Credit Survey*. Board of Governors of the Federal Reserve System, Washington, D.C., 1978.

Gonczy, Anne Marie. "ABC's of Figuring Interest." *Business Conditions*, Federal Reserve Bank of Chicago, September 1973, pp. 3–11.

Modigliani, Franco, and Brumberg, Richard. "Utility Analysis and the Consumption Function: An Interpretation of Cross-Section Data." In K. K. Kurihara (Ed.), *Post Keynesian Economics*. New Brunswick, N.J.: Rutgers University Press, 1954.

Osburne, Dale K., and Wendel, J. "A Note on Concentration and Checking Account Prices." *Journal of Finance*, March 1981, pp. 181–186.

Peterson, Richard L. "Consumer Lending by Savings and Loan Associations." In *Savings and Loan Asset Management under Deregulation*, proceedings of the Sixth Annual Conference of the Federal Home Loan Bank of San Francisco, December 1980, pp. 175–203.

Peterson, Richard L. "Factors Affecting Bank Credit Card and Check Credit Growth." *Journal of Finance*, May 1977, pp. 553–564.

Peterson, Richard L. "The Impact of General Credit Restraint on the Supply of Commercial Bank Consumer Installment Credit." *Journal of Money, Credit, and Banking*, November 1976, pp. 527–535.

Simonson, Donald, and Marks, P. "Breakeven Balances on NOW Accounts: Perils in Pricing." *Journal of Bank Research*, Autumn 1980, pp. 187–191.

Sullivan, A. Charlene, and Johnson, R. "Value-Pricing of Bank Card Services." *Working Paper No. 34*, Credit Research Center, Purdue University, West Lafayette, Ind., 1980.

Whitehead, David D. "MMDA's and SuperNOW's: The Record So Far." *Economic Review*, Federal Reserve Bank of Atlanta, June 1983, pp. 15–23.

19 Pricing Business Credit

Anthony M. Santomero

In this chapter the determinants of bank loan policy are discussed in a conceptual manner. The approach taken is the view necessary for senior management to achieve best results from the loan portfolio. It abstracts from the mechanics of pricing a particular loan in favor of an analytic framework. The treatment centers on two issues, each of which is independently important. First, the objectives of management are discussed and evaluated. Here it is suggested that optimal loan pricing should be viewed as a multiperiod and multiproduct problem where the bank's goal is the maximization of the firm's market value.[1] This converts to a decision rule that requires the bank to devise a pricing system for its loan applicants that is based on their effect on the bank's long-run returns. Estimating the total stream of returns that is obtained from the loan customer is a complex but necessary part of the investigation. Here it is argued that the applicant's demand for the bank's entire set of products should be estimated and included in the pricing decision. This is both important and difficult. It requires the computation of effective return from the customer account rather than the unbundled loan. It also requires the existence and availability of a central information file within the bank, and a sensitivity to the customer relationship that is difficult to obtain.

The second area of loan pricing investigated is the pricing convention, with special reference to indexing loans or, more generally, the loan portfolio, to market rates. This section examines the payoffs from both fixed- and variable-rate lending, as well as the appropriate level of prime-based pricing in the bank's balance sheet. The benefits and costs of both pricing mechanisms are discussed and the appropriate place for both types of lending is treated explicitly.

Taken as a whole, this chapter argues that rational loan pricing is both necessary and possible for bank profitability. A successful pricing regime, however, does contain a set of difficult issues that must be faced and resolved. It also requires a broader view of profitability than just the earnings effect of a single loan application on one quarter's "bottom line."

BANK MANAGEMENT'S PERSPECTIVE IN LOAN PRICING

It is assumed that the ultimate goal of bank management is the maximization of market value or ownership interest in the bank. This is accomplished by obtaining a set of customers that, other things equal, yields a stream of earnings over time that maximizes the value of the institution. This stream of earnings is evaluated by investors, or potential investors, by discounting the future earnings stream to obtain the net present value of the profits obtained by lending activity.

The Valuation of Earnings Streams

At first glance, the computation of present value is straightforward. The cash flow from a loan is evaluated by discounting the future stream of returns, including interest and amortization. However, a correct computation involves somewhat more subtlety. For each loan or loan class, one must compute the likelihood, or probability, that the loan will not be repaid in full. Under a default situation, the likely return to the bank must be computed as well. The expected return to the loan is obtained by computing the probability of complete repayment times the contracted return and the returns that will be obtained in the default case and the probability of nonperformance.

Obviously, the more severe the credit screen used to evaluate a loan proposal, the lower the default probability. This also implies that the returns obtained from the loan portfolio will be closer to the contractual return. However, competition is most fierce for the very best customers, so that the firm will find that restricting its loan portfolio to only the very best borrowers is likely to result in a small portfolio in which the margin above the cost of funds to the institution is minimal. Accordingly, the bank will accept at least some risk of default to improve its return stream. For some time, adding customers with somewhat higher default probabilities will add to the value of the firm by increasing the profit flow by more than enough to compensate the equity holders for the additional risk associated with the reduction in "quality" of the loan portfolio. At some point, however, the substitution of return for additional risk is no longer profitable. The gain in expected profit is more than offset by the effect of the uncertainty of returns due to a decline in the quality of the loan portfolio on the bank's overall value to the stockholder.

One will note that it is the effect of the loan's quality on the riskiness of the overall loan portfolio that is important. Additions to the portfolio that aid in the diversification of the bank's assets may, in this sense, actually reduce riskiness in the overall portfolio. On the other hand, loans that are identical to those already contained in the portfolio do little to reduce overall riskiness but may be offered because of a special expertise associated with previous lending in the industries involved. This concern for and weighing of diversification and specialization motivations for loan expansion is a healthy part of the evaluation of lending policy (see Flannery's chapter in this volume).

It is incumbent upon each institution to decide where the critical point in the expansion of the loan portfolio exists. The volume of total credits will ultimately depend upon two factors. First, the bank's market, defined geographically or perhaps by industry concentration, will dictate loan quantity. The competitive situation within the market area dictates both the extent to which a bank may extract a preferred return from its customer base and its ability to do so. It also dictates the degree to which the bank must be willing to increase risk in order to obtain additional loans and/or higher margins. Second, the capital market itself dictates the extent to which the bank may absorb risk for return. As noted above, the optimal trade-off between return and asset quality will be dictated by the valuation of the bank's returns by the investor, who must compare this earnings stream with others in the marketplace. In this sense, bank management must always remember that it is the market that will determine acceptable risk and return, and bank value. Once again, the privately held firm must realize the alternative opportunities open to the investor's funds.

Estimating Total Earnings

Accepting value maximization as a goal of management leads directly to the question of how to obtain estimates of the true earnings stream associated with the loan portfolio. Using a superficial, totally unbundled approach, the costs of funding are subtracted from the loan receipts to obtain the earnings stream. However, this assumes that such an arbitrary division of the clients' activity in the bank is both feasible and appropriate. Many would argue that such a procedure is inconsistent with the *banking relationship,* which should be viewed as a multiproduct and multiperiod association. Using this approach leads to two questions. First, what revenues should be included in gross return? Second, what is the expense profile of the portfolio? Frequently, these are combined under the rubric *loan profitability* analysis.

Loan profitability analysis is an attempt to integrate the revenues and costs associated with a customer in a uniform manner to obtain an estimate of the customer's overall contribution to bank earnings (see Flynn, 1978, and Mason, 1979). It involves the collection of all revenues obtained from the customer or customer-related accounts in the institution, as well as total costs. This is accomplished by deriving the contributions to the bank's balance sheet and the attendant profit and loss statement.

The usefulness of this method of cash flow analysis, an example of which is contained in Figure 19.1, has been the subject of much debate in the industry. Some argue that the advent of unbundling and product-by-product purchases in the financial industry has made this relationship approach obsolete. Further, proponents of this line of reasoning contend the current wave of deregulation has accelerated the already quickening trend toward specific and single-product purchasing.

However, these arguments miss an essential point in the use of customer analysis. At its heart it is an information-gathering process. If, in fact, the client firm is "cherry picking," that is, purchasing a series of unbundled services, this will be illustrated by the customer profile. On the other hand, if the firm conducts a wider range of activities with its bank, this higher degree of involvement and profitability will also be evident. The latter will prove valuable information when the bank is under competitive pressure from other industry participants.

Recent trends in unbundling product pricing have reduced the importance of customer analysis, it must be admitted. Yet, items such as free balances, commitment fees, and ancillary fee services remain an important part of bank relationships. Consequently, the insights gained from tracking customer contributions continue to be relevant and valuable. Indeed, this is most true in the lucrative "middle market" where the banking relationship has not been so keenly watched by corporate treasurers.

In Figure 19.1, the first half of the form consists of balance sheet contributions. The balance sheet entries in the customer analysis include the balances provided net of uncollected funds and required reserves. Demand and time deposits, RPs, and other liabilities purchased by the customer are included here. On the asset side, the average loan balance outstanding over the period is computed. The difference represents net funds used or furnished by the customer.

The second half of the form concentrates on revenues and expenses. Income includes loan income, fees on credit commitments, and other income sources. Line-of-credit income appears in the second category for those firms that regularly obtain such arrangements in anticipation of pos-

Account: The XYZ Company Date: _____
Affiliated Accounts: _____ Period Ending: _____
      _____ Type of Loan: _____
      _____ Pricing Convention: _____

Sources and Uses of Funds		Last 12 Months
1. Average Loan Balance		$ _____
2. Average Collected Demand Balance	$ _____	
2'. Investable Balances	$ _____	
3. Average Time Balances	$ _____	
3'. Investable Balances	$ _____	
4. Total Investable Balances		$ _____
5. Net Borrowed (or Invested) Funds		$ _____

Income Statement Revenues		
6. Gross Interest Income on Loans		$ _____
7. Fees on Line		$ _____
8. Fees Generated by Services		
a. Service Charges	$ _____	
b. Other	$ _____	
9. Total Income		$ _____

Expenses		
10. Interest on Balances		$ _____
11. Costs of Services Provided		
a. Demand Deposit	$ _____	
b. Cash Management	$ _____	
c. Other Funds Transfer	$ _____	
d. Loan and Other Credit Related	$ _____	
e. Other Costs	$ _____	
Total		$ _____
12. Total Expenses		$ _____
13. Income before Cost of Funds		$ _____
14. Transfer Price of Funds		$ _____
15. Profitability		$ _____

Figure 19.1. Customer Analysis Form

sible needs.[2] Likewise, firms that generate (and pay for) substantial transactions volume would be credited with service charge income. Other fee
services, inasmuch as they are relevant, would also appear in this category.

From the income total, both direct and indirect expenses are subtracted.
Some of these are readily available. Others are conceptually easy to define,
but difficult to obtain, for technical or accounting reasons. (In the treatment
at hand, capital costs are assumed to be incorporated in the costs of ser-

vices provided.) Interest paid on time deposits or other liabilities is in the first category. Likewise, direct operating costs are also obvious deductions. The frequently difficult areas are the operating costs associated with the loan and deposit balances. This problem results from the frequent absence of good operating cost accounting data at the bank level. Functional cost accounting data have been improving in the industry, but this remains a difficult area in which to obtain quality statistics. In the interim, many banks may be forced to use only rough approximations.

Taken together, this view of the client relationship results in a fuller understanding of a customer's profit (or loss) to the bank. To see this point, Figure 19.2 expands on the customer analysis to include the hypothetical case of the XYZ Company. This firm obtained a fixed-rate (12%) one-year loan on January 1, 1983. Its profile indicates that on average 8.8% of the loan was financed by its own balances, and the fees on an outstanding loan commitment contributed an additional $25,000 per annum. Operating expenses directly associated with the customer's services were $1,900, resulting in a net income before cost of funds of $143,100. Taken as a percentage of net borrowed funds, this is equivalent to 15.7% (143,100/ 912,000), which compares favorably to the simple 12% lending rate. The difference, obviously, is due to the value of balances, and the fee income from the outstanding line of credit. By incorporating these, the bank increases the effective rate of return by 3.7% or more than 20% of the loan rate.

Banks applying this methodology should be cautious in converting this historical record into future periods. Once customer profitability measures are obtained, it is easy to assume that the problem of estimating the future earnings stream has been solved. However, this is a very static view of the customer relationship and the financial markets. Abstracting from the volatility of interest rates, it assumes that balances on deposit during the preceding period, services provided to customers, and their cost of delivery are all constant. Current-period behavior can only be projected into the future if all three of these items are fixed. However, there are clearly reasons to suspect that this would not be the case.

Specifically, there is no obvious reason to assume that balances on deposit last period are indicative of average balances over the future loan horizon. The bank must be assured of this either by making these balances part of the loan agreement or by examining the historical pattern of the borrower to determine whether or not these represent normal or average behavior. Even in the latter case, the advent of electronics suggests that this concept of normal balances is suspect for all loan agreements beyond very short-run lending.

Operating costs should also be scrutinized. These costs have been rising

Account: The XYZ Company	Date: __January 15, 1984__
Affiliated Accounts: __none__	Period Ending: __December 31, 1983__
_____	Type of Loan: __Inventory__
_____	Pricing Convention: __Fixed 12%__

Sources and Uses of Funds		Last 12 Months
1. Average Loan Balance		$ __1,000,000__
2. Average Collected Demand Balance	$ __100,000__	
2′. Investable Balances	$ __88,000__	
3. Average Time Balances	$ __—__	
3′. Investable Balances	$ __—__	
4. Total Investable Balances		$ __88,000__
5. Net Borrowed Funds		$ __912,000__
Income Statement Revenues		
6. Gross Interest Income on Loans		$ __120,000__
7. Fees on Line		$ __25,000__
8. Fees Generated by Services		
a. Service Charges	$ __—__	
b. Other	$ __—__	
9. Total Income		$ __145,000__
Expenses		
10. Interest on Balances		$ __—__
11. Costs of Services Provided		
a. Demand Deposit	$ __1,400__	
b. Cash Management	$ __—__	
c. Other Funds Transfer	$ __500__	
d. Loan and Other Credit Related	$ __—__	
e. Other Costs	$ _____	
Total		$ __1,900__
12. Total Expenses		$ __1,900__
13. Income before Cost of Funds		$ __143,100__
14. Transfer Price of Funds		$ __110,000__
15. Profitability		$ __33,100__

Figure 19.2 Customer Analysis Form

precipitously in banking. Accordingly, the profitability of customers with a high volume of transactions may prove suspect in the near future. Of course, fees have become a more important part of transactions services so that increasing operating costs could be offset in this manner. However, the need for such escalation in service charges should be recognized when earnings streams are estimated.

The final entry on the cost side is the cost of funds, or transfer price, for the loan. It should be clear that a retrospective report that records the historical cost of funds, however constructed, is an irrelevant guide to current pricing policy (see Watson, 1977). Once the customer profile has been updated and examined, the prospective earnings stream must be compared with a current cost of funds or transfer price, which captures target rates of return, leverage, and the inherent risk of the loan or loan category. The latter factors together derive a set of transfer prices to be used as part of loan valuation.

Appropriate transfer prices are crucial to any loan pricing system. Constructing these rates involves three independently important considerations: namely, the cost of borrowed funds to finance the loan, the target rate of return for the loan function, and the inherent risk of the project. The first of these, for fixed-rate lending, is fairly straightforward. The cost of borrowed funds can easily be obtained from CD, Euro, or Fed funds quotes depending upon the applicable maturity and funding options open to the bank. For loans with well-defined repricing terms, for instance, loans priced off three-month LIBOR or CD rates, the direct cost of funds is also easily estimable. For prime-based loans, the process is somewhat more difficult. Here, it is common to develop a funding strategy to finance prime and to allocate the cost of this pool of funds to the prime portfolio. This approach of pool rate pricing is fairly standard in the industry.

The second element of the transfer price is related to the leverage of the bank and the target return on equity. If the bank is to obtain the required return on capital that is dictated by its strategic plan, recognition of the needed margin above the cost of borrowed funds must be incorporated into the transfer price. Given the planned leverage, this equity contribution margin is easy to calculate.

The final element in the funds cost area is a compensation for the probability of default associated with the lending type. Here, recognition of loss rates can be incorporated directly into the pricing scheme so that compensation for loss probability adjusts the overall profitability of the loan to both the bank and the lending officer. This risk adjustment factor should incorporate both the expected loss rate associated with a particular type of lending and a compensation for absorbing such risk. The latter can be viewed as either an increase in return for bearing greater than average risk, or, equivalently, a differential allocation of capital across types of loans.

Combining these three factors yields a funding transfer price, as is indicated in Figure 19.2, line 14. In the example, the net profit of the loan relationship is $33,100. This represents a 3½% return on net borrowed funds after all expenses and demonstrates more fully the attractiveness of the hypothetical customer. This example illustrates the value of the customer analysis. On an unbundled basis the customer had a margin of only 1%.

It is the responsibility of the commercial lending officer to construct the terms of the loan contract so as to assure at least some degree of bank profitability in the customer relationship. This is accomplished by incorporating information from the customer profile into the loan evaluation, and selecting loan terms that best fit the circumstances of the borrower. Loan terms should be selected in a manner that makes the loan desirable to the lender and at the same time feasible and profitable to the bank as a whole. It is this aspect of commercial lending that is discussed in detail in the next section.

LOAN CONTRACT TERMS

Along with the customer's earnings stream and its potential profitability to the bank, the pricing mechanism used for a proposed loan agreement must be consistent with the borrower's needs and capability. This section evaluates two interrelated issues surrounding pricing of commercial loans. The first of these is the effect of loan pricing on project performance and returns. Here, the characteristics of the loan returns under different lending contracts will be examined explicitly. The second issue addressed is the determinants of appropriate terms for the entire set of loans in the bank's portfolio. The questions of who should be granted fixed and variable lending terms will be analyzed, as well as the question of appropriate percentages of each in the bank's portfolio.

The background of these issues is fairly obvious. There have been increased interest in and use of variable-rate lending in banking over the last decade. In fact, recent statistics suggest that prime-based or cost-of-funds-based loan contracts now account for a majority of commercial lending activity (see Gendreau, 1983 and Santomero, 1983). This trend can be traced rather directly to the increased variability of bank liability costs over the same period. Banks have argued that the uncertainty of funding costs has made the fixed-rate loan increasingly less attractive to the bank, since it forces the lender to accept both credit risk and greater interest rate risk in one loan contract.

However, these arguments often fail to consider the implications of shifting interest rate risk to the customer. This alteration in loan terms will have an effect on the performance characteristics of the borrower. Different lending terms will alter the pattern of earnings associated with any project and the economic value of the investment. This fact is frequently neglected in discussions of loan pricing, as it is usually assumed that nothing has changed as a result of the shifting of interest rate risk from the lender to the borrower. Here, the characteristics of the loan returns under different lending contracts will be examined explicitly.

As interest centers here upon the choice between fixed- and variable-rate pricing, these two pricing methods will be considered in turn. Any number of composite or blended pricing formulas can be constructed from these two extremes. Specifically, a partially indexed loan will have characteristics consistent with both versions below; variable-rate lending with caps will approximate either one of these two loan types depending upon the extent of rate movement. The latter is a fully variable-rate loan until it reaches a limit value, at which time it has fixed-rate loan characteristics.

It will be assumed that the bank has at least some funds available to it of both a short- and long-term fixed-rate nature. However, these funds may be limited. Therefore, the bank may wish to shift some of its borrowers into a particular kind of lending contract, more appropriately to match its liability structure. The bank, of course, does have the option of altering its liabilities to some extent or engaging in futures market activity toward the same end. Yet, the positioning of the loan portfolio, in terms of interest rate sensitivity, is so significant a part of overall bank asset management that it requires careful consideration. Toward this end, let us consider the effect of loan contracts on the return stream.

The Fixed-Rate Contract

Consider the stream of earnings from a fixed-rate contract first. These loans, by definition, are priced at an interest rate that does not change over the period of the loan. The rate charged reflects the cost of funds for the term of the loan, capital contribution, and loss probability, as discussed above. Note, however, that appropriate pricing requires that the contract rates for loans of various terms correspond to the market price of funds for different maturities. Specifically, one should require that longer-term loans exceed short-term rates when the yield curve is significantly upward sloping and vice versa in a declining-rate environment (see Van Horne, 1978). This price differential merely reflects the fact that funding costs, on the liability side, differ according to maturity, and this differential must be incorporated into the bank's pricing scheme. In any case, prepayment fees should be established at the outset, so that the bank does not find itself with a significant amount of prepayments of long-term fixed-rate loans when rates suddenly move downward. Failure to do so leaves the bank in the unenviable position of bearing funding costs in an unexpectedly high-rate environment, but not gaining in the lower-rate one.

The return on the loan will differ from the contracted amount to the extent that the borrower is incapable of abiding by its terms, that is, in the case of default. Presumably, default occurs because the return from the project for which the loan was granted or the overall profitability of the firm in the case of working capital borrowing was significantly below what had been expected. Indeed, default will only occur when the difference between the return on the project and the contracted payment to the bank exceeds the equity capital of the firm. In the case of working capital lending, default occurs when the value of the firm declines so precipitously that default becomes a desirable option.

For loans that have been defined initially as higher in risk, the likelihood of default is greater by definition. However, after the investment evaluation, the return to the project is very much at the mercy of circumstances. Consequently, the returns may not, indeed will not, parallel the expected pattern of losses. Over the longer run, however, one should expect the project evaluation rankings, at least by broad categories, to be representative of loss experience.

The Variable-Rate Contract

The variable-rate contract differs from the above in that the exact price of the loan is unknown at the time that the loan is granted. Variable-rate loan returns have both default (credit) uncertainty and interest rate uncertainty, both of which will affect the actual earnings from the loan. By definition, the interest rate charged is set after the initial contract by a prearranged procedure such as prime-based or LIBOR-based pricing schemes.[3] In addition, the project returns are uncertain and may lead to situations where the investment returns are sufficiently low to cause default.

Intuitively, a default problem will occur in either one of two situations. In one case, the project returns plus firm equity are not sufficiently high to repay the loan commitment in spite of a certain interest cost on the loan. On the other hand, a second case could arise where the project returns are reasonably strong. Yet, given an abnormally high rate of interest on the variable-rate loan contract, the project goes into default. The point to recognize is that there are two separate factors that affect repayment: project success and interest rate movement. Interestingly, default for either reason listed above is labeled *credit risk,* as the observed phenomenon is the inability of the firm to repay the loan in full. This is true even if the actual reason for default is an unexpectedly high interest cost on the project, arising from unanticipated market rate increases.

Consider an extreme example of this situation. Suppose the firm in our example above, XYZ Company, sought funding for an investment project that has an expected return of 14%. Further, assume that the range of outcomes is 12% to 16%. At the time it approached the bank for a loan, the "going rate of interest" for a fixed-rate loan was 12%, which is the rate indicated in our Figure 19.2. The cost of a variable-rate loan would, of course, depend upon future levels of rate, but it is expected to be equal to the 12% fixed-rate figure. If the variable-rate loan was granted, rather than the fixed contained in our previous example, the firm has a possibility of default that could not have occurred if a fixed-rate loan was made (unless, of course, material *dis*inflation took place). Indeed, if interest rates moved upward during the course of the loan, the firm would default and the write-off would be defined as a credit risk loss. In fact, the loss was completely due to interest rate risk that was transferred to the firm by the bank in the loan agreement. This firm could not have defaulted on a fixed-rate contract if it had been offered.

Choosing Loan Terms

The preceding suggests that loan terms will have an impact on reported profitability of a loan portfolio and that the use of variable-rate loans adds uncertainty to those returns. In spite of this effect, the number of variable-rate or short-term rollover loans has increased continuously over the last two decades. This is presumably due to banks' preference for an increased percentage of loans in the variable-rate category, resulting from their inability to obtain a sufficiently large portion of their liabilities in the fixed-rate area. The continued move toward deregulation of short-term liabilities has accentuated this trend.

Faced with this imbalance, the institutions must determine both which loans to shift into the variable-rate category and, at the bank level, the aggregate total of fixed- versus variable-rate loans. In the following two sections, both of these questions are addressed.

Determining which loans to offer a variable-rate loan contract is an important issue. Yet, this issue has received very little attention in the industry. One is left with the view that the bank is free to shift any loan to the variable-rate category, regardless of its characteristics. However, as illustrated above, not all firms can absorb the variation in lending cost associated with an indexed pricing scheme equally well. Specifically, firms having cash flows that are relatively fixed in nominal terms would be particularly vulnerable to a variable-rate loan agreement. In these cases, variation in loan cost, precipitated by a change in the cost of funds to the bank, must be absorbed out of the profit from the project, or, ultimately, the capital of the firm. The bank essentially deceives itself in believing that the economic basis for granting the loan is unaffected by the alteration in rate charged to the borrower when market conditions changed. And, as pointed out above, it is surprised by the increase in defaults associated with its attempt to garner a larger portion of a relatively fixed return stream.

This scenario is considerably different for other projects. For loans used to finance investments that have a cash flow that varies with the level of interest rates, the variable-rate loan is an appropriate lending contract. If the firm's cash flow responds significantly to the forces that lead to higher interest rates, the borrower is better prepared to absorb the increased cost of a higher interest rate when an environment of higher rates occurs.

Reference to the recent past will make this point more clearly. Over the last two decades, a substantial portion of interest rate movement can be accounted for by variations in inflation (see Van Horne, 1978). Economists since Irving Fisher have contended that the level of expected inflation is a key determinant of the observed rate of interest. Some would contend it is the only major factor that has caused the substantial variation of interest rates over the last 20 years (see Fama, 1975). This contention aside, few would deny the existence of the link between inflation and the level of rates. This has interesting implications for loan terms. It argues that projects whose returns are closely related to the level of inflation will have returns highly correlated with open market interest rates. These will be prime candidates for variable-rate lending. On the other hand, projects or firms with returns that are relatively fixed in nominal terms should be the first group to be offered fixed-rate contracts. This would reduce the possibility that a high-rate environment, caused by an upward movement in the level of inflation, would drive firms into bankruptcy.

Operationally, this concept of lending term choice requires that the bank examine the implication of price and interest rate movements on the viability of the projects of firms seeking funding. Returning to our hypothetical loan, the bank should examine the funding request to determine the extent to which the firm can absorb loan-rate movements. XYZ Company expects returns in the 12% to 16% range. The bank wishes to determine whether or not the higher range of returns from the loan occurs when rates are expected to be high. If this is the case, the company is a better candidate for variable-rate lending than those firms that have no such relationship between profitability and interest rates. At the other extreme, if the borrower's fortunes are adversely affected by high-rate environments, the bank should resist the temptation to shift interest rate risk to the firm. To determine into which category a particular borrower falls requires an examination of the loan proposal submitted to the bank and its sensitivity to differential rate environments.

Choosing Portfolio Composition

The determination of how many projects should be in either the fixed- or variable-rate category goes beyond the firm and project specifics. It involves two different yet fundamentally important issues in bank management. The first of these is an analysis of the underlying structure of the bank's balance sheet, including both asset and liabilities, to determine the bank's existing interest rate exposure. The second issue is the implication on profit and loss of absorbing interest rate risk beyond the bank's capacity, given its liability structure. This second issue involves an analysis of the cost and benefits of interest rate exposure. The latter is consistent and interrelated with the discussion above concerning the bank's willingness to bear credit risk.

On the first point, the bank's balance sheet will dictate the extent to which fixed-rate lending can be financed with bank liabilities of similar fixed-rate duration. Institutions with a larger percentage of fixed-rate core deposits will be in a better position to offer fixed-rate lending than their counterparts in the industry.[4] Likewise, institutions with a small fixed-rate investment portfolio have a greater capacity to offer fixed-rate lending terms.

Beyond the ability to match the portfolio composition of assets and liabilities, the bank must determine the extent to which it wishes to deviate from a hedged balance sheet. Much has been written recently about the advisability of such hedging via gap management or futures activity. However, these arguments should not be oversold. In fact, it may not be desirable for the typical bank to immunize itself completely from interest rate risk, as is so often suggested. To determine appropriate balance sheet composition, the bank must weigh the benefits of absorbing some interest rate risk in its loan portfolio, in terms of the larger anticipated spreads, against the profitability of other types of risk bearing. The bank ought to be willing to accept some reasonable amount of interest rate risk in its portfolio, via offering a fixed-rate loan financed by variable-rate lending. The only real questions are how much interest rate risk will be borne and how this risk can be allocated among interested borrowers.

The previous section answered the latter question. It argued that variable-rate lending terms should be offered to firms that have a project return, or cash flow, that is likely to be related to interest rate movements. These are the firms that can most afford the rate uncertainty and will, accordingly, be the least likely to suffer excessively from such contract terms. On the other hand, fixed-rate terms are most efficiently offered to firms with relatively fixed returns, as well as firms with project returns that are not at all related to the factors that cause interest rate movement.

The quantity of mismatching in the portfolio, that is, the fraction of loans made with terms that differ from the financing mode, depends upon the likely returns from such mismatching, the riskiness of such activity, and the bank's willingness to bear such risk. For example, as the expected gain associated with offering a fixed-rate intermediate-term loan, financed by short-term CDs, increases, the bank should be more willing to acccpt more of such loans. On the other hand, as the uncertainties of the rate environment increase, as has the variability of rates over the last several years, the quantity of mismatched lending should decline. The latter is what we have seen over the last decade.

Equally important, however, is the recognition that the bank is in the business of bearing risk, albeit prudent and carefully considered. It makes little sense for it to absorb credit risk and completely shy away from interest rate risk. It makes no sense for it to have a portfolio that has fairly substantial projected loan loss figures, while at the same time trying to obtain a perfectly immunized interest rate position. The firm must look at both forms of risk, interest rate risk and default risk, and determine how both should be borne so as to achieve the best performance for the institution's market value. This means it must stand ready to absorb both types of risk if the benefits outweigh the cost of increased variability in its profit figures. Indeed, it should trade off the benefits of bearing credit risk with those associated with bearing interest rate risk. Some firms will find that performance and market value would benefit by improving the quality of their loan portfolios while at the same time increasing their interest rate exposure.

This argument does not imply that institutions should move headlong into interest rate mismatching. Indeed, much can be said, and has been written, on the advisability of limiting interest rate risk to the short end of the maturity spectrum and to a small portion of the portfolio. Prudence is always warranted. However, prudence does not call for completely eliminating interest rate risk, while at the same time bearing considerable credit risk in the loan portfolio. It requires the balancing of these two in the overall portfolio position so as to achieve the best possible return for bank stockholders.

SUMMARY AND CONCLUSIONS

The determination of the quantity, nature, and price of the loan portfolio requires an understanding of management's ultimate objectives of long-term value maximization. This has direct effects on loan portfolio structure and composition as these relate to this goal. Careful analysis of the entire loan relationship is needed to determine the nature of the return stream or earnings to be obtained from prospective or existing customers as they seek loan financing. This is an extremely difficult task to perform and, yet, fundamentally important. Its relevance in the competitive environment of the 1980s is likely to grow as this information allows the bank more adequately to evaluate the profitability of customer groups, and keep their best customers.

Finally, the discussion turned to loan terms per se. Appropriate decision making, at the bank level, requires more careful consideration of the trend toward variable-rate pricing. For some projects or firms, such pricing schemes do little more than reclassify interest rate risk as credit risk, because some firms cannot adequately absorb such loan price variability. Recognition of this phenomenon suggests that loan terms should be set only after due consideration of the project's nature. Loan pricing should fit the firm's ability to pay.

On an aggregate portfolio level, the determination of final loan portfolio composition involves knowledge of the bank's total balance sheet and its willingness to absorb risk. The latter is important, because ultimately interest rate risk is merely another dimension of uncertainty associated with the bank's earning stream. As such, it should be evaluated in the same manner as other types of risk. Equally important, however, it should be evaluated along with other sources of uncertainty so that the benefits and costs of each are equalized. This suggests that it is generally in the best interest of the firm to absorb at least some interest rate risk, for its expected profit, just as it is appropriate to bear some credit risk. Both types of risk should be evaluated carefully, of course, and accepted conservatively for their potential contribution to earnings.

NOTES

1. Closely held firms, and those with thin markets, should also strive for value maximization. Given the alternative financial assets available to the owners, the bank must pursue an efficient financial strategy to remain a desirable investment.

2. Firms that use the bank's lines of credit for backup or standby purposes primarily should be viewed as purchasers of a fee service, rather than true loan customers. Accordingly, it would be misleading to use a loan form to derive a rate-of-return figure for these customers.

3. The choice between these two options, that is, a prime-based pricing scheme versus some form of cost plus pricing as in LIBOR-based contracts, is of intense interest. For a review of this debate, see Gendreau (1983).

4. Even banks in this category should be aware that deregulation will ultimately erode their level of demand and personal savings. Therefore, some care should be taken when these funds are invested in longer-term assets.

REFERENCES

Agmon, T., Ofer, A. R., and Tamir, A. "Variable Rate Debt Instruments and Corporate Debt Policy." *Journal of Finance,* March 1981, pp. 113–125.

Edmister, R., and Schlarbaum, G. "Credit Policy in Lending Institutions." *Journal of Finance and Quantitative Analysis,* June 1974, pp. 335–356.

Fama, E. "Short-Term Interest Rates as Predictors of Inflation." *American Economic Review,* June 1975, pp 269–282.

Fisher, I. *The Theory of Interest.* New York: Macmillan, 1930 (reprinted by A. M. Kelley, 1965).

Flynn, T. "Loan Profitability—A Method to the Madness." *Journal of Commercial Bank Lending,* March 1978, pp. 3–11.

Gendreau, B. "When Is the Prime Rate Second Choice?" Federal Reserve Bank of Philadelphia, *Business Review,* May–June 1983, pp. 13–21.

Hafer, R. W. "The Prime Rate and the Cost of Funds: Is the Prime Too High?" Federal Reserve Bank of St. Louis, *Review,* May 1983, pp. 17–21.

James, C. "An Analysis of Bank Loan Rate Indexation." *Journal of Finance,* June 1982, pp. 809–825.

Mason, J. *Financial Management of Commercial Banks.* New York: Warren, Gorham, and Lamont, 1979.

Santomero, A. "Fixed versus Variable Rate Loans." *Journal of Finance,* December 1983, pp. 1363–1380.

Van Horne, J. *Financial Markets: Rates and Flows.* Englewood Cliffs, N.J.: Prentice-Hall, 1978.

Watson, R. "The Marginal Cost of Funds Concept in Banking." *Journal of Bank Research,* Autumn 1977, pp. 136–147.

20 Pricing Mortgage Credit

Kevin E. Villani

CONTEXT

Accurately pricing mortgage credit has become increasingly important in the 1980s. The post-Depression pattern of housing finance was for whole mortgage loans to remain in the portfolio of the lender until the borrower repaid. Pricing the loan in this environment was simply a matter of establishing mortgage coupon rates above the lender's cost of funds.

Housing finance is currently undergoing a revolution. Portfolio lending no longer dominates the mortgage market, as the origination and servicing functions are being separated from the financing function. Institutional barriers are also crumbling; commercial banks are entering savings and loan markets and vice versa, private mortgage insurers are creating secondary markets, and investment bankers are branching into all these areas.

The 1970s trend of sales of mortgage originations accelerated in the 1980s. Sales of existing mortgages also exploded in the 1980s. In 1982, about $22 billion in existing mortgages was "swapped" for pass-through securities with Freddie Mac, and another $11 billion with Fannie Mae.

Much of the material for this chapter comes from papers and articles coauthored by others, particularly Patric Hendershott. These are listed in the references. Also, this author would like to express his appreciation to Beth Preiss for her valuable assistance in the preparation of the manuscript and to Ahni Vanek for typing text and equations from an occasionally illegible draft.

The Federal Home Loan Mortgage Corporation, as a matter of policy, is not responsible for any private publication or statement by any of its employees. The views expressed herein are those of the author and do not necessarily reflect the views of the corporation.

When trades of existing pass-through securities and direct placements are counted, over $100 billion in existing mortgage securities is estimated to have been traded in 1982 alone.

What does all this imply for pricing mortgage credit? No longer is it simply a matter of determining a markup of the coupon rate over the cost of funds. Rather, the price is being determined in capital markets in competition with all other investments. How well these prices are determined is of vital concern to sellers, investors, secondary market conduits, and ultimately, home mortgage borrowers.

Capital markets have worked out fairly efficient pricing mechanisms for debt instruments. For pricing purposes, there are two key parameters to debt issues: maturity and risk. The first has been simplified in that bonds pay semiannual interest only, and pay principal at a prespecified date. The second has been addressed by the bond-rating agencies, which distill all the information regarding risk and categorize debt securities. Thus, pricing bonds essentially requires applying straightforward pricing formulas, plugging in the appropriate maturity and risk parameters.

These procedures are applied to mortgage pricing with only limited success. While the pricing concepts are the same, the technical complexity is significantly greater. There are three general areas of concern, listed in increasing order of importance:

1. *Adminstrative.*   Mortgages have more expensive servicing, accounting, legal review, and so on; and some firms can do this more efficiently than others.
2. *Default Risk.*   The risk exists that the borrower will not meet all the terms and conditions of the contract. Mortgage default underwriting is conceptually and empirically unrelated to other default risks in capital markets; it is linked to locally produced and available information and therefore is more expensive to obtain.
3. *Cash Flow Uncertainty.*   Mortgage cash flow is unknown, unpredictable, and often adverse to the economic interests of the lender, because a borrower can prepay the loan at any time before it matures.

The development of alternative mortgage instruments in the 1970s and their proliferation in the 1980s have compounded the pricing problem. No longer simply a financing instrument, the mortgage is now being designed to address the problems of all the parties to the transactions: Portfolio lenders face interest rate risks, households face affordability constraints, and investors face numerous financial and regulatory risks. Alternative mortgage designs—the adjustable-rate mortgage (ARM), the graduated-payment mortgage (GPM), the shared appreciation mortgage (SAM), the balloon payment loan, and so on—require special treatment to capture the pricing implications of their characteristics.

Social housing policy also has serious implications for mortgage pricing. Congress and various government agencies influence what provisions may or may not be included in the loan document. Sometimes, as in the case of the "due-on-sale" clause, state courts and legislatures rule these provisions unenforceable, even retroactively on existing contracts. The terms of the mortgage contract and their enforceability are of vital importance to the pricing of mortgage credit.

Secondary mortgage market institutions have vastly simplified mortgage pricing in several ways. In addition to standardizing loan documents, they have standardized many pricing parameters, including risk (e.g., by providing underwriting standards and guarantees). They have established markets with information generally available. They foster active trading, revealing market prices to participants and nonparticipants and serving as a barometer to the rest of the market. But there are still many instruments not actively traded and for which price data are scant.

READER'S GUIDE

This chapter provides a framework for pricing mortgages and mortgage securites that is sufficiently broad to encompass the general areas of concern outlined above, yet provides formulas for pricing. The discussion proceeds in the context of mortgage securities for simplicity, but is directly applicable to pricing individual mortgages. The section called Valuing Mortgage Pools with Known Cash Flows provides the basic algebra for mortgages. It is essentially patterned after the approach to pricing debt instruments. The section called Known or Actuarially Determined Premiums treats in greater detail the pricing of mortgage characteristics that typically have a bond counterpart and that are fairly straightforward. In the section on The Economics of Mortgage Termination, economic models of the refinancing and assumability options are developed and simulated to illustrate the importance of these characteristics for valuing mortgage securities. The section on Valuing Mortgage Contracts with Uncertainty provides the basic model for pricing the standard level-payment, fixed-rate mortgage, taking into account its numerous characteristics. This analysis is expanded in the section on Pricing Alternative Mortgage Instruments to adjustable-rate, graduated-payment, shared appreciation, and balloon payment mortgages. Finally, the section entitled Some Recent Evidence: Treasury Securities versus Ginnie Maes, Freddie Mac PCs, and Primary Mortgage Loans provides some evidence from secondary market trading on how well mortgages are being priced (or alternatively, how well these models do in pricing mortgages). For a more detailed discussion of the material in the second and fourth sections, see Hendershott, Hu, and Villani (1983); for the fifth section, see Hendershott and Villani (1981); and for the last section see Hendershott, Shilling, and Villani (1982).

SUMMARY AND IMPLICATIONS FOR THE FUTURE

Financial debt instruments with known characteristics trade relatively infrequently, and trades are not generally motivated by a difference in the perception of value. If the income stream is known, then both buyer and seller typically make the same calculation. In this environment, trades typically occur because of changes in the preferences of buyers and sellers.

Trading claims on real assets, for instance, equities (and houses), is much more complex. Basically, investors (and home buyers) must make judgments about what they expect the future income stream to be by weighing a great deal of information. Formulas can generate prices based on a particular set of information. However, buyers and sellers will make different judgments regarding the probability that a given set of information will turn out to be correct. Hence, their calculations of value will differ; those who value investments more will buy from those who value them less. The more uncertain investors are, the more trades take place.

Mortgages historically behaved more like debt than equity instruments. However, since October 1979, when the focus of monetary policy shifted from controlling interest rates to controlling monetary aggregates, interest rate volatility has increased. As a result, mortgage cash flow has become more difficult to predict than equity cash flow. The primary reason for the difference is that mortgage borrowers have the right to repay, although there are other reasons, as mentioned above. Valuing mortgages has thus become a matter of judgments. The more uncertain investors are regarding these judgments, the more mortgages will trade.

This chapter does not make the judgments for the reader. It cannot, as these change daily. Rather, it provides a framework for valuing mortgages, based on the probabilities attached to different outcomes by the investor. How well these formulas work depends on the quality of the information utilized. Unfortunately, there is very little good historical information on which to base expectations of future behavior. On a more positive note, much research is currently underway in this area, and our information is getting better all the time.

VALUING MORTGAGE POOLS WITH KNOWN CASH FLOWS

This section provides formulas for pricing expected mortgage cash flow. First, it provides basic value and pricing formulas. Next, it explains two approaches equivalent to that taken below. Finally, it discusses how interest rate uncertainty may affect the yield curve.

Scheduled Payment and Principal

We begin with the simple model in which it is known with certainty when a loan will terminate. The formula for the scheduled payment on a level-payment mortgage with an initial principal of X dollars is

$$\mathrm{PAY}^s = iX \left[\frac{(1 + i)^M}{(1 + i)^M - 1} \right] \tag{20.1}$$

where M is the maturity of the loan (the period over which the loan is amortized), and i is the mortgage coupon rate. The factor in brackets captures the amortization of the mortgage. The scheduled outstanding principal at time t on this mortgage is

$$\mathrm{PRIN}_t^s = X \left[\frac{(1 + i)^M - (1 + i)^t}{(1 + i)^M - 1} \right] \tag{20.2}$$

The above expressions hold for whatever unit of time is chosen $(\mathrm{PRIN}_o = X)$. These expressions also hold for variable-rate mortgages if interest rates are expected to be unchanged in the future. It is worth noting that the decline over time in the scheduled principal of level-payment mortgages results exclusively from amortization.

Our next step is to value a mortgage with these scheduled payments. However, mortgages are most often terminated well before maturity for reasons explained below. If at the time a loan is originated, we knew exactly when the loan would terminate, we could use the payment formula above and simply plug in the actual termination date. Not only is this information not available to lenders, but even borrowers do not know when they will terminate their loans.

What is typically done is to price a particular mortgage loan based on the expected maturity. The concept is that if the average is correct, then the formulas will work for the lenders' portfolio overall. Actual realized yields on particular mortgages may be more or less than expected, depending on whether the mortgages terminate earlier or later than average.

We could denote the probability that a mortgage will terminate at time t as ϕ_t. A more sophisticated approach than using the average is to consider the subjective probability that a mortgage will pay at a particular point of time. Consider the value of a pool of N loans. Then let ϕ_t^c denote the fraction of the loans in the pool that will terminate at time t (the c superscript indicates that the values are viewed as certain). These fractions implicitly form a probability distribution, but this approach facilitates the direct use of historical data on mortgage terminations as proxies for these probabilities. The total payment on the mortgage pool in period t contingent on ϕ_t^c is then

$$\text{TMPAY}_t^c = \phi_t^c \, N\text{PRIN}_t^s + (1 - \phi_T^c) \, N\text{PAY}^s \tag{20.3}$$

where

$$\phi_T^c = \sum_{j=1}^{t-1} \phi_j^c \quad \text{and} \quad \phi_{M+1}^c = 1$$

because all mortgages are terminated by period M. That is, the payment is simply the principal termination plus the scheduled payment (interest plus amortization) on the remaining principal outstanding.

Now consider the value of an existing pool k periods after origination. Q_k is the fraction of the N mortgages in the original pool that are still outstanding, that is

$$Q_k = 1 - \sum_{j=1}^{k-1} \phi_j^c$$

The fraction of mortgages that will terminate in each period t subsequent to k is defined as $_k\phi_t^c$ and the cumulative fraction of mortgages that will be terminated by time $t - 1$, after period k, is denoted by

$$_k\phi_T^c = \sum_{j=k}^{t-1} {}_k\phi_j^c$$

The total payment in time t (contingent on $_k\phi_T^c$) on a portfolio of mortgages $k - 1$ periods old is then

$$_k\text{TMPAY}_t^c = {}_k\phi_t^c \, Q_k \, N\text{PRIN}_t^s + (1 - {}_k\phi_T^c) \, Q_k \, N\text{PAY}_t^s \tag{20.4}$$

The most direct way to value this pool is to consider the present value of the payment stream. The value of this mortgage pool, utilizing this present-value approach, is simply the discounted present value of the total cash flow it generates, or

$$_kV^c = \sum_{t=k+1}^{M} \frac{_k\text{TMPAY}_t^c}{(1 + y_{t-k})^{t-k}} \tag{20.5}$$

Because we have assumed for our current purposes that these payments will definitely be made, the appropriate discount rates are the yields on risk-free, pure-discount securities of the matching maturity. That is, y_{t-k} is the yield on a riskless pure-discount bond of maturity $t - k$. Although such yields are not directly observable in the securities markets as coupon rates, capital markets will implicitly determine a unique spectrum of these yields, which form a yield curve when plotted.

Calculating a yield curve requires price and coupon data for a spectrum of securities that vary in maturity but are otherwise comparable. These data exist only for Treasury securities. Let i_j be the coupon rate on a par-value Treasury of maturity j. Calculating the yield curve then requires solving M equations of the form

$$1 = \sum_{t=1}^{j} \frac{i_j}{(1 + y_t)^t} + \frac{1}{(1 + y_t)^j} \qquad j = 1, \ldots, M \tag{20.6}$$

for the relationship between the M pure-discount yields (y_j) and the M coupon yields (i_j) on par-value bonds. Each pure-discount yield is a weighted average of the Treasury coupons of maturity less than or equal to that of the pure-discount security.

Prices

While prices for securities are generally quoted as a percent of par value, we shall express prices as a fraction of par. Thus the price at time k of a portfolio of securities is

$$_kP = \frac{_kV^c}{Q_k\,\text{PRIN}_k^s} \tag{20.7}$$

That is, the quoted price at time k is the market value at time k as a fraction of the principal still outstanding at time k.

Table 20.1 shows how this equation is translated into daily published

Table 20.1. Price and Yield on GNMA Issues

Rate	Bid	Asked	Yield
8.00%	80.28	81.4	10.96%
9.00	85.30	86.6	11.16
9.50	88.11	88.19	11.28
10.00	90.9	90.17	11.48
11.00	95.11	95.19	11.67
11.50	97.16	97.24	11.83
12.50	102.13	102.21	12.03
13.00	103.25	104.1	12.30
13.50	104.20	104.28	12.65
14.00	105.19	105.27	12.97
15.00	105.30	106.6	13.86
16.00	106.13	106.21	14.73

SOURCE: *Wall Street Journal,* March 24, 1983. Midafternoon over-the-counter quotations for March 23, 1983. Decimals in bid and asked represent 32nds; that is, 101.1 means 101 1/32.

price quotes. It shows the prices that dealers will pay (bid) and sell (ask) for Ginnie Mae issues with coupon rates ranging from 8 to 16% and the resulting yields. Prices are quoted as a fraction of the par value of the outstanding pool, not as a dollar amount. Of course, these quotes do not reflect the certain world described above. Instead, they reflect investors' expectations about the full range of payment options available to borrowers, as well as the transaction costs of participating in the market.

In later sections we will expand the pricing model to incorporate numerous possibilities, including uncertainty about when a mortgage will terminate. In addition, the pricing of alternative mortgage instruments will be considered.

Alternative Pricing Models

There are essentially three equivalent ways to value mortgage securities. The approach thus far is simply the discounted-present-value approach. While this first approach has obvious theoretical appeal, it is not the one most analysts have used. Perhaps this is because the yield curve is a hypothetical construct of yields on risk-free, pure-discount bonds that is not directly observable in the marketplace. Here we discuss two alternative ways of valuing mortgage pools and their equivalence to the straightforward discounted-present-value approach.

Many analysts have termed the difference between mortgage and bond cash flows on the one hand and a pure-discount zero-coupon bond on the other as *coupon bias*, and have valued this bias. This is a variant of the pure-discount approach. Implicitly, it assumes that the recipient of the mortgage cash flow invests in a pure-discount security when the payment is received, to mature at M. The basic approach is to figure out the value of these payments at maturity, and then to calculate a different yield curve from the Treasury coupon rates i_j by solving M equations of the form

$$1 = \frac{\sum\limits_{t=j}^{M} i_j(1 + a_t)^{M-i} + (1 + a_t)^{M-j}}{(1 + y_M)^M} \tag{20.8}$$

where a refers to the accumulation (as opposed to the discount) rate.

This is essentially the coupon bias approach. It utilizes the same price and coupon information as the more straightforward discount approach, but solves for reinvestment yields rather than discount yields. Another way to look at this is that it is the accumulated future value, as opposed to the discounted present value. Ultimately, the present value of these future pure-discount bonds must be calculated for this approach to have much intuitive appeal. But this produces the same result as the discounted-present-value approach. This conclusion is intuitively obvious when one considers that both approaches utilize the same information, but in algebraically different ways.

The most straightforward, market-oriented approach to rational pricing of mortgage pools is to assume that Treasury securities are priced appropriately, and to determine a price for a mortgage pool that will yield the same, after appropriate adjustments for differences in characteristics. This approach utilizes the observed price and coupon rate information and does not require that actual pure-discount yields be defined or calculated as an intermediate step. The premise is that two competing investments generating identical cash flows should have the same price. The procedure is to calculate the price of a portfolio of Treasury securities that would have the same cash flow as the mortgage pool. This approach may be termed the *comparable bond portfolio* approach.

The payments (principal plus interest) in period t on a portfolio of new-issue Treasury bonds with maturities $j = 1$ to M, carrying coupons of y_j, and having an initial value of X_B are

$$\text{TBPAY}_t = (\gamma_t + \sum_{j=t}^{M} \gamma_j y_j)X_B \qquad t = 1, \ldots, M \tag{20.9}$$

where γ_j is the fraction of the portfolio maturing in period j. The principal repayment analog is $\gamma_t X_B$, and the summation term captures the coupon payments on that part of the portfolio still outstanding. The comparable price (P) of the mortgage portfolio is

$$_kP = \sum_{j=1}^{M} \gamma_j X_B \tag{20.10}$$

where γ_j is determined by setting $\text{TMPAY}_j = \text{TBPAY}_j, j = 1, \ldots, M$.

This utilizes the same basic information, but solves for the equivalent portfolio maturity distribution of bond debt, as opposed to the pure-discount yields.

The Yield Curve

Even if the cash flows of the pool are certain, interest rate uncertainty could affect the value of the pool through its effect on the discount rates. The yields on pure-discount, default-free securities might contain interest rate risk or term premiums if the marginal investor is averse to the risk that future rates might differ from those currently anticipated. The magnitude of these premiums will reflect the degree of uncertainty. Thus, for example, "flat" interest rate expectations might generate an upward-sloping yield curve, where the degree of slope reflects uncertainty about future interest rates and investor aversion to this uncertainty. Because our focus is on the impact of interest rate uncertainty on the relative values of mortgage pools and competing instruments, for ease of exposition and with no loss of generality we assume that term premiums are zero. Thus, a flat yield curve implies constant interest rate expectations.

KNOWN OR ACTUARIALLY DETERMINED PREMIUMS

In the discussion above, loans are valued as if the borrowers' payments are made directly to the investor according to a certain schedule. Here we consider three adjustments to these payments that must be made to determine the value of the mortgage security to an investor. The first is the cost of loan servicing. The second is marketability, which determines the ability of the investor to resell the security and the expected proceeds upon sale. Finally, we consider default and the implications for investor proceeds.

Servicing

Fees for mortgage origination are often charged up front as discount points. The originator typically continues to service the loan contract over the life of the loan, charging an additional fee. Traditionally, this fee has been 0.375% of the outstanding principal balance. Residential Funding Corporation, a new private secondary-market conduit, will provide servicing of the loans it purchases for 0.25%. In the notation used above, the servicing fee, deducted from the investor's yield, is $f\text{PRIN}^s$ for each loan remaining in the pool, where f is the servicing fee. The remainder of this discussion relates to the servicer's cost in relation to this fee.

As a general rule, high-balance loans are more profitable than low-balance loans due to the existence of fixed servicing costs. A corollary is that, because of amortization, servicing becomes less profitable over the life of the loan. However, this conclusion is modified to the extent that servicing costs decline and servicing benefits increase over the life of the loan.

In addition to a one-time setup cost, there are recurring costs in five areas: payment processing, loan accounting, escrows, collections, and customer servicing. After an initial period, collection costs tend to decline over time (in real terms) as delinquency and default become less likely. Accounting costs may also decline with technological advances. Once a loan is 10 years old, servicing is a routine and largely automated process.

In addition to the servicing fee, servicers may generate float income from the borrowers' principal and interest payments that they hold each month before passing them on to the investor (or conduit). Even if the funds are placed in a non-interest-bearing custodial account, implicit interest is earned. This is because depository institutions will compete for these funds. For example, other borrowing costs may be reduced. This income does not decline as the loan amortizes because the total of scheduled principal and interest is constant. Servicers also benefit from controlling escrow accounts. These may increase over the life of the loan if property taxes and insurance payments increase.

On balance, it may be that servicers have a negative cash flow as mortgages are paid off. In other words, they are paid in previous years for a service performed later. The investors face any adverse consequences of this arrangement. It is noteworthy that the occurrence of servicers' defaulting on contracts to avoid servicing unprofitable loans is extremely rare. We also note that from the investor's viewpoint, having the servicing performed for a fee by someone with expertise in that area is generally well worth the cost. Processing and accounting for mortgage-backed securities (MBSs) are even easier than for individual whole loans. We now turn to two other benefits of MBSs: their marketability and risk managment.

Marketability

The central point of the theory underlying mortgage-backed securities is that undivided interests in a pool of mortgages can be made more attractive to investors than can individual whole loans. One reason this is the case is that an undivided interest in the pool is typically more marketable than the underlying whole loans. In general, the greater the volume of trading securities of a homogeneous risk class, the smaller the spread between bid and asked prices and, therefore, the greater the marketability. One problem with whole-mortgage loans is that a costly search is usually needed to determine the adequacy of the underwriting standards on each loan. This increases the time such loans remain in dealer inventory, and thus increases the bid–ask spread.

Establishing uniform underwriting standards for pooled mortgages makes interests in different pools more homogeneous. Additionally, ratings by an independent rating agency can establish comparability among issues of different mortgage originators, thereby expanding the market and improving marketability. The keys to marketability are homogeneity and the volume of trading, which largely determine the cost of trading. Two ingredients are necessary for a large volume: a sufficient number of issues and a way of evaluating risk cheaply. For further discussion, see Van Order and Villani (1981).

We define marketability as the ability to sell quickly for the discounted present value of a security. Our measure is the difference in price between what a dealer in the security will pay (bid) and sell (ask). This dealer spread shrinks with increases in volume that shorten the average time the securities are held in inventory. To the extent investors, at the margin, are concerned about the need to sell, a marketability "premium" based on this spread will be charged in the form of a higher coupon rate.

For investors who frequently sell securities that are not very marketable, this premium will fail to compensate them for the discount below the present value of the security. For investors who rarely or never sell, this premium raises yields. It should be just sufficient to compensate the marginal investor, given the propensity to sell.

Default

Recent high rates of delinquency and foreclosure have focused attention on default risk. The increase in national delinquency rates for conventional loans since 1974 is shown in Table 20-2. Economic studies have generally identified the loan-to-value ratio as the ultimate determinant of default. Events such as unemployment and family problems may change the ability or desire of a household to meet its mortgage payments. At this point,

Table 20.2.   National Delinquency Rates for Conventional Loans (seasonally adjusted)

Quarter	30 Days Past Due	60 Days Past Due	90+ Days Past Due	Total Past Due	Foreclosures Started
1974.1	1.87	0.45	0.24	2.56	0.08
.2	1.83	0.40	0.27	2.50	0.06
.3	1.82	0.41	0.25	2.48	0.08
.4	1.81	0.41	0.27	2.49	0.09
1975.1	1.91	0.44	0.30	2.65	0.10
.2	1.94	0.45	0.31	2.70	0.10
.3	1.93	0.47	0.33	2.73	0.09
.4	1.95	0.47	0.35	2.77	0.09
1976.1	1.95	0.45	0.33	2.73	0.07
.2	2.00	0.49	0.38	2.87	0.08
.3	2.04	0.47	0.35	2.86	0.08
.4	1.97	0.48	0.33	2.78	0.09
1977.1	1.92	0.46	0.32	2.70	0.08
.2	2.00	0.48	0.32	2.80	0.08
.3	1.98	0.47	0.31	2.76	0.07
.4	1.99	0.46	0.30	2.75	0.07
1978.1	1.98	0.46	0.29	2.73	0.06
.2	1.95	0.43	0.28	2.66	0.06
.3	1.98	0.42	0.28	2.68	0.06
.4	2.00	0.40	0.26	2.66	0.07
1979.1	2.01	0.41	0.24	2.66	0.07
.2	1.95	0.36	0.25	2.56	0.06
.3	2.36	0.43	0.25	3.04	0.06
.4	2.12	0.44	0.26	2.82	0.06
1980.1	2.30	0.47	0.27	3.04	0.07
.2	2.28	0.51	0.28	3.07	0.07
.3	2.28	0.52	0.31	3.11	0.08
.4	2.26	0.53	0.33	3.12	0.09
1981.1	2.27	0.48	0.32	3.07	0.09
.2	2.35	0.55	0.34	3.24	0.11
.3	2.50	0.58	0.35	3.43	0.11
.4	2.39	0.57	0.35	3.31	0.11
1982.1	2.52	0.58	0.42	3.52	0.13
.2	2.55	0.65	0.48	3.68	0.13
.3	2.61	0.66	0.52	3.79	0.14
.4	2.63	0.65	0.53	3.81	0.14

SOURCE: Mortgage Bankers Association, "National Delinquency Survey."

they may consider selling the property or defaulting on the loan. In theory, the decision is based on their net equity, or the proceeds they would have after paying the costs of a sale. Market conditions such as the inventory of other houses for sale and interest rates affect the outcome.

These factors may also affect the investor's loss in the event of a default. It is not just the probability of loss that is important, but this probability times the resulting economic loss. That is, the yield equivalent realized loss is λ = (PSALE) (EL), where PSALE equals the probability of a foreclosure and EL is the economic loss when sold. However, there are very little data available on economic loss.

By investing in mortgage-backed securities instead of individual whole loans, investors reduce their risk of default losses in a number of ways. A mortgage-backed pass-through security is analogous to a mutual fund in that both reduce risk to the investor through diversification. Thus, all other things equal, risk-averse investors should prefer a mortgage pass-through security to a whole loan. But there is still some overall default risk to the investor in straight mortgage pass-throughs, which is a reflection of the riskiness of the underlying mortgages. This riskiness has been limited in mortgage pass-throughs in several ways, including strict underwriting requirements, FHA insurance and VA guarantees, and private mortgage insurance. Typically, private mortgage insurance is required for conventional loans with loan-to-value ratios over 80%. As a result, default loss is, for the most part, only of concern to investors in the sense that catastrophic events could lead to the failure of the mortgage insurance system.

An additional approach to reducing investor risk is the modified pass-through, which involves some guarantee of principal and interest payments regardless of whether they are paid by the borrower. The timely receipt of these payments may also be guaranteed. For currently traded MBSs, the backing of the guarantees ranges from the full faith and credit of the U.S. government to the financial strength of private companies.

Summary

Before proceeding, consider how these three factors affect the payments to investors. The marketability premium, to the extent it is charged, is embedded in the security's coupon rate (but the price for this higher coupon may be paid in the form of discounted proceeds if sold). The servicing fee and the expected loss from default are deducted from expected investor proceeds. Equation 20.4 may be modified to produce an expression for an actuarially expected cash flow as

$$_k\text{TMPAY}_t^c = (_k\phi_t^c - f - \lambda) \, Q_k\text{NPRIN}_t^s + (1 - {}_k\phi_T^c) \, Q_k\text{NPAY}_t^s \quad (20.11)$$

THE ECONOMICS OF MORTGAGE TERMINATIONS

This section develops the economics of household mortgage terminations. It discusses why this should be of importance to investors. It describes the approach based on historical experience with FHA mortgages. It also develops the models explaining the economics of the refinancing and assumption decisions. Having identified the variables influencing these decisions, we simulate the models for different parameter values to determine under what specific conditions households will refinance or assume. The analysis assumes level-payment, fixed-rate financing.

Some Implications of the Borrower's Termination Option

The termination schedule on a mortgage pool is a random variable that depends in a rather complex way on the initial subjective (joint conditional Bayesian) probabilities that the individual mortgages will terminate in each subsequent future period. We define the "most likely" termination schedule as the collection of termination rates that are given the highest initial subjective probabilities.

The timing of mortgage repayments is irrelevant to the valuation of pools only if (1) the yield curve is flat, and (2) the mortgage pool is trading at par. Consider two pools, both carrying coupons equal to the current new-issue coupon. If the yield curve is upward sloping, indicating that future interest rates are expected to be higher, then faster-repaying pools will be valued above slower-repaying pools. And the converse is true if the yield curve is downward sloping. On the other hand, even if the yield curve is flat, faster- and slower-repaying pools with equal coupons will be valued differently if this coupon differs from the current new-issue coupon. For example, if the new-issue coupon exceeds that on the existing pools, then both existing pools will trade below par, with the slower-paying pool being further below par.

The fact that the termination rate is not known a priori would not be of concern if these rates were unrelated to economic variables and investors were indifferent to this uncertainty. One could simply project the "most likely" rates from past experience and calculate the value of mortgage pools as if terminations were known, based on these rates. However, mortgage terminations reflect the exercise of the borrowers' option, which is generally related to the course of interest rates. The systematic relationship between interest rates and termination experience causes investors to care about the uncertainty of termination rates.

The dependency of mortgage terminations on interest rates operates through three channels. First, the willingness of homeowners to sell their houses depends on current mortgage rates relative to the rate on their existing mortgages. For example, if rates are currently high, then homeowners will be reluctant to forego the implicit capital gains they have on their existing mortgages. Reduced mobility means fewer mortgage terminations. Second, even if homeowners do sell, in some cases the mortgage will be assumed by the new buyer. All FHA/VA mortgages are assumable, and while the standard deed of trust for conventional mortgages generally does not allow assumptions, some do occur. For loans originated before October 15, 1982, due-on-sale clauses cannot be enforced for certain types of lenders in many states. Third, even when no house sale occurs, the existing mortgage can be terminated. If mortgage rates decline below the coupon rates on existing mortgages by enough to outweigh the costs of refinancing, including closing costs, prepayment penalties, and any additional points charged the borrower, then mortgages may be terminated and refinanced at the current lower rates.

FHA Experience

The termination rate for mortgages is akin to the mortality rate used by life insurance companies. A "mortality table" has in fact been calculated for FHA experience (see Herzog, 1981). Termination rates are often expressed as some multiple, say 200%, of actual (and projected) FHA repayment experience for mortgages issued during a given period. For example, if one believed that the prepayment pattern would mirror FHA experience, but the rate would be more rapid, one could express this as a multiple of past FHA experience. Most generally,

$$\phi_t^w = \frac{w\phi_t^{100} (1 - \phi_T^w)}{100 (1 - \phi_T^{100})} \qquad (20.12)$$

where

$$\phi_T^w = \sum_{j=1}^{t-1} \phi_j^w$$

Thus the fraction of the pool still outstanding $(1 - \phi_T^w)$ that is repaid in a given period ϕ_t^x is $w\%$ of the fraction of a pool with actual FHA experience that would be repaid in that same period, that is,

$$\frac{\phi_t^{100}}{1 - \phi_T^{100}}$$

Refinancing

Just like corporations, households may be expected to repay (call) existing debt and refinance if it is financially advantageous to do so. In the following model, a mortgage will be called when the present value of expected benefits exceeds the costs. The model considers only these financially motivated refinancings. It does not address, for instance, a household's desire to borrow more.

The payment on a level-payment mortgage of principal amount X and maturity M carrying a fixed rate i_o, where o denotes the period the mortgage was originated, if it is refinanced at rate i_k for the remaining maturity $M - k$, is

$$\text{PAY}\ [i_k,\ \text{PRIN}\ (i_o,\ X,\ M,\ k,\ M - k)]$$

$$= i_k\ \text{PRIN}\ (i_o,\ X,\ M,\ k) \left[\frac{(1 + i_k)^{M-k}}{(1 + i_k)^{M-k} - 1} \right] \quad (20.13)$$

If the initial loan had a maturity of 30 years and is refinanced after five years, then the new loan is assumed to equal the outstanding loan and to have a maturity of 25 years. Note that the new payment is identical to the original payment if $i_k = i_o$.

If the borrower expects to maintain the mortgage for L additional periods $(L \leqslant M - k)$ and i_k represents the appropriate discount rate for all future periods, then the present value of the expected benefit of refinancing in period k is

$$\text{br}_k = \sum_{t=k+1}^{L} \frac{\text{PAY}\ (i_o,\ X,\ M) - \text{PAY}\ [i_k,\ \text{PRIN}\ (i_o,\ X,\ M,\ K),\ M - k]}{(1 + i_k)^{t-k}} +$$

$$\frac{\text{PRIN}\ (i_o,\ \ldots\ ) - \text{PRIN}\ (i_k,\ \ldots\ )}{(1 + i_k)^{L-k}} \quad (20.14)$$

The last term, which is 0 if $L = M$, reflects the difference in amortization rates of the two mortgages. The benefits of refinancing are greater the larger the decline in i, the greater the amount of original mortgage (X), the larger the remaining principal (the lower k is), and the longer the borrower expects to maintain the mortgage (the larger L is).

The cost in period k of refinancing the remaining balance of the mortgage is

$$cr_k = (u + v)\ \text{PRIN}\ (i_o,\ X,M,k) \quad (20.15)$$

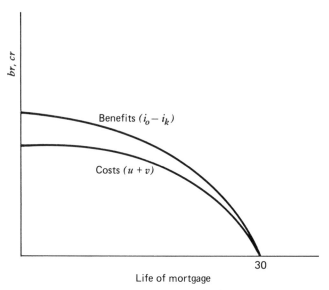

Figure 20.1. Benefits and costs of refinancings.

where the first term in parentheses reflects normal closing costs and re-payment penalties (u) plus any additional points that may be charged the borrower (v) to provide a below-market coupon rate. The v term includes points paid by the buyer and points paid by the seller but built into the price of the house, and both u and v are expressed as a percentage of principal. Refinancing will be profitable in period k if $br_k - cr_k > 0$.

If there is a significant probability that a call will be substantially more beneficial at some future period, even after discounting the interim cost, refinancing may be postponed.

The benefits and costs of refinancing are plotted in Figure 20.1 as a function of k. The height of cr_k depends solely on the initial principal and the cost parameters, $u + v$. The cr_k schedule declines monotonically, although quite slowly at first, as the mortgage amortizes. The height of the br_k schedule depends on the expected holding period L and the decline in $i(i_o - i_k)$, as well as the initial principal. The br_k schedule also declines monotonically with the amortization of the existing mortgage. Because the shapes of the schedules are so similar, the refinancing decision is quite insensitive to k. Either the decline in the mortgage rate is sufficient to trigger refinancing, given L and $u + v$, or the decline is not. The schedules are drawn such that the household will refinance.

Assumptions

Just as large declines in interest rates tend to shorten the average life of outstanding mortgages, increases in interest rates can lengthen the life of these mortgages dramatically. All FHA/VA mortgages contain assumability clauses. While most conventional loans written since 1970 contain due-on-sale clauses (an explicit prohibition of the assumability provision), state law and court decisions made these clauses unenforceable for loans originated by state-chartered lenders before October 1982 in certain states. Moreover, due-on-sale and assumability clauses only apply on the transfer of title; homeowners can choose not to move precisely to avoid terminating the mortgage contract. This may be thought of as an "implicit assumption" by the existing owner. From the investor's perspective, it is identical to an assumption by a new buyer.

The benefits to the assumption, explicit or implicit, of an existing loan are exactly analogous to the benefits of refinancing; the present value of the expected benefits of an assumption is the discounted savings from making payments on the outstanding principal at the lower old rate rather than at the higher current rate. In fact, we can simply write $ba_k = -br_k$.

The cost of an explicit assumption is the discounted extra outlays made on the financing of the remainder of the house purchase that would otherwise be financed at the current mortgage rate, i_k. If the house (and th'is the "normal" loan) has risen in value at rate π (inflation net of depreciation) and the financing rate for the "loan" in excess of the assumption is i_k^{sm} (for second mortgage), then the payments are

$$\text{PAY } (i_k^{sm}, \pi, X, M, k)$$

$$= i_k^{sm} \left[(1 + \pi)^k X - \text{PRIN } (i_o, X, M, k) \right] \left[\frac{(1 + i_k^{sm})^{M-k}}{(1 + i_k^{sm})^{M-k} - 1} \right] \quad (20.16)$$

The expression for the payment on this loan if it were financed at i_k, PAY (i_k, π, X, M, k), has an identical form but with i_k replacing i_k^{sm}. The costs of assumption, then, are

$$ca_k = \sum_{t=k+1}^{L} \frac{\text{PAY } (i_k^{sm}, \pi, X, M, k) - \text{PAY } (i_k, \pi, X, M, k)}{(1 + i_k)^{t-k}} + \\ \frac{\text{PRIN } (i_k^{sm}, \ldots) - \text{PRIN } (i_k, \ldots)}{(1 + i_k)^{L-k}} \quad (20.17)$$

Of course, if the household can borrow the incremental funds (effectively use its own resources) at the rate on first mortgages ($i_k^{sm} = i_k$), then there are no costs to assumption, and assumable mortgages will be assumed if mortgage rates rise at all. On the other hand, the second mortgage rate could be so high that the combined monthly mortgage payment on the assumed and second mortgages exceeds that on a new first mortgage. The combined payment could be higher, even if the average interest rate on the assumed and second mortgages is less than that on the first mortgage, because of the shorter remaining term of the assumed mortgage and the typical short term of second mortgages.

The costs and benefits of assumption at a given point in time are plotted in Figure 20.2 as functions of k. The ca_k schedule rises (from 0) initially as the amount of the second mortgage rises owing to $\pi > 0$ and amortization of the first mortgage. However, at some point (roughly $k = M/2$) the costs decline, due to the shorter period (remaining expected loan life) over which the costs will be paid. The height of the ca_k schedule is largely determined by $i_k^{sm} - i_k$. The ba_k schedule declines monotonically as the period over which the benefits are cumulated becomes progressively shorter. Its height depends primarily on how far interest rates have risen since the original mortgage was obtained ($i_k - i_o$). The schedules are drawn so that the mortgage will be assumed if the underlying house is sold prior to period k. Prior to this period, $ba_k > ca_k$; later, $ba_k < ca_k$.

The difference between ba_k and ca_k is the net value of the old mortgage that is received by the seller. This value obviously depends upon $i_k^{sm} - i_k$, a spread that is determined in the relevant local market for assumed mortgages. This determination is illustrated by the supply and demand schedules for a standard unit of significantly (say 2 %) "below-market" assumable mortgages drawn in Figure 20.3. The standard unit is defined as a combination of principal, maturity, and below-market coupon rate such that the present value of the stream of interest savings is $1,000. Thus, ba_k equals $1,000 for the unit. The supply curve in Figure 20.3 is the number of these units made available to the market by sellers in a given period. The higher the price paid for each unit, the greater the number offered. The demand depends on the liquidity or cash flow constraints of households that desire to purchase houses. For households with no constraint (they can easily supply their own equity for the entire difference between the sale price and the amount of an assumable mortgage), the demand is horizontal at ba_k. At a sufficient supply, households facing constraints must be drawn into the market by lower prices; thus the demand curve eventually falls off. The higher the level of interest rates, the more binding are cash flow constraints, and the greater the falloff in demand.

The solid schedules in Figure 20.3 could refer to the situation at the end of 1977. The supply is limited because virtually no mortgages were

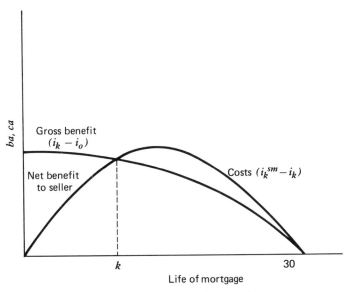

Figure 20.2. Benefits and costs of assumptions.

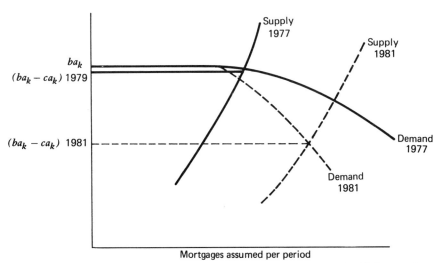

Figure 20.3. Determination of the net benefit of assumption of a standard below-market mortgage.

issued in the 1969-to-1977 period at a rate significantly below the late 1977 rate of 9%. As a result, $i_k^{sm} - i_k$ was low for the marginal investor, as was ca_k. Thus, the net benefit of assumptions was close to the gross benefit.

The sharp jump in mortgage rates from 1977 to 1981 had an enormous impact on the net benefit. First, the use of below-market, assumable mortgages grew substantially. Second, many potential home-buying households became severely cash flow constrained. The net result is a sharp drop in the net benefit ($ba_k - ca_k$) relative to the gross benefit (ba_k).

The Addition of Taxes

Taxes alter the above expressions in a fairly straightforward manner. Let the interest payment of the relevant household be deductible at rate θ. First, the discount rate becomes an after-tax rate, $(1 - \theta)i_k$. Second, the difference in the streams of tax savings on interest payments must be subtracted. For br_k, the difference is

$$- \sum_{t=k+1}^{L} \frac{\theta \left[i_o \, \mathrm{PRIN} \, (i_o, t - 1) - i_k \, \mathrm{PRIN} \, (i_k, t - 1) \right]}{[1 + (1 - \theta) \, i_k]^{t-k}} \qquad (20.18)$$

For ca_k, i_k^{sm} replaces i_o.

We also must change the expression for the cost of refinancing. If points charged the borrower to provide a below-market rate are the only deductible costs, then the correct expression is

$$cr_k = [u + (1 - \theta)v] \, \mathrm{PRIN}(i_o, X, M, k) \qquad (20.19)$$

Simulation Results

In the following pages the net gains (benefits less costs) from refinancings and assumptions for various values of the key parameters are computed. These values are selected to enable us to deduce how far interest rates had to fall from peak levels in 1981 in order to (1) trigger massive refinancings, and (2) deter the continued assumption of old mortgages (those carrying 8% and 9% coupons) upon the sale of the underlying houses.

Refinancing.   The parameters key to the refinancing decision are the after-tax difference between the original and current mortgage rates, $(1 - \theta) (i_o - i_k)$, and the up-front fees and points, $(u + v)$. The higher the points, the more the mortgage rate must decline in order to make refinancing profitable. In fact, the relationship is virtually a linear one. With a holding period of 12 years, a mortgage life of 30 years, and an initial mortgage rate of 15%, the issuer will gain from refinancing if

$$(1 - \theta) (i_o - i_k) \leq \frac{1}{4} [u + (1 - \theta)v] \qquad (20.20)$$

within the first 20 years of the mortgage life. For example, if u were $- 0.02$ and v were 0, then the mortgage rate need only decline to $14\frac{1}{2}\%$. In contrast, if $v = 0.08$, a decline to $12\frac{1}{2}\%$ is required. This approximation is roughly correct for tax rates of 0 and 0.3.

The calculation is most influenced by the decline in the mortgage rate and the up-front charges. The calculation is also sensitive to the effective remaining holding period if this period is short. The impacts of variations in the initial maturity of the loan, its effective remaining holding period, and the difference between original and current interest rates are illustrated in Table 20.3. In the first three rows, the remaining effective holding period is assumed to be the remaining life of the mortgage, $L = M - k$. A $1\frac{1}{2}$-percentage-point decline in the mortgage rate (from 15 to $13\frac{1}{2}\%$ and assuming up-front fees equal to 6% of the mortgage) will produce profitable refinancing if the decline occurs before the remaining maturity falls below 10 years, regardless of the original maturity of the mortgage. This result holds for household marginal tax rates of 0% and 30%.

The last three rows of Table 20.3 illustrate that the refinancing decision is sensitive to the expected holding period, and that the household tax rate may have some effect. In these calculations, the original maturity of the mortgage is 30 years, and the effective holding period is seven, six, and five years, respectively. With a six-year holding period, even

Table 20.3.   The Refinancing Decision: Initial Mortgage Rate (i_o) of 0.15 and Up-Front Fees ($u + v)^o$ of 0.06

New Mortgage Rate (i_k)	Original Maturity of the Mortgage	Effective Holding Period Remaining	Refinancing Will Occur Prior to This Year of Mortgage Life	
			$\theta = 0.0$	$\theta = 0.3$
0.135	20	$20 - k$	10	10
0.135	25	$25 - k$	15	15
0.135	30	$30 - k$	20	20
0.135	30	7	17	16
0.135	30	6	0	0
0.130	30	5	21	20

the 1½-percentage-point decline in the mortgage rate (from 15%) will not trigger refinancing. With a two-percentage-point decline, refinancing will again be induced, as shown in the last row of the table. With a five-year effective holding period, households who take the standard deduction ($\theta = 0.0$) will refinance if the decline occurs before 21 years after origination. For households in the 30% tax bracket, the number is 20 years. A sharper decline in interest rates may be needed for households in higher tax brackets.

Assumptions. Recall that the trade-off driving the assumption decision is the lower costs of the existing mortgage vis-à-vis the extraordinary costs (second mortgage rate greater than first mortgage rate) of the second mortgage. The greater the increase in mortgage rates since the mortgage was issued, $i_k - i_o$, the more profitable the assumption. On the other hand, the greater the excess of the second over the first mortgage rate ($i_k^{sm} - i_k$), and the larger the portion of the total financing taking the form of the second (the greater the net inflation rate, π, and the time since the original mortgage was issued, k), the less profitable the assumption.

In the calculations presented below, the rate on the second mortgage has been set two percentage points above the rate on the first mortgage. This constant difference reflects two offsetting factors. On one hand, we would expect the difference to rise as the maturity of the second rises because lenders tend to charge higher rates on longer-term second mortgages. On the other hand, the longer the maturity of the second, the less likely the combined cash flow on both the assumed and second mortgage is to pose a problem for the borrower. The original mortgage is assumed to carry a 9% coupon and have a life of 30 years.

The data in Table 20.4 indicate how increases in new-issue mortgage rates raise the desirability of assumption. In the upper half of the table, the gross benefit of assumption is reported for households with interest payments deductible at 0% and 30% tax rates, assuming a 7% net inflation rate, roughly the rate in the United States between 1972 and 1981. The percentage capital gains four, eight and 16 years after origination from assuming a 9% coupon, 30-year mortgage are listed for different values of the new-issue mortgage rate. As can be seen, with new-issue yields in the 15-to-17½% range, the capital gains are enormous. For mortgages issued in 1978, the gain in 1982 is 30 to 40% of the original value; for mortgages issued in 1974, the gains are only 4% less. In 1990, the gains would still be in the 20-to-25% range. In general, the gains are 3% less for those itemizing deductions in the 30% tax bracket than for those taking the standard deduction.

The data in the lower half of Table 20.4 refer to the net benefit of as-

Table 20.4.   The Assumption Decision: Initial Mortgage Rate (i_0) of 0.09 and Original Maturity (M) of 30 Years

| | A.   Gross Benefit: Inflation Rate (π) = 0.07 | | | | | |
| | Tax Rate (θ) = 0.0 | | | Tax rate (θ) = 0.3 | | |
New-Issue Mortgage Rate (i_k)	Percent Gain after 4 Years	Percent Gain after 8 Years	Percent Gain after 16 Years	Percent Gain after 4 Years	Percent Gain after 8 Years	Percent Gain after 16 Years
0.100	8	6	4	6	6	3
0.125	23	20	13	20	17	11
0.150	34	30	20	31	27	17
0.175	42	38	26	39	34	22

| | B. Net Benefit: Tax Rate (θ) = 0.0 | | | | | |
| | Net Inflation Rate (π) = 0.07 | | | Net Inflation Rate (π) = 0.12 | | |
New-Issue Mortgage Rate (i_k)	Last Year Mortgage Will Be Assumed	Percent Gain after 4 Years	Percent Gain after 8 Years	Last Year Mortgage Will Be Assumed	Percent Gain after 4 Years	Percent Gain after 8 Years
0.100	5	2	0	3	0	0
0.125	12	18	9	7	14	0
0.150	15	29	21	10	26	11
0.175	18	38	30	12	35	21

sumption. The last year in which the mortgage will be assumed is reported, as are the percentage net gains on the old mortgage that will exist after the fourth and eighth years. The results are reported for two net (of depreciation) inflation rates. Of course, the higher the inflation rate, the smaller the net gains from assumption upon sale of the underlying house because a larger portion of the sale price is financed at the higher second mortgage rate.

The reported results are for households taking the standard deduction and are little different for households in the 30% tax bracket. Consider first the results for a 7% net inflation rate. A one-percentage-point increase in the mortgage rate to 10% will induce an assumption only if the house sale occurs within four years after the mortgage was first originated. An increase from 9 to 15%, in contrast, will lead to an assumption if the sale occurs within the first 15 years of a 30-year mortgage (12 years of a 20-year mortgage). If the sale occurs at the end of the fourth year (1982 for a mortgage originated in 1978), the gain to the house seller is 29% of the face value of the mortgage. At the end of the eighth year, the gain is still 21%.

With a net inflation rate of 12%, assumption is less attractive; assumption will occur only about two-thirds as far into the life of the mortgage as was the case for a 7% net inflation rate. To illustrate, with a new-issue mortgage rate of 15%, assumption would occur through the tenth year; the net gain after eight years is 11%.

The above calculations explain both the passions that were generated by the due-on-sale controversy and the growth in owner financing. There were enormous gains at stake. Sellers with low-rate mortgages wanted to avoid giving up the gains (to the lenders from whom the gains were received). Special financing terms (based on the favorable terms on the existing mortgage) increased the volume of sales, and maintained the list house price (upon which brokers' fees are earned). If due-on-sale clauses were rigidly enforced, then many households who moved might have maintained their existing homes. (For further discussion of due-on-sale see Preiss and Van Order, 1981 and Preiss, 1983.)

VALUING MORTGAGE CONTRACTS WITH UNCERTAINTY

The basic purpose of this section is to incorporate the termination behavior described in the previous section into mortgage valuation and pricing formulas. The first part develops a valuation model based on investor expectations. The second part provides some examples of their implications. The third part develops a methodology for calculating the implied market price for this option.

Inflation and Mortgage Rates

While the most likely termination schedule is a useful concept, there is a large array of schedules that might occur with significant probability—at least one for every inflation/interest rate scenario. Moreover, each scenario implies a different set of discount rates. Assume that there are R viable inflation/interest rate scenarios that are expected to occur with probabilities $p_1, \ldots, p_R$, where

$$\sum_{j=1}^{R} p_j = 1$$

Denote the total mortgage payment and discount rate vectors associated with the jth scenario (and its termination schedule) by TMPAY(j) and $Y(j)$, respectively. Then, the value of a pool of mortgages in the uncertainty case can be expressed as

$$_kV^u = \sum_{j=1}^{R} p_j \sum_{t=k+1}^{M} \frac{_k\text{TMPAY}\,(j)_t}{[1 + y\,(j)_{t-k}]^{t-k}} \tag{20.21}$$

By substituting $_kV^u$ from this equation into Equation 20.7, we obtain an expression for the efficient market price of mortgage contracts. Conceptually, one could test for market efficiency by comparing this to observed prices. Empirically, this requires knowledge of the market's subjective probabilities of various interest rate scenarios (the $y(j)$'s) and the relationship between ex post interest rates and cash flows (the $_k\text{TMPAY}(j)$). Because we do not currently have such information, such a test is beyond the scope of this chapter.

With TMPAY and y based on the m (most likely) inflation/interest rate outcome and $p_m = 1$ (the probability that this outcome will occur is one, that is, the event is certain), Equation 20.21 reduces to Equation 20.5, the certainty case. Comparison of these expressions is instructive. An inflation rate higher than the most likely one lowers the present value of a given payment stream relative to the most likely rate by raising the discount factors; a lower than most likely inflation rate raises the present value. When the payment stream is independent of the inflation/interest rate outcome, one would expect $_kV^u = {_kV^c}$ for the same mortgage coupon rate. That is, mortgage values—like security values generally—would be affected by deviations in observed inflation/interest rate outcomes from those originally expected, but not by changes in the degree of uncertainty regarding these outcomes.

However, the payment stream and thus mortgage values are not independent of these outcomes. A higher than most likely inflation rate reduces mobility by creating capital gains on existing mortgages and increases the assumption of existing mortgages by buyers when moves do occur. The lower termination rate magnifies the decline in present value caused by higher discount rates. A lower than most likely inflation rate increases mobility by reducing existing capital gains and encourages refinancing of existing mortgages. Now, however, the higher termination rate mitigates the rise in present value caused by lower discount rates. Because of the asymmetric variation in termination rates, $_kV^u < {_kV^c}$ for mortgage pools based on the same mortgage coupon rate. Further, $_kV^c - {_kV^u}$ will be disproportionately greater the larger the variability of expectations regarding inflation, and thus the greater both the likelihood of and the resultant loss from adverse terminations. Conceptually, the difference in price should be the present value of the expected losses.

The termination option allows borrowers to repay at faster rates (re-financings) or slower rates (assumptions), depending upon which is to their economic advantage (and thus to lenders' disadvantage). Borrowers will have to pay for this option either once in the form of a front-end fee when the mortgage is issued or annually in a higher coupon. When the front-end fee is employed, the price of the option is known. When the higher coupon method is utilized, computation of the annual premium is a straightforward application of Equations 20.5 and 20.21 for the case of newly issued mortgage pools ($k = 0$). Equation 20.21 is solved for $_oV^u$, and then Equation 20.5 is employed to determine the coupon rate that would equate $_oV^c$ to $_oV^u$. This is the coupon that is required in the certainty case. The difference between the actual coupon and the certainty coupon is the annual premium of the termination options.

The default premium in the coupon rate can be calculated similarly. First, Equation 20.21 is solved for $_oV^u$ on the assumption that all payments will be made on schedule. Second, the ø's are altered to reflect expected defaults; the left side of Equation 20.21 is set equal to the value obtained assuming no default; and the coupon i^d is solved for. This is the coupon including the default premium. The implied default premium embedded in the mortgage coupon yield is $i^d - i$.

Mortgage Values and Coupon Rates: Some Examples

Consider how uncertainty may affect mortgage value by comparing two cases: when termination rates are exogenous (unrelated to changes in interest rates) and endogenous (refinancings and assumptions). Here we illustrate the effects of this distinction on capital values. For simplicity, assume that there are three possible interest rate patterns: rates rise, fall, and remain the same. We denote the patterns by $y(U)$, $y(D)$, and $y(C)$, where U denotes up, D down, and C constant. If the probability of rates rising is $\bar{p}$ and of rates falling is also $\bar{p}$, then the probability of rates being constant is $1 - 2\bar{p}$. The value of the mortgages is then

$$V^u = \bar{p}VU + (1 - 2\bar{p}) VC + \bar{p}VD$$

where

$$V^* = \sum_{t=1}^{M^*} \frac{\text{PAY} + \theta\, i\, \text{PRIN}_{t-1}}{\prod_{k=1}^{t} [1 + (1 - \theta)y(*)_j]} + \frac{\text{PRIN}(*)}{\prod_{k=1}^{M^*} [1 + (1 - \theta)y(*)_j]} \tag{20.22}$$

for $* = $ U,C,D, where M^* is the date the mortgage terminates in each scenario.

The arguments in the PAY and PRIN functions are dropped, except for the prepayment date. Note that interest payments are deductible at the lender's tax rate θ and that after-tax discount rates are employed.

Consider the case where the prepayment (termination) of a 30-year mortgage is assumed (by the lender) to be independent of future interest rates and is expected to occur at the end of the twelfth year. Assume further that the mortgage and discount rates are both 15% and that interest rates are expected with probability p to average 15½, 16½, and 17½% in the next three periods and to average 18% thereafter. Assume further that rates are expected, again with probability p, to average 14½, 13½, and 13 in the next three periods and some percent thereafter, say 12.64. If $p = 0.2$, then a mortgage loan of X will be valued at X by tax exempt investors. The data in the "exogenous" row of Table 20.5 indicate how the changes in interest rates affect the value of the given mortgage payment stream. The value when interest rates are constant at 15% is set at unity. When rates rise, the payment stream based on a 15% coupon falls in value to 0.89, or by 11%. The decline in interest rates is specified such that the increase in the value of the payment stream is also 11%.

Now let the prepayment decision be endogenous. More specifically, assume that the mortgage will be prepaid (refinanced) at the end of the third year if interest rates decline, but at the end of the twenty-first year (assumed until then) if interest rates rise. These responses are consistent with the refinancing and assumption calculations made above. The data in the second row of Table 20.5 demonstrate the impact of endogenous terminations on mortgage value. When the mortgage life shortens to three years with the decline in interest rates (refinancing occurs), the increase in mortgage value is only 3%. That is, the termination response wipes out 70% of the capital gain that occurred when the mortgage life was fixed at 12 years. Moreover, the capital loss in response to an increase in interest rates is exaggerated by the lengthening of mortgage life to 21 years (assumptions occur). Here, however, the impact is not large; the loss is increased by about 15%.

Table 20.5. Interest Rate Changes and Mortgage Value for Mortgages with a 15% Coupon

| Terminations | Prepayment Year and Value of Payment Stream | | | | | | Total Value ($p = 0.2$) |
| | Rate = 12.64% | | Rate = 15% | | Rate = 18% | | |
	Year	Value	Year	Value	Year	Value	
Exogenous	12	1.11	12	1.0	12	0.89	1.0
Endogenous	3	1.03	12	1.0	21	0.87	0.980

Table 20.6. Interest Rate Uncertainty and the Premium in Mortgage Coupon Rates

	Tax Rate = 0.0			Tax Rate = 0.3		
p	y (percent)	Total Value (par = 1.0)	Mortgage Premium (basis points)	y (percent)	Total Value (par = 1.0)	Mortgage Coupon (basis points)
0.1	12.94	0.990	19	12.80	0.990	24
0.2	12.79	0.980	41	12.65	0.980	50
0.3	12.74	0.969	66	12.60	0.969	80

The last column in Table 20.5 indicates that the value of the mortgage falls by 2.0%. This is the cost to the lender of giving the borrower the option of terminating the mortgage. An up-front fee of two points (or 2% of par mortgage value) would offset the decline in mortgage value. That is, it would equate the expected yield on the mortgage to that on a "mortgage" which terminates with certainty at the end of the tenth period.

The Total Value columns of Table 20.6 show how changes in the probability of significant increases or decreases in interest rates (in p) affect mortgage value for lenders in 0% and 30% tax brackets. The relationship between p and value is negative and approximately linear. Mortgage lenders can charge borrowers for the termination option over time via a higher mortgage coupon rate and thus greater monthly payments rather than a single up-front payment. The results of converting the single payments into higher coupon equivalents are listed in the Mortgage Premium columns of Table 20.6. These calculations determine how high the mortgage coupon rate would have to be to maintain mortgage value at par even when adverse terminations were expected. The results indicate, for example, that a 41-basis-point premium in the mortgage rate (a rate of 0.1541) would be appropriate when p = 0.2 for tax-exempt investors. The premium is approximately a linear function of p, and the premium is about 20% greater for investors in the 30% tax bracket.

The Market Value of the Option Premium

An interesting issue is what the market charges for the option premium in mortgage contracts. Computationally, the front-end option price is just the difference between the value of a mortgage pool with certain cash flow ($_oV^c$ from Equation 20.5) and that of a mortgage pool with uncertain cash flow ($_oV^u$ from Equation 20.11). The difference between the actual coupon and the certainty coupon is the annual premium of the termination option. Unfortunately, there are no mortgages with certain termination rates; that is, Equation 20.5 cannot be utilized.

Nevertheless, it is possible with one key assumption to obtain estimates of the termination premium in some mortgage coupon rates. The assumption is that there exist mortgage pools and bonds whose only difference in the eyes of investors is the uncertainty regarding the timing of the cash flows (the termination schedule) of the pool. Given that the incomes from the pool and the portfolio are taxed similarly and are subject to the same zero default risk, this assumption would seem to be a reasonable working hypothesis for Ginnie Mae pools and a comparable maturity portfolio of U.S. government bonds. With this assumption, the bond portfolio is equivalent to a mortgage pool with a certain termination schedule, and the difference between the actual coupon rate on the pool and the "effective" coupon on the bond portfolio is the termination premium. A comparable maturity bond portfolio has cash flows that are equal to those on a mortgage pool (based on the most likely termination schedule) after netting out the termination option premium in the mortgage coupon.

The most likely payment on a mortgage in period t, after netting out the option price in the mortgage coupon, ρ, is obtained from substituting the equations for scheduled payments and principal (20.1 and 20.2) into the equation for the total scheduled payment on the mortgage pool (20.11).

$$\text{TMPAY}_t^m = \frac{(\phi_t^m - f - \lambda)(E^M - E^t) + (1 - \phi_T^m)(i - \rho) E^M}{E^M - 1} Q_k NX$$

$$(20.23)$$

where the "most likely" termination rates (ϕ_t^m) have replaced the certain termination rates (ϕ_t^c), and $E = 1 + i - \rho$.

A bond portfolio that is comparable to a mortgage pool with expected net payments TMPAY^m is one in which the γ_t are chosen such that

$$\text{TBPAY}_t = \text{TMPAY}_t^m (1 + i_t^1)^{1/3} \qquad (20.24)$$

for all t.

The $(1 + i_t^1)^{1/3}$ factor adjusts for the fact that mortgage payments accrue roughly one-third of a semiannual period prior to the payments on the bonds; i_t^1 is the one-period rate expected to exist in period t. The i_t^1 are determined from the yields on pure discount bonds as $(1 + i_t)^t/[(1 + i_{t-1})^{t-1} - 1]$. Equation 20.24 represents $M - k$ equations that, along with the identity $\Sigma \gamma_t = 1$, determine $M - k$ γ's and ρ for the given ϕ, i^1, f, $_kP/Q_kNX$, and i.

Actually, it is possible to solve for ρ without determining the γ's. Substitution of Equation 20.23 into 20.5 and the result into 20.7 yields, after cancelling $PRIN_k^s$ and X, which are equal for newly issued pools $(k \sim 0)$, and incorporating the mortgage payment timing adjustment

$$_kP = \sum_{t=k+1}^{M} \frac{\frac{(\phi_t^m - f - \lambda)(E^M - E') + (1 - \phi_T^m)(1 - \rho)E^M}{E^M - 1}}{(1 + i)^{t-k}(1 - i_t^1)^{-1/3}}$$

(20.25)

where $E = 1 + i - \rho$.

Given the ϕ^m, f, i, i^j, and $_kP$, this equation can be solved for ρ. We note here that the appropriate discount rates are still the yields on risk-free pure discount securities of the matching maturity because the cash flows are, after adjusting for termination uncertainty, risk-free equivalents. Equation 20.25 provides a way to calculate what the market charges for uncertainty. It does not provide a way to test whether these options are efficiently priced, or whether they are worth the cost to borrowers or the risk to investors. To do this requires applications of option pricing models for stock options beyond the scope of the current discussion.

PRICING ALTERNATIVE MORTGAGE INSTRUMENTS

The discussion thus far has considered only fixed-payment mortgages. The basic framework for pricing alternative mortgages is the same, but the formulas can vary widely. Here we consider three types of alternative mortgage instruments that illustrate these differences:

1. Those with adjustable rates and payments, for example, adjustable-rate mortgages (ARMs)
2. Those with fixed rates but adjustable payments, for example, graduated-payment mortgages (GPMs)
3. Those with payments indexed, but not to interest rates, for example, shared appreciation mortgages (SAMs)

Adjustable-Rate Mortgages

The value of an ARM depends on the index it is tied to, the frequency of adjustment, and whether there are limitations to this adjustment. These factors affect scheduled cash flow and termination (default, assumption, and refinancing) probability.

We begin with a simplifying case, without termination risk, in which interest rates adjust each year, and are tied to the one-year Treasury rate.

Investors in these mortgages are essentially buying a series of one-year securities. The mortgages would be expected to trade at or near par. This expectation would be modified to the extent that the loans have high or low margins, that is, spreads between the contract rate and the index rate.

If the rate adjusts every year and is tied to a longer-term rate (e.g., an average mortgage commitment rate), investors are essentially buying a series of one-year instruments, but at the going 30-year rate. The discount or premium they will pay will depend on the relative yields of one- and 30-year funds. With a normal, upward-sloping yield curve, a premium might be expected. The borrower is paying the risk premium built into long-term rates, but still takes the risk of fluctuating interest rates. As with fixed-rate mortgages, investors will not pay a premium if the mortgage is likely to be prepaid (at par).

The desire of borrowers to refinance should be reduced or eliminated with ARMs because their payments will automatically fall with interest rate adjustments. However, some indexes may not fall as rapidly as the rate available on a new (fixed- or adjustable-rate) mortgage. This may be due to the choice of index (for example, an average commitment rate may be greater than the rate at which most loans close) or delays in data collection and rate adjustment.

Termination rates due to default may also be different than with fixed-rate mortgages. Borrowers face increases in monthly payments that can motivate the decision to default. These increases are modified if the index is slow to adjust, or the increases in payments are capped. However, empirical evidence is not available on the increase in default probability with ARMs.

To develop value formulas, one could simply utilize those for fixed-payment loans with the appropriate adjustments. In the extreme case where the discount yields equal the coupon rates, the value would go to par. Where a particular ARM mortgage falls on the value spectrum between par and the 30-year fixed-rate mortgage depends on how constrained the interest rate adjustments are, both in frequency and in magnitude.

Graduated-Payment Mortgages

In the early 1970s, substantial concern arose regarding problems created for first-time home buyers by the use of level-payment mortgages (LPMs) during an inflationary period. Not only are house prices pushed up by inflation, but expected inflation is built into mortgage coupon rates. This double whammy can sharply raise the ratio of the initial mortgage payment to income for households relative to the ratio in a noninflationary environment. One solution to this "tilt" problem is the graduated-payment mortgage. In general, GPMs are long-term, fixed-rate loans. The scheduled payments are fully known at the outset. In the most popular program, payments rise by 7½% for each of the first five years. The initial monthly payments are below those of an LPM with the same term to maturity and interest rate. This difference is borrowed, and added to the principal balance (negative amortization). As a result, the level payments at the end of the loan (e.g., from years six to 30), are at an amount greater than for the LPM.

GPMs have greater "assumability" risk for lenders than do LPMs because lenders agree to increase the principal on the former relative to the latter. If interest rates should rise, then the opportunity cost of investing in GPMs will exceed that of investing in LPMs. To compensate for this possible greater cost, lenders will charge a greater termination premium. This will, of course, tend to raise the ratio of the initial mortgage payment to the borrower's income.

Because the expected cash flows associated with GPMs are different than with LPMs, the formulas for their value are also different. The purpose of this section is to extend the methodology employed above to GPMs, to compute the termination premiums in coupon rates on pools of GPMs. These premiums will then be compared with those for LPMs.

GPM plans specify that payments will rise from an initial level $PAYG_o$ at a rate g for h periods. Thus

$$PAYG_t = \begin{array}{ll} PAYG_o (1 + g)^t & \text{for } t < h \\ PAYG_o (1 + g)^h & \text{for } t \geq h \end{array} \qquad (20.26)$$

The initial payment $PAYG_o$ on a GPM is computed, like that on a level-payment mortgage, as the payment that will fully amortize the mortgage over the given maturity, M, and will yield the investor a rate of return equal to the mortgage coupon rate i (plus 0.5% for FHA/VA mortgages in Ginnie Mae pools). With a "pure" GPM, $t = M$ and the initial payment is easily expressed in terms of i, M, g, and the size of the mortgage, X.

The result is

$$PAYG_o = \frac{(i - g) X (1 + i)^M}{(1 + i)^M - (1 + g)^M} \qquad (20.27)$$

With the FHA programs currently in place, payments rise for either the first five or the first ten years. In the most popular option, payments rise at an annual rate of 7½% for the first five years of the mortgage. For this plan, we solve

$$X = \sum_{t=1}^{10} \frac{\text{PAYG}_o \, (1.037)^t}{(1+i)^t} + \sum_{t=1}^{60} \frac{\text{PAYG}_o \, (1.037)^{10}}{(1+i)^t}$$

(semiannual payments are assumed and i is the semiannual equivalent of the coupon rate). The result is

$$\text{PAYG}_o^s = \frac{iX}{\left[1 - \left(\dfrac{1.037}{1+i}\right)^{10}\right]\left(\dfrac{i}{i - 0.037}\right) + \left(\dfrac{1.037}{1+i}\right)^{10}\left[1 - \dfrac{1}{(1+i)^{50}}\right]}$$

(20.28)

The outstanding principal at any time is

$$\text{PRING}_t^s = (1+i)\,\text{PRING}_{t-1} - \text{PAYG}_t \qquad (20.29)$$

From this point on, the analysis follows that of the level-payment mortgage. The total payment expression is the same, with GPM payments and principal replacing those of the LPM; the value equation is simply the discounted value of the total GPM payments; and price is the ratio of value to initial principal. The equation to be solved for ρ_g, the call premiums in coupon rates on GPMs, is obtained by substituting into those price equations, adjusting for the difference in the timing of bond and mortgage payments, and replacing i with $i - \rho_g$.

The GPM may be riskier than the LPM, thereby requiring a greater default premium. Because the GPM negatively amortizes, there is a greater probability, other things being equal, that the distressed home buyer will find it more advantageous to go to foreclosure than sell. There is very little empirical evidence, however, because for the most part, FHA has required much larger down payments on GPMs than on LPMs.

Shared Appreciation Mortgages

The shared appreciation mortgage differs from the standard fixed-rate mortgage in that the lender offers a reduced contract rate in return for a share of the house's appreciation when the house is sold or the mortgage is terminated. Thus, the ex post return on the lender's—as well as the borrower's—investment is partially indexed to the price of the house being financed.

High interest rates and extreme volatility in mortgage markets during 1979 and 1980 helped push SAMs rapidly through the design stage into implementation. The mortgage banking industry began offering SAMs in mid-1980. This was soon followed by the Federal Home Loan Bank Board's proposed regulations to allow federally chartered S&Ls to originate SAMs. In August 1982, final regulations gave the S&Ls authority to offer a wide range of alternative mortgage instruments, including SAMs.

In this section, we consider how SAMs should be priced. We present a simple formula for determining the equity share due the lender for a given interest rate reduction. We look at how sensitive the split is to changes in various parameters (e.g., expected inflation, loan term, and loan-to-value ratio). In addition, we compare actual and expected yields on SAMs and fixed-rate mortgages (FRMs) under different inflation scenarios. A more complete discussion is included in Dougherty, Van Order, and Villani (1982).

As previously specified, the nominal return on an FRM is simply the rate of discount that equates the present value of the payment stream to the price. For an FRM issued at par, the nominal discount rate equals the mortgage coupon rate. The return on a SAM is calculated using the same approach, the difference being that the SAM has a much larger end payment.

Our purpose is to compare returns on SAMs and FRMs. For simplicity we ignore adjustments to the payment stream, for example, servicing costs, that affect both types. We also abstract from default risk.

Denote the total mortgage payment for a shared appreciation mortgage and the discount rate vectors associated with scenario j (and its termination schedule) by $TSAMPAY(j)$ and $Y(j)$, respectively. Substituting Equations 20.1 and 20.2 into 20.3, and introducing uncertainty, we obtain

$$
\begin{aligned}
TSAMPAY\ (j) = \ &\phi_t^j\ NX\ \frac{(1 - \alpha i)^M - (1 + \alpha i)^t}{(1 + \alpha i)^M - 1} \\
&+ (1 - \phi_t)\ N\ \alpha i\ X\ \frac{(1 + \alpha i)^M}{(1 + \alpha i)^{M-1}}
\end{aligned} \tag{20.30}
$$

That is, αi substitutes for i in Equations 20.1 and 20.2, where α is 1 minus the percent discount on the SAM. For example, if the lender offers a one-third rate reduction, α equals two thirds.

Following Equation 20.21, the value of a pool of SAMs is

$$
\begin{aligned}
_kVSAM^u = \ &\sum_{j=1}^{R} p_j \sum_{t=k+1}^{M} \frac{_kTSAMPAY(j)_t}{[1 + y(j)_{t-k}]^{t-k}} \\
&+ \beta\left(\frac{X}{LTV}\right) \frac{\prod_{t=1}^{n}(1 + \pi)_t - 1}{[1 + y(j)_{t-k}]^n}
\end{aligned} \tag{20.31}
$$

The last term is simply the present value of the lender's share (β) of the capital gain earned in period n when the house is sold, or when the gain becomes contractually due, whichever is first. ($X/(LTV)$ is the initial value of the property, where X is the initial loan balance and LTV the initial loan-to-value ratio, and π is the net of depreciation rate of appreciation on the house the mortgage finances.)

We now look at the expected returns on a SAM and compute the terms necessary to make a SAM have the same expected present value as an FRM. Calculations of the required share of capital appreciation for a one-third reduction in the contracted mortgage rate are provided for three different scenarios in Table 20.7. These are meant to approximate the conditions of the mid-1960s, mid-1970s, and 1980. The calculations assume for simplicity that the lender's marginal tax bracket for mortgage interest is constant at 25%.

The conclusion from these examples is that the share of appreciation required to compensate the lender is generally greater than the one-third reduction in the mortgage rate assumed in this example. In other words, borrowers do not appear to be paying (in an expected present value sense) for the cash flow benefits of these SAMs, and lenders appear to be accepting "below-market" expected returns.

The exception is the mid-1970s scenario. During this period the anticipated inflation rate was quite large relative to the mortgage rate. Consequently, a smaller share of the inflation-induced appreciation is required to raise the yield to that of an FRM. The mid-1970s scenario may be considered a historical anomaly. After taxes, the expected real rate is negative ($9\% [1 - 0.25] - 8\% = -1.25\%$). The experiences of the mid-1960s and 1980 are more typical, with expected after-tax real rates of 1.50% and 1.25%, respectively. In both cases, the required equity share is significantly

Table 20.7. Share of Appreciation Due Lender to Equate Expected Yields of a SAM and an FRM (SAM with one-third rate reduction)[a]

Mortgage Life	Mid-1960s (3% inflation, 6% mortgage rate)	Mid-1970s (8% inflation, 9% mortgage rate)	1980 (10% inflation, 15% mortgage rate)
2½ years	0.53	0.29	0.40
5 years	0.53	0.28	0.41
7½ years	0.53	0.27	0.41
10 years	0.52	0.26	0.42

SOURCE: A. Dougherty, R. Van Order, and K. Villani, *Housing Finance Review*, 1982, *1*, 361.

[a] Assumes a 20% down payment (80% loan-to-value ratio) and a 30-year amortization.

greater than the percentage reduction in the mortgage rate. Moreover, the required equity share is much greater in the mid-1960s than in the 1980 scenario.

This observation points out a more general conclusion of the SAM pricing formula: The greater the anticipated inflation rate given the real rate (and, as a consequence, the smaller the proportion of the real to total mortgage rate), the smaller the required equity share necessary to earn the FRM yield.

Several words of caution are warranted regarding the above discussion. There are many parameters whose effects are not displayed. In addition, there is no reason to believe that the rates at which SAMs terminate will approximate rates on fixed-payment loans.

Thus far, we have considered only expected yields. But the SAM's outstanding characteristic is the indexing of deferred interest to house price inflation. In the absence of indexing, the SAM would simply be a negatively amortizing level-payment mortgage with a balloon payment. The difference in outstanding principal between a SAM and a fully amortizing level-payment mortgage would reflect the deferred interest.

One way to compare actual returns on SAMs and FRMs is to consider "unexpected" outcomes, and then recalculate the equity share that would equate the return from the two types of investments. Table 20.8 displays the ex post equity share required to equate a SAM and an FRM when inflation is 5% less than or greater than anticipated. If the house price appreciates 5% faster than anticipated, the required equity share is cut in half. If the house price appreciates 5% slower, the required equity share more than doubles.

The SAM, however, is indexed to the rate of increase in the price of a particular house, not the general inflation rate. Here the lender's risk

Table 20.8. Share of Appreciation Due Lender to Equate Ex Post Returns of a SAM and an FRM (SAM with one-third rate reduction)[a]

Mortgage Life	Actual Inflation is 5% Less Than Anticipated ($\pi = 0.05$)	Actual Inflation Equals Anticipated Inflation ($\pi = 0.10$)	Actual Inflation Is 5% More Than Anticipated ($\pi = 0.15$)
2½ years	0.87	0.40	0.25
5 years	0.94	0.41	0.24
7½ years	1.04	0.42	0.23
10 years	1.14	0.43	0.21

SOURCE: A. Dougherty, R. Van Order, K. Villani, *Housing Finance Review*, 1982, *1*, 361.

[a] The assumptions are those made for the 1980 case; that is, one-third reduction in interest coupon rate, 80% loan-to-value ratio, 10% expected inflation, and 15% mortgage rate.

is substantial. Although increases in house prices outpaced prices generally during the last decade, there is no reason to expect this to continue. Moreover, there is likely to be considerable adverse selection against lenders. Households with the least capital gains potential may be most likely to choose the SAM. Finally, Community Reinvestment Act considerations may limit lenders' ability to differentiate terms to reflect differences in expected appreciation rates among neighborhoods.

Comparing columns 2 and 3 in Table 20.8 indicates a decline in the equity share necessary to make a lender indifferent between a SAM and an FRM when actual inflation exceeds anticipated inflation (the equity share needed drops from 41% to 24% for a five-year term when inflation is 5% greater than anticipated). This is due to the partial hedging characteristics of a SAM compared with an FRM, which offers no hedge against unanticipated inflation. SAM lenders will still dislike unanticipated inflation, but less so than FRM lenders.

Balloon Payment Mortgages, Growing Equity Mortgages, and Others

If interest rate forecasts are uncertain, then investors will charge a premium both for the uncertainty of mortgage cash flow and for the maturity. Shortening the maturity distribution of the payment stream directly increases value (if long-term rates exceed short-term rates) and reduces the risk of adverse terminations, thereby reducing the option premium. A number of mortgage instruments have been designed to capitalize on the concept that investors are more certain about interest rates in the shorter term than in the more distant future.

The balloon payment mortgage contractually requires prepayment prior to the life of the loan. The pricing formulas for standard fixed-rate mortgages apply directly to these loans. The difference is in the projected termination pattern. That is, it is known in advance that all balloon payment loans will terminate by some preset date B, where $B < M$.

The growing equity loan is really a variant on the balloon payment loan. Rather than require the entire amount due in advance, however, it schedules additional equity payments over the life of the loan. Pricing the GEM requires manipulation of Equations 20.1 and 20.2 to capture the growing equity aspect.

RECENT EVIDENCE: TREASURY SECURITIES VERSUS GINNIE MAES, FREDDIE MAC PCs, AND PRIMARY MORTGAGE LOANS

As noted previously, if capital markets price mortgage securities efficiently, and if all participants have the same information and make the same judgments, then the risk-adjusted, after-tax, expected yields available to investors will be the same, on the margin, for all securities. Here we consider the yields on three financial instruments—Treasury securities, Ginnie Mae mortgage-backed securities (known as Ginnie Maes), and Freddie Mac Mortgage Participation Certificates (known as PCs)—and the yield required by primary mortgage lenders. In so doing, we utilize some historical information on mortgage performance and consider whether relative yield spreads are at least consistent with, if not fully explained by, the theory and formulas of the prior discussions. The analysis considers potential differences in yields from differences in marketability, default risk, term to maturity, refinancing/assumption options, and taxes. The following discussion pertains specifically to new-issue markets.

Investor Yields

Treasury securities and Ginnie Maes are the most marketable financial instruments. Since the middle of 1976, the bid–ask spread on Ginnie Maes and Treasuries, both new-issue and seasoned, has been roughly equal. (The spread on new issues has generally been a quarter of a point.) Black, Garbade, and Silber (1981) report evidence that an increase in the marketability of Ginnie Maes resulted in over a one-percentage-point decline in the yield on Ginnie Maes relative to Treasuries over the period from 1972 to mid-1978. Presumably this decline occurred prior to the middle of 1976. Freddie Mac PCs are less actively traded than Ginnie Maes; as a consequence, PC yields may contain a larger marketability premium. On a scale of one (for whole loans) to 100 (for Ginnie Maes), Guttentag (1982) rates the marketability of PCs as 50.

Default is another concern of mortgage investors. Ginnie Maes have virtually no default risk because even the timely payment of principal and interest on the underlying FHA/VA mortgages is guaranteed. Moreover, this guarantee is backed by the full faith and credit of the U.S. government. Freddie Mac PCs are backed by the Federal Home Loan Mortgage Corporation. It guarantees the timely payment of interest and ultimate collection of principal. Moreover, the underlying mortgages generally must have loan-to-value ratios less than 80% or private mortgage insurance covering 25%. We assume here that conventional loans with 25% down do not convey default risk to investors. Nonetheless, investors may require a slight yield premium to compensate for uncertainty about the timing of principal return in the event of default.

The expected cost to investors of prepayments and assumptions depends on the particular refinancing and assumption provisions in the different types of mortgages. These expectations should not have been markedly different for Ginnie Maes and PCs for the time period studied. In terms of prepayments, FHA/VA mortgages may be refinanced without penalty. Prepayment charges cannot be collected for mortgages purchased by Freddie Mac after December 31, 1979. For mortgages closed after this date, prepayment charges are not provided for in the standard Freddie Mac mortgage documents. FHA/VA mortgages generally have more up-front points than conventional mortgages, which reduce the incentive to refinance. While conventional mortgages have historically been prepaid more often and more rapidly than FHA/VA mortgages, we have no evidence that refinancings are more likely on conventional than on FHA/VA loans in response to given economic incentives; the more rapid paydown may simply reflect greater mobility on the part of conventional borrowers. Conventional loans in Freddie Mac pools generally contain due-on-sale clauses—in contrast to the full assumability of FHA/VA mortgages—but before July 1, 1983, these clauses were not enforced unless the new borrower was not creditworthy. Consequently, Ginnie Maes and Freddie Mac PCs should be considered roughly comparable in this regard.

The final source of the difference in yields accounted for in the analysis is taxes. While the three instruments being considered are treated similarly at the federal level, interest from Treasury securities is exempt from state and local taxes; interest from mortgage-backed securities has no general exemption. If the combined state and local income tax rate were τ, then the before-tax expected yield on Treasuries would equal $1 - \tau$ times the expected yield on private securities.

The above observations are summarized in Table 20.9. Yields (the q_i) equal the risk-adjusted expected yields after state and local taxes (the r_i) plus, potentially, adjustments for marketability, default, and call provisions. Just as net yields to investors should be equal after adjusting for technical differences in the securities, so should the net cost to the borrower. The spread between investor yields and borrower costs reflects conduit fees.

The FHA/VA mortgages underlying Ginnie Mae pools have interest rates 50 basis points above the coupon rate on the securities. Of these 50 basis points, the issuer (the mortgage originator) receives 44 basis points as a servicing fee and as compensation for the risk of advancing principal and interest when borrowers' payments are late. Ginnie Mae keeps the remaining six basis points as its guarantee fee.

Freddie Mac acts as packager and seller of its mortgage securities. Over the time period studied, it did not charge a fixed fee for this service, but rather bid for the loans at auction (it now posts required yields daily). The difference between the bid price on the mortgage and the rate on the PC reflects Freddie Mac's costs and its equity return.

Table 20.10 summarizes the relationship between borrower costs and yields to investors. Borrower costs (z) equal the yield to investors (q) plus both the cost of the conduit and the fees of the originator. For Treasuries,

Table 20.9. The Relationship between Yields (q_i) and Risk Adjusted Expected after State and Local Tax Yields (r_i)

	Treasury Bonds (B)	Ginnie Maes (G)	Freddie Mac PCs (F)
Marketability premium (m_i)	Small	Small after late 1976	Somewhat larger
Default effect (d_i)	Zero	Zero	Very small
Term effect (t_i)	Varies	Varies	Varies
Call premium (c_i)	Zero	Positive	Positive
yield (q_i)	$q_B = r_B + m_B + t_B$	$q_G = \dfrac{r_G}{1-\tau} + m_G + t_G + c_G$	$q_F = \dfrac{r_F}{1-\tau} + m_F + d_F + t_F + c_F$

Table 20.10   The Relationship between Borrower Costs (z_i) and Yields to Investors (q_i)

	Treasury Bonds (B)	Ginnie Maes (G)	Freddie Mac PCs (F)
Prices charged by conduits (f_i)	Treasury auction	Servicing fee to originators: 50 basis points	Set at auction: minimum is 37½ basis points for whole loans
Prices charged by originators (o_i)	Treasury auction	Varies, set loan by loan	Varies by institution
Financing cost to borrower (z_i)	$z_B = q_B + x_B + y_B$	$z_G = q_G + f_G + o_G$	$z_F = q_F + f_F + o_F$

the difference between q and z is negligible. For Ginnie Maes and PCs, the differences may be significant.

Empirical Evidence on Mortgage–Bond Yield Spreads

The Ginnie Mae–Treasury Bond Spread.   The spread between the yields on Ginnie Maes (which do not include the origination fee, o_G) and those on Treasuries (which do not include servicing fees, f_B, or origination fees, o_B) can be obtained using the expressions for the q_i in the bottom row of Table 20.9. Given that the marketability premiums are equal (after mid-1976) and that $r_G = r_B$ (risk adjusted, after state and local tax expected yields to investors must be equal), we obtain

$$q_G - q_B = t_G - t_B + c_G + \frac{\tau}{1 - \tau} r_B \qquad (20.32)$$

The yield spreads actually explained empirically are those after all appropriate adjustments. The technique employed is the computation of the difference between the internal rate of return on the mortgage pool and that on a "comparable portfolio" of U.S. Treasury securities, taking into account the coupons on the full-maturity structure of Treasuries. The yield spread, so adjusted, is denoted by SGB and equals

$$SGB = c_G + \frac{\tau}{1 - \tau} r_B \qquad (20.33)$$

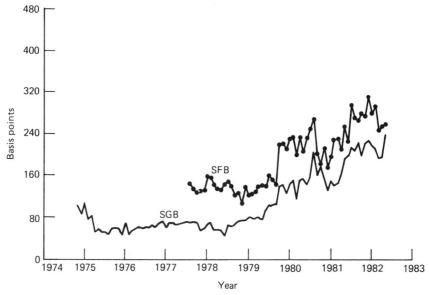

Figure 20.4. Ginnie Mae and Freddie Mac true spreads compared to Treasuries.

The spread is plotted in Figure 20.4. As can be seen, the spread falls in early 1975, is basically flat until the middle of 1979, and then rises on a sharp upward trend through early 1982 (with a dip in late 1980).

Estimation of the equation above requires selecting a proxy for c_G, the value of the call or termination option. We use the spread between the coupons on new-issue, high-grade, 20-year utility and industrial bonds. Utility bonds are ordinarily not callable for five years after issue, while industrial bonds are usually protected for 10 years. Thus the utility rate should exceed the industrial rate by enough to compensate lenders for the lesser call protection given investors. Because these securities have equal maturity and at least near equal default risk, the dominant source of movement in the difference in these coupons should be changes in the value of the extra five years of call protection. The value of the call option given mortgage borrowers, denoted by CALL, should be at least roughly correlated with this spread. CALL rose sharply in 1980 and 1981, in response to a sharp increase in interest rate volatility and thus uncertainty that increased both the likelihood and the cost of calls. As a result, CALL should contribute to an explanation of the SGB spread. The annual averages, in basis points, of CALL for 1976 to 1981 were 38, 31, 28, 49, 93, and 133. The monthly values ranged from 20 to 163 basis points. The data are for the first day of the month and are published by Salomon Brothers.

Table 20.11. Explanation of the True Spread between Ginnie Maes and Treasuries (SGB), July 1976–February 1982

	Constant	CALL	r_{10}	Correction for Auto-Correlation	$\overline{R}^2$	Standard Deviation of Equation	Durbin Watson
(1)	− 53.9	0.376	0.140		0.857	21.1	0.87
	(17.1)	(0.153)	(0.026)				
(2)	− 37.5	0.307	0.128	0.555	0.627	17.2	
	(20.4)	(0.130)	(0.025)	(0.101)			
(3)		0.758	0.062		0.830	22.5	0.86
		(0.099)	(0.008)				
(4)		0.434	0.084	0.547		17.7	
		(0.115)	(0.009)	(0.102)			

With the use of the 10-year Treasury bond yield for r_B, the estimation equation is

$$SGB = \beta_0 + \beta_1\,CALL + \beta_2\,r_{10}$$

$$\text{where } \beta_0 \sim 0 \qquad\qquad (20.34)$$
$$\beta_1 > 0$$
$$\beta_2 = \tau/(1 - \tau) > 0$$

Moreover, β_2 should not exceed 0.11 ($\tau \leq 0.1$).

Estimates are reported in Table 20.11 for the 68 months from July 1976 to February 1982. The coefficients suggest that the value of the call or termination option increased by between 45 and 80 basis points from the second half of 1978 to the second half of 1981 because CALL increased by 105 basis points.

The Freddie Mac–Treasury Bond Spread. The following expression for the Freddie Mac–Treasury bond spread is obtained much the way the expression for the Ginnie Mae–Treasury bond spread was obtained:

$$SFB = c_F + \frac{\tau}{1 - \tau}\,r_B + d_F + m_F - m_B \qquad (20.35)$$

The plot of the spread is also shown in Figure 20.4. The difference between SFB and SGB lies within the 42 to 86 basis point range during

47 of the 58 months plotted. Assuming that the call and state and local tax effects are the same as those for the Ginnie Mae–Treasury bond yield spread, this difference reflects the differential default and marketability premiums (as well as measurement error) during this time period. Given the extremely favorable default experience of the Freddie Mac portfolio and the dramatic increase in issues in 1982, this spread may be expected to erode.

The Conventional Commitment–Treasury Bond Spread

In this part, we wish to explain the spread between a mortgage borrower's cost of funds and the yield on Treasury securities. This examines the efficiency of mortgage pricing in primary markets given the presumption that Treasury securities are efficiently priced. The yield we use for the cost of mortgage funds is the average commitment rate offered by major lenders (savings and loans, mutual savings banks, commercial banks, and mortgage bankers) on 25% down, 25-year conventional mortgages as computed by the Federal Home Loan Bank Board. Given the large down payment, it seems reasonable to assume that the default risk parameter is negligible. The conventional yield will include the costs of servicing and originating conventional loans, f_C and o_C. After substitutions and adjustments, an expression quite similar to the Freddie Mac–Treasury bond spread is obtained for the conventional commitment–Treasury bond spread (net of servicing)

$$\text{SCB} = c_C + \frac{\tau}{1 - \tau} r_B + d_C + m_C - m_B + o_C \qquad (20.36)$$

If the calls are equal ($c_C = c_G$) and if $d_C = 0$, we have

$$\text{SCB} = \text{SGB} + m_C - m_B + o_C \qquad (20.37)$$

As can be seen from Figure 20.5, this spread is considerably more volatile than that between Ginnie Maes and Treasuries. Examination of the periods in which the spread was especially volatile suggests that the cause is sharp changes in interest rates to which some lenders apparently adjusted commitment rates with a lag. To illustrate, when interest rates fell sharply in late spring of 1980, the mortgage commitment rate lagged. As a result, the spread between this rate and that on Treasuries widened. This lagged response can be captured in the empirical analysis by including current and lagged values of Δr_{10} as regressors, expecting their coefficents to be negative in the spread equation.

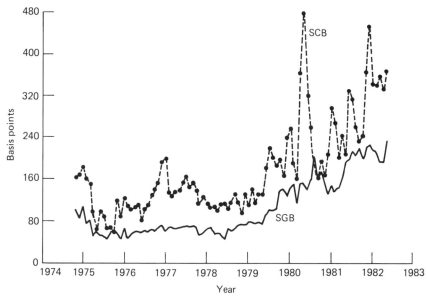

Figure 20.5. Ginnie Mae and conventional commitment true spreads compared to Treasuries.

The charge for originating conventional loans may depend on the availability of funds for investment at savings and loans or, more generally, on competition among all originators. This availability is measured as the sum of gross savings flows and mortgage repayments deflated by the average price of single-family houses sold in that month. To allow for lags and cumulative impacts, the average values of the variable during the previous six months are reported. As an alternative, we employ the percentage of major lenders that are offering the 25%-down, 25-year mortgage at the relevant time (the percentage varies between 70 and 90 during the estimation period) less 90. The origination variable is denoted by ORIG. The more available funds are, or the more lenders are offering commitments, the lower should be the conventional rate.

With these specifications and those described earlier, we can write the estimation equation as

$$SCB = \beta_0 + \beta_1\, SGB + \beta_2\, \Delta r_{10} + \beta_3\, \Delta r_{10-1} + \beta_4\, ORIG$$

$$\text{where } \beta_1 \sim 1 \tag{20.38}$$
$$\beta_2 < \beta_3$$
$$\beta_4 < 0$$

Table 20.12. Explanation of the True Spread between Conventional Mortgage Commitments and Treasuries (SCB), July 1976–February 1982

Origination Variable	Constant	SGB		Δr_{10}	Δr_{10-1}	ORIG	Correction for Auto-Correlation	$\overline{R}^2$	Standard Deviation of Equation	Durbin Watson
(1) Funds in last six months	121.7 (61.1)	1.038 (0.225)		−0.726 (0.078)	−0.134 (0.078)	−365 (332)		0.846	34.6	0.63
(2) Percent offering commitments—90	59.0 (112.2)	1.064 (0.128)		−0.710 (0.077)	−0.166 (0.078)	−2.464 (1.233)		0.852	33.8	0.60
(3) Funds in last six months	228.6 (58.1)	0.607 (0.208)		−0.669 (0.050)	−0.132 (0.050)	−898 (340)	0.665 (0.091)	0.801	24.2	
(4) Percent offering commitments—90	64.9 (112.7)	0.759 (0.148)		−0.656 (0.048)	−0.174 (0.050)	−4.257 (1.263)	0.670 (0.090)	0.812	23.5	
(5) Percent offering commitments—90	40.3 (126.8)	EXP 1.157 (0.238)	UNE 0.505 (0.180)	−0.712 (0.053)	−0.206 (0.050)	−3.105 (1.337)	0.687 (0.088)	0.825	22.7	

The estimates for the period July 1976 to February 1982 are reported in Table 20.12. In the last row of the table, the spread variable (SGB) is divided into the explained (by the CALL and r_{10} variables) and unexplained components. For this purpose, we use the coefficients of Equation 19.36 from Table 20.11. Thus, the explained component is

$$\text{EXP} = 0.434\text{CALL} + 0.084r_{10} \tag{20.39}$$

and the unexplained is

$$\text{UNE} = \text{SGB} - \text{EXP} \tag{20.40}$$

Given that the percentage of lenders offering commitments varies between 70 and 90, this equation implies that the conventional commitment rate has been 60 basis points higher when mortgage money has been tight than when it has been easy. The pattern of coefficients on the change in the Treasury yield suggests that lenders set the commitment rate with roughly a month lag. (More specifically, about three-fifths set it with a one-month lag and another fifth with a two-month lag).

To summarize this section, the rate mortgage borrowers are charged can differ from that earned by investors in comparable-maturity Treasury securities for a variety of reasons. First, even with efficient capital markets, it is the risk adjusted, expected after state and local tax yield on mortgages that is equated to the yield on comparable-maturity Treasuries. As a result, the spread between yields will vary with the level of interest rates (the effect of the state and local tax rate), interest rate uncertainty (the value of the termination option given borrowers), and possibly other factors (e.g, default risk), depending on the particular mortgage rate series being examined. Second, there is a wedge between the rate that borrowers commit to pay and the return promised ultimate investors. The wedge depends on origination and servicing costs. The former, in particular, could vary over time as conditions in local origination markets change. It is here that the availability of funds at housing finance institutions could matter.

The empirical results document these sources of differences in the spread between quoted yields on mortgages and Treasuries. Two spreads are explained. The first is between the promised returns to investors on Ginnie Mae pass-through securities and Treasuries. These are returns to investors (servicing fees and origination costs are not included) and there are no differences in default risk (zero) or marketability (the spreads between bid and ask prices are equal). As a result, the only sources of the spread are the value of the termination option given mortgage borrowers and the exemption from state and local taxes given investors in Treasury securities. The former is proxied by the spread between the yields on 20-year, new-issue, AA-rated utility and industrial bonds (industrial bonds have 10 years of call protection, while utilities have only five). The value of the tax exemption varies linearly with the level of interest rates, assuming a constant state and local tax rate. The estimates suggest that 45 to 80 basis points of the jump in this rate spread between late 1977 and late 1981 can be attributed to an increase in the value of the termination option, caused by the increase in interest rate uncertainty. A roughly equal amount was due to the general increase in interest rates.

The second spread analyzed is the difference between the commitment rate on 25% down, 25-year conventional mortgages and comparable-maturity Treasuries. Because the estimated coefficient on the spread between Ginnie Maes and Treasuries is roughly unity, the impacts of the termination option and state and local taxes on the two spreads are the same. The conventional commitment Treasury bond spread also depends on lags (about one month on average) in the setting of the commitment rate and on variations in the extent of competition in the origination market as proxied by the percentage of major lenders offering to make commitments at any point in time. The latter explains a roughly 60 basis point increase in the commitment rate between late 1977 and the late 1981.

There are two general observations from this empirical evidence. First, mortgage market participants seem to be pricing based on the formulas presented above. Second, when interest rates are volatile, judgments will differ regarding the probability distribution of income streams, that is, mortgage terminations.

Some Evidence of Option Prices in Graduated-Payment Mortgage Coupons

Beginning-of-month data were collected from Merrill Lynch for prices and coupons on graduated-payment mortgages for the 15-month period from July 1980 to September 1981. The same ϕ function and other data that were employed in calculating the termination premiums for level-payment mortgages were utilized in the calculation for the GPMs. The resulting termination premiums, as well as those computed for LPMs and the difference between them, are listed in Table 20.13.

For these 15 months, the premiums for GPMs averaged 226 basis points, about a one-half percentage point, or 30% greater than that for LPMs. While the correspondence between the GPM and LPM premiums is far from perfect, there is a tendency for them to move together. To illustrate, when the LPM premiums were at their peak in the last six months (190 basis points or higher and averaging 202 basis points), the spread between

Table 20.13.   Termination Premiums for Graduated-Payment and Level-Payment Mortgages

Date (first of month)		GPM	LPM	Difference
July	1980	250	202	48
August	1980	220	158	62
September	1980	258	176	82
October	1980	186	152	34
November	1980	188	128	60
December	1980	186	146	40
January	1981	172	136	36
February	1981	164	142	22
March	1981	206	160	46
April	1981	214	190	24
May	1981	266	194	72
June	1981	298	210	88
July	1981	252	202	40
August	1981	306	220	86
September	1981	248	198	50

the GPM and LPM premiums averaged 60 basis points. In the previous six months, the LPM premiums averaged only 144 basis points, and the spread was only 40 basis points.

Whether 30%-greater premiums in yields on GPMs compared to those in yields on LPMs are excessive is unclear. One guide to this issue is a comparison of the duration of GPMs with that of LPMs. After all, the greater duration of GPMs is the source of the anticipated larger termination premiums.

The duration of a pool of mortgages is the ratio of the time-weighted present value of the pool's future cash flows divided by the unweighted present value of those flows. That is,

$$
\mathrm{DUR} = \frac{\dfrac{\sum\limits_{t=1}^{M} t\mathrm{CF}_t}{(1 + i_t)^t\,(1 + i_t^1)^{-1/3}}}{\dfrac{\sum\limits_{t=1}^{M} \mathrm{CF}_t}{(1 + i_t)^t\,(1 + i_t^1)^{-1/3}}}
$$

where CF is the cash flow after netting out the termination premiums (after replacing i with $i - \rho$ or $i - \rho_g$). For our 15-month period, the average duration for GPMs is nearly 10 years; for LPMs the average is just over 5½ years. Given the much greater duration of GPMs, a 30% greater premium does not appear excessive.

Glossary of Notation

PAY	Mortgage payment
$PRIN_t$	Outstanding principal at time t
TMPAY	Total payment on pool of mortgages at time t
X	Initial mortgage loan amount
M	Initial mortgage loan maturity
N	Number of mortgages in pool
V	Value
P	Price
i	Coupon interest rate
i^d	Mortgage coupon rate reflecting expected default
i_k^1	One-period interest rate expected to exist in period t
i_k	Before-tax coupon rate for mortgage originated at period k
y_t	Yield on riskless pure discount bond of maturity t
Y	Vector of discount rates
a	Accumulation rate
Q_k	Fraction of mortgages in pool still outstanding k periods after origination
ϕ_t	Fraction of loans in pool that terminate at time t
ϕ_T	Cumulative fraction of loans in pool that terminate by time $t - 1$
$_k\phi_t$	Fraction of loans that terminate at time t after period k
$_k\phi_T$	Cumulative fractions of loans that terminate by time $t - 1$ after period k
TBPAY	Total payment on a portfolio of Treasury bonds
X_B	Initial bond amount
γ_j	Fraction of bond portfolio maturing in period j
θ	Tax rate
γ	Yield-equivalent default loss
ρ	Termination option price in mortgage coupon
ba_k	Benefit to borrower of assumption in period k

ca_k	Cost to borrower of assumption in period k
br_k	Benefit to borrower of refinancing in period k
cr_k	Cost to borrower of refinancing in period k
u	Closing costs and repayment penalty incurred to refinance
v	Additional points charged for new mortgage loan
π	Rate the house increases in value (inflation net of depreciation)
L	Length of time the borrower expects to hold a mortgage that has been refinanced at time k
R	Number of inflation/interest rate scenarios
p_j	Probability of inflation/interest rate scenario j occurring
p_m	Probability of most likely scenario
U	Up (rates)
D	Down (rates)
C	Constant (rates)
$PAYG_t$	Payment on GPM at time t
$PRING_t$	Outstanding principal on GPM at time t
g	Rate at which payments on GPM rise
h	Number of periods payments on GPM rise
TSAMPAY	Total payment on pool of SAMs
α	One minus interest rate discount on SAM
z	Borrower costs
q	Yield to investors
r	Risk-adjusted expected yields after state and local taxes
τ	State and local tax rate
c	Call premium
d	Default premium
f	Servicing fee
m	Marketability premium
o	Origination fee
t	Term effect
SGB	True spread between Ginnie Maes and Treasury bonds
SFB	True spread between Freddie Mac PCs and Treasury bonds

SCB   True spread between conventional commitments and
               Treasury bonds

	Superscripts		Subscripts
s	Scheduled	G	Ginnie Mae
c	Certain	B	Treasury bond
u	Uncertain	C	Conventional commitment
sm	Second mortgage	t	In period t
m	Most likely	o	At origination
		k	(left) After period k

REFERENCES

Black, D. G., Garbade, K. D., and Silber, W. L. "The Impact of the GNMA Pass-through Program on FHA Mortgage Costs." *Journal of Finance*, May 1981, *36*, pp. 457–469.

Dougherty, A. J., Van Order, R., and Villani, K. E. "Pricing Shared Appreciation Mortgages." *Housing Finance Review*, October 1982, *1*, pp. 361–375.

Guttentag, J. M. "Mortgage Pass-throughs: Structure and Policy." Prepared for the Mortgage Insurance Companies of America, June 1982.

Hendershott, P. H., Hu, S., and Villani, K. E. "The Economics of Mortgage Terminations: Implications for Mortgage Lenders and Mortgage Terms." *Housing Finance Review* April 1983, *2*, pp. 127–142.

Hendershott, P. H., Shilling, J. D., and Villani, K. E. "The Determination of Home Mortgage Rates: Empirical Results for the 1975–81 Period." Presented at the American Finance Association/American Real Estate and Urban Economics Association meetings, December 1982.

Hendershott, P. H., and Villani, K.E. "The Call Premium in Mortgage Coupon Rates: Evidence on the Integration of Mortgage and Bond Markets." National Bureau of Economic Research Working Paper Number 738, August 1981.

Herzog, T. N. "Bayesian Graduation of FHA/HUD Single Family Home Mortgage Insurance Contracts—Section 203." Mimeographed, May 1981.

Preiss, B. "The Garn-St Germain Act and Due-on-Sale Clause Enforcement." *Housing Finance Review*, October 1983, *2*, pp. 369–377.

Preiss, B., and Van Order, R. "An Economic Analysis of Due-on-Sale Clauses." A report to Congress by the Office of Policy Development and Research, U.S. Department of Housing and Urban Development, April 1981.

Van Order, R., and Villani, K. E. "A Study of a GNMA Conventional Mortgage Pass-through Security Program." In *Occasional Papers in Housing and Community Affairs*, U.S. Department of Housing and Urban Development, March 1981, *9*, pp. 155–191.

21 The Securities Activities of Commercial Banks

George G. Kaufman

Commercial banks (and other depository institutions) are intermediaries that borrow money from savers in the form of deposits and relend them to ultimate borrowers by making loans or buying securities. Investment banks are intermediaries that assist borrowers in raising funds directly from savers by: (1) advising in the design and origination of the securities to be sold; (2) underwriting the securities by buying them from the borrowers; and (3) distributing the securities by reselling them to investors. Thus, investment bankers deal in the securities originated by the issuer and, except for a brief period while they may be in inventory, do not own the securities. They are not investors. In contrast, commercial banks are investors buying and holding the securities originated by others. They finance these holdings by effectively transforming the original securities of the borrower into securities (deposits) on themselves that have different characteristics in terms of maturity, denomination, risk, and so on and selling them to different investors. Investment bankers also provide liquidity for securities issued by others by making a secondary market in them, buying the securities back from investors who wish to sell them before maturity and reselling them to other investors or helping sellers locate buyers.

Besides the basic differences in their operational techniques, commercial and investment banking have traditionally differed in the maturity of the funds raised. Commercial banks have focused primarily on borrowing and lending short term; investments banks have focused primarily on helping borrowers satisfy their longer-term needs for financial capital.

661

Because of these broad differences, commercial and investment banking tended to develop separately. But because they both dealt with the same raw material—money—they also provided some overlapping services. The extent of overlap has differed from country to country and even from time to time in a given country, depending on economic and political circumstances.

In the United States, commercial and investment banking have for the most part been conducted by different institutions, at times voluntarily and at other times by statute. The Banking Act of 1933, popularly referred to as the Glass-Steagall Act, largely separated the two functions, following a period in which they had been integrated to a considerable extent. The separation of commercial and investment banking is in the British tradition. In other countries, such as Germany and France, the two kinds of banking are frequently conducted by the same institution (see Daskin and Marquardt, 1983). In recent years, commercial and investment banks in the United States have increasingly provided the same or similar services, and the differences between the two types of institutions have narrowed. This process has been largely the result of two forces: advances in the technology of collecting, transferring, and manipulating information (data as well as funds) that have made it easier to bypass legal and regulatory barriers; and changes in the economic environment that have both altered and increased the public's need for financial services.

Commercial and investment banks each have established successful positions in markets in which they had been sheltered by law or by regulation from competition from the other. As may be expected, some of these institutions have resisted the efforts of the other class to penetrate their markets. Indeed, the battle for turf between commercial and investment banks is being hotly contested in national and state legislatures and regulatory agencies, as well as in the marketplace.

This chapter traces the development of commercial and investment banking in the United States, discusses the domestic investment banking or securities activities in which commercial banks engage—other than for the bank's own investment (portfolio) or the securities issued by the bank or its affiliates, examines the issues underlying the arguments for and against the separation of traditional commercial and investment banking, and considers future developments in the area.

OVERVIEW

Commercial banks have engaged in some securities activities (investment banking) virtually throughout their history. The particular kind of activity has changed through time depending upon federal and state legislation, judicial review, and the policies of the chartering agency of the particular bank; the aggressiveness and innovativeness of bank management; available technology; and the prevailing economic environment. The securities activities in which commercial banks currently engage expanded greatly in recent years and are likely to expand further in the future. This reflects a number of factors. The demand for all financial services, including securities services, has increased. Greater economic wealth has increased the financial resources of households and business firms; longer life expectancies have increased both the magnitude and complexity of financial needs; higher rates of inflation have increased the importance of financial management; higher rates of interest have increased the cost of holding funds in accounts paying below-market rates; and more volatile interest rates have increased financial risk. At the same time, many costs of providing these services have decreased. Advances in computer technology have permitted funds and information to be collected, transmitted, and manipulated cheaply and quickly. Indeed, such advances have opened financial markets to a variety of new participants (see Kaufman, Mote, and Rosenblum, 1983).

For many years, statutes and regulations have restricted the kinds of activities in which different classes of institutions may engage and the prices and interest rates that they may pay or charge for their services. The restrictions had been imposed to deal with the problems of an earlier age, primarily the depression years of the 1930s. They promoted safety by discouraging competition. Many of the regulations restricted (or were perceived to restrict) the ability of commercial banks to provide a number of financial services. As a result, other financial institutions (existing or entirely new) stepped in to fill the void. Their job was made easier by the evolution of new communications and computer technology that increasingly eased circumvention of the intent of the legal and regulatory barriers. Investment banking and other firms not only were able to offer many new products, but also were able to offer products closely resembling traditional banking products—such as deposit-type securities (shares in money market funds) and general-use consumer credit cards. In time, the commercial banks responded by lobbying to have the laws changed, challenging the restrictive regulations with the regulatory agencies and in the courts, and, perhaps most important, increasing their own aggressiveness and innovativeness.

Commercial banks, particularly larger banks, are well positioned to expand their securities activities. They possess large customer bases for financial services, large staffs of trained personnel, and computer systems programmed for financial services. These provide the potential for significant economies of both scale and scope by adding activities that are closely enough related to their current activities to enable building on existing facilities. In addition, some banks engage in a full range of investment banking overseas, where U.S. statutes permit equal treatment with local banks. Thus, they also have experience in providing such services. Although there is little evidence of excess profits or insufficient competition in those securities activities that appear to have been prohibited for banks, it is likely that the market for some of these services would be enlarged by bank entry and that, at least, some banks would succeed in attracting market shares from nonbank competitors. Thus, commercial banks view additional securities activities both as generating potentially high revenues on little additional outlays and as rounding out the package of financial services they could offer customers to attract more of their overall financial business.

The statutory and regulatory restrictions on domestic securities activities by commercial banks appear not to be as carefully spelled out as many believed only a few years ago. As recently as the mid-1970s, students of banking were reasonably certain about which securities activities commercial banks could or could not conduct. But the events of recent years have badly shaken this perception. Activities perceived as barely permissible 10 years earlier are common practice today, and some perceived as nonpermissible are being introduced by more aggressive institutions. In addition, some of today's securities did not exist (e.g., money market funds), were not widely used (e.g., financial futures), or were not of sufficient importance (e.g., municipal revenue bonds) to be clearly covered in extant legislation or regulation. As a result, the permissibility (or lack thereof) of many of the activities has been determined on a case-by-case basis, either by a bank application to engage in the new activity or by challenge to a bank's involvement in a particular activity. The determination of the legality of many of the services was eventually tested (or is now being tested) in the courts, most involving lengthy appeals and, not infrequently, final review by the U. S. Supreme Court.

Moreover, hardly any specific banking legislation or regulation concerning securities activities or regulation applies equally to all commercial banks. Most frequently, one statute or regulation applies to national banks and one or more others will apply to state-chartered banks, depending upon whether they are insured by the Federal Deposit Insurance Corporation (FDIC), members of the Federal Reserve System, and/or in which of the 50 states they are chartered. Indeed, the FDIC has ruled that most of the provisions of the Glass-Steagall Act do not apply to insured banks that are not members of the Federal Reserve. Nevertheless, the activities of these banks remain subject to the laws and regulations of the states in which they are chartered, which also spell out permissible security activities. Even when regulations apply equally to large groups of banks, it is unlikely that all banks will be affected equally. Securities activities are primarily engaged in by the larger banks. Smaller banks tend to offer a more limited number of these services. In addition, although thrift institutions are rapidly becoming more similar to commercial banks, they remain subject to different statutes and regulation.

HISTORY

Unlike commercial banks, investment banks need not obtain special charters. Until recently, most investment banks were not even incorporated. Even today, many investment banking houses are organized as partnerships. Because they were not incorporated—and therefore were not subject to the regulations that apply to corporations—the early investment banks could engage in any activity they wished and have offices in any location. Owing to the nature of their business, investment banking houses developed almost exclusively in major financial centers. Many offered deposit banking as well as underwriting services, although their investment banking activities (raising long-term funds for business firms and governments) tended to dominate their commercial banking activities.

The early investment banks were generally organized by people who had made private fortunes as brokers or foreign exchange dealers or in nonfinancial lines of business and found that they could put these funds to profitable although risky use by underwriting and distributing new security offerings.[1] Outstanding financial securities had been traded for commissions in New York City since 1793. (The New York Stock Exchange was established for this purpose in 1817.) But new securities were sold directly to investors by the issuing firm itself. As the needs of firms and governments for new capital increased, direct sales to investors became increasingly less efficient and the need for specialists developed.

Many of the larger early investment houses in the United States were branches or affiliates of large banks in Europe, particularly in Great Britain, that had considerable underwriting experience and could distribute U.S. securities to their customers in Europe and provide the U. S. affiliate with new European securities. The golden era of investment banking was the period immediately after the Civil War, when the great banking houses of J. P. Morgan, Lehman Brothers, Kuhn Loeb, and Goldman Sachs were established. These houses helped raise the capital, both in the United States and abroad, that financed the rapid industrialization of the country in the period between the Civil War and World War I.

The earliest commercial banks in the United States were chartered exclusively to issue notes (and later to accept fixed-value deposits) and make primarily short-term, self-liquidating business loans (e.g., inventory loans repaid as the inventory was sold). This was in accordance with the "real bills" doctrine of banking that was popular at the time and justified money creation only if collateralized by short-term, self-liquidating real assets. Through the years, however, states began to permit their state-chartered banks to make longer-term loans and to enter into various aspects of investment banking, although they were not permitted to own common stocks for their own accounts. At the same time, trust companies to manage the funds of wealthy individuals in a fiduciary capacity were organized in many states under general incorporation laws that gave them broader powers than commercial banks. In the process, they became involved in the trading of existing securities for their customers and then in underwriting new securities. In time, many trust companies requested and were granted deposit powers. By the beginning of the twentieth century, many trust companies were indistinguishable in their banking operations from both state-chartered commercial banks and investment banks.

In the meantime, the National Bank Act of 1864 granted the newly created national-chartered banks "incidental powers as shall be necessary to carry on the business of banking." This was initially interpreted by both the Comptroller of the Currency and the courts as prohibiting most aspects of investment banking other than investing in government securities. However, competitive pressures from state banks soon forced increasingly broader interpretations. National banks were permitted to underwrite and trade securities, although initially they were restricted primarily to issues of the federal government and municipalities in which they were permitted to invest for their own portfolios. Over time, to permit them to remain competitive with state banks, this authority was extended first to corporate bonds and then to corporate equities. National banks were also permitted to organize security affiliates under state charters. Unlike their parent commercial banks, however, these affiliates could have branch offices in any state and engage in full-service investment banking.

In 1927, the McFadden Act was enacted to equalize competitive conditions between national and state banks. National banks were permitted to branch in the states in which they were headquartered on approximately the same basis as state-chartered banks and to underwrite and trade directly almost all types of securities. By 1930, commercial and investment banking were almost fully integrated, and commercial banks played an increasingly important role in the securities markets. In 1930, commercial banks, trust companies, and bank affiliates underwrote an estimated 60% of all new bond issues, up from 37% only three years earlier.

The Banking Act of 1933

For reasons to be discussed later, the Banking Act of 1933 (Glass-Steagall Act) effectively separated commercial and investment banking.[2] The act did the following:

1. It prohibited, with certain exceptions, commercial banks that are members of the Federal Reserve System from underwriting, distribution, and dealing as principals in stocks, bonds, or other securities. The exceptions were federal government bonds, municipal bonds collateralized by the full faith and credit—that is, taxing power—of the issuer (general obligation, or GO, bonds), and deposit-type securities such as CDs.
2. It limited purchases of securities for a commercial bank's own account to debt securities approved by the bank regulatory agencies.
3. It prohibited commercial banks that are members of the Federal Reserve System from affiliating with investment banking firms.
4. It prohibited firms and individuals engaged in investment banking from simultaneously engaging in commercial banking.[3]

Banks were given the choice of being one or the other, but not both. Almost all primarily commercial banks chose to remain commercial banks, and almost all primarily investment banks chose to remain investment banks. They divested themselves of the prohibited activities. National City Bank (a predecessor of today's Citibank), Chase National Bank (a predecessor of Chase Manhattan Bank), and Harris Trust and Savings Bank of Chicago dissolved their securities affiliate. The First National Bank of Boston spun off as a separate entity its affiliate, First Boston Corporation, a major investment banking firm.

Lehman Brothers Kuhn Loeb was one of the investment banks that discontinued their deposit business. J. P. Morgan and Company was one of the few investment banks that chose to retain their deposit business and discontinue their securities activities. Some senior officers left, however, to establish the investment banking firm of Morgan Stanley. J. P. Morgan reorganized as the Morgan Bank, first as a private deposit bank and then incorporated as a state-chartered commercial bank. Today it is the Morgan Guaranty Trust Company.

Reasons for the Banking Act

The Glass-Steagall Act was a product of its time—the depression, widespread bank failures, and severe loss of public confidence in the stability of the economic and political system. Its purpose was threefold:

1. To restore confidence in the commercial banking system by separating commercial from investment banking. Many investment banks experienced severe financial difficulties at the onset of the depression. The attempts by some banks to come to the aid of their troubled securities affiliates were widely viewed as weakening their already precarious capital positions. There was a widespread belief that the securities activities of the banks increased their susceptibility to financial strains and had contributed significantly to their financial troubles. (This occurred before the introduction of FDIC insurance, and depositors probably had good cause to be anxious about the ability of their banks to meet deposit demands at full par value.)

2. To prevent a channeling of funds from "legitimate" commercial uses to "speculative" uses. Such channeling was considered easier if commercial banks could engage in securities activities and were able to advise their deposit customers to purchase securities. Increased credit flows into the securities markets were believed to have increased the instability of the financial system and to have contributed greatly to the cumulative nature, and thus the severity, of the 1929 stock market crash. Many bank customers had bought stock on credit, provided by the bank, and when the market price of the shares declined below the value of the associated loan, the banks were forced to sell the stocks. These forced sales exerted further downward pressure on stock prices.

3. To eliminate the conflicts of interest and self-dealing that may be inherent in the marriage of commercial and investment banking. A number of such abuses had received national publicity in congressional hearings and, coming at a time of massive bank failures, had created a public outcry for strong and immediate remedial action. (The alleged abuses are described later in this chapter.)

CURRENT SECURITIES ACTIVITIES OF COMMERCIAL BANKS

A listing of many of the securities activities presently offered by commercial banks and the year in which they were introduced appears in Table 21.1. Some of these activities are discussed below.

Underwriting and Distributing U.S. Government Securities

Commercial banks have traditionally helped to underwrite (purchase from the issuer) and distribute (resell to investors) new securities issued by the

Table 21.1 Commercial Bank Securities Activities

Activity	Year Started
Underwriting and distributing	
U.S. Treasury securities	always
U.S. federal agency securities	various years
Municipal securities	
General obligation	early 1900s[a]
Some revenue bonds	1968
Trading	
U.S. Treasury securities	always
U.S. federal agency securities	various years
Municipal securities	
General obligation	early 1900s[a]
Some revenue bonds	1968
Financial and precious metal futures	1983
Private placements	always
Sponsor closed-end funds	1974
Offshore dealing in Eurodollar securities	always
Mergers and acquisitions	always
Trust investments	
Individual accounts	always
IRA commingled accounts	1982
Automatic investment service	1974
Dividend investment service	always
Financial advising	
Closed-end funds	1974
Mutual funds	1974
Other	always
Brokerage	
Limited customer	always
Retail	1982
Securities swapping	always

[a] National banks; always for most state banks.

U. S. Treasury. Over time, this role was extended to securities issued by federal and official international agencies, including the Federal Home Loan Bank board and its affiliates, the Farm Credit System and its affiliates, the Government National Mortgage Association (GNMA), Federal National Mortgage Association (FNMA), the Student Loan Marketing Association, and the World Bank (IBRD). A complete list of eligible federal and international agencies is shown in Table 21.2.   All Treasury securities

Table 21.2.   Securities Eligible for Underwriting and Dealing by Commercial Banks, 1983

U.S. Treasury Department

General obligations of states and political subdivisions thereof

Washington Metropolitan Area Transit Authority

Federal Farm Credit Banks

Federal Home Loan Banks

Obligations insured by the U.S. Department of Housing and Urban
  Development

Federal National Mortgage Corporation

Government National Mortgage Corporation

Federal Financing Bank

Environmental Financing Authority

Student Loan Marketing Association

International Bank for Reconstruction and Development

Inter-American Development Bank

Asian Development Bank

African Development Bank

Revenue obligations of states and political subdivisions and agencies for
  housing, university, or dormitory purposes

Tennessee Valley Authority

U.S. Postal Service

Federal Home Loan Mortgage Corporation

are publicly sold at competitive auctions by the Treasury Department to the highest bidders in amounts up to the total amount of the particular issue for sale. Banks bid for Treasury securities both for their own investment accounts and for redistribution to other investors at a higher price. Generally, the largest banks bid to resell to other investors, including other banks, and act as security dealers. Individual commercial banks bid for these securities in competition with nonbank security dealers, other financial institutions, and investors in general. Like other bidders, commercial banks may submit competitive or noncompetitive bids for the new securities. In competitive bids, the securities are generally awarded to the highest bidders in order of their ranking from highest price down, until the Treasury has sold its desired amount. Bidders may generally submit as many different bids as they wish. Because successful bids are awarded at the price bid, all winners do not pay the same price. Although high bidders may win many securities, they may not be able to resell them at a profit as investors may go to other winning bidders, who paid a lower price, or purchase substitute securities in the secondary market. Banks may also submit noncompetitive bids up to a limited dollar amount in which they offer to buy the securities at the average price. Noncompetitive tenders are filled in full. But because of the small permissible amounts, noncompetitive bids are used only by relatively small investors.

Because the Treasury designs its own securities, banks act only as underwriters and distributors; they do not participate in origination, although representatives of commercial banks serve on a standing committee that advises the Treasury in its debt management.

The issuance of securities by federal agencies differs from that by the Treasury. As do most issuers, other than the U.S. Treasury, federal agencies select one or more commercial banks or other security dealers to serve as financial advisers or fiscal agents. Assistance covers determination of credit needs, security design (amount, maturity and coupon characteristics, collateral requirements, and any special option features such as call, put, or convertibility options), and preparation documentation about the issue to be provided to potential investors. In addition, the adviser analyzes market developments and interest rate movements and recommends the timing for the sale. Unlike Treasury issues, most federal agency issues are sold by negotiation rather than by competitive bid. Some are also underwritten on a "best effort" basis in which the underwriter does not buy the entire amount of the issue but promises only to make a best effort to sell as many of the new securities as possible at the agreed-upon price within a specified period of time.

Trading in U.S. Government Securities

Commercial banks are important makers of secondary markets for securities of the U.S. Treasury and federal agencies. They may act both as dealers, buying as principals for their own account and selling from their inventory, and as brokers, buying and selling as agents for the accounts of others. As dealers, they generate revenues by selling the securities at a higher price than the price at which they were purchased; as brokers, banks collect commissions from either or both the seller and buyer. Because interest rates may move unfavorably while securities are held in inventory, dealers tend to assume greater risk than brokers.

Only the very largest commercial banks make active markets in Treasury securities. Of the 36 dealers that made sufficiently broad and continuous markets to be required to report their activities to the Federal Reserve Bank of New York in 1983, 13 were commercial banks. They are:

Bank of America N.T. & S. A. (San Francisco)
Bankers Trust Company (New York)

The Chase Manhattan Bank, N.A. (New York)
Chemical Bank (New York)
Citibank, N.A. (New York)
Continental Illinois National Bank and Trust Co. (Chicago)
Crocker National Bank (San Francisco)
First Interstate Bank of California (Los Angeles)
The First National Bank of Chicago
Harris Trust and Savings Bank (Chicago)
Manufacturers Hanover Trust Company (New York)
Morgan Guaranty Trust Company (New York)
The Northern Trust Company (Chicago)

In 1982, these banks accounted for about 30% of all recorded dealer trans-actions. Treasury securities are by far the most actively traded security on the secondary markets. Most dealers will make markets for all Treasury securities, although markets tend to be more active for shorter-term issues.

Banks also make secondary markets in the securities of federal agencies. However, many banks tend to specialize, making more active markets for the securities of the agencies that they serve as financial advisers or underwriters.

Bank Dealer Operations.   Dealers generate profits from their trading and from increases in the value of their inventories. Their trading profits are derived from selling securities at a higher price (lower interest rates) than the price at which they bought the securities. The difference between the selling (asked) and buying (bid) price at any moment of time is termed the *spread*. Dealers hold inventories of securities—termed *positions*—for the same reason any merchant holds inventory—to have stock on the shelf when a customer comes to buy—and their inventory strategy is bas-ically the same as for other merchants. The amount and composition of inventory a dealer holds depend on:

1.   The estimated volume of sales in each issue or maturity grouping
2.   The cost of financing
3.   Expected interest rate changes
4.   Shape of the yield curve

The larger are predicted sales in the next period of a particular security or all securities, the larger will be the inventory held in that or all securities. Dealers can sell securities they do not have by quickly purchasing the security elsewhere or by selling short and borrowing the security until it is purchased, but these strategies involve greater risks and costs.

The securities held in inventory must be financed. Banks typically provide funds for their trading departments at a price. The price varies from bank to bank but is generally at or close to the daily federal funds rate. While held in inventory, securities yield a return to the bank. The difference between the market return on a security and the cost of financing paid by the bank or the trading department is referred to as the carry. The carry may be either positive or negative depending on the shape of the yield curve (term structure of interest rates). If the yield curve is upward sloping, so that yields on longer-maturity bonds are higher than those on shorter-maturity bonds, the carry on most Treasury securities tends to be positive and to become bigger with increases in maturity. If the yield curve is downward sloping, the carry on some of the securities will be negative and become more negative the longer the maturity.

The decision as to how much inventory to hold is also dependent on the direction and magnitude of expected movements of interest rates. If rates are expected to decline (so that bond prices will rise), dealers will build up their positions relative to expected trading volume. Conversely, if rates are expected to increase, dealers will run down inventories. Because changes in rates affect the prices of longer-term securities more than short-term securities, interest rate expectations will also affect the maturity composition of inventories.

Lastly, some dealers will take into account the shape of the yield curve. If the yield curve is upward sloping, they will buy longer-term securities, hold them as their maturities become shorter and their yields lower, and then sell them before maturity at the lower yield. This strategy is referred to as riding the yield curve. The profit potential from this strategy is greater the more steeply upward sloping the yield curve and the closer the maturities of the securities are to the point on the yield curve at which the slope changes the most.

In sum, dealers will hold greater overall inventories:

1. The greater are expected sales
2. The lower is the cost of financing and the more positive the carry
3. The more interest rates are expected to decline
4. The more positively sloped is the yield curve

These factors will also affect the maturity composition of the inventory. The last two factors tend to entail more risk than the first two. If interest rates move contrary to expectations or the yield curve becomes less positively sloped (or even negatively sloped), dealers may experience losses on their inventories. In recent years, dealers have made increasing use of the futures market to hedge their positions and to reduce their exposure to interest rate risk.

Underwriting and Distributing Municipal Securities

National banks have been permitted to underwrite and distribute debt issues of state and local governments collateralized directly or indirectly by the full faith and credit of the issuer (general obligation, or GO bonds) since the early 1900s and state-chartered banks in most states even longer. Banks are permitted to underwrite only a limited number of municipal revenue bonds.

Unlike many other types of securities activities, commercial banks of all sizes underwrite some municipal bonds, particularly the new issues of the government units in areas in which the banks are located. Most general obligation bonds are sold by the issuer to the underwriter by competitive bid, although some are sold by negotiation in which the underwriter is selected by the issuer before the sale. Most revenue bonds are sold by negotiation. In competitive bids, the issuer awards all the bonds to the lowest bidder. The profit to the underwriter comes from selling the bonds to investors at higher prices. In negotiated sales, the price paid to the issuer by the underwriter and frequently also the underwriter spread, or difference between the underwriter's purchase price and intended reoffering price, are prearranged through negotiation, although the issue price reflects expected market conditions.

New municipal bond issues are typically sold to underwriters in serial form. A serial issue is a package of bonds containing individual bonds having different maturities. Serial issues may contain bonds with as few as two different maturities or as many as 50. The package is sold to an underwriter as a unit at one price. The underwriter unbundles the package and reoffers each maturity individually to investors. The bonds are generally resold before their issue date so that inventories need not be financed.

Frequently, the dollar size of a new issue is too large for any one underwriter to handle singly, both in terms of the risk of not being able to resell the bonds at the expected prices (thus not realizing the target spread) and in terms of the ability to market the bonds to investors. For such issues, individual underwriting firms join together in temporary syndicates to bid or negotiate for particular issues. The syndicates frequently include both commercial banks and investment banks. The size of the syndicate may vary from two firms for small issues to over 50 firms for very large issues of nationally recognized issuers.

The ability to distribute the issue successfully depends in part on the familiarity of the investors with the issuer. Thus, small issuers appeal primarily to local investors and progressively larger issuers to progressively more distant investors. The largest issues have national markets. Individual underwriting firms join different syndicates for different issues, although they typically remain in the same syndicate for all issues of the same issuer. Within the syndicate, the bidding and pricing strategies as well as any origination assistance to the issuer are provided by one or more firms that also took the lead in organizing the syndicate. These firms are referred to as managers, and their names appear first and in bold print on any advertisements—called tombstones—of the sale. Managers are reimbursed extra from the syndicate for their services. The other syndicate members share in any profits proportionately both to the underwriting liability they assume and to the amount of bonds they sell.

Commercial banks as a whole underwrite about 50% of the total dollar volume of GO municipal bonds, although the percentage appears to have been declining in recent years. Some analysts attribute banks' declining share of the GO market to their inability to deal in municipal revenue bonds and thus to be in a position to offer customers a full line of tax-exempt securities.

Banks are permitted to underwrite and distribute only those municipal revenue bonds—bonds collateralized solely by the revenues derived from the capital project financed by the bonds—that are issued for housing, dormitory, or university purposes. Commercial banks had been prohibited from underwriting and distributing any revenue bonds by the Glass-Steagall Act. Until then, national banks had been permitted to underwrite and distribute all municipal revenue bonds since about 1900 and most state-chartered banks even longer. In those days, revenue bonds accounted for a very small proportion of total new municipal bonds issued. In the 1930s, the dollar amount of revenue bonds accounted for only an estimated 10% of total new municipal issues. Since 1960, however, revenue bonds have accounted for progressively larger percentages of total new municipal issues. By 1982, these bonds accounted for three-quarters of the total dollar volume, spurred by an increasing reluctance by taxpayers to authorize generalize obligation bonds financed by general taxes, the increasing use of user costs to finance projects, and the growing tendency of local governments to enter into services previously provided by the private sector and amenable to similar methods of financing.

The Housing and Urban Development Act of 1968 permitted commercial banks to underwrite and distribute municipal revenue bonds issued for housing, dormitory, and university purposes. In 1982, these accounted for almost 50% of the dollar volume of all new municipal revenue issues, although they have accounted for considerably smaller percentages in other years.

Trading Futures Contracts

Banks may trade futures contracts for securities and precious metals that they are permitted to trade on the cash or spot markets. They may also furnish customers with advice in connection with these transactions. Futures contracts are contracts for the delivery of a security or asset at a specific date in the future at a fixed price determined today. Because payment for a contact typically occurs concurrent with delivery, payment is also deferred. Futures trading occurs on organized futures exchanges according to the rules and regulations of the exchange. Contracting for future delivery may also be made directly between two parties according to their own negotiated rules on the forward market. These contracts are referred to as forward contracts. Banks have long operated in a number of forward markets, notably foreign currencies. Futures contracts may be traded for the bank's own account and for customers. Bank trading is permitted in futures contracts for gold, foreign currencies, Treasury securities, certificates of deposit, and other contracts on futures exchanges for securities in which banks are permitted to trade on the spot market. Banks typically become members of futures exchanges and trade directly, although they could conduct such transactions through other dealers as brokers. The trading entity must be approved by and registered with the Commodity Futures Trading Commission as a Futures Commission Merchant (FCM) and be subject to its regulation. The trading personnel must be registered representatives.

Banks have been permitted to trade futures contracts for customers only since 1982. In that year, the Board of Governors of the Federal Reserve (hereinafter Federal Reserve Board) permitted J. P. Morgan & Company, the parent holding company of the Morgan Guaranty Trust Company, to organize a futures trading affiliate, and the Comptroller of the Currency authorized the North Carolina National Bank to establish a futures trading subsidiary of the bank. The Commodity Futures Trading Commission gave approval to these units to begin trading shortly thereafter. Since then, FCMs have been organized by other banks, and in 1983 the Federal Reserve Board approved futures commission merchants as a generally permissible activity to bank holding companies under Regulation Y.

Trust Investments

Commercial banks may provide trust services either as part of the bank or as a subsidiary of itself or its parent holding company. Trust customers encompass a wide range including individuals, pension programs of business firms, nonprofit organizations, and labor unions, endowment funds, such as universities and hospitals, and so on. At year-end 1982, 4,041 commercial banks operated trust departments and managed assets totaling $689 billion.

As a fiduciary, the bank may purchase and sell any type of security at the request of the customer or, with the approval of the customer, at its own discretion. At first, banks managed each trust account separately. But over time, it became evident that significant cost savings were possible, particularly for smaller trusts, if the accounts were pooled for investment purposes and managed as larger common funds with the same investment objectives. Commingling of trust accounts for such purposes has been permitted as long as the commingling is not used to solicit accounts for primarily investment purposes rather than for the fiduciary services generally associated with a trust account. That is, banks may pool trust accounts as long as the service is sold to customers primarily as a fiduciary trust service and not as an investment service. The later activity was defined first by the Federal Reserve Board and then, over the objection of the Comptroller of the Currency, by the U.S. Supreme Court to represent the sale of securities in mutual funds, which is prohibited by the Glass-Steagall Act.[4] (The question of bank selling of mutual funds is addressed later in this chapter.)

In a recent ruling, the Comptroller permitted Citibank to invest funds in separate Individual Retirement Accounts (IRAs) collectively in common trust funds managed by the bank. Because of the retirement and pension characteristics of IRAs, Citibank and the Comptroller consider the management of these accounts as primarily fiduciary services rather than investment services and thus permissible within the Supreme Court's interpretation of the Glass-Steagall Act.[5] This interpretation has been challenged in the courts by the Investment Company Institute, the trade association for investment companies and mutual funds. Citibank offers three accounts—an equity fund, an income fund, and a money market fund. These funds are registered with the Securities and Exchange Commission. Since then, a number of other national banks have filed registration statements to offer similar accounts. The FDIC has proposed permitting banks under its primary jurisdiction to offer money market–type mutual funds (see FDIC, 1983).

Private Placements

Private placements represent the sale of a new securities issue directly by the issuer to one large investor or a small group of them. This process is often cheaper than public underwriting, since it bypasses some or all of the middlemen, does not require SEC registration, and can be completed quickly. Registration is waived because large investors are presumed to be sufficiently knowledgeable and informed about the issue, from their own investigations as well as their negotiations with the issuer, and to be aware of the risks involved. Security issuers often use the services of an intermediary to help design the security, locate promising investors, and negotiate financing terms. Larger banks have increasingly offered this service at a fee. A 1977 survey found that only some 30 large banks offered private placement services, however, and the dollar amount of such placements by these banks accounted for less than 10% of total private placements (see Board of Governors, 1977, and Comptroller, FDIC, and Board of Governors, 1978). Both the Federal Reserve Board and the Comptroller of the Currency have ruled this activity permissible within Glass-Steagall as the banks do not purchase the securities for their own accounts. Banks increased their activity in placing commercial paper after the U.S. Supreme Court ruling in mid-1984 that such paper was not exempt from the Glass-Steagall prohibitions against underwriting and dealing in securities (see section on nonpermitted securities activities).

Sponsoring Closed-End Investment Funds

Closed-end investment companies sell shares to investors and use the funds raised to purchase investment securities for their own portfolios. The shares of investment companies are generally less risky for investors than those of the individual firms in which the fund invests because the fund can reduce risk through both diversification (by pooling funds) and professional management. Closed-end funds issue shares when they are first organized and may issue additional shares at times thereafter. After initial issue, a fund's shares may be traded by individual investors on the secondary market, but the fund may not repurchase its own shares until liquidation. Thus closed-end funds differ from open-end (or mutual) funds, which stand ready to repurchase their outstanding shares at any time at their net asset value and also to issue additional shares at any time at this price upon demand. Because of the limited issuance of these funds, the courts have ruled that closed-end funds are not principally engaged in the issuance or public sale of securities and the management of such funds is not an activity that is prohibited commercial banks by Section 20 of the Glass-Steagall Act. In 1972, the Federal Reserve Board authorized nonbank affiliates of bank holding companies to sponsor and manage closed-end funds subject to its Regulation Y (see *Federal Reserve Bulletin,* February 1972, pp. 149–151). In 1981, the courts upheld this interpretation (see Pitt et al., 1983).

Investment Advice

Commercial banks themselves and their holding company affiliates may offer economic, financial, and investment advice, management, and counseling to a wide range of clients including open-end (mutual) investment companies, closed-end investment companies (including those sponsored by the bank), mortgage or real estate trusts, households, business firms, and state and local governments. Such services may include assisting issuers of securities to design and market new issues (short of actual underwriting and distribution), economic forecasts, and portfolio and budgeting assistance. Banks charge fees for such services. Recently, some banks have established cooperative undertakings with mutual fund sponsors to create and market "private label" mutual funds to bank customers. The bank would provide the fund with initial customer contact. The fund sponsor would sell and repurchase the securities and either the bank or the sponsor would manage and advise the fund. The two partners share the revenues. Most of the revenues are derived from managing the fund. The first major bank to engage in such an arrangement for a fund marketed to the general public was Security Pacific, which arranged with the Dreyfus Fund to create, underwrite, market, and deal in a family of six no-load mutual funds carrying the name Pacific Horizon. (The funds may not carry the bank's name.)

Security Mergers and Acquisitions

Banks have always been permitted to advise client firms on mergers and acquisitions. This service includes searches for candidate firms having the characteristics desired by a client, recommendations on the advisability of a particular merger or acquisition, development of financial strategies, an intermediary role between merging companies, and advice on how to prevent a merger or acquisition with an unwanted suitor. Banks are in a favorable position to furnish such advice because of their close contacts with business customers to whom they provide credit and other services. Large, international banks also are favorably positioned to assist in international acquisitions, particularly in those countries in which they have a presence.

The fee for advising on mergers and acquisitions is based on the value of the assets involved. A typical fee schedule is referred to as the "Lehman formula," used by the investment banking firm of Lehman Brothers Kuhn Loeb. It entails 5% of the first $1 million of assets involved, 4% of the next $1 million, 3% of the third million, 2% of the fourth million, and 1% of the remainder (see McMurray, 1983).

Security Brokerage Activities

The role of commercial banks in providing brokerage services is one of the most controversial and rapidly changing areas. Until the enactment of the Glass-Steagall Act, security trading as an agent (broker) and as a principal were generally treated alike. But Glass-Steagall distinguished between the two. Section 16 of the act states that for national banks: "The business of dealing in securities and stock by the association shall be limited to purchasing and selling such securities and stock without recourse, solely upon the order and for the account of customers, and in no case for its own account, and the association shall not underwrite any issue of securities and stock." There are a number of provisions permitting dealing in debt securities backed by the full faith and credit of the federal, state, and local governments—and in some municipal revenue bonds. As stated in note 5, these restrictions are made applicable to banks that are members of the Federal Reserve System through another section of the act. Bank powers to underwrite securities and to deal in securities as principals have been reviewed earlier. Unlike dealers, brokers do not buy and sell for their own account but receive commissions from trades between buyers and sellers arranged through their assistance. Brokerage is a pure agency relationship. Until recently, banks regarded transacting as agent as a convenience service provided to good customers. It was not actively publicized or promoted. Indeed, a ruling by the Comptroller of the Currency in 1936 stated that brokerage-type services had to be provided at cost without profit and that the customer must already have had a nonsecurities relationship with the bank. In 1948, the Comptroller liberalized the restriction against profits, and it was removed altogether in 1957 (see Pitt et al., 1983).

The major effort by banks to engage in brokerage began in 1981, when BankAmerica Corporation applied to the Board of Governors to acquire the Charles Schwab Corporation and operate it as a nonbank affiliate. Schwab was the largest "discount" broker in the country. It traded securities at low commissions, extended margin credit, and provided custodial services. Schwab did not offer investment advice, its salespersons were paid a straight salary and did not receive commissions, and customers did not have a personal broker. Although headquartered in San Francisco, the firm had a number of branch offices throughout the country. Through the use of a toll-free telephone number and aggressive advertising and pricing, Schwab solicited customers nationwide.

Before the Federal Reserve could act on this application, Security Pacific National Bank (Los Angeles) announced a cooperative venture with the Fidelity Group, a large sponsor of mutual funds and a registered dealer–

broker firm, in which Fidelity would execute and clear trades and maintain accounts for Security's customers on a contract basis. Shortly thereafter, Security Pacific received permission from the Comptroller of the Currency first to establish a de novo subsidiary of the bank itself to provide brokerage services, then to purchase an established discount broker and operate it as an affiliate of the bank, and finally to form a subsidiary to provide "back-office" brokerage support to other banks.[6] In January 1983, the Federal Reserve Board approved BankAmerica's application to purchase Schwab and, later in the year, added brokerage services as an activity permitted all bank holding companies under Regulation Y. The authority of commercial banks to solicit retail security brokerage business from the general public was challenged in the courts by the Securities Industry Association, but was upheld by the U.S. Supreme Court in 1984.

Brokerage services can also be offered by a bank without establishing a subsidiary. Although such an arrangement restricts the service to bank locations, it avoids the need to register as a broker with the Securities and Exchange Commission. The Securities Exchange Act of 1934 requires that all security brokers and dealers register with the commission but exempts commercial banks. Brokerage subsidiaries of a bank or a bank holding company are not exempt. Registration involves compliance with SEC regulations for the protection of investors and oversight of operations and practices by both the commission and designated self-regulatory organizations of the national security exchanges (on which the broker–dealer trades) and the National Association of Security Dealers (NASD). The regulations and oversight focus on advertising; customer solicitation; truthfulness of promotional materials and reports; disclosure of relevant information concerning both the broker–dealer and the securities traded; the character, supervision, and competency of employees, including the establishment of qualification requirements evidenced by training, experience, and examination; the power to revoke registration and suspend violators from securities participation; record-keeping requirements, examination, inspection, and internal controls; the adequacy of execution and confirmation of orders; minimum bonding requirements; and customer protection against insolvency, including minimum capital requirements. Although exempt from direct SEC supervision, brokerage activities of a bank itself are supervised by the bank regulatory agency having primary jurisdiction and are subject to similar regulations. In November 1983, the Securities and Exchange Commission proposed that because bank brokerage services have expanded greatly since the exemption was initially granted and banks now actively solicit public business, they should be required to register with the SEC and be subject to its jurisdiction even if the activity is one conducted jointly with an already-registered broker–

dealer (see *Federal Register* 1983; U.S. Senate, 1977; and Greene et al., 1983).

Banks have moved actively into brokerage business in all four basic forms—through the bank itself, through an affiliate of the bank, through an affiliate of bank holding company, and jointly with an established broker–dealer firm. By year-end 1983, some 2,000 banks were offering brokerage services, mostly through cooperative arrangements with nonbank broker–dealers.

Precisely what kinds of brokerage services may be provided by national and state-chartered Federal Reserve member banks is unclear, particularly since the approvals of these services through affiliates until mid-1983 were on a case-by-case basis rather than by general regulation. Almost all bank brokerage commission fees are below those charged by full-service brokers for comparable transactions and are similar to those of nonbank discount brokers. While generally this reflects the fewer services bundled into the package sold, not all bank brokerage services or nonbank discount brokers offer the same package. Some offer only trading services. Other add custodial services, a designated "personal" salesperson, margin credit, investment advice, 24-hour service, newsletters, portfolio analyses, and insolvency insurance. As a result, prices and "discounts" vary. As noted, Schwab traditionally has not offered advice nor a personal broker, nor has it paid its brokers a volume-related commission. This appeared in BankAmerica's application and became the service approved by the Federal Reserve Board. Obviously, these characteristics need not apply to all brokerage services approved. For example, Security Pacific's application to the Comptroller for a de novo security brokerage affiliate did not address the form of compensation to salespersons or whether customers would receive a personal salesperson. The Federal Reserve Board has indicated that it is prepared to consider investment advice and other services. In late 1983, the Comptroller permitted a bank to establish a subsidiary to provide investment advice to its customers, including buy and sell advice on individual securities and an investment advisory letter (see *American Banker,* 1983). The subsidiary will be registered under the Investment Advisers Act with the SEC. The bank already had a discount brokerage subsidiary. Although the two subsidiaries will be separate, their activities will be coordinated and security advice by the advisory service will be offered broker customers on a nonexclusive basis. The Securities Industry Association is challenging this ruling.

Banks that prefer to offer brokerage services in conjunction with a registered nonbank broker can do so in a number of ways (see Smith, 1983). Because discount brokerage services involve relatively large fixed costs and relatively small variable costs, the primary consideration in selecting an arrangement is expected sales volume. In low-volume plans, the broker provides most of the services. The bank incurs little cost. It publicizes the service, opens new accounts, receives payment from customers for security sales as an agent for the broker, and may provide custodial services. The broker typically furnishes the bank customers with an 800 telephone number; answers inquiries; accepts orders; executes; clears and confirms trades; finances margin credit; maintains customer records; and prepares and mails periodic statements. The bank receives a small percentage of the commissions generated by its customers' transactions. The commission fee schedule for the customer is determined by the brokerage firm.

In higher-volume plans, the bank provides more of the services, incurs more of the costs, and keeps more of the revenues generated. The bank typically markets the service and provides all customer contact, including opening and maintaining accounts, answering inquiries, accepting orders, receiving and making payments, providing margin credit, providing custodial services, confirming trades, and mailing periodic statements. The bank also determines the customer commission fee schedule. The broker basically executes and clears trades upon order of the bank, for which it is paid either a fixed fee per transaction or a percentage of the commissions. Because all customer contact is with the bank and the statements received have only the bank's name, the broker is effectively an invisible partner. Alternative plans falling between these two extremes may be negotiated between the bank and the nonbank broker. A growing number of nonbank brokers are providing these services for commercial banks.

Banks that operate their own broker subsidiary generally do not own a seat on security exchanges and contract with a firm that does to execute the transactions and frequently also to clear the securities. Whether banks that offer brokerage services in conjunction with a registered broker–dealer will be required to register with the SEC if the SEC's proposed rules are adopted is likely to depend on the extent of involvement in arranging the transactions and in custodial services. The greater the involvement, the more likely the requirement to register.

As noted earlier, both the FDIC and the FHLBB have ruled that institutions under their direct regulatory jurisdiction are not subject to Glass-Steagall and thus may operate in a wide array of securities activities, including more complete broker–dealer operations. In 1982, the FDIC issued proposed rules covering permissible securities activities. Comments were received and the proposal modified in 1983, but (as of year-end 1983) it had not yet been issued in final form (see FDIC, 1983). To that date, no commercial bank has applied to the FDIC for these powers. This is in part because many banks conduct their new securities activities through holding company affiliates, which are subject to Federal Reserve juris-diction and thus indirectly to the restrictions of Glass-Steagall. It is also in part because only smaller banks that provide fewer securities activities are under the sole jurisdiction of the FDIC, and their activities must still conform to state laws that, on the whole, prohibit a wide range of securities activities. The FHLBB has approved a number of full-service broker op-erations, including dealer activities, to affiliates of savings and loan as-sociation service corporations, which in turn are affiliates of S&Ls or S&L holding companies and have broader authority than S&Ls. The larg-est of these is INVEST, a separate full-service securities firm cooperatively owned through their service corporations by some 100 savings and loan associations.

Agency Investment Plans

Banks have traditionally offered on an agency basis a variety of security investment plans, generally through their trust departments. In automatic investment services (AIS), a prearranged amount approved by the cus-tomer is deducted regularly (e.g., monthly) from a participating customer's account. The bank prepares a list of a limited number of large, well-known firms in which the bank is willing to make share purchases, but individual recommendations are not made. The customer selects the company and amount of periodic purchases and becomes the sole owner of the securities. The customer benefits from any lower brokerage fee the bank pays from purchasing the stocks in larger quantities. The bank profits from higher brokerage activity or shares in the brokerage commissions directed at other brokers.

Banks also offer dividend reinvestment plans. Basically, these plans provide for the automatic reinvestment of all or part of the dividends re-ceived by customers in additional shares of the paying firms. The attraction of these plans is that customers may share in any commission cost savings the bank may experience through pooling funds and purchasing in larger quantities. In addition, some firms offer to sell shares purchased through dividend programs at discounts from current market value.

The oldest dividend reinvestment plans involve the establishment of a custodial account, placing customers' securities in the account, and or-dering the bank to reinvest a designated percentage of the dividends of the paying corporation in additional shares of that firm. More recently, banks have established automatic reinvestment dividend plans with cor-porations for whom they provide other securities services, such as dividend paying agent or transfer agent. Shareholders in these firms, customers or not, can arrange to have all or part of the dividends on their holdings of the particular firm to be sent to the bank for reinvestment in shares of these firms. In 1982, Congress exempted dividends paid by public utilities from federal income taxes up to $750 annually per taxpayer if reinvested in the shares of the paying utility. Banks provide this service for utility firms who are their customers. The bank again profits from increased brokerage activity, shares in the brokerage activity directed to other brokers, or may be paid a fee by the firms whose dividends are reinvested.

Security Swaps

The higher rate of price inflation in recent years was accompanied by higher and more volatile rates of interest. As a result, many lenders became increasingly reluctant to commit funds for long periods of time at fixed rates of interest. For their part, many borrowers became reluctant to accept an interest rate that could increase during the term of the loan, that is, variable- or floating-rate securities. Thus, frequently mismatches occur where lenders and borrowers find themselves with securities they do not prefer. Some financial intermediaries have found it profitable to seek out such "discontented" market participants and to assist them in swapping their securities for more suitable securities. As long as the intermediary bank does not buy or sell the securities for its own account but acts solely as an agent charging a commission, such assistance is a permissible activity for commercial banks.

NONPERMITTED SECURITIES ACTIVITIES

Most commercial banks are not permitted to engage either directly or through holding company affiliates in securities activities currently considered to be banned by the Glass-Steagall Act, by the Bank Holding Company Act (for not being "so closely related to banking or managing or controlling banks as to be a proper incident thereto"), or by state provisions. The clearest prohibition is against stock in almost all activities but investment as a fiduciary or in sponsored closed-end funds and the purchase and sale as an agent on commission for customers. With only infrequent exceptions, such as investment in venture capital, commercial banks are prohibited from investing in corporate stock for their own account, from underwriting and distributing new stock issues, and from trading in stock as principals. Nor may they sell shares directly in mutual funds or pooled trust funds in which fiduciary services are not the major component.

Similar prohibitions apply to corporate debt, including commercial paper, but banks are permitted to invest in investment-grade corporate bonds and notes, including convertible bonds for their own portfolio, and may underwrite, distribute, and deal as principals in bankers' acceptances and large-denomination commercial paper. Banks may also not underwrite, distribute, or trade in municipal revenue bonds, except those issued for housing, dormitory, or university purposes.

As a result of a June 1984 decision by the U.S. Supreme Court, commercial banks may not underwrite and deal in third-party commercial paper (unsecured short-term promissory notes issued by large business firms and typically having initial maturities less than nine months in order to be exempt from registration with the Securities and Exchange Commission). In its decision, the Court held that commercial paper is a "security" under Glass-Steagall. Although commercial banks are major investors in commercial paper, they apparently did not underwrite or distribute such paper on the primary market nor trade it in on the secondary market in significant volume until 1978. In that year, the Bankers Trust Company began to deal in commercial paper of third parties. This activity was challenged as a Glass-Steagall violation. Subsequently, the Federal Reserve Board (in this instance, as the regulator of state member banks such as Bankers Trust) reaffirmed its position that third-party sales of commercial paper were permissable within Glass-Steagall because commercial paper was not a "security" (see Board of Governors, June 28, 1979). A.G. Becker, a large investment banking firm, then brought suit against the Federal Reserve Board. In 1981 a district court upheld Becker's challenge, ruling that commercial paper was a security as defined in the Glass-Steagall Act and Bankers Trust's activities were therefore nonpermissible. The Federal Reserve Board appealed this decision, and in 1982 a court of appeals reversed the lower court's decision, ruling that commercial paper closely resembled a bank business loan and was not a security under Glass-Steagall. The appeals court noted, however, that its ruling applied only to large-denomination commercial paper sold to large, informed investors and that is might not be equally applicable to smaller-denomination paper sold to the general public. In response, the Federal Reserve Board promulgated specific regulations covering commercial banks dealing in commercial paper (see Board of Governors, 1981, and Pitt et al., 1983). It should be noted that the 1984 Supreme Court decision did not affect the status of CDs or bankers' acceptances, which are not considered securities under Glass-Steagall. Commercial banks have long traded bankers' acceptances (one of the oldest financial instruments) and have traded third-party CDs almost since their inception in the early 1960s.

Under Section 20 of the Glass-Steagall Act, Federal Reserve member banks also may not be affiliated with firms "engaged principally in the issue, flotation, underwriting, public sale or distribution at wholesale or retail or through syndicate participation of stocks, bonds, debentures, notes or other securities." Section 32 of the act prohibits an officer, director, or employee of a firm "primarily engaged" in these activities to be an officer, director, or employee of a Fed member bank. But recent interpretations of these sections by the Comptroller of the Currency and the FDIC (over the objections of the Federal Reserve) have permitted investment companies, such as Dreyfus, and mutual fund advisers and investment banking firms, such as J. & W. Seligman, to acquire commercial banks. The two agencies have been assisted in implementing these rulings by a provision in the Bank Holding Company Act of 1970 that defines a commercial bank for purposes of Federal Reserve jurisdiction over bank holding company affiliates as a bank "which (1) accepts deposits that the depositor has a legal right to withdraw on demand, and (2) engages in the business of making commercial loans." To avoid Federal Reserve jurisdiction, the applicant banks proposed to discontinue either offering demand deposits or making commercial loans. These banks are referred to as "nonbank banks."[7] In addition, the Comptroller has also ruled recently that income obtained by an investment firm from advising or managing mutual funds is not income from the sale of securities in determining whether these firms are primarily or principally engaged in the sale of securities. Because advising is the major activity and source of income for most investment firms and advisers do not control mutual funds, these firms may own national banks.[8] Investment banks and mutual funds, as well as other financial and non-financial firms not eligible to combine with commercial banks, affilate with nonbank banks for a number of reasons, including access to federally insured time deposits (particularly MMDAs, which are otherwise similar to money market funds), demand deposits, the national payments clearing system, and wider trust powers.

The FDIC has proposed regulations that would permit banks that it supervises to underwrite investment quality corporate debt and equity, as well as mutual funds that invest exclusively in such securities. It also proposes to permit these banks to underwrite all securities, including corporate equities and mutual funds, on a best effort basis in which the bank purchases neither all nor the unsold securities for its own accounts (see FDIC, 1983).

Until mid-1983, the Federal Home Loan Bank Board had also approved the affiliation of both investment banking firms and investment companies with savings and loan associations on the basis that the Glass-Steagall Act does not apply to savings and loan associations. At that time, it adopted a moratorium on further applications for such combinations.

In addition, banks have moved aggressively to participate in cooperative ventures in which the apparently prohibited activity is undertaken by another, independent firm and the revenues are split. Thus, for example, some banks entered the retail brokerage business in this way when the legitimacy of this activity was still in doubt and maintained this arrangement afterwards as a matter of efficiency. As stated earlier, banks have recently entered into such arrangements with mutual fund sponsors. A bank provides its customer base and investment advice, the sponsor sells the "private label" mutual fund, and the two share in the revenues. The Comptroller has recently ruled that national banks may lease space on bank floors, including their public lobbies, on an arm's-length basis to firms that engage in activities prohibited the bank itself (such as full-service security brokerage and dealer activities, insurance, and real estate) and collect rental fees based on a percentage of the firm's gross revenues and income from that activity at that location. The leased space does not have to be separated from the bank's space by walls, although some indication of separate entities must be provided.

ARGUMENTS FOR AND AGAINST COMMERCIAL BANK PARTICIPATION IN SECURITIES ACTIVITIES

The arguments for and against liberalizing commercial bank activities in the securities markets can be grouped under four headings: competition, economies of scale and scope, bank stability, and conflicts of interest.[9]

Competition

Banks have argued that their failure to provide customers with full-service investment banking puts them at a competitive disadvantage with nonbank security dealers. Those who favor increased commercial bank participation in securities activities further contend that because investment banks have expanded into some traditional commercial bank areas, it is only fair to permit commercial banks to retaliate and invade some traditional investment bank areas. They say also that bank entry would increase the number of firms, thereby enhancing competition and improving the quality of service to seller (borrower) and buyer (investor) alike. This would be particularly true for the underwriting of municipal revenue bonds and corporate securities issued by smaller, regional firms. Commercial banks are located in almost every community and take a close interest in the financial welfare of the community. Many smaller cities do not have offices of investment banking houses. And when they do, they are few in number and mostly likely are retail branches of firms headquartered elsewhere, frequently in other states. Commercial banks would provide alternative, local bidders. Larger banks would also provide better-capitalized competition for more highly leveraged large investment bankers.

A number of studies have provided evidence that bank participation makes a difference in the prices paid on new issues. (For a review of the arguments, see Bierwag et al., 1984.) As noted earlier, commercial banks may bid on new municipal GO bonds but on a restricted number of new municipal revenue bonds. These studies show that on average, new GO bonds have received more bids and have sold at lower interest rates than did revenue bonds with the same credit rating. They conclude that permitting banks to bid on new revenue issues would increase the number of bids and lower the interest yields, thereby providing significant cost savings to state and local governments. Similar savings would accrue to private corporations in the underwriting of their new securities and to individuals and institutions in the sale of newly issued securities on the primary market as well as outstanding securities on the secondary market.

Opponents of greater bank participation in the securities markets argue that commercial banks have an unfair advantage over investment banks. They have more intimate knowledge of the financial conditions of many firms and government units, acquired in the process of providing lending and deposit services to these customers; they have superior access to low-cost funds through their deposit activities and the discount window at the Federal Reserve; and they have a ready, "captive" market for the securities they underwrite regardless of the price in their own portfolios, in those of their correspondent banks, and in those of their trust accounts. As a result, according to opponents, although bank entry may intensify competition in the short run, in the longer run it would lead to the failure and exit of many investment banks and result in a lower number of firms and reduced competition. As evidence of the importance of these advantages, the opponents point to the very rapid increase in the percentage of new securities underwritten by the commercial banks in the late 1920s, after national banks had been given approval to engage in these activities, and to their eventual domination of this market shortly before the enactment of the Glass-Steagall Act.

Those opposing greater securities powers for commercial banks are not impressed by the studies claiming that interest rates would be lowered on municipal revenue bonds if commercial banks could bid on them. They assert researchers did not hold enough other things constant. General obligation bonds of a given credit rating are not equivalent in default risk to revenue bonds of the same credit rating. The ratings are relative for each class of bonds. Generally, an Aa-rated revenue bond has a greater risk of default than an Aa-rated GO bond. Permitting banks to underwrite revenue bonds would not transform them magically into GO bonds of the same rating. As a result, the number of overall bids and interest rates would remain unchanged; commercial banks might simply take a share of the market from investment banks.

The opponents of greater powers for banks argue that because of the all-pervasive nature of money, concentration in the financial markets is even more undesirable than concentration in other markets. They argue that less than 2% of the total number of commercial banks hold fully one-half of all bank deposits, and 2% of all banks hold two-thirds of the dollar amount of assets held in bank trust accounts (see Girton, 1981). If commercial banks drive investments banks out of business, concentration in all financial services would be greatly increased. The evidence from countries in which commercial and investment banking are fully integrated suggests such higher degrees of concentration. In addition, in some countries, banks have acquired significantly greater political power as well as economic power.

Moreover, opponents say that bank entry may not even increase competition in the short run. Instead of entering the new lines of activity as separate entities (de novo), commercial banks may combine in ownership or in bidding (in the form of a temporary syndicate) with investment banks. As evidence of this, opponents note that the percentage of the dollar volume of new municipal GO bonds, on which both commercial and investment banks may bid, that is underwritten by the largest firms is only a little smaller than that for municipal revenue bonds, on which generally only investment banks may bid. Commercial banks frequently combine with investment banks in syndicates in submitting bids on GO bonds. It may be argued, however, that if commercial banks were authorized to bid on all municipal revenue bonds, they would be more willing to incur the heavy start-up costs required to have their own marketing and distribution system and more apt to increase the number of bidding syndicates.

Finally, opponents argue that commercial banks have other unfair advantages over investment banks. Deposits provide them with an artificially low cost of funds, both because they are insured by a federal government agency and because (until recently) their funding costs were in part held down by ceilings. By contrast, investment banks must obtain many of their funds through bank loans, on which banks charge a markup over their own costs. In addition, commercial banks may deduct most interest costs for tax purposes regardless of whether they own tax-exempt municipal bonds in their portfolios, whereas investment banks may not deduct interest on funds borrowed to purchase municipal securities.

Economies of Scale and Scope

Advocates of expanded commercial bank powers argue that corporate underwriting, brokerage, and complete money management services are not significantly different from many of the financial services currently offered by commercial banks. Commercial banks already possess trained and qualified personnel and much of the capital equipment necessary for these activities. Adding the new services would result in lower average costs to consumers through economies of scale and scope. Moreover, the greater convenience that would be provided consumers by offering these services at some 55,000 commercial bank offices throughout the country would reduce their effective cost and increase the demand for these services further. Consumers would be able to satisfy all their financial needs at one place, and commercial banks could truly offer full-service banking (see Benston et al., 1982).

Opponents argue that significant economies and lower costs are unlikely to be realized. Personnel trained in lending activities or in underwriting government securities cannot be shifted readily to analyzing equities or underwriting corporate securities without considerable retraining. Investment banks are equipped to handle the total volume of underwriting and money management currently prohibited for commercial banks. Transfer of some of this business to commercial banks would leave investment banks with excess capacity. Any cost saving at commercial banks would be offset by higher costs at investment banks. To the extent that this makes investment banks less effective competitors, commercial banks would not be forced to pass through to their customers any economies they might realize.

Bank Stability

Commercial banks tend to have higher capital–asset ratios than do investment banks. Proponents of wider commercial bank securities powers argue that bank entry would strengthen the degree of competition in the new areas without weakening the commercial banks. Indeed, investment banks may be encouraged to augment their capital positions in order to match the aggressiveness of the commercial banks. This would decrease the likelihood of failure and increase the stability of the financial sector overall. Moreover, to the extent that the variability in investment banking earnings is not perfectly correlated with that in commercial banking, diversification and full-service investment banking could stabilize commercial bank earnings.

Not so, argue the opponents. The securities business is far more risky than most commercial banking activities, as reflected both in the variability of earnings and in the number of failures. As a result, current levels of bank capital appropriate for their current activities would be inadequate and the possibilities of bank failure increased. Moreover, whether investment banking is in fact riskier, many depositors perceive it as such, through its close association with the stock market. If commercial banks enter investment banking full scale, these depositors may lose confidence in their banks and withdraw some of their funds, FDIC insurance notwithstanding. Although this would be unlikely to lead to a crisis such as that in the 1930s, it would increase the degree of instability in the financial system and reduce the efficiency of the national payments system. Lastly, if a securities affiliate were to get into financial difficulties, it is argued that a commercial bank is likely to come to its rescue by providing resources in order to maintain the bank's reputation. Proponents of this line of reasoning point to this experience in the early 1930s and more recently (in the mid-1970s) when many banks came to the rescue of affiliated, and even nonaffiliated but similarly named, real estate investment trusts (REIT).

Conflict of Interest and Other Abuses

Opponents of permitting commercial banks increased power to participate in securities markets point to the abuses prior to enactment of the Glass-Steagall Act. Congressional hearings disclosed numerous instances of serious conflicts of interest and self-dealing. Many commercial banks were accused of having forced securities they had underwritten on their customers, their own trust departments, or their correspondent banks without regard to risk or the interests of the buyers (see Schotland, 1983, Peltzman, 1983, and the two contributions by Carosso, 1970). Many of these buyers suffered subsequent losses. At times, banks themselves purchased securities to prevent underwritings from being unsuccessful.

Some commercial banks were found to have paid large additional salaries and bonuses to their officers who were also officers of the banks' securities affiliates in the 1920s. One bank set aside 20% of its annual net earnings for this purpose. These payments, which were viewed to be excessive, reduced the capital base of these banks and increased their vulnerability to the financial crisis that occurred a short time later.

Congress also focused on other potential conflicts inherent in conducting commercial and investment banking under the same roof. Many of the banks' transactions were not independent or at "arm's length," that is, determined solely on their economic merits. Firms that agreed to use a bank's underwriting facilities might be provided credit on more liberal terms than otherwise, and firms that used other underwriters might be denied credit. Customers might be provided more liberal credit on securities underwritten by the bank, particularly on those the banks had difficulty selling. Good loan customers of the banks might be given preferential treatment in the underwriting and marketing of their securities. The sale of new equity securities might be recommended to capital-deficient loan customers, and the proceeds used to repay the loans and protect the quality of the banks' loan portfolio.

Moreover, in the conduct of their business, commercial banks are apt to acquire information not available to others about a customer that is important in evaluating the customer's financial prospects. Thus, for example, a bank may obtain information on a loan customer that would affect its decision to underwrite or invest in the customer's securities, or on a customer whose securities it had underwritten that would affect the bank's decision to extend credit to the firm. Such "inside" information may lead to both conflicts of interest between departments within the bank and a comparative advantage over firms that engage in only one of these activities.

Proponents of broader commercial bank securities powers concede that abuses did occur, but they contend that legislation enacted since the 1930s has greatly reduced the possibilities of a recurrence. Among the legislative actions, they cite the establishment of the Securities and Exchange Commission, numerous disclosure requirements and investor-protection provisions enacted by the Securities Act of 1933 and the Securities Exchange Act of 1934, the introduction of margin requirements on stock purchases, and the increased regulation of commercial banking affiliates by the Federal Reserve under the Bank Holding Company Act. In addition, bank regulatory agencies have been provided with additional powers to discover, halt, and penalize abusers. Bank examination practices have also been upgraded.

These proponents recognize that not all potentials for abuse can be eliminated from commercial banking any more than from any other industry. They argue that with proper protection, however, the public can obtain the benefits of greater bank participation in securities activities without exposure to the problems of the earlier era.

EFFECTIVENESS OF STATUTES AND REGULATIONS LIMITING SECURITIES ACTIVITIES OF COMMERCIAL BANKS

How effective have the statutes and regulations been since 1933 in restricting the securities activities of commercial banks? The answer appears to be that it depends on the time and the place. As indicated earlier, banks have increased their activities in securities functions significantly in recent years, without major or even many minor changes in legislation. The interpretation of the existing statutes by the courts and, in particular, by the regulators has changed, however. Perhaps even more important, the aggressiveness of commercial banks has also changed, intensifying and waning as economic conditions and competition have changed.

Until recently, on the whole banks were cautious in reentering the securities activities apparently forbidden them by the Glass-Steagall Act.

When decisions had to be made by regulators, the Comptroller of the Currency has tended to interpret the regulations more broadly and the Federal Reserve more narrowly. The Comptroller permitted banks to offer limited mutual funds through pooled trust funds after the Federal Reserve Board had ruled against such activity—before the ruling was overturned by the Supreme Court (Camp vs. the Investment Companies Institute, 1971). The Comptroller also authorized limited combinations with mutual funds and security dealers, over the objection of the Federal Reserve (Dreyfus National Bank and J. & W. Seligman Trust Company, N.A., 1983). The FDIC has ruled that the restrictive securities provisions of Glass-Steagall do not apply to insured banks that are not members of the Federal Reserve and has proposed rules for a broad range of securities activities (including underwriting) by such banks. In 1983, it approved insurance for state-chartered banks purchased by Prudential-Bache Securities (in Georgia) and organized de novo by the Fidelity Mutual Fund Group (New Hampshire) and E. F. Hutton (Delaware). These banks do not offer both demand deposits and business loans and therefore are not defined as banks under the Bank Holding Company Act for purposes of Federal Reserve supervision.

Even the Federal Reserve has occasionally provided broad interpretations extending banks' securities powers, such as those covering commercial paper and private placements. In many cases, however, the regulators did not act until forced to do so by the banks and even then acted narrowly solely on the description of the activity provided by the applicant bank. Thus, the scope of the permissible activity has been delineated only a step at a time and still does not appear to be completely specified. A good illustration of this sequence of events is bank entry into the general brokerage business.

The limitation on bank involvement in broad retail brokerage activities appears to have been mainly self-imposed, at least since 1970. It is doubtful that either the Comptroller or the Federal Reserve would have evaluated an application by Security Pacific or BankAmerica Corporation much differently in 1972 than in 1982. True, before May 1975 minimum retail brokerage commissions were fixed by the New York Stock Exchange, which would have made it harder for banks to capture market share from full-service investment banking firms. Nevertheless, banks did not lobby actively for the removal of this barrier. On the whole, banks did not find accommodation brokerage services very profitable. In 1976, Chemical Bank in New York began to offer broader brokerage services and advertised their availability (see U.S. Senate, 1977). The program did not appear to be as successful as expected, however, and was terminated not long afterwards.

The current restriction against banks combining brokerage services with investment advice to the same customers also appears to be primarily self-imposed. Because Schwab did not provide customers with investment advice before its proposed acquisition by BankAmerica, permission to offer such advice was not sought in the BankAmerica-Schwab application to the Federal Reserve, nor was it included in the Security Pacific application to the Comptroller to begin security brokerage services de novo. Nor is advice mentioned explicitly in Glass-Steagall as an activity that is prohibited—that is, a bank in dealing in securities and stock "shall be limited to purchasing and selling such securities and stock without recourse, solely upon the order, and for the account of, customers." Does providing advice on particular stocks imply that the bank and not the customer is taking the initiative in placing the order and thus produce a violation of the above clause? Is giving investment advice on brokerage activities "so closely related to banking or managing or controlling banks" that the Federal Reserve Board would not consider it an appropriate activity for affiliates of bank holding companies? The Board has already permitted bank holding company affiliates to engage in a wide range of investment advice to an equally wide range of bank customers. As noted, in 1983 the Comptroller permitted a national bank to have both a discount broker and an investment advisory affiliate. How significantly does this service differ from that of a full-service broker?

Similarly, the banks have complained that regulations did not permit them to offer a product competitive with Merrill Lynch's cash management accounts (CMA) until the authorization for money market deposit accounts (MMDAs) in December 1982. CMAs usually combined five separate services: consumer credit line, a credit card, security trading, a sweep money market account, and check writing—all incorporated in a single accounting statement. But commercial banks were always able to offer consumer credit lines and credit cards and to deal in federal and many municipal securities. As argued above, they also could have provided general retail brokerage services.

Before the authorization to offer MMDAs in December 1982, paying market rates of interest on deposits had been a severe problem for the commercial banks when market interest rates climbed above Regulation Q ceilings. The sale by banks of money market funds not subject to interest rate ceilings has been considered a sale of securities and therefore not permissible under the Glass-Steagall Act. It is clear, however, that the problem was due to Regulation Q, not to the Glass-Steagall Act, insofar as it prevented banks from offering a deposit account paying market interest rates. Yet, until recently, however, few banks (other than the largest) actively lobbied for the repeal of Regulation Q. In addition, banks could have provided customers with repurchase agreements. Although these are not insured, neither are money market mutual funds. Lastly, as a few banks did shortly before the authorization for MMDAs, they could have joined with money market funds in cooperative agreements to offer "private label" funds to their customers where investments were heavily in bank CDs.

Check-writing facilities are not a problem, of course. Indeed, money market funds use commercial banks for this service. But check writing on deposits paying market rates was difficult for banks themselves. They could have offered such services through cooperative ventures with money market funds, and it would have been technically possible for banks to tie check writing with repurchase agreements through some form of overdraft provision. Although the latter arrangements were likely to have encountered resistance from the Federal Reserve, they were not often tried. Had they been combined with earlier lobbying against Regulation Q, changes might have occurred before December 1982.

In sum, it would appear that the limitations on commercial banks' activities in providing securities and ancillary services are to a large extent the fault of the banks themselves. They were inhibited, for good or for bad reasons, as much by internal, self-imposed constraints (including lack of imagination) as by external constraints. At first, the lack of aggressiveness by the banks may have reflected the cautious attitude after the depression and its bank failures, coupled with the unfavorable public attitude to bank involvement in securities activities that resulted in the enactment of Glass-Steagall. But in more recent years, it more likely reflected commercial bank involvement in other activities that they considered potentially more profitable, to the neglect of securities activities.

THE FUTURE OF BANK SECURITIES ACTIVITIES

As discussed earlier, some commercial banks, particularly larger banks, may enjoy potential economies of scope by engaging in securities activities. Nevertheless, throughout U.S. history charges of increased risk, undue concentration of power, and abusive conflicts of interest have resulted in banks being periodically stripped of some of their securities powers. Over time, however, the banks have generally been successful in regaining some—if not all—of the lost powers. Except for severely restricted purposes, at least, national banks in this country have not been permitted to own common stock for their own investment account. In 1933, the Glass-Steagall Act appeared to deprive them also of the powers to deal in almost all but government securities that are fully collateralized by the full faith and credit of the issuer. In recent years, these prohibitions have become less onerous. The boundaries to bank participation in securities activities, once regarded as carefully circumscribed by law and regulation, began to be perceived as amorphous. What activities could and could not be undertaken began to be increasingly probed by more aggressive institutions willing to incur the substantial legal expenses necessary to fight the permissibility of the activity through the regulatory agencies, and, if challenged, the courts.

In 1968, Congress permitted commercial banks to deal in municipal revenue bonds issued for housing, dormitory, and university purposes. In the early 1970s, the Federal Reserve Board permitted banks through their holding company affiliates to become advisers to both open- and closed-end investment funds and to sponsor closed-end funds, and the Comptroller permitted national banks to provide automatic investment services. In the late 1970s, the Federal Reserve Board permitted banks to continue to deal in commercial paper (until overruled by the Supreme Court in 1984) and to assist in private placements. In 1982, the Federal Reserve Board and Comptroller both permitted banks to engage in general retail brokerage activities; the Comptroller permitted the sale of commingled IRA investment accounts that closely resemble mutual funds; and the Federal Reserve Board approved trading in financial futures. In addition, in areas where authorization for an activity was in doubt, banks have started to engage in cooperative arrangements with firms already operating in the area—for example, securities brokerage with established brokers and mutual funds with established mutual fund sponsors—and to share in the revenues.

As a result, many larger banks have increased their investment banking activities. A number of these banks have centralized all or most of their securities activities in investment banking or capital markets departments that are designed to resemble nonbank investment firms. These banks have also emphasized their international scope and their operation of full-service investment banking in a number of major foreign countries. This permits them to open the international capital markets to their clients through the sale of Eurodollar or foreign currency securities. In addition, smaller state-chartered banks that are not members of the Federal Reserve System are being offered wide securities powers by the FDIC, although they may still be restricted by state law. The FHLBB has no general policy concerning the securities activities of its member associations, other than to note they are not subject to the provisions of the Glass-Steagall Act.

The major setback in the banks' expansion into securities activities was the 1970 ruling by the Supreme Court that overturned the Comptroller's authorization for banks to offer commingled trust funds as a retail investment vehicle. Even this may not be a lasting restriction, in light of the Comptroller's ruling on pooling IRA accounts and a willingness by banks to offer mutual funds in conjunction with nonbank fund sponsors.

At the same time, investment banking firms have been reasonably successful in offering commercial banking–type services. In the late 1970s, money market funds were ruled not to be deposits. In the early 1980s, investment banks were permitted to establish new commercial banks under limited circumstances. Thus, commercial and investment banks have begun to become more similar again, much as they had done in the 30 years before the enactment of Glass-Steagall. Legislation has been proposed in recent years to extend the reach of both commercial and investment banks into the other's turf. Except for relatively minor areas, however, these proposals have received little support and their chances for early enactment appear small. Too many powerful groups are asked to share their private turf in exchange for what they view to be inadequate compensation in terms of new turf. (By contrast, legislation has greatly expanded the commercial banking powers of thrift institutions, and regulatory initiatives have greatly expanded their investment banking powers.)

While enactment of sweeping new banking legislation is improbable, a continued nibbling away of the elements of separateness between commercial banking and investment banking does seem likely. This process will reflect efforts by both industries with the periodic assistance of one or more regulatory agencies. Indeed, it is not too farfetched to predict that Glass-Steagall will be no more effective in maintaining a separation between commercial and investment banking in a few years than the McFadden Act and the Douglas Amendment to the Bank Holding Company Act have been in preventing interstate commercial banking. The new securities activities of commercial banks and new commercial banking activities of investment banks, for the most part, will be organized less efficiently than in the absence of the act. Indeed, it appears from most recent events that aggressive commercial banks or aggressive investment banks could offer almost as many "prohibited" activities as they wish as long as they are willing to incur the potentially large legal expenses involved. The major exceptions are likely to be full corporate security ownership (including underwriting) for commercial banks and full transactions deposit services for investment banks.

NOTES

1. Examples of histories of the development of investment and commercial banking include two by Carosso, 1970; Kaufman, 1983; Medina, 1954; Perkins, 1971; Redlich, 1951; and Sametz et al., 1979.

2. The Banking Act of 1933 also introduced federal deposit insurance. The act combined Representative Steagall's House bill establishing federal deposit insurance with Senator Glass's bill separating commercial and investment banking.

3. The sections of the Glass-Steagall Act of 1933, as amended, that deal with the securities activities of commercial banks are:

Section 16

The business of dealing in securities and stock by the (national) association shall be limited to purchasing and selling such securities and stock without recourse, solely upon the order, and for the account of, customers, and in no case for its own account, and the association shall not underwrite any issues of securities or stock: Provided [specifies securities qualified for the association's own investment account]. . . . The limitations and restrictions herein contained as to dealing in, underwriting and purchasing for its own account, investment securities shall not apply to [specifies securities exempted].

[Section 5 extends these restrictions to Federal Reserve member banks.]

Section 20

No member bank shall be affiliated in any manner . . . with any corporation, association, business trust, or other similar organization engaged principally in the issue, flotation, underwriting, public sale, or distribution at wholesale or retail or through syndicate participation of stocks, bonds, debentures, notes, or other securities.

Section 21

It shall be unlawful . . . for any person, firm, corporation, association, business trust, or other similar organization, engaged in the business of issuing, underwriting, selling, or distributing, at wholesale or retail, or through syndicate participation, stocks, bonds, debentures, notes, or other securities, to engage at the same time to any extent whatever in the business of receiving deposits subject to check or to repayment upon presentation of a passbook, certificate of deposit, or other evidence of debt or upon request of the depositor.

Section 32

No officer, director, or employee of any corporation or unincorporated association, no partner or employee of any partnership, and no individual, primarily engaged in the issue, flotation, underwriting, public sale, or distribution, at wholesale or retail, or through syndicate participation, or stocks, bonds, or other similar securities shall serve the same time as an officer, director, or employee of any member bank except in limited classes of cases in which the Board of Governors of the Federal Reserve System may allow such service by general regulations when in the judgment of said Board it would not unduly influence the investment policies of such member bank or the advice it gives its customers regarding investments.

4. *Investment Co. Institute v. Camp,* 401 U.S. 617 (1971). See also U.S. Department of the Treasury, 1975; Pitt et al., 1983; U.S. House of Representatives, 1983.

5. Comptroller of the Currency, "News Release," October 28, 1982, with accompanying documents.

6. A U.S. District Court judge ruled recently that brokerage subsidiaries of a bank are subject to the interstate branch prohibitions of the McFadden Act. This ruling is under appeal, and it has important implications for the location of other subsidiaries of national banks (see Rosenstein, 1983).

7. For a discussion of nonbanks see Bradfield (1983). To reduce the incentive to create nonbanks, the Board of Governors expanded the definition of commercial lending in December 1983 to encompass almost all types of loans and investments including the purchase of CDs and bankers' acceptances. The definition of deposits subject to withdrawal on demand was expanded to include NOW accounts. Nonbanks organized before December 1982 were grandfathered and are not subject to these provisions. In 1984, however, a federal appeals court in Denver ruled that NOW accounts are not demand deposits.

8. See Board of Governors, 1983; Comptroller (Seligman decision), 1983; and Comptroller (Dreyfus decision), 1983. The definitions of *principally* and *primarily* as well as the base activities to which these measures should be applied are in dispute among the regulatory agencies. The courts have held that *principally* requires greater involvement than *primarily*. The Federal Reserve Board has defined *primarily* as representing 10% or more of gross income. The Board has also ruled that the management of a mutual fund by itself represents a principal engagement in the issuance of securities in violation of Section 20. The Comptroller, in contrast, considers a principal engagement only if the gross revenues from the issuance of securities represents at least 10% of the consolidated gross revenues of the overall organization, including subsidiaries if any.

The Federal Reserve Board objected strenuously to the Seligman approval and threatened to fine the bank if it remained a member of the System. The Seligman bank subsequently withdrew from membership by surrendering its national bank charter and was rechartered by New York state as a nonmember state bank.

9. This section draws heavily from Kaufman, 1983.

REFERENCES

American Banker. "Ruling Allows Bank to Offer Investment Advisory Service." September 14, 1983, pp. 4, 6, 14.

Benston, George J., Hanweck, Gerald A., and Humphrey, David B. "Operating Costs in Commercial Banking." Federal Reserve Bank of Atlanta, *Economic Review,* November 1982.

Bierwag, G. O., Kaufman, George G., and Leonard, Paul H. "Interest Rate Effects of Commercial Bank Underwriting of Municipal Revenue Bonds: Further Evidence." *Journal of Banking and Finance,* forthcoming, 1984.

Board of Governors of the Federal Reserve System. "Commercial Bank Private Placement Activities." *Staff study,* June 1977.

Board of Governors of the Federal Reserve System. *Commercial Bank Private Placement Activities.* June 1, 1978.

Board of Governors of the Federal Reserve System. *Commercial Paper Activities of Commercial Banks: A Legal Analysis.* June 28, 1979.

Board of Governors of the Federal Reserve System. Letter to C. T. Conover, Comptroller of the Currency (concerning pending application of Dreyfus). December 14, 1982.

Board of Governors of the Federal Reserve System. "Policy Statement on Sale of Third-Party Commercial Paper by State Member Banks." *Federal Reserve Bulletin*, June 1981, pp. 494–495.

Bradfield, Michael. "Statement before the House Subcommittee on Commerce, Consumer, and Monetary Affairs." July 21, 1983. *Federal Reserve Bulletin*, August 1983, pp. 609–611.

Carosso, Vincent P. *Investment Banking in America: A History.* Cambridge, Mass.: Harvard University Press, 1970.

Carosso, Vincent P. "Washington and Wall Street: The New Deal and Investment Bankers." *Business History Review*, Winter 1970, pp. 425–45.

Comptroller of the Currency, Federal Deposit Insurance Corporation, and Board of Governors of the Federal Reserve System. *Commercial Bank Private Placement Activities.* June 1, 1978.

Comptroller of the Currency. "Decision of the Comptroller of the Currency on the Application to Charter J. & W. Seligman Trust Company N.A." February 1, 1983.

Comptroller of the Currency. "Decision of the Comptroller of the Currency to Charter Dreyfus National Bank and Trust Company." February 4, 1983.

Daskin, Alan J., and Marquardt, Jeffrey C. "The Separation of Banking from Commerce and the Securities Business in the United Kingdom, West Germany, and Japan." *Issues in Bank Regulation*, Summer 1983, pp. 16–24.

Federal Deposit Insurance Corporation. "Proposed Rule to Govern Securities Activities of FDIC-Supervised Banks." May 16, 1983.

Federal Register. "Proposed Rules." November 15, 1983, pp. 51930–32.

Girton, Lance. "Concentration of Financial Power." In exhibits to *Written Statement of the Investment Company Institute before the Senate Committee on Banking, Housing, and Urban Affairs on S. 1720, 97th Congress, First Session*, October 22, 1981.

Greene, Edward F., Murphy, John C., Jr., and Norman, W. Caffey, 3d. "A Vote against the SEC's Proposed Bank Rule." *American Banker*, December 13, 1983, pp. 4–9.

Kaufman, George G. "The Separation of Commercial and Investment Banking." In *The U.S. Financial System* (2nd ed.). Englewood Cliffs, N.J.: Prentice Hall, 1983.

Kaufman, George G., Mote, Larry R., and Rosenblum, Harvey. "The Future of Commercial Banks in the Financial Services Industry." *Staff Memoranda*, 83–5, Federal Reserve Bank of Chicago, 1983.

McMurray,Scott. "Morgan Guaranty Takes Aim at Wall Street." *American Banker*, July 8, 1983, pp. 1, 3, 5, 6.

Medina, Harold R. *Corrected Opinion: United States of America v. Morgan Stanley, et al.* U.S. District Court, New York, February 4, 1954.

Peltzman, Sam. "Commentary." In Franklin R. Edwards (ed.), *Issues in Financial Regulation*. New York: McGraw-Hill, 1979, pp. 155–161.

Perkins, Edwin J. "The Divorce of Commercial and Investment Banking: A History." *Banking Law Review*, June 1971, pp. 483–528.

Pitt, Harvey L., Schropp, James H., and Williams, Julie L. "The Evolving Financial Services Industry: Statutory and Regulatory Framework and Current Issues in the Banking/Securities Arena: An Outline." Working paper, Washington, D.C., May 1983.

Redlich, Fritz. *The Molding of American Banking: Men and Ideas* (Vols. I and II). New York: Hafner Publishing Co., 1951.

Rosenstein, Jay. "Interstate Barriers Applied to Bank Brokerage." *American Banker*, November 4, 1983, pp. 1, 14.

Sametz, Arnold W., Keenan, Michael, Bloch, Ernest, and Goldberg, Lawrence. "Securities Activities of Commercial Banks: An Evaluation of Current Developments and Regulatory Issues." *Journal of Comparative Corporate Law and Securities Regulation*, November 1979, pp. 155–193.

Schotland, Roy A. "Conflicts of Interest within the Financial Firm: Regulatory Implications." In Franklin R. Edwards (Ed.), *Issues in Financial Regulation*. New York: McGraw-Hill, 1979, pp. 123–154.

Smith, Robert H. "Discount Brokerage—Alternative Delivery Systems." Federal Reserve Bank of Chicago, *Proceedings of a Conference on Bank Structure and Competition*, May 2–4, 1983.

U.S. Department of the Treasury. *Public Policy Aspects of Bank Securities Activities: An Issues Paper*. November 1975.

U.S. House of Representatives, Committee on Government Operations. *Confusion in the Legal Framework of the American Financial System and Service Industry: Hearings*. 98th Congress, 1st Session, July 19–21, 1983.

U.S. Senate, Committee on Banking, Housing and Urban Affairs. *Bank Securities Activities of the Securities and Exchange Commission* (Committee Print). 95th Congress, 1st Session, August 1977.

22 Fundamentals of Mergers and Acquisitions

Arnold A. Heggestad

The financial services industry is going through revolutionary change. The industry is experiencing dramatic increases in the volatility of prices and interest rates. Furthermore, deregulation, sweeping technical innovations, and innovations in financial products are affecting the way services are delivered. Suppliers of financial products operate in an environment that is substantially different from that of only a few years ago.

These changes are especially challenging for commercial banks and thrift institutions, which have been heavily regulated with respect to the products they may offer, the prices of their services, and the geographic markets in which they operate. Depository institutions are characterized by large numbers of relatively small, locally limited firms. For example, there are over 14,000 commercial banks and almost 4,000 savings and loan associations. As a result of the series of changes that are now taking place, institutions are now facing strong threats and new opportunities.

One important manifestation of change has been an increase in merger activity. Indeed, there are the beginnings of major consolidation movements. Many surviving companies are making acquisitions to obtain larger size, to obtain access to new markets, and to be better able to compete in the new environment. Others are selling out, often because they do not feel they can remain viable. It is evident that this trend will continue—indeed, will probably accelerate in future years.

This chapter analyzes the merger and consolidation movement. It considers both the motivations of buyers and sellers in the acquisition process and the role of the regulatory agencies. Finally, it discusses the financial aspects of mergers. The financial aspects are shown to be critical in the determination of the structure of the transaction, in the valuation process, and in the ultimate viability of the combined firms.

RECENT TRENDS IN CONSOLIDATIONS

Mergers and acquisitions have been relatively common in banking (broadly defined). Over the past two decades, there have been over 5,000 bank mergers and acquisitions and 1,800 combinations of savings and loan associations. In 1981 and 1982, voluntary savings and loan mergers were double the previous high experienced in the early 1970s. Bank mergers reached an all-time high in 1982, as can be seen in Table 22.1. Since 1982 the rate of activity has increased further.

This recent surge of merger activity may be attributed to several factors. First, the uncertainty brought about by deregulation and by innovations in financial markets has accelerated the perceived benefits to small firms from affiliation with larger companies. It is commonly believed that larger companies with greater management depth and diversification, and greater capital resources, have a competitive advantage in an uncertain environ-

Table 22.1   Mergers and Acquisitions of Commercial Banks and Savings and Loan Associations

Year	Commercial Banks	S&Ls	Year	Commercial Banks	S&Ls
1963	141	34	1974	323	132
1964	140	38	1975	154	111
1965	158	35	1976	166	85
1966	153	40	1977	170	44
1967	154	50	1978	109	44
1968	160	42	1979	118[a]	37
1969	245	83	1980	185[a]	—
1970	294	118	1981	323[a]	108
1971	257	132	1982[b]	450[a]	217
1972	308	102			
1973	387	124			

SOURCE: Commercial banks, 1960–1979: Stephen A. Rhoades, "Federal Reserve Decisions in Bank Mergers and Acquisitions During the 1970's," Staff Study, Board of Governors of the Federal Reserve System, Washington, D.C., August, 1981; 1979–1982: Financial Structure Section, Board of Governors of the Federal Reserve System. S&Ls: Federal Home Loan Bank Board, *Journal,* selected issues.

[a] Indicates revised statistical series that is not comparable with earlier years.
[b] Voluntary acquisitions for commercial banks and savings and loan associations.

ment. Second, liberalization of branching laws within many states has opened markets to larger entities. They have generally expanded through acquisition rather than de novo.

Partly in response to the first two factors, there has been a liberalization by the regulatory agencies and by the courts of their attitudes toward mergers. Regulatory agencies, including the Department of Justice, are required to rule on the permissibility of mergers, taking into consideration the effects on competition and the financial viability of the combination. In the past few years, significantly fewer mergers have been denied on these grounds, especially because of competitive factors. Consequently, depository institutions have attempted larger and more innovative mergers than earlier in the decade.

Interstate Banking and Mergers

Over the past several years, the pressure for interstate banking has been growing. Savings and loan associations are now able to branch interstate as the result of rulings by the Home Loan Bank Board and by the Garn-St Germain Act of 1982. A number of states have already passed legislation to permit reciprocal or specialized interstate banking within their states.[1] While it seems unlikely that Congress will deal with interstate banking at the federal level in the near future, further action at the state level seems to be in the offing.

Interstate banking, however formulated, will substantially increase the number and size of consolidations in banking. Large banks that receive interstate banking authority to expand into new markets will grow through acquisitions and mergers just as they have within their respective states in earlier periods. Within the states, other institutions will combine in an attempt to increase their size and effectiveness in competing with large out-of-state banks. Finally, interstate banking will drop most of the regulatory barriers to a significant consolidation movement.

PUBLIC POLICY TOWARD MERGERS AND ACQUISITIONS

Mergers and acquisitions are limited by the antitrust laws and by legislation, including the Bank Holding Company Act and the Bank Merger Act.[2] This legislation prohibits any merger that will lead to a reduction in competition in any line of commerce in any section of the country. Since the analysis of the effect of a merger requires an estimate of its future consequences, there is room for interpretation on any individual merger.

The interpretations will depend on assessments of the lines of commerce, the geographic market, the competitive environment in which the firms operate, and patterns of behavior in the industry. Recent court rulings, as well as statements by the regulatory agencies and the Department of Justice, have signaled—through redefinitions of the line of commerce and geographic markets—a relaxation on the types of mergers that would be challenged.

All bank mergers and acquisitions must be approved by the Federal Reserve Board, the Office of the Comptroller of the Currency, or the Federal Deposit Insurance Corporation, depending on the charter class of the surviving institution and the type of transaction. All mergers of savings and loan associations must be approved by the Federal Home Loan Bank Board. The U.S. Department of Justice is required to challenge within 30 days any anticompetitive acquisition. In 1982, the Department of Justice and the Federal Reserve Board released guidelines detailing the conditions under which they would expect a bank merger to have an anticompetitive effect, given current legal interpretations. They are likely to deny or to challenge mergers that exceed these guidelines.

The Federal Reserve guidelines are directed at market extension mergers, and the Department of Justice guidelines are directed at horizontal mergers. Market extension mergers involve the combination of two banks operating in different geographic markets. For example, the merger of two banks operating in different cities would be a market extension merger. Horizontal mergers involve the combination of two firms operating in the same market.

The Federal Reserve guidelines state that the Board is unlikely to find an antitrust violation by any merger unless several criteria are met: that the acquiring firm is an important probable future entrant to the market; that the market is highly concentrated; that there are few other potential entrants; and that the acquisition is of a dominant firm in the market (see Table 22.2). Under current judicial interpretation, unless *all* of these criteria are met, it is unlikely there will be a reduction in competition sufficient to warrant a denial.

Mergers that meet all the criteria for challenge specified by the Federal Reserve Board are rare. Most market extension mergers will fail to meet at least one of the criteria, even under current regulations. Consequently, the probability of an antitrust challenge of a market extension merger, which normally represents a major barrier to bank mergers and acquisitions, is very low at this time.

The Department of Justice has set up similar criteria under which it would find a violation in a horizontal merger involving direct competitors.

Table 22.2. Proposed Criteria for Federal Reserve Challenges of Market Extension Bank Mergers

1. The market of the firm to be acquired is highly concentrated. The three-firm concentration ratio of total deposits exceeds 75%.
2. There are six or fewer other firms not operating in the market that are capable of entry.
3. The market of the firm to be acquired is a metropolitan area and has a growth rate in deposits higher than the average of its state or the average of the nation.
4. The firm to be acquired must be one of the three largest in the market and have more than 10% of the bank deposits.

SOURCE: Board of Governors of the Federal Reserve System, *Proposed Statement of Policy on Bank Acquisitions,* February 26, 1982.

These conditions are detailed in Table 22.3. The tests are based on the Herfindahl-Hirschman Index as a measure of market concentration.[4] The guidelines are significantly less stringent than the previous Justice Department guidelines (in place since 1968), especially in markets with low to moderate concentration (see Guerin-Calvert, 1983).[5] As a consequence, even mergers of two banks within their own markets are possible now, whereas most horizontal mergers would have been out of the question only a few years ago.

In summary, conditions are in place to lead to a significant consolidation movement. Restrictions on branching and interstate expansion are being lifted, with the high probability of further changes in interstate banking in the near future. At the same time, antitrust restrictions, as defined by

Table 22.3. U.S. Department of Justice Merger Guidelines

Change in HHI[a]	Level of Postmerger HHI		
	HHI < 1000	1000 < HHI < 1800	HHI > 1800
50 or less	No challenge	No challenge	May challenge
50 to 100	No challenge	No challenge	May challenge
Over 100	No challenge	May challenge	Challenge

SOURCE: U.S. Department of Justice, *Merger Guidelines,* issued June 14, 1982.

[a] The HHI is the sum of market shares squared of all firms in the market. For example, in a market with five banks with market shares of 40%, 30%, 20%, 7%, and 3% respectively, the premerger HHI would be 2,958. A merger of the two smallest firms would increase the postmerger HHI of 3,000 by 42 and would not be challenged. A merger of the largest two banks would increase the postmerger HHI of 5,358 by 2,400 and would be challenged.

court decisions and by the U.S. Department of Justice, have been liberalized, lifting a major barrier to consolidation.

MOTIVATIONS FOR MERGERS AND ACQUISITIONS

The objective of management in a free market environment must be to maximize the value of its stock. Management serves as an agent for its shareholders. Consequently, for any major corporate action, including a merger or acquisition, to take place, it must be expected ex ante that the merger will increase the wealth (stock price) of the stockholders of both the acquiring and the acquired firm. Of course, what is expected ex ante may not always happen.

To approve a merger proposal, stockholders of the acquiring firm must perceive that a merger will increase the level of earnings of the combined firm, increase the growth in its earnings, or reduce its risk level. As a result of the merger, the trade-off between earnings levels, earnings growth, and risk must be expected to become more favorable. This would have the effect of increasing the price of their stock. Similarly, stockholders of the acquired firm must receive a premium for their stock relative to its expected value in the future if the merger did not take place.

The management of the acquiring entity may have goals in addition to or other than the maximization of stockholders' wealth. These may include the desire to maximize market share or growth, or the desire to achieve a critical size large enough to reduce the probability of unfriendly takeover by individuals or by other large banks. (For a discussion of other motivations see Rhoades, 1983.) Accordingly, they may undertake mergers that sacrifice shareholders' wealth to achieve other goals. In the long run, such actions would depress the value of their stock, ultimately increasing pressure for a change in management or even leading to the possible takeover of the firm by an outside group.[5]

Similarly, management of the acquired firm may also have goals other than the simple maximization of share price for their stockholders. This could lead them to resist merger proposals, fight unfriendly takeovers, or recommend acceptance of offers lower than the highest price. Their motives may be a wish to align themselves with a company with a similar management style, to protect their own employment, or to protect their employees. Because of imperfect information regarding the value of merger offers, management has some control over the ultimate merger partner, although markets are sufficiently competitive to prevent major divergences from the maximum stock price. Consequently, managers of publicly owned companies have only limited ability to resist merger proposals where a premium is offered over the existing price of the stock.

STRUCTURE OF THE TRANSACTION

Most bank mergers and acquisitions are made by bank holding companies or their subsidiaries. The holding company structure gives management considerable latitude in setting the legal form of transaction. Management will wish to structure the legal form of the transaction so as to minimize the after-tax cost. This will involve a determination of the type of merger or acquisition, how it will be financed, and the form of payment to stockholders of the acquired firm. A major cost of a merger is to arrive at an agreement and then encounter delay or even denial by a regulatory agency. By manipulating the type of transaction, the acquiring company has some control over what agency will rule on the merger, and this is important because there are significant differences among the agencies in their methodologies and criteria used to evaluate proposed acquisitions. An application that might possibly be denied by one agency could easily be approved by another.

There are several types of transactions that may be used. They are depicted in Figure 22.1. Panel A illustrates a typical transaction, in which a bank holding company acquires a target bank. Payment to stockholders may be made with stock of the acquiring holding company or with cash or other securities. The target bank will become a subsidiary of the bank holding company. In this transaction, the Federal Reserve Board will rule. Under the Bank Holding Company Act, the Board has primary authority over the acquisitions of bank holding companies.

The transaction may be structured to avoid an application to the Federal Reserve Board by merging the target bank into a subsidiary of the acquiring company. In this type of transaction, depicted in Panel B, which also may be accomplished by transfer of cash, securities, or stock, the merged bank's balance sheet and income statement reflect the impact of the merger. Any adjustments to the assets or liabilities of the acquired target bank will be reflected in the balance sheet of the merged bank. The major benefit of this form of transaction is that the regulatory authority that will rule on the acquisition is the one that will have primary authority over the surviving bank after the merger is consummated. If the surviving bank is a national bank, the Office of the Comptroller of the Currency will rule on the merger application. If the surviving bank is a state-chartered, Federal Reserve member bank, the Federal Reserve will have authority. Fi-

Panel A   Direct acquisition

Panel B   Merger into a subsidiary bank

Panel C   Phantom bank merger

Panel D   Merger or acquisition of two holding companies

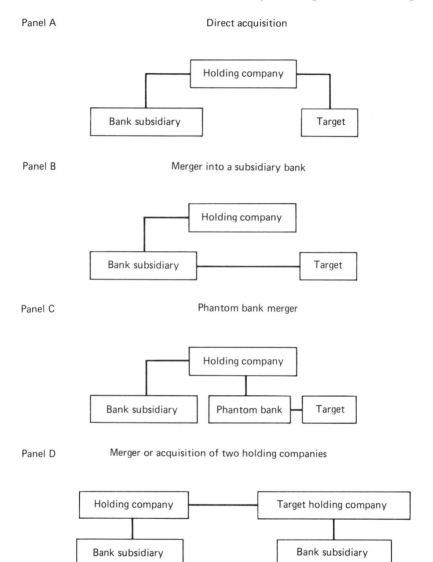

Figure 22.1.   Alternative legal structure of mergers and acquisitions.

nally, if the surviving bank is a state-chartered bank, but not a member of the Federal Reserve, the Federal Deposit Insurance Corporation will have primary authority on the merger. (The FDIC rules on all acquisitions involving the merger of an uninsured bank into an insured bank.) On all mergers, the Department of Justice may challenge an agency approval within 30 days.

If a direct merger into a subsidiary is not possible, a triangular merger may be constructed. In a triangular merger, such as that depicted in Panel C, the holding company obtains a charter for a new phantom bank and merges the target bank into the phantom bank. The phantom bank is chartered for the sole purpose of facilitating the merger. The target bank then operates as a subsidiary of the holding company. There may be reasons to accomplish a reverse triangular merger, in which the phantom bank is merged into the target bank. For example, a reverse triangular merger could be used to maintain the charter of the target bank. In either case, the acquired bank's balance sheet is adjusted to reflect the merger and the regulatory agency will be determined by the charter of the surviving bank.

The final major type of transaction involves the merger or acquisition of another holding company, as shown in Panel D. In this transaction which is becoming increasingly common, the target holding company will disappear and its subsidiaries will become subsidiaries of the acquiring company. The Federal Reserve will have primary authority in this instance.

Choice of the regulatory authority may be very important, especially in cases that have some probability of denial. Denial normally occurs because the merger would have a significantly adverse impact on the capital adequacy of the acquiring firm, from excessive debt, or because of anticompetitive effects. Capital adequacy considerations become especially important when acquisitions are financed by new debt with no corresponding increases in equity. If a premium is paid, it must be shown as good will, and regulatory authorities discount intangible assets in capital adequacy determinations.

The Federal Reserve has been more conservative in its interpretations of both financial and competitive criteria and has been less likely to approve acquisitions than other regulatory agencies in recent years. Consequently, there is presently a tendency to structure acquisitions to avoid the jurisdiction of Federal Reserve. As mentioned previously, the different regulatory authorities employ different analytic procedures and use different geographic and product market definitions in their competition evaluation. This may affect their conclusion on any merger. In future years, economic conditions or the relative philosophies of the regulatory agencies may change, making other agencies more restrictive. Consequently, the structure of the transaction must be considered in each instance and close watch must be maintained for signals of changes in agency policies.

FINANCING THE ACQUISITION

How an acquisition will be financed is obviously a major transaction issue. Will funds be obtained through the issuance of debt, stock, or the sale of assets? How will the stockholders of the acquired firm be reimbursed? Should the acquisition be a tender offer in which the acquiring holding company will allow minority stockholders or should it require a merger and 100% control? These decisions have implications for the tax liabilities of the target bank's stockholders, for the tax liabilities of the combined firm after the merger, and for capital adequacy. Basically, the merger may be consummated by the exchange of stock, by the payment of cash that the holding company obtains by issuing debt, by the transfer of debt instruments, or by some combination of these approaches. It may be consummated with full control or with part ownership.

An exchange of stock is the most common form of acquisition. After determining the price to be paid for a share in the acquired firm, the appropriate exchange ratio is fixed. For example, if each share of the target bank is to be purchased at $25, and the acquiring firm's stock sells for $100, holders of the target bank will receive one share of the acquiring bank for every four shares they hold in the target. Under certain conditions, this form of merger will allow the stockholders of the acquired firm to defer any capital gains tax liability until they sell the newly acquired stock.

Alternatively, the price may be set at $25 and the exchange ratio be determined at the date of sale. If the acquiring firm's stock appreciates to $125, the exchange ratio would fall from one share for every four shares of the acquiring bank to one share for every five.

There is often a long delay between the signing of an agreement and final regulatory approval in bank mergers, which makes the choice of a fixed exchange ratio or a fixed price critical. If the final agreement is based on a fixed exchange ratio, any increase in stock price of the acquiring firm benefits both groups of stockholders and effectively increases the price of the merger to the acquiring company. Similarly, if the stock price of the acquiring firm falls, the effective price of the merger is reduced and the decrease in value falls on both groups of shareholders. If the price of the acquired firm's stock is fixed and the exchange ratio is allowed to vary, stockholders of the acquired firm are insulated from any increases or reductions in the market value of the acquiring firm's stock. Given that several months may elapse before regulatory approval is obtained, subsequent changes in stock prices may be unrelated to the merger transaction.

A transaction funded through an exchange of stock may be treated as a pooling of interest for tax purposes. This gives certain advantages to the acquiring bank, including the ability to utilize any desirable tax attributes of the acquired bank—such as operating loss carry-forwards and investment tax credit carry-forwards. Further, it does not necessarily lower the capital/asset ratio.

The primary disadvantage to the acquiring bank of this form of transaction is the likelihood that the new stock will dilute the earnings per share of its current stock, especially if a premium is paid for the acquired company (see Brigham, 1982). The effect of this could be to drive down the price of its existing stock.

The alternative to an exchange of stock is a direct purchase. A purchase of shares or the assets of the acquired firm may be financed from cash held by the acquiring firm or through the issuing of new debt or equity capital. If funds are obtained by issuing debt, without corresponding increases in equity, the capital/asset ratios of the acquiring firm would be reduced. This may evoke regulatory criticism and, in extreme cases, may cause the regulatory agency to deny the merger. It is also likely to cause an increase in the cost of debt and a reduction in the price of the stock as the financial markets perceive the company as having greater leverage and risk.

A direct purchase may be desirable for the acquiring bank because it opens the possibility of using purchase accounting for tax purposes (see Koch and Baker, 1983). Under purchase accounting, as recently modified by the Tax Equity and Fiscal Responsibility Act of 1982 (TEFRA), the acquiring bank is able to write up the book value of real estate to market value, and receive higher depreciation tax cash flows from the assets. By the same token, however, it must also adjust (often downward) the value of fixed-rate financial assets to reflect market values.

A disadvantage of purchase accounting is the need to classify as good will any premium above the net market value of bank assets. Good will must be amortized and charged against earnings over a period of years, but it is not a tax-deductible expense. Since it is not, its impact on earnings is significant. To avoid this, many banks have placed an economic value on the deposit base of the acquired bank. This is netted out of the reported good will. This deposit premium value is an intangible asset that may be depreciated and is a tax-deductible expense.

The value of the deposit premium is derived from two factors. First, the cost of the core deposits in the acquired bank is below the cost of funding in the wholesale markets. The ability to obtain low-cost funds is

Table 22.4. Accounting Implication and Allocation of Future Benefits of Payment Alternatives

Method of Payment	Accounting Method	Future Benefits	Capital Adequacy Difficulties
Cash	Purchase	Acquiring stockholders	Yes
Debt securities	Purchase	Acquiring stockholders	Yes
Stock exchange at fixed price	Purchase or pooling	Acquiring stockholders	No
Stock exchange at fixed exchange ratio	Purchase or pooling	Acquiring and acquired stockholders	No
Combination of cash, debt securities, and stock	Purchase	Acquiring and acquired stockholders[a]	Yes

[a] Acquired stockholders receive all future benefits if the stock transaction is at a fixed exchange ratio.

an asset with economic value. Second, core deposits are more stable and are less likely to leave the bank in a period of financial distress. Consequently, the funds may be invested in somewhat less liquid assets that offer a higher return. Even though the cost factor will soon be eroded by deregulation, the deposit stability will not. Consequently, the deposit base premium will be increasingly used in the future.

Many transactions are now structured to include both an exchange of stock and a cash purchase. In this type of transaction, the acquiring firm may tailor the mix between stock and debt to minimize dilution of its earnings per share and maintain sufficient capital. In addition, stockholders of the acquired firm may choose to be paid in stock or in cash, depending on their own need for liquidity and tax position.

The impact of the form of transaction is illustrated in Table 22.4. Only if there is a combination in which the price is set at a fixed exchange ratio will the acquired stockholders receive any benefits beyond the initial offer. In other cases, future benefits accrue to the stockholders of the acquiring firm.

Valuation of the Acquisition

For the acquiring company, the valuation of an acquisition is a complex and difficult process. It requires the calculation of benefits to be derived from the acquisition. Benefits may be derived from cost reductions through greater efficiency, from increased revenue generated by better management of the acquired bank's portfolio, from the repricing of the bank's services, or from increased leverage. Moreover, as mentioned previously, the tax consequences of the acquisition may be very important. The target bank may have favorable tax attributes such that the merger will be partially subsidized by reduced taxes (see Burke, 1982).

The acquiring bank cannot ignore the implications of the merger for its key financial ratios and future earnings. It will most likely have to pay a premium over existing value to obtain the approval of the acquired bank's shareholders. In a direct purchase, this premium will have to be amortized, leading to a drain on future earnings. Further, it will generally finance the acquisition with additional debt. Increased debt may force the leverage ratios beyond regulatory limits and place pressure on the holding company to issue new equity. In an exchange of stock, issuance of new stock may dilute earnings per share in the company and conceivably force down the price of its stock. These factors will play major roles in the estimation of the value of the bank to be acquired.

The final selling price will be determined by negotiation of management of the acquiring and the acquired firms. The price will depend on each management's assessment of the target bank's value as an independent firm, and their estimates of its likely contribution to the value of the combined firm, as well as the relative negotiating strength of both parties.

Assume that banking organization A is negotiating to acquire target banking organization B. For the merger to take place under normal conditions, the following must hold. The expected value of the combined firm, $V(AB)$, must exceed the expected value of the two firms operating separately—$V(AB) > V(A) + V(B)$. Under normal conditions, this means that there must be a synergistic relationship between the two organizations when they combine.

Individual mergers may take place without true synergies if the acquiring firm has goals other than the maximization of its stockholders' wealth. In that case, the acquiring firm would be willing to acquire companies that provided no synergistic value. However, in the long run, such a strategy would depress the stock price of firm A and provide pressure for a change in management. Similarly, B may be willing to accept a price below its value. This would make the merger profitable for A, even though it provided no synergistic effects.

If the stockholders of B receive only $V(B)$, A is paying them their value as an independent company and sharing none of the synergistic benefits. There is no premium for the acquisition. Depending on the means of payment, however, shareholders of B may still benefit. Any gains from the merger will go to the owners of A in a cash transaction. Specifically, the owners of A will receive $V(AB) - V(B)$. However, if the acquisition is accomplished as a stock transfer, some of the benefits could go to the shareholders of B if the exchange ratio were fixed prior to the announcement of the merger. Their stock in the combined firm would appreciate in value to the extent that the financial markets valued the combined firm at greater than the sum of their separate values. Alternatively, if the exchange ratio were allowed to vary, and the price were fixed, the stockholders of A would receive all of the gains, just as in a cash transaction. On the other hand, if the stockholders of B were paid $V(AB) - V(A)$, they would receive all of the benefits of the combination. The owners of A would be no better off than before the merger.

These extreme values set the range for negotiations. In most cases, the actual transfer price will fall in this range. However, it is possible that because of superior negotiating skills, a lack of information on the value of B as a separate entity or of $V(AB)$ by one of the two parties, or non-value-maximizing goals by either party, the actual price may fall outside of the range. In this event, there is an effective transfer of wealth from the stockholders of one firm to the stockholders of the other firm.

The expected value of the combined company will depend on the benefits to be derived from the merger. These benefits may come from two sources. First, management of A may be better able to manage the operations or finances of the acquired firm B and increase its revenue or lower its costs, thereby increasing its earnings and its value as part of a larger organization. Second, the increased size of the combined firm (AB) may make the entire operation more efficient or better able to generate revenue. Consequently, A also becomes more efficient or more profitable from the merger. Although these two effects are conceptually separable, in practice it is difficult to separate them.

The most commonly cited benefit from mergers is increased efficiency. As the result of economies of scale, a larger combined firm may be able to operate more efficiently than the two separate companies. Unit costs will fall due to the elimination of duplication of effort and the utilization of a more efficient plant size and equipment that is only available for large production units. Although this motive for bank mergers is widely cited, most studies of costs and economies of scale in banking have found these benefits to be fairly small. (see Benston et al., 1982, and David B. Humphrey's chapter in this volume). Further, many of the benefits of large size are lost in multioffice operations, which will usually be the result of a merger. If there are any benefits from economies of scale, they are likely to accrue to mergers and acquisitions of small companies with total combined assets of less than $100 million. After this size is achieved, the available evidence suggests these benefits are exhausted.

The acquiring bank may be able to reduce the operating costs of the bank it acquires, however. One source of greater efficiency is improved management. Management of the acquired bank may not have been sufficiently concerned with operating costs, or may not have used new financing techniques or operating technology. Management may have had goals other than profit maximization. By making management place greater stress on efficiency, costs may be lowered.

The most important single expense of a commercial bank or thrift institution is its cost of funds. When it is part of a larger organization, the cost of funds to the acquired bank is likely to fall, at least at the margin. Larger banks have greater flexibility in obtaining funds, as they have access to short-term and long-term national and international financial markets. These markets are only accessible indirectly through correspondents for the smaller banks. In addition, larger multioffice banks are more diversified geographically. Hence, they have a more stable source of deposit liabilities. They may be able to expand their deposit base in lower-cost areas more readily than a smaller bank. Access to these sources of funds may reduce the cost of funds to the acquired bank.[6]

Management may be able to take advantage of its larger size in the management of the invested assets of the acquired bank. Larger size and greater deposit supply stability obtained from diversification across deposit and other liability markets mean that the merged bank need hold less funds in cash and other liquid assets as a reserve against unexpected deposit outflows. By reinvesting the funds in less liquid assets, returns are increased. Similarly, managers of the portfolio of the acquired bank may be able to take advantage of its greater diversification and increase the risk exposure of the portfolio without any increase in risk to the combined firm. This will increase the revenue to be obtained from investing the assets of the acquired bank.

The combined firm may also be able to increase its leverage as a result of the merger. This leverage advantage is significant in banking for several reasons. Banking is already highly leveraged. Small differences in leverage have large impacts on return on equity. This effect is compounded by the regulatory structure. Deposit insurance guarantees all deposits under $100,000. In addition, it is widely felt that the regulatory agencies will never permit the largest banks to fail. This effectively guarantees all of their liabilities. Consequently, there is no significant market penalty in the form of higher interest costs for banks with higher leverage.

The firm with greater leverage has the ability to underprice its competitors. Spreads between interest revenue and interest costs are very narrow in banking. The firm with more leverage is able to maintain a smaller spread between interest revenue and costs, and still earn a comparable return on its equity. Therefore, in the highly competitive commercial lending markets and money markets, it can pay slightly more for funds or charge less on loans, and still earn a higher return. This could provide a substantial competitive advantage.

In summary, there are many possible synergistic gains from a merger. Operating costs may be lowered or revenues increased. Regulatory capital constraints may be avoided. In any case, there is considerable potential for the value of the combined firm to be increased. The relative importance of these factors will play an important role in the determination of the final price.

The relative bargaining strength of the two parties will also be quite significant in the determination of the price of the acquisition. The bargaining strength will primarily be determined by the number of potential buyers and sellers. These are limited by the existing structure that restricts acquisitions of banks by nonbank companies and that restricts interstate banking. However, this is likely to change. Interstate banking should materially increase the number of potential buyers in the market and effectively increase prices of acquisitions. In addition, recent legislation and regulatory action that permit thrift institutions to be acquired by banks, and vice versa, will expand the potential number of buyers and sellers in the market, as would any revision in the Glass-Steagall Act. Of course, the uncertainty of deregulation and increased competition will also increase the number of sellers.

Table 22.5 illustrates the critical interaction of synergies and purchase price in allocating the benefits of the merger. In all examples, it is assumed the merger is consummated by the exchange of stock. Consider the merger of banks A and B. Assume both have capital/asset ratios of 5% and that both are earning 1% on assets, after taxes. Assume further that the acquiring bank, A, has either "safer" earnings or a higher expected earnings growth rate. Its price/earnings ratio is 6.25, while B's is 4.0. Consequently, A's stock is selling at $2.50 and B's at $0.80.

Case 1 assumes there are no synergistic increases in the level or expected growth in earnings, nor their risk as a result of the merger. It also assumes a fixed-rate exchange of stock, and a purchase price of two times book value. Stockholders of B will receive stock in A worth $2.00 for every share they own. This represents a premium of 2.5 times the market value of their stock, which had been selling below book value.

Bank A must issue 80 new shares of stock to give to B. After the merger, earnings per share on its 330 shares will be $0.36. If the price/earnings ratio had remained at 6.25, a share of stock would fall to $2.25. At a 6.25 ratio, the holders of A are worse off, since the share price has fallen from

Table 22.5.   Hypothetical Merger Transactions

	Firm A	Firm B	Combined Firm (AB)		
			Case 1[a]	Case 2[b]	Case 3[c]
Total assets	10,000	2,000	12,000	12,000	12,000
Net income	100	20	120	132	120
Equity (book)	500	100	600	600	600
Stock (shares)	250	100	330	330	290
Equity per share	2.00	1.00	1.82	1.82	2.07
Earnings per share	.40	.20	0.36	0.40	0.41
Price–earnings	6.25	4.00	6.25	6.25	6.25
Stock price	2.50	.80	2.25	2.50	2.56

[a] Case 1: No synergies present. Price is twice book value. Stock transaction at exchange ratio of 0.8.
[b] Case 2: Synergies present increase earnings by 10%. Price is twice book value. Exchange ratio is 0.8.
[c] Case 3: No synergies present. Price is book value. Exchange ratio is 0.4.

$2.50 to $2.25. The owners of B are even better off, as they have received 80% of $2.25, or $1.80, for every share of B they held (previously worth $0.80). This estimate of the increase in stock price is probably too high. By assumption, the underlying growth prospects and risk levels are unchanged. Consequently, it is unlikely the combined price/earnings ratio will remain at the 6.25 level, which represents A's potential. It will be forced down to a level consistent with the greater risk or lower earnings growth prospects of the combined firm, which will be an average of A and B. It is likely the price/earnings ratio will fall below 6.25, because in this example there have been no benefits in terms of increased growth prospects or reduced risk of earnings.

In Case 2, it is assumed that there is a synergistic effect that increases the earnings level of the combined firm by 10%. If the same price were paid, earnings per share of the combined firm would be $0.40. A constant price/earnings ratio of 6.25 would mean that a share of stock in the combined firm would sell for $2.50. Owners of A are no better off than before the merger. Owners of B will receive 80% of $2.50, or $2.00 for every share. They receive effectively all of the benefits of the merger. A further increase in earnings or improvement in the growth or risk prospects of the combined firm would make all stockholders better off.

In Case 3, it is assumed there are no synergies, but the price of B is set at book value per share, which still represents a premium over its market price. The exchange ratio is 0.4. In this case, Bank A must issue only 40 new shares. Earnings per share of the combined firm increase to $0.41. If the price/earnings ratio remains at 6.25, there is a capital gain for shareholders in A, as the price of their stock increases. Owners in B receive 40% of $2.56, or $1.02, for every share they held in B worth $0.80.

The critical factors are the impact of the merger on earnings per share and the impact on the price/earnings ratio. Earnings per share is affected by the change in earnings resulting from the merger and by the number of shares that must be issued, or the premium. The price/earnings ratio is affected by the impact of the merger on the riskiness of earnings and on the expected growth of the combined company.

Valuation Approaches

The valuation ranges are relatively easy to determine in principle. The value of the target company is simply the discounted stream of earnings that the firm will generate in the future as an independent entity. Similarly, its value to the combined firm is the discounted stream of incremental earnings it will bring to the combination.

This approach is difficult in application, however. It requires the development of projections of future revenues and expenses in a very uncertain environment. The appropriate discount rate that equates future uncertain income to the present must be determined. For the acquiring firm, in evaluating the merger, the discount rate will depend on the riskless rate of interest and an adjustment for the risk of the incremental cash flows of the combined firm. In the valuation of B as an independent entity, the discount rate will reflect the riskiness of future cash flows from B. The two discount rates are likely to differ, unless there are no gains from reduced risk in the merger.

Alternative approaches and rules of thumb have developed as a result of the difficulties in valuing incremental cash flows. Most have evolved around the valuation of the target firm, B, as an independent firm, and using the value as a target or lower bound for negotiation.

A common approach is to set the value of B at its book value and then to negotiate the price as a multiple of book value. In its simplest form, book value is the difference between the adjusted purchase price or book value of the bank's assets and the book value of its liabilities. This target value would not be totally unreasonable in a period of low inflation and stable interest rates. However, in a period of unstable rates, it can lead to serious errors. If interest rates increase unexpectedly, as they did in 1979–1982, the book value approach will overstate the value of the bank. Longer-term fixed-rate financial assets, when sold at market, would be worth far less than the value at which carried on the books. On the other hand, fixed-rate real assets will have appreciated. For most depository institutions, real assets are significantly smaller in magnitude than financial assets. Moreover, a comparable market adjustment to liabilities would not change their values in the same magnitude as liabilities must be paid at book value. Thus in all likelihood adjusted book value will be below reported book value.

Book value can be adjusted and used as a basis for valuation. Financial as well as real assets may be placed at their market values. Intangible assets may be discounted. The adjusted book value will more correctly reflect the true value. Adjusted book value, however, is a liquidation value concept, rather than a going-concern concept. That is, it does not consider the value and risk of future earnings of the acquired organization. Because of improper diversification (including a poorly balanced asset–liability maturity structure), one bank may be substantially riskier than another. It should be worth less than a safer company with the same adjusted book value, but with more stable expected future earnings.

Market value, as determined by the stock market, is another way to determine the value of the acquired company. The value of the firm's equity is simply the stock price multiplied by the number of shares. However, since there is no active market for the stock of many smaller institutions, there is a possibility of significant error. The price set on the last trade may not reflect adequately a current assessment of earnings, risk, and growth of the company. Similarly, if the markets suspect an acquisition, the current stock price will reflect the expected merger price rather than the value of the company as an independent.

Premiums on Bank Acquisitions and Mergers

In a recent paper, Bullington and Jensen (1981) analyzed the prices paid for a sample of banks in five states in 1980. The results are reproduced in Table 22.6 and Table 22.7. The sample was not scientifically drawn, however, and one cannot generalize from these statistics to all bank mergers and acquisitions. Nevertheless, their results are reasonably indicative of recent merger activity. They found considerable disparity in the prices being paid for banks in the five states. Prices per share relative to earnings per share ranged from 6.3 to 63.5. Similarly, price per share relative to book value per share ranged from 1.0 to 3.4.

These numbers have considerable potential for error, as the authors note in their study. Earnings in the year prior to acquisition, which served as a base for price/earnings ratios, may not be indicative of expected future earnings. If earnings were low the year prior to acquisition, but

Table 22.6. The Price of Selected Recent Bank Acquisitions

State	Number of Combinations	Multiple of Earnings		Multiple of Book Value	
		Mean	Range	Mean	Range
Florida	11	14.7	6.3–25.9	1.9	1.0–2.3
Michigan	7	14.2	9.3–23.8	1.5	1.1–1.8
Missouri	11	26.7	8.0–63.5	1.9	1.1–2.8
Ohio	7	13.4	8.7–17.0	1.9	1.3–2.3
Texas	14	17.8	7.4–30.4	2.1	1.5–3.4

SOURCE: Robert A. Bullington and Arnold E. Jensen, "Pricing a Bank," *Bankers Magazine,* May–June 1981, pp. 94–98.

were expected to improve, this measure would overstate the premium on earnings. Similarly, book value measures are very difficult to interpret. In 1979, a bank with a portfolio dominated by long-term fixed-rate mortgages and other investments would have an adjusted book value significantly less than the reported value. Consequently, the premium over book is understated in these banks.

Even given these qualifications on the data, the surprising result was the lack of differences in premiums among the various states. Average premiums over book value were the same in Florida, Missouri, and Ohio, although growth rates and potential earnings are significantly higher in Florida. On the basis of these numbers, it is questionable whether many of the acquisitions in slower growth states such as Missouri or Ohio will be profitable.

Table 22.7. The Past Performance of Selected Recent Bank Acquisitions

State	Combinations	Return on Equity (percentage)		Five-Year Growth Record (percentage)	
		Mean	Range	Mean	Range
Florida	11	13.7	7.3–19.9	21	2–50
Michigan	7	10.9	5.4–19.9	11	3–30
Missouri	11	10.5	4.2–16.8	17	6–28
Ohio	7	14.3	9.3–19.0	13	10–15
Texas	14	14.8	5.5–25.1	13	6–16

SOURCE: Robert A. Bullington and Arnold E. Jensen, "Pricing a Bank," *Bankers Magazine,* May–June 1981, pp. 94–98.

SUMMARY

In summary, mergers and acquisitions will reflect a wide range of adjustments by depository institutions over the next decade. The combination of deregulation and technical and financial product innovations will increase pressures on management. At the same time, the regulatory agencies are likely to be less restrictive on mergers.

Financial factors play a critical role in the merger process. Great care must be taken in determining the price to be paid and the means of payment. The purchase price relative to any change in earnings after the merger is the critical factor. However, the ultimate viability of the merger will also be determined by tax considerations, the method for financing the merger, and the medium of exchange. These financial factors provide the ultimate test of the merger. There must be sufficient benefits of the merger relative to the price paid, or the stockholders of the acquiring firm will suffer.

NOTES

1. By 1982, these states included New York, Massachusetts, Maine, Alaska, South Dakota, Washington, and Delaware (see Eisenbeis, 1983).
2. The primary legislation is the Bank Merger Act, 12 U.S.C. (1976, 1980), and the Bank Holding Company Act, 12 U.S.C. (1976, 1980).
3. Federal Reserve System, 12 CFR11, *Statement of Policy on Bank Acquisitions,* February 26, 1982 and U.S. Department of Justice, *Merger Guidelines,* June 14, 1982, Washington, D.C. For guidelines on S&L mergers, see 48 *Federal Regulation* 170–189 (January 3, 1983).
4. The Herfindahl-Hirschman Index (HHI) is the sum of all market shares squared. Its possible values range from a maximum of 10,000 in a market with one firm with 100% to a minimum approaching 0 with a very large number of very small firms.
5. Hostile takeovers are not as common in banking as in many other industries, perhaps because of the reporting and regulatory burdens imposed by the Change in Bank Control Act.
6. An excellent discussion of the benefits of diversification in obtaining funds is contained in Citicorp, 1977.

REFERENCES

Benston, George J., Hanweck, Gerald O., Humphrey, David B. "Scale Economies in Banking: A Restructuring and Reassessment." *Journal of Money, Credit and Banking,* November 1982, pp. 435–456.

Brigham, Eugene F. *Financial Management: Theory and Practice* (3rd ed.). Chicago: Dryden Press, 1982, pp. 731–754.

Bullington, Robert A., and Jensen, Arnold E. "Pricing a Bank." *Bankers Magazine,* May–June 1981, pp. 94–98.

Burke, Jon R. "Financing Interstate Expansion: NCNB as a Case Study." *Bank Acquisition Report,* November 1982, pp. 5–7.

Citicorp, *Annual Report,* 1977.

Eisenbeis, Robert A. "Regional Forces for Interstate Banking." *Economic Review,* Federal Reserve Bank of Atlanta, May 1983, pp. 24–31.

48 *Federal Regulation* 170–189 (January 3, 1983).

Guerin-Calvert, Margaret E. "The 1982 Department of Justice Merger Guidelines: Applications to Bank Mergers." *Issues in Bank Regulation,* Winter 1983, pp. 18–25.

Harris, Charles E. "Motivating Factors in Financial Institutions Mergers and Acquisitions: The Motivation to Buy." *Bank Acquisitions Report,* August 1982, pp. 4–7.

Harris, Charles E. "Motivating Factors in Financial Institutions Mergers and Acquisitions: The Motivation to Sell." *Bank Acquisitions Report,* April 1982, pp. 1–4.

Koch, D. L., and Baker, R. M. "Purchase Accounting and the Quality of Bank Earnings." *Economic Review,* Federal Reserve Bank of Atlanta, April 1983, pp. 14–22.

Rhoades, Stephen A. *Power, Empire Building, and Mergers.* Lexington, Mass.: Lexington Books, 1983.

23 Strategic Planning in a World of Regulatory and Technological Change

Edward J. Kane

Existing patterns of deposit institution regulation are disintegrating as dramatically as medieval city walls in an earthquake. Just as in ancient times survivors labored to rebuild the walls around their cities and towns, however, during the 1980s state and federal legislators hope to erect new and less quake-prone regulatory structures.

In 1984, authorities have only begun the process of planning this regulatory reconstruction. Deposit institution managers must incorporate the regulatory risk this implies (i.e., uncertainty as to what statutory materials and architectural forms will ultimately be chosen) into every decision they make. Allowing for alternative futures is the stuff of strategic planning.

FORCES UNDERMINING THE INTENDED SEGMENTATION OF FINANCIAL SERVICES COMPETITION

The regulatory structures that are crumbling today served the goal of segregating different types of institutional competitors into homogeneous neighborhoods. A network of state and federal regulations evolved to maintain narrow product lines and restricted geographic orbits for financial services firms. For this purpose, legal constraints were imposed on competition between:

725

1. *Bank and Nonbank Types of Depository Firms.* Federal and state regulations establish different asset and liability powers for commercial banks, savings banks, savings and loan associations, and credit unions.
2. *Deposit Institutions in Different States.* The relevant federal laws are the McFadden Act and the Douglas Amendment to the Bank Holding Company Act.
3. *Securities Firms and Depository Institutions.* The single most relevant federal law is the Banking Act of 1933.
4. *Financial and Nonfinancial Firms.* State and federal laws restrict the entry of commercial, communications, and data processing firms into financial services activity and of financial firms into nonfinancial forms of commerce.

For financial services firms, the intended cartellike segmentation of competitive opportunities disintegrated in two stages. Change first occurred in the so-called wholesale sector, where financial services are offered to larger business and government customers. Only later was it extended to the retail sector, where parallel services are delivered to smaller entities and to households. In each sector, inherited patterns of financial services production and delivery were undermined by two forces: (1) increases in the opportunity cost of deposit balances whose explicit returns were subject to government regulation; and (2) declines in the costs to customers of searching out alternative financial outlets and of executing transactions. Within the wholesale sector, the breakdown of market segmentation was accelerated by state-of-the-art innovations in computers and telecommunications, which lowered financial shopping costs, made it possible to pay implicit interest in the form of improved record keeping, and made the physical distance between the offices of nonfinancial firms and suppliers of financial services increasingly less relevant. Loan production offices made it possible for banks to take more initiative in competing for the business of out-of-state customers. At the same time, technological change made it easier for a nonfinancial firm to expand the number of banks with which it maintained an ongoing relationship and to collect multiple quotes for the loan or deposit business it wished to transact. Competition from nonbank sources of funds (such as commercial paper dealers) and nonbank cash management services further extended the range of quotes that a nonfinancial firm could readily collect.

As innovations mature, unit costs fall. Hence, after a lag, the application of any technological improvement to lower-balance and lower-volume retail customers becomes economical. In this way, technological changes in retail banking are foreshadowed by arrangements developed earlier for business customers. Such developments as money market funds, brokerage cash management accounts, automated credit scoring, prenegotiated credit lines, deposit institution sweep accounts, and real-time balance inquiry all parallel cash management arrangements (such as automated repurchase agreements, computerized financial statement analysis, and real-time balance and activity reporting) that were available much earlier for corporate customers.

In the long run, efficient producers expand at the expense of inefficient ones. Even in a regulated industry, the structure of competition adapts—through entry, exit, and market share adjustment by individual competitors—to permit products to be produced and delivered at minimum average resource cost. Regulation tends to slow this process, while technological change helps to accelerate it. The breakdown of the inherited segmentation of financial competition provides evidence of what are called economies of scope (Panzar and Willig, 1981): opportunities to reduce the costs of financial services by producing these services in combination rather than on a stand-alone basis.

Telecommunications and computer record keeping create obvious economies of scope in executing and keeping track of varied types of customer transactions. These scope economies lie at the heart of the rapid progress toward homogenization of function observed for such traditionally distinct financial institutions as commercial banks, thrift institutions, brokerage firms, and insurance companies and even for nonfinancial firms engaged in data processing and communications. The quest for productive efficiency leads managers of these firms to find ways to expand their product lines into one another's preexisting domains.

The Financial Services Firm

Homogenization in the product lines of formerly specialized financial institutions is captured in the concept of the all-purpose financial services firm: a generic reconceptualization of financial industry boundaries broad enough to encompass the range of activities being undertaken by evolving institutional competitors. The financial services firm (FSF) produces informational and transactional products to a base of customers with whom it has established relationships. To deliver any financial service, an FSF must exchange information with its customers. Customers and FSFs exchange information by means of information media, which besides person-to-person contacts today include: paper evidences (such as loan agreements, checks, and deposit slips); telephonic messages; magnetic entries on striped plastic cards, tapes, or discs; and keyboard-actuated video displays. These media specifically connect the customer with the particular

FSF product that is desired. In future years, these media may include electronic text, digital imagery, and digitized voice.

Increasingly, financial services register on and occur through an electronic transactions and record-keeping system. This system employs three kinds of productive processes: (1) techniques for maintaining and communicating with remote data bases; (2) techniques for executing transactions; and (3) techniques for delivering services to customers. Because the first and second types of technology are known collectively as back-office technology, the third type is frequently described as front-office technology. Elements of front-office technology appear before the customer every day: brick-and-mortar offices, automated teller machines, drive-in teller windows, and home-based electronic equipment such as telephones and computer terminals.

Among the elements that do not appear before the customer are the complicated interfaces that connect the financial services firm that plugs him or her into the transactions system with the rest of the financial services industry. Efficient production requires that FSFs share customers and equipment in various ways. This means that FSFs belong to networks in which they both compete with and serve one another. For example, at the same time that brokerage firms and correspondent banks act as wholesalers of back-office services to FSF customers, they compete with these customers for front-office business. Federal Reserve Banks not only supply correspondent and communications services to the firms they compete against, but they are even empowered to regulate their competitors' activities. Moreover, as regulators they compete against other federal agencies and state banking departments.

Clearly, conflicts of interest inherent in these interfaces are hard to resolve. Sharing customers and equipment increases the potential for unethical business practices. Wholesale purchasers of back-office services risk servicer expropriation of proprietary information about their customer base. At the same time, widespread sharing creates an environment in which agreements to limit competition are easier to reach and to enforce. For this reason alone, government regulation of financial services firms is sure to survive. Moreover, regulation of financial services firms is expected to serve other public-policy purposes as well. State and federal governments maintain a system of banking regulation to assure a stable, sound, and efficient deposit institution system, and also to accomplish an important hidden objective. Besides its strictly economic purposes, deposit institution regulation serves as an instrumentality for redistributing wealth in politically preferred ways. It seeks to move funds and opportunities from designated victims to recipients designated as deserving. Regulation of deposit institutions serves a purpose akin to handicapping in high-stakes horse races. The weights assigned in process of regulatory change are selected by means of political struggles to redistribute wealth away from the distribution that would be established by market forces. Although industry lobbyists claim only to want a "level playing field" vis-à-vis their competitors, they battle politically to assure—at a minimum—that the wind is at their backs.

Traditionally, these battles have been fought by agent trade associations formed to promote the common interests of similarly situated firms. An important political effect of the ongoing desegmentation of the financial services industry is a noticeable unraveling of preexisting communities of lobbying interest among traditional institutions. This splintering of long-standing coalitions is renewing the competitive fervor of financial trade associations, all of whom must labor to refashion a viable membership base. Homogenization of FSF functions is expanding the boundaries of traditional trade associations. This expansion is exemplified by the 1983 merger of the National Savings and Loan League into the National Association of Mutual Savings Banks to form the National Council of Savings Associations and by the renaming of the National Consumer Finance Association as the American Financial Services Association. These moves reposition competing associations to attract a broader class of institutional members.

Whether political advantages are gained in the regulatory process, market forces reshape financial opportunities to unload the *intended burdens* of regulation from the backs of the targeted victims of regulation. This adaptation explains why statutory changes prove much less important in the long run than they appear at first blush. Omnibus depository institution reforms passed in 1980 and 1982 may be portrayed as the culmination of a long political struggle between banks and thrift institutions. But a rational observer must reject the hypothesis that deregulation is truly in the offing. Neither Congress nor state legislatures have suddenly discovered a light at the end of their tunnels of financial regulation. Regulators and legislators reap enough political advantages from regulation and remain sufficiently in the dark about market forces that it is unreasonable to expect the meandering tunnels they dig ever to reach the outside.

Competition among Regulators

In the face of technological change, competition among financial services firms is enhanced by competition among regulators. Regulated players' ability to switch regulatory affiliations permits them to engage in what we may call *structural arbitrage:* changes in an institution's form of organization that permit it to pursue opportunities for profit that the old form foreclosed. This arbitrage puts economic pressure on bureaucrats to alleviate the burdens that, in a changing marketplace, inherited regulations would otherwise impose on regulated firms and their customers. Duplicate regulatory functions and overlapping administrative boundaries provide opportunities for regulated firms to shrink the domains (and therefore the budget resources) of regulators whose responses to the evolving needs of the institutions or markets they supervise are habitually shortsighted or inflexible.

The institutional structure of financial regulation expresses a series of contradictory political preferences: for self-regulation over government regulation; for state regulation of local activities and federal regulation of national ones; for parallel regulation of all institutions involved in a given functional activity; and for parallel regulation of all institutions of a given type. At both the state and federal level, collisions occur not only between alternative providers of specialized regulation for deposit institutions, but also between these interests and the interests of functional regulators such as the Securities and Exchange Commission (SEC) and Commodities Futures Trading Commission (CFTC).

With the liabilities of deposit institutions backed up by a system of federal deposit insurance that does not explicitly price default, maturity, and leverage risk, federal deposit institution regulators must concern themselves with limiting risk taking by insured firms. This concern leads them to constrain and supervise a deposit institution's position in futures contracts as well as any risky activities undertaken by any holding company affiliates. Conflicts over regulatory turf are heightened by cross-industry merger activity and product-line expansion by brokerage and deposit firms. Innovations in the production and delivery of financial services are increasingly extending the boundaries of regional competition and sweeping the activities of individual deposit institutions into new states and into the orbits of securities and futures market regulators. These same forces are simultaneously thrusting the activities of securities and futures market firms into the orbits of state and federal deposit institution regulators.

These changes create incentives for individual state legislatures to compete against each other in relaxing the regulatory rules under which state-chartered banks and holding company affiliates can play in their states. Banking lobbies are able to hold out to a cooperative legislature a promise of jobs, tax revenues, and crisis-free absorption of failing institutions in exchange for portfolio powers that Congress has not yet seen fit to give them.

Bureaucratic competition for regulatory jurisdiction is part and parcel of the American way. Although it makes for messy organization charts and an overabundance of government agencies, this form of competition improves the long-run adaptive efficiency of government regulation. It is a manifestation of the system of checks and balances that keeps political power from being exercised arbitrarily and assures us that future patterns of government regulation must ultimately mirror long-run equilibrium patterns of competition.

Over the short run, however, structural arbitrage can generate bureaucratic crisis. Today, bureaucratic competition for jurisdiction is leading state and federal regulators to promote forms of structural arbitrage that undermine the viability of the inherited system of federal deposit insurance. Although this arbitrage is vastly increasing the risk exposure of the FDIC and FSLIC, political pressures and competition from other regulators have so far prevented the deposit insurance agencies from bringing these new risks under administrative control.

CONCEPTS AND DISTINCTIONS USEFUL IN UNDERSTANDING FINANCIAL CHANGE[1]

To incorporate the interplay of such broadly gauged forces into a framework for strategic planning, it is necessary to establish an evolutionary perspective on the process of financial change. Financial innovation is impelled by adaptations of two general classes: (1) those that regulated and unregulated competitors make to observed changes in the technological, market, and regulatory constraints under which they operate; and (2) those that regulators make to ensuing changes in opportunities for carrying out their agencies' economic missions and to changing opportunities for strengthening their agencies bureaucratically and politically.

Three Preliminary Distinctions

Three distinctions help to make the diffusion of financial innovations more intelligible. The first is the Schumpeterian distinction between invention and innovation. By an invention, we mean an unfolding technological opportunity. An inventor is a person clever enough to devise a way to do something that has never been done before or to accomplish an old task in a better way. The technological state of the art limits what can be done at any cost. Innovation is the act of applying an invention: putting an inventive idea into profitable operation. Inevitably a lag occurs between the appearance of an invention and its embodiment in an innovation. We call this delay the innovation lag.

Weather forecasters use lagged prediction models in ways that illustrate how knowledge about innovation lags can help make technology forecasts for financial services competition. Just as modern weather forecasters use orbiting satellites to study yesterday's weather in upwind areas, innovation lags in retail applications of financial services technology make it possible to forecast the technology of future competition for household customers merely by observing the techniques used in wholesale financial and data processing applications today. The lag reflects the time it takes to reduce the operating costs of a new technology to a level where it can be offered profitably to retail customers. Future products and delivery systems can be anticipated for retail accounts by examining what is available today for wholesale ones. For example, the techniques used to record and clear airline reservations could be applied to retail financial services. The airline reservation system is just a centralized electronic accounting system. It distributes information on reservations and unfilled seats to would-be users all over the world. Because access to this system is automated more thoroughly than are existing ATM networks, it is reasonable to expect deposit institution networks to move in this direction.

Two other distinctions serve to develop a framework for classifying innovations. One of these contrasts autonomous innovations with induced innovations. An innovation occurs autonomously when a profitable new business opportunity is put into place without the innovator's having been moved to search for it by prior shifts in market or regulatory constraints. The last distinction focuses on differences in the motivation for induced innovations, recognizing a regulation-induced and a market-induced category.

In financial services competition, invention may be treated as an autonomous development. Few financial firms operate on the cutting edge of technological development. Most financial innovations are induced by regulatory policies or by disturbances in the market environment.

Environmental Developments That Induce Adaptation

Two sets of adaptations drive the process of financial innovation: market adaptation to environmental change and regulatory adaptation to market developments. During the 1970s and early 1980s, financial adaptation responded predominantly to three environmental forces:

1. Technological change
2. Volatility of inflation and interest rates
3. Preexisting patterns of financial regulation, which affect the adaptive efficiency of different institutions

Market adaptation to regulation consists of an array of *avoidance* activities. To confront the avoidance they observe, regulators need to address the task of reregulation. They must realign their control network either to bring innovative products and organizations into their regulatory net or to lessen the handicaps they impose on regulated players.

Deposit institution adaptations are responses to changes in the constraints under which they operate. When the constraints facing an institution change, managers must adapt their behavior to make the best of their new circumstances. Three types of constraint apply: regulatory, technological, and market.

Regulation delimits the set of business opportunities that are legal. Technology delimits what opportunities are profitable. Technology bounds what a firm could do if the law and the market did not pose objections. Regulatory and market constraints reflect behavioral forces. Shifts in any of a firm's threefold constraints lead managers of a well-run firm to reconsider business strategies and tactics.

It is sometimes forgotten that regulatory agencies are also constrained by technology, laws, and markets. Most regulatory change is adaptive rather than exogenous. Regulatory adaptation occurs when regulators find that changes in their own opportunity sets make it advisable to adjust their patterns of regulation—that is, to reregulate.

The Regulatory Dialectic

An evolutionary perspective on contemporary financial innovation seeks to identify and to sort out the economic forces behind the institutional transformations taking place in the financial sector. The guiding vision is what I call the *regulatory dialectic*. This conception highlights the conflict between governmental attempts to force competitors to obey rules that implicitly impose a tax on the activity of regulated institutions and the interests of regulated parties, their customers, and their competitors. Managers of regulated institutions and their competitors face market incentives to minimize the regulatory burdens that their customers ultimately have to bear. Financial innovation is impelled by regulated and unregulated institutions' adaptation to observed changes in regulatory, technological, and market constraints and by regulatory adaptation to the resulting changes in regulators' own opportunity sets.

Evolutionary perspectives are often dialectical in nature. The dialectic in financial services innovation focuses on the way that exogenous shifts in technological, market, and regulatory constraints play themselves out when the players possess different adaptive capacities. *Dialectic* is merely a high-sounding philosophical term for a struggle model. In such a model, events are moved by two forces that act in direct opposition to each other.

Each force works reflexively to undo the effects of the other. The basic idea corresponds to the mechanics of a seesaw. In the regulatory dialectic, regulators and regulatees are counterpoised on either side of the seesaw, driving it up and down as they pursue their own goals.

The regulatory dialectic has three stages thar recur in sequence repeatedly. When we think of a regulatory action as initiating the process, we may label the three stages in the adaptive sequence regulation, avoidance, and reregulation. When technological improvements or structural changes in regulated markets act as a triggering force, the sequence becomes one of innovation, reregulation, and avoidance. In both sequences, two critical elements exist: (1) a conflict between creative and hard-to-forecast economic efforts to undo the effects of regulatory activity and political efforts to assert or reassert regulatory control; and (2) the hypothesis that the second or third stage of any given sequence may also be interpreted as the first stage of a new sequence.

In the regulatory dialectic, political processes of regulation and economic forces of avoidance adapt continually to each other like riders on a seesaw. Although continual, this alternating adaptation is not continuous. Rather, it develops as a series of lagged responses. Moreover, because of essential differences in the capacity for creative adaptation (i.e., in the *adaptive efficiency*) possessed by regulators, regulatees, and unregulated competitors, avoidance lags tend to be shorter than regulatory lags.

Regulation may be conceived as an implicit tax: governmental restrictions withhold profitable opportunities from a body of affected parties, the regulatees. As any rational taxpayer must do, regulatees search for ways to lighten their implicit tax burden among what would, in the absence of taxation, be discarded opportunities. Regulation converts what were formerly inefficient ways to compete into efficient ones. Regulatory avoidance is much like tax avoidance. In filling out income tax returns, taxpayers develop records designed to minimize the final tax bill. To behave as passively as governmental conceptions of regulation presume that a regulatee should act, far from minimizing tax, an individual would have to fill out his or her return to help the government extract the greatest amount of funds possible. Governmental conceptions emphasize what a regulation is intended to do, without acknowledging that affected parties adaptively recast the burden that regulation proposes to place on them.

Regulation is seldom more effective than parental efforts to use expandable wooden fences to keep unsupervised toddlers away from staircases and rooms containing breakable or hazardous furnishings. Children learn to surmount such fences almost as soon as they are put in place. The point is that regulatory fences are surmounted in the marketplace, too. To predict the effect of a regulation, an analyst must examine both the marginal costs of avoidance activity and its marginal benefits.

The regulatory dialectic emphasizes that decisions taken by regulators and regulatees jointly condition each other. As in a chess game, each player must anticipate the behavior of players that operate on the other side of the regulatory board. The model is essentially dynamic and strategic, in the sense that it does not predict a stationary state nor tell us much about the details of future play beyond the next move in the game.

Differential Lags Reflect Differences in Adaptive Capacities

Differences in the adaptive capacities of regulators, regulatees, and less-regulated players make for differential lags in responding to exogenous changes in technological opportunities or market conditions. On average, regulatory lags are longer than avoidance lags. It generally takes longer to close loopholes than to open them. This traces partly to a difference between bureaucratic and profit motivations and partly to asymmetries in the flow of useful information. Regulatees and their less-regulated competitors receive better and more timely information about events in the marketplace and about the flow of new inventions than regulators do.

Although it takes time to ascertain the most efficient way to avoid any set of regulations, the search for avoidance opportunities begins as soon as a regulation is imposed. Differences in response time help to explain why deposit institution avoidance proceeded so far during the 1970s. The principal burdens from which institutions sought relief were those of deposit rate ceilings, capital adequacy regulation, activity restrictions, takeover barriers, and restrictions on branching.

At least three sets of players operate on the supply side of the financial services game: regulatees, regulators, and less-regulated operators. Regulatees are institutions to whom the federal government has assigned a specialized regulatory agency. For example, compared with deposit institutions, most other types of financial firms are less extensively regulated. Securities firms are subject to specific regulation by state commissions and to general disclosure and antitrust regulation by the Justice Department and the Securities and Exchange Commission. When less-regulated players choose to jump into regulated markets, as money market funds did from 1974 on, they are apt to show unusually high adaptive capacities. Such firms are often organized to exploit a new technology. Their managers represent a population of competitors selected for their aggressiveness. These managers have chosen to risk their careers on a chancy prospect.

Differences in lags ultimately reflect differences in players' capacities for responding adaptively to changes in regulations, in technologies, and in market pressures. Although regulatees are often instructed about emerging opportunities by less-regulated competitors, their profit motivation leads them to remain alert to opportunities for successful innovation.

By contrast, regulators' instincts are to maintain a preexisting system of regulation as long as they can. In the case of interest rate ceilings, regulators fought change for almost two decades. Avoidance lags shorten over time, as familiarity with a slowly changing regulatory system helps regulatees to develop a good eye for what we may call loophole productivity. For regulatees, an innovation may be profitable even if it is not useful technically. Its productivity may consist merely of creating a loophole that lets managers legally avoid a government-imposed burden.

REREGULATION

Regulatory Inertia Fades over Time

Less-regulated competitors in one market are often highly regulated players in another market, as (for example) when a securities firm fashions a new deposit substitute. Although less-regulated players and new entrants take advantage of traditional players' inertia, their advantage is largely temporary. Over time, their success forces the traditionally regulated players to quicken their responses to defend their market shares.

In the short run, federal and state regulatory agencies tend to be frozen into near inaction by political crossfire from contending interests. It takes an economic, political, or bureaucratic crisis to override the tendency of legislators and bureaucrats to postpone a difficult decision. No matter how many holes the market punches in the existing structure of regulation, as long as they can figure a way to keep it standing a little longer, regulators have a propensity to patch and make do.

Political myopia translates into regulatory inertia. But this inertia can be overcome by any of three events: (1) an unraveling of the political coalition that a given framework of regulation is intended to serve; (2) a substantial loss by traditional clients of funding or lending opportunities to less-regulated players (such as by deposit institutions to money market mutual funds); or (3) a clear and present danger of widespread institutional collapse.

Such events awaken bureaucrats and politicians to the long-run impact of regulatee problems on their own regulatory dominions. In the 1980s, politicians and regulators are helping their traditional clients to extend their product lines and geographic reach, precisely because such innovations promote politician's and bureaucrats' own welfare. Actions that strengthen the economic position of their traditional clienteles fortify their own political positions both against the continued success of less-regulated competitors and against the threat of a financial panic. No matter how comfortable legislative committees and bureaucrats may have been with the old framework of regulation, they cannot fail to see advantages in encouraging their beleaguered clients to experiment with new products, new technologies, new organizational forms, and new pricing schemes. Unless these clients find a profitable combination of financial services to produce for the long run, the tax revenues, agency budgets, and employment they have previously supported will wither away.

An Emergent Era of Reregulation

Precisely because avoidance activity predominated in the 1970s, the 1980s promise to go down as a decade of reregulation. During the last five years, omnibus deposit institution legislation has started a process of consolidating regulatory functions across and within federal agencies.

In the late 1970s, an interagency Federal Financial Institutions Examination Council was established to standardize supervisory forms and examination procedures. In 1980, a second interagency body—the Depository Institutions Deregulation Committee—was set up to dismantle interest rate ceilings on time and savings accounts. The same piece of legislation greatly extended the portfolio powers of thrift institutions and gave the Federal Reserve System, for the first time, authority to levy reserve requirements on nonmember banks and thrifts. In 1982, the Garn-St Germain Depository Institutions Act expanded FDIC and FSLIC authority to aid troubled institutions and broadened their conservatorship powers vis-à-vis state banking supervisors. More recently, Congress is considering consolidation of these federal deposit insurance funds, the possible imposition of risk-rated deposit insurance premiums, and the imposition of new restrictions on the acquisition of deposit institutions by nondepository firms.

Continuing advances in telecommunications and robotics make *intraagency* consolidation appropriate as well. The Office of the Comptroller of the Currency has already closed half of its regional offices. In the future, it is doubtful that the nation will need as many Federal Reserve Banks, Federal Home Loan Banks, and regional FDIC offices as it has needed in the preelectronic era.

Scope economies threaten regulator-imposed segmentation on other fronts. Prohibitions against interstate banking and restrictions on permissible deposit institution activities have been massively circumvented by foreign banks and by deposit institutions' use of service corporations, holding companies, and charter conversions.

So far, Congress has authorized interstate takeovers only in the case of failing institutions for which in-state interests are strongly outbid. Congressional resistance to interstate banking contrasts sharply with state legislatures' open pursuit of affiliate, subsidiary, and branch operations of out-of-state deposit institutions. Among state-approved interstate acquisitions, the takeover of Washington's Seafirst Corporation by California's BankAmerica Corporation looms by far the largest and most significant. For two such extensive branching systems to merge makes a mockery of current federal restrictions.

Recognizing that these laws are unworkable over the long run, many bank holding companies have achieved broader interstate expansion in three complementary ways. First, they have developed a national presence by building a network of limited-service financial offices in states outside their home state. Second, they have purchased nonvoting preferred stock that becomes convertible into common stock if and when interstate banking is allowed. Third, they have made permissible 4.9% "toehold" common stock investments in out-of-state banks and bank holding companies. So far, however, only a few banks and bank holding companies have been able to exploit a loophole in the Bank Holding Company Act (one that has been widely used by nonbanking firms) to establish or acquire so-called "nonbank bank" subsidiaries in other states. These subsidiaries have bank charters, but an out-of-state nonbank parent may operate without registering with the Federal Reserve under the Bank Holding Company Act so long as the subsidiary elects not to exercise either commercial lending or demand deposit functions. Only to a limited (and still fluid) extent have banks and bank holding companies been able to take advantage of the nonbank bank loophole.

Even though the 1980 and 1982 acts make distinctions among traditional types of deposit institutions less meaningful, they also make an institution's charter type an important element of structural arbitrage. Responding to competition among regulators meant to attract regulatees from one another's dominion, managers of a growing number of deposit institutions are investigating whether some kind of charter conversion (perhaps leading ultimately to affiliation with a holding company) would be advantageous. Among the conspicuous benefits of charter conversion are enhanced opportunities to expand the firm's product line and the possibility that it could increase the effective value of the subsidy that a firm receives from deposit insurance (Buser, Chen, and Kane, 1981). Charter conversions are taking place on three fronts:

1. Conversions between federal and state charters
2. Conversions from mutual to stock charters
3. Conversions from one type of deposit institution to another.

As deposit institutions directly and indirectly expand their product lines and geographic reach, and as brokers, insurance companies, data processing, and communications firms establish firmer and firmer footholds in such traditional deposit institution bailiwicks as cash management, the political case against permitting deposit institutions to engage directly in investment banking, insurance, and information processing activities becomes increasingly less tenable.

Arbitrage Pressure and Long-Run Equilibrium

Structural arbitrage sees to it that in the long run financial services are made available at minimum resource cost. In financial markets, regulation creates opportunities for structural arbitrage because, especially in the face of modern information processing and communications technologies, financial products have an unlimited number of potential substitutes. Introducing restrictions on any set of financial opportunities immediately increases the demand for substitute products.

As falling information and transactions costs have driven entry costs toward zero, potential competitors have imposed more and more discipline on deposit institution markets. Because they ignore potential entry by unconventional competitors, inherited paradigms for regulating deposit institution markets are ill-adapted for managing the continuing evolution of the financial services industry. Inherited patterns of regulation reinforce cartellike behavior that invites out-of-state depository competitors and differentially regulated institutions of other types to find ways of structurally arbitraging themselves into regulatorily protected markets. Structural arbitrage proceeds by developing new legal forms (such as holding company subsidiaries) and substitute financial products. In the long run, shortsighted regulation induces financial innovation that diverts business away from traditional competitors. During the last 30 years, structural arbitrage has helped to deflect commercial loans to out-of-state banks, consumer loans to finance companies and travel-and-entertainment credit card firms, and household savings to money market funds.

Inherited regulatory paradigms treat industry structure as an exogenous determinant of competitor performance and define structure in terms of market shares held by one of several narrowly conceived lines of financial services in a localized geographic market. Considerable emphasis is placed on constraining strategic elements in deposit gathering, interposing barriers to deposit institution entry into nondepository activities, and preventing horizontal combinations that would concentrate a large share of the market in the hands of a few firms. Although banking regulators and the Justice Department have finally learned to take account at least of the competitive impact of nonbank deposit institutions in the local area and of potential entry by other in-state banks, the Supreme Court has repeatedly rejected this view.

Specialized regulators see the need for adapting the inherited structure–performance paradigm and have done so implicitly by allowing holding company acquisition to function as a way of circumventing market-narrowing restrictions on deposit institution takeover activity, office locations, and diversification of product line. Because they serve to equalize prospective rates of returns across previously segmented markets, such acquisitions may be regarded as a form of structural arbitrage.

However, structural arbitrage is a two-way street. The existence of patterns for circumventing regulatory restrictions on deposit institution activities makes deposit institutions more attractive candidates for takeover by nondepository firms. Just as deposit institution holding companies can acquire nondepository firms, nondepository financial institutions (such as Merrill Lynch, Dreyfus Corporation, and Prudential Insurance) and even nonfinancial firms (such as Sears Roebuck, J. C. Penney, National Steel, and the Parker Pen Company) can acquire a stockholder-owned deposit institution. If the acquired firm is a thrift institution or is converted into one, its parent can avoid specialized federal oversight at the holding company level as long as it meets the definition of a unitary savings and loan holding company. If the acquired firm is a bank, spinning off the commercial loan side of the business makes it possible for the parent firm to elude regulation as a bank holding company. The hybrid operation that results is known popularly as a nonbank bank, because its charter gives it the power to gather deposits and to have these deposits insured by the FDIC.

To some deposit institution regulators and trade associations, the freedom afforded nonbank banks and unitary S&L holding companies represents a glaring pair of loopholes in the legislative fabric of depository holding company regulation (Eisenbeis, 1983). In April 1983, Federal Reserve Board Chairman Volcker, citing the growing threat to the traditional separation of banking from commerce and from investment banking, urged Congress to pass a temporary moratorium on nondepository acquisitions of deposit institutions and on state and federal actions that allow different types of financial services firms to expand beyond their traditional lines of business. Congressional reluctance to legislate in this area and an unsuccessful attempt by the Comptroller of the Currency to impose a moratorium on nondepository acquisitions of national banks make it likely that Congress will permit structural arbitrage to set the future parameters of financial services competition. Without strong Congressional backup, federal banking regulators can do little to arrest the industry realignments generated by structural arbitrage.

PLANNING FOR STRUCTURAL ARBITAGE

Financial reregulation is cooperating with competitive forces to destroy longstanding patterns of institutional specialization in American capital markets. Fast-growing financial institutions are increasingly those that spread their operations into broader geographic regions and additional product lines.

For deposit institutions, the emphasis is no longer on inventing new ways to offer implicit interest to deposit customers. The day of underpriced services and unprofitable but conveniently located institutional offices is past. Increasingly, account-holder service departments have to generate sufficient fee income to support themselves. To adapt to the electronic era, unprofitable branch offices have to be consolidated.

A deposit institution's explicit interest margin is again playing a straightforward role in determining its rate of return on shareholder capital. To exploit economies of scale and scope, the average size of deposit institutions is growing, with many individual firms merging themselves out of existence. Politically, as small deposit institutions lose political muscle and as securities firms improve their foothold in retail banking markets, the lines of financial institution trade associations and lobbying pressure are adapting accordingly.

Initiating and coping with structural arbitrage must be the major focus of management efforts at strategic planning. Strategic planning is a process for making timely reappraisals of a firm's evolving business options. To take maximal advantage of unfolding opportunities, an institution's strategic planners should establish a research group to search continually for loopholes in the fabric of regulation and to evaluate their potential profitability. At least once a year, this group should formally reassess the net regulatory and tax benefits of every feasible type of charter conversion and every practicable acquisition, spinoff, and relocation of existing operations. The purpose of these ongoing reassessments is to make certain that market opportunities opened up by the latest acts of competitive reregulation will be explored in timely fashion. The research group should report even more regularly on how, on the one hand, emerging technologies might be used to circumvent burdensome state or federal regulations and how, on the other hand, these technologies might facilitate the entry of unaccustomed competitors into the firm's traditional markets. At the same time, new technologies must be studied for evidence that scope economies may exist between specific new products and the firm's existing product line. In carrying out these tasks, the task force needs to focus on identifying opportunities for product and organizational substitution that can permit unregulated processes and products to take the place of regulated ones.

In the financial services industry, great rewards have gone to innovators such as money market funds that have substituted parallel but unregulated production processes and financial contracts for preexisting regulated ones.

Strategic planning should be tied to efforts to monitor and influence changes in tax and regulatory laws in Congress and in relevant state legislatures. At regular intervals, formal projections of alternative regulatory scenarios and of their consequences for the firm should be prepared.

Deposit institution managers must recognize that initiating and coping with structural arbitrage are major activities at successful financial services firms. They must establish a framework of strategic planning that keeps their firm alert to opportunities to extend its product line and customer base, to potential competition from nontraditional sources, and to the lagged interplay of legislative and regulator self-interest in framing patterns of reregulation. The economic case for consolidating and simplifying financial services regulation along functional lines is a strong one. Especially in the short run, however, it will be difficult to overcome the disintegrating force of the political constituencies that stand behind existing regulatory entities.

In the long run, to maintain the efficiency of financial services production and distribution, many deposit institutions will be taken over and many others will convert themselves into diversified financial services firms. Nevertheless, extensive diversification is not strictly necessary for an *individual* deposit institution's survival. To survive economically, a small firm need not produce in house the full gamut of traditional and emerging financial products, nor need it join a network of firms to offer their customers direct (as opposed to indirect) access to a full line of financial services. Although the progressive diminution of regulatory and technological barriers to entry threatens to shrink the market share of limited-purpose financial institutions, specialized banks and thrifts can position themselves to exploit three areas in which they have comparative advantages over nonlocal and nondepository firms: (1) customer loyalty and inertia; (2) the information base they can employ in credit analysis; and (3) their capacity to offer tailored financial advice. At such institutions, special attention must be devoted to the financial needs of the evolving customer base and to the need to maintain a product line that (with the back-office support of outside vendors such as correspondent banks) can be produced at least as cheaply as that of the lowest-cost competitor.

NOTES

1. The next two sections draw closely on Kane (1983).

REFERENCES

Buser, Stephen A., Chen, Andrew H., and Kane, Edward J. "Federal Deposit Insurance, Regulatory Policy, and Optimal Bank Capital." *Journal of Finance,* March 1981, *36,* pp. 51–60.

Eisenbeis, Robert A. "Policy Issues Raised by the Expansion of Nonbank Banks." Chapel Hill: University of North Carolina, mimeographed, 1983.

Kane, Edward J. "Metamorphosis in Financial-Services Delivery and Production." In *Strategic Planning for Economic and Technological Change in the Financial Services Industry.* San Francisco: Federal Home Loan Bank of San Francisco, 1983, pp. 49–64.

Panzar, John C., and Willig, Robert D. "Economies of Scope." *American Economic Review,* May 1981, *71,* pp. 268–272.

24 Costs and Scale Economies in Bank Intermediation

David B. Humphrey

The process of intermediating liabilities (e.g., deposits and purchased funds) and equity capital into assets (e.g., loans, security holdings, and other investments) is the basic business of depository institutions. The profitability of the intermediation process depends upon the operating income and costs of this "production process"; the losses that could be realized from intermediating shorter-term liabilities into longer-term assets (interest rate risk); and the losses arising from loan defaults (credit risk). In this chapter we focus on the operating costs of the intermediation process.

This chapter concentrates on analytical issues that concern the definition, measurement, and estimation of scale economies at commercial banks. Similar analyses exist for S&Ls and credit unions (but not MSBs); where appropriate, these are briefly noted. How the analytical issues are approached and resolved, it turns out, often predetermines or biases the scale economy conclusions. This fact has not been understood adequately in the past and has led most previous researchers in this area to form misleading conclusions. Results from a recent reexamination of the scale economy issue are used to illustrate these assertions and to restructure the scale economy conclusions.

My colleague Allen Berger has made many helpful comments and suggestions that have improved this chapter. Oscar Barnhardt performed all data manipulations in deriving the tables. The views expressed here are the author's and are not endorsed by the Federal Reserve System.

The remainder of this chapter is organized as follows. The first section describes the composition of bank liabilities and assets and the average or unit cost of production of each as reported by banks in the Federal Reserve's *Functional Cost Analysis* (FCA) reports. It also discusses the potential for substantial cost reduction through the use of new and developing payment technologies. In the section called Scale Economies in Banking Operations, analytical issues are described concerning scale economies in the provision of deposit and loan services. The results of a number of earlier studies are summarized. It is shown how some misleading consensus results concerning scale economies were previously derived because of certain methodological problems, and how most of these problems have been resolved today. The third section notes the analytical issues that remain unresolved, and the next section discusses some policy conclusions that can be drawn from the scale economy results. A summary of conclusions is presented in the last section.

COMPOSITION AND COSTS OF PRODUCING LIABILITIES AND ASSETS

The most detailed data available on financial institution operating costs and income are the Federal Reserve's annual compilation of commercial bank cost accounting data—the *Functional Cost Analysis* (FCA) reports. These data, which cover over 600 banks in both unit and branch banking states, are not generally made available to the public, except in a highly aggregated form. Some results are summarized for nine size classes of unit and branch state banking institutions. The deficiencies of these data are: (1) that the largest banks in the United States are underrepresented; and (2) that other types of depository institutions (S&Ls, MSBs, credit unions) are not covered. As it turns out, neither problem is very important. First, data on the largest banks in the U.S. are consistent with those for large banks in the FCA data. Second, where cost accounting data have been available on nonbank financial institutions, the average operating costs and income flows by type of liability or asset category have been found to be close to those experienced by commercial banks. The scale economy results have also been similar, although to date these studies have not always been correctly implemented or interpreted.

Composition of Bank Liabilities and Assets

The percentage composition of unit and branch state bank liabilities and assets is shown in Table 24.1.[1] This dollar-value composition differs only slightly between similar-sized unit and branch banks, so we display the

Table 24.1. Percentage Composition of Bank Liabilities and Assets, 1981 (unit and branch state banks together)[a]

Deposit Size Class (in millions of dollars)	Demand Deposits	Savings and Small Time Deposits	Purchased Funds	Securities and Investments	C&I and Other Loans	Installment Loans	Real Estate Loans	International Loans
< 10	0.36	0.46	0.15	0.36	0.24	0.17	0.10	0.00
10–25	0.30	0.55	0.13	0.35	0.21	0.15	0.17	0.00
25–50	0.30	0.54	0.15	0.37	0.21	0.13	0.18	0.00
50–75	0.27	0.55	0.16	0.36	0.21	0.13	0.19	0.00
75–100	0.26	0.54	0.18	0.36	0.21	0.14	0.17	0.00
100–200	0.28	0.48	0.23	0.37	0.22	0.11	0.17	0.00
200–300	0.28	0.46	0.25	0.37	0.21	0.11	0.17	0.00
300–400	0.29	0.41	0.29	0.31	0.23	0.14	0.15	0.01
> 400	0.32	0.39	0.29	0.33	0.25	0.12	0.12	0.02
Average	0.29	0.47	0.23	0.35	0.22	0.12	0.16	0.01

SOURCE: Computed from Federal Reserve FCA data.

[a] Rows do not add to 100% for liabilities or assets since certain liability and asset categories were not included.

1981 aggregate FCA data for all 625 banks together.[2] However, there are marked differences across bank size classes, most of which may be seen in Table 24.1. These differences are expected and relatively well known. In terms of percentage composition, they are as follows:

Bank Liabilities	Bank Assets
Large banks purchase twice as much funds (federal funds plus large CDs) as do small banks.	Small banks hold more government securities as assets than do large banks.
Small banks rely more on savings and small time deposits than do large banks.	Small banks hold over 10 times more agricultural loans.
Large banks are less capitalized than small banks.	Large banks fund more construction loans and make virtually all of the international loans.
	Small banks have more assets tied up in buildings and equipment.

These differences in percentage composition between small and large banks are primarily due to different liability–asset management behavior, location, and risk preferences.[3]

Large banks practice liability management where, in addition to traditional liabilities, purchased money (large CDs) is used to fund new loans. This permits large banks to grow faster than if reliance were placed solely on the growth of internally generated deposit funds, as had been the case prior to the late 1960s. In addition, as illustrated when scale economies are discussed, purchased money is likely to be a cheaper way to fund loan growth than reliance on increasingly costly deposit funds as banks grow larger. Large banks, of course, have greater access to these markets than smaller banks. Federal funds purchases by large banks appear to play an equilibrating role by permitting a cost-effective response to unexpected daily deposit flows and asset fluctuations (such as unanticipated loan takedowns).[4]

In contrast, small banks are often important suppliers of purchased funds to large banks. These banks still manage their portfolio position through secondary reserves management. Holdings of government securities are altered to fund new loans or accommodate unexpected deposit flows.[5] Small banks do not rely heavily on liability management as large banks have increasingly done since the late 1960s.

Differences in loan composition between small and large banks are primarily due to geographical location—being close to the borrower—and to regulatory limits imposed on loans to a single borrower. Loan limits are tied to capital levels so that loans that have an inherently higher average size—like construction, commercial and industrial, and international loans—are concentrated at the larger banks. Large banks' practice of selling smaller banks' participations or a share in large loans, however, is an offsetting factor. Loans with a smaller average size—like consumer installment loans and most agricultural loans—would be more likely spread evenly across bank size classes. This typically occurs for consumer installment loans. However, for agricultural loans this is not the case; small banks have a geographical (and therefore informational) advantage due to their generally rural location.

Small banks also have higher capitalization ratios than large banks, primarily due to the fact that they have more assets (per dollar of total assets) tied up in buildings and equipment. Higher capitalization has also often been attributed mainly to more conservative risk-taking behavior by small banks compared to their large bank counterparts in money centers that rely on higher leverage[6] ratios in an attempt to reduce funding costs. In addition, loan limits to a single borrower may provide an incentive for small banks to hold larger amounts of capital, raising their capital ratios.

Costs of Producing Liabilities and Assets

Liability and asset operating costs and the interest cost of liabilities are examined for seven broadly defined bank functions that "produce" the following liabilities or assets. The liabilities are: (1) demand deposits (business and consumer); (2) savings and small time deposits; and (3) purchased funds (large CDs and federal funds). The assets are: (4) securities and investments; (5) commercial and industrial (C&I) and other loans; (6) installment loans; and (7) real estate loans. These costs are first shown per dollar of liabilities raised or assets funded. They are then shown as a cost per account in each of these functions.

Operating Costs per Dollar.   Total operating costs, which exclude any interest expense, are divided by the dollar value of liabilities raised or assets funded in each of the seven categories shown in Tables 24.2 and 24.3. This expresses operating costs in terms of cents per dollar in each account category. For example, the average operating costs per demand

Table 24.2. Unit State Bank Liability and Asset Operating Costs per Dollar, 1981 (in cents per dollar)

Deposit Size Class (in millions of dollars)	Demand Deposits	Savings and Small Time Deposits	Purchased Funds	Securities and Investments	C&I and Other Loans	Installment Loans	Real Estate Loans	Number of Banks in Sample
<10	3.7¢	1.0¢	3.5¢	0.3¢	2.6¢	2.7¢	2.1¢	7
10–25	3.4	0.6	1.9	0.4	2.5	2.7	1.1	31
25–50	3.2	0.6	1.3	0.2	1.8	2.6	0.8	89
50–75	2.8	0.5	0.7	0.1	1.3	2.5	0.7	47
75–100	3.0	0.6	0.6	0.1	1.9	2.2	0.7	34
100–200	2.6	0.6	0.4	0.1	1.4	2.6	0.7	48
200–300	2.2	0.7	0.3	0.1	1.3	2.7	0.7	5
300–400	1.6	0.5	0.3	0.1	1.6	1.1	0.6	4
>400	1.4	0.7	0.0ᵃ	0.6	0.9	2.7	1.3	2
Average	2.6	0.6	0.5	0.1ᵇ	1.5	2.4	0.7	(267 total)

SOURCE: See Table 24.1.

[a] Numbers less than 0.05 were rounded down to 0.0.

[b] Numbers more than 0.05 were rounded up to 0.1, giving an average value in this column that looks to be incorrect but is not.

Table 24.3. **Branch State Bank Liability and Asset Operating Costs per Dollar, 1981 (in cents per dollar)**

Deposit Size Class (in millions of dollars)	Demand Deposits	Savings and Small Time Deposits	Purchased Funds	Securities and Investments	C&I and Other Loans	Installment Loans	Real Estate Loans	Number of Banks in Sample
<10	4.6¢	1.8¢	2.3¢	0.3¢	2.0¢	3.0¢	1.1¢	8
10–25	3.6	0.8	1.6	0.2	2.1	2.9	0.7	35
25–50	3.3	0.8	1.3	0.2	1.9	2.6	0.6	97
50–75	3.5	0.6	1.2	0.1	1.9	2.6	0.7	56
75–100	3.3	0.7	0.7	0.1	1.7	2.5	0.5	47
100–200	3.2	0.6	0.7	0.1	1.7	2.6	0.5	59
200–300	3.6	0.8	0.7	0.1	1.7	2.9	0.8	19
300–400	3.6	0.9	0.5	0.1	1.4	2.7	0.6	14
>400	3.8	0.9	0.4	0.3	1.8	3.0	0.7	23
Average	3.6	0.8	0.6	0.2	1.7	2.8	0.6	(358 total)

SOURCE: See Table 24.1.

deposit dollar in 1981 for unit state banks were 2.6¢ while for branch state banks they were 3.6¢. For savings and small time deposits, the per-dollar costs were 0.6¢ versus 0.8¢, respectively. As seen in Tables 24.2 and 24.3, operating costs per dollar for the average branch state bank institution are almost always higher (except for real estate loans) than those for unit state banks. However, this observed cost difference does *not* by itself lead to the conclusion that branch banking is necessarily less efficient than banking in unit banking states. Only if all other influences on costs, such as bank size, wage rates, average account size, and so on, were "held constant" or were not significantly different between banks in unit and branch banking states would such a conclusion be warranted. The typical way this "other things constant" comparison between unit and branch state banks is made is to use regression analysis to separate out *statistically* the various influences on bank costs and then compare the results for these two different types of banking organizations. When this is properly done, as illustrated below, these two forms of banking organizations appear very similar in terms of cost efficiency and scale economies. Thus, the per-dollar cost differences shown in Tables 24.2 and 24.3, as well as those shown next per account in Tables 24.4 and 24.5, are not indicative of any inherent cost difference between unit and branch bank organizational forms. The main point of interest concerns the variation in costs (per dollar or per account) *across* bank size classes, not *between* unit and branch state banks.

On a per-dollar basis, operating costs for unit and branch state banks start high and fall as bank size increases. In many cases, however, this reduction in per-dollar or unit operating costs is reversed at larger banks, giving a slight "U" shape to the average cost curve that would result if the numbers in Tables 24.2 and 24.3 were graphed. This "U" shape is most noticeable for the asset side of the balance sheet. The liability side shows either a very weak "U" shaped average cost relationship or none at all.

We address below the question of whether, when "other things are held constant" in a regression model, this "U" shape persists. This, of course, is the basic scale economy question for financial institutions. Other studies have addressed this question, and the answer has typically been that the estimated bank average operating cost curve is *not* "U" shaped but rather falls over the entire range of bank size classes. This result indicates that scale economies appear to exist for all banks regardless of size. Although some researchers have not found this result for the largest-sized banks, these limited results have generally been ignored in favor of more well-known research results showing scale economies for all bank size classes. However, these well-known statistical results may have come about because of the use of inappropriate research methods. Because earlier researchers have not always adequately addressed the analytical issues surrounding the measurement of scale economies, they may have been misled in their conclusions. To be fair, it should be emphasized that some of the tools now used to address these analytical issues properly have only recently been developed.

Operating Costs per Account.   An alternative way to express how operating costs vary across bank size classes is to divide operating costs by the number of deposit or loan accounts rather than by the dollar value in these accounts. This is done in Tables 24.4 and 24.5. The entries for purchased funds and securities and investments are excluded because numbers of accounts are not relevant measures for these categories. On a per-account basis, average costs for both unit and branch state banks have a strong "U" shape. Economies of scale seem to exist—average costs fall as banks get larger—but these economies are quickly reversed, usually when a bank reaches the fourth size class (above $50 million in deposits). This yields a more distinctive "U"-shaped cost curve compared to that when average operating costs are expressed in terms of per-dollar liabilities raised or assets funded as in Tables 24.2 and 24.3.

Although they are different, either way of expressing operating costs is basically correct. The choice between them depends on how one wishes to view the output of banks or the financial intermediation process. The output produced by a financial institution might be viewed primarily as the *number* of deposit and loan accounts "produced," since most banks' operating costs are incurred by the processing of deposit and loan documents as well as by the debiting and crediting of deposit and loan accounts. Some control factor for differences in the average sizes of accounts across different-sized banks would also be appropriate here if this output definition were used. This approach, which relates operating costs to number of accounts, is analogous to that used to investigate scale economies in manufacturing firms where emphasis is on the production and measurement of output in physical units, like weight, volume, or numbers of units produced.

An alternative view of bank output focuses on the *dollars* in each account rather than the number of accounts. This view argues that while banks do indeed produce deposit and loan accounts, the production process is more closely associated with the costs incurred per dollar in that account. That is, although scale *diseconomies* may exist at larger banks in the direct production of the number of, say, deposit liability accounts, the extra cost per account is acceptable if it is fully (or more than fully) offset by having proportionally more dollars in the account. In this sense,

Table 24.4. **Unit State Bank Liability and Asset Operating Costs per Account, 1981 (in dollars per account)**

Deposit Size Class (in millions of dollars)	Demand Deposits	Savings and Small Time Deposits	Purchased Funds	Securities and Investments	C&I and Other Loans	Installment Loans	Real Estate Loans
<10	$ 99	$64	a	a	$ 354	$191	$600
10–25	65	26			305	88	204
25–50	42	12			174	68	89
50–75	67	30			274	76	174
75–100	83	32			510	79	168
100–200	103	35			522	87	226
200–300	101	40			646	103	291
300–400	115	28			944	72	284
>400	143	74			2,031	205	571
Average	75	25			381	82	168

SOURCE: See Table 24.1.

NOTE: See Table 24.2. Number of banks in the sample for Tables 24.2 and 24.3 is the same as that for Tables 24.4 and 24.5.

a Costs per account are not shown since the number of accounts is not available (Securities and Investments) or when available (Purchased Funds) has little meaning.

Table 24.5. Branch State Bank Liability and Asset Operating Costs per Account, 1981 (in dollars per account)

Deposit Size Class (in millions of dollars)	Demand Deposits	Savings and Small Time Deposits	Purchased Funds	Securities and Investments	C&I and Other Loans	Installment Loans	Real Estate Loans
<10	$ 73	$35	[a]	[a]	$178	$ 88	$182
10–25	69	24			170	88	126
25–50	75	25			207	80	133
50–75	82	26			232	85	150
75–100	78	26			236	79	125
100–200	81	24			298	80	127
200–300	97	26			328	92	134
300–400	103	28			347	93	171
>400	128	34			597	102	123
Average	98	28			344	89	133

SOURCE: See Table 24.1.
[a] See Table 24.4.

diseconomies of scale per account produced can coexist with scale economies per dollar intermediated.

It is not surprising that the issue of the "appropriate" definition of bank output—accounts produced or dollars intermediated—has been much discussed in the literature. But this conflict becomes a moot point if it can be shown that regardless of the definition used, the same general scale economy conclusions apply. We demonstrate this below by showing that the average cost curve for banks is "U"-shaped when either definition of bank output is used. The point at which the average cost curve reaches its minimum is different between these two alternative definitions of bank output, of course, but the robustness of the "U" shape in the average cost curve is clearly demonstrated.[7]

Interest Expenses plus Operating Costs.   Adding interest expenses to operating costs gives the full cost of funds intermediation. This is done in Table 24.6 where both operating costs and operating costs plus interest expenses are expressed on a per dollar and per account basis for both unit and branch state banks. These expenses are aggregated over the five deposit and loan account categories shown in Table 24.5 and, as such, reflect the "total" average cost relationship for virtually the entire banking organization. Three results stand out:

1. The "total" average cost relationship is always "U"-shaped (the values printed in bold in Table 24.6 show where average costs reach their minimum point).
2. The minimum point on the average cost curve occurs at a smaller size class when number of accounts is used to reflect bank output (columns 3, 4 and 7, 8) than when dollars are used (columns 1, 2 and 5, 6).
3. The cost curve becomes more "U"-shaped with a minimum point at a smaller size class when interest expenses are added to operating costs (last four columns) than when only operating costs are used (first four columns).

Along with the two alternative definitions of bank output, there are two corresponding definitions of average cost: cost per account (the production approach) and cost per dollar in the accounts (the intermediation approach). In terms of Table 24.6, the production approach gives average cost as only operating costs per account (columns 3 and 4) while the intermediation approach yields operating plus interest costs per dollar in the account (columns 5 and 6). The intermediation approach always includes purchased funds when costs are expressed per dollar in the ac-

Table 24.6. **Unit and Branch State Bank Total Operating Costs and Operating plus Interest Costs per Dollar and per Account, 1981**

Deposit Size Class (in millions of dollars)	Total Operating Costs				Total Operating Plus Interest Costs			
	Per Dollar		Per Account		Per Dollar		Per Account	
	Unit	Branch	Unit	Branch	Unit	Branch	Unit	Branch
<10	2.3¢	2.7¢	$130	$65	9.0¢	7.8¢	$ 499	**$187**
10–25	1.9	1.8	70	**59**	8.2	**7.7**	309	255
25–50	1.6	1.7	**38**	62	**8.1**	8.0	**194**	299
50–75	1.3	1.6	68	68	8.5	7.8	428	337
75–100	1.5	1.5	78	66	8.5	8.2	452	352
100–200	1.4	**1.4**	96	64	9.7	8.4	650	370
200–300	1.4	1.7	105	71	10.0	8.8	762	362
300–400	**1.2**	1.7	103	75	9.7	9.3	870	406
>400	1.3	2.0	192	99	11.3	9.5	1,836	469
Average	1.4	1.7	71	76	9.2	8.8	459	387

SOURCE: See Table 24.1.

NOTE: The values printed in bold show where average costs reach their minimum point.

counts. Columns 1, 2, 7, and 8 are included for illustrative purposes since they show how average cost would look if either approach were altered (e.g., looking only at operating costs per dollar and adding interest to operating costs per account). This interpretation is significant since it demonstrates that when the intermediation approach to bank output (columns 5 and 6) is contrasted with the production approach (columns 3 and 4), the average cost curve results are very similar. All four of these cost curves are "U"-shaped with a minimum point at banks with between $10 and $50 million in deposits and occur at the same point for unit or branch state banks. Average cost curves based on data for all 14,000 banks in the U.S., using the intermediation approach, confirm the "U"-shape result (so use of FCA data does not distort this conclusion).

To summarize, either view of bank output or average costs—the production or the intermediation approach—appears to lead to the same basic conclusion, and that is that smaller-sized banks appear to experience falling average costs for all five services taken together until they reach some critical size, at which time unit (or average) costs rise. This result holds across different definitions of bank output, across unit and branch state banks, and whether or not interest costs are added to total operating costs. A definitive answer to the scale economies associated with these cost curves will, however, have to wait until the results of regression analyses (which hold "all other things constant") are discussed below.

Operating Income.   Bank operating income is derived almost entirely from interest income and fees on loans plus the return from holding investments (government and municipal securities). With the exception of fee income from checking accounts (3% of total income), no liability category generates more than 1% of the income flow. The percentage composition of operating income across bank size classes is shown in Table 24.7.[8] Because few differences in this composition exist between unit and branch state banks (other than those noted above when liability and asset composition was discussed earlier in the chapter), the aggregate composition for these two categories of banks is shown in Table 24.7. The compositional changes across bank size classes closely resembles that shown in Table 24.1, which presented the percentage composition of assets and liabilities. As banks expand, income from securities, federal funds, checking accounts, and consumer and agricultural loans generally falls while income from C&I and construction loans generally rises.

New Payment Methods: Potential for Bank Cost Reductions.   A number of new payment methods have been developed and put into use in recent years. These range from electronic payments via automated clearinghouses

Table 24.7. Percentage Composition of Bank Operating Income, 1981 (unit and branch state banks together)

Deposit Size Class (in millions of dollars)	Demand Deposits	Securities and Investments	C&I and Other Loans	Installment Loans	Real Estate Loans	International Loans
<10	5%	35%	30%	17%	10%	0%
10–25	4	33	28	17	15	0
25–50	4	33	25	15	16	0
50–75	3	32	30	15	16	0
75–100	3	32	29	16	15	0
100–200	2	34	32	12	14	0
200–300	3	33	30	12	15	0
300–400	2	27	33	15	14	1
>400	2	29	34	12	10	2
Average	3	31	32	13	13	1

SOURCE: See Table 24.1.

NOTE: Rows do not add up to 100% because some functions that generate operating income have been excluded.

(ACH) to account transfers and withdrawals through automated teller machines (ATMs) and cash dispensers (CDs). These, as well as other new payments delivery methods, can affect bank costs by reducing future check payment processing costs (i.e., substituting electronic check payments for current reliance on processing paper checks) and by reducing future capital and labor expenses incurred in providing certain payment or account services (i.e., substituting ATMs, CDs, telephone bill payment, and/ or home banking for brick-and-mortar offices and teller services).

Existing usage studies of ATMs and CDs indicate that high volumes are required to generate cost savings compared to continued reliance on brick-and-mortar office delivery methods. Moreover, many installations of ATMs and CDs are located at existing bank office sites, so that primarily teller labor costs, not building costs, may be saved. However, since one of the main reasons that consumers choose one bank over another is locational convenience, installation of an "after banking hours" CDs may improve market share at a lower overall—bank plus customer—cost than reliance on branch office delivery methods. The large volumes needed to produce some direct operational cost savings for banks are now being realized, and ATMs and CDs are being used as a marketing tool to improve market share (or used defensively to retain it). Market share is improved since convenience benefits to customers are increased, lowering the costs incurred by customers in using banking services.

A possible future development with the greatest potential for payments cost reduction is a shift of the delivery of virtually all payment-related banking services to the point at which sales are made—the point-of-sale (POS) or debit card approach. These electronic payment systems have the potential to turn banking offices into deposit accounting and loan production offices, rather than on-site providers of retail payment services. However, POS systems are not likely to experience rapid growth until two important issues are resolved. These are:

1. *The Delivery System Access Issue.*   Whether the system is proprietary or franchised by banks versus owned and franchised by retail stores.
2. *The Float Issue.*   Consumers give up float in substituting a POS debit card for a check.[9]

These problems are yet to be satisfactorily resolved and, as a consequence, the potential for bank cost savings inherent in this approach is not likely to be realized soon.

Finally, there is the area of the much-forecasted shift from paper check processing to processing of electronic payment at ACHs. ACHs appear to have scale economies, while check processing seems to experience scale diseconomies at the largest offices,[10] but the forecasted shift to electronic processing has yet to be felt in any meaningful way. ACH payments currently account for less than 2% of the total payment value made by check. Even if current growth rates continue—around 30% a year for ACH but only 5% for paper checks—the price and cost-level differences still favor paper over electronics.[11] Only with the most optimistic estimated growth and scale economy projections have researchers been able to forecast ACH unit costs to be lower than paper-check-processing unit costs in the next five to seven years.

Overall, the potential for significant cost reductions in bank payments delivery methods and payments processing procedures has yet to be substantially realized using the new payment methods discussed above. It is likely that these developments will slowly continue to improve in cost effectiveness and that changes in bank processing costs will be evolutionary, not rapid. Consequently, the conclusions reached earlier regarding the "U"-shaped nature of bank average cost curves are unlikely to be altered in the near future due to technological advancement in providing payments services. Moreover, there is no reason to expect significant changes in the cost of providing loan services. Thus the scale economy results (presented next) are likely to be representative of what can be expected in the near and foreseeable future.

SCALE ECONOMIES IN BANKING OPERATIONS

Results of and Problems with Earlier Studies

A survey of the most frequently cited earlier banking and thrift institution scale economy studies would reveal the following:

1. Scale economies exist and are statistically significant for *all* size classes of institutions.
2. The scale economy value for the total of all bank services probably lies between 0.82 and 0.95.[12]

These results have been relatively consistent across different time periods and definitions of bank output. While some earlier studies have not fully supported these results, this conflict has not been emphasized in the literature. The existence of scale economies for most or all bank services is part of the conventional wisdom surrounding the operation of financial institutions, and these results are regularly cited in economic textbooks. The purpose of this part of the chapter is to provide a critical review of the main analytical issues regarding these well-accepted results. This review shows that the nature of the earlier scale–economy results is critically dependent on how researchers have chosen to approach and resolve these issues. Put differently, the design of the "experiment" used to measure bank scale economies has, in large part, predetermined the results obtained. Design the "experiment" differently, and the scale economy conclusions change dramatically. Since it can be shown that one "experiment" is superior to another, the new conclusions displace the earlier ones.

The analytical issues that have led to this reversal in scale economy results concern:

Issue	Before	Now
Cost model used to estimate scale economy values.	Cobb-Douglas model—can only show scale economies, constant costs, or scale diseconomies; can*not* show all three (i.e., cannot show a "U"-shaped average cost curve).	Translog model—can show all three cost curve relationships, giving a "U"-shaped cost curve if it exists in the data.
	Assumes that scale economies are the same for all size classes of banks and equal to the average scale economy value measured.	Allows scale economies to vary across different size classes of banks.
Confusion between *plant*- and *firm*-level scale economies.	Did not distinguish scale economies at the single branch office or *plant* level from those for all offices together—the *firm*.	Separates branch from unit state banks and distinguishes *plant* from *firm* scale economies.
Coverage of larger banks in the sample.	Heavily concentrated on samples containing very small banks.	Includes a greater size dispersion of banks—larger (but not the largest) banks are included.

Of these three analytical issues—the cost model used, the confusion between *plant* and *firm* scale economies, and the coverage of the sample—the second is new and basically unrecognized.[13] These analytical issues, and others of lesser weight, are now discussed in their (likely) order of importance.

Analytical Issues in Determining Scale Economies

Cost Model Used. Most of the earlier studies used a Cobb-Douglas cost or production function to estimate bank scale economies (c.f. Bell and Murphy, 1968; Benston, 1965a).[14] The Cobb-Douglas cost model can be expressed as:

$$\begin{matrix} \text{Bank} \\ \text{operating} \\ \text{cost} \end{matrix} = a + b \left(\begin{matrix} \text{bank} \\ \text{output} \end{matrix} \right) + c \left(\begin{matrix} \text{price} \\ \text{of} \\ \text{labor} \end{matrix} \right) + d \left(\begin{matrix} \text{price} \\ \text{of} \\ \text{buildings} \end{matrix} \right) + \begin{matrix} \text{random} \\ \text{error} \\ \text{term} \end{matrix}$$

where all variables in this regression equation are measured in natural logarithms and the terms a, b, c, and d are parameters to be estimated statistically. Because the preceding equation is in logarithms, the scale economy measure is simply:[15]

$$SCE = \text{percent change in costs/percent change in output} = b$$

Including the prices of labor and capital in the first equation, along with influences such as holding company affiliation, number of branch offices, and other control variables, serves to hold "other things constant" so that the cost effect of only varying bank output is (assumed to be) reflected in SCE.[16] Scale economies are determined from the size of the SCE according to:

SCE < 1.0   Scale economies (falling average cost)
SCE = 1.0   No scale economies or diseconomies
                (average cost is constant)
SCE > 1.0   Scale diseconomies (rising average cost)

For purposes of illustration, the average cost curves are plotted for the sum of branch and unit state banks in Figure 24.1. These curves reflect the production and intermediation approaches to viewing bank output; the data are from columns 3, 4 and 5, 6 of Table 24.6 and use the per-

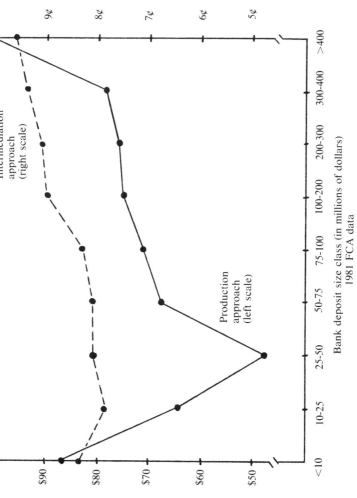

Figure 24.1. Average cost curves by bank size class: the production and intermediation approaches to measuring bank output. (Production approach: solid line, costs per account; intermediation approach: dashed line, costs per dollar in the account.)

account and per dollar definitions shown there. Although Figure 24.1 is in arithmetic terms, the slopes of these average cost curves indicate the extent to which SCE $\gtrless$ 1.0 if all effects on costs except output were zero. As seen, either method of expressing average costs—the production or intermediation approach—yields cost curves with a "U"-shape.

Since SCE $= b$ in the Cobb-Douglas model—the first equation—and is a constant across all sizes of banks, it can show scale economies, diseconomies, or constant costs but not all three at the same time. Although the average cost curve has a clear "U"-shape, it is possible that the Cobb-Douglas model in the first equation would give $b = 1.0$.[17] One would conclude, incorrectly, that constant costs existed for all banks at all output levels when in fact they only existed for the *average* bank in the data set. With average cost curves similar to those shown in Figure 24.1 (using 1978 data), the Cobb-Douglas form in fact gives $b = 1.01$ and constant costs are estimated for all output levels for branch and unit state banks together. Thus the Cobb-Douglas cost model used to estimate scale economies:

1. Cannot estimate a "U"-shaped averge cost curve even if one exists in the data
2. Can conclude that constant costs exist when the average cost curve is "U"-shaped like those shown in Figure 24.1
3. Assumes that the value of SCE $= b$ is constant across all sizes of banks

Because of these drawbacks with the Cobb-Douglas form, more recent investigators have used a different cost function form—the *translog cost function*—which avoids all of these three problems.[18]

The translog model is complex and will not be shown here. (See Benston, Hanweck, and Humphrey, 1982 for a description of this model.) However, the scale economy results from the Cobb-Douglas and this newer model, for unit and branch state banks separately, are shown in Table 24.8. The production approach is shown here using 1978 FCA data.[19]

For branch state banks, the SCE value using the Cobb-Douglas model was 0.93 and showed statistically significant scale economies. For unit state banks, the Cobb-Douglas result was SCE $= 1.07$ and showed statistically significant scale diseconomies. For branch and unit state banks aggregated together the Cobb-Douglas model gave SCE $= 1.01$ and reflected constant costs.

The translog results are quite different from those of the Cobb-Douglas model. Measurements from the translog model (Table 24.8) indicate that small unit and branch state banks both experience scale economies (see

Table 24.8.   Production Approach: Bank Scale Economies Using the Cobb-Douglas and Translog Cost Models[a] (1978 FCA data)

Deposit Size Class (in millions of dollars)	Unit State Banks		Branch State Banks	
	SCE	SCE*	SCE	SCE*
	Cobb-Douglas Model			
All bank size classes	1.07^b	Undefined	0.93^b	Undefined
	Translog Cost Model			
<10	0.95	0.89	0.81^b	0.97
10–25	1.01	0.99	0.89^b	1.05
25–50	1.07^b	1.07^b	0.93^b	1.09^b
50–75	1.11^b	1.12^b	0.93^b	1.10^b
75–100	1.13^b	1.14^b	0.92^b	1.11^b
100–200	1.19^b	1.20^b	0.94	1.12^b
200–300	1.19^b	1.20^b	0.92	1.14^b
300–400	1.24^b	1.24^b	0.93	1.15^b
>400	1.23^b	1.23^b	0.92	1.16^b
Average	1.09^b	1.09^b	0.92^b	1.10^b

SOURCE: (Benston, Hanweck, and Humphrey, 1982) and working paper cited there.

[a] Bank output is here measured as an operating cost share weighted average (or Divisia Index) of the number of accounts in the following five banking functions: demand deposits, small time and savings deposits, C&I and other loans, installment loans, and real estate loans. These Divisia Index results are almost identical to those obtained by defining bank output as a simple sum of the numbers of accounts in these five banking functions.

[b] Indicates a SCE or SCE* value different from 1.0 (constant costs) at the 95% confidence level.

the columns headed by SCE). These economies become diseconomies at unit state banks as bank output rises. For branch state banks, scale economies are observed for all size classes but, as discussed next, this is an artifact of not properly distinguishing between *plant* and *firm* scale economy effects. When this correction is made (see the columns headed SCE*—discussed below), the scale economies observed for larger branch state banks become scale diseconomies, like those experienced for unit state banks, and the associated average cost curve is "U"-shaped.

The intermediation approach is shown in Table 24.9. A "U"-shaped average cost curve with significant scale diseconomies is observed for unit state banks. In contrast, a much flatter cost curve exists for branch state banks, with a corresponding decrease in the incidence of scale diseconomies. While the production and intermediation approaches both yield estimates of scale diseconomies in the provision of banking services,

Table 24.9. Intermediation Approach: Bank Scale Economies Using the Translog Cost Model[a] (1978 FCA data)

Deposit Size Class (in millions of dollars)	Unit State Banks SCE*	Branch State Banks SCE*
<10	.96[c]	1.01
10–25	.95[b]	1.02
25–50	.96[b]	1.02[b]
50–75	.98[b]	1.02[b]
75–100	1.00	1.01[b]
100–200	1.02	1.01
200–300	1.09[b]	1.00
300–400	1.13[b]	.99
>400	1.13[b]	.99
Average	.97[b]	1.02[b]

SOURCE: See Table 24.8.

[a] Bank output is measured as the total dollars in the five deposit and loan account categories plus purchased funds. Total costs are total operating plus total intrest costs.
[b] Indicates a SCE* value different from 1.0 (constant costs) at the 95% confidence interval.
[c] Indicates significance at the 90% level of confidence.

this result is less severe when the intermediation approach is used, as implied by Figure 24.1.

Confusion between *Plant* and *Firm* Scale Economies.   Virtually all the earlier studies of bank scale economies have overstated the extent to which branch banking organizations experience scale economies.[20] These earlier studies have employed the economic textbook definition of scale economies, which envisions a single firm (banking organization) producing output at a single plant (banking office). This condition is met exactly only for unit banks (wherever located) and closely met for banks in unit banking states.[21] It is not met for branch banking organizations, since output is produced by more than a single plant, and this is the source of the problem.

Scale economies reflect how operating costs are affected as output expands. In the case of unit banks, output can only be expanded by producing *more* of various banking services at a *single* office—plant scale economies. Since this single office also fully describes the entire unit banking organization, scale economies of the firm are the same as those of the plant.[22]

In a branch banking organization, scale economies for one office—the plant SCE—happen to be quite different from those for the entire organization or all offices together—the firm SCE. This is because branch banks can expand output by either: (1) adding new accounts or deposits to existing branch offices in a given market area; or (2) adding new offices, which attract new accounts and deposits, in new market areas. The SCE measure used by all previous researchers only considers the first method of output expansion (SCE in Table 24.8). This is appropriate only for unit banks or banking organizations with very few branches. For larger banking organizations with more offices, it turns out that the second method of output expansion is predominant. This result is seen in Table 24.10, which shows the number of accounts and deposits for unit and branch state banking organizations and the average number of accounts and deposits per office (for banks in branching states). For the smallest three size classes in Table 24.10, branch state banks expand output primarily by adding new accounts to a small number of offices (last column), and the average number of accounts and deposits per office rises (columns 3 and 6). But after a branch banking organization achieves a certain size—$25 to $50 million in total deposits—the average number of accounts or deposits per office is relatively stable. This indicates that adding new offices, rather than adding new accounts to existing offices, is the primary method of expansion for larger branch banking organizations.

There is a good economic reason for this behavior by larger branch banks. The reason is that expansion by opening new offices keeps the average number of accounts or deposits at each office relatively low and very close to what appears to be the optimal (or lowest-cost) size for unit banks; namely not expanding branch offices beyond an average of $10 to $25 million in deposits or beyond 7,000 accounts. These offices appear to be of optimal size because unit state banks with the same number of accounts or deposits (Table 24.10, columns 1 and 4) are also those that do not experience the scale diseconomies shown in Table 24.8. That is, unit state banks with more than $25 million in deposits or 7,000 accounts experience scale diseconomies, so keeping the average size of a branch office below this size reduces the apparent inefficiencies involved in branching. The inefficiencies that are observed for branching—scale diseconomies at the firm level—may only exist because of our inability to measure consumer benefits from investments in branch offices. If consumer benefits more than offset the extra costs of branching (or setting up new unit bank offices), then there is no overall economic inefficiency, even though scale diseconomies may be observed when only bank cost data are used in the regression model.

In summary, unit banks expand by servicing a larger number of accounts at a single office, which eventually results in scale diseconomies. Branch banks, in contrast, service a larger number of accounts by opening more offices; by keeping the average number of accounts at each office low, they generally do not experience significant scale diseconomies at the office

Table 24.10. Number of Accounts and Deposits at Unit and Branch State Banking Organizations and at the Average Branch Office, 1981

Deposit Size Class (in millions of dollars)	Number of Deposit and Loan Accounts (in thousands of accounts)			Value of Total Deposits (in millions of dollars)			Number of Offices at Branch State Banks
	Unit State Banks	Branch State Banks	Average Branch Office	Unit State Banks	Branch State Banks	Average Branch Office	
<10	3	4	2.7	8	6	4.0	1.6
10–25	7	10	4.4	17	19	7.8	2.2
25–50	26	17	4.9	37	37	11.0	3.4
50–75	22	25	5.2	63	63	13.2	4.8
75–100	28	35	6.1	88	87	15.1	5.7
100–200	35	53	5.9	132	140	15.4	9.1
200–300	58	93	6.2	240	226	15.1	15.0
300–400	72	140	6.0	335	340	14.5	23.4
>400	59	202	5.6	475	568	15.8	36.0
Average	26	46	5.6	74	118	14.3	8.2

SOURCE: See Table 24.1.

or plant level. Consequently, the usual calculation of scale economies, which attempts to hold the number of branches constant in the regression equation, is only appropriate when a contrast of scale economies at the average plant or office of unit or branch state banks is desired. The SCEs for the average office across different-sized banking organizations (and therefore office sizes, too) are shown in columns 1 and 3 of Table 24.8. These SCEs are inappropriate for comparisons of scale economies at the firm level when the entire banking organization is considered. At the firm level, a more appropriate measure is one that permits *both* output and branches to vary, all else held constant.

Such an augmented scale economy measure has been defined as SCE*, and the results are shown in columns 2 and 4 of Table 24.8.[23] Taking the two sources of bank expansion into account leaves the unit state bank scale economies virtually unchanged, as expected. But for branch state banks, scale economies (SCE) at the plant or office level change to scale diseconomies (SCE*) at the firm or total organization level. In fact, the augmented scale economies for unit and branch state banks are very close together, indicating that these two banking organizational forms are quite similar when proper consideration is given to how output expansion actually occurs. This similarity is also evident when average costs between unit and branch state banks are compared after adjusting for differences in the types of customers served and labor and building costs faced.[24]

Overall, the resolution of the earlier confusion between plant and firm scale economies has led to two conclusions: (1) that virtually all previous scale economy results have been biased toward finding scale economies at the firm level (where none may in fact have existed at larger banks) whenever branch banks have been examined separately or commingled with unit state banks; and (2) that there appear to be no large inherent "cost efficiency" differences between unit and branch bank organizational forms when scale economies are measured properly. These conclusions, and the size of the augmented scale economy values shown above, have important policy implications, which are briefly outlined below.

Coverage of Larger Banks in the Sample.   Most of the earlier studies of bank scale economies used samples of unit or unit and branch banks in which larger banks were not included or were underrepresented (e.g., Gramley, 1962; Benston, 1965b). With such limited coverage the Cobb-Douglas and translog cost function estimating forms will both yield results that show only the scale economies that exist at the smaller banks used in the sample. In a number of studies the size of the sampled banks only occasionally exceeded $100 million in deposits. Limiting the 1981 FCA sample to such smaller banks—the data points shown at the left-hand side in Figure 24.1—would clearly remove or reduce the "U"-shapedness of the average cost curve being fitted statistically, making it more likely to find scale economies for the average bank in the sample.

Reporting Scale Economy Results Only for the Average Bank. A related problem is the earlier practice of reporting scale economies only for the *average* bank in the sample. This practice understates (overstates) the scale economies that exist for the smallest (largest) banks when the average cost curve is "U"-shaped. For the 1978 FCA sample shown in Table 24.8 and the 1981 FCA sample in Table 24.10 and Figure 24.1, the average bank size is small and lies between $50 and $75 million in deposits. The particular restrictiveness involved in reporting only average bank results would not be overcome even if the earlier studies had included the larger banks.[25] This problem is compounded, as noted above, when the Cobb-Douglas form is used since a "U"-shaped cost curve could not be fitted even if one existed in the data.

Other Analytical Issues: Measurement of Bank Output and Specification of Branch Offices. Other difficulties were faced by earlier studies even when larger banks were better represented in the sample. Indeed, even if larger banks are perfectly represented and the Cobb-Douglas form is not used, there is a strong bias toward finding scale economies where none may exist when total assets (or total deposits, loans, or deposits plus loans) are used to represent bank output in the first equation given earlier.[26] Since these studies typically express scale economies in terms of how *operating costs* change as total assets (or the other dollar measures of bank output) change across bank size classes, they neglected to correct for the fact that operating costs per dollar of assets will always fall as higher proportions of purchased funds are used to finance assets. Thus what appears to be falling average operating costs per dollar of assets, or economies of scale, can in fact be the result of increased reliance on purchased funds. Statistical results that may have otherwise indicated constant costs or scale diseconomies at larger banks can be turned into scale economies when the dollar measure of bank output (here total assets) is used to explain variations in only operating costs, and interest costs are excluded.

As noted above, the dollar measure of bank output is valid when one wishes to focus on the intermediation function of financial institutions, rather than on the scale economies surrounding the "production" of deposits and loans. But to describe properly the intermediation relationship, the interest costs of "produced" deposits plus purchased funds should be added to operating costs before it is regressed on bank output (and other variables) to estimate scale economies. This would give an estimate of the scale economies involved in the intermediation process, rather than the production process.

The specification of the number of branch offices in earlier studies was often performed with dummy variables[27] or simply using the number of offices each bank had. These seemingly reasonable specifications, however, imply that the operating cost of a branch is a constant and uniform percentage of a bank's total operating costs regardless of the size of the branch banking organization. A more general (e.g., quadratic) specification would have allowed these percentages to vary across size classes. The translog cost function represents such a specification and, not surprisingly, these percentages were found to vary significantly across different sizes of banking organizations.

A related issue concerns using unit and branch state banks in the same sample, a common practice in earlier studies. It has been shown that such aggregation cannot be supported, however, even though the (augumented or SCE*) scale economy results between these two groupings of banks are very similar.[28]

These last three additional analytical issues have concerned:

1. The bias toward finding operating cost scale economies when bank output is measured as total assets or some other dollar value (because the role of purchased funds and their interest costs are neglected)
2. The assumption (an incorrect one) that the cost of a branch office is a constant percentage of total operating costs regardless of bank size
3. The inclusion of unit and branch state banks (incorrectly) in the same sample

Of these issues, only the first one has likely had any real significant impact in misleading researchers to conclude that scale economies, if properly measured as SCE*, exist at all banks regardless of size.

UNRESOLVED ANALYTICAL ISSUES IN MEASURING SCALE ECONOMIES

The basic purposes of this chapter have been: (1) to provide a critical review of the analytical issues involved in determining scale economies in banking; and (2) to show how the resolution of these issues can predetermine or bias the statistical measurement of these economies. While many issues were raised and discussed, some have not yet been mentioned and are still unresolved. These unresolved issues concern:

1. The difficulty in generalizing the existing scale economy results to the very largest banks, since they are not covered in the FCA data[29]

2. The extent to which scale economy values have been misrepresented because economies of scope—the cost economies due to producing many different outputs—have not been accounted for

3. The extent to which scale economy values are biased because of the inability to account properly for the separate role played by technology and differences in labor productivity across bank size classes

Only partial information exists on these three issues. First, the very largest banks do not appear to have markedly different ratios of total operating plus interest costs per dollar of assets compared to the largest banks in the FCA sample. In addition, for both unit and branch state banks, a "U"-shaped cost curve is observed when all 14,000 banks in the U.S. are contrasted with the around 600 banks in the FCA sample used here. This comparability, using the intermediation approach to scale economy measurement, suggests that such similarity may also exist for operating costs and numbers of accounts (the production approach to measuring scale economies). Second, preliminary studies indicate that scope economies in banking, when statistically significant, are quantitatively small. Their inclusion and estimation using new multioutput cost function models have not had a significant effect on either the value of the scale economies estimated or the basic conclusions outlined above.[30] One reason for this (preliminary) result may be seen in Table 24.11, which shows the operating cost shares for five bank functions for both unit and branch state banks. Operating cost shares show how operating costs for one function, as a percentage of the operating costs for all five functions, vary across bank size classes.[31] As seen, while there is some variation by size class (especially for C&I and other loans), the variation is not great. This indicates that, on average, bank product mix does not have much variation and thus is consistent with the preliminary conclusion that including scope effects has little effect on measured scale economies. Even if there are very strong cost incentives that influence the composition of bank output, regression analysis will have a difficult time identifying them since the equilibrium position will be observed in the data. Since this position is seemingly very similar across bank size classes it may not turn out to be statistically significant in a regression equation. Alternatively, it could be that this similarity in bank output composition (as measured by the cost shares in Table 24.11) merely reflects the homogeneity of the users of bank services—a demand side influence—rather than the result of cost economies from scope effects that dictate a given and similar output mix across bank size classes—the supply side influence. At the present time,

Table 24.11. Unit and Branch State Bank Operating Cost Shares for Five Bank Functions, 1981 (in percentages)

Deposit Size Class (in millions of dollars)	Demand Deposits		Savings and Small Time Deposits		C&I and Other Loans		Installment Loans		Real Estate Loans	
	Unit	Branch	Unit	Branch	Unit	Branch	Unit	Branch	Unit	Branch
<10	40%	46%	13%	23%	25%	12%	15%	17%	7%	3%
10–25	39	42	14	18	25	16	17	19	5	6
25–50	42	43	15	18	21	16	16	18	6	6
50–75	41	43	15	16	19	16	18	18	6	7
75–100	39	41	16	17	21	19	17	19	6	5
100–200	42	43	14	17	24	17	16	17	5	6
200–300	41	44	14	18	25	17	14	17	6	7
300–400	38	45	11	18	31	18	14	18	6	5
>400	37	48	11	14	30	15	17	15	4	4
Average	41	45	14	16	23	17	16	17	6	5

SOURCE: See Table 24.1.

774

it is not possible to sort out which influence—demand or supply—is dominant here. In addition, the level of detail that is observed in the data does not permit a convincing analysis of, say, the jointness or scope effects of producing domestic and international loans. The banks covered in the FCA data are too small to represent fairly a large bank's international operations.

Lastly, considering the availability of the most recent technological equipment to both large banks (through purchase) and small (through rental or franchise), it is unlikely that the technological and productivity differences that still exist among banks would have a large effect on the measured scale economies. These assertions regarding the likely importance or unimportance of these unresolved analytical issues, of course, are tentative and may be altered depending on the results of future research in this area.

POLICY CONCLUSIONS FROM SCALE ECONOMY RESULTS

Two policy issues traditionally have been associated with the measurement of financial institution (bank) scale economies. These are: (1) cost efficiency and competitive effects of relaxing existing state and federal restrictions on intra- and interstate branching; and (2) effects of financial institution mergers and acquisitions on the operating costs of the institutions requesting permission to merge. These two issues are closely related since both concern what may happen to average operating costs as a financial institution gets larger by branching (within a state or across state lines) or by merging with another institution. In both cases, the answer from the average cost and scale economy data presented above is that after a banking institution reaches a certain minimum size—around $50 million in deposits (see Tables 24.6 and 24.8)—the costs per account or per dollar of funds intermediated no longer fall but appear to rise. Because of this, it is unlikely that relaxing existing state and federal restrictions on intra- and interstate branching would result in a rapid or even a substantial consolidation of financial institutions as a result of scale economies alone. Anecdotal information on institutional structure in branching states lends support to this view; that is, very small single-office banks coexist with exceptionally large branch banking organizations in California, New York, and other branch banking states. Since intrastate branching has not eliminated small banks, neither should interstate branching. Although some consolidation will undoubtedly occur following a relaxation of interstate branching restrictions, it will not be primarily motivated by the cost economies of doing so since these costs economies, on average at least, do not appear to exist.

The average cost and scale economy results also imply that, on average, cost reduction is not the primary incentive for bank mergers or bank holding company acquisitions. Mergers between banks above $50 to $75 million in deposits should raise costs per account or per dollar of funds intermediated, not lower them. Thus expansion into market areas by merger would seem to be most cost effective if restricted to de novo entry or through mergers between very small institutions, not through mergers among large institutions.

The scale and scope economy results also have implications for bank pricing and product development. The fact that preliminary studies at times find statistically significant scope effects, even though the scale economy results are largely unchanged, implies that there are significant joint or shared costs in providing different bank services. In such a situation, a bank's competitive position is best maintained by not unbundling services, except to defensively match what a successful competitor is doing. If unbundled, however, the price of the service should at least cover variable costs and make some contribution to fixed costs. Pricing, whether through explicit fees or implicit balances, should be done in accordance with the perceived elasticity of demand of the customer. That is, prices should be higher than average costs where demand is relatively insensitive to price (inelastic demand) and lower than average costs—but above average variable costs—when demand is very sensitive to price (elastic demand).[32]

The scale economy results imply that large banks have no cost advantage in supplying bank services to customers compared to small banks. Thus, from a cost or supply standpoint, one bank would seem to have few advantages over another, apart from the (unmeasured) effect of customer convenience. Correspondingly, if customers are to be attracted to one bank over another the important factors appear to be customer convenience and product differentiation, whether real or merely perceived. Since true product differences seem to have a short lifetime in banking, because some banks always seem willing to franchise a new product to other banks (e.g., ATM network access), the importance of advertising is correspondingly increased. When products are essentially the same, advertising will emphasize perceived rather than actual differences. Thus essentially homogeneous financial institutions will appear to be specialized and thereby reduce the elasticity or price responsiveness of consumers.

If Operating Cost Scale Economies Do Not Exist for Larger Banks, Why Do They Merge?

Mergers have been an important source of bank growth. One study indicates that, of the 20 largest U.S. banking organizations, mergers accounted for some 75% of the current size of these institutions (Rhoades, forthcoming). Ask bankers and thrift executives why they wish to merge and become larger and almost all of them at some point in the discussion will say, "To take advantage of economies of scale." This is also an often stated reason behind wanting to engage in interstate banking. But why merge and get larger if operating cost scale economies don't seem to exist? The above discussion has rather conclusively demonstrated that, as institutions become larger, on average their operating cost per account serviced or operating and interest cost per dollar in these accounts rises, rather than falls.

If operating cost scale economies are nonexistent at larger banks, then there must be some other motivating factor for these institutions to merge and become larger. Some of the other reasons most often mentioned are:

1. Larger banks, particularly those in money centers, appear to be able to operate (without strong regulatory interference) using greater leverage—more (cheaper) deposits and debt per dollar of (expensive) equity capital.
2. Larger regional and money-center banks face somewhat lower costs of purchased funds (CDs, federal funds, Eurodollars) and, because sellers of these funds generally set higher position limits when selling to larger institutions, greater amounts of purchased funds can be obtained.
3. Larger institutions are seemingly better able to diversify their assets and reduce risk as well as to offer a broader range of services to customers and play a role in many different markets (e.g., domestic versus international).
4. Larger institutions typically have higher levels of executive compensation than smaller institutions.

The first three reasons—greater leverage, lower cost of purchased funds, and risk and product diversification—should all lead to higher profits and hence represent a good logical reason for merging and becoming larger.

But larger banks are not in fact more profitable; they are either less profitable or only just as profitable as smaller banks. When profits (net income) are measured as a rate of return on assets (net of loan loss reserves), banks with less than $100 million in assets had an ROA of 1.10% as a five-year average over 1977–1981. This falls to 0.91% for banks with $100 million to $1 billion in assets. It falls further to 0.54% for money-center banks with more than $1 billion in assets (Opper, 1982). Measured as a rate of return on assets, larger banks are less profitable than smaller banks.

However, one of the above benefits of being a large bank is higher leverage, so equity capital is a smaller percentage of total assets at large banks. Thus when profitability is measured as a rate of return on (the book value of) bank equity, the three size classes of banks show very similar profitability rates; specifically 13.5, 13.1, and 13.2%, respectively.

This result—that large banks are not more profitable than small banks—is very unsatisfying. Neither operating cost scale economies nor the three profitability-related reasons listed above seem to be good explanations for bank mergers. One is left with the behavioral reason that executives prefer the higher compensation accorded to managers of larger firms and the other nonmonetary benefits associated with working for and in a large institution (Rhoades, 1983). That increased profitability or internal operating efficiency does not seem to be the primary motivation behind mergers is not unique to banking. A recent study of nonbank merger activity across five European countries, the United States, and the United Kingdom came to the same conclusion (Mueller, 1980). Overall, the standard reasons cited in the financial press regarding the motivation for bank mergers are not found to be realized upon examination. Clearly, this subject deserves further study.

SUMMARY OF CONCLUSIONS

The following is a brief listing of the results of the analyses presented in this chapter:

1. The average cost curve underlying the production of the sum of the main components of bank services—demand deposits, time and savings deposits, C&I loans, installment loans, and real estate loans—is "U"-shaped. Smaller banks experience falling average costs until they reach some critical size (around $50 million in total deposits), and then average costs start to rise.

2. The "U"-shaped average cost curve: (a) exists for banks in both unit and branch banking states; (b) holds when bank "output" is defined on a per account basis or in terms of the dollar value of funds raised and intermediated; and (c) applies even when interest expenses are added with operating costs.

3. New developments in payment methods seem to offer little in the way of making the "U"-shaped cost curve flatter (i.e., lowering costs at high output levels) in the near future.

4. Scale economies exist in banking but are apparently limited to the smaller-sized institutions. Large institutions experience statistically significant scale *diseconomies* (when the scale economy measure for a branch banking organization is properly formulated).

5. The cost and scale economy results imply that relaxation of current state and federal restrictions on intra- and interstate branching would not lead to much consolidation in the banking industry on the basis of cost effects alone. Although consolidation will occur, it will not be primarily due to the cost advantages faced by larger banking organizations since these advantages (on average) do not exist.

Most of these results are contrary to conventional wisdom in banking. As noted in the chapter, this is because most earlier studies of scale economies in banking were limited in several important respects and these limitations resulted in misleading scale economy estimates. In our view, the most important limitation was that the earlier models used to estimate scale economy values could not allow for the average cost curve to be "U"-shaped. Because of this, the average scale economy value estimated in these earlier models was applied to all banks regardless of size. More recent analyses have used less restrictive models and have found that the scale economy results differ markedly across different sizes of banks. Correspondingly, the policy conclusions to be drawn from these newer studies of bank scale economies are quite different from the conclusions based on the earlier analyses.

NOTES

1. All banks in unit banking states are here called a *unit state banks,* even though some of the banks are allowed to have limited-purpose branches, and sometimes full-service branches, under certain conditions. All banks in states that allow limited or full branching are termed *branch state banks.* This includes unit banks in branching states, whose size is typically very small.

2. The basic differences between unit and branch state banks were that unit state banks had a slightly higher percentage composition of purchased liabilities (federal funds and large [> $100,000] CDs), more agricultural and construction loans, but less real estate and consumer loans than do branch state banks.

3. These same differences are evident when small and large banks were contrasted by percent composition of numbers of accounts across the same nine size classes, rather than by the dollar-value composition shown in Table 24.1. The differences in capitalization by bank size are not presented in Table 24.1 but are evident in the FCA data.

The same holds for agricultural and construction loans, which are included in the broad aggregates shown in Table 24.1.

4. The substitution between bank liabilities and the equilibrating role played by federal funds have been modeled and directly estimated in Humphrey (1981).

5. Secondary reserves management is discussed and extensively modeled in Hester and Pierce (1975).

6. Leverage typically is measured as the ratio of total deposits and debt to bank equity and reserves.

7. One potentially important cost that can not be readily measured and has never been adequately included in the empirical analysis involves the cost of "delivering" bank output to the customer. In unit banking states, this transportation cost is borne by the customer to some degree while in branch banking states it is to some (unknown) extent assumed by the bank and represents one cost of branching. These "delivery" costs are likely to be important, since customer convenience issues often dominate in the choice of which bank to deal with (according to customer surveys).

8. Only those FCA asset–liability categories that comprised more than 1% of the operating income flow are shown in the table.

9. The pricing and/or elimination of Federal Reserve float has reduced the benefit of float to both consumers and banks. However, substantial (mail and check-processing) float remains so this issue is still important.

10. ACH and check-processing scale economies are discussed in Humphrey (1982).

11. This is true now and will be even more important when the current Federal Reserve subsidy to ACH costs is fully removed in 1986.

12. A scale economy value of 0.95 means that for each 10% increase in bank output, total operating costs only rise by 9.5%, so that average cost (i.e., total cost/bank output) falls as output expands. More formally stated, the scale economy value is the elasticity of total cost with respect to changes in output.

13. The only exceptions may be Longbrake (1974) and Benston, Hanweck, and Humphrey (1982).

14. For S&Ls the definitive earlier study is by Benston (1970). Credit unions were analyzed in Wolken and Navratil (1980).

15. Formally, $SCE = \partial\ln(\text{operating cost})/\partial\ln(\text{bank output}) = b$, which also equals the ratio (marginal cost/average cost).

16. Correspondingly, the cost effect of only changing these other influences are (assumed to be) measured in the other parameters estimated in the first equation.

17. In many earlier studies, the Cobb-Douglas model yielded results in which $b < 1.0$, indicating scale economies, even though the cost curve, as shown in Figure 24.1, was "U"-shaped overall. This result likely occurred because of under representation of larger banks in the sample, an issue discussed below.

18. Some earlier investigators (e.g., Greenbaum, 1967; Kalish and Gilbert, 1973) also used model specifications—typically adding the term $(\text{bank output})^2$ to the first equation— which could have avoided these problems as well. But because of the popularity of the Cobb-Douglas form and because of somewhat inconsistent scale economy results— namely, that some bank functions showed scale economies while others showed dis-economies—these earlier results were not taken as seriously as perhaps they should have been.

19. The translog model has also been recently used to examine scale economies at S&Ls (McNulty 1982). These estimates show S&Ls to have "U"-shaped average cost curves.

20. The same criticism applies to existing studies of scale economies at S&Ls.

21. Some banks in certain unit banking states have a small number of full-service or limited-service branches. The number of these branches is sufficiently small so that their existence has little effect on the properly computed scale economy measure (discussed below).

22. The term *banking organization*, as used here, refers to the bank and all of its branches (if any) and does not include any of its nonbank subsidiaries.

23. The usual SCE measure was defined above as SCE = ∂ln (operating cost)/∂ln (bank output) or SCE = ∂lnTC/∂ln$Q$. Let B equal the number of branch offices. The augmented measure is obtained from the total derivative $d$lnTC = (∂lnTC/∂ln$Q$)$d$ln$Q$ + (∂lnTC/∂ln$B$)$d$ln$B$. Dividing both sides of this expression by $d$ln$Q$ gives the augmented measure as SCE* = $d$lnTC/$d$ln$Q$ = SCE + SCB ($d$ln$B$/$d$ln$Q$), where SCB = ∂lnTC/∂ln$B$ and is a measure of the economies obtained by adding new branches. The last term in parens is weight, which vary by size class.

24. These results are not shown here but were presented in Benston, Hanweck, and Humphrey (1982, p. 450).

25. Only if these larger banks experienced such large scale diseconomies that they created a "U"-shaped cost curve where the right side of the "U" is much higher than the left side would the scale economy result be reversed. In this instance, however, the Cobb-Douglas form would give results that indicated that scale *diseconomies* existed for all banks regardless of size class, an incorrect result here as well.

26. See Langer (1980) for a recent example.

27. For example, a dummy variable is equal to 1.0 if the bank in question has branches but is 0.0 if no branches exist.

28. While unit banks in unit banking states should not be aggregated with branch banks in branch banking states, the aggregation of unit and branch banks in branch banking states did not have a statistically significant effect on the regression results and therefore is "permitted."

29. This difficulty relates only to measuring scale economies in *producing* various types of deposits and loans.It does not apply to the intermediation approach of determining scale economies since the dollar values of deposits and loans at all banks and total operating and interest costs are regularly reported and publicly available.

30. This area of research is quite new, and only two banking studies exist: Gilligan, Smirlock, and Marshall (1984) and Benston, Berger, Hanweck, and Humphrey (1983). Scope economies were found in a study of Canadian credit unions by Murray and White (1983).

31. For example, row 1 in Table 24.11 shows that demand deposits account for 40% of the total operating costs for the five functions at unit state banks. Each row in the table, for unit and branch state banks separately, adds up to 100% (except for rounding error).

32. These pricing "rules" represent optimal deviations from marginal cost pricing when a firm has to match revenues with costs plus a reasonable return to equity holders (Baumol and Bradford, 1970). Such pricing is also called Ramsey pricing in the economics literature.

REFERENCES

Baumol, William J., and Bradford, David F. "Optimal Departures from Marginal Cost Pricing." *American Economic Review*, June 1970, pp. 265–289.

Bell, Frederick W., and Murphy, Neil B. *Costs in Commercial Banking: A Quantitative Analysis of Bank Behavior and Its Relation to Bank Regulation*. Research Report No. 41, Federal Reserve Bank of Boston, 1968.

Benston, George J. "Branch Banking and Economies of Scale." *Journal of Finance*, May 1965a, pp. 312–331.

Benston, George J. "Economies of Scale and Marginal Costs in Banking Operations." *National Banking Review*, June 1965b, pp. 507–549.

Benston, George J. "Cost of Operations and Economies of Scale in Savings and Loan Associations." *Study of the Savings and Loan Industry*, Federal Home Loan Bank Board, Washington, D.C.: U.S. Government Printing Office, 1970, pp. 677–761.

Benston, George J., Hanweck, Gerald, and Humphrey, David B. "Scale Economies in Banking: A Restructuring and Reassessment." *Journal of Money, Credit, and Banking*, November 1982, Part 1, pp. 435–456.

Benston, George J., Berger, Allen, Hanweck, Gerald and Humphrey, David B. "Economies of Scale and Scope in Banking." *Proceeding of a Conference on Bank Structure and Competition*, Federal Reserve Bank of Chicago, May 1983.

Board of Governors of the Federal Reserve System. *Functional Cost Analysis*, 1978 and 1981.

Gilligan, Thomas, Smirlock, Michael, and Marshall, William. "Scale and Scope Economies in the Multiproduct Banking Firm." *Journal of Monetary Economics*, May 1984, pp. 393–405.

Gramley, Lyle E. *A Study of Scale Economies in Banking*. Monograph, Research Department, Federal Reserve Bank of Kansas City, November 1962.

Greenbaum, Stuart I. "Banking Structure and Costs: A Statistical Study of the Cost–Output Relationship in Commercial Banking." *National Banking Review*, June 1967, pp. 415–434.

Hester, Donald D., and Pierce, James L. *Bank Management and Portfolio Behavior*. Cowles Foundation Monograph No. 25. New Haven: Yale University Press, 1975.

Humphrey, David B. "Intermediation and Cost Determinants of Large Bank Liability Composition." *Journal of Banking and Finance*, June 1981, pp. 167–185.

Humphrey, David B. "Costs, Scale Economies, Competition, and Product Mix in the U.S. Payments Mechanism." *Staff Studies*, No. 115, Federal Reserve Board, Washington, D.C., April 1982, pp. 1–18.

Kalish, Lionel, and Gilbert, R. Alton. "An Analysis of Efficiency of Scale and Organizational Form in Commercial Banking." *Journal of Industrial Economies*, July 1973, pp. 293–307.

Langer, Martha J. "Economies of Scale in Commercial Banking." Working paper, Banking Studies Department, Federal Reserve Bank of New York, December 17, 1980.

Longbrake, William A. "Differential Effects of Single-Plant, Multi-Plant and Multi-Firm Organizational Forms on Cost Efficiency in Commercial Banking." FDIC Working paper No. 74-7, Washington, D.C., 1974.

McNulty, James E. "Economies of Scale: A Case Study of the Florida Savings and Loan Industry." Federal Reserve Bank of Atlanta, *Economic Review*, November 1982, pp. 22–31.

Mueller, Dennis C., ed. *The Determinants and Effects of Mergers: An International Comparison.* Cambridge: Oelgeschlager, Gunn and Hain, 1980.

Murray, John D., and White, Robert W. "Economies of Scale and Economies of Scope in Multi-Product Financial Institutions: A Study of British Columbia Credit Unions." *Journal of Finance,* June 1983, *28,* pp. 887–902.

Opper, Barbara N. "Profitability of Insured Commercial Banks." *Federal Reserve Bulletin,* August 1982, pp. 453–465.

Rhoades, Stephen A. "The Role of Mergers in the Growth of the 20 Largest Banks and Industrials." *Antitrust Bulletin* (Forthcoming).

Rhoades, Stephen A. *Power, Empire Building, and Mergers.* Lexington, Mass.: Lexington Books, 1983.

Wolken, John D., and Navratil, Frank J. "Economies of Scale in Credit Unions: Further Evidence." *Journal of Finance,* June 1980, *35,* pp. 769–777.

Index